Preface

The second European Distributed Memory Computing Conference, EDMCC2, was held at Technische Universität München, April 22-24, 1991 and organized by the relevant Technical Committees of the German Associations for Informatics (GI) and for Information Technology (ITG) and the German Science Foundation (DFG) in cooperation with IFIP Working Group 10.3. The first conference focused on hypercube architectures and was held in Rennes, France, in 1989.

Even though a number of specialists in computer science since the mid-1970s have predicted that multiprocessor systems will gradually replace the classical pipelined vector-supercomputers, this has not happened yet on a large scale. On the other hand, after a large number of research projects and scientific prototypes of distributed memory computers, several commercial products in the field have become a success all over the world. The perfect distributed memory architecture still does not exist, and the field is characterized by large research efforts. The organizing research group (Sonderforschungsbereich 342 "Methods and tools for the use of parallel computer architectures") consisting of about 80 academic staff at Technische Universität München and Siemens Corporate Research is only one example of such activity. Whereas in the past decade, research has been oriented towards systems hardware, interconnection, processor and memory structure, it is now felt that the ease of use offered by the systems software, programming model, development tools and application-oriented program libraries will decide the success of such architectures. Again, new hardware architectures are in development that aim at virtualizing the concurrency of the underlying hardware to the user in the sense that the user will be offered compatibility up to object-code with conventional (sequential) computers: virtual shared memory, virtual distributed I/O, virtually completely interconnected multiprocessors, etc. On the way to this ambitious goal, (semi-)automatic tools for parallelizing compilers, load balancers, etc., are in development.

On the other hand, it is very well known that the best sequential algorithm is not necessarily a good algorithm to be executed on a parallel machine. Therefore, research for good parallel algorithms in all areas of computer applications is needed. Where new software for parallel architectures is beeing created, unconventional programming languages, execution paradigms (dataflow, reduction machines, neural nets, etc.) will be used. These last topics have been ruled out of the scope of the conference by the program committee. This decision reflected the fact that far more than 100 contributions were submitted to the conference, only some of which could be accepted as full papers in order to keep the conference within reasonable size and the proceedings readable. The interest in distributed memory computing is still growing and a number of very challenging research topics are to be solved in the future.

The conference was sponsored by:

GI FB 3.2.1	Gesellschaft für Informatik, Parallel-Algorithmen, Rechnerstrukturen und Sprachen
GI FB 4	Gesellschaft für Informatik, Informationstechnik und Technische Nutzung der Informatik
ITG FA 4.1	Informationstechnische Gesellschaft, Rechner und Systemarchitektur
SFB 0342	Sonderforschungsbereich "Methoden und Werkzeuge für die Nutzung paralleler Rechnerarchitekturen" (Deutsche Forschungsgemeinschaft)
ERCIM	European Research Consortium for Informatics and Mathematics

I would like to thank the sponsoring organizations and Technische Universität München for their support, the invited lecturers, the authors of papers and posters and the exhibitors for their contribution, the members of the program committee, the other reviewers, the chairpersons of the sessions for their help in preparing this event, the attendants of the conference for their interest in the field, and last but not least, all the members of the organizing committee of the Institut für Informatik and SFB 342 at TU München who have helped make this event a success.

München, Spring 1991 — Arndt Bode

Program committee members

C. Addison
F. André
K. Antreich
T. Bemmerl
A. Bode
W. Brauer
R. Chamberlain
M. Cosnard
E. Dagless
W. Giloi
W. Händler
R. Hempel
F. Hofmann
C. Jesshope
B. Kågström
P. Leca
P. Müller-Stoy
J. Nehmer
T. Priol
P. Quinton
K. Reinartz
G.L. Reijns
D. Roose
T. Schwederski
M. Valero
M. Vanneschi
J.P. Verjus
K. Waldschmidt
C. Whitby-Strevens

Reviewers

C. Addison
F. André
K. Antreich
E. Ayduade
F. Baiardi
G. Balbo
J.-P. Banatre
T. Bemmerl
A. Bode
G. Bolch
K. Borg
R. Chamberlain
J. Cook
M. Cosnard
E. Dagless
L. Edblom
J. Eriksson
W. Ertel
J.S. Fakis
G. Fritsch
U. Furbach
A. Gonzalez
M. Gutzmann
W. Händler
R. Hempel
D. Herman
F. Hofmann
H.-C. Hoppe
G. Howard
C. Jard
M. Jazayeri
Y. Jegou
T. Jeron
C. Jesshope
J.M. Jezequel
P. Joubert
B. Kågström
M. Kunde
C. Labit
K.-J. Lange
E. Lindström
P. Ling
F. Malucelli
A.C. Marshall
E. Masson
F. Mattern
A. McKeeman
H. Mehl
H. Mierendorff
P. Müller-Stoy
J. Nehmer
A. Niestegge
T. Orci
P. Quinton
J.-L. Pazat
J. Peters
B. Plateau
D. Pretolani
T. Priol
G.L. Reijns
K.D. Reinartz
W. Reisig
H. Ritzdorf
J.L. Roch
B. Rochat
D. Roose
M. Schäfer
A. Schüller
Ph. Schwebelen
A. Strey
E. Tärnvik
T. Tensi
D. Trystram
M. Valero
M. Valero-García
M. Vanneschi
K. Waldschmidt
D. Watson
C. Whitby-Strevens
T. Wiberg

Organizing committee members

T. Bemmerl (chairman)

P. Braun

D. Hampel

H. Klaskala

B. Ries

T. Treml

R. Wismüller

Session chairpersons

Session 1.1 "Virtual Shared Memory":	T. Priol
Session 1.2 "Tools" (1):	B. Kågström
Session 2.1 "Interconnection Problems" (1):	K. Waldschmidt
Session 2.2 "Applications" (1):	D. Roose
Session 3.1 "Systems Software":	F. Hofmann
Session 3.2 "Tools" (2):	R. Chamberlain
Session 4.1 "Programming Languages and Algorithms":	W. Brauer
Session 4.2 "Alternative Execution Models":	W. Händler
Session 5.1 "Applications" (2):	M. Cosnard
Session 5.2 "Tools" (3):	P. Müller-Stoy
Session 6.1 "Operating Systems and Related Topics":	J. Nehmer
Session 6.2 "Systems" (1):	C. Jesshope
Session 7.1 "Interconnection Problems" (2):	T. Schwederski
Session 7.2 "Systems" (2):	K. Reinartz
Session 8.1 "Tools" (4):	F. André

Contents

Interconnection Problems

Applications

Systems Software

Programming Languages and Algorithms

Alternative Execution Models

Operating Systems and Related Topics

Systems

The New Age of Supercomputing

Justin Rattner

Intel Fellow
Director of Technology
Intel Corporation
Supercomputer Systems Division

Summary

The solutions to today's foremost scientific challenges require order-of-magnitude increases in computing power. The route to TeraFLOP computing lies in parallel multi-computers that exploit advances in microprocessor technology.

As the only manufacturer of both advanced microprocessors and parallel supercomputers, Intel Corp. plays a unique role in the drive toward TeraFLOP computing. The Touchstone Program, a joint effort by Intel and the U.S. Defense Advanced Research Projects Agency (DARPA), already has led to the development of the world's fastest supercomputer, a 32-GigaFLOP, distributed memory, mesh interconnection machine installed at the California Institute of Technology (Caltech). The machine, called DELTA, will be used by member institutions of the Concurrent Supercomputing Consortium for research on the so-called Grand Challenges of Science, identified by the U.S. Office of Science and Technology Policy, and other projects.

The Need for a New Era in High Performance Computing

From Charles Babbage's eighteenth-century compute engine through the mechanical calculator to today's multi-GigaFLOP supercomputers, computation has become a fundamental instrument of science. Increasingly, computation supplements, and even replaces, the role of experimentation in advancing scientific knowledge.

Powerful though they are, today's supercomputers are nontheless inadequate for many of the foremost questions facing scientists today. For example, a majority of the Grand Challenge problems depend for their solution on the availability of TeraFLOP levels of computing performance - nearly 1.000 times faster than current conventional supercomputers. Grand Challenge problems are not only of theoretical importance; they include areas such as human genome mapping and global climate modelling, which will have far-reaching economic and sociological impact (Figure 1).

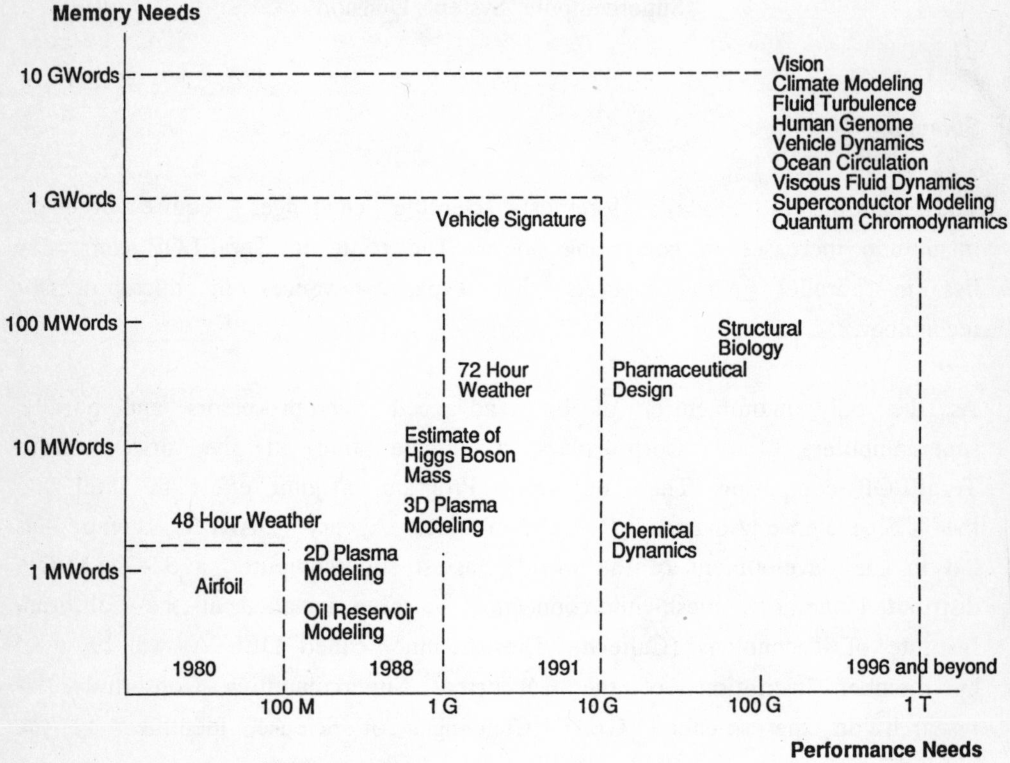

Figure 1: Computing performance requirements for Grand Challenge problems

Entering the New Age

While the need for higher computing performance is critical, the traditional path to high performance computing is, at best, rocky and circuitous, and at worst, dead-ended. Conventional vector supercomputers face limits of physics and thermodynamics that make performance increases increasingly difficult to attain, within realistic contraints of time and budget. A single Cray Y-MP

CPU, for example, has only twice the peak performance of the original Cray-1 processor introduced in 1976. The Y-MP's small-scale multiprocessing (up to eight CPUs) affords a sixteenfold aggregate performance increase over the original system, but speedups of the CPU itself have been relatively slight.

Microprocessor technology, in contrast, continues on a smooth path to higher performance. During the decade in which Cray CPU performance barely doubled, microprocessor performance improved a hundredfold. A single microprocessor, the i860, introduced by Intel in 1989, equals the power of a Cray-1 computer.

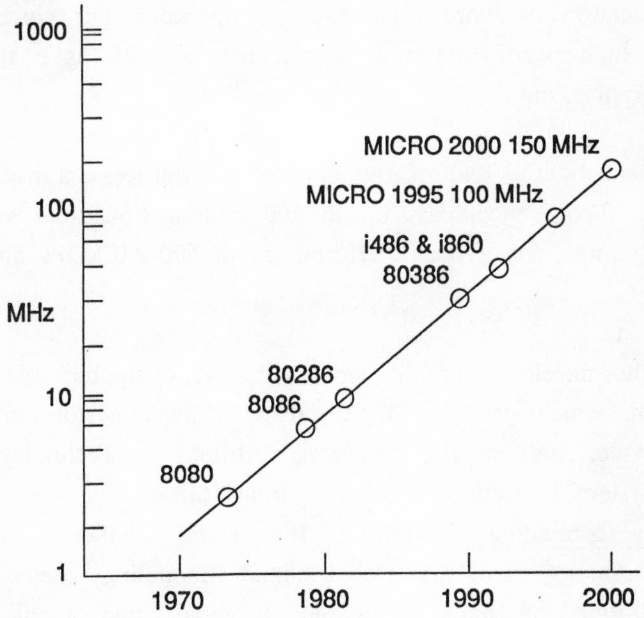

Figure 2: Microprocessor Performance

According to Intel studies, in particular Intel's *Micro 2000* report, microprocessor performance will continue to double every two years through the end of this century (Figure 2). Thus, massively parallel, microprocessor-based multicomputers will far outstrip traditional supercomputers in performance. As a result, we have entered a new age of supercomputing, in which both current and future needs for high performance computing will be met by massively parallel computers.

Intel's Role: Superchips to Supercomputers

Intel Corp. designs and manufactures both advanced microprocessors and parallel multicomputers. As a result, Intel will play a leading role in moving the computing industry toward the TeraFLOP levels of computing required to solve Grand Challenge problems.

Intel's million-transistor i860 microprocessor has opened the door to microprocessor-based, high-performance numeric computation. The i860 operates at 40 MHz, has a 64-bit bus, and provides a superscalar architecture that allows execution of more than a single operation per clock cycle. The i860 integrates high-speed code and data caches, as well as a floating point unit and a 3-D graphics unit.

Intel projects that by the end of the decade, microprocessors will, on a one-inch square of silicon, encompass up to 100 million transistors and four 250 MHz processing units, for a peak performance of 500 MFLOPs and 750 VAX MIPS.

Intel is also the developer of the world's fastest computer: the Touchstone DELTA System, which provides 32 GigaFLOPs peak performance and was installed in March, 1991 at the California Institute of Technology (Caltech). The DELTA System is used by the fourteen institutions and companies of the Concurrent Supercomputing Consortium for Grand Challenge research and other projects. Among them are global climate modeling, chemical reactivity studies, visualization of data from the Magellan and Galileo satellites, aerospace simulations, human genome research, and the study of molecular processes.

Unlike earlier Touchstone prototypes, which use a hypercube interconnection scheme, DELTA employs a two-dimensional mesh with a bisection bandwidth approaching 1 Gbyte/sec. Using a mesh router chip from Caltech and a backplane-routingplane arrangement designed by Intel, DELTA scales to 512 nodes. Aggregate peak performance exceeds 30 double-precision GigaFLOPs and 17.000 VAX MIPS. System memory scales as well, reaching a maximum of over 8 Gbytes.

The DELTA System was developed as part of the Touchstone Program, a comprehensive, three-year effort to accelerate the progress toward Tera-FLOP-level computing by achieving order-of-magnitude improvements in key aspects of high-performance, distributed-memory, message-passing multicomputers. Touchstone is funded by a total of $ 27 million (US) from Intel Corp. and the U.S. Defense Advanced Research Projects Agency's Information Science and Technology Office (DARPA/ISTO).

The Touchstone Program aims for order-of-magnitude price/performance advantages over conventional high-performance computing systems. Research tracks address the full range of hardware, software and applications issues: node performance and capability; the performance, bandwidth, latency and scalability of multicomputer interconnection schemes; I/O performance; packaging; operating systems; programming tools; ease of use; and applications development.

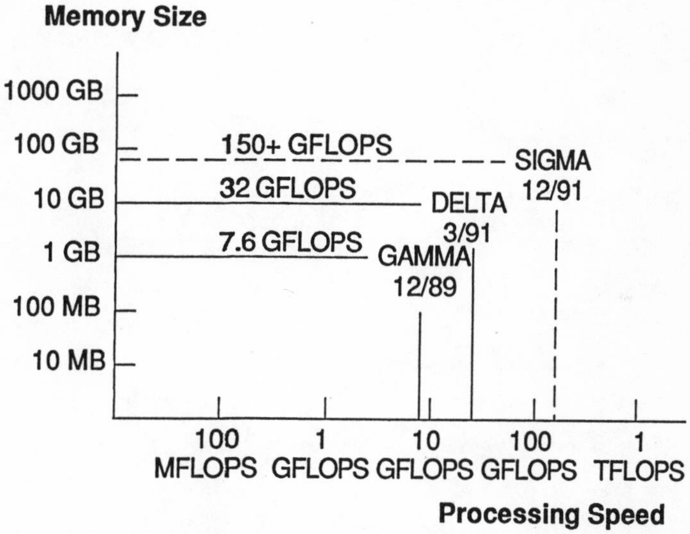

Figure 3: Touchstone Prototypes

In 1992 Intel will demonstrate SIGMA, the fourth and final Touchstone prototype (Figure 3). SIGMA will incorporate technologies developed for earlier Touchstone systems, along with new ones such as scalable visualization facilities and an integrated development-tool architecture. SIGMA will scale to at least 2,048 nodes with 64 GBytes of main memory and half a Terabyte of online storage, providing aggregate performance in excess of

150 GFLOPs and 100.000 VAX MIPS. The system will incorporate high-density packaging that quadruples the packaging density of the previous prototypes.

Conclusion

While conventional supercomputers have slowed in their rate of progress, the performance horizon for microprocessor-based systems seems virtually unlimited. By focusing on the synergies among advances in silicon technology, microprocessor architectures and parallel multicomputing architectures, Intel is reframing the question of Tera FLOP computing, turning from "will we?" to "when?" and bringing closer the day when the computing power needed for Grand Challenge problems is both at-hand and affordable.[1]

Intel, iPSC and i860 are trademarks or registered trademarks of Intel Corp. Other trademarks used are the property of their respective owners.

The Next Generation Transputers and Beyond

David May
Inmos Limited, 1000 Aztec West
Almondsbury, Bristol, UK

Abstract

The Inmos transputer family is a range of VLSI components for concurrent processing systems. Transputers are used in applications such as communications, real-time control, image processing, robotics, databases, graphics and animation. New, software compatible, transputer products will exploit parallelism in instruction execution to provide greatly increased processor performance. New communications components will allow the construction of message-routing networks; these can be used in conjunction with the new transputers to provide high speed system-wide communication.

Experience with existing transputer based machines - and theoretical considerations - suggest several promising approaches to the architecture of scalable *general purpose* concurrent computers. An important requirement is a communications architecture supporting system-wide communication and memory access. This will allow more flexible - and more portable - programming styles. Further developments in architecture and programming techniques will open the way to portable parallel software - and make general purpose parallel computing a reality.

1 Transputers

VLSI technology enables a complete computer to be constructed on a single silicon chip. The Inmos T800 transputer introduced in 1987 [1], integrates a central processor, a floating point unit, four kilobytes of static random access memory, an interface for external memory, and a communications system onto a chip about 1 square centimeter in area.

The T800 contains a simple integer processor and a compact floating point unit; peak performance is about 30 MIPS and 4 (scalar) MFLOPS. In 1991, a new transputer developed within the Esprit PUMA project (and currently known as the H1) will increase this performance to a peak of 150 MIPS and 20 (scalar) MFLOPS. The increased performance comes partly from the use of a more advanced manufacturing process and partly from the use of more parallelism in the execution of instructions.

Transputers have the ability to communicate directly with each other via their communication links; this enables transputers to be connected together to construct multiprocessor systems to tackle specific problems. The communication links of the T800 transputer provide a total communication throughput of about 10Mbytes/second. For the H1 transputer, the throughput of the links is 80Mbytes/second, maintaining the balance between processing throughput and communication throughput. The effect is that the H1 can be used in exactly the same way as the T800 transputer, and will provide a substantial increase in overall system performance.

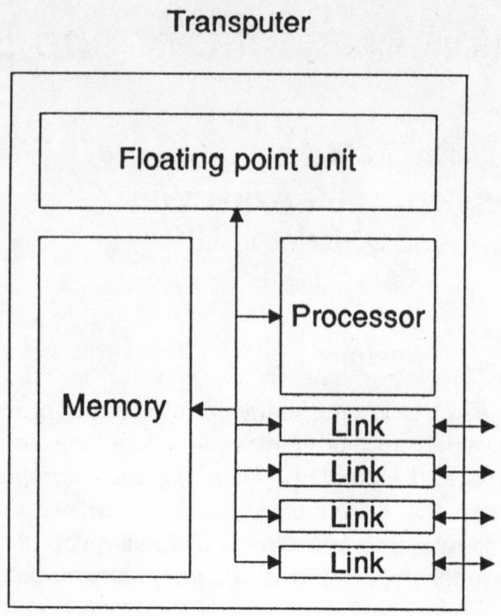

Each transputer includes a hardware kernel with the ability to execute many software processes at the same time, to create new processes rapidly, and to perform communication between processes within a transputer and between processes in different transputers. All of these capabilities are integrated into the hardware of the transputers, and are very efficient. Kernel operations (process scheduling, communication) take about 1 microsecond, in contrast to the 100 microsecond overheads typical of software kernels.

The concurrent processing architecture of the transputers follows the the concepts of concurrency and communication embodied in the occam programming language [2]. The occam language allows an application to be expressed as a collection of concurrent processes which communicate via channels. Each channel is a point-to-point connection between two processes; one process always inputs from the channel and the other always outputs to it. Communication is synchronised; the first process ready to communicate waits until the second is also ready, then the data is copied from the outputting processes to the inputting process and both processes continue. Transputer systems can be programmed directly in occam, or alternatively in an ordinary sequential programming language extended with the processes and channels of occam. In many applications a combination of languages has been used, with occam used to write concurrent programs in which the individual sequential processes are written in ordinary sequential languages.

Occam provides direct access to the functions provided by the hardware kernel. The kernel includes a process scheduler which allows the transputer to share its time between a number of processes. Communication between processes on the same transputer is performed using the local memory; communication between processes on different transputers is performed using a link between the two transputers. Consequently, an occam program can be executed either by a single transputer or by a collection of transputers connected in a network. Three different ways of using transputers to execute the component processes of a typical occam program are shown below.

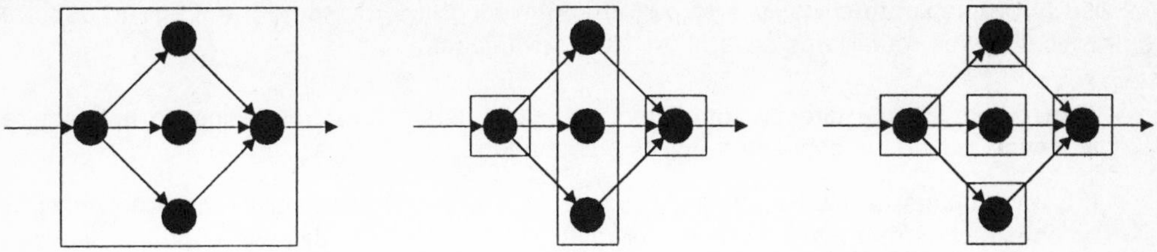

This picture shows the same collection of processes executed on three different specialised networks. In the first network, which is a single transputer, each communication channel connecting two processes is implemented by the local memory of the transputer. In the other examples each channel is implemented by a physical link between different transputers.

Transputers have also been used to construct a number of general purpose machines, which all consist of an array of transputers connected together in a network. In some machines the network can be configured by software, for example by connecting the links via a crossbar switch. Many applications have been successfully ported to these machines and have demonstrated efficient parallel processing.

One of the problems with existing general purpose machines is that the need to carefully match algorithms to the interconnection networks of specific machines results in a lack of software portability. It has become clear that a standard architecture is needed for these general purpose message-passing machines. An attractive candidate is a collection of transputers connected by a high throughput, low delay communication network supporting communication channels between processes anywhere in the network.

2 Routers

There are many parallel algorithms in which the number of communication channels between processes on different transputers is much greater than the number of physical links available to connect the transputers. In some of these algorithms, a process executed on one transputer must communicate with processes on a large number of other transputers. These requirements for system-wide communication between processes can be met by:

- the new H1 transputers which include hardware to multiplex many channels along a single physical link
- the new C104 VLSI message-routing chips which can be used to construct efficient communication networks

This new communications architecture allows communication channels to be established between any two processes, regardless of where they are physically located. This simplifies programming because processes can be allocated to transputers after the program is written in order to optimise performance. For general purpose message-passing machines, a further benefit is that processes can be allocated to transputers by a compiler, which effectively removes configuration details from the program, thereby enhancing portability.

The use of two separate chips, one to perform computing (the transputer) and one to perform communication (the router) has several practical advantages:

- Transputers can be directly connected without routers in systems which do not require message routing, so avoiding the silicon cost and routing delays.
- It allows routers to have many links (eg 32 on the C104) which allow large networks to be constructed from a small number of routers, minimising the delay through the network. For example, 48 such routers can connect 512 terminals with only 3 routing delays, as in figure 1.
- It avoids the need for messages to flow through the transputer, reducing the total throughput of the chip interface. This reduces the pin count, power consumption and package costs of the transputer.
- It supports scalable architectures in which communication throughput must be balanced with processing throughput. In such architectures, it is known that overall communication capacity must grow faster than the total number of processors - a large machine must have proportionately more routers.

3 Virtual Links

In the T800 transputers, each point-to-point physical link between transputers provides two communication channels, one in each direction. In the new H1 transputers, each physical link provides an arbitrary number of point-to-point *virtual links*. Each virtual link provides two channels, one in each direction. Hardware within the transputer multiplexes virtual links onto the physical links.

A message is transmitted through a virtual link as a sequence of packets. Each packet starts with a *header*, which is used to route the packet to an inputting process on a remote transputer. Packets are restricted in length to a maximum of 32 data bytes.

The splitting of messages into packets, each of which is acknowledged before the next is sent, has several important consequences:

- It prevents any single virtual link from hogging a physical link
- It prevents a single virtual link from hogging a path through a network
- It provides flow-control of message communication and provides the end-to-end synchronisation needed for synchronised process communication
- It requires only a small buffer to be used to avoid blocking in the case that a message arrives before a process is ready to receive it

An important feature of the H1 is that the multiplexing of virtual links onto physical links is performed by a hardware virtual channel processor which operates concurrently with the processor. This ensures that that communication via virtual links is very efficient, and that virtual link operations do not consume any processor time.

4 Message Routing

Where system-wide message routing is required, a collection of transputers can be interconnected by a routing network constructed from routers.

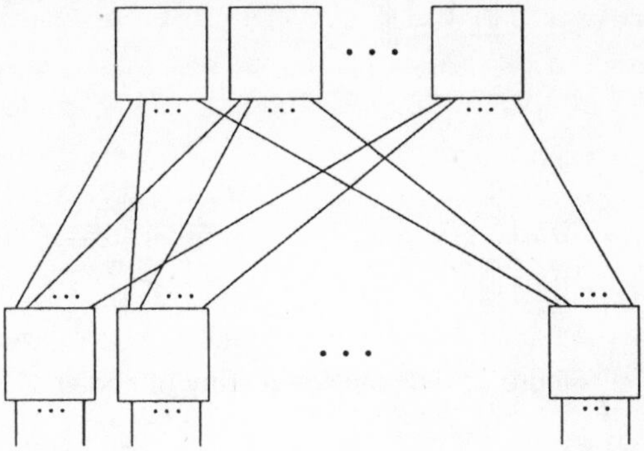

Figure 1: Clos network constructed from routers

In some cases, it is convenient to construct a network from routers and attach transputers to its terminal links. An example is the clos network shown in figure 1. An alternative is to construct a network such as a hypercube or an array from a number of nodes, each node consisting of a transputer and a router as shown in figure 2.

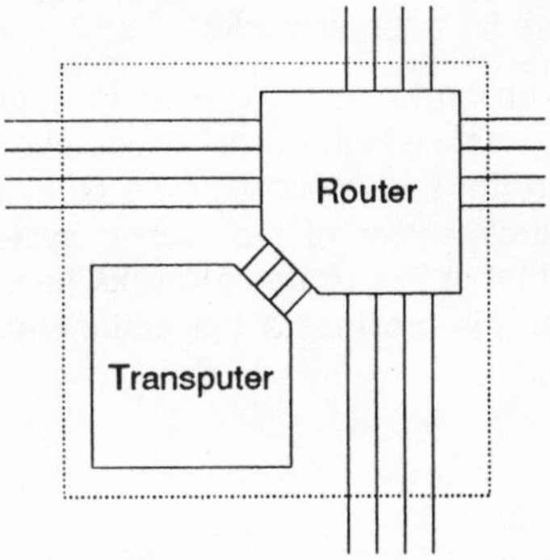

Figure 2: Node combining a transputer and a router

Each router has a number of communication links and operates as follows:

- It uses the header of each packet arriving on a link to determine the link to be used to output the packet
- It arbitrates between two (or more) packets which must both be output through the same link, and causes them to be output one after another
- It starts to output each packet as early as possible (immediately after the output link is determined, provided that the output link is not already in use for another packet)

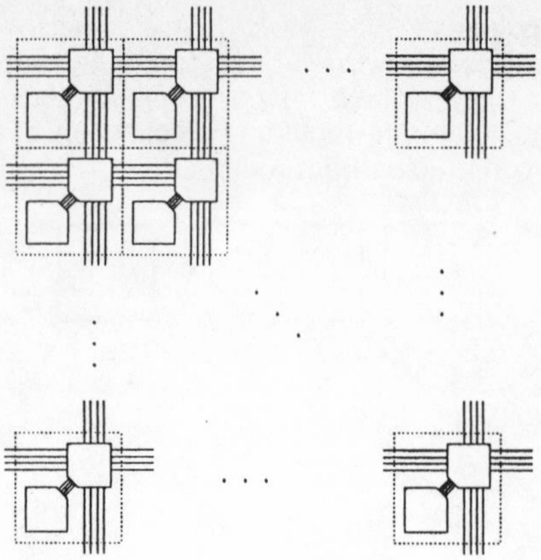

Figure 3: 2-dimensional array of nodes

The ability to start outputting a packet whilst it is still being input can significantly reduce delay, especially in networks which are lightly loaded. This technique is known as *wormhole routing*. In wormhole routing, the delay through the switch can be minimised by keeping headers short and by using fast, simple, hardware to determine the link to be used for output.

The first router to be introduced (the C104) incorporates 32 links. As each link provides bidirectional communication at 10 Mbytes/second in each direction, the total throughput of the C104 is 320 Mbytes/second. Delay through the C104 is less than 0.5 microseconds, provided that the outgoing link is not already in use for another packet.

For some purposes, it may be useful to combine a router together with each transputer in a single module or package. One example is the construction of a two dimensional array of simple transputers for image processing (for this application, no off-chip memory is needed, and most communication is local). The architecture of the routing system makes such a combination possible, as in figure 3. Notice that in this example 4 links have been used in parallel for each connection between two routers; this provides a bidirectional throughput of 80 Mbytes/second along each (parallel) link.

4.1 Addressing

Every packet must carry with it the address of its destination; this might be the address of a transputer, or the address of one of a number of virtual channels forming input channels to a transputer. As a packet arrives at a router, the destination address must be inspected before the outgoing link can be determined; the delay through the router is therefore proportional to the address length. Further, the address must itself be transmitted through the network and therefore consumes network bandwidth.

It is therefore important that this address be as short as possible, both to optimise network latency and network bandwidth. However, it is also important that the destination link can be derived from the address quickly and with minimal hardware. An addressing system which meets both of these requirements is *interval labelling*.

An *interval labelling scheme* [6] assigns a distinct label to each transputer in a network. For simplicity, the labels for an N transputer network can be numbers in the range $[0, 1, \ldots, N-1]$. At each router in the network, each output link has an associated *interval* - a set of consecutive labels. The intervals associated with the links on a router are non-overlapping and every label will occur in exactly one interval. As a packet arrives at a router, the address is examined to determine which interval contains a matching label; the packet is then forwarded along the associated output link.

The main disadvantages of the interval labelling system are that it does not permit arbitrary routes through a network, and it does not allow a message to be routed through a series of networks. These problems can be overcome by a simple extension: *header deletion.* Each outgoing link can be set to delete the header on every packet which passes through it; the result is that the data immediately following becomes the new header as the packet enters the next node.

Header deletion can be used to minimise delays in the routing network. To do this, an initial header is used to route the packet to a destination transputer; this header is deleted as it leaves the final router and enters the transputer. A second header is then used to identify the virtual link within the destination transputer. As the number of transputers is normally much less than the number of virtual links, the initial header can be short, minimising the delay through each router.

4.2 Summary

The techniques described so far provide efficient deadlock free communications and allow a wide range of networks to be constructed from a standard router. Packets are delivered at high speed and with low latency provided that there are no collisions between packets traveling through the same link.

Unfortunately, for general purpose concurrent computers, this is not enough. In any sparse communication network, some communication patterns cannot be realised without collisions. Such collisions within the network can reduce system performance drastically. For example, some parallel algorithms require that all messages from one phase of a computation are delivered before the next phase starts; the late arrival of a single message delays *all* of the processors. In the absence of any bound on message latency it is difficult - and in many cases impossible - to design efficient concurrent programs. The problem of constructing general purpose concurrent computers therefore depends on the answer to the following question:

Is it possible to design a *universal* routing system: a realisable network and a routing algorithm which can implement all communication patterns with bounded message latency?

5 Universal Routing

A universal routing system allowing the construction of scalable general purpose parallel computers was discovered by Valiant [3] in 1980. This meets two important requirements:

- The throughput of the network scales with the number of nodes
- The delay through the network scales slowly with the number of nodes ($O(log(p)$ for p nodes)

Notice that the aim is to maximise capacity and minimise delay under heavy load conditions - a *parallel* communications network is a vital component of a parallel computer. This is not the same as, for example, minimising delay through an otherwise empty network.

A p-node hypercube has a delay of $log(p)$ if there are no collisions between packets. This is an unreasonable assumption, however, as all of the transputers will be communicating via the network simultaneously. An important case of communication is that of performing a *permutation* in which every transputer simultaneously transmits a message and no two messages head for the same destination. Valiant's proof [4] demonstrates constructively that permutation routing is possible in time $O(log(p))$ on a sparse p-node network even at high communication load.

To eliminate the network *hot-spots* which commonly arise when packets from many different sources collide at a link in a sparse network, two phase routing is employed. Every packet is first dispatched to a randomly chosen intermediate destination; from the intermediate destination it continues to its final destination. This is a distributed algorithm - it does not require any central co-ordination - so it is straightforward to implement and scales easily. Randomisation does not, in fact, guarantee a delivery time less than $O(log(p))$ - but it gives it a sufficiently high probability to achieve the universality result. The processors will occasionally be held up for a late message, but not often enough to noticeably affect performance.

5.1 Randomising Headers

When a packet enters a randomising network, it must be supplied with a random header; this header will be used to route the packet to a router which will serve as the intermediate destination. Each input link of a router can be set to *randomise* packets as they arrive. Whenever a packet starts to arrive along such a link, the link first generates a random number and behaves as if this number were the packet header. The remainder of the packet follows the newly supplied random header through the network until the header reaches the intermediate (random) destination.

At this point, the first (randomising) phase of the routing is complete and the random header is removed to allow the header to progress to its final destination in the second (destination) phase. The removal of the random header is performed by a *portal* in each router which recognises the random header associated with the router. The portal deletes the random header with the result that the original header is at the front of the packet, as it was when the packet first entered the network. This header is now used to route the packet to its final destination.

6 General purpose transputer machines

Universal routing overcomes one of the major difficulties in constructing scalable general purpose transputer machines. Ideally, a general purpose machine should be able to execute any program designed for a specialised transputer network, and should achieve similar performance (to within a small constant factor).

The performance of a general purpose message passing computer depends on two major factors:

- The balance between the throughput of the communications network and the computational throughput of the transputers
- The delay through the network

The importance of achieving a good balance between computation and communication can be understood by considering a simple example. Suppose that a two dimensional image is to be processed by an array of transputers. Each transputer stores and processes a portion of the image. Each step of the computation involves updating every element of the image in parallel. Assume that at every step of the computation, every element of the array `a[i,j]` is to be updated to:

```
f(a[i,j], a[i-1,j], a[i+1,j], a[i,j-1], a[i,j+1])
```

and that function `f` involves 4 operations. The following table shows the operations performed for each item communicated for four possible mappings.

elements/transputer	operations/communication
1	1
4	2
16	4
256	16

If we chose a mapping which allocates one element to each transputer, we would need each transputer to perform one operation in the same time that it can communicate one data item. This is often referred to as *fine grain* processing. If, on the other hand, we allocate a large number of processes to each transputer, the communications requirements are small. This is often referred to as *coarse grain* processing. It can be seen from the example that as the grain is decreased, the communications capability becomes the limiting factor. At this point, it is impossible to use more transputers to increase performance, but easy to use more transputers to process a larger image.

Specialised transputer configurations can often be used to provide fine grain processing. In the above example a two-dimensional array of transputers could be used, as communication is required only between adjacent transputers in the array. However, a general purpose machine should be able to provide fine grain processing for a wide variety of algorithms, and for software portability it should allow automatic allocation of processes to transputers. To do this it must support a high rate of *non-local* communication, which can be achieved with a suitable network of routers.

Another important factor affecting the performance of parallel computers is the *delay* in communication. A transputer may idle awaiting data from another transputer even though the communication rate between the transputers is adequate. This is normally achieved by using extra parallelism in the algorithms to *hide* communication delays. Instead of executing one process on each transputer, we use the transputer process scheduler to execute several processes on each transputer.

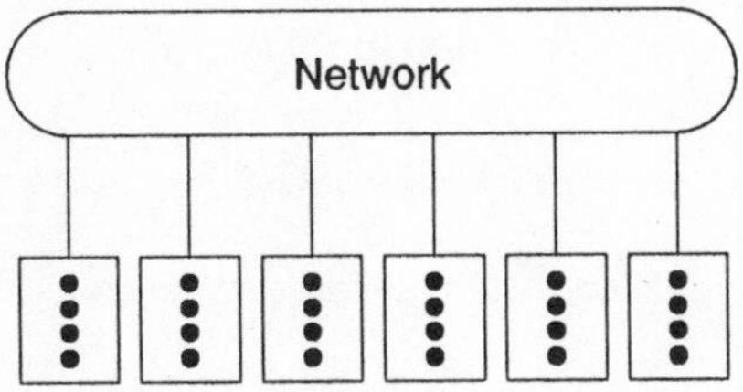

Excess concurrency in the algorithm can hide interconnect delays

Whenever a process is delayed as a result of a communication, it is descheduled and the transputer activates another process. This in turn will eventually become descheduled as a result of a communication. Execution proceeds in this way through several processes. Whenever a communication completes, the corresponding process is rescheduled ready for subsequent execution. Provided that there are sufficient processes, the transputer will never idle as a result of communication delays.

To understand the use of excess parallelism, consider the following simple *worker* process suitable for use in a processing farm. In a typical farm a controller process would hand out packets of work to many such worker processes.

```
local data, result
loop
{ input ? data
  result := compute (data)
  output ! result
}
```

This process performs input (?) to a local variable, computation and output (!) from a local variable sequentially. Any delay in performing communication will be directly reflected in the time taken for each iteration of the loop.

Provided that the result output at each iteration of the loop is not used (by the controller) to produce input for the next two iterations, this process could be replaced by the following version which allows input, computation and output to take place in parallel.

```
local data, nextdata, result, nextresult
loop
{ parallel
  { input ? nextdata
    nextresult := compute (data)
    output ! result
  }
  data, result := nextdata , nextresult
}
```

Here delays in communication will affect the total time taken for the loop only if one of the communications takes longer than the computation. Even larger delays in communication can be tolerated by executing several such processes in each transputer, as in the following version. The n processes are all independent of each other, and each operates on its own local variables (data, nextdata, result).

```
parallel i = 1 to n
{ local data, nextdata, result, nextresult
  loop
  { parallel
    { input[i] ? nextdata
      nextresult := compute (data)
      output[i] ! result
    }
  data , result := nextdata , nextresult
  }
}
```

Here every communication can be delayed by up to n computation steps. An algorithm of this kind can be efficiently executed even in the presence of long communication delays.

This leads directly to the conclusion that algorithms must contain large scale parallelism. Provided that there is sufficient parallelism, we can hide delays in communication. Thus, there are two requirements of the communication network. Firstly, it must be predictable in the sense that there is a known upper bound on the delay - otherwise it will not be possible to determine how many processes should be executed on each transputer. Secondly, it must provide adequate communication throughput in relation to the processing throughput of the transputers.

The excess concurrency is the price to be paid for the ability to use implementable communication networks. Networks in which every transputer is connected to every other transputer have minimal delay but are not implementable for large numbers of transputers. However, there are several networks with delay $O(log(p))$ which are implementable in current technology. One of these (the binary n-cube, or *hypercube*) also meets the requirements of overall communication capacity - this must grow as $p \times log(p)$. However, the best choice of network will normally depend on the machine size; a machine with a few transputers requires only a single router!

The need for $log(p)$ excess parallelism means that if we want to provide algorithms which can be used on machines with up to 1000 transputers, they will need to have 10,000 concurrent processes. Such algorithms will run on machines with up to 1000 transputers with performance scaling with the number of transputers.

7 General purpose parallel computers

The H1 transputer and C104 routers developed within the Esprit PUMA project will be used in a further Esprit project (*General Purpose MIMD* project) to construct scalable *universal message passing machines*. These machines will be designed to maintain a balance between processing throughput and interconnect throughput independent of the number of processors; they will also be designed to ensure that system-wide communication latency grows slowly ($log(p)$ for a p-processor machine). This will allow the development of scalable, portable parallel algorithms. To ensure program portability in addition to algorithm portability, concurrent programming languages and language extensions will be standardised and defined in an *application support interface*.

The components developed within the PUMA project will allow general purpose *message-passing machines* to be constructed. They will not support common memory operations (or global synchronisation) in hardware. However, it is clear that a truly *general purpose* parallel architecture must efficiently support both common memory operations and message passing. Indeed, it seems likely that the two architectures will converge as both of them depend on the existence of high-performance interconnection technology. Recent theoretical developments provide a basis for the design of components for scalable general purpose multiprocessors. Of particular importance is the theory of general purpose parallel machines based on the *Parallel Random Access Machine* (PRAM) model [4].

An important consequence of supporting both message-passing and common-memory operations is that most (perhaps all) of the common parallel processing paradigms will be supported by the machine architecture. The most common alternative to message passing is the combination of *barrier synchronisation* together with common memory access. These parallel processing operations are supported by a combination of hardware and software (making them relatively slow) on some experimental common-memory multiprocesors.

Recent work on general purpose parallel computers has identified several important requirements for future parallel processing components:

- The ability to construct interconnection networks with high throughput and low delay (for processor-processor and processor-memory interconnect).
- A processor architecture which provides fast process switching, so that execution can continue when a process is delayed by communication through the interconnect (this technique is known as *latency hiding*).
- Highly parallel algorithms - and support for them in standard programming languages.

Unlike existing transputer-based multiprocessors, these machines will support common memory multiprocessing as well as message passing; unlike existing common-memory multiprocessors they will scale easily.

7.1 Processor architecture

A processor architecture must combine high sequential performance together with the ability to support efficient concurrent processing. Several projects now aim to provide high performance processors by executing several instructions at once. Examples are:

- *Very Long Instruction Word* processors, which operate a collection of function units in lock-step. Instructions are allocated to the function units by the compiler. These machines have fairly simple hardware but complex compiler technology.
- *Dynamic Instruction Scheduling* processors, in which the instruction dispatcher dynamically issues instructions to the function units. These machines have simple compilers but complex hardware.

For the construction of concurrent computers, it is important that the processor be able to provide latency-hiding in large multiprocessors by efficient hardware scheduling of processes or *threads*. Further, by allowing the processor to take instructions from the instruction streams of several processes at the same time, it is possible to keep a collection of function units busy, with instructions being dynamically allocated to the available function units. It may be possible to use such processors to support fast sequential processing, using a compiler which can find small amounts of parallelism sequential programs. However, it seems likely that further parallelism can be provided by allowing more than one instruction from each stream to be executed at once. It is therefore reasonable to expect that future components for multiprocessors should:

- provide fast context switching between a collection of processes; this collection should be large enough to support latency hiding in large multiprocessors (but would also be useful with smaller numbers of processors but longer communication delays).
- execute several instructions simultaneously. When executing multiple processes, the processor should select instructions from the instruction streams of different processes (minimising inter-dependence between the instructions). However, it should also be capable of initiating several instructions from the same instruction stream to allow performance on sequential instructions to be maximised (even in a multiprocessor, this is useful during the initial and final stages of a computation, when there is limited available parallelism).

7.2 Memory system architecture

An important issue in the design of a VLSI processor architecture is the memory system. The constraints imposed by packaging and power dissipation severely restrict the speed at which addresses and data can be transferred between the processor and the memory system. Most existing microprocessors do not allow memory requests to be pipelined; the processor is delayed until each request is completed with the result that the performance is limited by the access *latency*. In contrast, for an architecture which allows memory accesses to be pipelined and overlapped with other operations, performance can be increased until the overall *throughput* of the memory system becomes the limiting factor.

The objective of any new architecture should be to ensure that, as far as possible, performance is be limited by *throughput* rather that *latency*. This has major benefits: .

- The fast context-switching supported in the processor can be used to hide delays both in memory access and in message passing
- High performance can be achieved using slow, cheap memory systems
- High throughput is much easier to achieve than low latency: it simply requires deeply pipelined memory access. In addition it is possible to support parallel access to many words of memory; this fits well transfers of cache lines between cache and main memory

The use of a large on-chip cache means that off-chip memory operations can take place primarily in reads and writes of cache-lines, rather than words. This reduces throughput requirements: one address must be transferred for each cache-line, rather than one for each word. The on-chip access to the cache can be optimised to meet very high access rates from the multiple on-chip sources. There are significant opportunities for performance enhancement through innovative cache designs.

Another method of reducing the memory throughput is to use an instruction set designed for compact program representation. The compacted instructions can be translated into a form suitable for execution when the instructions are loaded into the instruction cache (or even as the instructions are executed). The instruction sets of conventional RISC architectures have not been designed for compactness and provide very bulky program representation - with instruction-level programs larger then most CISC architectures and twice as large as the transputer. A compact instruction representation can easily halve the memory throughput required for instructions, and significantly increase the effectiveness of the instruction cache.

7.3 PRAMs

When an access is made to a location which is not within the local memory at all (neither on-chip nor off-chip), a request must be made to the common memory system. This will be made via the processor-memory interconnect.

Common memory machines have been classified in terms of an idealised abstract machine: the *parallel random access machine*, or PRAM. A PRAM is a synchronous parallel machine in which, at each step of the computation, every processor can make an access to a common memory. It is useful to distinguish three different types of PRAM:

In a *seclusive* PRAM, no two processors access the same memory module in the same 'step' of the computation. Seclusive PRAM operations involve a series of permutation routing steps, which can be implemented by an interconnect based on Valiant's random-routing algorithm.

In an *exclusive* PRAM, no two processors access the same memory location in the same step, but more than one procesor may access the same memory module. In this case, access delays can arise as a result of many (possibly all) of the processors accessing the same memory module; this will obviously degrade performance. This problem can be partially solved by careful allocation of the data to the memory modules. However, it is also possible to hash the address space so as to distribute data (and accesses to it) throughout the memory modules. Certain hash functions can be shown to provide efficient data-distribution, eliminating the need for explicit allocation or complex compilation techniques. An obvious possiblity is to implement these hash functions in hardware.

In a *concurrent* PRAM, more than one processor may access the same memory location in the same step (indeed, *all* of the processors may access the same memory location). In this case the communications network must be enhanced by a combining capabilty. This combines multiple accesses to the same store location into a single access. This operation can also be viewed as a sorting operation: the simultaneous accesses from all of the processors are sorted in order of their addresses with the result that accesses to the same location are grouped together. The groups of accesses can then be merged to produce a set of accesses all to distinct locations, which can be implemented by an exclusive PRAM. It has recently been demonstrated that this technique can be used to implement concurrent PRAM operations on a bulk synchronised seclusive PRAM with combining software. A bulk synchronised machine is one in which the processors are synchronised every few operations; this is much more appropriate to VLSI technology than synchronising the processors for every operation. Notice that the processors in a binary n-cube can be synchronised in $O(n)$ local synchronisation steps. It therefore seems feasible to implement concurrent PRAM operations on a multiprocessor in which the underlying interconnect provides only local synchronisation and does not support combining.

An important consideration in the design of the memory architecture is the extent to which the local memory is used to cache common memory data. Obviously, the programs and local data (pointers, temporaries, stacks) will normally reside in the local cache: these are not updated by other processors. However, if common data-structures are transferred to the local cache, their local values will become inconsistent with their values in the common memory. In the PRAM machines, it is assumed that data in the common memory will be consistent at the start of each *step* of the computation; in the bulk-synchronised PRAM this step can be many operation times. For PRAM programs, it would be sufficient to ensure that common-memory data is flushed at each synchronisation point.

The significance of the PRAM work is that it provides a theoretical basis for the development of general purpose parallel computers, and complements work based on simulation or on the construction of experimental machines. Further work is needed to establish whether the proposed algorithms are implementable and efficient enough to be used in practical machines, but initial simulations are promising. It is becoming clear that ideas such as randomising, hashing and combining are not restricted to the construction of tightly synchronised PRAMs, and can equally be applied to the development of efficient scalable interconnects for asynchronous concurrent computers.

7.4 VLSI Interconnect

The extent to which future VLSI can enhance interconnect capability is still unclear. The VLSI routing chips under development in the PUMA project each deliver total throughput of about 320 Mbytes/second. It is becoming clear that by fully exploiting VLSI, unprecedented interconnect performance can be achieved. It now seems likely that interconnect will become one of the major consumers of commodity VLSI. For parallel machines, the next obvious development is to design chips suitable for scalable processor-memory interconnects.

The total throughput of a routing node is limited primarily by packaging constraints. Even in present VLSI technology, it is possible to construct large crossbar switches (32×32) on a single chip, and deadlock-free routing algorithms with very small silicon implementations are known. Simply by increasing the channel width and increasing the pin-count, it would be easily possible to provide chips with over 1 Gbyte/second throughput.

The delay through the node is limited by the time taken to select an output on the basis of the first few bits of the message (provided the selected output is not busy). In fact, for certain interconnect structures, it is possible to make this decision on the basis of only the first bit of the message.

8 Conclusions

Concurrent machines can be constructed from two components: transputers and routers. Transputers can be connected via their links to form dedicated processing systems in which communication takes place only between directly connected transputers. They can also be connected via routers allowing system-wide communication.

The provision of system-wide inter-process communication simplifies the design and programming of concurrent machines. It allows processes to be allocated to transputers after a program is written in order to optimise performance or minimise cost. It ensures that programs will be portable between different machines, although their performance will vary depending on the capabilities of the specific communications network used.

Transputers and routers can be used to build machines in which a balance is maintained between communication throughput and processing throughput. Universal routing can be used to achieve bounded communication delay, and fast process scheduling within the transputers allows this communication delay to be hidden by a small amount of excess parallelism. An immediate possibility is the development of a standard architecture for general purpose message-passing machines.

Further developments of the transputer will extend the use of fast process scheduling to hide delays in both message passing and memory operations. Routers suitable for the construction of processor-memory interconnects will allow the construction of *scalable general purpose parallel computers.* These machines will combine the main features of message-passing machines and common memory machines. By investing sufficently in system-wide communication capacity, new levels of programmability and sofware portability will be achieved. These developments are central to the creation of a parallel software industry, and to the widespread use of parallel computers.

References

[1] M. Homewood, D. May, D. Shepherd, R. Shepherd, *The IMS T800 Transputer*, IEEE Micro, Volume 7 Number 5, October 1987

[2] INMOS ltd., *occam2 reference manual*, Prentice Hall, 1988

[3] L. G. Valiant, *A scheme for fast parallel communication*, SIAM J. on Computing, 11 (1982) 350-361

[4] L. G. Valiant, *General Purpose Parallel Architectures*, TR-07-89, Aiken Computation Laboratory, Harvard University

[5] L. G. Valiant, G, J. Brebner, *Universal Schemes for Parallel Communication*, ACM STOC (1981) pp. 263-277

[6] van Leeuwen, J., and Tan, R.B. *Interval Routing* The Computer Journal **30**(4) 298-307, 1987

A DISTRIBUTED IMPLEMENTATION OF SHARED VIRTUAL MEMORY WITH STRONG AND WEAK COHERENCE*

by

W. K. Giloi, C. Hastedt, F. Schoen, W. Schroeder-Preikschat

GMD Research Center for Innovative Computer Systems and Technology
at the Technical University of Berlin, Germany

Abstract

A *virtual shared memory architecture* (VSMA) is a distributed memory architecture that looks to the application software as if it were a shared memory system. The major problem with such a system is to maintain the coherence of the distributed data entities. *Shared virtual memory* means that the shared data entities are pages of local virtual memories with demand paging. Memory coherence may be *strong* or *weak*. *Strong coherence* is a scheme where all the shared data entities look from the outside as if they were stored in one coherent memory. This simplifies programming of a distributed memory system at the cost of a high message traffic in the system, needed to maintain the strong coherence. The efficiency of the system can be increased by adding a *weak coherence* scheme that allows for multiple writes by different threads of control into the same page. The price of the weak coherence scheme is the need for explicit program synchronizations, needed to reestablish at the end the strong coherence of the result. For the computer architect, the challenging question is how to implement a VSMA most efficiently and, specifically, by what architectural means to support the implementation. In the paper a new solution to this question is presented based upon an innovative distributed memory architecture in which communication is conducted by a dedicated communication processor in each node rather than by the node CPU. This will make the exchange of short, fixed-size messages, e.g., invalidation notices, very efficient. Therefore, it becomes more appropriate to minimize the overall administrative overhead, even at the cost of more message traffic. On that rationale, a novel, capability-based mechanism for both strong and weak coherence of shared virtual memory is presented. The weak coherence scheme is built on top of the strong coherence, utilizing its mechanisms. The proposed implementation is totally distributed and based on a strict need to know philosophy. Consequently, the elaborate pointer lists and their handling at runtime typical for other solutions is not needed.

Keywords: Distributed memory architecture, virtual shared memory architecture, strong and weak data coherence, communication hardware, parallelizing compilers

1. INTRODUCTION

Shared memory architectures offer the advantage that an application program can be automatically parallelized by the compiler, while dynamic load balancing may be done jointly by the operating system and the runtime system and supported by appropriate hardware [1]. This allows applications to be programmed as if the system were a conventional single processor architecture.

---

* This work was partly sponsored by the Ministry of Research and Technology of the German Federal Government, grant No. ITR 90022

However, large MIMD systems cannot be realized in any reasonable way other than as *distributed memory architecture*. For any sizable number of processors the access contentions to a shared memory would severely degrade the performance of the system. Moreover, only distributed memory systems are scalable. Scalability means that with the same hardware and system components one can realize the entire spectrum ranging from superworkstations to supercomputers with hundreds or thousands of nodes [2]. In a distributed memory architecture the nodes communicate through message-passing via the *interconnect*. This leads to a programming model consisting of a large number of cooperating processes that communicate through appropriate inter process communication protocols (IPC). There exist no global data objects; rather, data are encapsulated into processes. We recognize here one of the basic constituents of *object-oriented programming.*

However, conventional programming languages such as Fortran, Lisp, Ada, and C, have the view of *shared data objects* existing in a global address space and being accessible by various procedures. Computation is seen as a succession of state changes of scalar memory objects. Parallel processing is viewed in the same manner, with the proviso that now several memory states are transformed simultaneously in different *threads of control* (TOC). Consequently, parallelism is the fine grain parallelism of the primitive statements of the programming language. If one wants distributed memory architectures to become accepted by the majority of programmers, one must find ways to reconcile them with the conventional programming style.

The ideal solution would be to have a superbly intelligent compiler which performs a global data flow analysis over the entire program, parallelizes the program so that an optimal workload distribution is achieved, and puts the *send* and *receive* constructs needed for the communication among the cooperating processes and the synchronization of their activities into the right place. However, such a compiler is at least years way. For the time being it is a more practical solution to make the distributed system look to the application software as if there existed a global sharable memory. Hence, by building a *Virtual Shared Memory Architecture* (VSMA) on top of the distributed (physical) system [3], the advantages of the distributed memory architecture can be reconciled with the conventional programming style.

Independent of the question of programming style, VSMAs have an important advantage over distributed memory system: In the latter data are encapsulated into processes which, in turn, are statically distributed over the nodes of the system, whereas in the former data migrate dynamically to the site where they are needed. This advantage must be paid for by a loss in efficiency caused by the virtual shared memory overhead. Thus, it becomes a major challenge for the computer architect to make that overhead as small as possible.

Since in a VSMA copies of shared data items may be distributed over a number of nodes, the main problem is how to maintain the consistency of the shared data. This problem is analog to the well-known cache coherence problem in multi-cache architectures: The virtual shared memory takes the role of the main memory, and the local memories of the nodes take the role of the caches [3]. Several solutions to this problem have been proposed in the literature [4],[5],[6] and software solutions have been implemented in commercial multicomputer systems [7]. In this paper, we propose the novel solution of a capability-based implementation of shared virtual memory with strong data coherence. It will be shown how one can build on top of a strongly coherent shared virtual memory a *weak coherence mechanism* to improve the efficiency of the VSMA. By these mechanisms and in combination with innovative architectural support we expect to obtain a very efficient VSMA realization.

Our solution takes the *Shared Virtual Memory approach* introduced first by Kai Li [3], i.e., using as shareable entities the *pages* of the local virtual, demand-paging memories of the nodes. This approach has been much refined by adding a novel *weak coherence mechanism* in coexistence with the strong coherence scheme. This new approach has found an innovative, highly efficient implementation that is supported by appropriate architectural measures. Consequently, our scheme is expected to be orders of magnitude faster than a pure software solution [8].

2. DATA COHERENCE IN VSMAs

2.1 The Need for Synchronization

A program written for a shared memory system is not guaranteed to run correctly unless it contains synchronization constructs that enforce the appropriate order of data access as determined by the data dependencies in the program. In physically shared memory systems data access synchronization may be carried out implicitly by putting the memory accesses into the right order. However, in VSMAs with their many concurrent threads of control, which all may read and write the same data entities, it is safer not to assume a particular sequence of events but to synchronize the data accesses explicitly by *critical regions*.

That way the danger of incorrect program execution is avoided -- specifically when taking the weak coherence approach discussed below.

Locking and unlocking critical regions requires indivisible semaphor operations. Implementing a lock by agreement between N sharing nodes of a distributed system requires 2*(N-1) messages [9]. Thus, when executed by software the data access synchronization through critical regions in the VSMA program induces a considerable overhead that may readily exceed the IPC protocol overhead in distributed memory architectures. Consequently, specific architectural support should be provided to increase the efficiency of VSMAs. The most important single measure is to minimize the message passing overhead. Messages must be exchanged for two purposes: (i) to synchronize the concurrent threads of control of the VSMA program and (ii) to synchronize the data accesses. The latter is needed to obey the *data dependencies* in the program and to maintain the *data coherence* in the distributed system. The virtual shared memory is called *coherent* if the value fetched by a read operation is always the value written by the most recent write operation to the same location.

For efficiency reasons, the nodes of a VSMA operate on their own copies of a shared *primary data entity*. There exist synchronization points in the program (usually the beginning or end of critical regions) at which the consistency of the primary entity and its copies must be ensured. The thread of control (TOC) that has access to the primary entity is called its *owner*, and the TOCs that have copies of it are called *copy holders*. Data coherence may be *strong coherence* or *weak coherence* [10].

2.2 Data Coherence

First we introduce the general notion of a data entity and discuss afterwards details such as the appropriate granularity of entities and their representation.

DEF: Data entity

A data entity or, simply, *entity* is a set of data such that (i) the entire set resides in one and the same node and (ii) it forms an entity with respect to access capabilities. Entities may be private or shared. Under certain conditions several replicas of a shared entity may reside in the system, distributed over different nodes.

Strong coherence means that the coherence of the virtual shared memory is maintained at all times. In a VSMA, the node memories can be viewed as "caches" containing copies of certain data entities in the virtual shared memory. As in the case of caches, a coherence problem arises as soon as one of the copies is modified by a write access. In a VSMA, this happens whenever a TOC is granted write access to a data entity. The analogy to the cache coherence problem suggests the use of the *write-invalidate* technique usually employed to achieve cache coherence [3]. In a cache architecture, this is done by a *snoop logic* which monitors the instructions on the memory bus, detects write instructions, and consequently invalidates the cache lines involved. In a distributed memory system this must be performed by message passing.

Instead of the write-invalidate approach described above, a write-update scheme could be employed. In that case, rather than destroying all copies except for the primary entity, one only renders them temporarily inaccessible, updates them before the owner has handed the write capability for the primary entity back, and then uses them again. This approach reduces the copying overhead at the cost of increasing considerably the message passing overhead. In connection with the Shared Virtual Memory approach discussed below, the write-invalidate method is more efficient [3].

In many applications, shared data entities are the carriers of values exchanged between different nodes. This causes the need for alternating writes by different TOCs into the same entity. Strong coherence, however, does not allow for multiple writes by different sharers. This may lead to a situation where the data item must be copied back and forth among the sharers[3]. On the other hand, strong coherence among multiple reads and writes performed by different TOCs is not required if the programmer enforces the correct order of access between concurrent computations by appropriate synchronization activities (e.g., locks and unlocks). Assume that the several tasks of a parallel program are coherent within itself but not in relation to the others, unless this is enforced by explicit synchronization in the program. This situation is called *weak coherence* [10].

2.3 Using Pages as Data Entities: Shared Virtual Memory

While most data entities in a VSMA are private (owned by only one of the TOC), there exist also a number of shared entities. For each shared entity access rights must be issued for every entity. Performing this at the granularily of the single memory word would make a system overly inefficient. Therefore, one must look for a more suitable choice of data entities. Choices proposed in the literature are:

* the page of a demand-paging virtual memory [3]
* the cache line [11].

One question to be addressed is why one does not choose the objects of the high-level programming language directly as entities. This has the following reasons. Object types in von Neumann languages typically are scalars (single memory words), arrays, and structures. In our opinion, none of these types is very suitable for being introduced as an entity in the sense of the definition above. As was pointed out above, scalars are too small. Arrays, on the other hand, may easily be too large. Therefore, array operations are typically carried out on message-passing architectures by decomposing the array into subarrays and distributing the subarrays over the nodes of the system, to have them processed in parallel [12].

The solution to this problem is to base the virtual shared memory on the common virtual memory organization with demand paging [3]. In this case, the representation of data entities in the system is the *page*, i.e., a logical entity, the access right control of which can be readily integrated into the func-tionality of the memory management. The superposition of a virtual shared memory on a distributed memory system with virtual memory organization in the nodes is called *Shared Virtual Memory* [3].

The advantage of the shared virtual memory solution is that its management can be combined with the demand paging mechanism of the private node memory [4]. Copies of an entity that must be destroyed as soon as a process is granted the write capability for it can simply be tagged as invalid in their page descriptor. Any attempt to access an invalid page leads to a page fault in the same manner as if the page were not existent in the local memory. In both cases, the effect is that a new copy of that page must first be loaded into the private memory before computation can continue. This can be handled uniformly by the operating system in connection with the demand-paging virtual memory management unit (PMMU) in the node.

In contrast, the cache line is an arbitrary physical entity that does not have any meaning in the abstract machine model. We believe that one should prefer a meaningful logical entity (the page) over an arbitrary physical entity (the cache line) as the unit of access.

3. A CAPABILITY MECHANISM TO ENFORCE STRONG DATA COHERENCE

3.1 Rules for Granting Access Capabilities

3.1.1 Access Capabilities

Based upon the rationale given above, pages of the demand-paging virtual memories of the nodes of a VSMA are used as the shared data entities. In our approach, access to shared pages are controlled by granting access capabilities as defined below.

DEF: Access Capability
An access capability to a shared page is a quadruple:
(*page_id, access_right_specification,owner_id, copy_set_list_pointer*).

DEF: Access rights
An access right is either *read access* or *write access*. The read access is either *valid* or *invalid*.

DEF: Owner of a shared page with strong coherence
Each shared page has exactly one owner, which is the TOC that was the last one to have written into it. The page for which the owner holds the write capability is called a *primary page*. Replicas of the primary page for which other TOCs may have a read capability are called *copies*. The owner of a page lists in a *copy set list* all the other TOCs which have copies of that page.

3.1.2 Rules for Strong Coherence

In the following we present the two rules that guarantee that no TOC can read a page while another TOC is writing into it [3]. The rules also guarantee that a write capability cannot be taken away from a TOC while it is in a critical region.

Write Capability Grant Rule:
A write capability to a shared page can be held by only one TOC at a time, i.e., there is only one owner. On occurrence of a write fault in a TOC, the TOC will request the write capability from the current owner. As long as the owner is in a critical region, it can ignore the request; else it must honor it. Before granting the write capability, the current owner must change its capability from *write* to *read*. Subsequently, it sends the write capability together with the copy set list to the requestor. Before the new owner can exercise the write capability received, it must invalidate all other copies of that page by sending out invalidation notices to the TOCs in the copy set list.

Read Capability Grant Rule:
A read capability may be simultaneously requested from the owner by any number of TOCs. As long as the current owner is in a critical region, it can ignore the request; else it must honor it. Before sending the read capability, the current owner must change its capability from *write* to *read*. Subsequently, it sends the read capabilities together with a copy of the page to the requestor.

4. SHARED VIRTUAL MEMORY IMPLEMENTATION

4.1 The Linked List Solution

A solution proposed for the implementation of a VSMA is to have in each node an operating system server called *page manager*. The page manager administers the pages of the node and their access rights and requests access capabilities to additional pages in the case of page faults. Therefore, the page manager operates on a data structure called *page table* which has an entry for each sharable page containing [3]:

* the *owner field*, indicating the node that owns the page (executing the TOC that has most recently written to it);
* the *copy set* field, listing all nodes that have copies of the page;
* the *access right* field, defining the access right the node has to the page;
* the *lock field* used for synchronization of access to the page.

Changes of ownership of a page occurring during program execution can be handled by the following mechanism [3]. If the page addressed as the owner in a page fault request is not the owner any more, it forwards the request to the node designated by its owner field. That way, the current owner will eventually be reached.

Another approach is to have in each node for every shared entity a doubly linked list connecting the owner with the copyholders [5],[7]. That way the owner knows where to send invalidation messages, and the copyholders know where to get an updated page from after an invalidation. In case of a change of ownership, the linked list is extended accordingly at the site of the old owner; therefore, the copy-holders need not be notified about the change [3].

These list structures are very elaborate. If all sharable pages can be shared by all existing TOCs, than a copy of the page table for all sharable pages must exist in every node. Fortunately, this is not the normal case; typically, each TOC shares only a certain subset of the set of all sharable pages. In this case the page table in each node must contain only entries for the subset of pages shared by that node. The typical way to implement such a table is by hash coding.

The page table solution minimizes the amount of messages to be exchanged at the cost of having to store large lists in the node memory and burdening the node CPU with managing them. Nevertheless, it may be the appropriate solution if the startup time penalty for a message exchange is high, i.e., in the order of magnitude of several hundred microseconds typical for a fast software solution [13].

4.2 Innovative Architectural Support for the VSMA

In [14] we have shown that the communication startup time problem of message-passing systems can be greatly reduced by equipping each node with a dedicated *communication processor* (CP). This holds true specifically in the case that the node operating system must support multitasking. Multitasking, however, is a requirement for making a distributed memory system scalable and reconfigurable. In VSMAs there is another strong reason for multitasking: Since one cannot afford to let the system idle whenever a page fault occurs, there must be other tasks ready to be activated.

The communication between the CPU and the CP of the node takes place via *send* and *receive queues* as illustrated in Figure 1. When the CPU encounteres a send instruction, it only puts the send request into the send queue and goes on with its work. The CP, on the other hand, polls the send queue and executes the send requests. Another task of the CP is to put messages received from another node into the receive queue. On executing a receive instruction, the CPU goes to the receive queue and takes the message out. Thus, the CPU need not be interrupted. Moreover, in a multi-tasking environment, the CPU need not perform environment switches whenever communication takes place.

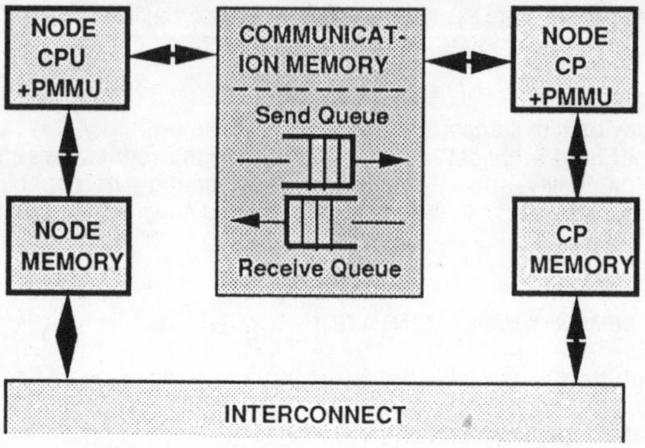

Figure 1 Communication between CPU and CP

Thus, a very efficient communication of short, fixed size messages is provided. The same mechanism is employed to establish the *rendezvous* needed to perform a secure data exchange between the address spaces of the different TOCs of the application program [13]. The data communication is supervised by an appropriate *lightweight* operating system process, supported by hardware DMAs in both the sending and the receiving node [13].

The CP in the node of a VSMA can readily perform also the functions of the page manager as described below. The copy set table the page manager must maintain for every page owned can be realized as a hash-coded associative memory. In this case, these tables can be stored in the private memory of the CP, and the CP may execute the hash function. Moreover, the CP -- rather than dedicated special hardware as proposed in [1] -- may support the node CPU in dynamically scheduling the concurrent execution of the tasks inside the node.

It can be shown that a very favorable interconnection structure for highly parallel MIMD systems is the hierarchy of crossbars, e.g., the *Simple TICNET* or the *Extended TICNET* [15]. Networks of this type combine a high connectivity (low probability of blocking) with a high transmission bandwidth and low cost of realization [15]. The specific demands on the interconnect put forth by VSMAs is the need for a very fast mechanism for conveying very short, fixed size messages from node to node. The very favorable blocking behavior of a hierarchical crossbar interconnect helps to meet that demand.

4.3 The Capability-Based Strong Data Coherence Mechanism

The capability-based strong data coherence mechanism implements the two governing rules given in Section 3.1.2, the *write capability grant rule* and the *read capability grant rule*. Capabilities follow the definition in Section 3.1.1 with the provise that in the case of a read capability the copy set is empty and need not be considered. As postulated by the rules, the owner of the page is responsible for sending a write or read capability to a requestor. In case of a read request, the owner node (more specifically, its CP) will just send a *read capability message* followed by a copy of the page. In case of a write request, the owner will send a *write capability message* followed by the copy set list. The new owner then must first send *invalidation messages* to all the nodes in the copy set. All three kinds of messages can be packed into one fixed message format, consisting of

$$(page\_id,\ op\_code,\ owner\_id).$$

The receiving CP uses the message to update the appropriate page table entry for the identified page in the demand-paging memory management unit (PMMU). The PMMU page table entries and the copy set lists are the only data structures needed in our approach.

Note that in our scheme strong data coherence is maintained at all times, regardless of whether a TOC that has a read capability to a page really is reading it. Our rationale is that if one has a very fast way of passing short messages, it is simpler and more efficient not to have to manage complex data structures and not to have to know anything about the state of the TOCs in other nodes. Short messages are exchanged directly between the CPs of communicating nodes, while larger blocks of data, e.g., pages or copy set lists, are transferred by a mechanism called *high volume data transfer* (HVDT) and described in [14]. For larger blocks of data the hardware (DMA) supported HVDT mechanism is the most efficient way of communication.

5. ADDING A WEAK COHERENCE MECHANISM

The weak coherence scheme allows for multiple writes by several TOCs into *different locations of the same page.* Some first implementations of the weak coherence scheme have been proposed in the literature [7], [16]. We present here a novel implementation which is implemented by aid of the strong coherence mechanisms defined above. Hence, strong coherence and weak coherence may coexist in a program. Our implementation is optimized for the VSMA described in Section 4.2.

We assume that a program block in which a multi-write is allowed is declared as a *weak block,* indicated, e.g., by a **begin_weak** - **end_weak** construct. In all program sections not declared as weak block the strong coherence protocol is obeyed by default. During execution of a weak block the ownership of the shared pages may arbitrarily change; i.e., when the weak block is left, the owner of a shared page may be the TOC who owned it on entering the block or it may be any other sharing TOC.

On entering the weak block the owner will send on request a *weak write capability* to any number of other TOCs. Inside the weak block all these TOCs can write the page concurrently. Eventually, on leaving the weak block, the different copies must be *merged* into one updated primary page that reflects all the changes made by the participating TOCs. Note that the weak block is entered from and left in a state of strong coherence.

This can be efficiently mechanized in the following way. Let $P_o = \bigcup_i p_{io}$ be the value of the original primary page. Let $P = \bigcup_i p_i$ be the value of the page after a multiple write. The new value P can be expressed by the identity

$$P = P - P_o + P_o = [\bigcup_i (p_i - p_{io})] + P_o$$

That is, the multiple writers form the differences $(p_i - p_{io})$ between the elements p_{io} of the primary page and the modified elements p_i. Each such difference can be viewed as an *update mask.* The updated page P is obtained by adding all the update masks to the original primary page P_o. Since different TOCs must not write into the same location there exists the additional condition:

$$[\bigcup_i (p_i - p_{io})] \cap [\bigcup_k (p_k - p_{ko})] = \emptyset,$$

if $\bigcup_i (p_i - p_{io})$ and $\bigcup_k (p_k - p_{ko})$ are the update masks of any two different writers and ø is the empty set.

The TOC that requests a weak write capability for a shared page receives from the owner a copy of the primary page P_o. As a first step, the CP of the receiving node duplicates that page. One copy will be used as *working copy,* the other one will be kept by the CP as *local reference copy.* From now on, the TOCs can concurrently write into their working copies.* At the end, they will subtract the local reference copy from the result to obtain the update mask. Subsequently, they will request the *strong write capability* from whoever the current page owner is at that time and update the page received. After the last sharer has done this, the result is the updated primary page in the sense of strong coherence. This mechanism allows the merge of all update masks to be performed in a distributed, pipelined fashion, rather than having one specific "page master" perform all the merges. Thus the potential bottleneck of a sequential merge is avoided.

It should be mentioned that any other strategy can be pursued in the merge operation; e.g., in certain applications it may be more efficient to perform a tree-structured merge. Unlike the solution described above, such a strategy will now require that the owner, who at the beginning distributes the multiple write pages, will also notify each writer where to send the result at the end. This information is readily available in the owners copy set list.

---

* Note that of N sharers only N-1 nodes need an extra local reference page.

6. CONCLUSION

The paper demonstrates that all the hardware support needed to implement the VSMA concept efficiently is to have a dedicated, fast communication processor in each node and to organize the private memory of the node as a virtual memory based on demand paging. Whether a broadcast capability would yield an additional gain (e.g., by broadcasting the invalidation messages) is a question for a more detailed investigation. One must consider that in the case of strong program locality broad-casting may not gain much; moreover, broadcasting does not go very well with the demand for a secure communication, i.e., a protocol with positive acknowledgement.

All the functionality of a VSMA with shared virtual memory, including the execution control of concurrent tasks, can readily and efficiently be provided by appropriate routines of a dedicated communication processor in the node. This leaves on the software side as the main effort the compiler issue. Specifically, the compiler for a VSMA should provide a favorable initial distribution of TOCs and data as well as a satisfactory page utilization of the shared virtual memory. Thus, the implementation of VSMAs raises a challenge as far as the compiler is concerned, presenting the opportunity for new, interesting research and innovative solutions.

Strong coherence can be maintained in a transparent manner without compiler support. This advantage must be paid for by a high page traffic because of the frequent page invalidations. *Weak coherence* lowers the page traffic considerably, however, requires explicit synchronization through the definition of *weak blocks.* This leaves the yet unanswered question to what extent this will put the programmer into the same situation as with distributed memory architectures, namely to have to explicitly program data access synchronization. There is one advantage with VSMAs, however: In the worst case, the user can fall back to working with strong coherence only, at the cost of a decrease in efficiency. The unique implementation proposed in the paper supports this by building a weak coherence scheme on top of a strong coherence mechanism, thus allowing both forms of coherence to coexist in the program.

References

[1] Anonymous: *PAX Standard Concurrency Control Architecture,* Revision 2.4 (Sept. 1989), Intel Corp. and Alliant Computer Systems Corp.

[2] Giloi W.K.: *Development of Future Supercomputer Architecture -- The Challenge of the Nineties,* Proc. 6th German-Japanese Technology Forum (1990)

[3] Li K.: *Shared Virtual Memory on Loosely Coupled Multiprocessors,* Ph.D.thesis, Yale University 1986

[4] Li K. and Schaefer R.: *A Hypercube Shared Virtual Mermory System,* Proc. 1989 Internat. Conf. on Parallel Processing, IEEE Catalog No. 89CH2701-1, 125-132

[5] Lenoski D. et al.: *Stanford DASH Multiprocessor,* paper submitted for publication 1990

[6] Haridi S., Hagersten E.: *The Cache Coherence Protocol of the Data Diffusion Machine,* in Odijk E. et al.(eds.): PARLE ´89 Parallel Architectures and Languages Europe, LNCS 365, Springer 1989, 1-18

[7] McBryan O.: *Aktuelle Entwicklungen im Parallelen Rechnen in den USA,* GMD Spiegel 1/89

[8] Stumm M., Zhou S.: *Algorithms Implementing Distributed Shared Memory,* COMPUTER (May 1990), 54-64

[9] Ricart G., Agrawala A.K.: *An Optimal Algorithm for Mutual Exclusion in Computer Networks,* CACM 24 (Jan. 1981), 9-17

[10] Dubois M., Scheurich C., Briggs F.: Memory Access Buffering in Multiprocessors, Proc. 13th Internat. Symp. on Comp. Architect., IEEE Publication No. 86CH2291-3, 434-442

[11] Cheriton D.R. et al.: *Multi-Level Shared Caching Techniques for Scalability in VMP-MC,* Proc. 16th Annual Internat. Symposium on Computer Architecture (June 1989), 16-24

[12] Kennedy K. and Zima H.P.: *Virtual Shared Memory for Distributed-Memory Machines,* Proc. 4th Hypercube Conference 1989

[13] Schröder W.: *Overcoming the Startup Time Problem in Distributed Memory Architectures,* Proc. Hawaii Internat. Conf. on System Sciences (Jan. 1991), IEEE publication

[14] Giloi W.K., Schroeder W.: *Very High-Speed Communication in Large MIMD Supercomputers,* Proc. 3rd. Internat. Conf. on Supercomputing (June 1989), ACM Order No. 415891, 313-321

[15] Giloi W.K., Montenegro S.: *High-Bandwidth Interconnects for Highly Parallel MIMD Architectures,* Proc. 24th Hawaii Internat. Conf. on System Sciences (Jan-.1991), IEEE publication

[16] Bisiani R., Nowatzyk A., Ravishankar M.: *Coherent Shared Memory on a Distributed Memory Machine,* Proc. 1989 Internat. Conf. on Parallel Processing, IEEE Catalog No. 89CH2701-1, 133-141

Store coherency in a parallel distributed-memory machine

Lothar Borrmann, Petro Istavrinos

Siemens AG, Corporate R&D, ZFE IS SYS 33
Otto-Hahn-Ring 6, D-8000 München 83, West Germany
Phone:++ 49 89 636 42350, E-Mail: borrmann@ztivax.siemens.com
Phone: ++ 49 89 636 45274, E-Mail: istavrin%isar@ztivax.uucp

1 Introduction

The European Declarative System (EDS) project, supported by the Esprit program, is concerned with the development of a scalable multiprocessor technology and with the implementation of a prototype to demonstrate the system. The underlying hardware for EDS is a message-passing machine supporting up to 256 processing elements (PE) with large private memories. The PEs are connected by a high speed delta network [War90].

It is the aim of the project to provide not only the parallel hardware but also some prototypical applications, parallel language subsystems, a parallel relational database and an efficient system software environment. The system software [Ist90] will also support a distributed virtually shared memory (DVSM).

There has been previous research activity to provide the shared memory programming model for distributed-memory parallel systems too [Abr85, Hsu89, Li86, Ram88, War88]. The usefulness of such a scheme has been discussed and is widely accepted [Bis88, Stu90]. In the following, we concentrate on those algorithms which are based on replication of memory objects. The basic scheme is to introduce a cache-like copying protocol for the memory objects, allowing several processors to access distributed memory without any communication overhead on subsequent accesses. This may lead to a situation where multiple instances of one memory object exist, raising a coherency problem.

While most approaches aim at achieving the coherency semantics of shared memory architectures with a shared bus by adopting some hardware cache protocols, we first investigate the coherency requirements of parallel applications. We distinguish three basic types of coherency: *strong ordering*, *sequential consistency* and *weak coherency*. We then explain the semantics of weak coherency and show different models of their realization on the EDS machine.

The models are discussed and the results of a preliminary implementation on a testbed will be presented.

2 Basic scheme

As a parallel program spreads its processes over several processing elements (PEs), shared data must be made available to the different PEs. The shared data may be allocated to one or more PEs. By dividing the address space in (MMU-supported) pages, the shared memory programming model can be implemented easily by sending read/write-requests to the PE where the page with the accessed data resides. To reduce the overhead involved with frequent request messages a cache-like copying protocol may be introduced, allowing a remote processor to do subsequent accesses without any communication overhead. With this scheme, each PE that reads from a certain page keeps a local copy of that particular page to speed up memory access (fig. 1). For our discussion only the algorithms based on replication of memory objects are considered as only this approach has the potential of reducing the average cost of remote read/write operations. Replication may lead to a situation where multiple instances of one memory object exist, which does not cause any problem as long as there are solely read operations. But as soon as write operations occur, different instances of one page will have different values stored in them, raising a coherency problem.

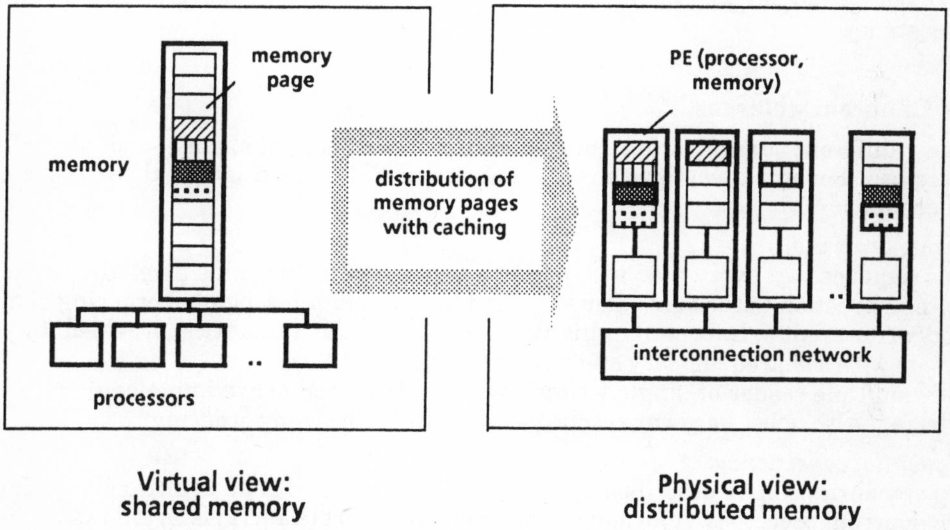

Figure 1: Memory distribution and caching

One of the best known schemes to deal with this problem is Kai Li's implementation of distributed shared memory on a ring of Apollo workstations [Li86] and on the Intel Hypercube [Li89]. The algorithms used realize a "multiple reader or single writer" protocol with exclusive *write ownership*. The scheme implies that any processor trying to issue a write must first acquire write ownership of the page and must ensure that all existing copies are invalidated, such that there is only one single copy during a write. This guarantees that all subsequent read accesses will refer to this up-to-date copy and will see the writer's modification. To allow multiple writers, ownership may be migrated among the nodes in the system. Similar schemes have been adopted for a number of implementations [For88, Roz88, War88, Cox89].

The basic restriction here is that exclusively one processor is allowed to update a piece of data only while no other processor is updating or reading it. This is ensured by invalidating all replicated memory objects. Thus global synchronization as known from a central bus must be established explicitly here. This can lead to a vast amount of synchronisation messages.

As a consequence, contention problems can arise. One writer will obstruct multiple readers by frequent page invalidations and the writer will be obstructed by frequent change of page properties from single writer to multiple readers. If there are concurrent writers to the same page, they will compete for write ownership and page thrashing is likely to occur. As the unit of "caching" is rather large (a page), the probability of "false sharing" is high, due to the fact that the same page may contain different data structures which are used independently.

The root of this problem is the approach to really emulate the behavior of a physically shared memory system. Such a high degree of coherency is actually not needed for parallel applications to run properly [Che86, Bis88, Ram88]. So in the next paragraph we will have a look at the semantics of memory coherence and consistency.

3 Coherency classes

Many different classifications of coherency have been published and formally described. For our investigations we found it useful to distinguish three types of coherency:

Strong ordering:
This requires that every read instruction always returns the value given by the last write instruction to the same address. Formally this implies a global ordering of all read/write-events. Informally this corresponds to the semantics provided by a system with a shared memory and a shared bus.
The "multiple reader or single writer" protocol described above implements strong ordering. Also, most hardware cache protocols provide strong ordering.

Sequential consistency:
The semantics can be described by a sequential system with an arbitrary ordering of concurrent processes. A formal definition by Lamport [Lam79] is as follows:

> "[A system is sequentially consistent if] the result of any execution is the same as if the operations of all the processors were executed in some sequential order, and the operations of each individual processor appear in the order specified by its program."

Every process thus observes the same sequence of events. In contrast to the first definition a process on a read access may not get the latest value written.

For multiprocessor systems without physically shared memory, this definition still imposes many restrictions and will produce performance trade-offs. So relaxing the coherency requirements is a broad research topic and some proposals have been issued discussing weak coherency [eg. Adv90, Hut90].
In the following section we will present our view on the requirements of store coherency and explain the semantics of weak coherency. A more formal treatment of this aspect is given in [Bo90].

4 Weak coherency

Our first observation is that in all parallel programs some form of synchronization is needed. The cooperating concurrent processes of the program have to take care of their synchronizations explicitly if a certain ordering of operations is required. Depending on the programming language used and the corresponding paradigm, synchronizations are explicitly included by the programmer, or they are invisible to the application program and implicitly included by the compiler or run time system. Even in uniprocessor systems with quasiparallel processes this synchronization is required.

In a DVSM system, we can exploit those synchronizations for the control of memory coherency. Thus we separate synchronization from exchange of data.

In a distributed system like the EDS machine, it is reasonable to base synchronization primitives on a message passing scheme. Semaphores and other synchronization mechanisms can be implemented using message-passing. Even in implementations which enforce strong ordering [Li86], synchronization mechanisms were realized on top of message-passing for performance reasons. We conclude that use of shared variables for synchronization purposes is not required.

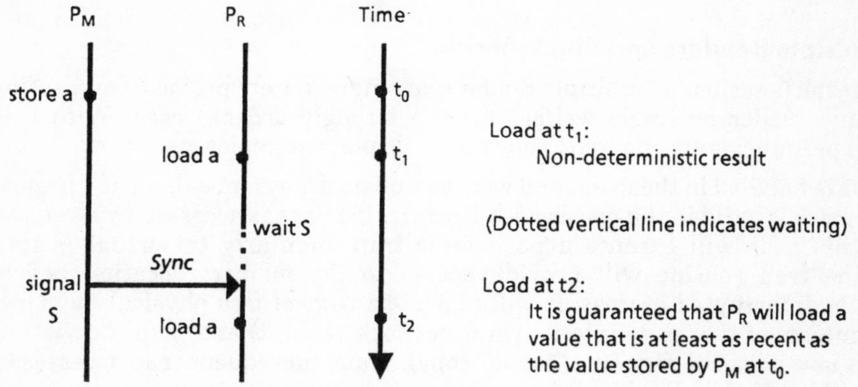

Figure 2: Coherency after Synchronization

Now let us consider two processes P_M and P_R using a shared variable a. Assume that there is no synchronization between them, except the one at S as depicted in figure 2. Hence, it is not decidable whether the first load operation of P_R will happen before P_M's store or after it. Thus, the load instruction will read a non-deterministic value, depending on the ordering of execution. From this we can conclude that even in the case depicted in the figure (load happens after store), it is not semantically incorrect, if the load operation reads the old value of variable a.

Thus, the propagation of the value stored by P_M can be postponed until an explicit synchronization establishes an ordering between the two processes, such that the load operation happens definitely after the store operation. This is true for the second load operation of P_R. The synchronization ensures that all operations after the *wait* call cannot be executed before P_M's *signal* call. In this case, it can be expected that P_R will see P_M's modification.

The above considerations show that updates to shared variables need not be made globally visible until an explicit synchronization requires this. Remember that synchronization itself does not rely on shared variables. Based on this insight, we can design a DVSM system using a *lazy update* strategy. Updates or invalidations are postponed until visibility of the newly written values is required. This does not only reduce the update and invalidation rate, but also allows a scheme where multiple processes can concurrently read data from a page that is being updated by a writer at the same time. It also permits multiple writers to the same page and thus provides a solution to the "false sharing" and thrashing problem.

4.1 Implementation models

The weak coherency model has a number of advantages for an efficient implementation. Updates to a memory location need not be made visible immediately. Only after an explicit synchronization from the writer to the reader, the writer's modifications have to be visible at the reader's site. The visibility of updates is undefined until guaranteed by a synchronization. In the following this synchronizations are called "coherency establishing synchronizations" (CES). Due to space restrictions, we can not discuss all options broadly, but will concentrate on two models that will be implemented for the EDS project.

4.1.1 Multiple Readers and Single Writer

This paragraph describes a "multiple reader *and* single writer" protocol contrasting to "multiple reader *or* single writer" for the strongly ordered case. With this protocol we permit exactly one write copy but multiple read copies per page.

Read access is handled in the usual and well-established way. Initially, each page of virtual memory is valid in the *owner node* P_O only. If a page is accessed by a remote node P_R, this node will execute a page fault trap. Similarly to virtual paging systems, the trap routine will provide access to the memory location before resuming the interrupted process. It will allocate a page of free physical memory, load the contents of the page into it (via a network request) and map the virtual page to this new physical page (the "cache" copy). Thus, subsequent read accesses to this page will be efficient local reads.

Like in the conventional implementation, it is only the write owner, which is allowed to update the page. Thus this is the node which owns the master copy of the page, i.e. the copy that incorporates the most recent changes. As the fundamental difference, multiple other nodes may read from their local copies while the master copy is being modified.

If the owner node alters a page, any other reader P_R will not see this modification immediately. To make modifications visible, the secondary copy has to be invalidated eventually.

Based on the requirements of weak coherency, these invalidations need not take place immediately. Instead, modifications are kept track of locally, and an accumulated invalidation message is sent out on initiating a CES. Multiple subsequent accesses to one page will only require a single invalidation message. Multiple accesses to different pages are also optimized as all invalidation information can be packed into a single message. In the course of a CES, all secondary copies of a page will get invalidated. Further accesses to that page will cause a new copy to be fetched from the master copy.

This lazy invalidation technique avoids effort to promote updates where it is not really needed. It avoids the obstruction of writers which are not concerned by the modifications in progress and thus is able to improve the exploitation of potential parallelism where the conventional scheme introduces unnecessary blocking.

The implementation can be similar to the one for strongly ordered systems, described by Kai Li [Li86]. Write-requests are sent to the PE which has the write ownership. This PE then replies with a copy of the page and then sets its own local page to read-only. Suitable algorithms are available to find the PE with write ownership, as this ownership may move. In the distributed scheme, the page tables are extended by an additional attribute *probable owner*. This attribute gives a hint on the location of the owner. If a PE receives a request for a page of which it is not the owner, it forwards the request according to the hint from its page table. The hint is updated under certain conditions, eg. when a request is forwarded.

An alternative solution avoids this non-determistic message routing by introducing a static *page manager*: While write ownership may move, there is one node, which is responsible for dispatching page ownership for a particular page. The page manager keeps track of the copied pages and grants write ownership to exactly one PE, it always "knows" which PE has the master copy. When another PE wants to write to that page, the manager forwards the request to the page owner, which in turn passes the write privilige together with an up-to-date copy of the page to the requestor. Thus page-requests are always send to the page manager first. Note that the job of managing pages is distributed for different pages. One page server per PE takes over the managing task for a number of pages. For the EDS implementation, we consider to have one manager for all pages of a *region* (a region is a contiguous area of virtual address space allocated by the user).

This scheme has the benefit that it is easy to implement and it scales well. It solves one of the major problems in the conventional approach, enabling multiple nodes to read from a page that is being modified. The problem of concurrent writers, however is still present.

4.1.2 Multiple Readers and Multiple Writers

This model attacks the problem of concurrent writers to one page. Our proposal retains the notion of a *page owner* for each page of memory. The page owner is the one PE that maintains the primary (most recent) copy of a particular page. Nevertheless, other PEs are allowed to update the page. To keep the master copy up-to-date, modifications have to be propagated to the page owner via the network.

Write Accesses of the owner of a page are directly executed on the master page. If a remote update to a page occurs, say on node P_M, data is written to the local copy *and* an update message is sent to the master copy (*write through*). Further nodes which may hold a local copy of that page are *not* notified. Thus all modifications will be collected in the master page. The remote writer P_M has to keep track of all pages modified.

The basic strategy for the implementation of the "multiple reader *and* multiple writer" protocol can be summarized as follows:

- All write accesses to a secondary copy update that copy and perform a *write through* to the master copy which is located at the owner PE.
- Each node keeps track of all write accesses of a task on a page basis.
  This has to be done only if either a secondary copy is accessed or the master copy is accessed and a remote copy of this page exists.
- When a thread initiates a CES then a list of the modified pages (invalidation list) is sent out by multicast.
- At an arbitrary time between reception of an invalidation list and the next resumption after a CES, all pages referenced by the invalidation list are invalidated by resetting a bit in the page table. The pages of physical memory that held the copies are returned to free memory.

This model does not require ownership to migrate, as the ownership is not associated with write access any more. However, as write accesses are more efficient when done by the owner, it is still worth while to provide for changing ownership as an optimization.

A difficulty that occurs on implementation of this model is the realization of the *write-through* mechanism if there is no particular hardware support. The software that implements the coherency protocol (eg. a DVSM-server) has to be informed when a write access to a replicated page happens. The method normally used is to set the page status to read-only forcing a page fault on each write access. This page fault is propagated to the DVSM-server. Now the update has to be performed on the local copy. One solution is to make the page writeable, then execute a single step of the faulting process and then set the page to read-only again and resume the process. This involves considerable software overhead.

An alternative solution is to have the DVSM server execute the write access. To be able to do this, the server must know the fault address and the value to be written. The efficiency of this method depends on the hardware support provided by the processor, ie. how easy this information could be obtained.

5 Applicability

We have shown that the weak coherency semantics are better suited for distributed shared memory than the traditional coherency semantics. It is evident that every parallel algorithm can be easily implemented based on weak coherency. Hutto et al. [Hut90] have shown how a number of algorithms can be implemented in a weakly coherent environment. Carter [Ben89] uses weak coherency in an object-oriented parallel programming system. In the Myrias system, weak coherency is exploited for the implementation of parallel loops ("parallel do" [Myr90]).

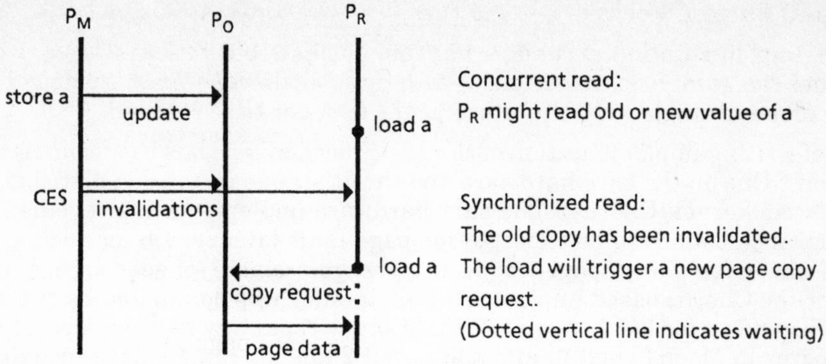

Figure 3: Coherency mechanism (P_O is the page owner)

In the scope of the EDS project it has been shown that weak coherency is well suited for the implementation of a parallel Prolog-like language [Ver90]. In the same project, a parallel extension of Common Lisp has been designed, which allows the expression of parallelism with the future construct [Ham90, Rad90]. It is also based on the weak coherency model. Synchronization points (CES) are included at the start and termination of a future. This is transparent for the application programmer.

6 Related work

Distributed memory implementations are strongly related to cache coherency schemes. The idea of utilizing weak coherency and the basic analysis of coherency requirements also emerged in this field of research [Sch87]. As simulations have shown [Tor90, Cha90] the performance gain for weak coherency is in the area of 10 to 30 % when used with directory based cache coherency schemes.

There are however some basic differences between the two disciplines:
- The unit of replication is usually a page for distributed shared memory systems (4 - 8 KByte) whereas cache coherency schemes operate on small cache lines (8 - 64 Bytes).
- As a consequence the distributed shared memory schemes show a higher degree of sharing thus leading to increased competition on memory objects.
- Due to the large memory objects, ownership schemes cause a higher load on the network and longer delays if conflicts occur.
- Cache coherency schemes are designed to be simple and implementable by hardware thus not utilizing all potential benefits of weak coherency. In general they exploit latency masking for write operations but do not adopt techniques like accumulating update messages.

Therefore we expect even better performance improvements in distributed shared memory systems.

7 Status and Future Work

A prototype implementation is under way on a small bus-based system with M68030 nodes to gain first experience with the weak coherency model. The "multiple reader and single writer" protocol is the first one to be realized.

At the time of writing implementation of the basic mechanisms has been completed in two versions: One on the bare hardware and the other one on top of a distributed operating system kernel (Chorus). The bare hardware implementation reveals the upper performance bounds to be expected for page fault latency: 1,8 ms including handling of the page fault, page request message, remote page copying and mapping. For the Chorus based implementation, latency was dominated by system overhead. We got 6ms for local page fault handling without any network operation (which compares to Mach [You89]) and additional 20ms for remote page copying. This comparison indicates that the integration of these schemes into operating system kernels is a crucial point which needs further investigation.

Ongoing efforts are targeted at the comparison of various DSVM implementation schemes to gain empirical evidence for the strengths of the weakly coherent model.

The target system for EDS, a 64-node system using Sparc processors but special-purpose hardware for network interfacing and remote memory accesses is currently being designed. The hardware will provide highly efficient message handling and support for page copying without CPU intervention on the owner node [War90].

Acknowledgements

We owe special thanks to Nic Holt of ICL, Manchester for the constructive discussions and all other members of EDS work packages 2 and 6, who participated in the design of the model and the implementation concept.

We are also indebted to the EC for sponsoring the work within project ESPRIT EP 2025.

References

Abr85 D.A. Abramson, J.L. Keedy "Implementing a large virtual memory in a distributed computing system", *Proc. of the 18th Annual Hawaii International Conf. on System Sciences 1985*

Adv90 Adve S.V., Hill M.D.: "Weak ordering - A new definition", *Proc. 10th Int'l Conf. on Distributed Computing Systems, Paris May 1990*

Bis88 Bisiani, R. et al. "Coherent Shared Memory on a Message Passing Machine" *Report CMU-CS-88-204, Carnegie-Mellon University*

Bo90 Borrmann L., Herdieckerhoff M.: "A Coherency Model for Virtually Shared Memory", *Proc. Int'l Conf. on Parallel Processing, St. Charles, Ill. August 1990*

Cha90 Chaiken D.: "Weak Ordering versus Multiple Contexts" MIT, Lab for Computer Science, July 1990

Che86 Cheriton, D.R. "Problem-oriented Shared Memory: A Decentralized Approach to Distributed System Design" *Proc. 6th Int. Conf. on Distributed Computing Systems, May 1986*

Cox89 Cox A.L., Fowler R.J.: "The implementation of a coherent memory abstraction on a NUMA multiprocessor: Experiences with PLATINUM", *acm operating systems review Vol. 23 No. 5, 1989*

Ham90 Hammer C., Henties T.: "Parallel Lisp for a Distributed Memory Machine", Proc. EUROPAL Workshop, Twickenham UK, 1990

Hsu89 Meichun Hsu, Va-On Tam "Transaction Synchronization in Distributed Shared Virtual Memory Systems" *Report TR-05-89*, Harvard University, Center for Research in Computing Technology, (1989)

Hut90 Ahamad M., Hutto P.W., John R.: "Implementing and Programming causal distributed shared memory", report Georgia Institute of Technology, GIT-CC-90-49, 1990

Ist90 Istavrinos P., Borrmann L.: "A process and memory model for a parallel distributed memory machine", *Proc. of the Joint Conf. on Vector and Parallel Processing, September 1990*

Lam79 Lamport, L. "How to Make a Multiprocessor Computer That Correctly Executes Multiprocess Programs", *IEEE Trans. on Computers*, Vol. C-28, No 9, (Sept. 1979)

Li86 Kai Li, Paul Hudak "Memory Coherence in Shared Virtual Memory Systems" *Proc. 5th ACM Symp. on Principles of Distributed Computing*, (Aug. 1986)

Li89 Kai Li, Richard Schaefer "A Hypercube Shared Virtual Memory System" *Proc. of the 1989 Int. Conf. on Parallel processing*, (Aug. 1989)

Myr90 Myrias Research Corporation, System Documents, Alberta, Canada

Rad90 Radlhammer M: "The Future of Futures", Proc. EUROPAL Workshop, Twickenham UK, 1990

Ram88 U. Ramachandran, M. Ahamad, M.Y.A. Khalidi "Unifying Synchronization and Data Transfer in Maintaining Coherence of Distributed Shared Memory" *Technical Report GIT-ICS-88/23*, Georgia Institute for Technology, School of Information and Computer Science, (1988)

Roz88 Rozier, M. et.al. "CHORUS Distributed operating systems", *Tech. Report CS/TR-88-7.6*, Chorus Systems, (1988)

Sch87 Scheurich C., Dubois M.: "Correct memory operations of cache-based multiprocessors", *14th Int. Symp. on Computer Architecture Conf Proc. 1987*

Stu90 Stumm M., Zhou S.: "Algorithms implementing distributed shared memory", *IEEE Computer May, 1990*

Tor90 Torrellas J., Hennessy J.: "Estimating the performance advantages of relaxing consistency in a shared-memory multiprocessor", ICPP proceedings, 1990

Ver90 Veron A., Xu J., Noye J.: "Using distributed shared memory for building complex applications: the Elipsys case", Esprit report EDS.WP.3E.DPS93, 1990

War88 David H.D. Warren, Seif Haridi "Data diffusion machine - a scalable shared virtual memory multiprocessor" *Proc. of the International Conf. on Fifth Generation Computer Systems 1988*, (1988)

War90 Ward M., Townsend P., Watzlawik G.: "EDS Hardware Architecture", *Proc. of the Joint Conf. on Vector and Parallel Processing, September 1990*

You89 Young M. W., "Exporting a user interface to memory management from a communication-oriented operating system", report CMU-CS-89-202

Using a Weak Coherency Model for a Parallel Lisp

Carsten Hammer, Thomas Henties
Siemens AG, ZFE IS SOF 22
Corporate Research and Development
Otto-Hahn-Ring 6
D-8000 Munich 83, Germany

Abstract The parallel language EDS Lisp has been designed for distributed memory machines. In this respect, it presupposes only a minimal required coherency in the storage view of parallel processes. This paper describes the coherency model of EDS Lisp and shows how the requirements of EDS Lisp can be realized using a weak coherency model on the parallel distributed memory EDS machine.

1 Overview

The objective of the Esprit project EP2025 EDS (European Declarative System) is to develop a highly parallel machine together with a parallel relational database subsystem and parallel versions of Prolog and Lisp. The system aims at supporting large knowledge based systems. Because the system is designed for a large number of processors, a distributed memory scheme had to be chosen. The design of hardware, operating system kernel, and the language subsystems went hand in hand to achieve a coherent hardware and software architecture. This paper focuses on the storage coherency aspect of the parallel EDS Lisp subsystem.

We will give a short overview of the parallel features of EDS Lisp in section 2. This section also describes the minimal requirements that the language demands for a consistent view of parallel accesses to shared variables. The minimal requirements are defined more formally in Section 3. They are given as weak coherency conditions of EDS Lisp and are used as an interface between the language and the machine. Section 4 describes those properties of the EDS machine that are relevant for the implementation of the coherency conditions. In the last section, we will show how the weak coherency conditions are used by the EDS Lisp parallelism constructs, and how these conditions can be guaranteed by the EDS machine.

2 The Language EDS Lisp

The language EDS Lisp [HaHe 90] is an extension of Common Lisp [Steele 84]. Common Lisp was chosen because it constitutes a de-facto standard and is used by large application programs. The extensions allow access to the parallel relational database of the EDS system and they provide explicit parallelism. The language has been designed for distributed memory systems. The main result of this design decision is the support of explicit large grain parallelism rather than automatic detection of low grain parallelism and a storage model that presupposes only a minimum of hardware support to run efficiently.

2.1 Language Constructs for Parallelism

EDS Lisp contains a single construct to spawn parallel processes, the *future* construct[Hal 85]. This construct is also used in different variations in other parallel Lisp dialects. The main idea of the future construct is that it immediately returns a placeholder for the result of the spawned process, before the spawned process starts execution. In functional languages, many operations can be applied to the placeholder without knowing the explicit result computed by the spawned process. If some process really needs the result instead of the placeholder, that process waits implicitly until the result is available. Neither the mechanism of the placeholder nor the implicit synchronisation is visible to the programmer.

Consider for example the following piece of Lisp code:

```
(setq x (future foo arguments))
```

Here, a parallel process is spawned to apply a function *foo* to its arguments. The placeholder of this function is immediately returned and then assigned to the variable *x*. Many operations can now be applied to the placeholder, such as assignments of *x* to other variables or list operations with *x*. Only if a strict function (i.e. one that needs the value itself, e.g., an arithmetic operation) is used, then the process performing this function waits implicitly.

The future construct is simple but powerful. It is not only used to spawn one parallel process at a time but can also be applied - using standard Common Lisp constructs - to lists of functions which will then all be evaluated in parallel.

A *wait* construct is provided for those cases where the user wants explicit synchronisation, for example if s/he wants to be sure that all side effects (like output) of a process are finished before another process continues. An example of this is

```
(wait x)
```

with *x* from the example above. EDS Lisp also provides mechanisms for critical sections (called exclusive functions or x-functions) and message passing via mailboxes [HaHe 90].

2.2 The Store Model of EDS Lisp

EDS Lisp assumes an indefinite number of processes with a common address space. On the language level this means that a child process inherits its parent's environment and thus can access its parent's data. In addition, spawned processes can of course have their own local variables. Note however, that a common address space does not necessarily imply a shared memory architecture.

The language definition of EDS Lisp states that the result of parallel write accesses to a shared variable is undefined. On the other hand we must guarantee a minimum of coherency for accesses from parallel processes. The language guarantees, for example, that a write access to a shared variable from a spawned process is available after (implicit or explicit) synchronization with that process.The example in figure 1 highlights this behaviour. A main process sets the variable *x* to zero and then spawns a child process. The child process can access the variable *x* with the value 0. In the child process, this variable is then set to 5. It is undefined which value is seen by the main process, because the relative speed of the processes is undefined. In particular, it is not defined if the value is immediately written through to

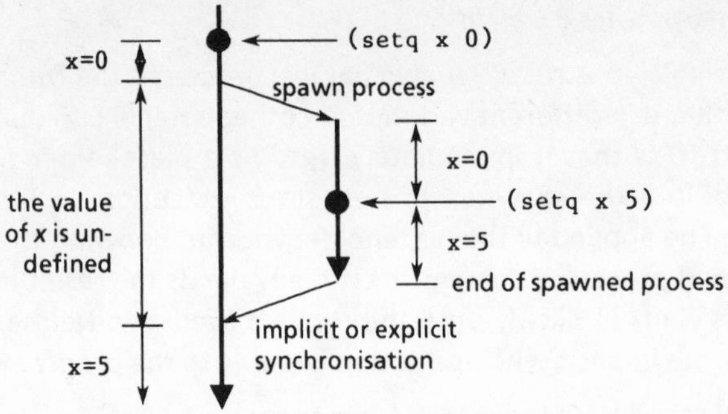

Figure 1: Unsynchronised parallel use of variables

the variable seen by the main process, or if the update is postponed. Only after a synchronisation between the two processes it is guaranteed that the main process sees the changed value of *x*.

3 The Weak Coherency of EDS Lisp

The weak coherency model defined in this section is a more precise description of what may happen to shared variables in EDS Lisp.

Because we have a parallel share-nothing architecture on the EDS machine, there is no global unique time valid for all concurrent processes. As usual, we can define a partial order between events in different processes that relies on the "*happens before*" relation defined in [Lamp 78]. The "*happens before*" relation (denoted by "$A \rightarrow B$") means that it is possible that event A causally affects event B. *Happens before* is defined as follows [Lamp 78]:

(1) If A and B are events in the same process, and A comes before B, then $A \rightarrow B$.

(2) If A is the sending of a message by one process and B is the receipt of the same message by another process, then $A \rightarrow B$.

(3) If $A \rightarrow B$ and $B \rightarrow C$ then $A \rightarrow C$.

Two distinct events are said to be *concurrent* (denoted by "$\|$") if neither $A \rightarrow B$ nor $B \rightarrow A$ is true.

In a synchronous shared memory system *happens before* is defined between any two events. Even in a distributed memory system there may be more *happens before* relations than are visible on language level (eg. reading a page that is local to another processor). Let "$\ll$" be a relation on language level such that $A \ll B$ implies $A \rightarrow B$. The semantics of "$A \ll B$" are that the user forces that event A to happen before event B (e.g., by implicit or explicit synchronisation, or by sending mail via a mailbox). With this relation we define the following weak coherency conditions.

Let W, W',W'' be write accesses and R a read access that denote accesses (potentially from different processes) to the same virtual address. The *weak coherency conditions* can then be defined as follows:

(1) write happens before read

If $W \ll R$

and there is no intermediate write access W': $W \ll W'$ and $W' \ll R$

and there is no concurrent write access W'': $W \parallel W''$

then R reads the value written by W.

(2) read happens before write

If $R \ll W$

then R does not read the value that is written by W.

(3) concurrent write and read

If $W \parallel R$

then it is undefined whether or not the reader will see the writers modification.

(4) concurrent writers

If $W' \parallel W$ (i)

and $W \ll R$ (ii)

then it is undefined whether R will read the value written by W or by W'. It may read either of those values.

Remark: If $W' \parallel R$ then (3) applies.

If $W' \ll R$ then no distinction can be made between W and W'.

$R \ll W'$ is impossible because (ii) and $R \ll W'$ implies $W \ll W'$, which contradicts (i).

The definition of "$\ll$" leads us to the term *synchronisation*. Some of the new language constructs allow the user control the ordering of events in different processes. A synchronisation between two processes is now defined to be an action that ensures that the "$\ll$-relation" between two events is defined and the weak coherency conditions hold.

A synchronisation is always anti-symmetric because it *orders* two events. If a synchronisation is defined between events E_1 and E_2 where $E_1 \ll E_2$ then E_1 is called *synchronisation initiating event* and E_2 is called *synchronisation receiving event*.

In this sense, uses of future results are synchronisations, as are passing messages via mailboxes and the spawning of a future itself. Here, the $\ll$-relation states that the environment of the spawning process (before spawning) is visible to the spawned process.

The memory model of EDS Lisp has been defined such that it can be supported on a wide range of memory architectures. Any coherency model that is stronger than the minimal model demanded by EDS Lisp can also be used.

We will show in section 5.1 how the different EDS-Lisp parallelism constructs can make use of the weak coherency requirements defined above. Thus we do not need to implement different coherency establishing mechanisms for each language construct, but we need only implement the $\ll$-relation. In section 5.2 we will describe how the $\ll$-relation can be implemented on the EDS machine.

4 System Support of the EDS Machine for Lisp's Storage Model

The main point of this section is the storage mechanism of the EDS system used to support the weak coherency model of EDS Lisp. Before we define this, we will give an overview of the relevant features of the EDS hardware and the EDS process and store model.

4.1 The EDS System

The EDS system is a homogeneous share-nothing, multiprocessor architecture. It can consist of any number of processing elements (PEs), a prototype will have 64 PEs. The processing elements are connected via a high-bandwidth delta network. The system is intended as an accelerator for one or more host processors also connected to the delta network. Specialised elements, such as I/O processors or a diagnostic node, can be connected to the network instead of PEs. Each PE of the prototype has 64 MByte local memory which can be extended up to 4 GByte per PE [WTW 90].

The EDS operating system supports a four level process model, that manages - in decreasing level of granularity - *jobs*, *tasks*, *teams* and *threads* [IsBo 90].

An EDS Lisp program is a task. A task provides a common virtual address space for all of its teams. For each Lisp task there is at most one team per PE. A task has at least one team, and a team consists of one or more threads. The threads are associated with processes on the language level, or are system threads (e.g., controlling access to critical sections or handling errors). The threads of one team are executed in a coroutine like manner, because they share one CPU.

When new processes are created by the future function, the relevant information to execute the future's body is first held locally on the PE where the spawning process resides. Depending on system load the future's body will be executed by a thread of the same team, or fetched by another team that is searching for work. Using this mainly passive scheme, high locality is achieved after a startup phase where new threads are stolen by teams on a lightly loaded CPU.

A team (i.e. a thread/process belonging to that team) allocates virtual memory on the PE where the team is located. This PE is called the *owner* of the allocated virtual memory pages, all other PEs are called *remote* PEs with respect to these memory pages. The physical memory associated with each PE is logically divided into two parts, one for owned pages and one for copies of remote pages.

Threads that belong to different teams of the same task never share physical memory. Instead, pages are copied to the PEs where they are needed. A caching like coherency mechanism for copied pages allows reading remote addresses without any communication overhead on subsequent reads. This approach is well suited for functional programming. But because Common Lisp (and thus EDS Lisp) is far from being a purely functional language, remote write accesses to shared variables whose owner is a different PE can occur. A simple classification of memory pages leads to different schemes that are used to handle remote accesses.

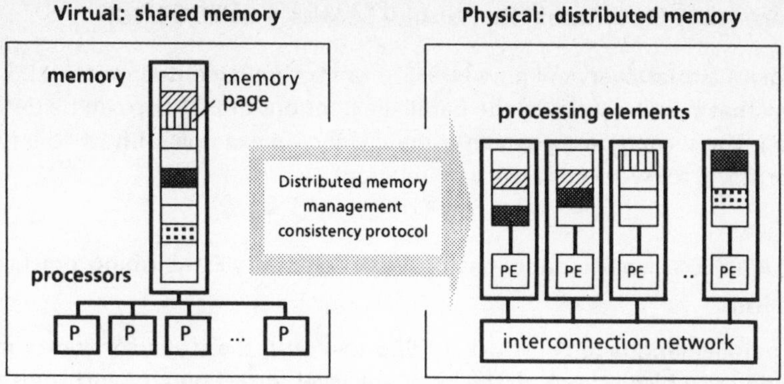

Figure 2: Store Model

4.2 EDS Lisp upon the EDS Store Model

To support the EDS Lisp store model (fig. 2) we make use of the read and write protection capabilities of the EDS machine. We have defined three properties *noncacheable*, *cacheable-with-update* or *cacheable-without-update* which are used if pages are accessed by remote PEs. Each page has one of these properties. Cacheable-without-update pages can be copied to other PEs but cannot be changed there. These pages are used for compiled code or constants. Noncacheable pages cannot be copied to other PEs and are used, for example, for future data structures [Radl 90]. Cacheable-with-update pages can be copied to other PEs where they can be changed. These are used for normal data including shared variables.

We have to distinguish between read and write accesses to remote pages. The mechanism for remote *read accesses* depends on the page property. If a page is accessed by a PE that is not owned by this PE and no copy exists on this PE then a page fault occurs. An exception thread then gets control and sends a message to the owner of the requested page. Before the owner of the page transmits that page, it insures that all previously received *write-throughs* (see below) to this page have been completed. If the page is noncacheable, only the demanded value is used. Otherwise the page copy is stored in the local memory. The page table is modified, so that further accesses to this address immediately use local accesses. Finally, the exception thread returns control to the interrupted program.

Write accesses to remote pages use the following mechanism. First, an exception thread gets control. If the data to be updated is present the modification will be made in the local copy. A so-called *write-through* message is sent to the owner. It causes the owner of the modified page to update the original. Both actions are performed in an arbitrary order by the exception thread, but it is an atomic operation to the user thread. Depending on the coherency protocol, other copies of this page may be invalidated at once, or after a synchronisation. If the page to be modified is not present only a write-through is performed.

Following the philosophy of lazy update, performing a write-through may be postponed until a subsequent synchronisation occurs.

Note that as long as there are no side effects in an EDS Lisp program, no write accesses will occur to cacheable-with-update pages.

5 Implementation Outline of the Parallel Features of EDS Lisp

This section gives a brief overview how EDS Lisp can be implemented on the EDS machine. First, we show that the semantics of the parallel extensions of EDS Lisp can be defined with the ⋖-relation. The second part gives an overview and an example of how to implement a consistency protocol for weak coherency (⋖-relation).

5.1 How to Map EDS Lisp Semantics onto a Weak Coherency Establishing Synchronisation Mechanism

To map the parallel language constructs of EDS Lisp onto the weak coherency model, we only need to define which actions on the language level correspond to synchronisation initiating and synchronisation receiving events.

Consider first the spawning of a future. A synchronisation takes place between the process that spawns a future and the future evaluating process (① in fig. 3). The synchronisation initiating event is the call of the future function. The future's body will be executed by some other process. The beginning of this execution is the synchronisation receiving event.

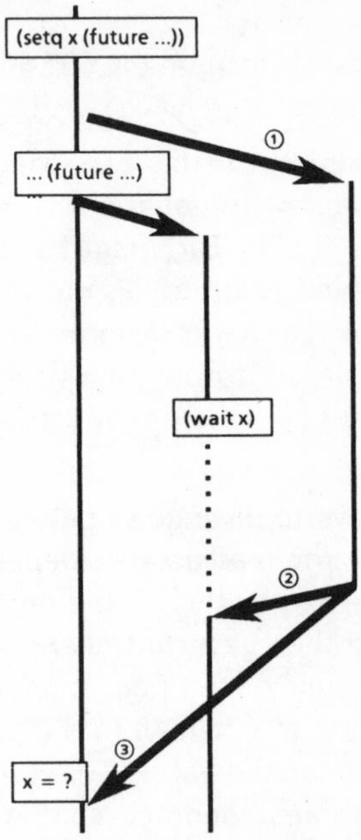

Figure 3: Synchronisation semantics for future

Further on, the execution of the future's body must be completed before a strict function can use the future result. Because side effects of the future are defined to be completed when the future result is available to other processes, the weak coherency conditions must hold between all actions done during execution of the future's body and all actions performed in any process subsequently to a strict access of a future result (③ in fig. 3). The weak coherency conditions are also satisfied if the access to a future result is not implicit but explicit (② in fig. 3) as in `(wait x)`. In other words, the end of an execution of a future body (that is, when the future result is stored), is a synchronisation initiating event. The implicit or explicit access to the future result is the synchronisation receiving event.

For mailboxes, a send operation is the synchronisation initiating event, and the receipt of this message is the synchronisation receiving event. Thus

`(send messagel mailbox)` ⋖ `(receive mailbox)`

holds, if the result of the receive is `messagel`.

For the other parallel extensions of EDS Lisp the synchronisation initiating and receiving events can be defined in a similar straightforward way.

If synchronisation events are expressed implicitly (e.g., the end of a future computation, usage of a concurrently evaluated value), it is not self-evident how control can be passed so that the intended synchronisation actions will be performed. All implicit synchronisation events are combined with an access to a future result. As already mentioned future results are stored in noncacheable pages. Every access to future results (incl. local accesses) cause invocation of an exception thread. The exception thread can access all information required to perform the synchronisation actions (e.g., the location of the process that tried to evaluate this particular future result). This is described in more detail in [Radl 90, HaHe 90].

5.2 Implementation Variants for Weak Coherency

As shown above the semantics of all EDS Lisp constructs concerning different processes can be described by synchronisations. In this section, an example shows how a synchronisation mechanism can be implemented for the EDS machine. In general there are four possibilities where actions may be performed to guarantee the weak coherency conditions:

(1) when writing to a shared location,
(2) when initiating a synchronisation,
(3) when receiving a synchronisation,
(4) when reading a shared location.

If most of the work is done at (1) this leads to a strong coherency model where "a processor is allowed to update a piece of data only while no other processor is updating or reading it" [LiHu 86]. If all the work is done at (4) this is close to performing an RPC (remote procedure call) for each memory access. In this case each virtual memory location is physically present only once, and therefore this is another way to achieve strong coherency.

In our approach we focus on coherency establishing strategies where the major part of the work is done in (2) or (3). We have worked out two different strategies for implementing a protocol that fulfills the weak coherency conditions. The main difference between the protocols is whether the invalidation of page copies is controlled by the synchronisation receiving process or by the synchronisation initiating process.

A sketch of the second protocol is given below, where we focus on the cacheable-with-update pages, because this is the important case concerning weak coherency. A more detailed description of the protocol and a general discussion of virtual shared memory can be found in [Bols 90].

For write accesses to remote pages a write through is performed. If other copies exist, an invalidation message is sent to all PEs holding a valid copy of this page. The invalidation messages are performed and acknowledged asynchronously. When the owner eventually receives all acknowledge messages, a final asynchronous message is sent to the PE where the write through occurred. Of course invalidation must also be done if an owner writes to a local page that has valid copies.

When a synchronisation is initiated it is checked that all invalidations corresponding to previously performed write throughs are acknowledged. It is ensured that there are no pending write-throughs to owned pages.

In this protocol the receiver of a synchronisation has nothing to do, because all necessary invalidations are already completed (and acknowledged). A subsequent access to invalidated shared data is the same as if the data were not present: a new copy must be fetched from the owner.

This protocol guarantees the weak coherency conditions. Assume some data is written in one process and read by another process after a synchronisation. If there does not exist a copy of the data at the PE where the reading process runs, a new copy is fetched from the original. The update of the original must be completed, because a write through is an atomic operation (as is a local write). Therefore the new copy contains the desired value unless another write changed it in the meantime, but in this case a deterministic value is not required by the weak coherency conditions.

A copy of the page containing the data that is changed cannot "survive" a synchronisation. That is because the synchronisation initiator waits until all invalidations of previous changes are acknowledged. Therefore a valid copy on the PE must be fetched after the invalidation, and therefore after the data was changed.

Synchronisation initiating always *happens before* synchronisation receiving. Either both events take place on the same PE (and condition (1) of *happens before* holds) or synchronisation relies on message passing (condition (2) of *happens before* holds).

Now it is obvious that the second weak coherency condition holds. A read access, a subsequent synchronisation initiation, the corresponding synchronisation receipt and a subsequent write is a sequence of events where *happens before* is defined. That means that the write access is physically later than the read access, and therefore cannot affect the value that was read before.

The third weak coherency condition holds trivially, because it does not require a unique result. As already shown before, the fourth condition can be reduced to the conditions one to three.

The protocol above shows how weak coherency can be established on the EDS machine. Additionally a strong coherency model will be provided. This will be helpful for debugging of schedule dependent errors, as well as measuring the performance benefit of weak coherency.

6 Comparison to Other Parallel Lisp Systems

Almost all other parallel Lisp systems have been developed for shared memory machines. One exception is Butterfly Lisp [SABS 86] which runs on the distributed memory Butterfly machine where a shared memory view is supported by hardware (called "non uniform shared memory"). Therefore Butterfly Lisp needs not care about the problems dealing with distributed memory.

Top Level Common Lisp [TL 90] can specify different grain sizes for running processes with shared or own environment. Virtually shared memory is not supported. Different grain sizes can therefore have different semantics with respect to accesses to global variables. In addition, the semantics for global accesses may change with the scheduling. In EDS Lisp, semantics of global variable accesses is independent of process scheduling.

A more detailed comparison of EDS Lisp to other parallel Lisp systems can be found in [HaHe90].

7 Summary

EDS Lisp is an extension of Common Lisp that has been designed for parallel distributed memory machines. The language guarantees the visibility of changes to shared variables only after an implicit or explicit synchronisation. We have defined weak coherency conditions that describe this behavior. Using these conditions, it is explicitly stated whether accesses to shared variables are deterministic or nondeterministic. These conditions serve as an interface between the parallelism constructs of EDS Lisp and the EDS system. We have shown how the weak coherency conditions can be satisfied by the EDS system. Any coherency model that is stronger than the minimal model demanded by EDS Lisp can also be used.

References

[BoIS 90] L. Borrmann, P. Istavrinos: "Store Coherency in a Parallel Distributed Memory Machine"; submitted to the Second European Distributed Memory Conference (EDMCC2), Münchem April 1991

[HaHe 90] C. Hammer, Th. Henties: "Parallel Lisp for a Distributed Memory Machine"; Lisp Europal Workshop "High Performance and Parallel Computing in Lisp" London November 1990

[Hal 85] R. Halstead: "Multilisp: A Language for Concurrent Symbolic Computation"; ACM Transactions on Programming Languages and Systems, October 1985

[IsBo 90] P. Istavrinos, L. Borrmann: "A Process and Memory Model for a Parallel Distributed Memory Machine"; Joint Conference on Vector and Parallel Processing, Zürich Sep.1990

[Lamp 78] L. Lamport: "Time, clocks and the ordering of events in a distributed system"; CACM Vol 21 pp. 558-564 1978

[LiHu 86] K. Li, P. Hudak: "Memory Coherence in Shared Virtual Memory Systems"; 5th ACM Symp. on Principles of Distributed Computing, 1986

[Radl 90] M. Radlhammer: "The Future of Futures"; Lisp Europal Workshop "High Performance and Parallel Computing in Lisp", London November 1990

[SABS 86] S. Steinberg, D. Allen, L. Bagnall, C. Scott: "The Butterfly Lisp System"; Proceedings of the August 1986 AAAAI, Volume 2, Philadelphia, PA, pp. 730

[Steele 84] G. Steele: "Common LISP: The Language"; Digital Press, 1984

[TL 90] "Top Level Common Lisp Reference Manual"; Top Level Inc., Mass., USA, January 1990

[WTW 90] M. Ward, P. Townsend, G. Watzlawik "EDS Hardware Architecture" Joint Conference on Vector and Parallel Processing, Zürich Sep.1990

Flexible User-Definable Memory Coherence Scheme in Distributed Shared Memory of GALAXY

Pradeep K. Sinha, Hyo Ashihara, Kentaro Shimizu, Mamoru Maekawa

Department of Information Science,
Faculty of Science, University of Tokyo
7-3-1 Hongo, Bunkyo-Ku, Tokyo-113, Japan

1. Introduction

A *distributed system* is a collection of several autonomous processors having their own memory, secondary storage and other devices. Each processor with its memory, secondary storage and other devices is called a *node* of the distributed system. All the nodes of the system work cooperatively to execute the jobs to be processed by the system. One important scheme necessary for the creation of this cooperative working environment in a distributed system is the scheme for distributed shared memory coherence. Several proposals for this have been made in the past [1, 2, 3, 8, 9, 12, 13]. However the proposed schemes lack all or some of the following facilities which can be considered important from flexibility and efficiency points of view:

(a) Facility for dynamically defining or declaring variable-size of the shared storage space. This facility is necessary for the realization of flexible, uniform and simple but powerful structures for use by the various processes of the system.

(b) There are two basic data sharing mechanisms [3]: *copy sharing* and *original sharing*. The existing distributed operating systems such as IVY [13], Accent [3], V system [2], etc. do not necessarily differentiate between the two types of sharing mechanisms. Hence the users of these systems do not have the flexibility to choose and use the exact type of sharing mechanism desired to meet their particular application needs.

(c) In the existing distributed systems variables or storage spaces are either shared or unshared for the entire application program currently operating on the data. Their shared status cannot be changed dynamically within an application. It would be nice for the users if they had the flexibility to dynamically bind and unbind the shared storage spaces to meet the dynamically changing needs of their applications.

(d) Use of problem-oriented consistency of shared data for improving system efficiency was proposed by Cheriton [2] and subsequently used by some other systems [1, 9]. However, the proposals made in the past are either not precise or difficult for the users to apply. For example, Cheriton's [2] discussion is case by case and limited only to the system processes. Munin's [1] type-specific mechanism requires the users to specify the type of their application which may not be easy for the users to guess. In order to extract maximum benefit out of this facility, the best approach will be to provide this facility to the users in a manner which is easy for them to use.

(e) The existing systems also lack the facility to dynamically declare the subject (processes) to whom a consistent view of the shared data should be presented at any instance of time.

In this paper we present the concepts and mechanisms for designing a distributed operating system that provides all the above mentioned facilities to its users. The first three of these facilities are provided by the *copy*, *unify* and *split* primitives that basically help in constructing a flexible and uniform address space which is simple to use. The remaining facilities are provided by our relaxed consistency control mechanism which can be tuned to satisfy the varying needs of all types of applications. The most attractive feature of our approach is that all these facilities are thrown open to the users for selecting and specifying the most suitable approach for their particular application needs. Thus the users have their own choice to tune the efficiency of the system based upon the needs of their applications. The concepts and mechanisms proposed in this paper have been developed in the GALAXY distributed operating system [6, 10, 11] which we are now implementing.

2. GALAXY's Uniform Address Space

GALAXY's *uniform address space* is a network-wide virtual address space which covers all the nodes of the system. This address space is segmented where a segment is an object (primarily file) or a portion of an object mapped to the address space for use by one or more processes. For ease of implementation, segment sizes are in multiples of page size. Now to provide the facilities of original as well as copy sharing with dynamic binding and unbinding of variable size shared data segments, we provide the following primitives to the GALAXY users:

1. Copy(*src_object, src_address, dst_object, dst_address, npages, transfer_flag, real_flag*)

   Copy is the basic primitive for copy sharing in GALAXY. *npages* of data contained at the position *src_address* in the object *src_object* is copied to the position *dst_address* in the object *dst_object*. If *transfer_flag* is set, the data is transferred in which case the source area is not guaranteed to contain the same data after the copy. The copy primitive is implemented by copy-on-write for the copy within a local node and by copy-on-reference for the copy across the node boundaries. The copy-on-write or copy-on-reference mechanism is not applied when *real_flag* is set.

2. Unify(*src_object, src_address, dst_object, dst_address, npages, read_flag, real_flag*)

   Unify is our basic primitive for original sharing. It is basically used to dynamically bind the shared data areas which need to be consistent. The area specified by *src_address* and *src_object* are unified to the area specified by *dst_address* and *dst_object*. After the unification, they have the same contents and the data written to one area can be accessed from the other. An object (or part of it) can be unified to many objects. For implementation reasons, the unification cannot be recursive although it can be nested. Therefore, the unification yields a tree-structured relation among objects. If *read_flag* is set, *dst_object* becomes read-only even if both the objects are writable. The unification is implemented by physical sharing within a local node. If *real_flag* is set, this operation is limited to be local. Unification to a remote object is implemented by the mechanism of caching of the source object.

3. Split(*object1, address1, object2, npages*)

   This primitive allows dynamic unbinding of shared address spaces. Two objects *object1* and *object2* which have been already unified for the purpose of original sharing can be split by using this primitive. Note that the source area may be only a part of the unified object instead of the full object. In this case, the source is specified by the position *address1* in *object1* and the length of the area to be split is specified by *npages*.

3. GALAXY's Approach for Relaxing Consistency

In GALAXY strict coherency of shared memory is relaxed based on user specifications. The granularity of consistency relaxation is at operation level within an application instead of application level. By allowing dynamic binding and unbinding of shared spaces within an application through our unify and split primitives and then by further allowing operation level consistency relaxation within an application, we actually provide the facility of nested fine grained consistency relaxation within an application by our flexible memory coherence scheme. The methods of consistency relaxation identified by us for this purpose are as follows:

1. Time-t read: A time-t read operation requires that the read operation be carried out only if all the updates generated before time-t for the shared data have been carried out. That is, the read operation be blocked until these update operations have been carried out on the copy of the shared data being accessed for the concerned read operation. The data may or may not reflect the result of any operation carried out on the data after time-t. This is the same as the t-bound requirement defined by Garcia-Molina et. al. [4].

2. Time-t update: A relaxed consistency of degree time-t update means that the user application will not be affected if the current update operation is transmitted to all the other copies of the shared data at time-t. This type of consistency relaxation is normally useful in case of applications dealing with non-deterministic computation for simulations, numerical analysis, etc. in which every update operation need not necessarily be made immediately to all the copies of the shared data.

3. Process-group consistency: Unlike the above two methods which are for time-wise consistency relaxation, this method is for space-wise relaxation of consistency. A *process-group* is a set of processes which belong to a single group. Now a *process-group consistency* of a particular shared data requires that all the copies of the shared data have the same content at the time of any read operation that is carried out by any of the processes belonging to the process-group.

3. SYNCH Facility: SYNCH facility is basically used for the synchronized execution of two or more processes. Thus in this type of sharing of data, two processes do not access the shared data simultaneously. Rather a process uses it (probably updates it during use) and then sends a SYNC message to the next process that wants to use this data along with the information about updates carried out on the data. This update information is used at the next process's node to update its version of the data before starting to use it. Thus all update messages are accumulated and sent to the next process along with the SYNCH message. Note that the update messages need not be sent to all the processes sharing that data but the style of sharing requires that it be sent only to the next process that is going to operate on it. So the SYNCH facility is actually a combination of both time-wise and space-wise relaxation of consistency of shared data.

4. Basic Primitives for Consistency Control

1. process_group_id = define_process_group(*list of processes*)

This primitive is used by the users to define a process-group. A new process-group may also be defined in relation to one or more existing process-groups such as:

process_group_id_i - list of processes, process_group_id_j + list of processes, process_group_id_i + process_group_id_j, etc.

2. data = read (*object_id, offset, byte_count, time_t, unit_of_time, process_group_id*)

   Object_id specifies the desired object. *Offset* and *byte_count* specify the position and size respectively of the desired data within the object *object_id*. *Time_t* parameter specifies the time boundary for the relaxed consistency desired for the read operation. The specified time may be in absolute or relative form. For relative time specification which is always relative to the current clock time, second, minute or hour may be specified as the *unit_of_time* for the calculation of the exact point of time desired. If the time is relative, it always signifies a point of time before the current clock time. The *process_group_id* parameter specifies the processes which should have consistent values of the data when the shared data is read.

3. write(*object_id, offset, data_address, data_size, time_t, unit_of_time*)

   The *object_id, offset, time_t* and *unit_of_time* parameters have the same meaning as described for the read operation. However in this case if the time is relative, it always signifies a point of time after the current clock time. The *data_address* specifies the address of the new data to be written. The *data_size* parameter specifies the size of the new data to be written in number of bytes.

4. SYNCH(*next_process_id, object_id, update informations*)

   The *next_process_id* specifies the process to which the SYNCH message is to be sent. *Object_id* specifies the shared object and *update informations* specify the updates to be carried out on the shared object before it can be used.

5. Implementation Details of Distributed Shared Memory in GALAXY

The collection of memories of all the nodes in GALAXY is treated as a single virtual memory space. For ease of handling, GALAXY's memory space is paged. A page is the minimum unit of synchronization which migrates from one node to another on demand. There is a memory manager at each node of the system which is responsible for satisfying both local and remote requests and also for implementing the protocol for distributed shared memory coherence. When a reference to a page in the shared memory space is generated, the faulting process is blocked and the memory manager checks if the desired page is resident in its local storage. If the page is not stored locally, a network page fault is generated and the missing page is brought from a remote node. The process generating the page fault resumes execution only after the desired page has been acquired. Thus the first step in the management of distributed shared memory is the mechanism for page fault handling. GALAXY's page fault handling mechanism is built on top of its object locating mechanism. Thus before discussing about the mechanism of page fault handling, we will give a brief description of GALAXY's object locating mechanism.

5.1. Object Locating Mechanism

Object locating not being the subject of this paper, only the functionality of GALAXY's object locating mechanism that is felt necessary for this paper will be very briefly presented here. The details of our object naming and locating mechanisms are given in [11].

In addition to user defined names, every object in GALAXY has a system defined name called *Unique ID* (ID in short). An object's ID is unique in the entire system. In GALAXY, one object can have multiple replicas. All replicas of an object use the same ID irrespective of their locations. For mapping of IDs to the physical locations of replicas, all the IDs of the entire system are stored in a system-wide table called *ID Table*. An ID Table entry (called IDTE) contains all the information necessary for accessing the corresponding object. Out of these, the *replica list* plays an important role in our page fault handling mechanism. It basically returns all the locations of the desired object as a result of the object locating operation. In our method, the node number whose value is nearest to the value of the client's node is selected from the replica list for servicing the access request. This selection policy is based on the assumption that node numbers are assigned in our system on the basis of network topology. That is, the difference between the values of the node numbers of far off nodes is larger as compared to the difference between the values of the node numbers of nearby nodes. Sufficient gaps between node numbers are left at the time of assigning the node number values to various nodes in order to facilitate future expansion of the network.

In GALAXY, each node has a partial copy of the ID Table and an IDTE may be replicated on several nodes depending upon its possibility of use at a particular node. Our replication policy of the IDTEs at the various nodes ensures the direct locating of any object from any node given the object's ID. Thus when a process wants to access an object, it can know the replica locations of the desired object by searching only its local IDTEs and extracting the concerned object's replica list from the local copy of the ID Table.

5.2. Page Fault Handling

The main issue in page fault handling in distributed shared memory is the management of page ownership information for locating the current owner of a particular page at any instance of time. Li et. al. [8] proposed several algorithms for this purpose: centralized manager algorithm, fixed distributed manager algorithm, broadcast based distributed manager algorithm and dynamic distributed scheme based on the use of probable owners. These mechanisms suffer from one or more of the following problems: low efficiency, low reliability, limited to the use of very small networks, difficult to find a good static distribution function, etc. To overcome the limitations of these methods, GALAXY services a page fault by consulting one of the replica locations of the object to which the desired page belongs. For this, each node maintains a pages-in-use table (PIUT) having the following fields for each of its entries:

1. *Object_ID*: This is the identifier of the object to which the desired page belongs.
2. *Offset*: Gives the page location within the object. Its unit is number of pages.
3. *Owner*: Node number which is the current owner of the page.
4. *Memory address*: Location of the page in the local memory if the page is loaded in the memory of the local node else its value is NULL.
5. *Copy list*: If the local node is the owner of the page then this field contains the list of nodes having a copy of the page in their memory else its value is NULL.
6. *Lock*: It is used for locking the page to synchronize simultaneous accesses made by two or more processes to the page.

7. *Status*: It is used to keep track whether the page is invalid.

Now page faults in case of read and write operations are handled according to the algorithms given below.

Read fault handling: The following steps are carried out in this case:

1. Search the local ID Table entries to get the replica list for the desired object.
2. Let the client node be N_c. Select the node (say N_s) from the replica list which is nearest to N_c according to the policy mentioned in Section 5.1.
3. Send a request from node N_c to node N_s for the desired page of the object.
4. If the requested page is present in the PIUT of node N_s then this page is already in use. So go to step 9.
5. Otherwise this page is not yet in use. So the page is entered in the PIUT of node N_s with node N_c as its owner and the page is sent from node N_s to node N_c.
6. Node N_c enters information about this page in its local PIUT and enters its own node number in the owner and the copy list fields.
7. Using the replica list, node N_c sends a message to the other replica locations indicating its ownership of the page.
8. The replica locations use this message to create an entry for this page in their local PIUT and the fault handling process finishes.
9. The PIUT is consulted to get the owner node (N_o) of this page and a message is forwarded from node N_s to node N_o indicating the request made by node N_c.
10. Node N_o returns a copy of the desired page to node N_c and adds node N_c to its copy list.
11. Node N_c enters the details of the page and its ownership information in its local PIUT and the page fault handling process finishes.

Write fault handling: Steps 1 to 9 for write fault handling are the same as that for read fault handling. Steps 10 and 11 that are different from read fault handling are given below:

10. Node N_o sends the page along with its copy list to node N_c and changes its owner field in PIUT to node N_c. The copy list field of the PIUT in node N_o for this page is also reduced to NULL.
11. Node N_c sends a message to the nodes in the replica list which is used by those nodes to update the ownership information for this page in their PIUT. The write fault handling process finishes with this.

It may be noted that the copy list of a particular page is maintained only by the owner node. At any instance of time there can be only one owner node for any page that is in use and a node must obtain ownership right for a page before performing write operation on that page. Each replica location of an object maintains information about the owner node of any page which belongs to that object and which is in use. Thus consulting any one of the replica locations of the concerned object to which the desired page belongs gives the information about the owner of the concerned page. Whenever the owner of a page changes in the system, the concerned object's replica locations are informed to update this information in their PIUT. Note that in this mechanism if a page is already in use, every new page fault causes the page to be transferred from the owner node to the client node. Thus the updating of copy list at the owner node in this case only requires the addition of the client node number which is already available at the owner node in the request message.

5.3. Performing Read/Write Operations

Conventional distributed systems use the write-invalidate approach in which a node willing to perform a write operation on a page first invalidates all other copies of the page lying on other nodes before performing the write operation. So any node other than the one that carried out the most recent write has to recreate the page if it wants to perform a read/write operation on that page.

However in case of our relaxed consistency approach, there is no need to invalidate the page on all other nodes at the time of a write operation. Rather a particular node's page is invalidated only when it is found to be stale with respect to *time_t* for the particular read operation or when it is to be updated by a user on that node. To take care of this, we include the following additional fields in our PIUT:

T_1: Time when this copy of the page was last updated. Initially its value is the time of last update of this page on the node from where it was fetched.

T_2: Time when this page was last updated at any node of the system. Initially its value is NULL.

Now the write and read operations are carried out as follows:

WRITE: Let the node on which write operation is to be carried out be N_w.

Step 1: if (desired page already present on node N_w)
    if (N_w is the owner node for this page)
        nothing to be done in this case;
    else
        get the latest version of the page from
        node N_o along with the ownership right;
    fi;
else
    cause write page fault which automatically gets the
    latest version of the page along with ownership right;
fi;
Now node N_w becomes the owner node for the page.

Step 2: Node N_w sends a lock message to all the nodes having a copy of the page using the copy list and sends the value of T_2 for this update and its own node number to all these nodes along with the locking information. Using this information, the values of T_2 and owner fields are updated in the PIUT of all these nodes.

Step 3: Node N_w carries out write operation and updates the values of T_1 and T_2 to T_2 and NULL respectively in local PIUT and then releases the locks obtained for performing the write operation.

Thus each node having a copy of the page always has the information about the time of last update on this page and the node having the latest copy of the page. Note that no copy of the page is invalidated at the time of performing a write operation rather only the value of T_2 is updated in the entry corresponding to this page in the PIUT at all the nodes having a copy of the page.

READ: Let N_r be the node on which the read operation is to be carried out and let T_{read} be the absolute time calculated based on the time specified for relaxed consistency. The following algorithm is carried out at node N_r:

```
Step 1:  if (desired page already present on node Nr)
            nothing to be done in this case;
         else
            cause read page fault which automatically gets the
            latest version of the page and updates PIUT of node Nr;
         fi;

Step 2:  if (Tread <= T1)
            read operation is carried out on the local copy of the page;
         else
            if (T2 = NULL)
               means this node has the latest version of the page.
               So read is carried out on the local copy of the page;
            else
               local copy of the page is stale for the user application.
               So get the updated version of the page from node No and
               change T1 to new version's update time and T2 to NULL
               in local PIUT corresponding to this page;
            fi;
         fi;
```

To take care of delayed write operations, we use the concept of shadow page. Let T_{write} be the absolute time calculated based on the time specified by the user for delayed write operation. If T_{write} is greater than the current clock time then a copy of the page is created on the same node and the write operation is carried out on this copy known as the shadow page. All local read and write operations are carried out on this shadow page but for operations of other nodes on this page, the shadow page is invisible till time T_{write}. At time T_{write}, the original page is invalidated, the shadow page is made the original page and the other nodes having a copy of this page are informed about this update using global locking as already discussed. Thus in case of a delayed write, all operations carried out on the page up to time T_{write} are treated as a single transaction whose commit time is T_{write}. It may be noted here that a delayed write can be used only in case of applications where there is no danger of conflicts in updates made by other nodes during the time the write operation was executed and the time when it was propagated to other nodes.

For implementing the concept of process-group consistency, we use the time parameter T_1 of PIUT. If a read operation has a process-group consistency parameter associated with it, then the read operation locks all the copies of the page belonging to the processes within the process-group. Then the value of T_1 is checked for these copies of the page. If the value of T_1 is the same for all these copies then the read operation is carried out and the locks are released. On the other hand, if T_1 is not the same for all these copies then the updated version of the page is copied on all these nodes from node N_o, the PIUT entries are updated properly on all these nodes and then the read operation is carried out. Another way of satisfying this consistency requirement is to migrate the processes of the process-group to a single node so that all of them always access the same copy of the shared data. However this approach may severely limit the parallel processing operation. So we use the first method in GALAXY.

5.4. Page Replacement Policy

An invalid page is first selected for replacement and if there are no invalid pages, then the LRU policy is used for selecting a page to be replaced. When a particular page is replaced from the memory of a node N, then the following update operations are carried out:

1. If N is the owner node and if the copy list has any other node excluding the owner node then the owner node is deleted from the copy list and the node of the copy list that is nearest to N is made the new owner of the page and the copy list information is transferred from node N to the new owner node. A message is also sent to all the nodes in the copy list of PIUT and in the replica list of the ID Table of the concerned object to update the ownership information of this page in their PIUT. The entry corresponding to the replaced page is deleted from the PIUT of node N.
2. If N is the owner node and if the copy list has no other node except N then node N is the sole user of this page. So the corresponding page entry is deleted from node N's PIUT and a message is sent to all the replica locations of the corresponding object to delete this page entry from their PIUT.
3. If N is not the owner node of the page to be replaced then a message is sent to the owner node of this page to delete node N from its copy list and the entry corresponding to the replaced page is deleted from the PIUT of node N.

5.5. Clock Synchronization

For our time oriented relaxed consistency requirements, we have assumed that the clocks of the various nodes of the system are synchronized. To achieve this in our prototype system, a shared memory variable called *system-wide-clock* is used that is maintained by a network time server node. It is updated by the passage of time to always reflect the current time and can be read by all nodes. To achieve sufficient accuracy and consistency, each node caches a copy of the system-wide-clock variable and extrapolates it forward using the local periodic interrupts. Each node periodically receives the correct time from the network time server node whose time is considered to be standard for the entire system. This message is used to correct the cached system-wide-clock variable at each node if it deviates from the standard. The small mismatch in clock time of the various nodes is generally not discernible to the users and hence do not affect their applications. In future we plan to replicate network time server on several nodes for reliability and use one of the several clock synchronization algorithms [5, 7] to get these time servers to agree within a reasonable error bound.

6. Summary

In this paper we have described a user-definable memory coherence scheme for distributed shared memory that is flexible enough to meet the varying needs of a wide variety of user applications. We believe that the concepts presented in this paper will be useful for the design of other distributed systems.

References

1. Bennett, J. K., Carter, J. B. and Zwaenepole, W., "Munin: Distributed Shared Memory Based on Type-Specific Memory Coherence," *Proc. 2nd ACM SIGPLAN Symp. on Principles and Practice of Parallel Programming*, pp. 168-175, (1990).
2. Cheriton, D. R., "Problem-Oriented Shared Memory: A Decentralized Approach to Distributed System Design," *Proc. 6th Int. Conf. Distributed Computing Systems*, pp. 190-197, (1986).
3. Fitzgerald, R. and Rashid, R. F., "The Integration of Virtual Memory Management and Interprocess Communication in Accent," *ACM Trans. on Computer Systems*, Vol. 4, No. 2, pp. 147-177, (May 1986).
4. Garcia-Molina, H. and Wiederhold, G., "Read-Only Transactions in a Distributed Database," *ACM Trans. on Database Systems*, Vol. 7, No. 2, pp. 209-234, (June 1982).
5. Halpern, J., Simons, B., Strong, R. and Dolev, D., "Fault Tolerant Clock Synchronization," *Proc. 3rd Annual ACM Symp. on Principles of Distributed Computing*, pp. 89-102, (1984).
6. Jia, X., H. Nakano, K. Shimizu, and M. Maekawa, "Highly Concurrent Directory Management in Distributed Systems," *Proc. 10th Int. Conf. Distributed Computing Systems*, pp. 416-423, (1990).
7. Lamport, L. and Smith, P. M., "Byzantine Clock Synchronization," *Proc. 3rd Annual ACM Symp. on Principles of Distributed Computing*, pp. 68-74, (1984).
8. Li, K. and Hudak, P., "Memory Coherence in Shared Virtual Memory Systems," *Proc. 5th ACM Symp. on Principles of Distributed Computing*, pp. 229-239, (1986).
9. Minnich, R. G. and Farber D. J., "The Mether System: A Distributed Shared Memory for SunOS 4.0," *Proc. Summer 1989 USENIX Conf.*
10. Shimizu, K., M. Maekawa and J. Hamano, "Hierarchical Object Groups in Distributed Operating Systems," in *Proc. 8th Int. Conf. Distributed Computing Systems*, pp. 18-24, (1988).
11. Sinha, P. K., K. Shimizu, N. Utsunomiya, H. Nakano and M. Maekawa, "Network Transparent Object Naming and Locating in Distributed Operating Systems," Tech. Rep., Dept. of Info. Sc., Univ. of Tokyo, TR89-033, (1989).
12. Stumm, M. and Zhou, S., "Algorithms Implementing Distributed Shared Memory," *IEEE Computer*, pp. 54-64, (May 1990).
13. Tam, M. C., Smith, J. M. and Farber, D. J., "A Taxonomy-Based Comparison of Several Distributed Shared Memory Systems," *Operating Systems Review*, Vol. 24, No. 3, pp. 40-67, (July 1990).

Parallelization of Multigrid Programs in SUPERB

Michael Gerndt
University of Vienna
Institute for Statistics and Computer Science
Rathausstr. 19/II/3
A-1010 Vienna,Austria
EMAIL: A4424DAN@AWIUNI11.bitnet

Abstract

This paper describes the parallelization of Multigrid Programs with SUPERB. SUPERB is an interactive SIMD/MIMD parallelizing system for the SUPRENUM machine. We present multigrid oriented features of our data partitioning language and discuss interprocedural aspects in the parallelization of these programs. One of our results is that interactivity is inherent to the parallelization of these programs.
Keywords: multiprocessors, analysis of algorithms, program transformations

1 Introduction

SUPERB (Suprenum ParallelizER Bonn) is a semi-automatic parallelization system developed at the University of Bonn within the framework of the SUPRENUM project [Trott 86]. The target machine is the SUPRENUM supercomputer which is a loosely-coupled hierarchical multiprocessor where each node processor has its own vector unit. SUPERB thus combines MIMD parallelization and vectorization. It is an interactive tool transforming Fortran 77 (F77) programs into parallel programs written in SUPRENUM FORTRAN, an extension of F77. SUPRENUM FORTRAN includes extensions for parallel programming and vector features in the style of FORTRAN 8x. The parallel programming model is based on asynchronous message passing.

Though SUPERB has been developed for the SUPRENUM supercomputer its ideas are not limited to this special machine. It can be seen as an parallelization tool for Distributed Memory Multiprocessors (DMP) which consist of a set of node computers with exclusively local memory and a host computer performing I/O. This machine model is typical for most existing DMP.

The general idea for parallelizing scientific programs for these machines is to decompose the domain of the application and to assign the parts to individual processes [Fox 88].

These processes perform the computation on their subdomain and have to synchronize if they need values computed by other processes. In terms of F77 programs, domain decomposition means distribution of arrays. In our approach this distribution is specified by the programmer. This strategy is also persued by other groups working in the field of parallelization for DMPs [CalKen 88, KoMeRo 88, PinRog 90, SCMB 90]. Very interesting alternatives to this approach are: to extract suitable distributions automatically from the input program [LiChen 89, KnLuSt 90] or to assist the user in this task with a tool which generates a performance prediction for a specified distribution [BFKK 90].

In this article, we describe the special features of SUPERB for parallelizing multigrid programs. Section 2 presents the overall parallelization process. We introduce the special charcteristics of multigrid programs written in F77 in Section 3 and discuss in Section 4 features of our data partitioning language dealing with the peculiarities of the data structures of multigrid programs. Section 5 presents interprocedural aspects of data partitioning.

2 Overall Parallelization Strategy

Data parallelism can be typically found in scientific applications. Many of these applications are grid-type problems. The central mathematical model of these applications are Partial Differential Equations (PDEs) which are solved by finite element methods, finite volumes methods or finite differences methods. Typical for grid-type problems are local computations in the points of a grid. The computations are called local since only certain points in the neighborhood of the computed point are needed.

Grid problems are parallelized manually for DMPs by decomposing the grid into parts, which are assigned to individual processes. The processes exchange points on their boundaries and compute new values for the points in their own part.

SUPERB provides special analysis services and transformations for automatic program restructuring according to the domain decomposition technique, e.g. program splitting, data partitioning, communication analysis, optimizing transformations and MIMD code generation. We illustrate the main transformations within the Restriction operation of multigrid programs, computing the right hand side (rhs) values of a partitial differential equation on a coarser grid from the defect on the finer grid.

Let the rhs of the partial differential equation on the coarse grid be implemented via array F2(65,65) and the values of the solution on the fine grid via array U1(129,129). The code of the Restriction operation is:

```
DO I=2,64
   DO J=2,64
      F2(I,J)= ...  - 4.0D0*U1(2*I,2*J)+U1(2*I-1,2*J)+U1(2*I,2*J-1)+
             U1(2*I+1,2*J)+U1(2*I,2*J+1)
   ENDDO
ENDDO
```

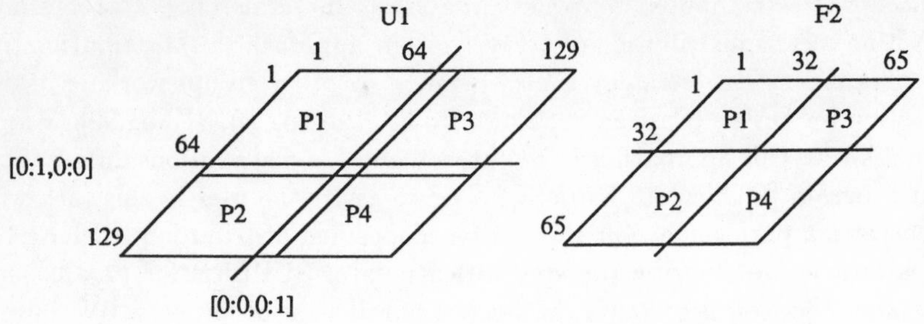

Figure 1: Distributions of U1 and F2 with Overlap Areas

Data Partitioning

The user specifies data distributions for some of the program's arrays interactively via commands. Each distribution characterizes the decomposition of an array into segments and the mapping of these segments to the processes. Variables assigned to a process are called *local variables.* The arrays U1 and F2 of the program's data domain are distributed among 4 processes by the commands: *part U1(2,2)* and *part F2(2,2).* The resulting distributions are shown in Figure 1.

Initial Adaptation

A process computes new values exclusively for local variables. Thus the system determines an appropriate mask for each statement of the node program. The mask suppresses the execution of a statement in a process if the written variables are non-local. If a process executes a statement, it may read local and non-local variables. For all references which may access a non-local variable a communication statement EXSR (EXchange Send Receive) is inserted which updates a copy of the variable if necessary.

```
DO I=2,64
   DO J=2,64
      EXSR (U1(2*I+1,2*J),[0:1,0:0])
      EXSR (U1(2*I,2*J+1),[0:0,0:1])
      owned(F2(I,J))→F2(I,J)= ...   - 4.0D0*U1(2*I,2*J)+U1(2*I-1,2*J)+
            U1(2*I,2*J-1)+U1(2*I+1,2*J)+U1(2*I,2*J+1)
   ENDDO
ENDDO
```

The communication statements are extended by an **Overlap Description**. This description determines an **Overlap Area** for each process which is a subset of the non-local variables. The resulting overlap areas of the example are shown in Figure 1. If the accessed variable belongs to the overlap area of a process a copy is updated via communication. For example, if U1(2*I+1,2*J) in the first EXSR statement accesses U1(65,4) in iteration (i=32,j=2), P1 receives a new value for its copy of U1(65,4) since this variable belongs to its overlap area. In the same iteration P2 sends the value of U1(65,4) because the variable is local to P2 and in the overlap area of P1.

The overlap descriptions are computed from the mask of the statement and the accessing reference. The resulting overlap area of each process is a conservative estimation of the non-local variables which may be accessed in this process via the reference. The overlap analysis, done in SUPERB, needs precise information about the distribution of the array in the mask and the array read.

Optimization

The initial masking and communication is usually not efficient. Thus the system tries to optimize the code. For example it may implement the masks by transforming the loop bounds. The communication is optimized by extracting communication from loops and thus combining messages.

```
EXSR (U1(*,*),[0:1,0:0])
EXSR (U1(*,*),[0:0,0:1])
DO I=max($L1,2),min($R1,64)
   DO J=max($L2,2),min($R2,64)
      F2(I,J)= ...   - 4.0D0*U1(2*I,2*J)+U1(2*I-1,2*J)+U1(2*I,2*J-1)+
             U1(2*I+1,2*J)+U1(2*I,2*J+1)
   ENDDO
ENDDO
```

The program is parameterized according to the data partition. The local segment of the executing process is F2($L1:$R1,$L2:$R2). The mask of the assignment is enforced in the loop bounds. Looking at process p1, for example, we see that it executes iterations 2 to 32 of the I- and J-loop. The EXSR statements describe all elements of the array as candidates for the updating. All of these variables which belong to the overlap area of a process are exchanged in a single large message.Combining messages is very important, since the start-up time for a message is typically high.

A more detailed description of these transformations can be found in [GerZi 87, ZBG 88, Gerndt 89b, Gerndt 90].

3 Multigrid Programs

One of the fastest known methods for solving partial differential equtions on general bounded domains is the Multigrid Method [StTr 82]. The differential equation is discretized on a grid with a fine mesh size; the solution process is a combination of standard relaxation methods and the computation of corrections on coarser grids. The multigrid method is based on a hierarchy of grids where grids on the higher levels are coarser than the grids on the next lower level (Figure 2(a)).

One possible solution procedure, the V-cycle, first performs some relaxation sweeps on the fine grid. Then the solution is corrected by the solution of another differential equation discretized on the next coarser grid. This equation is defined by the defect on the fine grid. Its rhs is computed in the Restriction operation from the defect. The solution

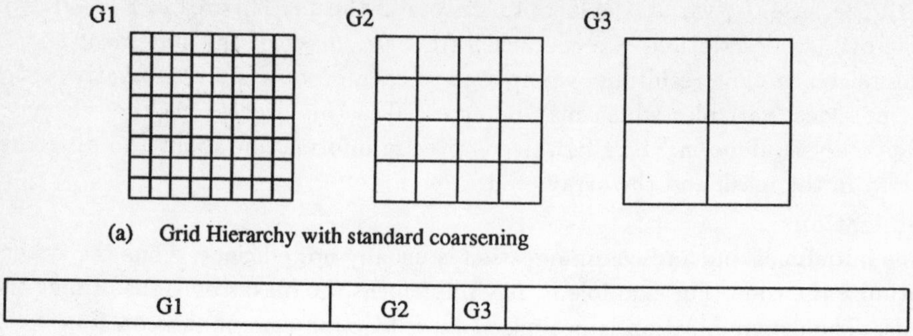

(a) Grid Hierarchy with standard coarsening

(b) Workarray

Figure 2: Grid hierarchy embedded in a workarray

computed on the coarse grid is taken to correct the solution on the fine grid. This step is called Interpolation. After this correction step, usually some more relaxation sweeps are performed on the finer grid. The procedure can be recursively applied to compute the solution on the coarser grid, until the coarsest grid is reached where the solution is computed by an exact solver.

In this article we do not go into more detail on the mathematical background. We now present the typical implementation characteristics of multigrid programs written in F77.

To solve partial differential equations with the multigrid method, different values have to be stored for a single grid point. In the simplest case, the value of the grid solution and the value of the rhs function. Thus, for each grid two arrays with the grid's shape are needed. Since F77 does not provide any language features to allocate arrays dynamically, these arrays are sequentially embedded into two workarrays declared in the program (Figure 2(b)). In the following we call the individual arrays of the grids *virtual arrays* since they are not explicitly declared.

All operations on grids are implemented via individual subroutines. Inside these subroutines virtual arrays are accessed via formal parameters (Figure 3). The formal arrays select exactly the storage in a workarray which belongs to a virtual array of a single grid. The virtual array is determined dynamically via the index of its first element in the workarray and an appropriate declaration which depends on the actual number of grid points in each dimension [1]. For example, the Restriction operation is now applied to each pair - fine grid, next coarser grid - in the grid hierarchy.

Usually the number of grids of a special run of the program is an input parameter. Since our approach is limited to static distributions, the arrays which are distributed, the number of processes and the actual distributions are fixed at compile time, we cannot deal with a varying number of grids for different runs. Thus the program has to be parallelized for one fixed grid hierarchy.

[1]We assume that the grids are squares.

Program Multigrid

```
REAL U(40000), F(40000)                    /* workarrays for solution and rhs */
INTEGER GrSt(20)                          /* First grid element in the workarray */
INTEGER NoPo(20)                           /* Number of points in one dimension */
   ...
DO i=1,Level-1
   CALL Relax(U(GrSt(i)),F(GrSt(i)),NoPo(i))
   CALL Restr(U(GrSt(i)),NoPo(i),F(GrSt(i+1)),NoPo(i+1))
ENDDO
Solve(U(GrSt(i)),F(GrSt(i)),NoPo(i))
DO i=Level-1,1
   CALL Interpol(U(GrSt(i+1)),NoPo(i+1),U(GrSt(i)),NoPo(i))
   CALL Relax(U(GrSt(i)),F(GrSt(i)),NoPo(i))
ENDDO
   ...
END
```

SUBROUTINE Restr(UF,NPF,FC,NPC)

```
REAL UF(NPF,NPF),FC(NPC,NPC)                        /* Grids on subroutine level */

DO I=2,NPC-1
   DO J=2,NPC-1
      FC(I,J)= ...  - 4.0D0*UF(2*I,2*J)+UF(2*I-1,2*J)+UF(2*I,2*J-1)+
            UF(2*I+1,2*J)+UF(2*I,2*J+1)
   ENDDO
ENDDO
END
```

Figure 3: Multigrid Program with V-cycle

4 Data Partitioning for Grid Hierarchies

The usual way to distribute an array among a set of node processes is to decompose the array into segments and then to map these segments to the processes. For the sake of efficiency [Gerndt 89a] of the resulting parallel program we restrict our distributions in three ways:

- Segments have to be always rectangular subarrays.
- The segments build a partition of the array.

- At most one segment can be assigned to an individual process but a single segment may be assigned to different processes.

Formal arrays inherit their distribution at runtime from the actual array. Again for efficiency reasons we enforce - via transformations - three restrictions on formal parameters:

- Formal arrays are always distributed or never.
- Distributed formal arrays have to start at the same location and must have the same size as the actual array.
- Formal scalar variables are always replicated, i.e. local to each process.

Due to these restrictions the specification of a distribution for the workarray is not the appropriate way to parallelize a multigrid program. Some processes will be assigned to parts of the workarray which are never used since the grid hierarchy is not so deep. Furthermore, only those processes which are assigned to the same grid really work in parallel, since the computations on different levels of the hierarchy cannot be executed in parallel. Multigrid programs are a typical example for Loosely Synchronous Computation [Fox 88].

Since the data parallelism is found inside the computation on one grid level, the best suited way to parallelize this application is to distribute each grid individually among the processes (Figure 1). This data decomposition strategy is made possible in SUPERB via an additional feature of the partitioning language: the **Workspace Concept**.

Before specifying the different distributions for the grids, i.e. for the virtual arrays implementing the grids, the user specifies the structure of the grid hierarchy or more precisely of the hierarchy of virtual arrays. For example, if the grid hierarchy includes five levels, e.g. G1(129,129), G2(65,65), G3(33,33), G4(17,17) and G5(9,9), the corresponding virtual array hierarchy is determined with the following commands:

WS Main.U: U1(129,129), U2(65,65), U3(33,33), U4(17,17), U5(9,9)
WS Main.F: F1(129,129), F2(65,65), F3(33,33), F4(17,17), F5(9,9)

Following this step, the individual virtual array can be distributed in the same way as normal arrays. For example, U1 is distributed in the way shown in Figure 1 via *part U1(2,2)*. This concept for data decomposition of multigrid programs is very flexible. For example, it is possible to decompose the two finest grids into 256 segments and to assign each segment of such a grid to an individual process. Since the decomposition of the coarser grids into 256 segments will not be efficient - the segments will be to small - and is impossible for G5, the coarser grids are decomposed into 16 segments which are then individually replicated to 16 different processes. The necessary commands based on a two dimensional process grid PROC(16,16) are:

part U1(16,16) with (i=1,16(j=1,16 (U1(i,j)→PROC(i,j))))
part U3(4,4) with (i=1,4(j=1,4(k=0,3(l=0,3 (U3(i,j)→PROC(i+k,j+l))))

The workspace concept presented here for multigrid applications is a powerful tool to supply domain specific structural knowledge to SUPERB and thus to the parallelization process. It is well suited for a lot of application programs since the lack of dynamic array allocation features results in the same methods to overcome this drawback in other applications. Extensions to the presented static concept are discussed in the Conclusion.

5 Interprocedural Partitioning Analysis

One of the main task of the initial adaptation step is the insertion of communication. Communication is implemented by EXSR statements which depend on a reference to a distributed array and an overlap description. This overlap description determines for each node process a superset of those non-local array elements accessed via this reference. The description is the criterion for updating a private copy of an accessed variable. If the accessed variable belongs to the overlap area of a process, its private copy is updated by the actual value of this variable in a process which owns it.

As discussed in Section 3 and in [Gerndt 89b] the quality of the overlap description depends on the knowledge about the distribution of the array in the mask, e.g. owned(FC(I,J)), the distribution of the referenced array and the subscript expressions in the array references. In the example in Section 3 the relevant arrays have a single fixed distribution at runtime, which is known at compile time. Thus it can be determined which part of U1 is accessed in the computation of the local part of F2 in a process.

In multigrid programs and usually also in other programs, formal distributed arrays have different distributions at runtime. This results from the fact, that subroutines are used to perform the same computation for different data structures. For example in the presented multigrid program, FC in subroutine RESTRICT will have the distributions of G2 to G5 in different incarnations and UF those of G1 to G4.

If there is no further information the overlap description has to be determined with respect to each pair of these distributions. This usually leads to an inprecise conservative approximation since most of the pairs are unpossible at runtime. Thus more precise information of the possible pairs is needed which is computed as the first substep of the initial adaptation.

For each subroutine a set of **Partition Vectors** is computed, which determine for each distributed array of the subroutine a single distribution. The distributions result from the distributed arrays bound to the formal arrays and thus are represented via the distributed arrays. For example, the partition vectors of RESTRICT are pv_1, pv_2, pv_3 and pv_4 with:

$$\begin{array}{ll} pv_1(UF) = U1 & pv_1(FC) = F2 \\ pv_2(UF) = U2 & pv_2(FC) = F3 \\ pv_3(UF) = U3 & pv_3(FC) = F4 \\ pv_4(UF) = U4 & pv_4(FC) = F5 \end{array}$$

The general procedure for the computation of partition vectors has been published in [Gerndt 89a]. It is performed in a single sweep over the callgraph of the node program.

A unit is visited only if all predecessors have been processed [2]. If the actual unit contains distributed formal arrays, the partition vectors are computed by inspecting all call sites and the partition vectors of the calling units. So the maximal set of possible partition vectors is build.

The specific problem in computing partition vectors in multigrid programs results from the workspace concept. At some points in the call chain the virtual arrays are selected at runtime from the workarray. In our example all six procedure calls are such points. At these points SUPERB cannot determine the following information:

1. Does a formal array always select exactly a single virtual array?
2. Does the formal array has the same shape as the virtual array selected in an incarnation?
3. Which virtual arrays are selected?
4. Which combination are possible at runtime?

As discussed above, the last two questions have to be answered precisely to parallelize the input program successfully. If the first question is not fulfilled, the workarray cannot be handled as a workspace with virtual arrays. Thus in this case the user is forced to parallelize the program with the standard data partitioning methods of SUPERB. If the second question cannot be proven to be fulfilled, the transformed code related to the formal array cannot be optimized and so will be inefficient but still correct.

Due to the fact that these questions cannot be answered automatically by SUPERB, the user has to supply the required information. Therefore SUPERB first prompts the user during the computation of the partition vectors and asks, if always exactly a single virtual array is selected and which combinations are possible. It presents some helpful information about the relevant arrays at the call site, e.g. the structure of the workspace, and the called procedure. The user then specifies the possible combinations.

For example, the system cannot determine automatically the partition vectors of subroutine RESTRICT. Therefore the user determines which combinations of virtual arrays are possible via the specification: *1-4 2-5*.

Each group of this specification determines the sequence of virtual arrays selected via a single formal array. The sequence of groups, e.g. 1-4 followed by 2-5, corresponds to the sequence of formal arrays in the parameter list accessing virtual arrays. From this specification, the combinations (1,2),(2,3),(3,4) and (4,5) are derived, and the partition vectors presented above are determined.

The user also has to answer the second question. In the example, SUPERB is not able to proof, that UF(NPF,NPF) has the same shape at runtime as the corresponding virtual array accessed in an incarnation of RESTRICT. Of course this condition is fulfilled, since we assume that array NoPo containes the correct value and that the correct array elements are selected at a call side.

There are two important results from this discussion: First, SUPERB has to be an interactive tool to be able to parallelize multigrid programs successfully and second, the user has to have a deep knowledge about his program to assist the system.

[2] We require that the input program is non-recursive, so that the callgraph is acyclic. If it is not, it is possible to transform it into an equivalent acyclic graph.

Inside subroutines working on grids, the formal distributed arrays can be handled as if they are distributed explicitly by the user. The only difference to those arrays is, that formal distributed arrays may have different distributions at runtime. This fact must be considered when determining overlap descriptions and optimizing the initial adapted code.

6 Conclusion

This articles gives an overview about parallelization of multigrid applications in SUPERB. One of the features of SUPERB is the workspace concept, which can be utilized to specify the structure of the application domain, e.g. a grid hierarchy. This structure is very important to parallelize these programs successfully. Data decomposition, the widely accepted technique for parallelization for Distributed Memory Multiprocessors, has to be applied to the grids. Since the grids are mapped to a single large workarray the structure of the grid hierarchy has to be supplied to SUPERB. Thus the user can specify a suitable data decomposition for the grids via distributions for the corresponding virtual arrays.

The second feature of SUPERB which assists the user in the parallelization of multigrid programs, is the interface where the users specifies the relevant combination of distributions of formal arrays. Without this feature effective parallelization of these programs will be impossible.

The workspace concept is as well flexible as it is restrictive. Its flexibility results from the fact that the virtual arrays can have any declaration which is possible in F77 for arrays. It is restrictive since the sequence of virtual arrays must be fixed at compile time. This characteristic corresponds to the general limitations of SUPERB. A specified data partition is fixed for the parallelized code and is independent of any runtime parameters such as the number of processors or the size of the data domain in a special run of the program.

An extension to this approach can be a high level data partitioning language, which includes features to describe a grid hierarchy [RupWi 89] and to generate distributions for the coarser grids from distributions of the finer grids.

More ambitious extensions will be to allow data distributions which depend dynamically on the number of processors and which may depend on input values of the program. Approaches which support these extensions via library routines are the Cubix system [Fox 88] and Express [Express 89]. Until now there are no parallelization tools which are able to handle these extensions.

References

[BFKK 90] Vasanth Balasundaram, Geoffrey Fox, Ken Kennedy, Ulrich Kremer, An Interactive Environment for Data Partitioning and Distribution, Fifth Distributed Memory Computing Confrerence, Charleston, S. Carolina, April 9-12, 1990

[CalKen 88] David Callahan, Ken Kennedy, Compiling programs for distributed-memory multiprocessors, J.Supercomputing, 2(2), 151-169,(Oct.1988)

[Express 89] ParaSoft Corporation, EXPRESS A Communication Environment for Parallel Computers, ParaSoft 1989

[Fox 88] Geoffrey C. Fox et al., Solving Problems on Concurrent Processors, Prentice Hall,Englewood Cliffs, 1988

[Gerndt 89a] H.M.Gerndt, Array Distribution in SUPERB, Proceedings of the 3rd International Conference on Supercomputing 1989, 164-174, ACM,(1989)

[Gerndt 89b] H.M.Gerndt, Automatic Parallelization for Distributed-Memory Multiprocessing Systems, Ph.D. Dissertation, University of Bonn, Informatik Berichte 75, (1989) and ACPC Technical Report Series, 1, 1990, University of Vienna

[Gerndt 90] H.M. Gerndt, Updating Distributed Variables in Local Computations, Concurrency: Practice and Experience, Vol.2(3), pp.171-193 (Sept. 1990)

[GerZi 87] H.M.Gerndt, H.P.Zima, MIMD parallelization for SUPRENUM, In: E.N. Houstis, T.S. Papatheodorou, C.D. Polychronopoulos (Eds.), Proc. 1st International Conference on Supercomputing, Athens, Greece (June 1987), LNCS 297, 278-293

[Karp 87] Alan H.Karp, Programming for Parallelism, Computer 20(5), 43-57, May 1987

[KnLuSt 90] Kathleen Knobe, Joan D. Lukas, Guy L. Steele, Data Optimization: Allocation of Arrays to Reduce Communication on SIMD-Machines, Journal of Parallel and Distributed Computing 8, 102-118, 1990

[KoMeRo 88] C.Koelbel, P.Mehrotra, J.Van Rosendale, Semi-Automatic Process Partitioning for Parallel Computation, International Journal of Parallel Programming, Vol.16, No.5, 1987, 365-382

[LiChen 89] Jingke Li, Marina Chen, Index Domain Alignment: Minimizing cost of Cross-Referencing Between Distributed Arrays, Yale University, Report YALEU/DCS/TR-725, November 1989

[PinRog 90] Keshav Pingali, Anne Rogers, Compiler Parallelization of SIMPLE for a Distributed Memory Machine, Technical Report, Department of Computer Science, Cornell University, No. TR90-1084, 1990

[RupWi 89] Ruppelt,Th.,Wirtz,G., Automatic Transformation of High-Level Object-Oriented Specifications into Parallel Programs, Parallel Computing 10 (1989),15-28

[SCMB 90] Joel Saltz, Kathleen Crowley, Ravi Mirchandaney, Harry Berryman, Run-Time Scheduling and Execution of Loops on Message Passing Machines, Journal of Parallel and Distributed Computing 8, 303-312 (1990)

[StTr 82] K. Stüben, U. Trottenberg, Multigrid Methods: Fundamental Algorithms, Model Problem Analysis and Applications, Proc. Conf. Multigid Methods, Lecture Notes in Mathematics, Vol. 960, Springer Verlag, 1982

[Trott 86] U.Trottenberg: SUPRENUM - an MIMD Multiprocessor System for Multi-Level Scientific Computing, In: W.Händler et al., eds.: CONPAR86, Conference on Algorithms and Hardware for Parallel Processing, LNCS 237, Springer, Berlin, 48-52

[ZBG 88] H.P.Zima, H.-J. Bast, H.M.Gerndt, SUPERB: A tool for semi-automatic MIMD/SIMD parallelization, Parallel Computing 6, 1988, 1-18

MAPPING GRAPHS ONTO A PARTIALLY RECONFIGURABLE ARCHITECTURE

Philippe Chrétienne
Université Pierre et Marie Curie, Laboratoire Masi
4, place Jussieu, 75252 Paris Cedex 05
Françoise Lamour
Onera, Division Calcul Parallèle
BP 72, 92320 Chatillon

Introduction

There are two main ways of mapping tasks from a graph onto a distributed architecture, which differ by the optimization criterion used. One quantitative method defines a cost function including the execution and communication times and other parameters, and then searches for a minimal-cost mapping [2,4]. The other method is qualitative, and its aim is to find a mapping that is as close as possible to the network topology [3,5,9,10,11].

In this paper we are concerned with the problem of finding a mapping that matches exactly a partially reconfigurable architecture called a Reconfigurable Transputer Ring Network (RTRN). A Transputer is a processor with four bidirectional communication links. Two links ensure the ring structure and the two others can be connected to other Transputers through a programmable link switch [7,8].

Our goal is to recognize the graphs for which such a topological mapping exists and to build a software tool that allows the simulation of the behaviour of a program according to this mapping.

The paper is organized as follows: Section 1 briefly describes the notation and definitions used in the paper and defines the problem. Section 2 gives the theoritical results about graphs that can be mapped onto the concerned architecture while Section 3 describes the software tool. Finally we end with a brief conclusion in Section 4.

1. Problem definition

First, let us recall some definitions. Let $G = (V, E)$ be a task graph with node set V and edge set E. $H = (V, F)$, $F \subset E$, is a partial graph of G. $\Gamma_G(x)$ denotes the set of the neighbors of a node x in G. The number of elements in $\Gamma_G(x)$ is the degree of x in G and is denoted $d_G(x)$. A graph is called r-bounded (resp r-regular) if for any node x, $d_G(x) \leq r$ (resp $d_G(x) = r$) [1].

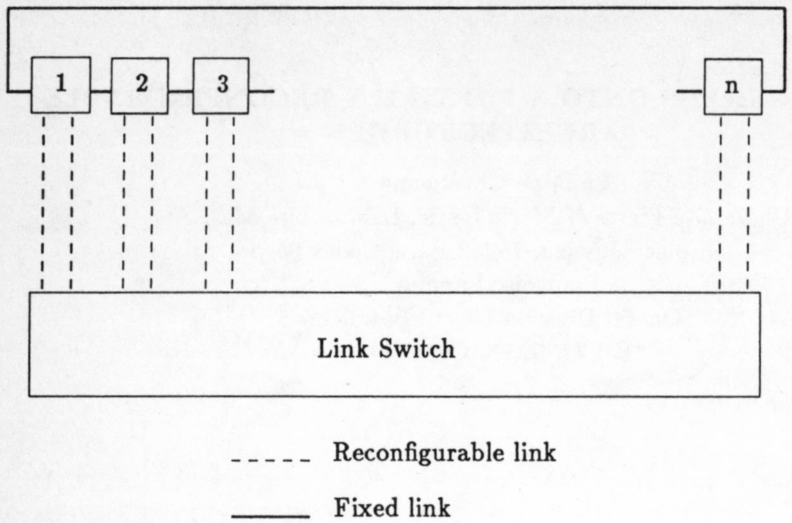

Figure 1: An RTRN with n processors.

One instance of this problem is specified by an RTRN N and a task precedence graph $G = (V, E)$. Figure 1 shows an RTRN of n processors.

Let $(1, 2, ..., n)$ be the processor sequence of an RTRN N. If i is a processor, the processors $(i - 1)$ *mod* n and $(i + 1)$ *mod* n are called the *ring neighbors* of i.

A *configuration* of N is a 4-bounded graph with node set $\{1, 2, ..., n\}$ and an edge set (corresponding to the active communication links) which is such that every processor i has at most two neighbors which are not *ring neighbors* of i.

A task precedence graph $G = (V, E)$ is *assignable* to N if there exists a one-to-one mapping function

$$f : V \longrightarrow \{1, 2, ...n\}$$

such that $\{(f(u), f(v)) \setminus (u, v) \in E\}$ is the edge set of a *configuration* of N.

Given a task precedence graph $G = (V, E)$ and an RTRN N, the problem is to decide if G is *assignable* to N.

Due to the one-to-one condition of the mapping, the tasks can be identified with the processors, and then the problem is to decide if G itself is a *configuration.* So we formulate the problem as follows:

Let $G = (V, E)$ be a task graph. Does there exist a partial graph $H = (V, F)$ of G such that :

a) for any node $v, d_G(v) - 2 \leq d_H(v) \leq 2$

b) H has no cycle with less than $|V|$ nodes.

The edges of H correspond to the active links of the ring. Condition b) ensure that the neighbors of i in H are *ring neighbors* of i while condition a) ensure that the number of neighbors of i in H is adequate.

The partial graphs of G that verify conditions a) and b) are called the *solutions* of the problem.

2. Theoritical results

In this section we characterize three classes of graphs which are *assignable* and we determine the absolutly necessary property which allows a 4-regular graph to be *assignable*. As it may be too long we give only the mains ideas of the proofs.

Theorem 1 *Every 3-bounded graph is assignable.*

Proof

Let us consider $G = (V, E)$ a 3-bounded graph and M a maximal matching of G.We build a *solution* by completing the matching M with additional edges.
The matching divides the set of nodes in two subsets : the subset the unsaturated nodes and the subset of the saturated nodes. We build the bipartite graph G' induced by $W \bigcup S$ where W is the set of unsaturated nodes of degree three and S of the saturated nodes. There exits a matching M' of G' for which any node of W is matched and then we can easily saw that $M \bigcup M'$ makes a *solution.*□

Theorem 2 *Every 4-bounded tree is assignable.*

Proof

Since $G = (V, E)$ is a tree, it is a bipartite graph. We build the solution in two steps. First we find a maximum matching M of G such that every node with degree four is matched. Then we consider $G' = (V, E - M)$, G' is a 3-bounded subgraph. Once again we find a maximum matching M' of G' for which any node of degree three is matched. We can easily saw that $M \bigcup M'$ is a *solution.* □

We briefly recall the recursive definition of a series-parallel graph (in short SP graph). A graph $G = (\{v\}, \emptyset)$ is an SP graph. The node v is both the input node and the output node of G. If the k graphs $G_1, G_2, ..., G_k$ (e_i and s_i being the input and output nodes of G_i) are SP graphs, the two graphs $S(G_1, G_2, ..., G_k)$ and $P(G_1, G_2, ..., G_k)$ defined by Figure 2 are SP graphs. The parallel construction $P(G_1, G_2, ..., G_k)$ produces two nodes, called *fork* node and *join* node, which are respectively the input and output nodes of the graph $P(G_1, G_2, ..., G_k)$.
We note that the nodes with degree at least three in a SP graph are *fork* and *join* nodes.

Theorem 3 *Every 4-bounded SP graph is assignable.*

Proof

First we introduce the following notations which make easier the proof.
A node of degree three (resp four) in G is *satisfied* if it is one endpoint of one (resp two)

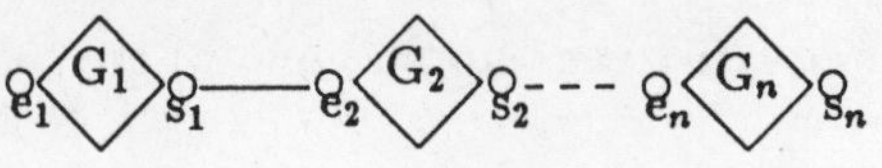

(a)

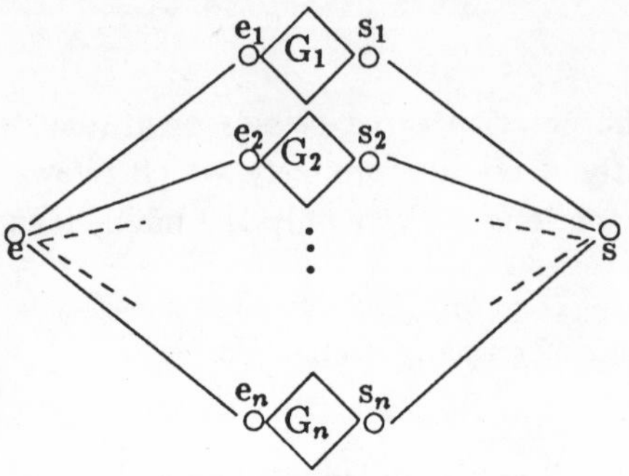

(b)

Figure 2: (a) The serial construction with graphs $G_1, G_2, .., G_n$. (b) The parallel construction with graphs $G_1, G_2, .., G_n$.

ring edge. A node of G is *fully-satisfied* if it is one endpoint of two ring edges already chosen to make a part of the *solution*. So a node can be *satisfied* if it has a sufficient number of neighbors which are not *fully-satisfied*. A node of G is *free* if it is not already one endpoint of a ring edge.

We first make up the prefix list $L = \{(e_i, s_i) \backslash i = 1 .. q\}$ ((e_i, s_i) being the i^{st} pair of *fork* and *join* nodes) of the rooted tree representing the sequence of parallel and serial construction that leads to G, a 4-bounded SP graph. Then we satisfy each pair of *fork* and *join* nodes by choosing, first, edges which have their endpoints *free*. □

The problem of deciding if a 4-regular graph is a *configuration* can be expressed now as follows:
Does there exist a partial graph H such that :
a) for any node $v, d_H(v) = 2$
b) H has no cycle with less than $|V|$ nodes.
Therefore, a 4-regular graph is *assignable* if and only it includes a hamiltonian cycle. So the problem of deciding whether a 4-regular graph is *assignable* is equivalent to the problem of deciding if such a graph is hamiltonian. An example of a 4-regular graph without hamiltonian cycle (so not assignable) is given in [12,pp 373]. □

3. Building a software tool

As we want to automatically determine the mappings of graphs and to visualize the solutions, we naturally build a software tool which simulates the chain of an auto-

matic paralleliser which converts a sequential program fragment in a parallel program running on an RTRN. The program fragment is in fact a Fortran loop and we simulate the pipelined execution of the iterations of the loop. The chain is in three parts which lead to the following results: computation of the task graph of the Fortran loop, determination of the mapping, simulation and visualization of the parallel execution of the loop, respectively.
We have used VATIL, a vectorizer developed at INRIA, to determine the task graph of a Fortran loop. We add to VATIL a phase of restructuration in the writing of the loop in order to obtain a dependance graph which is a data flow graph. We have also included to VATIL the algorithms which compute the mapping function of 3-bounded graphs or 4-bounded trees. So, after VATIL computes the task graph of the loop, the mapping function in the case of 3-bounded graphs or 4-bounded trees is automatically generated. The simulation and visualization of the execution has been realized with Transim and Gecko two products developed at the Polytechnic of Central London [6,14].
Transim is a tool which simulates the behaviour of an application written in OCCAM and running on a Transputers network, while Gecko allows the visualization of the simulation by animating network diagrams.
OCCAM is a langage specially build for parallel applications. An OCCAM program is a set of processes which can communicate with each others. Communications are done through a one-way chanel and are synchronised and unbeffered.
To be able to run, Transim needs that the user defines on one hand the application written in OCCAM and on the other hand the architecture on which the application has to run.
So we compute automatically the input files of Transim. The hardware description is realised by the commands NODE and LINK. The first one fixes the number of processors while the second one defines the topology by specifying for each processor the list of its neighbors. From the mapping function and the task graph we can give the complete description of the configuration of the network.
We automatically generate the software description by identifying each node v of the task graph with a labelled process p which receives (resp sends) data from (resp to) the processes corresponding to the predecessors (resp successors) of v. A process is divided in three parts : reception, calculation and broadcast. The processes are written in OCCAM, but the calculation phase does not need to be detailed and can be replaced by a counter which simulates the execution time. Each process must be labelled to make possible the correspondance between processes and processors.
Finally, the mapping is explicitly given by the command MAP which describes the correspondance function between labelled processes and processors.
The files generate by Transim are necessary inputs for Gecko. These files contain the informations on the hardware and software topologies, and on the activity to simulate. Gecko gives a visualization by animating on one hand the task graph and on the other hand the network. The diagrams are presented in separate windows where squares represente processors and cercles represent processes while communication are represented by triangles. The activity of processors is simulate by color. Gecko needs one more file

to be able to run. This file must define the graphical positionning for each processor in the hardware display and must be created by the user.
We automatically generate the file of the graphical coordinates from the graph which is arranged by level according to the predecessors. To each level, a vertical coordinate is associated, while to each node in a fixed level an horizontal coordinate is associated.
Figure 3 shows the simulation of the mapping of a 4-bounded tree.

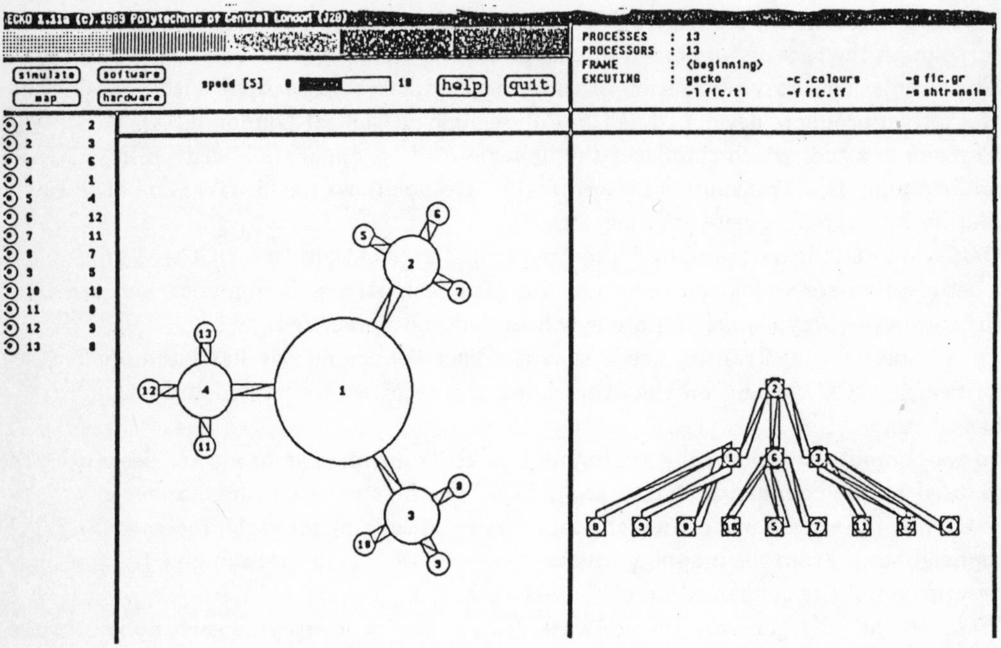

Figure 3: A 4-bounded tree and its *solution*

Conclusion

As we search for a mapping that will avoid the routing of data, our interest in this paper was to characterize the graphs for which there exits a topological mapping onto an RTRN and to simulate the behaviour of an application running onto this machine according to this mapping. After we have determined the kind of graph which is *assignable* we realize a software tool which simulates the execution of the tasks and which gives a graphical interpretation of the mapping.

References

1. Berge, C. Graphes et Hypergraphes. Dunod Université 1970.

2. Bokhari, S.H. A Shortest Tree Algorithm for Optimal Assignements Across Space and Time in a Distributed Processor System. IEEE Transactions on Software engineering Vol SE-7, n° 6, November 1981.

3. Bokhari, S.H. On the Mapping Problem. IEEE Transactions on Computers Vol C-30, n° 3, March 1981.

4. Bokhari, S.H. Partitioning Problems in Parallel, Pipelined, and Distributed Computing. IEEE Transactions on Computers Vol 37, n° 1, January 1988.

5. Fellows, M.R., and Langston, M.A. Processor Utilization in a Linearly Connected Parallel Processing System. IEEE Transactions on Computers Vol 37, n° 5, May 1988.

6. Gecko User Manual, Version 1, Polytechnic of Central London, March 1989.

7. IMS T800 Data Sheet April 1987.

8. IMS C004 Data Sheet April 1987.

9. Lee, I., and Smitley, D. A Synthesis Algorithm for Reconfigurable Interconnection Networks. IEEE Transactions on Computers Vol 37, n° 6, June 1988.

10. McDowell, C.E., and Appelbe, W.F. Processor Scheduling for Linearly Connected Parallel Processors. IEEE Transactions on Computers Vol C-35, July 1986.

11. Pinter, S.S., and Wolftahl, Y. On Mapping Processes to Processors in Distributed Systems. International Journal of Parallel Programming Vol 16, n° 1, 1987.

12. Sachs, H. Construction of non hamiltonian planar regular graphs of degrees 3, 4, and 5 with highest possible connectivity. Théorie des graphes ICC P.Rosientiehl ed Dunod Paris 1966.

13. Shen, C.C., and Tsai W.H. A Graph Matching Approach to Optimal Task Assignement in Distributed Computing Systems using a Minimax Criterion. IEEE Transactions on Computers Vol C-34, n° 3, March 1985.

14. Transim User Manual, Version 2, Polytechnic of Central London, March 1989.

SIMPLE: a performance evaluation tool environment for parallel and distributed systems

Bernd Mohr
Universität Erlangen-Nürnberg, IMMD 7,
Martensstraße 3, D-8520 Erlangen,
Federal Republic of Germany

email: mohr@immd7.informatik.uni-erlangen.de

Abstract. This paper describes SIMPLE: a performance evaluation tool environment for parallel and distributed systems based on monitoring of concurrent interdependent activities. We emphasize the tool environment as a prerequisite for successful performance evaluation. All tools use the data access interface TDL/POET which can decode measured data of arbitrary structure, format and representation. This makes the evaluation independent of the monitor device(s) used and the system monitored. It also provides a problem-oriented way of accessing the data. Therefore it is very easy to adapt SIMPLE to any kind of measured data and to understand the evaluation results.

1. Introduction

The .characteristic feature of parallel and distributed computer systems is that they share load and common resources among several processing nodes in order to increase performance and reliability of the overall system. Understanding the how and why of an achieved performance in an existing system is a must for tuning a system or improving the design of new systems. One successful way of getting the necessary insight is to monitor the real-time sequences of interesting activities in the system under investigation (the **object system**) and make their interactions visible. This results in an **event trace** which can be used to describe and reconstruct system activities and the dynamic behavior of the object system. In most cases, this approach results in excellent explanations of why the system behaves the way it does.

Monitoring parallel and distributed systems is a complicated task because of the asynchronous and sometimes unpredictable dynamic behavior of such systems. Normally this results in an enormous amount of measured data due to the often great number of processor nodes. In order to analyze these data one needs tools which have to be both powerful and easy to use. In the following we describe **SIMPLE,** a modular tool environment for performance evaluation, modeling and visualization of monitored event traces. The name SIMPLE indicates that it is easy to use. The acronym SIMPLE stands for Source related and Integrated Multiprocessor and -computer Performance evaluation, modeLing and visualization Environment.

There is already a great number of evaluation environments. But either they are integrated in a programming environment like TOPSYS [2] or they are build only for one special monitor system like for NETMON [13]. SIMPLE is the first (and only) performance evaluation tool environment which is independent of the monitor device(s) used and the system monitored. The crucial step forward to this independency was introducing the data access interface TDL/POET, which can decode measured data of arbitrary structure, format and representation, for all tools in SIMPLE. We will introduce the different tools in the next chapters guided by a walk through the main steps of processing measured data. There are eight categories of activities (supported by our tools) which contribute to solving the performance evaluation problem: preparing the measurement, supporting the measurement itself, accessing traces, generating an integrated view, validating traces, evaluating traces, visualizing traces and modeling the performance.

2. A walk through a measurement

Throughout this article we will use the following example to introduce and explain the properties and problems of the tasks to perform and the tools we use for them: Suppose we have a little program written in the programming language C which has to compute on a large amount of input data, therefore we distribute it among several processing nodes. The computation is repeated until the result is as exact as desired. After each computation step it is necessary to synchronize the single processors. The left side of figure 1 shows the skeleton of such a program.

```
main ()
{
   do {
      diff=Compute ();
      Sync ();
   } while (diff > epsilon);
}
```

Instrumentation →

```
main ()
{
   WriteEvent ('B');
   do {
      WriteEvent ('C');
      diff=Compute ();
      WriteEvent ('S');
      Sync ();
   } while (diff > epsilon);
   WriteEvent ('E');
}
```

Figure 1. Example C program

2.1 Preparing the measurement

Before doing any further steps, you should first ask yourself the following questions:

(1) **Why** should the measurement be taken and **what** is to be measured ?

(2) **How** to get the desired results ?

The first question is normally easy to answer; in our case we want some statements about how long it takes to compute the results and why it takes so long. The answer to the second question is a little bit more difficult. It normally depends on the hard- and software environment used. One successful way of getting the necessary insight is to monitor the real-time sequences of interesting activities in the object system and make their interactions visible. Whenever we reach an interesting point in our program (called **event**), we store a data record describing all properties of the event occurred. Therefore, we call such a data record event record or **E-record** for short. Storing the E-records continually in a file, one gets a sequence of E-records sorted according to increasing time. Such a sequence is called an **event trace** which can be used to reconstruct the dynamic behavior of the object system and also to compute some performance indices. So in this case question (2) can be read as

(2) **What** are the points of interest (events) in our program ?

This question is easier to ask if we use a model of the functional behavior of our program (the **functional model**) as a base for defining events of interest. Such a model describes the functional behavior of the program on a chosen level of abstraction. Using a model has not only the advantage of precisely defining events and a level of abstraction: adding timing, frequency and probability values to the functional model leads to a **performance model** [9] which can be used to study the functional and performance behavior of other (future) configurations of the program. The type of model can be chosen according to personal taste; normally graph models [12], CSP [4] or petri-nets[3] are used. Figure 2 shows the behavior of our example program as a petri-net. Each branch in the middle of the net corresponds to one processor used. The number n of tokens in the first place is the number of loops in our program.

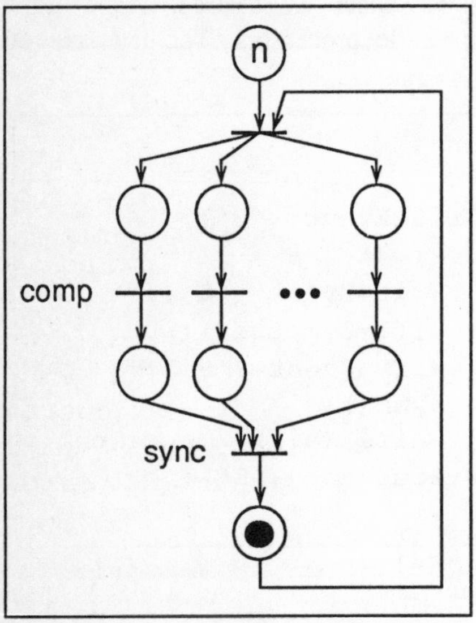

Figure 2. Petri net of example

The simplest way of recognizing the events is to insert some special measurement instructions in the object program. This is called **instrumentation**. These measurement instructions write an event identification to a hardware system interface where it is caught and stored by an external hardware monitor (**hybrid monitoring**), or together with a timestamp into a reserved memory area of the object system (**software monitoring**). Instrumentation can be done manually or by using the SIMPLE tool **AICOS** (Automatic Instrumentation of **C** Object Software). This tool provides an automatic instrumentation of procedure calls, procedure bodies and of arbitrary statements in object software written in the programming language C. The result of the instrumentation of our example program is shown in figure 1 on the right side. Here the routine `WriteEvent` is used as measurement instruction.

2.2 The measurement itself

As already stated, the dynamic behavior of computer systems can be described by event traces. But how can we get reliable event traces in a parallel or distributed computer system, where we have to record many (parallel) and independent event streams? The way mostly chosen is to build a distributed monitor system organized as master-slave-system. The single master station is used for central control and the evaluation of the measured data. The slaves (often called monitor agents) are connected to one or several nodes of the object system and record the event traces. Often, a global time base is provided by the monitor system because many parallel or distributed systems miss it. Examples of such monitor systems (among many others) are the ZM4 [5] and NETMON-II [13]. For a detailed description see the references. Sometimes other monitor systems like network or logic analyzers [5] or software monitors are used [6].

2.3 Uniform and problem-oriented event trace access

As seen is the last section, there are many ways of getting event traces. But the design and implementation of an evaluation system is too complex and expensive a task to be done for one special object or one monitor system only. Therefore we designed and implemented the event trace interface TDL/POET. The basic idea is to regard the measured data as an object as in object oriented programming languages. The evaluation system can access the measured data only via a uniform and standardized set of generic procedures. Using these procedures, an evaluation system is able to abstract from different data formats and representations and thus becomes independent of the monitor device(s) and of the object systems. So, a user can apply the same evaluation tools to different measurements. The tool consists of two components as shown in figure 3:

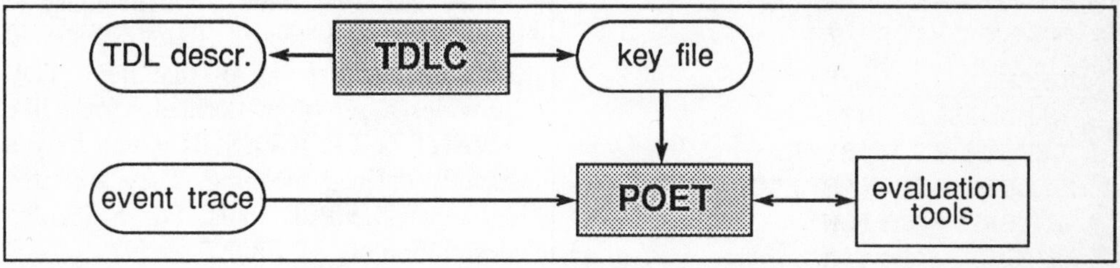

Figure 3. Data handling with TDL/POET

The **POET** library (**P**roblem **O**riented **E**vent **T**race interface) is a simple and monitor independent function interface which allows the user to access measured data stored in event traces in a problem-oriented manner. In order to be able to access and decode the different measured data, the POET functions use a so-called access **key file**, which contains a complete description of formats and properties of the measured data. In addition to describing data formats and representation of the single values, the access key file includes the user defined identifiers for the recorded values, thus allowing the demanded problem-oriented data access.

In order to make the construction of the access key more user friendly, we developed the language **TDL** (event **T**race **D**escription **L**anguage) which is especially well suited for a problem-oriented description of event traces. The access key is then produced by a TDL compiler TDLC which syntactically and semantically checks the user written TDL description. The development of TDL had two principal aims: the first was to make a language available which clearly reflects the fundamental structure of an event trace. The second was that even a user not familiar with all details of the language should be able to read and understand a given TDL description. By writing an event trace description in TDL one provides at the same time a documentation of the performed measurement.

The TDL description of our example is shown in figure 4. Suppose we run our program on three processors and we use software monitoring. Suppose also the measurement routine `WriteEvent` first writes out one byte indicating the processor on which it was invoked, then an event token (provided as parameter) and at last a global time stamp (in this case with a resolution of milliseconds). First, some global properties of the event trace have to be specified. In our case, it is the specification that the event trace is not segmented, i.e. the event records were continuously recorded and therefore the event trace has no gaps. Then the structure of one E-record is described. The processor and the event fields are declared as **TOKEN**. TOKEN record fields contain only values of a fixed

```
TRACE DESCRIPTION:
 TRACE IS UNSEGMENTED;
EVENT RECORD:
 TOKEN:
  NAME IS PROCESSOR;
  LENGTH IS 1 BYTE;
  VALUES ARE [1 .. 3];
  INTERPRETATION
    1 = 'Proc1',
    2 = 'Proc2',
    3 = 'Proc3';
 TOKEN:
  NAME IS EVENT;
  LENGTH IS 1 BYTE;
  VALUES ARE ['B','C','S','E'];
  INTERPRETATION
    'B' = 'Begin',
    'C' = 'Compute',
    'S' = 'Sync',
    'E' = 'End';
 TIME:
  NAME IS ACQUISITION;
  FORMAT IS (UNSIGNED*4, ms);
  MODE IS POINT;
```

Figure 4. Example TDL description

and well known range of constant values. Each value has a special, fixed meaning called **interpretation**. For TOKEN fields we have to specify the length of the field and all values and their interpretations. Record fields containing timing information are declared as **TIME**. Here we have to specify the format and the length of the field, the resolution and whether the value is a point in time or the distance to the last time value. A name must be given to each record field. It should indicate the meaning of that field. TDL provides a set of predefined names like **EVENT** or **PROCESSOR** which have a exactly defined meaning. They are used by other SIMPLE tools. For a detailed description of TDL/POET see [7].

Using TDL/POET for all tools of SIMPLE we are independent of all properties of a object system, especially of its operating system and the programming languages used. In order to adapt our environment to another kind of measurement, one only has to write a TDL description of the event trace to be analyzed. Being independent of the object system and the monitor device(s), the TDL/POET interface inherently has another advantage: As it provides a uniform interface, the evaluation of the data is independent of its recording.

2.4 Generating an integrated view

Sometimes the measured data is recorded at one central place only but using a distributed monitor system we get a set of more than one independently recorded event traces. The next step is to generate a global event trace in order to have an integrated view on the whole object system. It is necessary to have such an integrated view in order to detect and evaluate the interactions between the interdependent activities of the local object nodes. This task can be done by the SIMPLE tool **MERGE**. It takes the local event trace files and the corresponding access key files as input and generates the global event trace and the corresponding access key. The E-records of the local event traces are sorted according to increasing time.

This can easily be done if a monitor system providing a **global timebase** was used. However, most modern monitor systems provide it (e.g. TOPSYS [2], NETMON [13], ZM4 [5] and many others). Without a global timebase there is no assignment of absolutely valid time stamps, but sometimes, there are other aspects (e.g. send / receive) for partially ordering events.

2.5 Validation and plausibility tests

The next step, which is often forgotten, is to perform some validation checks on the recorded event trace in order to check whether all used monitor devices have worked correctly and whether the measurement was performed without errors. Of course it is no proof that everything went right with the measurement - but it takes little time and yet can save you hours or even days of useless work. The program **CHECKTRACE** performs some simple tests on the event trace given which can be applied to all event traces; e.g. it is checked whether the E-records are correctly sorted according to increasing timestamp or whether E-record fields with a fixed range of values contain these values only. For more detailed and application related validation checks the tool **VARUS** (**VA**lidating **RU**les checking **S**ystem) was designed. The user can specify some rules in a formal language (assertions) to validate the event trace in a measurement and object system specific manner. In the assertions we can use the names defined in the TDL description. Both tools generate a report which contains all errors detected.

```
ASSERT (EVENT=='Compute' AND PROCESSOR=='Proc1') ALTERNATING
  WITH (EVENT=='Sync'    AND PROCESSOR=='Proc1')
ELSE "sequence error on processor 1";

ASSERT NUMBER (EVENT=='Begin') == NUMBER (EVENT=='End')
```

Figure 5. Example VARUS file

Figure 5 shows a VARUS input file for our example. The first rule states that the 'Compute' and 'Sync' events on processor 1 should appear alternating. We should also define similar assertions for the other processors. The second rule specifies that the number of 'Begin' and 'End' events should be the same. If we do not specify an error message like in the second assertion, VARUS prints a standard message.

2.6 Evaluating event traces

The simplest form of analyzing event traces is the generation of a trace protocol readable by the user, which can be done by the program **LIST**. It has many options; the user even has the possibility to determine which E-record fields are to print and how. In figure 6 the output of LIST is shown with the data of our example measurement.

```
******* NEW GLOBAL SEGMENT ********************************

   NO     ACQUISITION     PROCESSOR  EVENT

   0:           0 [ms]    Proc1      Begin
   1:           1 [ms]    Proc2      Begin
   2:           3 [ms]    Proc3      Begin
   3:          54 [ms]    Proc1      Compute
   4:          56 [ms]    Proc2      Compute

                      ...

1390:      135075 [ms]    Proc2      End
1391:      135076 [ms]    Proc3      End
```

Figure 6. Trace protocol generated by LIST

Another tool quick and easy to use is **TRCSTAT**. It performs simple statistical computations on an event trace. It can count the frequency of token field values, compute the distance between the different occurrences of an event or the duration of activities defined by a start and an end event. TRCSTAT can perform all computations in parallel within one run through the event trace. On each line the output of the particular commands is marked with a unique prefix so that it can be easily separated using standard UNIX tools like *awk* or *grep*. Figure 7 shows the output of TRCSTAT invoked with the command to compute the duration between 'Compute' and 'Sync' for each processor for our example. It prints a list of all values computed and a summary of the values (the number of values, the minimum, maximum and mean value and the variance) at the end. It shows that the computation on processor 3 needs an average of 49 ms less than on the others processors.

```
#01H  DURATION 'Compute' 'Sync' PROCESSOR

#01S   461 [ ms ] on Proc3
#01S   523 [ ms ] on Proc1
#01S   527 [ ms ] on Proc2

                ...

#01S   520 [ ms ] on Proc2

#01T             Proc1    Proc2    Proc3
#01T    no:        231      231      231      693
#01T   min:        500      500      450      450    [ ms ]
#01T   max:        549      549      499      549    [ ms ]
#01T  mean:        524      524      475      508    [ ms ]
#01T   var:        207      215      216      748    [ ms ]
```

Figure 7. Output produced by TRCSTAT

The tools LIST and TRCSTAT are quite useful, but normally more complex computations have to be done. The user wants to analyze the measured data interactively, with graphics support and in a high-level environment. For this purpose we integrated the commercial data analysis package S from AT&T [1] in SIMPLE. S provides a high-level programming language for data manipulation and graphics. We extended the S package with some additional functions to access the event traces via the TDL/POET interface. We can now read the example data into S and compute the same duration values as we did for TRCSTAT. The necessary commands are shown in figure 8 (the character '>' is the prompt of the S system):

```
> initkey ("example.key")
> readtrace ("example.trc")

> e1 <- EVENT [PROCESSOR == ix("Proc1")]
> t1 <- ACQUISITION [PROCESSOR == ix("Proc1")]
> d1 <- t1[e1 == ix("Sync")] - t1[e1 == ix("Compute")]
> #***** the same for e2,t2,d2 and e3,t3,d3 *****

> boxplot (d1, d2, d3, names=interpret("PROCESSOR"))
```

Figure 8. S commands for boxplot below

The command `initkey` tells S which event trace description (stored in a key file) to use. The command `readtrace` transforms the event trace data into an internal form of the S package. The results are three vectors with the same names as the corresponding E-record field names and as long as the number of E-records in the event trace. The i-th value in a vector contains the value of the i-th E-record. Note that all commands work on the whole data objects (here: vectors) at once. Now we compute which events happened on processor 1 and the corresponding time stamps and store this in the vectors `e1` and `t1` ('<-' is the assignment operator in S). The function `ix` returns the internal coding of the names used and allows us to use the same names as defined in the TDL description. Now we compute the durations between the events 'Sync' and 'Compute' simply by subtracting vectors of the corresponding time stamps. Of course we have to do the same computations for the processors 2 and 3.

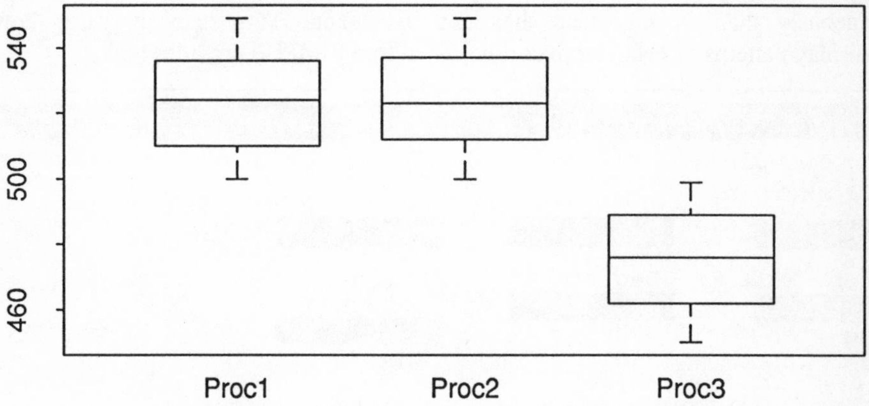

Figure 9. Boxplot diagram generated with S

Figure 9 shows the duration needed for computation (d1, d2, d3) as a `boxplot`, which is much more vivid than the table of numbers from TRCSTAT. The identifiers necessary for labeling can be achieved by the function `interpret`. A boxplot represents the data by a box showing the median and quartiles, and by "whiskers" out of the box to show the range of the data. This makes it easy to compare different distributions.

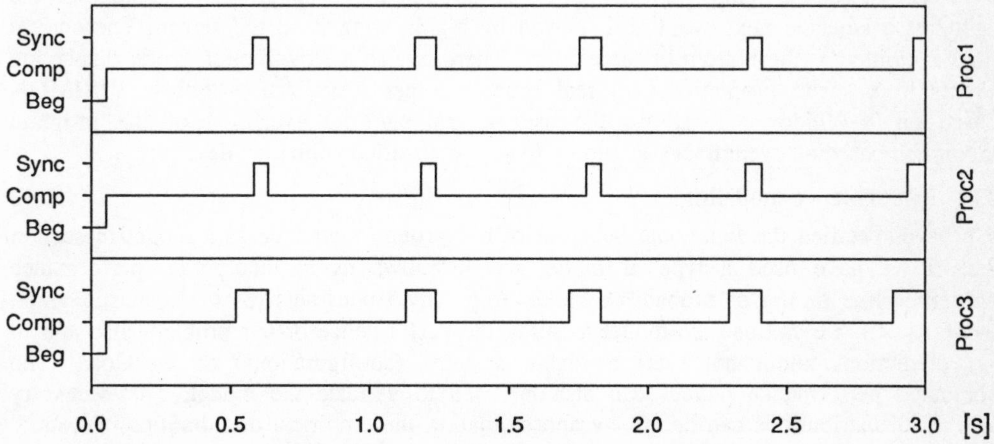

Figure 10. Gantt diagram generated with S

To visualize the dynamic behavior of concurrent activities we implemented the function `gantt` in S. As shown in the Gantt diagram in figure 10, the activities of a program are displayed over a common time axis. In the example only the first three seconds are shown. We can see the interdependencies between all processes very well, i.e. that all processes have to synchronize themselves after the computation phase and the relation between the duration of Compute and Sync. We can also see that processor 3 is faster in the computation phase and has to wait in the synchronization phase.

2.7 Dynamic trace visualization or execution animation

The dynamic visualization of an event trace presents the monitored dynamic behavior in a speed which can be followed by the human user, exposing properties of the program or system that might otherwise be difficult to understand or might even remain unnoticed. By only displaying a single instant of time, more state information can be displayed simultaneously than in time-state diagrams like gantt. Time-state diagrams however better display patterns of behavior over time. Therefore SIMPLE provides both.

```
S M A R T - Slow Motion Animated Review of Traces  Version 2.4 01.05.90
KEY: example
TRC: example

Proc1            Proc2            Proc3

Begin            Begin            Begin
Compute          Compute          Compute
Sync             Sync             Sync
End              End              End

VisEv [  7]                                      -->
RecNr [  6]            518 [ ms ]                Type ? for help
```

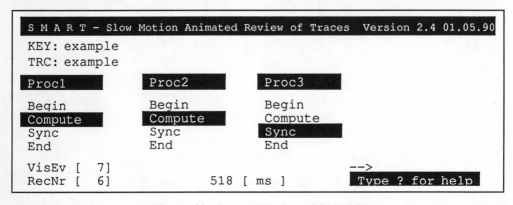

Figure 11. Screen snapshot of SMART

The simple visualization program **SMART** (**S**low **M**otion **A**nimated **R**eview of **T**races) can be used on any ASCII-terminal (see figure 11). A column represents the place of actions like processors or processes. The possible values of the E-record field EVENT are listed in each column. Now we can step through the event trace, i.e. whenever the user hits a key, the next event is displayed by highlighting it on the screen. The current time is printed at the bottom of the display. There is also a slow-motion mode displaying events in a speed proportional to real time. Another visualization tool is **VISIMON** based on X-Windows. It allows the user to animate the execution of the program monitored based on event traces according to a user specified animation description.

2.8 Performance modeling

We have specified the functional behavior of our program example as a model in section 2.1. If we have used a type of model which allows us to incorporate performance properties like timing or probability values (e.g. timed petri-nets [3] or stochastic graph models [12]), we can use the model to study the performance of our problem also and to get predictions about not (yet) available systems (configurations) or workload. The computed performance indices can also be used to validate the model. The necessary analytical distributions can be get by approximating the empirical distributions measured, e.g. the distribution for the transitions "comp" or "sync" of our example model in figure 2.

3. Conclusion

The performance evaluation tool environment SIMPLE is running under UNIX. The implementation of the basic tools like TDL/POET, LIST, TRCSTAT, CHECKTRACE, VARUS, AICOS, SMART and VISIMON and the integration of tools like S is completed. SIMPLE includes some more tools than described in this paper, e.g. a FILTER tool which make it possible to select E-records depending on the values of their record fields. For a more complete list see [8], for details [7]. We have now used our environment heavily over three years in many real world projects like support of the implementation of a UNIX multiprocessor operating system by accompanying measurements [11] or for different measurements of parallel programs on the DIRMU multiprocessor [5] or in transputer environments. It is also used in the European Networking Center (ENC) of IBM [10]. The experiences thereby gained led to extensions and improvements of our environment.

The performed tests show that it can successfully be used in practice and not only for small problems like the example we used throughout this article; nevertheless it is as easy as in the example to adopt our environment to a new measurement and to use it for performance evaluation. The only thing to do is to write a TDL description for the kind of event trace to be analyzed and from then on you can already carry out simple evaluations using the tools LIST, TRCSTAT or SMART. You can read the data into the S package and perform complex computations with a few commands in a high-level, problem-oriented language. All tools can be adapted to the new data and their requirements and to personal taste with some simple statements written down in a descriptor file. So we believe that the behavioral abstraction approach, and the SIMPLE tools supporting it, provide a valuable aid to developers and users of parallel and distributed systems.

References

[1] R. A. Becker, J. M. Chambers, A.R. Wilks, *The New S Language*, Wadsworth, 1988.

[2] T. Bemmerl, *The TOPSYS Architecture*, Proc. of the Int. Conf.: CONPAR 90 / VAPP IV, 1990.

[3] G. Chiola, *A Graphical Petri Net Tool for Performance Analysis*, Proc. of the 3rd Int. Workshop on Modeling Techniques and Performance Evaluation, Paris, 1987.

[4] C.A. Hoare, *Communicating Sequential Processes*. Prentice-Hall, NJ, 1985.

[5] R. Hofmann, R. Klar, N. Luttenberger, B. Mohr, G. Werner, *An Approach to Monitoring and Modeling of Multiprocessor and Multicomputer Systems*, Proc. of the Int. Seminar on Performance of Distributed and Parallel Systems, Kyoto, 1988.

[6] B.P. Miller, *IPS-2: The Second Generation of a Parallel Program Measurement System*, IEEE Transactions on Parallel and Distributed Systems, No. 2, 1990.

[7] B. Mohr, *TDL/POET - Version 5.2*, TR 7/89, University of Erlangen, IMMD 7, 1989.

[8] B. Mohr, Performance Evaluation of Parallel Programs in Parallel and Distributed Systems, Proc. of the Int. Conf.: CONPAR 90 - VAPP IV, Zürich, 1990.

[9] N. Luttenberger, Monitoring von Multiprozessor- und Multicomputer-Systemen, PhD thesis, University of Erlangen, 1989.

[10] N. Luttenberger, R.v. Stieglitz, Perf. Evaluation of a Communication Subsystem Prototype for B-ISDN, 2nd Workshop on Future Trends of Distr. Computing Systems in the 1990's, Kairo, 1990.

[11] A. Quick, Synchronisierte Software-Messungen zur Bewertung des dynamischen Verhaltens eines UNIX-Multiprozessor-Betriebssystems, Proc. of the 5th GI/ITG-Fachtagung MMB '89.

[12] F. Sötz, G. Werner, Lastmodellierung mit stochastischen Graphen zur Verbesserung paralleler Programme auf Multiprozessoren, ITG/GI Conf. Architektur von RS, 1990.

[13] M. Zitterbart, Monitoring and Debugging Transputer-Networks with NETMON-II, Proc. of the Int. Conf.: CONPAR 90 - VAPP IV, Zürich, 1990.

Interleaving Partitions of Systolic Algorithms for Programming Distributed Memory Multiprocessors

A.Fernández, J.M.Llabería, J.J.Navarro and M.Valero-García

Departament d'Arquitectura de Computadors, Universitat Politècnica de Catalunya
c/ Sor Eulalia de Anzizu, Mòdul D4. 08034 - Barcelona. SPAIN

Abstract

In this paper we present a systematic method for mapping systolizable problems onto Distributed Memory Multiprocessors. A systolizable problem is a problem for which it is possible to design a Systolic Algorithm. As a first stage, we design a Systolic Algorithm for the problem to be solved. Then, different transformations are applied to this Systolic Algorithm in order to adapt it to the available Distributed Memory Multiprocessor. One of these transformations is what we call band interleaving. This transformation which is the main contribution of this paper permits to increase the granularity of the parallel algorithm reducing in this way the communication requirements. We will show how the proposed transformations modify the original sequential code in order to obtain the parametrized code for each Processing Element of the Distributed Memory Multiprocessor. The method is illustrated with an example consisting in the design of a parallel algorithm to solve a triangular system of equations on a Distributed Memory Multiprocessor System with a ring topology. Some measurements of performance are presented for the case of a Transputer-based network.

1. INTRODUCTION

In this paper we propose a systematic method for mapping systolizable problems onto Distributed Memory Multiprocessors (DMM). A systolizable problem must be understood as a problem for which it is possible to design a Systolic Algorithm (SA).

In a DMM, each Processing Element (PE) has its own local memory. PEs communicate by message passing through an interconnection network based on point to point links. DMM are attractive in the context of massive parallelism due to their scalability. However, programming a DMM can be a difficult task. Both computation and data must be decomposed and distributed among PEs. That logic decomposition should match the physical interconnection topology of the DMM in order to minimize the communication cost of the final parallel algorithm.

During the last years, many papers have been published dealing with parallel algorithms for DMM [GeiH87] [LiCo88] [HeRo88]. However, just a few of these papers deal with systematic methods for mapping sequential algorithms into DMM [CalK88] [KinN89] [RamS89] [TorA90]. Some of these papers suggest the use of Systolic Algorithms (SA) as an starting point to design parallel algorithms for DMM [FerL89] [IbaS89] [Leng89].

A SA is a parallel algorithm specified on the basis of a set of processes (cells) which perform very simple operations and communicate frequently among them (fine granularity). The cells of the SA are connected in a regular and local way [KunL79]. SAs can be automatically derived from a formal specification of the problem to be solved (a system of recurrences [Quin84], a nested loops structure [Mold83], etc.).

The original problem to be solved should be specified using a nested loop structure like those considered in [Mold83]. From this specification, we design a SA for the problem. The SA is partitioned in order to adapt it to the size of the available DMM. Although the resulting parallel algorithm could be directly executed by the DMM, the high communication cost, due to the fine granularity of the algorithm, will not permit us to obtain a good system performance. So, in order to reduce the communication cost, we increase the granularity of the parallel algorithm.

* *This work has been supported by the Ministry of Education of Spain (CICYT) in program TIC 299/89, and ESPRIT PCA 4146.*

In order to carry out some of the stages of the proposed method (design and partitioning of the SA), we use techniques published in the literature. The contribution of our paper is the systematic procedure to increase the granularity of the partitioned SA and the procedure to derive the parametrized code for each PE of the DMM.

The proposed method is based on a data dependence classification that is used to derive a dependence graph among bands. Those bands are obtained by partitioning the SA. Then bands are executed in an interleaved way when they are independent or when the dependences among them are due to variables propagating through the bands. Finally, we show that a further partitioning of bands into subbands permits to increase the granularity of the parallel algorithm.

In section 2 we discuss each of the stages of the proposed method and describe the code transformations. In section 3 we present some performance measurements using a DMM based on Transputers [Whit85].

2. THE STAGES OF THE METHOD

In this section we describe each of the stages of the method proposed in this paper. In order to illustrate the stages, we use an example. This example consists in the design of a parallel algorithm to solve a triangular system of equations:

$$L \cdot x = b$$

where L is a lower triangular matrix, x is an unknown vector and b is a vector. This problem must be solved using a DMM with a ring topology.

The original problem can be specified by a nested loop structure. The specification for a triangular system of equations is shown in figure1a. The design of a SA for the original problem requires a uniform specification like that shown in figure 1b. In a uniform specification the indexing functions of the variables have the form:

$$f(I) = I - d$$

where I is a vector formed with the indices of the nested loop structure and d is a constant vector. For instance, the indexing function for S1 in figure 1b is f(j,i) = (j,i)-(0,1). The initial data are b(i, -1) = b(i) and the results are x(i, i) = x(i).

The uniformization is the first step in many SA design methodologies. The problem has been studied by several authors [ForM84], [VanQ88], [WonD88], but no general solution has been given yet. However, for the majority of the Linear Algebra operations (Matrix Multiplication, Triangular Systems of Equations, LU Decomposition, etc.), the uniformization is possible.

Starting from a uniform specification, our method proceeds in three stages: (a) Dependence classification and decomposition into segments; (b) SA design and partitioning; and (c) increase of granularity. In the following subsections, we discuss each of these stages.

(a)

```
do i=0,N-1
  do j=0,i-1
    b(i)=b(i)-l(i,j)x(j)
  enddo
  x(i)=b(i)/l(i,i)
enddo
```

(b)

```
do i=0,N-1
  do j=0,i-1
S1:   x(i,j)=x(i-1,j)                          SEG1
S2:   b(i,j)=b(i,j-1)-l(i,j)x(i,j)             (i, j)
  enddo
S3: j=i                                        SEG2
S4: x(i,j)=b(i,j-1)/l(i,j)                     (i, i)
enddo
```

Figure 1. (a) Nested loop specification for a triangular system of equations. (b) Nested loop structure after uniformization

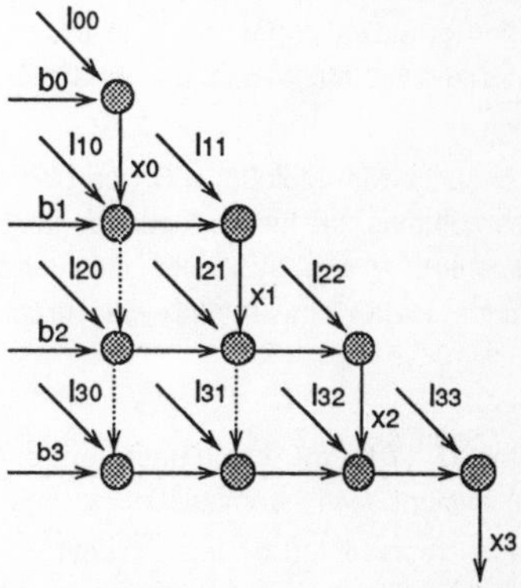

Figure 2. Dependence graph for the resolution of a triangular system of equations.

2.1 Dependence classification and decomposition into segments

The dependence vectors are those constant vectors d used in the indexing functions of the uniformized code. The dependence vectors allow to construct the dependence graph (DG) for the computation. In this DG, each node represents the computations performed in one of the iterations of the nested loops. The edges in the DG represent the data dependences among computations. The DG is regular because the dependence vectors are constant. The DG for our example is shown in figure 2.

In order to permit some of the transformations to be done in step (c), we identify two types of dependences: propagated dependences (P) and generated dependences (G). Dependences of type P arise from statements of the form V(I) = V(I-d), where d is one of the dependence vectors. This kind of dependences have been introduced during the uniformization of the original code. The rest of dependences are of type G.

After the uniformization of the code, each statement is surrounded by a subset of the nested loops and its execution can be subjected to some conditions on the indices of the nested loops. We call these conditions as guard commands. We define a segment as the set of statements surrounded by the same subset of nested loops and the same guard command. We associate a tuple with every segment. All those tuples have the same number of elements. This number is equal to the maximum number of nested loops in the uniform specification. The tuple associated with a segment also identifies the guard command and the rank for the values of the indices for that segment.

In our example, see figure 1b, we identify two segments: SEG1 and SEG2. The concept of segment will play an important role in step (c) of the proposed method (subsection 2.3).

Figure 3 shows a classification of the different dependences in our example. For each dependence we identify the statement in which the dependence is originated, the segment that statement belongs to, the name of the variable written in that statement, the associated dependence vector and the type of the dependence. In the DG shown in figure 2, dependences of type P have been identified by dotted arrows and dependences of type G by continuous arrows.

Statement	Segment	Variable	Dependence vectors	Dependence type
S_1	SEG_1	x	$d_1=(1, 0)^T$	P
S_2	SEG_1	b	$d_2=(0, 1)^T$	G
S_4	SEG_2	x	$d_3=(1, 0)^T$	G

Figure 3. Dependence vectors and associated information.

2.2 SA Design and Partitioning

For the design of the SA we use the method proposed in [Mold83] and for the partitioning of the SA we use the method proposed in [MolF86]. In this section we briefly review these methods, and indicate some criterion to select the SA that favours the band interleaving.

SA Design

As it is described in [Mold83] a SA can be obtained through a linear transformation of the dependence matrix D, whose columns are the dependence vectors d_i for the problem to be solved. The linear transformation can be represented by a m_by_m non_singular matrix T, where m is the maximum number of nested loops in the original code. Matrix T has the following structure:

$$T = \begin{bmatrix} \Pi \\ S \end{bmatrix}$$

Vector Π (1_by_m) establishes an ordering of the computations (temporal mapping). Matrix S ((m-1)_by_m) assigns every computation to one of the cells of the resulting SA (spatial mapping). Specifically, a computation represented by node $r=(x,y)^T$ in the DG is executed in cell $S\cdot r$ in cycle $\Pi\cdot r$. In order to preserve the dependences of the computation, vector Π must satisfy the following condition:

$$\Pi\cdot d_i > 0 \quad \forall d_i$$

The spatial mapping S determines the topology of the SA. Therefore, matrix S should be selected so that

(a)

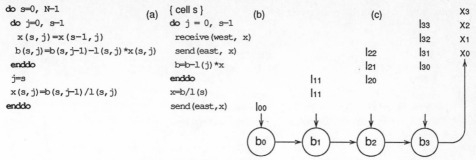

```
do s=0, N-1
  do j=0, s-1
    x(s,j)=x(s-1,j)
    b(s,j)=b(s,j-1)-l(s,j)*x(s,j)
  enddo
  j=s
  x(s,j)=b(s,j-1)/l(s,j)
enddo
```

(b)

```
{ cell s }
do j = 0, s-1
  receive(west, x)
  send(east, x)
  b=b-l(j)*x
enddo
x=b/l(s)
send(east,x)
```

(c)

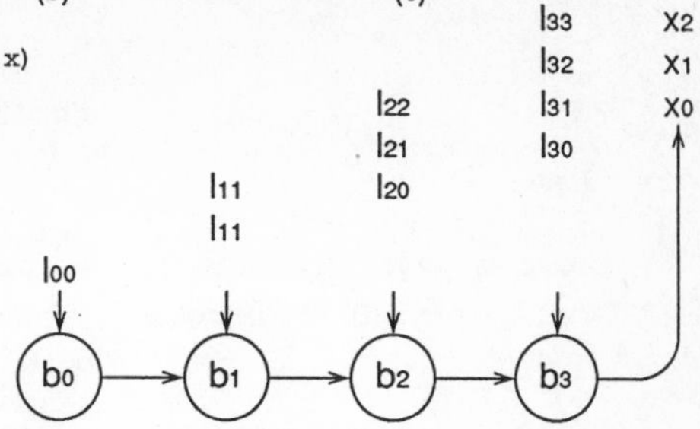

Figure 4. (a) Code obtained by applying transformation Ts. (b) Code for each cell. (c) Systolic Algorithm for Triangular System of Equations.

the resulting topology matches that of the DMM. In order to do that, a matrix P is used, which represents the topology of the communication links of each node in the DMM. Matrix S should be selected among the possible solutions of the diophantine equation:

$$S \cdot D = P \cdot K$$

Matrix K indicates how the communication links in the DMM must be used in order to satisfy the dependences of the algorithm. The elements of matrix K must satisfy the following condition:

$$\sum_j k_{ji} \leq \Pi \cdot d_i \quad \text{with } k_{ji} \geq 0$$

This expression indicates that the communication of data associated with dependence d_i, must be done using $\Sigma\, k_{ji}$ times the communication links.

Any matrix T which satisfies the previous conditions represents a different SA. In our method, the selection of matrix T will be guided by the following criterion: data flows moving from cell to cell in the resulting SA should be, if possible, those associated with propagated dependences. As we will see later, the procedure to increase the granularity of the parallel algorithm, in step (c), will benefit from this criterion.

For the problem we are using as an example, we are interested in a SA in which elements of vector b remain statics in the cells, and elements of vector x move through the array. Provided that the available DMM has a ring topology, matrix P is: P=[-1 1]. The selected matrix T is:

$$T = \begin{bmatrix} 1 & 1 \\ 1 & 0 \end{bmatrix}$$

For the code generation we assume an asynchronous system, that is, there is not a global clock which determines the computation cycles. Communication and synchronization among PEs is done by means of the send and receive primitives with a rendez-vous protocol. The code to be executed in each PE can be obtained by transforming the original code. The transformation can be represented by the matrix

$$T_s = \begin{bmatrix} e_i \\ S \end{bmatrix}$$

where e_i is a vector of the canonical basis, and $T = T_\Pi \cdot T_s$. On the other hand, we use the value $\Pi \cdot d_i$ (with $S \cdot d_i \neq 0$) to identify the size of the buffer between cells and the value $S \cdot d_i$ to identify the direction of the data flow. In our example, we have

$$T_s = \begin{bmatrix} 0 & 1 \\ 1 & 0 \end{bmatrix} \qquad (1\ 1) \cdot (1\ 0)^T = 1$$

Figure 4a shows the code obtained by applying transformation Ts. Now, applying the transformation T_Π to this code and parametrizing the code with the external loop we obtain the code execute by every PE. This code is shown in figure 4b. Figure 4c shows a graphic representation of the selected SA.

<u>SA partitioning</u>

The number of cells of the resulting SA depends on the size of the problem to be solved. In general, this number is greater than the number of PEs of the DMM. Therefore, the SA should be partitioned so that it can be executed in the DMM.

(a)

```
do m=0, P-1
  do Is=0, NN-1
    s=Is*P+m
    do j = 0, s-1
      x(s,j)=x(s-1,j)
      b(s,j)=b(s,j-1)-l(s,j)*x(s,j)
    enddo
    j=s
    x(s,j)=b(s,j-1)/l(s,j)
  enddo
enddo
```

(b)

```
{PE m}
do Is=0, NN-1
  do j=0, Is*P+m-1
    receive(west,x)
    send(east, x)
    b(Is)=b(Is)-l(Is,j)*x
  enddo
  j=Is*P+m
  x(Is)=b(Is)/l(Is,j)
  send(east,x(Is))
enddo
```

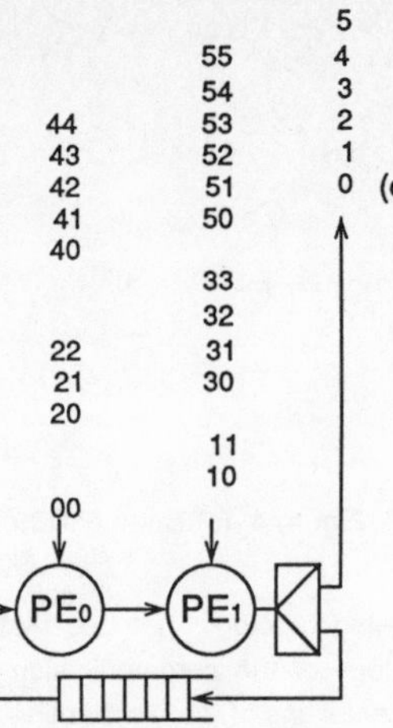

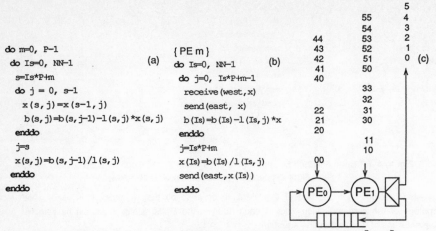

Figure 5. (a)Code after partitioning. (b) Code executed by each PE. (Note: NN = ⌈N / P⌉).
(c) Partitioned Systolic Algorithm.

For the partitioning of the SA we use the technique proposed in [MolF86]. According to that technique, the set of computations is decomposed in subsets called bands. The partitioning of the computations is specified by the matrix S (from transformation T). Each row of S should be viewed as the normal vector of a hyperplane that is used to cut the DG.

Any band is executed completely before initiating the execution of the following one. So, if band B_t is executed after band B_s, no computations in B_s should depend on computations included in B_t. This requirement imposes a condition to the partitioning hyperplanes, represented by the rows of S:

$$S_j \cdot d_i \geq 0 \ (\forall S_j) \ \& \ (\forall d_i)$$

Each of these bands can be executed by a SA with the same size than the DMM. The whole computation is carried out by chaining the execution of the different SAs.

Specifically, for the case of a 2D DG, computation r is assigned to band B_{I_p}, where:

$$I_p = \lfloor S{\cdot}r / P \rfloor$$

and P is the number of PEs of the DMM. Moreover, this computation will be performed by PE_m where:

$$m = (S{\cdot}r) \bmod P$$

It can be seen that this partitioning scheme assigns computations in the boundary of the bands to PEs in the boundary of the DMM. So, in order to chain the execution of the bands we need a link between the PEs in the boundary of the DMM and a buffer to store data. This link is available because the DMM has a ring topology.

Figure 5a shows the code obtained by partitioning the code in figure 4a. The dimension associated with the external loop, which represents the processor space is divided into bands of the same size. Those bands are executed in the lexicographical order. Figure 5b shows the code executed by every PE if we parametrize with index m. Note that rows of L are indexed with $Is=\lfloor s/P \rfloor$ instead of s. This is necessary if we assume that any two rows i and i+P of the original matrix L are adjacent in the same PE. As the bands are executed in a lexicographical order, the buffer between PE_{P-1} and PE_P is a FIFO queue. Figure 5c shows the partitioned SA.

Figure 6 shows the partitioning of our DG into bands, assuming P=3 and N=9. Each band can be executed in a 3 PE DMM using a SA like that shown in figure 4. The execution ordering for these bands is B_0, B_1, and B_2.

The parallel algorithm obtained in this way has a fine granularity. Because the DMM executes a series of SAs, PEs exchange short messages (a single element of x) and very frequently. Moreover, PE_0, must wait till PE_2 sends message before starting the computations in B_1 (idle time). So, the important communication requirements can lead to a poor performance when executing the algorithm in the DMM. The objective of the

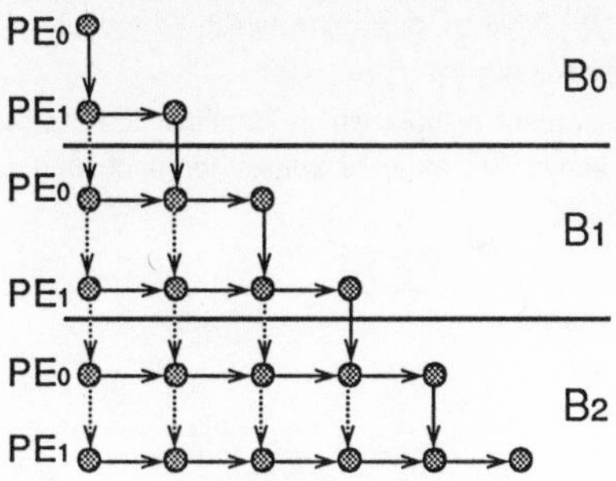

Figure 6. Dependence graph decomposition into bands.

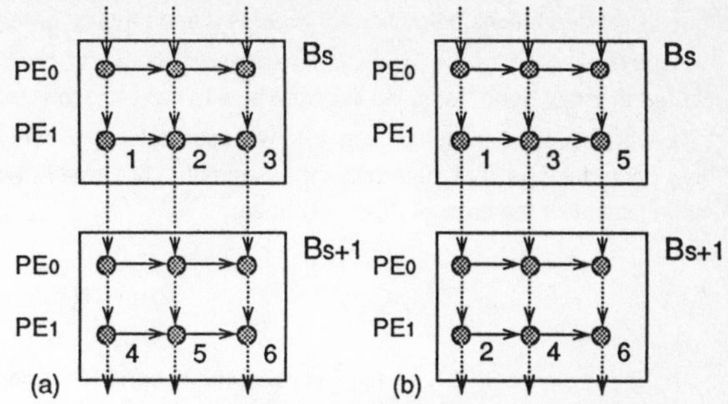

Figure 7. An example of band interleaving. (a) Execution ordering for operations assigned to PEs if bands B_s and B_{s+1} are executed one after the other. (b) Execution ordering if band are interleaved.

next stage is to increase the granularity of the algorithm, reducing in this way the communication requirements.

2.3 Increase of Granularity

The proposed procedure to increase the granularity of the parallel algorithm is based on the concept of band interleaving, that will be explained later in this subsection. But, first we have to define the concept of band dependences.

Band dependences

We say that there is a generated dependence between bands B_r and B_s if data produced in B_r is used in B_s. Analogously, there is a propagated dependence between B_r and B_s, if data used in B_r is also used in B_s, without modification.

If there is a generated dependence between B_r and B_s then B_r must be executed before B_s. If all the dependences between B_r and B_s are propagated then they can be executed in any order, and in particular, they can be executed in an interleaved way. Now, we explain what does this mean by means of a simple example.

Band interleaving

Figure 7 shows two bands B_s and B_{s+1} belonging to a given DG. If these bands are executed one after the other then PE_1 executes its computations in the order indicated in figure 7a. To perform each of these computations PE_1 must receive a data item from PE_0. Because the dependence between B_s and B_{s+1} is propagated, the data item received by PE_1 to perform operation (1) is the same that the one received later to perform (5). The same stands for computations (2) and (6), (3) and (7) and so on. The number of messages from PE_0 to PE_1 can be reduced if PE_1 executes operation (5) immediately after operation (1), using in both operations the received data item. Analogously, operation (6) is executed immediately after operation (2) and so on. The new execution ordering is show in figure 7b. In that case we say that bands B_s and B_{s+1} are executed in an interleaved way.

In general, a set of bands can be interleaved if all the dependences among them are propagated, or if the bands are independent. If bands are interleaved then the communication requirements of the algorithm are reduced because the contents of every message is used for computations in several bands. If bands are independent we cannot use the same data item for different bands. However, we can pack different data items into a simple message, reducing also in this way the communication cost. Selecting the SA according to the criterion proposed in subsection 2.2 the number of generated dependences between bands is minimized and so the number of bands that can be interleaved is increased.

Identify the type of dependences between bands

As we saw before, the dependences of an algorithm can be associated with the segment where they are originated. As an example, dependence d_2 in our example, of type G, is originated in SEG1. Therefore, any band containing computations belonging to SEG1 is a band that generates the dependence d_2.

In order to identify the type of dependences between bands we have to determine which segments are executed in every band. Now, we illustrate how to carry out this analysis in our example.

As we described in subsection 2.1, we associate with every segment a tuple which identifies the indices of the nested loops that determine the segment. Moreover, we know the range of values for each one of these indices. For the case of SEG1 we have:

$$(i, j)$$
$$0 \le i \le N-1$$
$$0 \le j \le i-1$$

An index point of SEG1, $r = (i, j)^T$ is executed in band B_{ls}, where:

$$l_s = \lfloor S \cdot r / P \rfloor = \lfloor i / P \rfloor$$

Taking into account the range of values for the indices of the nested loops, we conclude that computations belonging to SEG1 are executed in every band B_{ls} such that:

$$0 \le l_s \le \lfloor (N-1) / P \rfloor$$

That is, SEG1 is executed in all the bands. A similar analysis for SEG2 indicates that this segment is also executed in all the bands.

So, in the developed example, all the bands propagate dependence d_1 and generate dependences d_2 and d_3. Dependence d_2 corresponds to dependences between computations belonging to the same band. On the contrary dependences d_1 and d_3 correspond to dependences between bands. Therefore, we conclude that in our problem, there is a generated dependence between any two bands B_p and B_{p+1}, and bands cannot be interleaved.

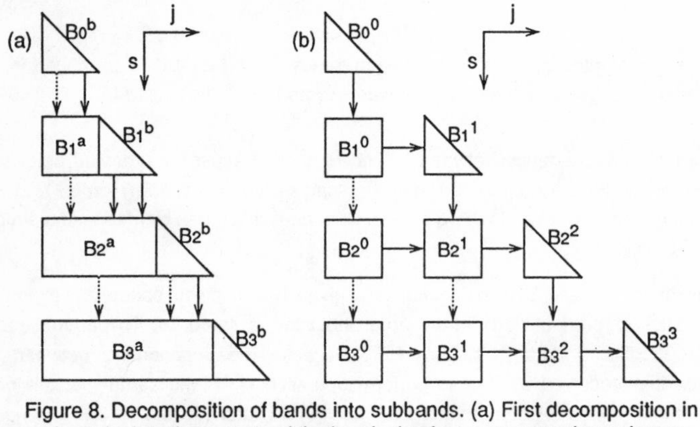

Figure 8. Decomposition of bands into subbands. (a) First decomposition in order to isolate those parts of the bands that just propagate dependences. (b)Final partitioning in order to obtain subbands with the same size.

<u>Further partitioning of bands</u>

In general, after the analysis of dependences between bands, we expect to identify the subsets of bands that can be interleaved. As we have seen, in our example no band interleaving is possible. However, a further partitioning of bands into subbands permits to increase the number of subbands that can be interleaved, increasing in this way the granularity of the algorithm.

A band that has been identified as a generator of a dependence may actually generate that dependence only during a part of the computations. Coming back to our example (see figure 6), during the first computations, band B_1 just propagates d_1 (because all these computations belong to SEG1). Only during the final computations, the band executes SEG1 and SEG2 and so, it propagates d_1 and generates d_3. The same stands for all the bands, except for band B_0. If we isolate that part of the computations where the band just propagate d_1 then these parts could be interleaved. This fact suggests a further decomposition of bands into subbands.

In order to determine the new partitioning we have to identify, for every segment, which part of each

```
do m=0, P-1
 do Is=0, NN-1                                  (a)
  s=Is*P+m
  do Ij=0, Is -1
    do j1=0, P-1
     j=Ij*P+j1
     x(s,j)=x(s-1,j)
     b(s,j)=b(s,j-1)-l(s,j)*x(s,j)
    enddo
  enddo
  Ij=Is
  do j1=0, m-1
   j=Ij*P+j1
   x(s,j)=x(s-1,j)
   b(s,j)=b(s,j-1)-l(s,j)*x(s,j)
  enddo
  j=s
 x(s,j)=b(s,j-1)/l(s,j)
 enddo
enddo
```

```
do m=0, P-1
 do Ij=0, NN-1                                  (b)
  do j1=0, m-1
   j=Ij*P+j1
   Is=Ij
   s=Is*P+m
   x(s,j)=x(s-1,j)
   b(s,j)=b(s,j-1)-l(s,j)*x(s,j)
  enddo
  Is=Ij
  j=Is*P+m
  s=j
  x(s,j)=b(s,j-1)/l(s,j)
  do j1=0, P-1
   j=Ij*P+j1
   x(s,j)=x(s-1,j)
   do Is =Ij+1, NN-1
    s = Is*P+m
    b(s,j)=b(s,j-1)-l(s,j)*x(s,j)
   enddo
  enddo
 enddo
enddo
```

```
{ PE m }
do Ij=0, NN-1                (c)
 do j1=0, m-1
  j=Ij*P+j1
  Is=Ij
  receive(west,x)
  send(east,x)
  b(Is)=b(Is)-l(Is,j)*x
 enddo
 Is=Ij
 j=Is*P+m
 x(Is)=b(Is)/l(Is,j)
 send(east,x(Is))
 do j1=0, P-1
  j=Ij*P+j1
  receive(west,x)
  send(east,x)
  do Is =Ij+1, NN-1
   b(Is)=b(Is)-l(Is,j)*x
  enddo
 enddo
enddo
```

Figure 9. (a) Code after the partitioning of the bands. (b) New code after loop exchange. (c) Code executed by each PE.

band contains computations belonging to that segment. We now illustrate how to carry out this analysis in the case of SEG1 and SEG2 from our example.

A band B_{Is} contains the index points (s,j) such that:

$$I_sP \leq s \leq I_sP+P-1$$
$$0 \leq j \leq i-1$$

We know that SEG1 is executed in the index points (s,j) such that:

$$0 \leq s \leq N-1$$
$$0 \leq j \leq i-1$$

and SEG2 is executed in the index points (s,j) such that:

$$s = j$$
$$0 \leq s \leq N-1$$

Intersecting these domains of index points we conclude that only for index points (s,j) such that $j \geq I_sP$, band B_{Ip} executes SEG1 and SEG2 and therefore, it generates d_3 and propagates d_1. During the rest of computations, this band just propagates d_1. So, each band can be decomposed into two parts: B_{Is}^a which propagates d_1, and B_{Is}^b which propagates d_1 and generates d_3. Figure 8a shows the result of this decomposition.

In order to determine the partitioning of the bands we intersect the domain of those index points of B_{Is+1} which propagate the dependences with the index points of B_{Is} (for all I_s). In our example, for each band B_{Ip}, the domain of index points which propagates the dependence is $j<I_sP$. Therefore we use the partitioning hyperplane represented by $S_0=(0,1)^T$. That hyperplane satisfies the condition $S_0 \cdot d_i \geq 0$ ($\forall$ d_i) and the size of the obtained subbands along the partitioning dimension is P. Figure 8b shows the final partitioning.

Figure 9a shows the code obtained by applying that new partitioning to the code shown in figure 5a. The loop has been unrolled because the number of iterations is not always a multiple of P. On the other hand, the unrolling permits to identify the bands that propagate the dependences and the bands that generate the dependences.

The analysis of propagated dependences determines the new execution ordering. This ordering is: B_0^0, (B_1^0, B_2^0, B_3^0), B_1^1, (B_2^1, B_3^1), B_2^2, B_3^2, B_3^3, where B_{ls}^{lj} represents band (ls,lj) and bands in parenthesis are executed in an interleaved way. Note that we interleave along direction $(1,0)^T$. Therefore, it is necessary to modify the lexicographical order specified in the code shown in figure 9a. The new ordering requires a loop exchange between l_s and $j=(l_j, j_1)$. This loop exchange can be represented by the transformation matrix:

$$T' = \begin{bmatrix} 001 \\ 100 \\ 010 \end{bmatrix}$$

The new code obtained by this transformation is show in figure 9b. Finally, the parametrized code for PE m is shown in figure 9c. Due to the new execution ordering for the subbands, the buffer between EP_{P-1} and EP_0 is not a FIFO queue. Once bands B_{ilj} (l_j < NN-1) have been executed it is necessary to empty the buffer.

3. EXPERIMENTAL RESULTS

The proposed parallel algorithm for solving Triangular System of Equations has been executed on a 16 PE DMM based on Transputers T414B and T800C. The results are plotted in figure 10. This figure shows the efficiency obtained varying the size of matrix L (N_by_N). The efficiency has been measured using the following expression:

$$\text{Efficiency} = \frac{T_{seq}}{P\, T_{par}}$$

where T_{seq} is the time required to solve the problem in a single PE, using the best serial algorithm, and T_{par} is the time required by P PEs.

The efficiency of the parallel algorithm with 320-by-320 matrices approaches the 75% using T414 processors and 40% using T800 processors. With 640-by-640 matrices the efficiency with T800 processors approaches the 50%. The plots reflect the different computations/ communications ratios in the T414 and T800 processors. Note that the efficiency of the interleaved algorithm, for the T800 processors, double the efficiency of the systolic algorithm (serial execution of the bands).

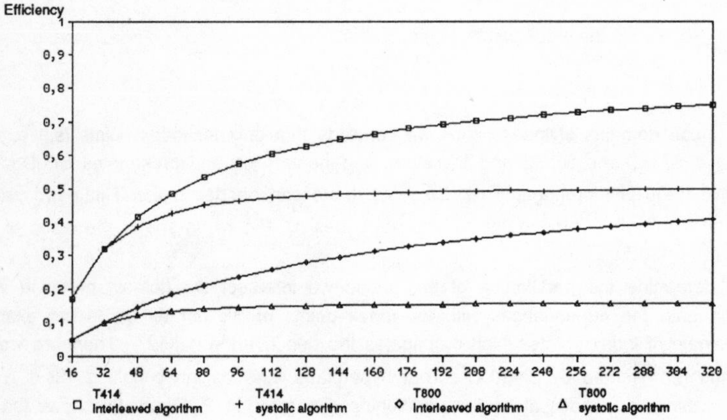

Figure 10 Experimental results when executing the obtained algorithm on a ring of 16 Transputers.

4.CONCLUSIONS

In this paper we have presented a systematic method for mapping systolizable problems onto DMM. The inputs to the method are a nested loop based specification of the problem to be solved and the interconnection topology of the DMM.

For the first stages of the method (design and partitioning of a SA for the problem) we use techniques proposed by other authors. The main contribution of the paper is the procedure to increase the granularity of the partitioned SA. This increase of granularity is necessary in order to reduce the communication cost of the algorithm. This issue is specially important when designing parallel algorithms for DMM, where the effects of communication between PEs cannot be neglected.

The method has been illustrated with an example consisting in the design of a parallel algorithm to solve a Triangular System of Equations on a DMM with a ring topology. We have obtained some promising results running the code on a ring of Transputers.

The method has been applied to map others problems like Matrix Multiplication or LU Decomposition on a DMM whit different topologies (ring, mesh, etc.). The resulting algorithms exhibit superior efficiencies (85% - 90%) than the one presented here, due to their greater level of intrinsic parallelism.

References

[CalK88] D.Callahan and K.Kennedy. "Compiling Programs for Distributed-Memory Multiprocessors". J.Supercomputing 2, october 1988, pp. 151-169, Kluwer Academic Publishers.

[FerL89] A.Fernández, J.M.Llabería, J.J.Navarro, M.Valero-García and M.Valero. "On the Use of Systolic Algorithms for Programming Distributed Memory Multiprocessors", Proc. Int'l. Conference on Systolic Arrays, Prentice Hall, pp. 631.640, 1989.

[ForM84] J.A.B.Fortes and D.I.Moldovan. "Data Broadcasting in Linearly Scheduled Array Processors", Proc. 11th Int'l Annual Symp on Computer Architecture, pp. 224-231, 1984.

[GeiH87] G. A. Geist and M. T. Heath. "Parallel Algorithms for Matrix Computations", The Characteristics of Parallel Algorithms, MIT 1987, pp. 233-251.

[HeRo88] M.Heath and C.Romine. "Parallel Solution of RTriangular Systems on Distributed-Memory Multiprocessors", SIAM J. Sci. Stat. Comput. 9 (1988), pp. 558-588.

[IbaS89] O.H.Ibarra and S.M.Sohn. "On Mapping Systolic Algorithms onto the Hypercube". Int'l Conf. on Parallel Processing, Vol.I, pp 121-124, 1989.

[KinN89] C.T.King, L.M.Ni. "Grouping in Nested Loops for Parallel Execution on Multicomputers". Int'l Conf. on Parallel Processing, Vol.II, pp 31-38, 1989.

[KunL79] H.T.Kung and C.E.Leiserson. "Systolic Arrays (for VLSI)", Sparse Matrix Proc. 1978, 1979, Society for Industrial and Applied Mathematics (SIAM), pp.256-282.

[Leng89] C.Lengauer. "Towards Systolizing Compilation: an Overview". Proc. Parallel Architectures and Languages Europe, PARLE'89. Lecture Notes in Computer Science 366, Springer-Verlag, pp. 253-272, 1989.

[LiCo88] G.Li and T.Coleman. "A Parallel Triangular Solver for a Distributed-Memory Multiprocessor", SIAM J. Sci. Stat. Comput. 9 (1988), pp. 485-502.

[Mold83] D.I.Moldovan. "On the Design of Algorithms for VLSI Systolic Arrays", Proc. of the IEEE, vol 71, no. 1, 1983. pp. 113-120.

[Mole86] C. Moler. "Matrix Computation on Distributed Memory Multiprocessors", Hypercube Multiprocessors 1986, pp 181-195.

[MolF86] D. I. Moldovan and J. A. B. Fortes. "Partitioning and Mapping Algorithms into Fixed Size Systolic Arrays", IEEE Trans. on Computers, Vol. 35, n. 1, 1986, pp. 1-12.

[Quin84] P.Quinton. "Automatic Synthesis of Systolic Arrays from Uniform Recurrent Equations", 11th Int'l Annual Symp. on Computer Architecture, pp.208-214, 1984.

[RamS89] J.Ramanujan and P.Sadayappan. "A Methodology for Parallelizing Programs for Multicomputers and Complex Memory Multiprocessors". Supercomputing 89, pp 637-646, 1989.

[TorA90] J.Torres, E.Ayguade, J.Labarta, J.M.Llabería, M.Valero. "On Automatic Loop Data-Mapping for Distributed-Memory Multiprocessors", Proceedings of the 2nd European Distributed Memory Computers Conference, Springer-Verlag (in this volume), 1991.

[VanQ88] V.VanDongen and P.Quinton. "Uniformization of Linear Recurrence Equations: a Step Towards the Automatic Synthesis of Systolic Arrays", Proc. Int'l Conf. on Systolic Arrays, pp. 473-482, 1988.

[Whit85] C. Whitty-Stevens. "The Transputer". Proc 12th Int'l Symp. of Computer Architecture, 1985, pp. 292-300.

[WonD88] Y.Won and J.M.Delosme. "Boadcast Removal in Systolic Algorithms", Proc Int'l Conf. on Systolic Arrays, pp. 403-412, 1988.

Partial Ordering of Synchronization Events for Distributed Debugging in Tightly-coupled Multiprocessor Systems

G.J.W. van Dijk and A.J. van der Wal

Eindhoven University of Technology, Department of Physics,
P.O. Box 513, 5600 MB Eindhoven, The Netherlands

Abstract

In this paper, a partial ordering of synchronization events for the debugging of distributed programs in tightly-coupled multiprocessor systems is defined. Techniques for the debugging of parallel programs require timestamping of events. The physical clocks of different processors are in general not suitable for time stamping events, because these clocks are not synchronized. Synchronization of the physical clocks of all processors in a multiprocessor system requires additional hardware mechanisms. In an alternative approach, a partial ordering of events can be derived using *logical* clocks for timestamping events with *virtual* time. The concept of virtual time has been used successfully to derive clock conditions in distributed systems, in which message-passing is the only form of interaction. In this paper, clock conditions are derived for tightly-coupled synchronization primitives in multiprocessor systems. Finally the concept is successfully used in the implementation of a distributed debugger in the EMPS multiprocessor system.

Introduction

In the development of software, programmers inevitably will be confronted with bugs, i.e. a departure of the expected program behavior. Programmers therefore need tools to trace these errors efficiently and correct the software. A debugger is such a tool. Various debuggers exist for tracing errors in sequential programs. However, only a small number of debuggers for parallel programs in multiprocessor systems have been developed and of these only a fraction has been implemented.

The usual techniques in the debugging of sequential programs are e.g. the halting of a program at prescribed points in its execution, the tracing of specified parts of the program, and the setting of watchpoints at variables in the program. Since sequential programs are ordered completely, these techniques are sufficient to trace program bugs. Parallel programs however have only *partial* ordering because of the communication and synchronization between the processes. Therefore, additional techniques are required for the debugging of parallel programs, especially if they are running on multiprocessor systems.

In general, three techniques are used for the debugging of distributed programs, viz. recording, replay, and behavior specification. The first technique records all events (i.e.

including the interactions between processes) of a distributed program [1,2,3]. The recording technique is used for off-line analysis of the execution order of a distributed program. The recording of events is time-consuming and requires ample storage resources for retaining the information. The replay technique is used to re-execute the distributed program starting from specific points [4]. The replay technique controls the order in which the events occur in such a way that the order of events is the same as during the original execution of the program. The user has interactive control over the execution of the program during replay. The information that is used for replay has been recorded during the original execution. The technique of behavior specification is used to compare the expected program behavior with the actual behavior [2,5,6,7,8,9,10]. A behavior specification consists of a number of events combined by simple, disjunctive, conjunctive, or time-linked relations. When a behavior specification is violated (i.e. the actual program behavior does not match the expected behavior), interactive control is transferred to the user. This technique can be time-consuming as well.

The techniques for the debugging of distributed programs require time stamping of events. The physical clocks of different processors are unsuitable for time stamping, since these clocks are generally not synchronized. Synchronization of the physical clocks of all processors in the multiprocessor systems requires difficult hardware mechanisms. Instead of physical clocks, logical clocks can be used for time stamping events with virtual time. These logical clocks do not have to be synchronized by hardware, but have to satisfy certain clock conditions. In this way, a partial ordering of events is achieved. Logical clock conditions for distributed systems, in which message-passing is the only form of interaction, are derived in [11,12]. In this paper, these logical clock conditions have been extended for synchronous message passing based on rendez-vous. In addition, logical clock conditions have been derived for distributed semaphore and eventflag primitives for process synchronization in tightly-coupled multiprocessor systems.

The organization of this paper is as follows: In Sec. 1, the concept of virtual time is introduced and logical clocks are used for time stamping message-passing events based on rendez-vous synchronization. Partial ordering of distributed semaphores and eventflag synchronization primitives in tightly-coupled multiprocessor systems will be defined in Sec. 2. In Sec. 3, some implementation implications for the multiprocessor architecture design are discussed. In Sec. 4, the conclusions of the paper are summarized.

1 Partial ordering of message-passing events

Techniques for the debugging of distributed programs require time stamping of events. Events cannot be ordered using physical time because the physical clocks of each processor in the distributed system are in general not synchronized. However, a partial ordering of events can still be derived by time stamping events with *virtual* time.

1.1 Virtual time

Usually a "happened-before" relation between two events can be justified using the concept of physical time. Although the physical clocks on different processors are generally not synchronized, yet happened-before relations exist between events of processes.

Happened-before relations exist between all events occurring in one process, because a process consists of a sequence of events. Happened-before relations also exist between interaction events, thus inducing a partial ordering of all events in the system.

The happened-before relation (denoted by $\rightarrow$) for distributed systems in which is assumed that message-passing is the only form of interaction between two processes, can be defined by the following three rules [11]:

R1 If A and B are events in the same process and A comes before B, then A $\rightarrow$ B.
R2 If A is the sending of a message by one process and B is the receipt of that message by another process, then A $\rightarrow$ B.
R3 Two distinct events A and B are said to be concurrent if A $\not\rightarrow$ B and B $\not\rightarrow$ A.

A clock condition is derived from these rules:
Clock condition. For any events A and B : if A $\rightarrow$ B, then C(A) < C(B)

In words: if A happened before B, then the (virtual) time stamp of event A is smaller than the time stamp of event B.

If each process in the distributed system is provided with a logical clock, the clock condition can be divided into two parts:

C1 If A and B are events in the process P_i and A occurs before B, then C_i (A) < C_i (B).
C2 If A is the sending of a message by process P_i and B is the receipt of that message by process P_j , then C_i (A) < C_j (B).

The logical clocks of all processes have to satisfy the clock conditions, although they do not have to be synchronized. At the occurrence of an event in a process, the logical clock of that process is incremented. When a message is exchanged between two processes, not only the logical clock of the sending process is incremented, but also the logical clock of the receiving process is updated according to the clock conditions. In order to achieve this, the time stamp of the sending event is transmitted as part of the message. The receiving process then updates it logical clock to a value greater than the time stamp contained in the received message.

1.2 Synchronous message-passing based on rendez-vous

In many distributed systems, synchronous message-passing based on rendez-vous is used for interprocess communication. Interprocess communication based on rendez-vous implies that whichever process (sender or receiver) is first, is required to wait until the other process is ready. Synchronous message-passing implies that the sending of a message can be subdivided into two parts, viz. initiating the message transfer and waiting for its completion. The receiving process notifies the sender that the message has been received. Synchronous message-passing adds a happened-before relation rule to the three previously mentioned rules:

R4 If B is the receipt of the message by the receiving process and C is the completion of the message transfer of the sending process, then B $\rightarrow$ C.

The following clock condition can be derived from this rule:

C3 If B is the receipt of the message by process P_j and C is the completion of the message transfer of process P_i , then C_j (B) < C_i (C).

The logical clock of a process can be implemented as a vector of integers, one element for each process in the distributed system. When a process P_i sends a message M to process P_j , the logical clocks of the communicating processes are updated according to the clock conditions using the following scheme:

1 Upon initiating the communication, process P_i increments the i-th element of its logical clock vector in order to satisfy clock condition C1. This time stamp T_M is transmitted as part of the message.
2 In the case that process P_j is ready to receive a message before process P_i has sent the message, the j-th element of the clock vector of P_j is incremented (C1), and P_j is suspended.
3 When the message M is actually received by process P_j , P_j first increments the j-th elements of its logical clock vector. Then, each element of the logical clock vector of P_j is compared with the corresponding element of the time stamp of the message T_M , and the smaller element is set equal to the larger one. Finally, the i-th element of the vector of P_j is incremented in order to satisfy clock condition C2. The resultant vector is the time stamp for the message receipt.
4 Process P_j notifies the sending process P_i of the message receipt by transferring the updated message time stamp T_M to P_i . Each element of the logical clock vector of P_i is compared with the corresponding element of T_M , and set to the larger one. Process P_i finally increments both the i-th and the j-th elements of its logical clock vector in order to satisfy clock conditions C1 and C3, respectively.

Fig. 1 shows an example of the time stamps of the events of three processes that interact with each other by passing messages based on rendez-vous synchronization. In order to determine whether event A in process P_i happened before event B in process P_j, the i-th element of the time stamp T_A is subtracted from the i-th element of T_B . If and only if the result is a positive number, it may be concluded that A happened before B. For example, from Fig. 1 we determine that H $\rightarrow$ M since 3-1 > 0. Events J and M are concurrent because J $\not\rightarrow$ M ((3-3)$\not>$0) and M $\not\rightarrow$ J ((0-2)$\not>$0).

2 Partial ordering of distributed semaphores and eventflags

In tightly-coupled multiprocessor systems, processes not only interact using message-passing communication. Processes also synchronize with each other using shared data structures, e.g. semaphores and eventflags. Also the synchronization events in processes are partially ordered. In this section, a partial ordering for distributed semaphores and eventflags will be derived.

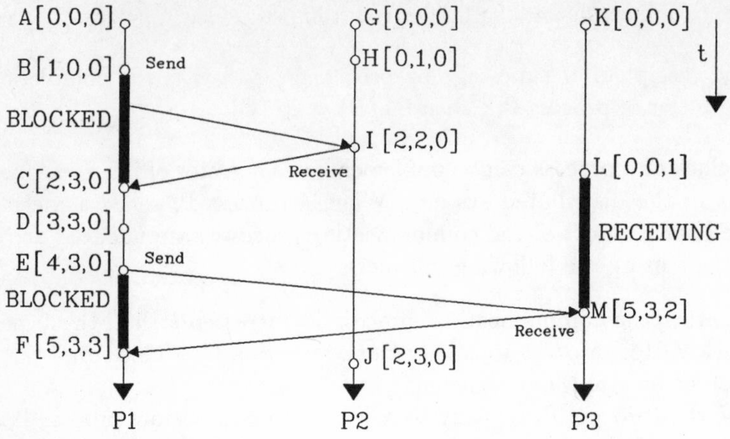

Figure 1: *A typical example of timestamping of communication events using the clock conditions C1, C2, and C3 for synchronous message passing based on rendez-vous. Process P1 sends a message to process P2 (event B) and is suspended since P2 is not yet ready to receive the message. When P2 executes a Receive operation (I), the message is actually transferred. The receiving process notifies the sender P1 that the message has been received (C). Event E is the sending of a message from process P1 to process P3. In this situation, the message is transferred immediately (M) since P3 has already executed a Receive operation.*

2.1 Semaphores

A semaphore is a common data structure, consisting of a non-negative counter and a queue, on which two operations are defined, viz. wait and signal. A process that executes a wait operation on a semaphore is suspended in the semaphore queue if the counter has a zero value. Otherwise, the process continues execution after the counter has been decremented. A signal operation either increments the semaphore counter if the queue is empty, or releases the first process from the semaphore queue. Semaphores are used to establish mutual exclusion between processes either executing on the same or on different processors.

The happened-before relation for wait and signal operations on a semaphore S can be summarized by the following two rules:

R5 If A and B are operations on the semaphore S by different processes and A occurs before B, then A $\rightarrow$ B.

R6 If A is a signal operation of process P_i on the semaphore S that releases process P_j from the semaphore queue, and B is the event of process P_j following the wait operation on S, then A $\rightarrow$ B.

The corresponding clock conditions are:

C4 If A and B are operations on semaphore S by processes P_i and P_j respectively, and A occurs before B, then C_i (A) < C_j (B).

C5 If A is a signal operation of process P_i on the semaphore S that releases process P_j from the semaphore queue, and B is the event of P_j following the wait operation on semaphore S, then C_i (A) < C_j (B).

A partial ordering for operations on semaphores is induced by associating a logical clock with each semaphore in the multiprocessor system. The logical clocks associated with the semaphore and the processes are updated according to the following scheme:

1 If process P_i executes an operation on a semaphore S, the i-th element of P_i is incremented, corresponding to clock condition C1.

2 Each element of the logical clock vector of process P_i is compared with the corresponding element of the logical clock vector of semaphore S and both elements are set to the larger one. Then, the i-th element of the logical clock vector of S is incremented. In this way, the clock condition C4 is satisfied.

3 Directly after a process P_i , that has been suspended in the semaphore queue, is released from that queue, and before execution of the first statement of P_i, the logical clock of P_i is equalized to the logical clock vector of semaphore S. In this way, clock condition C5 is satisfied.

An example of partial ordering of semaphore synchronization events is sketched in Fig. 2. The semaphore counter initially equals one. A wait operation that decrements the semaphore counter and a wait operation that suspends process P_i in the semaphore queue can be distinguished by examining the i-th element of the logical clock vector of P_i : In the case that the i-th element increases by more than unity between the wait event and the next event in process P_i , P_i was suspended in the semaphore queue; Otherwise the wait operation decremented the semaphore counter and P_i continued execution without being suspended.

2.2 Eventflags

An eventflag is a shared data structure, consisting of a flag and a queue, on which two operations are defined, viz. WaitForEventflag and SetEventflag. A process that executes a WaitForEventflag operation is *always* suspended in the eventflag queue. In contrast to the signal operation, the SetEventflag operation releases *all* pending processes from the eventflag queue at the same time. All processes that share an eventflag are partially ordered.

The happened-before relation for WaitForEventFlag and SetEventflag operations can be summarized by the following two rules:

R7 If A and B are operations on the eventflag E by different processes and A occurs before B, then A $\rightarrow$ B.

R8 If A is a SetEventflag operation that releases process P_i, P_j, P_k, ... from the eventflag queue, and B,C,D,... are the events of processes P_i, P_j, P_k, ... respectively, following the corresponding WaitForEventflag operations on E, then A $\rightarrow$ B, A $\rightarrow$ C, A $\rightarrow$ D, ...

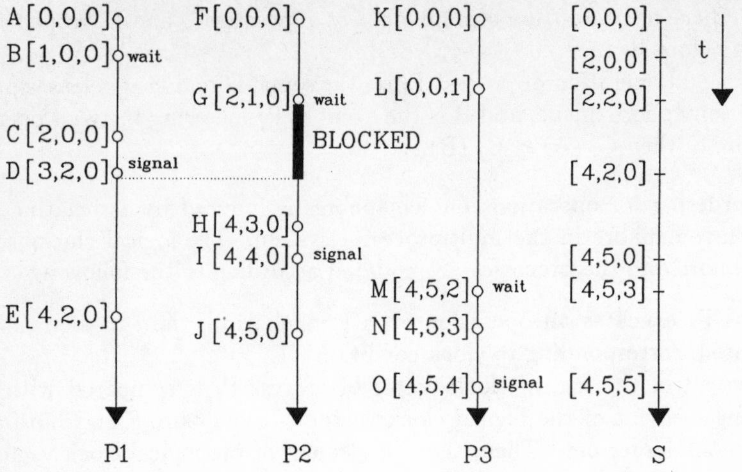

Figure 2: *An example of timestamping of semaphore events using the clock condition rules C4 and C5 for semaphore primitives. The semaphore S is used to establish mutual exclusion between the processes P1, P2, and P3. Initially the semaphore counter is set equal to one. Process P1 executes a wait operation on S (B) and enters its critical region. Process P2 is suspended in the semaphore queue by the wait operation (G). When P1 leaves its critical region, it executes a signal operation on S, thereby releasing P2 from the semaphore queue. Then P2 enters its critical region. It should be noted that the second element of P2 increases more than unity between the two successive events G and H. This implies that P2 was suspended in the queue of S.*

The corresponding clock conditions are:

C6 If A and B are operations on eventflag E by processes P_i and P_j respectively, and A occurs before B, then C_i (A) < C_j (B).

C7 If A is a SetEventflag operation of process P_i on the eventflag E that releases processes P_j ,P_k ,P_l ,... from the eventflag queue, and B,C,D,... are the events of P_j ,P_k ,P_l ,... following the WaitForEventflag operation on E, then C_i (A) < C_j (B), C_i (A) < C_k (C), C_i (A) < C_l (D), ...

A partial ordering for operations on eventflags can be defined by associating a logical clock with each eventflag in the multiprocessor system, and updating the logical clocks of the eventflag and the processes according to a similar scheme as for semaphore operations:

1 If process P_i executes an operation on an eventflag E, the i-th element of P_i is incremented, corresponding to clock condition C1.

2 Each element of the logical clock vector of process P_i is compared with the corresponding element of the logical clock vector of eventflag E and both elements are set to the larger one. Then, the i-th element of the logical clock vector of E is incremented, thus guaranteeing that clock condition C6 will be satisfied.

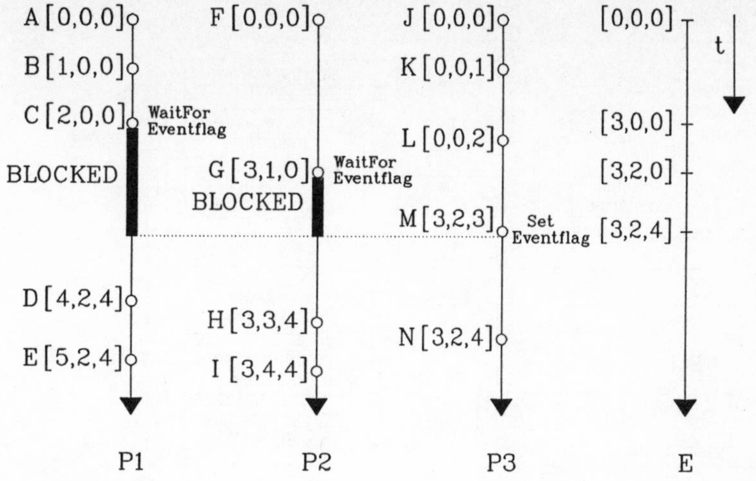

Figure 3: *An example of timestamping of eventflag events using the clock condition rules C6 and C7 for eventflag primitives. Process P3 executes a SetEventflag operation on E (event M), thereby releasing all processes (P1 and P2) that were suspended on a WaitForEventflag operation on E (C and G, respectively).*

3 For all processes P_i, P_j, P_k, ... that have been suspended in the eventflag queue, the logical clocks of P_i, P_j, P_k, ... are equalized to the logical clock vector of eventflag E on release. In this way, clock condition C7 is satisfied.

An example of the use of logical clocks for eventflag synchronization events is illustrated in Fig. 3.

3 Hardware support for distributed debugging

A microcomputer-based multiprocessor system (EMPS) has recently been developed at the department of physics of the Eindhoven University of Technology. The EMPS system is a homogeneous multiprocessor system based on Motorola MC68030 microprocessors. In order to realize the design objectives of flexibility and scaleability, general purpose computer, memory and local area network modules have been designed that can be used to construct the required hardware configuration for a given application. Several modules can be interconnected by means of a *cluster bus* to form a *cluster*. A *system bus* connects several clusters to form a *node* (Fig. 4). A detailed description of the EMPS system architecture can be found in [13].

The architecture of the EMPS multiprocessor system has been designed to support distributed debugging in the following ways: First, the computer modules of the EMPS system are equipped with three dedicated hardware registers (debug registers). A hardware facility for implementing distributed watchpoints is provided by these debug registers. The setup of a watchpoint corresponds to writing the address of a variable into

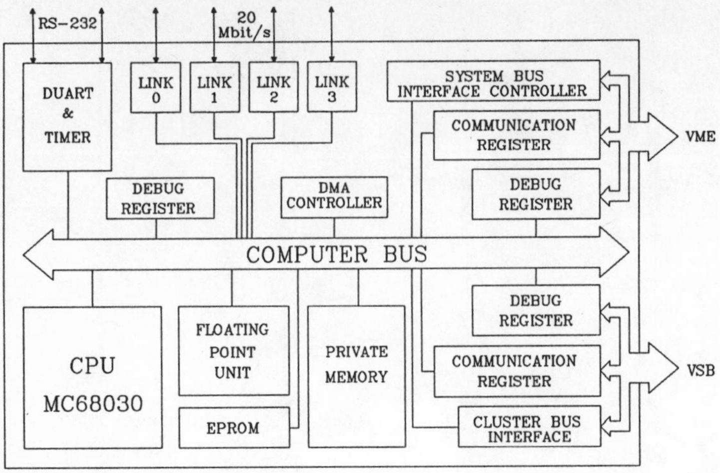

Figure 4: *The block diagram of the computer module of the EMPS multiprocessor system. The debug register is used to implement watchpoints on three different buses, viz. the computer bus, the cluster bus, and the system bus. The links are used to create a separate communication layer to debug the multiprocessor system.*

the debug register. If a watchpoint is set, a counter is decremented every time that this addresses is used. When the counter overflows, a local interrupt is generated at the computer module. Secondly, each computer modules is equipped with four serial links (20 Mbits/s). These links can be used to create a separate communication layer in hardware to debug the multiprocessor system. This separate layer prevents the debug processes from interfering with the interactions between user processes on different processors. In this way the hardware architecture offers facilities to supervise and debug true system behavior.

4 Concluding remarks

Parallel programs differ from sequential programs in that the temporal relationships between events are only partial defined. Therefore, the usual techniques for the debugging of sequential programs are insufficient for the debugging of distributed programs. The techniques for the debugging of parallel programs require a mechanism for time stamping of events. Even if physical time cannot be used for time stamping, a partial ordering of events can be achieved using logical clocks for time stamping events. In this way the concept of virtual time is introduced. The concept of virtual time has already been used successfully to derive clock conditions in distributed systems, in which message-passing is the only form of interaction between processes. In tightly-coupled multiprocessor systems, process synchronization is provided by common data structures, e.g. semaphores and eventflags. The operations on these common data structures also induce a partial ordering of events. The concept of virtual time can be used to derive clock conditions for these synchronization events in tightly-coupled systems, by providing each common data structure with its logical clock.

A multiprocessor architecture has been designed that supports the debugging of distributed programs by providing dedicated debug registers for implementing distributed watchpoints, and a separate communication layer that prevents the debug processes from interfering with the interactions between the user processes. The computer module of the EMPS multiprocessor systems, that contains these hardware facilities for the debugging of distributed programs, has recently become operational.

References

[1] H. Garcia-Molina, F. Germano, and W.H. Kohler. "Debugging a Distributed Computing System". *IEEE Transactions on Software Engineering*, **SE-10**(2), pages 210–219, March 1984.

[2] B. Lazzerini and C.A. Pete. "Event-driven Debugging for Distributed Software". *Microprocessors and Microsystems*, **12**(1), pages 33–39, Jan/Feb 1988.

[3] C-C. Lin and R.J. LeBlanc. "Event-based Debugging of Object/Action Programs". *SIGPLAN NOTICES*, **24**(1), pages 23–34, Jan 1989.

[4] I.J.P. Elshoff. "A Distributed Debugger for Amoeba". In *ACM workshop on Parallel Distributed Debugging*, pages 1–10, Madison Winconsin, U.S.A., May 1988.

[5] R. Cooper. "Pilgrim: A Debugger for Distributed Systems". In *Proceedings of the 7th International Conference on Distributed Computing Systems*, pages 458–465, Berlin, Sept 1987.

[6] R. J. Fowler, T.J. LeBlanc, and J.M. Mellor-Crummey. "An Integrated Approach to Parallel Program Debugging and Performance Analysis on Large-Scale Multiprocessors". *SIGPLAN NOTICES*, **24**(1), pages 163–173, Jan 1989.

[7] M.E. Garcia and W.J. Berman. "An Approach to Concurrent Systems Debugging". In *Proceedings of the 5th International Conference on Distributed Computing Systems*, pages 507–514, Denver, May 1985.

[8] P.K. Harter, D.M. Heimbigner, and R. King. "IDD:An Interactive Distributed Debugger". In *Proceedings of the 5th International Conference on Distributed Computing Systems*, pages 498–506, Denver, May 1985.

[9] B.P. Miller and J. Choi. "Breakpoints and Halting in Distributed Programs". In *Proceedings of the 8th International Conference on Distributed Computing Systems*, pages 316–323, 1988.

[10] F. Baiardi, N. De Francesco, and G. Vaglini. "Development of a Debugger for a Concurrent Language". *IEEE Transactions on Software Engineering*, **SE-12**(4), pages 547–553, April 1986.

[11] L. Lamport. "Time, Clocks, and Ordering of Events in a Distributed System". *Communications of the ACM*, **21**(7), pages 558–565, July 1978.

[12] C.J. Fidge. "Partial Orders for Parallel Debugging". *SIGPLAN NOTICES*, **24**(5), pages 183–194, Jan 1989.

[13] G.J.W. van Dijk and A.J. van der Wal. "EMPS: An Architecture for a Distributed Homogeneous Multiprocessor System". submitted to Microprocessors and Microsystems.

A Development Environment for Distributed Systems

S. Chaumette and M.C. Counilh
Laboratoire Bordelais de Recherche en Informatique*
Université Bordeaux I, LaBRI,
351, cours de la Libération
33405 TALENCE, FRANCE

Introduction

The programming of distributed computing systems requires specific development, debugging and analysis tools. The purpose of this paper is to present some features of a project carried out at **LaBRI** in this area. This project consists of defining a way of expressing massively parallel algorithms (**EDAM**) and designing an environment to aid the development of such algorithms (**ADAM**).

The underlying model of EDAM is that of a set of processes communicating by message-passing. EDAM's concepts aim to provide a programming method that is independent of the topology of the target machine and that leads to an efficient implementation for communications. These concepts are implemented in a Pascal-based language called **LCH** [8]. In this paper, we present the notion of a task defined in EDAM to introduce parallelism into the behaviour of a process.

The ADAM environment provides a tool for solving the mapping problem, a centralized **SIM**ulator-debug**GER** [6] at the language level (**SIMGER**) and a visualization and analysis tool of interprocess communications, **VICI** (achronym in French of "Visualisation Interactive des Communications Interprocessus"). SIMGER aims to assist the developer and serves as a basis for the debugging tools. We focus in this paper on the debug mechanisms supported by SIMGER and on the VICI software.

This paper is organized as follows:
we first briefly describe in section 1 the main concepts of EDAM. We then present in section 2 the notion of a task and look at a specific example of application. Section 3 describes the debugging tools provided by SIMGER and the VICI communication analysis system.

*Unité associée au Centre National de la Recherche Scientifique n^{0}1304

1 EDAM: basic concepts

1.1 Interprocess communication graph

In EDAM, programs are expressed in the form of a set of *processes communicating by message passing* on *channels.* A channel is an oriented link between an *ouput port* of a process (sender) and an *input port* of another process (receiver).

We call *interprocess communication graph of a program*, the graph where each vertex represents a process of the program and each edge a channel between two ports of two processes. This graph, which is machine-independent, is explicitly described in the *initialization part* of a program and is statically created during the execution of this part (*initialization phase*) by creating all the channels and processes which form it. This enables a pre-allocation of all the channels during the *loading phase* and leads to an efficient communication system [14] during the *process execution phase.*

So, the successive phases that precede the process execution phase and that take place on the host computer are: the program compiling, the initialization phase, the *mapping* of the communication graph on the graph describing the topology of the target machine (carried out by the ADAM software MAPP [1, 18]) and the loading phase.

1.2 Interprocess communication mechanism

Two communication mechanisms are available in EDAM: the *synchronous message-passing* (or CSP rendez-vous [11]), and the *k-synchronous message-passing.* The latter is a buffered, order-preserving, message-passing system which blocks the sender only if the buffering capacity k has already been reached. This mechanism can be used when full synchronization between the sender and the receiver is useless.
Hence, the programmer can create so-called *synchronous* and *k-synchronous channels* in the initialization part of his program. Yet, in order to optimize the setting-up, the buffering capacity k of a k-synchronous channel is chosen by the system during the loading phase and is therefore not known by the programmer.

In EDAM, as in most distributed languages [5], a process can execute a receipt among several possibilities and can therefore take into account the parallelism of its environment. In LCH, this is achieved by the nondeterministic function **ready** which takes as a parameter a set of input ports and which delays a process until a message can be received on one of the input ports of the set. Then, this function returns arbitrarily one such port.

2 Tasks in EDAM

EDAM, as for example the languages SR [2] and Lynx [20], allows a process to describe a *pseudoparallel* algorithm, the pseudoparallelism being here defined by the notion of lightweight process or *task.* A process, also called main task, can dynamically create tasks which are executed on the processor assigned to the process. More precisely, any task is allowed to create tasks during its execution, and a task is executed in pseudoparallel with the task which created it.

The notion of task is reflected in the LCH programming by declarations of tasks, which can be nested, and by instructions for task creation, authorised within the body of any task.

2.1 Intertask communication

Communication by message-passing The tasks of one process (that is, the main task and all the tasks directly or indirectly created by the process) can communicate by message-passing through synchronous or k-synchronous channels called *internal* channels in opposition to *external* channels between processes. The internal channels are dynamically created by the tasks of the process.
The tasks of two different processes can also communicate by message-passing using the external channels between these two processes.

Communication by shared variables The tasks of one process having access to a common memory, they are also allowed to communicate by shared variables. The tasks of one process, which share data, can synchronize their operations using the message-passing primitives and signals (cf. [8]).

Shared ports The tasks of one process can share their output and input ports and can so send, receive or monitor receipt of messages on the same internal or external channel. A message which is passed through a shared channel was sent by one of the tasks which share the output port and will be received by one of the tasks which share the input port (no multicasting).

2.2 Example

We now propose to illustrate the task notion using an example which corresponds to a particular implementation of ray-tracing where a scene is precut into volumes, and where a process is associated with each volume obtained. In order not to complicate our presentation, we limit ourselves to the functions of this application.

2.2.1 Description of the example

In the implementation under consideration, the graph describing the potential communication between the processes has the form presented figure 1.

Thus, each process G of the mesh (3×3 on the above figure) can communicate (send and receive) with its (2, 3 or 4) neighbours in the mesh, and can also send messages to F.

This application has a lot of data, spread out through the processes of the mesh which all have the same function. Each of these processes G has two roles:

- **role 1**: it makes a finite, known number of calculations of the same type (noted as *calcul_1*) on its local data (i.e. the data that describe the volume associated with it). After each calculation *calcul_1*, zero, one or several transmissions are possible. The message and the destination (one of its neighbours in the graph), determined during the calculation, can change for each transmission. We denote as *seq_1* the sequence of the two actions: *calcul_1* then transmission(s).
- **role 2**: it receives the messages which its neighbours on the mesh send to it, and for each message received, it makes a calculation (noted as *calcul_2*) which uses *both*

its local data and the received message. After each calculation *calcul_2*, zero, one or several transmissions are possible. As before, the message and the destination are determined by the calculation and can change for each transmission. We denote as *seq_2* the sequence of the three actions: receipt of a message, then *calcul_2*, then transmission(s).

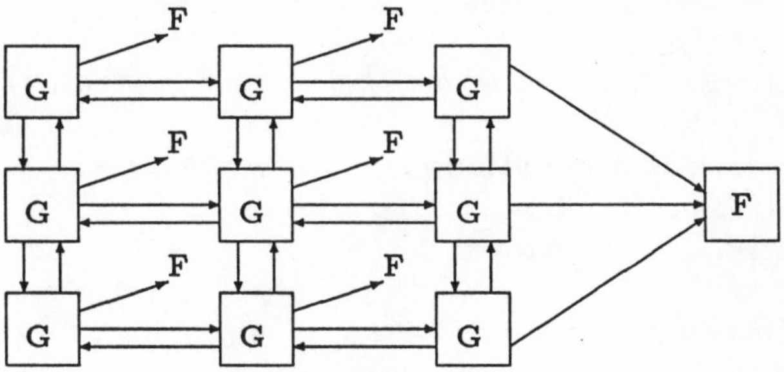

Figure 1

Moreover, the *internal* functioning of a process G has the following two properties:
Property 1: Calculations of the type *calcul_1* and *calcul_2* do not alter local data of the process. Moreover, all of the calculations of a process G are independent: in other words, a calculation (of type *calcul_1* or *calcul_2*) is independent both from another calculation of the same type and from a calculation of the other type.
Property 2: On a process G, transmissions and receipts can be done in any order.

Process F receives the messages sent by the processes G. For each message received, it makes a calculation (*calcul_3*) which contributes to the final result and which allows it to detect the end of the program. In this case, it stores the final result, kills all the other processes, then terminates.
Moreover, communications between processes are asynchronous, and messages exchanged are all of the same type.

We give below a programming in LCH of a process G. The complete program describes an interprocess communication graph which is exactly the one in figure 1. Moreover, we can use k-synchronous channels.

2.2.2 Programming in LCH

```
program example;
type                   (* ports type declarations *)
  t_message = ...      (* messages type *);
  t_in      = inport of t_message;      t_out     = outport of t_message;
  t_g_in    = array[1..4] of t_in;      t_g_out   = array[1..5] of t_out;

process G (n , nb : integer) % in : t_g_in; out : t_g_out %;
  task P;    (* task P declaration *)
```

```
  var i : integer;
  begin
  for i := 1 to n do
    begin    (* seq_1 *)
    calcul_1; transmission(s)     (* on out[1], or ..., or out[nb+1] *)
    end
  end;
  task T (m : t_message);      (* task T declaration *)
  begin
  calcul_2;  transmission(s)    (* on out[1], or ..., or out[nb+1] *)
  end;
  task R;      (* task R declaration *)
  var ens : set of t_in;     e : t_in;
      msg : t_message;       i : integer;
  begin
  ens := [];    for i := 1 to nb do ens := ens + [in[i]];
  while true do
    begin     (* seq_2 *)
    e := ready(ens);     recv(e,msg);      T(msg)
    end
  end;
begin     (* main task of process G *)
acquisition of data associated with the process;
P ;    R ;
end;
...     end.
```

2.2.3 Comments

The process G has four parameters *n*, *nb*, *in* and *out*. *n* is the number of sequences *seq_1* (cf. role 1) that it has to execute. *nb* is the number of input ports of the process (*nb* is also the number of its neighbours in the mesh), and its input ports (resp. output ports) are *in*[1], ..., *in*[*nb*] (resp. *out*[1], ..., *out*[$nb+1$]).

The main task of G is simple: after having executed an acquisition procedure of local data, it creates one instance of P and one instance of R. This programming of process G uses, first of all, the independence of its two roles, i.e. the independence of every action of a sequence *seq_1* compared to every action of a sequence *seq_2* (cf. properties 1 and 2). As a matter of fact, **role 1** is performed by task P which sequentially executes *n* sequences *seq_1*, and **role 2** is performed by task R and tasks T that R creates. This programming then uses the independence of sequences *seq_2* between themselves: the receipts (cf. role 2) are made by task R and each message received is handled by one instance of task T.

Task P and tasks T may need to send messages to the same neighbour of G (cf. role 1 and role 2). In LCH, this is easy to perform: the tasks are allowed to send on the same external channel using a shared output port (as described in 2.1).

Furthermore, the P and T tasks share the local data of the process, which they access in read mode only (cf. property 1).

3 Programming assistance for distributed memory machines: debugging and communication analysis tools

A centralized simulator at the level of the language has been developed (cf. [6] for extensive description). It aims to suppress limitations encountered in similar systems (e.g. limited capacity in terms of simulated processes encountered in Bsim [12]) and to be a basis for the tools described in what follows. A "trace visualizer" will also be presented. It should be noted that all of these tools aim to be non-intrusive. (For example, Parasight [3] is a non-intrusive system.) For further information, the reader is referred to [7].

3.1 Debugging tools

3.1.1 Solving the main problems

Naming: when multiple occurrences of the same process model exist, it is difficult to name any one of them. Compared to commonly used solutions (e.g. **UNIX**-like mapping dependent pathnames as in Helios O.S. [19]), ours is more user-friendly: it consists in displaying the interprocess communication graph (this is analogous to Poker's "Code Names View" [16]) so that the user can select a process or a channel by means of a pointing device.

Non-determinism: there are two kinds of non-determinism within a distributed program. They are explicit non-determinism due to programming (i.e. to the use of non-deterministic control structures, **ready** in the case of **EDAM**), and implicit non-determinism due to relative speeds of execution between processes (i.e. non-causally related events can happen in any order). Non-determinism implies that in order to debug a program, one must be able to replay an execution, that is, in our sense, to execute a program, preserving the partial order of the communications observed during a reference execution. This means "suppressing" explicit non-determinism (cf. [17] for our solution).

3.1.2 Classical tools

Classical tools are those one is accustomed to find in a centralized environment, for instance, the command equivalent to the **UNIX** "ps". But it also includes more sophisticated tools, such as a source-level debugger. Ours is based upon Gdb, GnuEmacs and its Lisp interpretor. We have augmented them with various filters and definitions built in GnuLisp so as to offer the user, within a multi-window environment, services such as occurrence-specific conditional breakpoints. (Most of the other debuggers in the same context - i.e. a centralized simulator using a sole process - enable one only to put a breakpoint in all of the occurrences of a process model.)

3.1.3 Distributed programming tools

General purpose tools such as termination- and deadlock-detection mechanisms have been implemented; such states of the system are detected "as soon as they arise" since these mechanisms are basically implemented within the scheduler of the (simulated) multi-tasking system which has to discover, every time it takes control, whether an executable process can be found or not.

Tools dedicated to communication are emphasised within our environment. They are accessed by means of a window-based dialogue (figure 2). For example, the user can decide on:

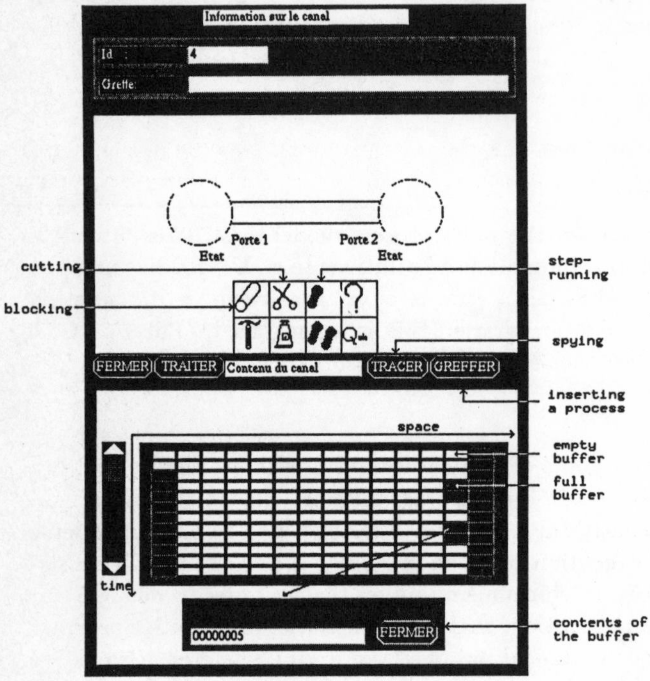

Figure 2: Communication dedicated tools

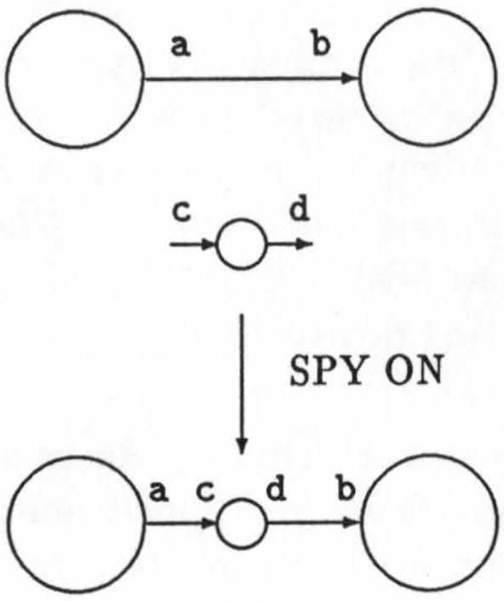

Figure 3: Spying on a channel

- Step-running a channel: every time a send to this channel or a receipt from it happens, the whole application blocks, until the user decides to unblock it;
- Putting a process within a channel: the user can decide to spy on or modify a message, or both at the same time. In order to do that, one has to write a process that is applied the operation depicted in figure 3, without needing to recompile the application. The types of the newly connected communication ports must match. It should be noted that this help may serve as a basis to debug communication since most of the other tools dedicated to communication can be designed by means of this one (this will not be detailed here); for instance:
  - Blocking a channel p: **send**(s,...) blocks the sender and **recv**(e,...) blocks the receiver (s and e are the ports by which channel p is accessed);

- Cutting a channel *p*: **send**(*s*,...) will never block the sender (the message is lost) but **recv**(*e*,...) blocks the receiver;
- Spying on a channel: all the buffers are displayed in a space-time manner, and their contents can be seen (figure 2).

This spying mechanism may also serve to implement similar things as Voyeur's "Views" [4].

3.2 VICI: a tool to visualize "execution traces" interactively

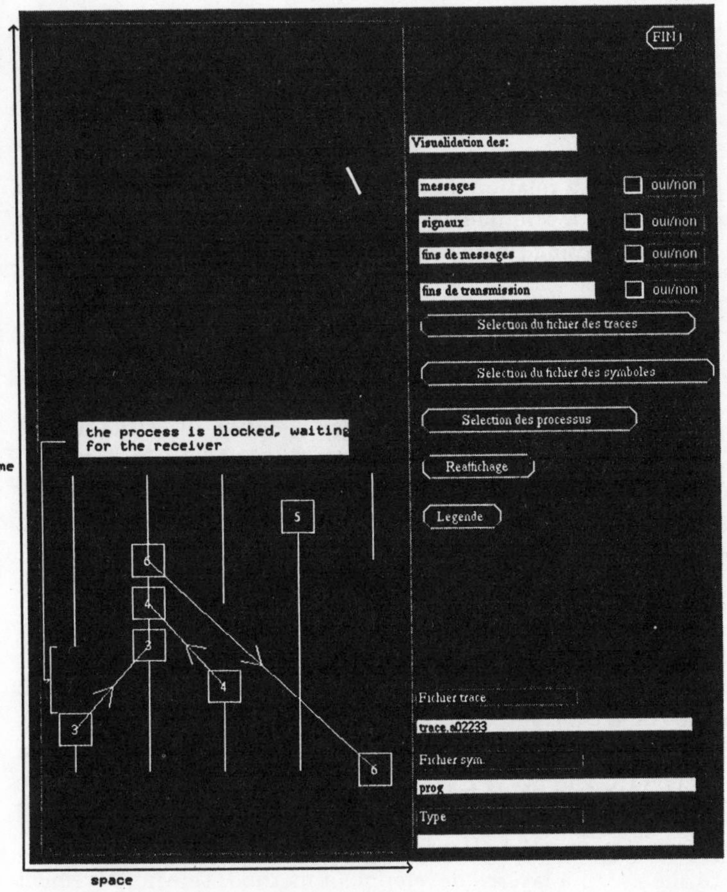

Figure 4.a: The observed communications

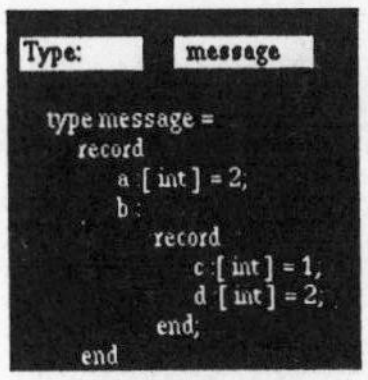

Figure 4.b: Message

It is likely that most often, the ability to check concretely the effectiveness of a communication and to see the exchanged information, would surely be sufficient to correct (or at least to identify) a buggy process among many others. **VICI** is a tool especially designed to examine communications that took place during the execution of a distributed application.

How to handle information related to communication ? Communications are difficult to examine using a classical debugger because non-determinism may lead to situations where they are so differently interlaced from one execution to the other that they cannot be "mind-handled" at run-time. Therefore, a global view is required, and an a posteriori analysis will be preferred.

The basic theory underlying VICI: the semantic foundation of **VICI** is Lamport's causality relation [13]. It leads to a partial order among the set of all events (in our case, events are communications), that matches the usual meaning of "happens before". It can also be viewed as a space-time diagram. The representation that is used within **VICI** is this: each process is associated with a vertical line representing its local time increasing upwards; each communication is represented as a line directed from the sender to the receiver. Alternative representations, emphasizing concurrency relation, also exist [21].

Example: figure 4.a shows a causality relation as displayed by **VICI**; the information that one of the channels carried during a communication can be seen in the syntax of the expression language (figure 4.b) by selecting (by means of the mouse) the line representing this communication.

Conclusion

These features are part of a global environment that aims to simplify all of the phases composing the life cycle of a distributed application. They are effectively used to develop, debug and test the applications studied at **LaBRI** in the area of scientific parallel programming (cf. [10]), where they have proven useful and time-saving; they are also used to support a course on parallelism.

In order to have a rigourous approach, we have described (cf. [9]), using the CCS model of Milner [15], the semantics of the LCH language; VICI and the debugging tools are also based upon theoretical models.

The compiler for the language **LCH** is under completion and the underlying communication system is being developed on a transputer-based distributed computer (**T.NODE**). The debugging and analysis tools available with the simulator have been implemented on a **SUN** workstation running **UNIX** and **X-WINDOW**; these tools will also be made available on distributed architectures. We are also thinking of simulating and providing all of these tools for other programming languages (for instance, those that can be found on the Intel **iPSC2**). Thanks to the use of a layered development method, this improvement requires only adapting the one layer of the simulator that ensures the link between the simulated language and the automata of the communication system implemented within the simulator.

Furthermore, research concerning higher-level parallelism expression modes is being carried out. Traces and communication primitives are also being investigated.

References

[1] F. André and J.L. Pazat. Le placement de tâches sur des architectures parallèles. *Technique et Science Informatiques*, 7(4):385–401, 1988.

[2] G.R. Andrews. The distributed programming language SR– mechanisms, design and implementation. *Software-Practice and Experience*, 12(8):719–753, 1982.

[3] Z. Aral and I. Gertner. Parasight: A high-level debugger/profiler architecture for shared-memory multiprocessors. *Comm. ACM*, pages 131–139, 1988.

[4] M.L. Bailey, D. Notkin, and D. Socha. Voyeur: graphical views of parallel programs. In ACM, editor, *Workshop on Parallel and Distributed Debugging.* SIGPLAN NOT. 24(1):206–216, 1989.

[5] H.E. Bal, J.G. Steiner, and A.S. Tanenbaum. Programming languages for distributed computing systems. *ACM Comput. Surveys*, 21(3):261–322, 1989.

[6] S. Chaumette. Etude et réalisation d'un simulateur et de son environnement pour le calculateur CHEOPS. Mémoire de DEA, Université de Bordeaux I, 1989.

[7] S. Chaumette. Programming assistance for distributed memory machines: simulation, debugging, test and analysis tools. Rapport Interne A paraître, Université de Bordeaux I, 1990.

[8] M.C. Counilh. *LCH: un langage pour la programmation du calculateur CHEOPS.* Thèse de l'Université de Bordeaux I, 1989.

[9] M.C. Counilh. Description de la sémantique du langage LCH. Rapport Interne 90-03, Université de Bordeaux I, 1990.

[10] M.C. Counilh and J. Roman. Expression for massively parallel algorithms- description and illustrative example. *Parallel Comput.*, 16, 1990.

[11] C.A.R. Hoare. Communicating Sequential Processes. *Comm. ACM*, 21(8):666–677, 1978.

[12] Intel Corporation. iPSC2 simulator manual. Intel, 1988.

[13] L. Lamport. Time, clocks and the ordering of events in a distributed system. *Comm. ACM*, 21(7):558–565, 1978.

[14] J.M. Lépine and F. Rubi. The CHEOPS operating system. In North-Holland, editor, *Proceedings of the first European Workshop on Hypercube and Distributed Computers (Rennes), Hypercube and Distributed Computers*, pages 161–174, 1989.

[15] R. Milner. A Calculus of Communicating Systems. *Lecture Notes in Comput. Sci.*, 92, 1980.

[16] D. Notkin, L. Snyder, et al. Experiences with Poker. In ACM, editor, *Proceedings of PPEALS.* SIGPLAN NOT. 23(9):10–20, 1988.

[17] J.L. Pazat. A control replay scheme for distributed systems. In North-Holland, editor, *Proceedings of the first European Workshop on Hypercube and Distributed Computers (Rennes), Hypercube and Distributed Computers*, pages 105–113, 1989.

[18] J.L. Pazat. *Outils pour la programmation d'un multiprocesseur à mémoires distribuées.* Thèse de l'Université de Bordeaux I, 1989.

[19] Perihelion Software Ltd. *The Helios Operating System.* Prentice Hall, 1989.

[20] M.L. Scott. Language support for loosely coupled distributed programs. *IEEE Trans. Software Engrg.*, SE-13(1):88–103, 1987.

[21] J.M. Stone. A graphical representation of concurrent processes. In ACM, editor, *Workshop on Parallel and Distributed Debugging.* SIGPLAN NOT. 24(1):226–235, 1989.

Monitor-Supported Analysis of a Communication System for Transputer-Networks

C.-W. Oehlrich
Informatik-Forschungsgruppe E, Universität Erlangen-Nürnberg, Martensstraße 3, D-8520 Erlangen, Germany

A. Quick, P. Metzger
IMMD VII, Universität Erlangen-Nürnberg, Martensstraße 3, D-8520 Erlangen, Germany

Abstract

Most parallel applications in a Transputer-network require a lot of communication between the processing nodes. For such applications the communication system TRACOS was developed to support data transfer between arbitrary Transputers in the network. To maximize the performance of the parallel system its dynamic internal behavior has to be analyzed. For this purpose event-driven monitoring is an appropriate technique. It reduces the dynamic behavior of the system to some important events, which are recorded by a monitor system and stored in event traces. In this paper the architecture of the communication system TRACOS and its analysis are presented. For the analysis a synthetic workload was instrumented and monitored with the distributed hardware monitor ZM4.

1. Introduction

The use of multiprocessor or multicomputer systems (e.g. Transputer-networks) for parallel applications (e.g. image processing or numerical applications) is quite popular today. In the context of this paper, image processing means manipulation of image data represented in a rectangular matrix of sample values received by a video camera or a scanner. Two conventional methods to parallelize image processing applications are data partitioning and functional partitioning. Both methods need image data to be transferred between processing nodes of the Transputer-network. For data transfer between arbitrary nodes of the Transputer-network, the packet-oriented communication system TRACOS, presented in section 2.1, was developed.

To maximize the performance of a parallel system the dynamic internal behavior and the interdependency between processes on different nodes have to be made visible. One of the most promising ways of gaining the necessary insight in parallel systems, e.g. Transputer-networks, is event-driven monitoring, a technique in which the real-time sequence of interesting activities is monitored and stored as event traces. Event traces can be used for qualitative and quantitative analysis of the internal behavior of the system under investigation. Such traces give the programmer excellent explanations of why the program behaves the way it does. Their evaluation can give valuable hints for program tuning and for the design and implementation of new programs.

Although there is an internal clock with the resolution of 1 μs in each Transputer, an external monitor, having a clock of its own is necessary to measure inter-Transputer communication like the packet transfer time.

In the next section an overview of communication in Transputer-networks is given. Some fundamentals about monitoring and the monitoring environment are presented in section 3. In section 4 the results of the monitor supported analysis are described.

2. Communication in Transputer-networks

With the development of the Transputer in 1987 [INM88] a simple way of building multiprocessor systems with distributed memory came up. The major attributes of the Transputer are:

- RISC architecture
- Integration of a complete computer on one chip
- Simple interconnection of Transputers via Links
- Built-in multitasking system kernel

Using Transputers as processing nodes for image processing the necessary interprocessor communication is typically be done over the Links. Links are bidirectional bitserial communication channels which operate at a speed of 20 Mbit/s. To access the Links, the hardware kernel offers a datatype called Channel and two instructions IN and OUT operating on Channels. The use of Channels is not limited to interprocessor communication over Links. They are also used for interprocess communication inside one Transputer. Therefore the Channels are implemented as variables in the Transputer memory, and the Channel variables associated with Links are located on dedicated memory addresses. Another feature of the Channel concept is the *rendezvous* process-coordination. If a process (sender) transmits data to another process (receiver) over a Channel it executes an OUT-instruction. This blocks the sender until the receiver is ready by executing an IN-instruction on the same Channel. If the receiver comes first with its IN it has to wait until the sender executes its OUT. Using the described mechanism on Links only two neighboring Transputers can communicate with each other. To establish communication between random processors in a Transputer-network the built-in Channel concept must be extended by a packet-oriented communication system realized in software.

2.1. TRACOS: A *TRA*nsputer *CO*mmunication *S*ystem

TRACOS is a communication system dedicated to image processing applications. It was implemented to avoid the overhead of commercial systems like HELIOS ([HEL89]).

The major task of TRACOS is the routing of packets inside the Transputer–network from the packet sender to the receiver. In each Transputer an instance has to exist that receives packets coming in from the Links. With the receiver of the packet being identified, the packet can be routed forward to the next neighboring Transputer on the way to the receiver. This procedure continues inside each Transputer on the way of the packet until the receiver is reached [Oeh89], [Geu89]. Figure 1 shows the structure of the packet-oriented communication system TRACOS that resides in each Transputer in the network.

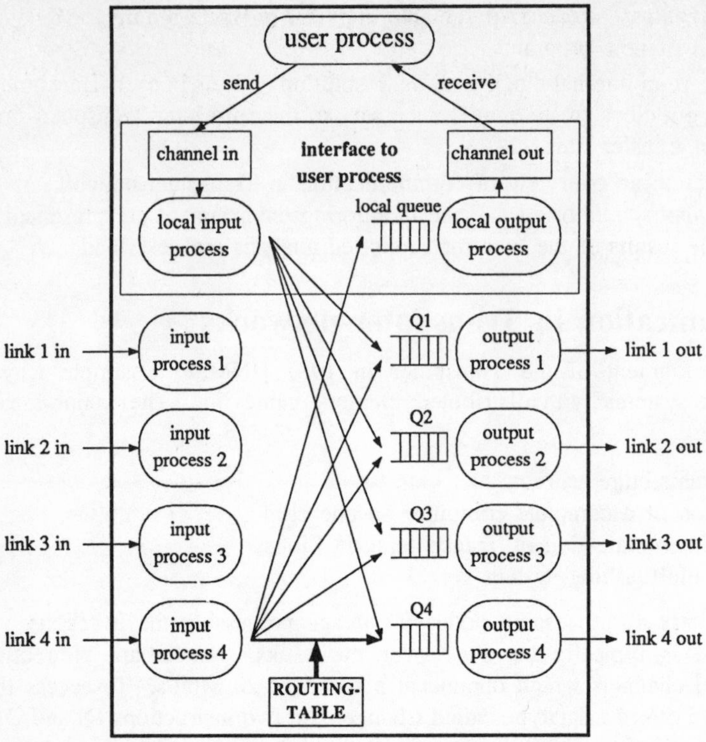

Figure 1: the structure of the communication system TRACOS

Each of the four high priority input processes (1–4) waits for incoming packets at one of the four Links. When a packet to be routed is received, it is put into one of the four output queues (Q1–Q4) with fixed length (in this case 50). A routing table provides the information to which queue the packet has to be forwarded. A high priority output process belonging to each queue transfers the packets from the queue to the corresponding output Link.

The user interface to the communication system consists of two additional processes, the local input process and the local output process. The local input process, which has the same functionality as the input processes 1–4, waits at an internal Channel variable (*channel in*) for packets from the low priority user process. On the other hand the local output process sends received packets over a Channel variable (*channel out*) to the user process. To speed up the data transfer between the user process and the communication system, only the pointers to the packets are transmitted over the internal Channels.

Before the user process is started, the network booter (see the WORM program in [Def88]) determines the configuration of the Transputer-network and distributes it to all processing nodes. Now each Transputer finds out the shortest communication path to all other Transputers in the network and stores it in its own routing table. The table consists of as many entries as Transputers are in the network. Each entry consists of a queue ID. If the system is up and a received packet has to be forwarded to Transputer N, the queue ID in location N of the routing table is fetched and the packet is put into the identified queue. Then the corresponding output process can transmit the packet to the next Transputer.

3. Event-driven Monitoring — Fundamentals and Tools

Event-driven monitoring completely reveals the dynamic behavior of program activities represented by events. An event can be defined as a particular value on a processor bus which is detected by a hardware monitor or as a certain point in a program where an instruction supporting measurement is inserted (instrumentation). The instrumentation defines which program activities are recognized by the monitor and establishes an abstraction of the system behavior [KQS91]. As in our case the intention of monitoring is to get a view of the functional behavior in the Transputer-network, reasonable events are entry and exit of functional building blocks. When monitoring a distributed system, like a Transputer-network, normally not only a single monitor, but rather a system of distributed monitors is needed (see fig. 2). The object system structure is apparently reflected in some way in the monitoring system structure. A single monitor can only cope with a limited number of event streams.

For reconstructing the dynamic behavior of all processes and their interactions in a Transputer-network it is not sufficient to monitor communication events like *send/receive*. Further characteristic points in the programs have to be instrumented and monitored. To get the temporal order and the exact timing of all these events a global time base is needed.

In our analysis hybrid monitoring [Kla85], a mixed form of software and hardware monitoring is used. With this monitoring technique instrumented event tokens are written to a dedicated monitor interface and recorded by a hardware monitor. For this the ZM4, a hardware monitor providing a global time base, was developed.

3.1. The Distributed Monitoring System ZM4

The ZM4[1] is a distributed hardware-monitor featuring a master/slave configuration of one central control and evaluation computer (CEC), an arbitrary number of distributed monitor agents (MA), and a monitor network (data channel and tick channel). In fig. 2 the monitor configuration and two different adaptation methods to a Transputer-network are shown.

The monitoring system is built from standard components as far as possible: the CEC is a UNIX minicomputer or workstation, and the monitor agents are personal computers (IBM-AT). The data channel which is used for transferring commands and setup parameters from the CEC to the monitor agents and measured data from the monitor agents to the CEC is an Ethernet with TCP/IP protocol. The event recognition and recording is done by the dedicated probe units (DPU). The tick channel is a twisted pair connection which is used to synchronize the local clocks of each DPU to the master clock of the measure tick generator (MTG). The monitor timebase has a resolution of 100 ns. The MTG and DPUs can be plugged into the monitor agents, they are our own development ([Hof90]).

For evaluating event-traces the performance evaluation environment SIMPLE, which allows evaluations under various aspects (statistics, graphics, trace-oriented evaluation, execution animation, etc.), was implemented ([Moh90]).

3.2. Hybrid-Monitoring in Transputer-networks

For event-driven monitoring, the programs under investigation have to be instrumented. The instrumentation defines which aspects and details of a program may be observed in terms of events.

---

1 ZM4 is the German abbreviation for counting monitor 4 (Zählmonitor 4).

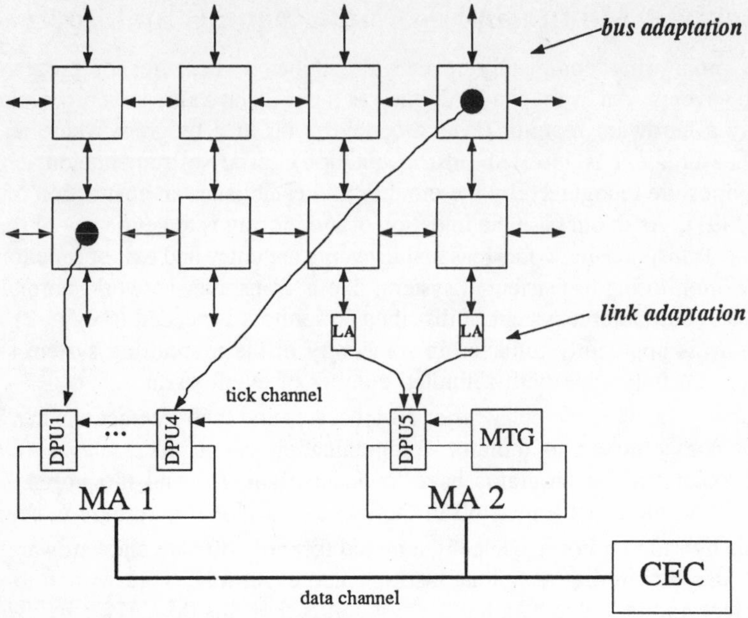

Figure 2: a small ZM4 monitor system and its adaptation to a Transputer-network

In hybrid monitoring, the event token instrumented must be written to a hardware interface dedicated for monitoring. In the following two different adaptation methods for hybrid monitoring in Transputer-networks are presented: **bus adaptation** and **Link adaptation.**

1. **Bus Adaptation**

   The event tokens are assigned to a reserved part of the memory, the *dedicated measurement memory*. The event recognition unit of the DPU has to watch the Transputer memory bus and to record the respective event token if there is an assignment to the dedicated measurement memory.
   This adaptation method only has marginal influences on the internal behavior of the Transputer, because there is only a minimal overhead for one measurement instruction of about 100 ns (one assignment instruction). Furthermore this method is flexible, as no Links must be dedicated to monitoring. A disadvantage of bus adaptation is that the hardware costs are higher than for Link adaptation.

2. **Link Adaptation**

   The event tokens are written out via a Link and stored by an INMOS Link adapter IMS C012 (LA in fig. 2), where they are recognized and recorded by a DPU.

   This adaptation can easily be implemented, but the influence on the internal behavior of the monitored system exceed that of bus adaptation, as the measurement instructions are treated as interprocessor communication (see section 2). If there is more than one process at each Transputer, process scheduling and dynamic behavior of the Transputer will change. In order to reduce these influences a special procedure for monitoring (*mon_out*) was implemented, resulting in an overhead of about 200 μs for each event. This procedure also uses interprocessor communication via a Link, but there is no more influence on internals like process scheduling. If there is only one process at each Transputer this overhead can be avoided, yielding an overhead of only 4 μs. Of course, Link adaptation is only possible if Links at the Transputer under investigation can be dedicated to monitoring (see fig. 2).

4. Monitoring Results

4.1. The Transputer Configuration

For our first analysis a small Transputer-network consisting of three Transputers was monitored (see fig. 3). The distributed hardware monitor ZM4 was adapted to all three Transputers via Link adaptation as there are Links available which can be dedicated to monitoring. Furthermore we assume one low priority user process at each Transputer so that there is no modification of process scheduling due to monitoring.

As the performance of the communication system TRACOS should be analyzed, a synthetic workload, consisting of three programs, was implemented and instrumented at significant points. At Transputer T_1 the sender (S) is running. This program has two configuration parameters (packet size and packet rate); it sends packets to the receiver (R) running at Transputer T_3. At Transputer T_2 the working process work (W) is just looping without any communication. This is an unrealistically behavior, as there are no communication activities, but it is well suited for analyzing the influence of TRACOS on this low priority user process.

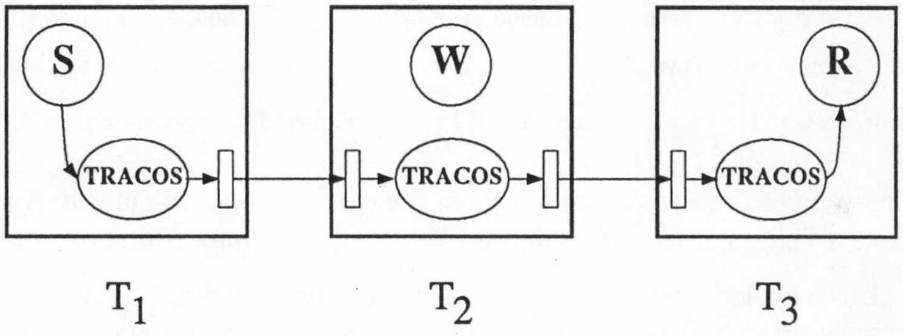

Figure 3: the monitored Transputer configuration (S: sender, W: work, R: receiver)

Instrumenting a synthetical workload with user-driven process communication between the sender and receiver depending on two parameters, an analysis of the communication system's behavior can be well done. In section 4.2 the performance of TRACOS and in section 4.3 the influence of TRACOS on the working process work are described.

With the global time base provided by each DPU of the ZM4, a global time stamp can be assigned to each recorded event token. An event token assigned with a time stamp is a so-called event-record. Since there is a global time base, a global event trace can be created from local event traces by sorting the event-records by increasing time. While monitoring all Transputers at the same time and with a global time base, for example, the packet transfer time **ptt** (time from event "*send_end*" at T_1 to event "*receive_end*" at T_3) can exactly be evaluated. The global event trace is the basis for further evaluations. The instrumentation of the synthetical workload and the monitoring results are described in detail in [Met90].

4.2. Performance of the Communication System TRACOS

In fig. 4 the interdependency between packet size and packet rate is shown (solid line). Long packets result in a low maximum packet rate, as the time for memory allocation and data transfer is greater for large packets than for short packets.

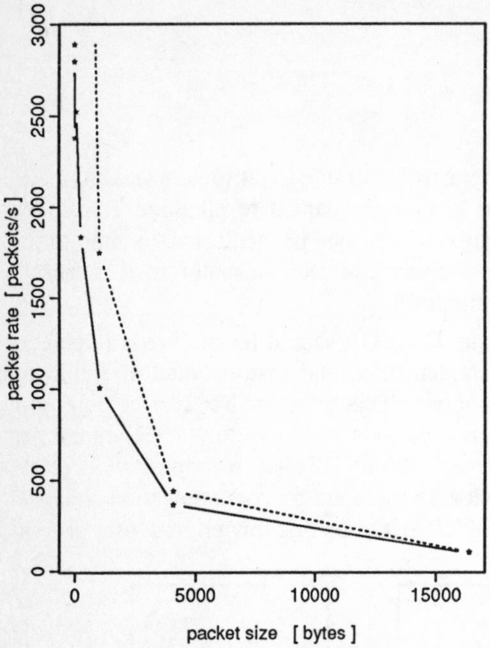

Figure 4: packet size vs. packet rate

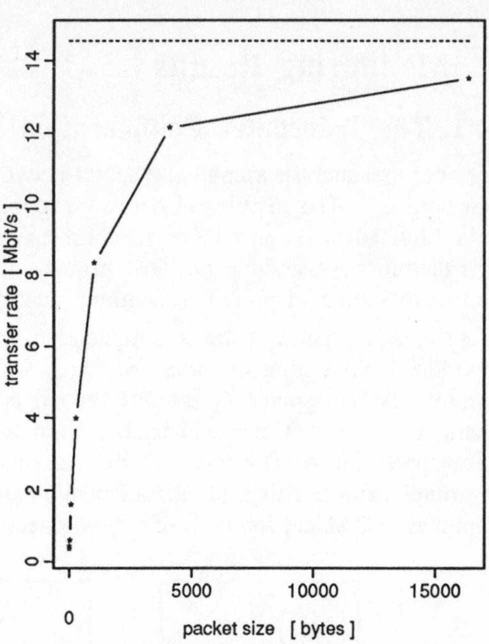

Figure 5: transfer rate of TRACOS

The difference between the theoretically possible packet rate, calculated from the link bandwidth (dotted line), and the monitored packet rate (solid line) results from two reasons:

- For packets smaller than 256 bytes the packet rate is limited by the time used for memory allocation and packet management. An unexpected behavior can be seen in fig. 4: the memory allocation needs more time for 16 bytes than for 64 bytes; therefore the maximum packet rate is greater for 64 byte packets than for 16 byte packets.
- For packets larger than 256 bytes the packet rate is limited by the bandwidth of the Links. The reason for the remarkable difference between the monitored and the theoretical value for 1 Kbyte packets depends on the implementation: in this case the possible parallelism between packet transfer and packet creation is not exploited. The difference is so great, because the duration for packet creation (408 μs) is nearly the same as the duration for data transfer (563 μs). When both activities are executed in parallel, a packet rate of 1775 packets/s could be achieved. This unsuitable implementation was discovered by monitoring and will be fixed.

Fig. 5 shows the packet size vs. the transfer rate of TRACOS (Mbit/s). The transfer rate is limited by the Link bandwidth to 14.5 Mbit/s, as each data byte is transmitted by 11 bits. As the packet management takes time, it is obvious that the maximum transfer rate will be reached with the maximum packet size allowed in the communication system, as in this case the lowest number of packets is to be managed. For short packets (up to 1Kbyte) there is an almost linear increase of the transfer rate.

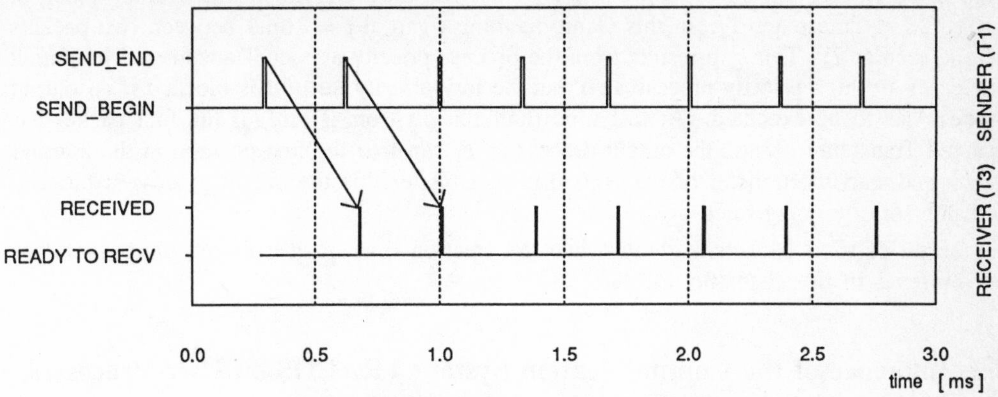

Figure 6: Gantt-diagram: packet size 0 byte

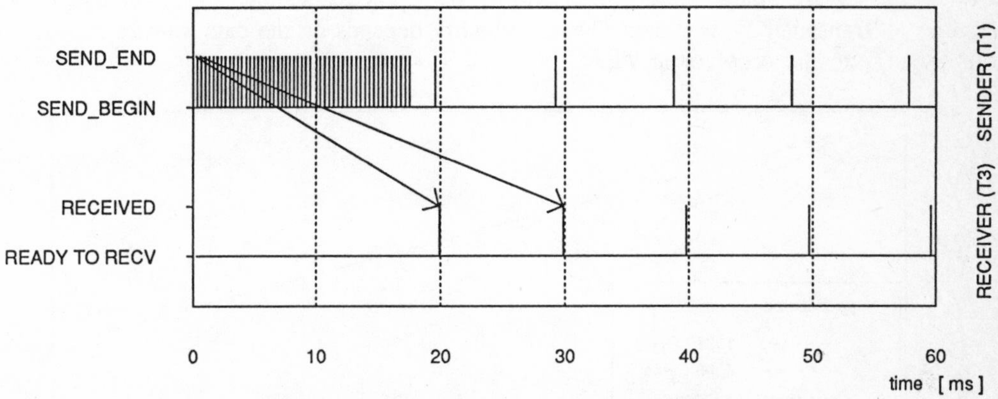

Figure 7: Gantt-diagram: packet size 16 Kbyte

In fig. 6 and fig. 7 the flow and interdependency between the sender and the receiver are shown in a trace-oriented manner with Gantt-diagrams (time-activity diagram). Gantt-diagrams are used to show the interdependencies of selected activities in parallel for qualitative and quantitative analysis. Here, the communication between Transputer T_1 and Transputer T_3 is shown. The packet rate depends on the packet size and can be found in Gantt-diagrams as the reciprocal value of the time between packet arrivals. For 0 byte packets the time between packet arrivals is limited by header management to about 350 μs (fig. 6); for 16 Kbyte packets this time is limited by the Linkspeed to about 10 ms (fig. 7).

Furthermore, the interdependency between sender and receiver is depicted and the packet transfer time between T_1 and T_3 via T_2 can also be found in the Gantt-diagrams: for 0 byte packets this time is constant (about 390 μs for each packet transfer); for 16 Kbyte packets more time, mainly for the Link data transfer time, is needed. Obviously, in the latter case the packet transfer time depends on the length of the internal packet queue.

Without using a communication system process communication is implemented following the *rendezvous-concept* (see section 2). With TRACOS buffering of packets is implemented, so that the sender does not have to wait until the packet has reached the receiver. This effect can be monitored while transferring long packets (fig. 7). Before the first packet is completely transferred from T_1 to T_3 via T_2, exactly 51 packets are buffered in the internal queue of TRACOS at Transputer T_1. In this Gantt-diagram a gap at $t = 10ms$ between two packets can be seen at T_1. This gap results from the process priority at each Transputer. The output processes are high priority processes so that the low priority sender is blocked if an output process has to be executed. At this time (half the ptt from T_1 to T_3) the first packet has reached Transputer T_2 and the output process at T_1 can free the first position in the internal queue and start the transfer of the second packet. After this the output process is blocked and the sender is activated again.

As the ptt of short packets is shorter than the creation time of one packet, the packets are not buffered in this case (fig. 6).

4.3. Influence of the Communication System TRACOS on User Processes

The CPU time used by the communication system to manage the packet transfer should be minimized so that the CPU-availability for application processes is as high as possible. In fig. 8 the CPU-availability for a low priority user process without any communication activities at Transputer T_2 is shown. The availability depends on the data transfer from the sender at T_1 to the receiver at T_3.

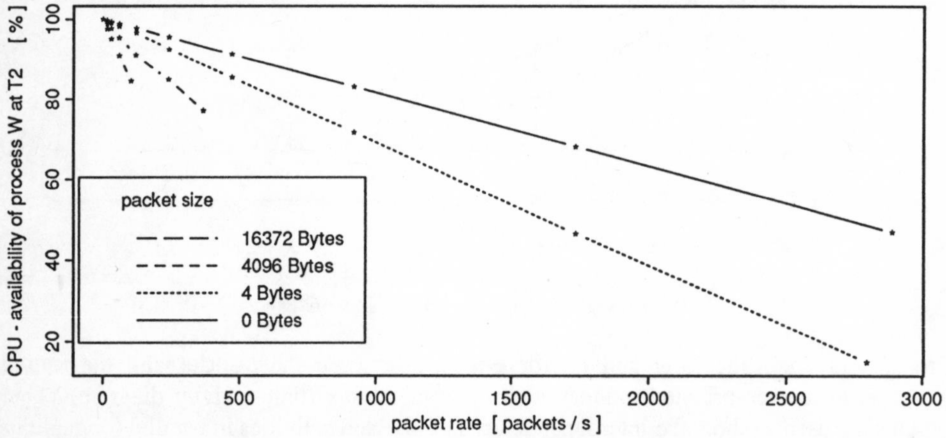

Figure 8: CPU-availability of the process work (W)

- For a given packet size the availability decreases linear to increasing packet rate, as the time for packet management and memory allocation is constant for each packet.
- For a given packet rate the availability decreases with increasing packet size. Although data transfer is a DMA process and hardly needs any CPU time, the memory bandwidth available for the CPU decreases with increasing packet size.
- For a given data rate (product of packet size and packet rate) the decrease of CPU-availability is minimal for long packets.

Therefore, the worst case for low priority user processes is the transfer of as many short packets as possible; in our analysis availability decreases to about 18% by transferring nearly 3000 4 byte packets per second. For analytical purposes packets of 0 bytes are also monitored.

As in this case only the packet header is transferred and no memory allocation is needed, the packet management time is shorter than in the 4 byte case.

5. Conclusions and Outlook

In this paper a packet-oriented communication system for Transputer-networks is described and analyzed by distributed event-driven monitoring. Monitoring results show that TRACOS is well suited for parallel applications in Transputer-networks. In typical image processing applications the average packet size is about 4 Kbyte with an average packet rate of about 50 packets/s. This leads to CPU-availability for a low priority user process of about 95% only, which is a satisfying result.

For improving the packet rate for 1Kbyte packets the internal behavior of TRACOS on a finer level of abstraction has to be analyzed. For this the high priority processes of TRACOS have to be instrumented. As there are a few instrumented processes, Link adaptation is no more sufficient. Therefore a bus adaptation for hybrid monitoring in Transputer-networks will be built. After this, measurements will be carried out under the operating system HELIOS in order to compare the performances of TRACOS and HELIOS.

References

[Def88] Definicon Systems Inc., Newbury Park, CA 91320, USA. *The Parallel Transputer System — Operation and Installation Manual, Release 2.0*, 2nd edition, 1988.

[Geu89] D. Geuder. Ein allgemeines Kommunikationssystem zur Unterstützung paralleler Bildverarbeitungsalgorithmen auf Transputerbasis. Master's thesis, Universität Erlangen–Nürnberg, Lehrstuhl für Technische Elektronik, 1989.

[HEL89] Perihelion Software LTD, Prentice–Hall, New York, London, Toronto, Sidney, Tokyo. *The HELIOS Operating System*, 1989.

[Hof90] R. Hofmann. Gesicherte Zeitbezüge beim Monitoring von Multiprozessorsystemen. In P. Müller-Stoy, editor, *Architektur von Rechensystemen, Tagungsband 11. ITG/GI–Fachtagung München, März*, pages 389–401, Berlin und Offenbach, 1990. vde–Verlag.

[INM88] INMOS. *The Transputer Databook*, 1988.

[Kla85] R. Klar. Das aktuelle Schlagwort — Hardware/Software–Monitoring. *Informatik–Spektrum*, 1985(8):37–40, 1985.

[KQS91] R. Klar, A. Quick, and F. Sötz. Tools for a Model–driven Instrumentation for Monitoring. In G. Balbo, editor, *Proceedings of the 5th International Conference on Modelling Tools and Performance Evaluation of Computer Systems*. Elsevier Science Publisher B.V., 1991.

[Met90] P. Metzger. Messungsunterstützte Analyse von Kommunikationsprozessen in einem Transputernetzwerk. Master's thesis, Universität Erlangen–Nürnberg, Oktober 1990.

[Moh90] B. Mohr. Performance Evaluation of Parallel Programs in Parallel and Distributed Systems. In *Proceedings of the Joint Conference on Vector and Parallel Processing*. Springer, LNCS, 1990.

[Oeh89] C.-W. Oehlrich. *Objektorientierte Methoden für massiv parallele Algorithmen*, pages 131–147. Arbeitsberichte des Instituts für Mathematische Maschinen und Datenverarbeitung 22/13. Universität Erlangen–Nürnberg, Oktober 1989.

An Integrated Environment for Programming Distributed Memory Multiprocessors[1]

Thomas Bemmerl and Arndt Bode

Lehrstuhl für Rechnertechnik und Rechnerorganisation, Institut für Informatik, Technische Universität München, P.O. Box 20 24 20, Arcisstr. 21, D-8000 München 2, FRG, Tel.: +49-89-2105-8240, -8247 bemmerl(bode)@lan.informatik.tu-muenchen.de

Abstract

A breakthrough of distributed memory architectures as general purpose programmable computers depends strongly on the ease of programming such machines. TOPSYS (TOols for Parallel SYStems) is an integrated environment for programming distributed memory multiprocessors. Its concepts and application on an iPSC/2 multiprocessor are presented. It is based on a simple message passing process model implemented in the operating system kernel MMK with a global object space. A smooth transition of parallelization methodology from manual to interactive (semiautomated) and finally to fully automated is provided with this environment. It uses several distributed monitoring techniques and offers various development tools ranging from specification to performance analysis. Fully transparent dynamic load balancing is being implemented.

1. Distributed Memory Architectures and Programming Environments

From the standpoint of performance, reliability and scalability, parallel systems with fully distributed resources including memory and I/O are most suitable. On the other hand, to keep the programming effort reasonable the introduction of as many virtual shared resources as possible is needed to achieve the goal of a universally programmable general-purpose parallel system [Bode90]. This virtualization may be obtained by hardware and/or software support. Although several projects attack this problem from different point of views (TOUCHSTONE [Rat91], iWARP [Rat91], PUMA/H1 [May91], GENESIS [BGS91], EDS [Bol91]) such systems are not widely used in production processes. The reason for this is the need for explicit parallelization, which makes the programming process more complicated, compared to sequential systems. A lack of adequate programming tools for parallel architectures boosts this effect.

2. TOPSYS Methodology and State of the Art

This gave us the motivation to work within the TOPSYS (TOols for Parallel SYStems) project toward a methodology for a more automatic way of using and programming scalable (distributed memory) parallel architectures [BBB90]. We try to overcome the difficulty of programming distributed memory multiprocessors with an integrated approach and virtual concepts. Only with the support of integrated tools and new programming methodologies will the programmers of distributed memory machines be able to handle the complexity introduced with massive parallelism. Future concepts in this field have to hide as many details of

1 partly funded by the German Science Foundation under contract number SFB 0342 (project A1)

the parallel machines as possible. The programming tools have to abstract from specific architectural details such as topology, physical interconnection network, configuration, number of processors, available amount of memory, distributed disk space, etc. One of the basic TOPSYS requirements is to introduce as many virtual concepts as possible to offer architecture independence.

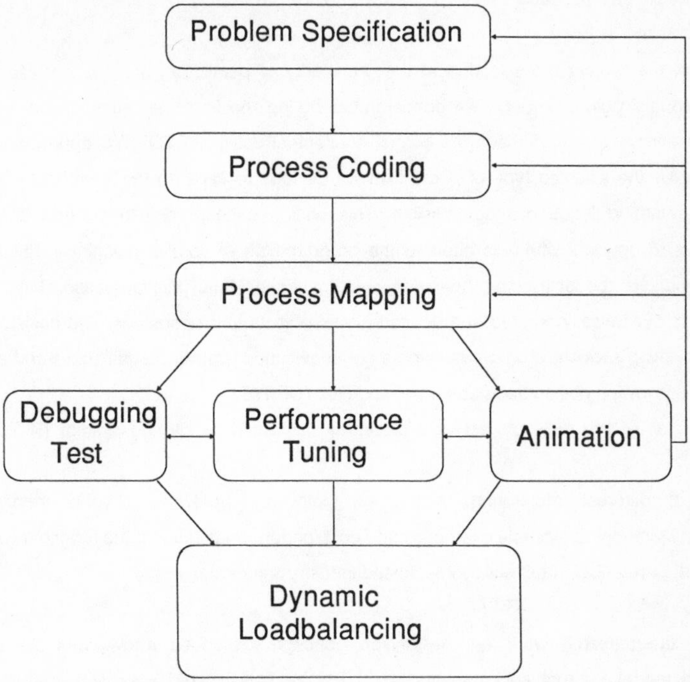

Figure 1: Parallelization methodology with TOPSYS supporting manual, interactive and automatic strategies

In the long term future, parallel architectures and in particular distributed memory multiprocessors will only survive, if it is possible to simplify the use and programming of these systems with more automatic concepts. As fully automatic parallelization in general is not feasible in the near future, we have introduced in the TOPSYS project a step which we call interactive or semiautomatic parallelization. In this interactive step the user gets tools for easy experimentation with different parallelization possibilities. With this methodology the programmer can change very quickly parallelization strategies and evaluate this parallelization with analysis tools. Figure 1 illustrates this interactive optimization and refinement cycle. In this first step of the project, interactive tools for specification, mapping, debugging and testing, performance tuning and visualization (animation) were developed. With these interactive tools the user still is involved in optimizing the parallelization. In the long term future this necessity will be eliminated by automatic schemes. One direction toward automatic parallelization is an application transparent and adaptive dynamic load balancing. In the second step of the TOPSYS project we develop an adaptive dynamic load balancing system for distributed memory multiprocessors. The idea for this adaptive load balancing algorithm was developed from the interactive methodology for using the TOPSYS tools. This adaptive dynamic load balancing scheme integrates the described optimization and refinement cycle into system software.

Only a few integrated development environments for parallel architectures are available. Well known research projects are PIE [Seg85], Poker [SuS86], PISCES [Pra87] and FAUST [Gua89]. Apart from these integrated environments, some tools for specific phases of the parallelization cycle are available.

3. The TOPSYS Integrated Approach

In an early stage of the project the selection of the granularity of parallelism and the corresponding process model was an important point. Although we concentrated during the implementation of the tool environment on coarse grain parallelism, we also made the overall conceptual design of TOPSYS appropriate for fine grain parallelism. To express the selected type of parallelism we decided to have a process model which is as close to sequential programming languages as possible. This design concept should support a programmer of sequential programs to upgrade with less effort to the programming of parallel machines. The implementation of this process model is the distributed operating system kernel MMK (Multiprocessor Multitasking Kernel) [BeL90] which offers dynamically created and deleted global objects and operations. The basics of the process model are communicating sequential processes where communication is done via mailboxes and synchronization via semaphores. The following design decisions were made for TOPSYS:

- implementation of all of the tools on top of a common distributed monitoring system [BLT90] for extensibility
- implementation of different monitoring techniques (software-, hardware-, hybrid monitoring) and a heterogeneous environment to evaluate overheads and cost/performance ratio for the monitoring system
- support of network based host-target environments and industry standards.

A major result of the research work on the design concepts described above was the definition of a hierarchical layered model for tool environments like TOPSYS. This layered approach is illustrated in figure 2. The figure shows the interfaces defined between the several subsystems of the development environment. The hierarchical model results mainly from the idea to use all tools together with all monitoring techniques, regardless of the implementation of the corresponding partner. Apart from the definition of some smaller interfaces, the integration idea has lead to the definition of two important interfaces - the monitor interface and the tool interface. The monitor interface is a command driven interface via which the upper layers of the tool model request the different monitors to deliver runtime information of the processor nodes. The monitors are duplicated and adapted or downloaded to the several processor nodes of the parallel target machine. All types of monitors of this distributed monitoring system offer the same functionality to the upper layers of the tool environment and they are therefore replaceable by each other. The monitor interface is based on virtual addresses and internal process identifiers of the MMK kernel.

In contrast to the monitor interface, the tool interface offers the abstraction level of the source program. All objects of this interface are referred to by their names in the source program, e.g. variable names, task names, etc. The tool interface is a procedural interface. Via this interface all tools can request runtime information about the dynamic behaviour of the parallel execution at the abstraction level of the source program. The advantage of the definition of this interface is the extendability of the tools' functionality without a modification of the lower layers. Within this phase of the TOPSYS project we have developed several tools with the following functionalities:

- The parallel debugging and test system DETOP for validating parallel programs at the source level.
- A performance analyzer called PATOP for performance tuning and performance measurement of parallel systems [BHL90].
- The visualization tool VISTOP for dynamic graphical animation of parallel executions.
- Interactive configurators, load generators and mapping tools for fast experimentations with different process/processor mappings (SAMTOP).
- The dynamic load balancer integrated into the operating system kernel MMK uses the runtime information collected via the monitor interface to establish more efficient process/processor mappings. The remapping during runtime is based on a paging oriented process migration scheme explained in [Tri90].

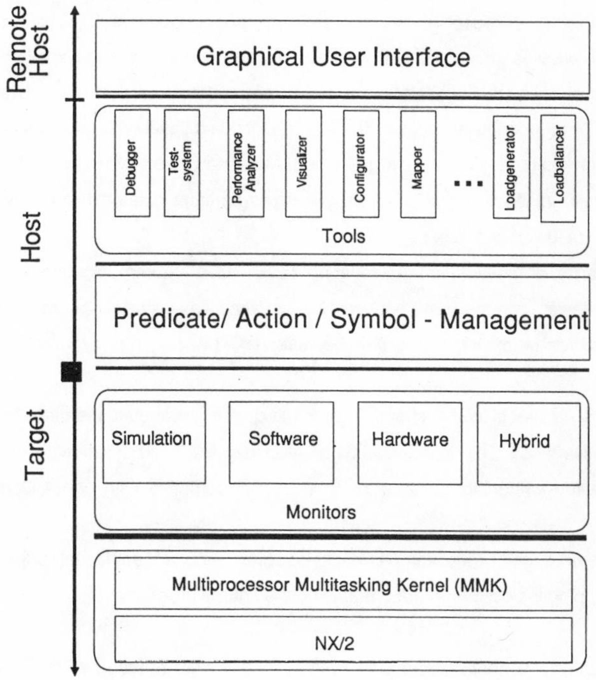

Figure 2: TOPSYS hierarchical tool model

As most of the tools implemented within the TOPSYS project are interactive tools, an important part of the project is the development of appropriate and easy to use interfaces. All tools of the tool environment have a graphic and menu-driven user interface with the same look and feel, i.e. with the same philosophy of usage. For the implementation of this common graphic user interface a specific graphics library on top of X-windows has been developed, which is used by all tools of the TOPSYS project.

4. The MMK Distributed Operating System Kernel

Various process models and implementations for distributed memory multiprocessors have been proposed in the literature. Two basic classes can be characterized. Firstly the process models used in writing real applications for today's distributed memory multiprocessors are based on system calls to the node operating system of the parallel machine ([Pie88], [Sch88]). System calls to deal with synchronization and communication of processor nodes are offered. An advantage of this approach is the close relation to conventional programming languages. A major drawback is the architecture dependency of these process models. The programmer normally has to know various architectural features of the parallel machine, like topology, physical number of nodes, number of communication channels, physical or logical processor numbers etc. Secondly another group of researchers have proposed completely new parallel programming languages. In this class of process models, programming paradigms for procedural programming [Whi88], object oriented programming [ACG86], functional programming [Hal87] and logic programming [Sha86] are enhanced with parallelism. Problems with these approaches are compatibility, performance and the effort to rewrite huge application packages. The process model of the MMK is an approach, which tries to find a compromise between the two explained classes [BBB90]. MMK abstracts from architectural features, while staying as close as possible to conventional programming languages. The features of this parallel process model are:

- MMK supports an object oriented style of programming based on fixed types of objects. The types of objects supported are tasks, mailboxes and semaphores. A programmer cannot define new types of objects, he can only use instances of the given types.
- A parallel program consists of multiple communicating tasks, where communication is implemented with message passing. The tasks communicate via mailboxes and synchronize via semaphores. Nearly all communication and synchronization structures can be built: 1:1, 1:n, n:1, n:n, synchronous, asynchronous, buffered, unbuffered, etc.
- All objects are available in a global name space implemented in a distributed manner and multiple objects can reside on each processor node. The objects can be created and destroyed dynamically during runtime.
- The bodies of the tasks are written in C, C++ or Fortran and compiled with conventional C-, C++- and Fortran-compilers.
- Mapping of the objects onto the processor elements is done using an additional object description file. With this approach, remapping is possible without modifying the source program.

The MMK is implemented as a distributed operating system kernel. The interface to the application program is implemented with calls to a library, which is linked to the application program.

5. Distributed Monitoring System

Besides the TOPSYS distributed monitoring system, there are several other projects in this area. The first class of projects deal with the fundamentals of concurrent and distributed systems. The main research topics of these projects are the order in time and consistent global states ([ChL85], [SpK88]). A second class of projects uses software monitoring, in most cases source code instrumentation or simulation to gather runtime information ([MLS86], [Seg85], [BSN88], [MiC88], [BaW88], [CuW82], [HHK85]). Only a small number of projects try to deal with the problem of nonintrusive monitoring. [HKL87] and [WyH88] use hardware and hybrid monitors respectively for performance analysis. Other projects ([BuM88], [GMZ86]) are limited to shared memory multiprocessors, which makes monitoring easier because of the existence of shared resources.

The monitoring system of TOPSYS is based on an event/action model. In this model the monitoring system monitors the execution of events. Based on the detection of events several conditional actions can be initiated. Three classes of primitive events can be evaluated by the monitoring system; control flow events which describe the execution flow of a program; data flow events which monitor the state changes of data objects (e.g. variables) and concurrency events which describe the relation between MMK objects (e.g. sending of messages). Multiple primitive events may be combined to generate more complex events. Two operators are available for event combination; a logical or and a sequence operator, which is used as "happened before". Upon detection of events several classes of actions may be initiated. Classes of actions are breakpoints for stopping several tasks or the whole system, traces on different activities and count/time measurements. The definition of events and actions is done at the logical task level. This means, that the programmer does not have to know the location of tasks and objects.

As during the mapping of applications multiple application tasks are mapped onto one processor node, the corresponding monitor tasks are grouped to a local monitor. One local monitor is responsible for the monitoring of the corresponding processor node. For monitoring events distributed over multiple processor nodes, the local monitors communicate via so called crosstriggers. A crosstrigger is used to inform other local monitors on the detection of events. This concept allows to implement global breakpoints, global consistent states and a global time base (only in the case of the hardware monitor).

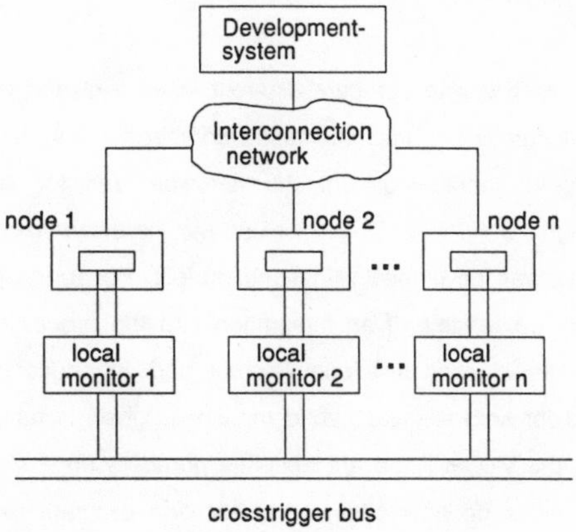

Figure 3: Distributed Monitor System of TOPSYS

The physical implementation of local monitors (see figure 3) and crosstriggers differs with respect to the instrumentation technique. For hardware instrumentation the local monitors and crosstriggers are implemented with extra hardware which is adapted to the corresponding processor chip and monitors the events and actions in parallel to the program execution. The software monitor uses software traps and monitor hooks, which are inserted into the object code of the running program. Crosstriggers are implemented in the software monitor by using message passing system calls to communicate with local software monitors of other processor nodes. A combination of hardware and software monitors is used for hybrid instrumentation. With this technique, software hooks inserted into the operating system kernel MMK are used to detect events and hardware is used to compare the events and initiate the corresponding actions.

Monitor-Hook-Handler			Software-Monitor	Hardware-Monitor
Performance-Trace	Task	run	188 µs	49 µs
		stop	185 µs	49 µs
	Mailbox	send begin	114 µs	51 µs
		send end	153 µs	85 µs
		receive begin	136 µs	45 µs
		receive end	139 µs	51 µs
	Semaphor	request begin	116 µs	45 µs
		request end	115 µs	42 µs
		wait begin	160 µs	46 µs
		wait end	143 µs	77 µs
		release end	142 µs	37 µs
Counter	Mailbox-Queue	wait begin	116 µs	11 µs
		wait end	115 µs	10 µs
	Semaphor-Queue	wait begin	148 µs	80 µs
		wait end	128 µs	60 µs
	RPC-Queue		118 µs	4 µs
	Ready-Queue		113 µs	4 µs
	Idle-Time		170 µs	58 µs
	Message-Length	remote send	117 µs	4 µs

Table 1: Program slow down by performance measurements

One important goal of the TOPSYS project was to compare different instrumentation techniques with respect to program retardation, measurement accuracy and implementation complexity. Only hardware instrumentation can offer the possibility of non-intrusive monitoring. But the hardware monitor lacks flexibility and its implementation complexity is very high. Only a VLSI version of the hardware monitor is acceptable. A comparator chip for hardware monitors was developed within the project. For future processor generations, the hardware monitor solution will only be feasible, if an integration into the processor ICs is offered. Software and hybrid monitoring are more flexible and less complex but both introduce program slow down to the application program. The overhead for software and hybrid monitor is given in table 1. When reading the table you have to keep in mind, that the values listed are absolute numbers measured on the iPSC/2. The total retardation of the application depends on how often the application program uses the several system calls (send, receive, etc.) of the operating system. Our experience shows that the total program slow down by the monitors for typical applications is far less than the figures given in table 1.

6. The Tools of the TOPSYS Environment

Based on the tool interface offered by the middle layers, several tools have been implemented. This section describes the functionality of the tools. All the tools may be used in an integrated manner at the same time with one application program. It is easily possible to switch between the tools by moving the mouse from one window to another. Following the TOPSYS development cycle, the tool used first is the Specification And Mapping TOol SAMTOP. SAMTOP is a graphic based specification, design and mapping tool. It allows a structured specification of parallel programs based on the method SA/SD of Tom DeMarco. Dataflow diagrams and control maps are used for a joint refinement top-down design. In addition object graphs can be used to specify concurrency on the base of the MMK programming model. The programmer can specify object graphs of parallel programs using graphical objects for tasks, semaphors and mailboxes. Operations on these objects are expressed by connections and arrows between their graphical representations. As many parallel programs for distributed memory multiprocessors are programmed with data partitioning, fragments of object graphs may be replicated to build up the complete object graph for data partitioned applications. Up to this step the specification of the parallel programm based on the MMK programming model is independent of the underlying system. The mapping of this logical object graph onto the physical multiprocessor architecture is supported with a specific programming language. Several mapping strategies are offered; manual, random and program controlled mapping. For making a decision on the mapping strategy, the programmer uses performance results generated by the other tools (e.g. PATOP, VISTOP). SAMTOP automatically generates the mapping file which is used during program generation by the MMK preprocessors. The design phase for parallel programs is supported by the automatic generation of code frames for each task.

After program specification the user has to write the sequential parts of each task using the MMK library calls. With a predefined makefile the parallel program is compiled, linked, mapped and downloaded to the processor node. For debugging these parallel programs the TOPSYS environment offers the parallel debugger DETOP. With this debugger the programmer gets a global view on the parallel system. All information is globally available; objects are referred to only by their name. The programmer does not need to know the mapping or the location of objects. The languages supported by all the tools until now are C and Fortran. In contrast to many other debuggers, this debugging tool is process oriented. DETOP knows all object types of MMK and can deal with single tasks or groups of tasks regardless of their processor location. From the functionality point of view for a single task the parallel debugger DETOP offers all the features well known from sequential sourceoriented debuggers extended for distributed memory systems. In addition DETOP offers a graphic user interface for simplified handling with on-line help and listing information. All the breakpoint options offer consistent breakpoints and consistent global states at the MMK level. The most important features are:

- inspection of program states, displaying the contents of data structures, the states of tasks, semaphores and mailboxes;
- modification of the contents of data structures;
- local and global breakpoints which can be triggered by control flow, data flow and concurrency events;
- trace collection on control, data flow events and concurrency events;
- program control via (re)starting of tasks and single stepping at the task level.

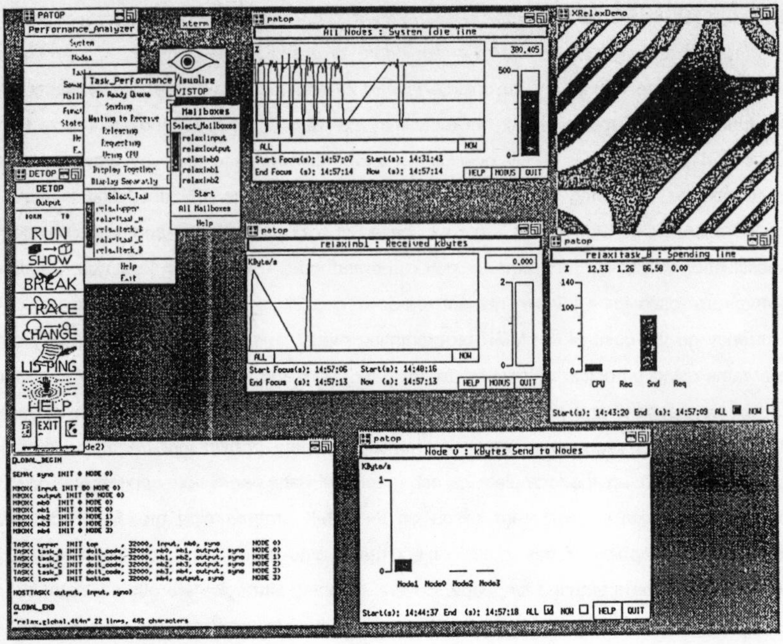

Figure 4: DETOP and PATOP screendump

With the debugging system the programmer can localize "normal" bugs in his program. For performance tuning of parallel programs the TOPSYS environment offers the performance analyzer PATOP. This tool is used for finding performance bottlenecks. Like all the other tools, the performance analyzer collects dynamic runtime information on the running parallel program via the TOPSYS tool interface. With PATOP the programer can specify multiple performance measurements. Using time stamps the performance measurements may be time correlated to get a consistent global overview on the performance of the parallel system. As all the tools within the TOPSYS environment are on-line tools, the performance analysis and display is done during runtime. PATOP supports four different levels of abstraction at which the programmer can get performance analysis. At the system level the performance measurements of all processor nodes are summed up to give a total system performance. At the node level performance measurements for each node are possible. To get insight into one node, the task level gives performance data of all MMK objects of a parallel program (task, mailbox, semaphore). At the finest level the programmer can look at the performance of one sequential task and can measure the execution of several procedures or statements. At each level of abstraction different performance values may be measured. Depending on the selected level these performance values are CPU (task), communication, synchronization or memory oriented. Examples are CPU utilization by specific tasks, amount of communication via mailboxes, CPU idle times, synchronization waiting times etc. The user can specify time and count measurements. The specification of measurements is supported with graphical menus where all the objects are refered by names independently of their processor localization. The performance values of each measurement are presented in a graphical way with two types of graphical representations; with time related diagrams and bargraphs. A screendump of a DETOP and PATOP session for a relaxation problem is given in figure 4.

With the specification tool SAMTOP the programmer is able to specify object interaction at the process level graphically. This gave us the motivation to work toward a graphical understanding and validation of the program execution. Therefore we have implemented based on the TOPSYS tool interface the graphical visualisation and animation tool VISTOP. This tool is able to visualize and animate parallel programs at the level of object graphs containing MMK objects and operations. Comparing this animation with the graphical specification the programmer can understand and validate his parallel programs using graphical representations. VISTOP is doing on-line animation during runtime of the parallel program. The runtime data via the TOPSYS tool interface using global breakpoints and state inspection system calls. Runtime data is collected and graphical animation are done concurrently. The animation can be controlled manually or executed automatically with a predefined update frequency. The animation of the objects selected by the programmer can be done forwards and backwards. During animation the states of the animated objects (tasks, mailboxes, semaphores) can be displayed. VISTOP is also usable with different monitoring techniques in contrast to many parallel animation systems which use only a simulation of the parallel system.

7. Adaptive Dynamic Load balancing

Two classes of strategies are described in the literature to achieve dynamic loadbalancing. The first strategy is an application dependent scheme, where the loadbalancing algorithm is implemented within the application program. The disadvantage of this approach is, that loadbalancing has to be considered during each application design explicitly which requires additional effort. A simpler strategy for the user is an application transparent dynamic loadbalancing scheme which is common to each application and which is offered by the operating system. We have chosen the second, application independent dynamic loadbalancing algorithm.

The idea for this adaptive loadbalancing algorithm was developed out of the interactive methodology for using the TOPSYS tools. With our adaptive dynamic loadbalancing scheme, we integrate the regulation cycle into system software. We have designed and implemented dynamic loadbalancing as a regulation cycle based on distributed monitoring starting with an initial mapping. This idea is comparable to well known schemes for virtual memory management and cache memories. There are three components to our procedure for dynamic load balancing. These components are performance measurement, control decision and process migration. This adaptive dynamic loadbalancing scheme is illustrated in figure 5. A migration and a performance measurement component is implemented for each node, while the decision and control component can be implemented in a centralized or distributed manner.

The control and decision component initiates some performance measurements. Reading the measured values it first has to decide whether a process migration is necessary at all. If the decision is made that it is necessary, a source and destination node for a migration has to be found. Finally an appropriate process to migrate (migration candidate), has to be selected. This decision may be made in combination with the search for an adequate source and destination node for the process migration. To make these decisions, further performance-measurements may be required. After the migration of a process systems performance changes and the regulation cycle starts again.

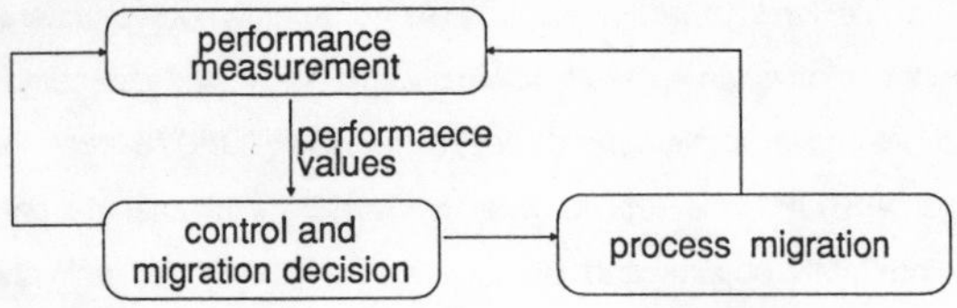

Figure 5: Adaptive dynamic load balancing as regulation cycle

For evaluating the overhead for the page-oriented process migration scheme we have measured the migration time for one page from one processor to another. This is the time between the occurrence of the page fault trap on the source node and the restart of the process to be migrated on the destination node processor. We have measured 2.7 ms for this migration time. This period of time is independent of the source and destination processor location because of the virtual fully interconnected topology of the iPSC/2 hypercube. Compared to the raw communication bandwidth of the iPSC/2 interconnection network, there is a very low overhead for organization. The raw communication time for a 4 KByte page from processor to processor is 2.2 ms. Therefore the organizational overhead for trap handling, process restart etc. is only 0.5 ms or 22%.

8. Applications of TOPSYS

TOPSYS tools for interactive program development are being evaluated by a number of users from different application areas. The iPSC/2 system is currently being used by more than 20 active users in a host-target-environment, where the target multiprocessor system is connected to the host workstation via a TCP/IP Ethernet. Host systems (workstations of all types) are local (within same building) or remote (up to several kilometer distance) and run remote hosting software and the TOPSYS tools. In this sense, the distributed memory multiprocessor is used in a computing center-like fashion offering several users a space-sharing environment for the target system. Amongst the application areas are:

- placement algorithm for VLSI CAD-tools using conjugate gradient method (GORDIAN)
- computational fluid dynamics (FLUBOX an QUADBOX)
- parallel simulation using the time warp approach
- simulation of neural networks based on Runge-Kutta methods
- sorting algorithms for parallel database application (MERKUR)
- parallel inference for a theorem prover system (PARTHEO)
- multigrid algorithms for engineering applications

9. Conclusion and future extensions

The TOPSYS tools for interactive program development are now being used and evaluated intensively on an iPSC/2 and ported to an iPSC/860. The transparent dynamic load balancing system testbed is currently being implemented. The overheads incurred by different migration decision strategies must be throughly measured for real applications. In future, additional tools will be integrated into TOPSYS, ranging from (semi-)automated parallelizers for dusty deck programs to specification and verification tools for parallel development. To be able to support fine grain parallelism, the implementation of virtual shared memory based on high speed communication networks will be investigated.

10. References

[ACG86] S. Ahuja, N. Camero, D. Gelernter: Linda and Friends; IEEE Computer 1986

[BaW88] P.C. Bates, J.C. Wileden: High Level Debugging of Distributed Systems: the Behavioral Abstraction Approach; Journal of Systems and Software 4, 3, 225-264, Dec. 1983

[BBB90] H.J. Beier, T. Bemmerl, A. Bode et al.: TOPSYS, Tools for Parallel Systems; Collected Papers, TU München, TUM-I9013, SFB-Bericht Nr. 342/9/90 A, 1990

[BeL90] T. Bemmerl, T. Ludwig: MMK - A Distributed Operating System Kernel with Integrated Dynamic Loadbalancing; CONPAR 90 - VAPP IV, Sept. 1990, Zürich, Switzerland

[BGS91] U. Bruening, W.K. Giloi, W. Schroeder-Preikschat: The Architecture of the European MIMD Supercomputer GENESIS; paper in this conference

[BHL90] T. Bemmerl, O. Hansen, T. Ludwig: PATOP for Performance Tuning of Parallel Programs; CONPAR 90 - VAPP IV, Sept. 1990, Zürich, Switzerland

[BLT90] T. Bemmerl, R. Lindhof, T. Treml: The Distributed Monitor System of TOPSYS; CONPAR 90 - VAPP IV, Sept. 1990, Zürich, Switzerland

[Bod90] A. Bode: Developments in Distributed Memory Architectures; Proceedings Microsystem'90, Strbske Pleso, CSFR, 1990

[Bol91] L. Borrmann, P. Istavrinos: Store coherency in a parallel distributed-memory machine; paper in this conference proceedings

[BSN88] M.L. Bailey, D. Socha, D. Notkin: Debugging Parallel Programs using Graphical Views; Proc. Int. Conf. on Parallel Proc., 46 - 49, Aug. 1988

[BuM88] H. Burkhart, R. Millen: Techniken und Werkzeuge der Programmbeobachtung am Beispiel eines Modula-2 Monitorsystems; Informatik Forschung und Entwicklung, 3, 6 - 21, 1988

[ChL85] K.M. Chandy, L. Lamport: Distributed Snapshots: Determining Global States of Distributed Systems; ACM TCS, 3, 1, 63 - 75, Feb. 1985

[CuW82] R. Curtis, L. Wittie: BUGNET: a Debugging System for Parallel Programming Environments; 3rd Int. Conf. on Distr. Comp. Syst., 18 - 22, 1982

[GMZ86] F. Gregoretti, F. Maddaleno, M. Zamboni: Monitoring Tools for Multimicroprocessors; EUROMICRO'86, 409 - 416, 1986

[Gua89] V.A. Guarna, D. Gannon, D. Jablonowski, A.D. Malony, Y. Gaur: Faust: An Integrated Environment for Parallel Programming; IEEE Software, 20 - 26, July 1989

[Hal87] R.H. Halstead: Multilisp and Multilisp-oriented Architectures; Proc. MIT/ZTI-Symposium, München, 1987

[HHK85] P.K. Harter, D.M. Heimbigner, R. King: IDD, An Interactive Distributed Debugger, 5th Int. Conf. on Distr. Comp. Syst., 498 - 506, 1985

[HKL87] R. Hofmann, R. Klar, N. Luttenberger, B. Mohr: Zählmonitor 4, ein Monitorsystem für das Hardware- und Hybrid-Monitoring von Multiprozessor und Multicomputer-Systemen; Proc. Messung und Modellierung von Rechensystemen, 79 - 99, 1987

[May91] D. May: The Next Generation Transputers and Beyond; paper in this conference proceedings

[MiC88] B.P. Miller, J.D. Choi: Breakpoints and Halting in Distributed Programs; Proc. Int. Conf. on Parallel Proc., 316 - 323, Aug. 1988

[MLS86] H. Mühlenbein, F. Limburger, S. Streitz, S. Warmhaut: MUPPET, a Programming Environment for Message-Based Multiprocessors, FJCC, Nov. 1986

[Pie88] P. Pierce: The NX/2 Operating System, Int. Hypercube Conf., 1988

[Pra87] T.W. Pratt: The PISCES2 Parallel Programming Environment, Int. Conf. on Parallel Proc., 439 - 445, 1987

[Rat91] J. Rattner: paper in this conference proceedings

[Sch88] W. Schröder: The Distributed PEACE Operating System and its Suitability for MIMD Message Passing Architecture; CONPAR 88, Manchester, 1988

[Seg85] Z. Segall, L. Rudolph: PIE: a Programming and Instrumentation Environment for Parallel Processing; IEEE Software, 22 - 37, Nov. 1985

[Sha86] E. Shapiro: Concurrent Prolog: a Progress Report; IEEE Computer 1986

[SnS86] L. Snyder, D. Socha: Poker on the Cosmic Cube: The First Retargetable Parallel Programming Language and Environment, Int. Conf. on Parallel Proc., 628 - 635, 1986

[SpK88] M. Spezialetti, J.P. Kearns: A General Approach to Recognizing Event Occurrences in Distributed Computations; Int. Conf. on Distributed Comp. Systems, 300 - 307, 1988

[Tri90] S. Tritscher: Dynamischer Lastausgleich auf dem iPSC/2 mittels Prozeßmigration; Diploma thesis, TU München, 15. Jan. 1990

[Whi88] C. Whitby-Strevens: Supernode: Transputer and Software; Int. Conference on Supercomputing, 1988

[WyH88] D. Wybranietz, D. Haban: Monitoring and Performance Measuring Distributed Systems during Operation; Proc. Org. u. Betrieb von Rechensystemen, 308 - 323, 1988

OPTIMAL MULTINODE BROADCAST ON A MESH CONNECTED GRAPH WITH REDUCED BUFFERIZATION

Abderezak TOUZENE , Brigitte PLATEAU
LGI-IMAG, Groupe Calcul parallèle, 46 avenue Félix Viallet
38031 Grenoble cedex France

Abstract : We present an optimal *all-to-all* communication procedure for a mesh connected topology of processors with wrap-around (a torus). This procedure is based on a spanning tree method and uses a reduced bufferization space.

1 Introduction

Mesh or torus topologies are well suited for solving numerical and matricial problems in distributed memory architecture. But even for adequate topologies, the communication cost of a parallel algorithm is a crucial factor to minimize. In this paper, we focus on one useful communication procedure, known as *all-to-all* or *multinode-broadcast* where every node receives data from every node of the topology. The need for broadcasting occurs for example in numerical problems where a vector is the result of a parallel computation and has its entries distributed over the network. Re-using the vector on each processor for the next step requires a multibroadcast procedure *(all-to-all)*. This happens in neural computation, iterative matrix procedure, etc.

In [2] [3] [4] [5], the proposed *all-to-all* solutions require a number of storage buffers which increases with the topology size. The procedure that we propose reduces the number of storage buffers to zero or one unit maximum. We limit our study to two dimensional square meshes with wrap-around (torus). For the *all-to-all* procedure we assume that the data length is the same at each node and we refer to it as the data unit.

In this paper the communication model is as follows : $T_{com} = \tau\, n$ where τ is the link bandwidth and n the data length. We assume that the links are bi-directional and that each processor can use its 4 communication links in parallel. This communication model is well suited for Transputer based architectures because the communication "start-up" time is small and neglected compared to the message transfer time. As an example, to send 100 bytes, the "start-up" time represents 2% of the total transfer time (this figure comes from measurements using a C with communication libraries).

We define a communication step as the simultaneous send/receive of a data unit on each node on its 4 links. For the *all-to-all* procedure, each node must receive p^2-1 data if p^2 is the total number of nodes in the mesh. Since each node has 4 links, at each step it can receive at most 4 new data. The minimum time to accomplish the *all-to-all* procedure is $\frac{p^2-1}{4}\tau n$, corresponding to $\frac{p^2-1}{4}$ communication steps.

In this paper, we present an *all-to-all* procedure reaching this lower bound of propagation time. In Section 2, we consider the case where meshes are $p \times p$ with p odd. In Section 3, we shall see how to perform the *all-to-all* when meshes are $p \times p$ with p even and Section 4 sketches an implementation.

2 All-to-all procedure on the mesh ($p \times p$) with p odd

2.1 Notation

Each mesh node is named by double index $(i,\ j)$ which is its mesh position (i=row number, j=column number). Throughout the paper the index computation are implicitly made modulo p. The four node links are named $North$, $East$, $West$, $South$ ($NEWS$). Node $(i,\ j)$ communicates with node $(i+1,\ j)$ by its $North$ link, with node $(i,\ j+1)$ by its $East$ link, with node $(i-1,\ j)$ by its $South$ link and with node $(i,\ j-1)$ by its $West$ link. Note that, if $(i,\ j)$ is connected to $(i+1,\ j)$ by its $North$ link, then node $(i+1,\ j)$ is connected to node $(i,\ j)$ by its $South$ link.

2.2 Problem overview

A spanning tree rooted at node $(i,\ j)$ of a connected graph G, is a partial graph of G noted $A_{(i,j)}$ which is connected and acyclic.

Broadcasting data on a spanning tree rooted at a node, consists in forwarding data from the root to each node along the spanning tree. In our approach, the *all-to-all* is a multinode broadcast. To solve a multinode broadcast, we need to specify one spanning tree per mesh node. We consider the parallel send from each mesh node $(i,\ j)$ along its rooted spanning tree $A_{(i,j)}$. The difficulty here is that some links may belong to several spanning trees at the same communication step. To solve this problem, we construct spanning trees $A_{(i,j)}$ that are time edge-disjoint i.e, at each step, a given mesh edge belongs to one and only one spanning tree $A_{(i,j)}$. We shall show further what a topological constraint on spanning tree structures is sufficient to obtain the time edge-disjoint property (see F_{NB} tree definition next).

The propagation time lower bound for the *all-to-all* procedure is $\frac{p^2-1}{4}\tau n$ corresponding to $\frac{p^2-1}{4}$ communication steps. The basic idea is to construct spanning trees of depth $\frac{p^2-1}{4}$. Spanning trees have p^2-1 nodes plus the root, so it is sufficient to consider such a spanning trees with 4 linear branches of depth $\frac{p^2-1}{4}$. We note F such a tree family.

Given that each mesh node has an even degree, the existence of an Eulerian cycle that can be decomposed in two distinct Hamiltonian cycles has been shown in [1]. Assume p^2-1 is divisible by 4 (p is odd). Choose a node (i,j) and give an orientation to the two Hamiltonian cycles. The first tree branch is the $\frac{p^2-1}{4}$ first nodes on the positive chain starting at node (i,j) of one cycle. The second one is the $\frac{p^2-1}{4}$ first nodes on the negative chain starting at node (i,j) of the same cycle. The third and the fourth ones cover respectively the $\frac{p^2-1}{4}$ nodes located on each side of node (i,j) on the second cycle. When p^2-1 is not divisible by 4, the number of nodes per branch cannot be the same. We have just shown that F is not empty. To accomplish the *all-to-all* in $\frac{p^2-1}{4}$ steps, we need a spanning tree $A_{(i,j)} \in F$ rooted at each mesh node $(i,\ j)$. The time edge-disjoint property of the trees will be shown to be a consequence of the following property :

Definition 1 *We define a family of spanning trees $F_{NB} \subset F$, called NEWS-Balanced trees. A tree is NEWS-Balanced if and only if : For all $d \in [1, \frac{p^2-1}{4}]$, the 4 nodes at depth d of the spanning tree are connected to the nodes at depth $d+1$ (on the same branch) by distinct links in the set L=(North, East, West, South) (figure 1).*

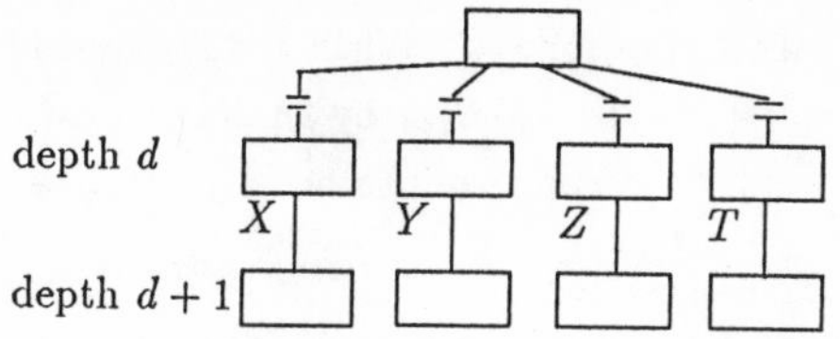

Figure 1: Connection at depth d of a F_{NB} tree, where (X, Y, Z, T) are distinct in L.

2.3 An example of a F_{NB} spanning tree for the mesh ($p \times p$) with p odd

To prove the existence of F_{NB} spanning trees, we show an example of such a tree. To construct a F_{NB} spanning tree rooted at node (i, j), we proceed in three phases. The first phase consists in partitioning the mesh nodes in 4 distinct areas plus the root node. In the second phase, we cover the nodes of one area with a chain which is one of the spanning tree branches. In the last phase, we deduce the other branches of the spanning tree, by rotation of the first branch.

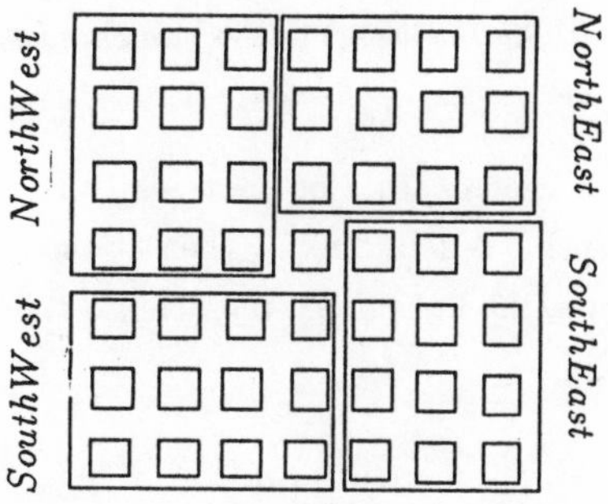

Figure 2: (a). Partitioning the mesh nodes.

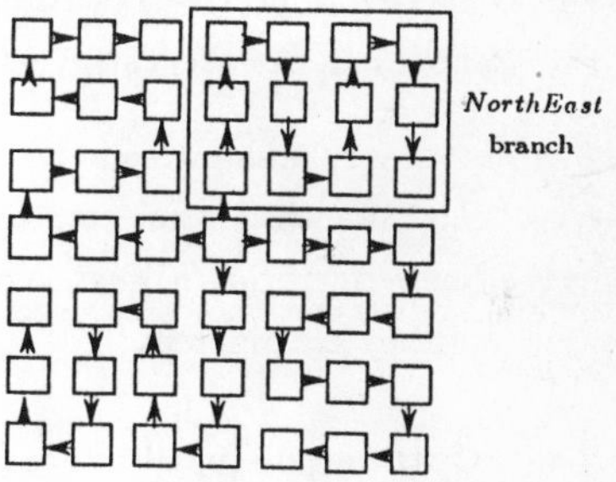

Figure 2: (b). A F_{NB} spanning tree.

- **First phase : partitioning the mesh nodes in 4 distinct areas**
  Let $m=\lfloor \frac{p}{2} \rfloor$. Define the four areas (*NorthEast*, *SouthEast*, *SouthWest*, *NorthWest*) surrounding node (i,j) such that (figure 2 (a)) :
  if $1 \le x \le m$ and $0 \le y \le m \Longrightarrow$ node $(i+x, j+y)$ belongs to the *NorthEast* area
  if $-m \le x \le 0$ and $1 \le y \le m \Longrightarrow$ node $(i+x, j+y)$ belongs to the *SouthEast* area
  if $-m \le x \le -1$ and $-m \le y \le 0 \Longrightarrow$ node $(i+x, j+y)$ belongs to the *SouthWest* area
  if $0 \le x \le m$ and $-m \le y \le -1 \Longrightarrow$ node $(i+x, j+y)$ belongs to the *NorthWest* area
  It is clear that such areas cover all mesh nodes except node (i, j).

- **Second phase : construction of the *NorthEast* branch** (figure 2 (b))
  The *NorthEast* branch is formed by the concatenation of $m+1$ sub-branches of m nodes,

the sub-branches are numbered from 0 to m (figure 2 (b)). We consider an orientation on this branch from the root node of the tree to the terminal node.
The sub-branch numbered k noted SB_k has the nodes $(i+x,\ j+k)$, with $1 \leq x \leq m$. The sub-branch nodes of SB_k with k odd are connected by a *North-South* connection. The sub-branch nodes of SB_k with k even are connected by a *South-North* connection. The $(m+1)$ sub-branches are connected as follows : When k is even, node $(i+m,\ j+k)$ of SB_k is connected to node $(i+m,\ j+k+1)$ of SB_{k+1} by an *East-West* connection. When k is odd, the node $(i+1,\ j+k)$ of SB_k is connected to node $(i+1,\ j+k+1)$ of SB_{k+1} by an *East-West* connection.

- **Third phase : deduce the other tree branches by rotation** (figure 2 (b))
  Denote T the mesh nodes set and the directions set L={*North*, *East*, *South*, *West* }, and define three applications : Let $R_{(i,j)}$ the $\frac{\pi}{2}$ rotation around node $(i,\ j)$. $R : R : T \longrightarrow T$, which associates to node x_1=$(i+i_1,j+j_1)$, node $R_{(i,j)}(x_1)$=$(i-j_1,j+i_1)$. Let $\Gamma_{(i,j)}$ be the graph homomorphism associated with $R_{(i,j)}$. Finally S is, $S : L \longrightarrow L$, which rotates the cardinal points of $\frac{\pi}{2}$: $S(North)$=$East$, $S(East)$=$South$, $S(South)$=$West$, $S(West)$=$North$.

  Remark that all nodes of the respective areas (*NorthEast*, *SouthEast*, *SoutWest*, *NorthWest*) have their images with $R_{(i,j)}$ respectively in the areas (*SouthEast*, *SouthWest*, *NorthWest*, *NorthEast*). We built by hand the *NorthEast* branch. The *SouthEast* branch is deduced from the *NorthEast* branch by $\Gamma_{(i,j)}$. Similarly the *SouthWest* branch is obtained from the *SouthEast* branch by $\Gamma_{(i,j)}$, and so on for the *NorthWest* branch. The root node $(i,\ j)$ is connected respectively by its links (*North*, *East*, *South*, *West*) to the branches (*NorthEast*, *SouthEast*, *SouthWest*, *NorthWest*).

The resulting spanning tree is NEWS-Balanced : at each depth d of the tree, if the node of the *NorthEast* branch is connected to the node at depth $d+1$ by link l_1, then at the same depth in the *SouthEast*, *SouthWest*, *NorthWest* branches, the links $S(l_1)$, $S \circ S(l_1)$, $S \circ S \circ S(l_1)$ are used and they are different.

2.4 Optimal all-to-all procedure on the mesh $p \times p$ with p odd

Back to the general case, we study the *all-to-all* procedure using F_{NB} spanning trees . Assume that the spanning trees rooted at each mesh node have the following property.

Property 1 : *Given a spanning tree $A_{(i_0,j_0)} \in F_{NB}$ rooted at node $(i_0,\ j_0)$, for any other node (i,j), $A_{(i,j)}$ is deduced from $A_{(i_0,j_0)}$ by a translation (graph homomorphism) of amplitude (i-i_0, j-j_0).*

Remember that our *all-to-all* procedure approach is based on the parallel broadcasts on spanning trees rooted at each mesh node. The *all-to-all* procedure involves a particular initializing step, where each mesh node sends its data to its four neighbors. Because the mesh topology, each node has to receive on each of its four links a different data. Then, the *all-to-all* procedure is seen as a succession of communication steps : if a given node (i,j) belongs to tree $A_{(i,j)}$ at depth d and is connected to node (i',j') (at depth $d+1$), then the $(d+1)$th communication step of this node includes a communication to node (i',j') .

In the next proof, we name the branches of a F_{NB} tree according to the link by which they are connected to the root node. We have the *North*, *South*, *East*, *West* branch for each tree. In the following, we prove that such a procedure is optimal, in the sense that it requires exactly $\frac{p^2-1}{4}\tau n$ time.

Lemma 1 *At the first step of the all-to-all (at depth 1 in the tree), each node belongs to 4 distinct spanning trees on different branches.*

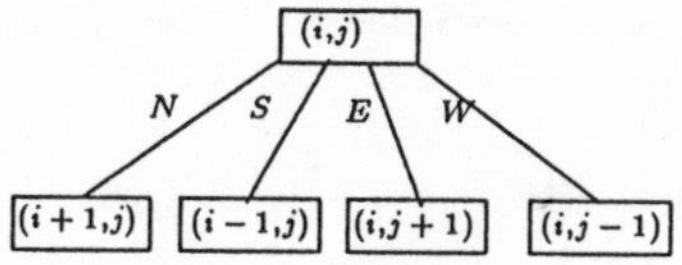

Figure 3: At depth 1 of a spanning tree.

Proof : given a node (i, j), we search all the trees which involve this node at depth 1. By construction, the trees rooted respectively in $(i\text{-}1, j)$, $(i\text{+}1, j)$, $(i, j\text{-}1)$, $(i, j\text{+}1)$ have node (i, j) respectively in their *North*, *South*, *East* and *West* branch (figure 3). This proves lemma 1.

Lemma 2 *At each depth $i \in [\,1, \frac{p^2-1}{4}\,]$ of a F_{NB} spanning tree, every node belongs to four distinct spanning trees in different branches.*

Proof : We proceed by induction. Let (H) be the induction assumption : At each depth of all spanning trees, each node belongs to exactly 4 distinct spanning trees in different branches.

(H) is true for depth $d = 1$ (lemma 1). We assume that (H) is true at depth d and we show that it is also true at depth d+1, $d+1 \leq \frac{p^2-1}{4}$.

(H) true at depth d, implies that every mesh node X belongs to 4 distinct spanning trees in different branches. This is true in particular for the four neighbors of node X, which we note VX_1, VX_2 , VX_3 , VX_4 .

At depth d node VX_1 is in four different branches of four distinct spanning trees. So it reaches node X on one of the four branches at depth $d+1$ (NEWS-Balanced structure). With the same reasoning applied to the spanning trees involving the nodes VX_j with j=2, 3, 4 at depth d, we deduce that at depth $d+1$, node X belongs to four spanning trees. Those trees are distinct, otherwise they are not spanning trees (two different branches of the same tree reaching the same node X) .

Let us prove that the branches are distinct: the trees rooted at different nodes are deduced by translation, so all *North* branches of each tree connect the node at depth d to the node at depth d+1 with the same direction (*North*, *East*, *West*, *South*). Moreover, the trees are NEWS-Balanced, which implies that the direction used by the depth- d -to-depth-$d+1$ characterizes the branch, for every d. X being reached by its 4 neighbors belongs to 4 different branches.

Theorem 1 *Given an F_{NB} spanning tree family, with one spanning tree rooted at each node and property 1 , then a multi-broadcast along these trees accomplishes the all-to-all procedure with an optimal propagation time $(\frac{p^2-1}{4})\ \tau n$.*

Proof : We have shown that at each depth $d \in [1, \frac{p^2-1}{4}]$ of this family of F_{NB} spanning trees, every node belongs to four distinct spanning trees in different branches. So at each communication step, each mesh node receives on its four links different data, because at any given depth of the spanning tree, distinct branches use distinct links (see F_{NB} definition). So there is no link contention at any communication step and the trees are time edge-disjoint. As the broadcasting trees have the depth $\frac{p^2-1}{4}$, the *all-to-all* procedure reaches the lower bound of propagation time $(\frac{p^2-1}{4})\ \tau n$.

Remark :

This *all-to-all* procedure has an optimal delay and uses no additional storage buffer. At each communication step, a node simply forwards what it has just received.

3 All-to-all procedure for a mesh $(p \times p)$ with p even

For a mesh, remember that an Eulerian cycle can be found. We decompose such a cycle as in Section 2. Similarly, a spanning tree is built with four linear branches rooted in node (i, j). Since $p^2 - 1$ is not divisible by 4, the number of nodes per branch is not the same . The spanning tree has 3 linear branches of length $\frac{p^2}{4}$, the fourth is $\frac{p^2}{4}$-1 long. For this type of tree, we were not able to find an edge-disjoint tree example (we could not prove either that it is impossible to find any). The idea to step over this difficulty is to cover a maximal subset $E(i, j)$ of mesh nodes by a spanning tree rooted at node (i, j) with an equal number of nodes per branch and with the edge-disjoint property : we note this tree family F^E_{NB}. Remark that the depth of such a tree does not exceed $\frac{p^2}{4}$-1. We note T-$E(i, j)$ the set of nodes not reachable from such a tree, the cardinality of this set is 3 maximum. In the general case, we have no criteria of choice for the T-$E(i, j)$ nodes. Next, we propose a spanning tree example where the choice of the T-$E(i, j)$ nodes is simple.

3.1 An example of a F^E_{NB} spanning tree for mesh $(p \times p)$ with p even

We present two types of spanning trees corresponding to the two cases : $m=\lfloor \frac{p}{2} \rfloor$ is odd or even. We show that for both cases, the *all-to-all* procedure using such trees is accomplished in optimal time and uses only one storage buffer at each node.

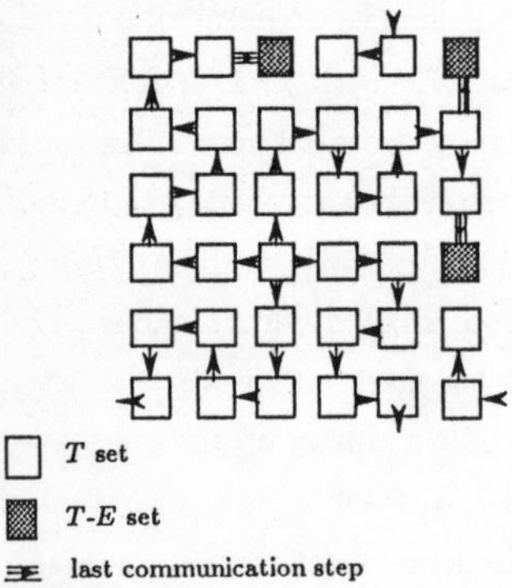

Figure 4: (a) F^E_{NB} tree for a mesh 6×6

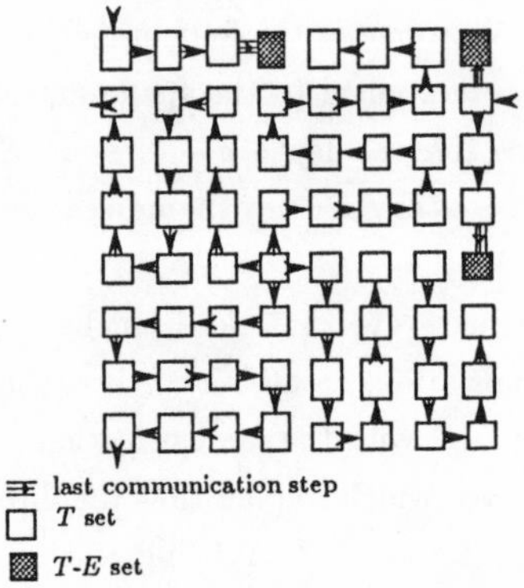

Figure 4: (b) F^E_{NB} tree for the mesh 8×8

- m odd : (figure 4 (a))
  As in Section 2.3, we construct the *NorthEast* branch of the tree and then we deduce the other by rotations. The *NorthEast* branch is the concatenation of $(m+1)$ sub-branches with $(m-1)$ nodes. Sub-branches are numbered from 0 to m. Sub-branch SB_k involves the nodes numbered $(i+x,\ j+k)$ with $1 \leq x \leq m-1$. The nodes of SB_k with k odd, are connected by a *North-South* connection. The nodes of SB_k with k even, are connected by a *South-North* connection. The $(m+1)$ sub-branches are connected as follows : The node $(i+m-1,\ j+k)$ of SB_k with k even is connected to node $(i+m-1,\ j+k+1)$ of SB_{k+1} by a *West-East* connection. The node $(i+1,\ j+k)$ of SB_k with k odd is connected to the node $(i+1,\ j+k+1)$ of SB_{k+1} by a *West-East* connection.

- m even : (figure 4 (b))
  First construct the *NorthEast* branch tree : The *NorthEast* branch is the concatenation of $(m-1)$ sub-branches of (m) nodes each, plus one sub-branch involving $(m-1)$ nodes. The sub-branch SB_k involves the nodes numbered $(i+k,\ j+x)$ with $0 \leq x \leq m-1$ for k=0, m-2 and $1 \leq x \leq m-1$ if k=m-1. The nodes of SB_k with k odd are connected by an *East-West* connection. The nodes of SB_k with k even are connected by a *West-East* connection. The $(m-1)$ sub-branches are connected as follows :

  The node $(i+k,\ j+m-1)$ of SB_k with k even is connected to the node $(i+k+1,\ j+m-1)$ of SB_{k+1} by a *South-North* connection. The node $(i+k,\ j)$ of SB_k with k odd is connected to the node $(i+k+1,\ j)$ of SB_{k+1} by *South-North* connection. Finally, the *SouthEast*, *SouthWest*, *NorthWest* branches are deduced by rotation from the *NorthEast* branch.

Remark that these trees are F_{NB}^E (branches deduced by rotation). Given that the depth of such trees is $\frac{p^2}{4}$-1, the set $E(i,\ j)$ is maximal because it is impossible to find spanning trees structured with linear branches and with an equal number of nodes per branch and exceeding depth $\frac{p^2}{4}$-1.

In the two cases, the set T-$E(i,\ j)$ has the 3 nodes $x_m = (i+m,\ j)$, $y_m = (i,\ j+m)$ and $xy_{2m} = (i+m,\ j+m)$. Nodes x_m, y_m are located at distance m from the root node $(i,\ j)$ and node xy_{2m} is $2m$ far (diameter) from the root node.

3.2 All-to-all procedure for the mesh $(p \times p)$ with p even

In the following, F_{NB}^E broadcast trees with property 1 are used as in the previous Section for a partial *all-to-all* . We show how to perform the entire *all-to-all* procedure to reach the T-$E(i,\ j)$ nodes, for all (i,j).

The broadcast procedure on tree $A_{(i,j)}^E \in F_{NB}^E$ is as follows:
The root data is broadcast along the tree $A_{(i,j)}^E$. At step $\frac{p^2}{4}$-1, the 3 remaining nodes must receive the data sent by the root node $(i,\ j)$. Because of the mesh topology, each one of these 3 nodes is connected to at least 1 node in $E(i,\ j)$. Denote respectively $E'(i,\ j)$=$(vxy_{2m},\ vx_m,\ vy_m)$ the neighbors of nodes $(xy_{2m},\ x_m,\ y_m)$ in $E(i,\ j)$. It sufficient to make an additional communication step, where 3 nodes of $E'(i,\ j)$ send the data to their neighbors of T-$E(i,\ j)$.

A good choice of $E'(i,\ j)$ is such that they use different link direction in *NEWS* (avoiding link contention for the last step). Such a choice gives an optimal *all-to-all* procedure in $\frac{p^2}{4}$ steps.

Moreover, the $E'(i, j)$ nodes should store the data sent by (i, j) at a given step, in the perspective to communicate it to the nodes of $T\text{-}E(i, j)$ at the last step. If they are terminal node of a branch they just forward it. We cannot prove in general the existence of such an $E'(i, j)$ with good properties. But for the example developed in Section 3.1, let us propose this $E'(i, j)$.

The two cases m even and odd are considered.

- m **odd** (figure 4 (a)) :
  1. $vxy_{2m} = (i+m-1,\ j+m)$ in the *NorthEast* branch, sends the data on its *North* link.
  2. $vx_m = (i+m,\ j-1)$ in the *NorthWest* branch, sends the data on its *East* link.
  3. $vy_m = (i+1,\ j+m)$ in the *NorthEast* branch, sends the data on its *South* link.
- m **even** (figure 4 (b)) :
  1. $vxy_{2m} = (i+m-1,\ j+m)$ in *NorthWest* branch, sends the data on its *North* link.
  2. $vx_m = (i+m,\ j-1)$ in *SouthWest* branch, sends the data on its *East* link.
  3. $vy_m = (i+1,\ j+m)$ in *NorthWest* branch, sends the data on its *South* link.

In the two cases, we emphasis that nodes vx_m, vy_m are located at depth $\frac{p^2}{4}$-1 of $A^E_{(i,j)}$ (terminal nodes) and node vxy_{2m} is located at depth $\frac{p^2}{4}$-m+1. At step $\frac{p^2}{4}$-m+1, node vxy_{2m} of each tree $A^E_{(i,j)}$ stores the data sent by node (i, j). Precisely at step $\frac{p^2}{4}$-m+1, every mesh node, stores the data just received on its *West* link if m is odd, *East* link if m is even and sends it on its *North* link at the last step. Nodes vx_m, vy_m are located at depth $\frac{p^2}{4}$-1 (corresponding to the last procedure step). They do not need to store the data and forward respectively on their (*East*, *South*) links the data which they just received on their (*West*, *North*) links in each $A^E_{(i,j)}$ tree. In the two cases, the *all-to-all* procedure finishes in $\frac{p^2}{4}$ communication steps and uses only one unit intermediate storage buffer on node vxy_{2m}.

Remark : We just showed that for avoiding the need of a storage buffer, we should choose $E'(i,j)$ nodes located at depth $\frac{p^2}{4}$-1 of $A^E_{(i,j)}$. The question is the following : Is it possible to find F^E_{NB} spanning trees such that the nodes of $E'(i, j)$ are all located at depth $\frac{p^2}{4}$-1. For the particular case of the mesh 4×4, the answer is yes. In the general case we have no answer to this question.

4 Implementation

Let us present an algorithm for our *all-to-all* procedure for a $p \times p$ torus where p is odd, with the trees built as an example in Section 2.3. Remember that m is the length of a sub-branch SB_k. Define the procedure $Communication(l_1, l_2, l_3, l_4 : \text{in } L)$ as :
In parallel :
- Send previous step data received on *North* link over link l_1.
- Send previous step data received on *East* link over link l_2.
- Send previous step data received on *West* link over link l_3.
- Send previous step data received on *South* link over link l_4.
- Receive data on links l_1, l_2, l_3, l_4.

And the procedure *FirstStep*() as :

In parallel :

- Send the local data on the 4 links.
- Receive data on the 4 links.

Algorithm at each node :

```
Procedure all-to-all()
{
FirstStep().
Communication(South, West, East, North);
k=0; /* sub-branch number */
m= (p-1)/2; /* number of sub-branch */
   While(k ≤ m)
      {
         for (i=1; i ≤ m-2; i++) /* Built sub-branch SB_k, k even */
          Communication(South, West, East, North);
         if (k < m)
         {
          k=k + 1;
          Communication(West, North, South, East); /* Change direction */
          Communication(West, North, South, East); /* Change direction */
          for(i=1; i ≤ m-2; i++) /* Built sub-branch SB_k, k odd */
           Communication(South, West, East, North);
          if (k < m)
          {
           Communication(East, South, North, West); /* Change direction */
           Communication(East, South, North, West); /* Change direction */
          }
         }
         k = k + 1;
      }
   }
```

The implementation of our *all-to-all* on a network of the Transputer result in a step by step procedure which requires synchronization at all step. This synchronization is naturally provided by the synchronous mode of communication (rendez-vous) of the Transputer. In this case the MIMD network is used as an SPMD network. If the network is running only the application using the *all-to-all* procedure, it performs it in almost synchronous mode. The local computation is reduced to counters increments and a few tests.

5 Conclusion

By using the spanning tree superposition method, we have reached the lower bound of propagation time of an *all-to-all* procedure. We have shown that this procedure uses in the worst case one buffer storage (0 for a square mesh with p odd, 1 when p even). The procedure is well suited when the data to exchange are large, avoiding memory requirement problem. In the literature [3] [4] [5], existing procedures use an increasing buffering space with the topology size. In [4] this buffer space is equal to p data unit where p is one dimension of the mesh. An extension of this work is the generalization of our *all-to-all* procedure to multidimensional meshes, which is on going work.

References

[1] Berge. *Théorie des graphes.* Gautiers-Villars, 1983.

[2] S.M. Hedetniemi, S.T Hedetneimi, and A.L. Liestman. A survey of gossiping and broadcasting in communication networks. *Networks*, 18, 1986.

[3] A M.Farley and A.Proskurowski. Gossip in grid graphs. *Journal of Combinatorics information and System Sciences*, 5(2), 1980.

[4] Y. Saad. Data communication in parallel architectures. *Parallel Computing*, (11), 1989.

[5] D.M. Topkis. All-to-all broadcast by flooding in communication networks. *IEEE Transactions on Computers*, 38(9), September 1989.

Adaptive Irregular Multiple Grids on a Distributed Memory Multiprocessor

J. De Keyser and D. Roose
Dept. of Computer Science, K.U.Leuven
Celestijnenlaan 200A, B-3001 Heverlee - Belgium

Abstract : We describe a tool that supports data-parallel programming on a distributed memory multiprocessor. Load balancing, based on an evolution algorithm, is integrated into this environment. Timing results for balanced Jacobi relaxation on an adaptive unstructured grid show that the encurred overhead is acceptable for calculation intensive applications.

1. Data Parallelism for Adaptive Multiple Grids

The principle of the parallel programming paradigm called *data-parallelism* is to distribute a problem's data items among the processors. The processors concurrently perform calculations on the data assigned to them. This technique is also called *geometrical parallelism* when the data represent information on a geometrical mesh.

This approach has been applied successfully to codes for computational fluid dynamics (Euler and Navier-Stokes equations) on distributed memory parallel computers, see e.g. [1,2]. These efforts were mostly restricted to software for regular meshes. Locally refined unstructured grids are used to resolve local solution features like shocks [7]. Multiple grid methods, including multigrid [5], have been applied to the Euler equations because their solution time is only linearly proportional to the problem size. This paper discusses the load balancing problems that arise when using adaptive irregular grids on distributed memory machines. We implemented grid generation and relaxation, and we present some timing results.

1.1 Basic Ideas

To introduce some basic concepts we sketch the data-parallel organization of the classical Jacobi iterative method for the solution of partial differential equations (PDE) on a regular grid (see [13]). In each iteration step an update has to be calculated in every gridpoint. This requires at each gridpoint the function values associated with the four neighboring gridpoints. The grid is divided into pieces, and each processor treats one of them. The updates can be calculated concurrently. However, to update the function value in a gridpoint at the border of a piece, values are needed that were assigned to a different processor. These values can be made available if we duplicate the values associated with gridpoints at the other side of the border. Each processor then performs the following algorithm :

```
while (solution not accurate enough) do {
    send the latest function values at gridpoints adjacent to the interfaces
        to the processes with adjacent pieces
    receive the copies of the function values from adjacent pieces
    calculate the new function values
}
```

The exchanging of messages between pieces to make the duplicated data consistent we call *flushing*. The communication pattern (figure 1) is regular and a priori known. In the case of irregular grids however this pattern can not be predicted. The quantity of exchanged data is proportional to the sum of the perimeters of all pieces, while the number of arithmetic operations is proportional to the number of gridpoints in each piece. This favors pieces as square as possible [3] and decompositions with the smallest number of them, a property called the *perimeter effect*. The *load imbalance* is defined as the relative processor idle time due to an uneven work distribution.

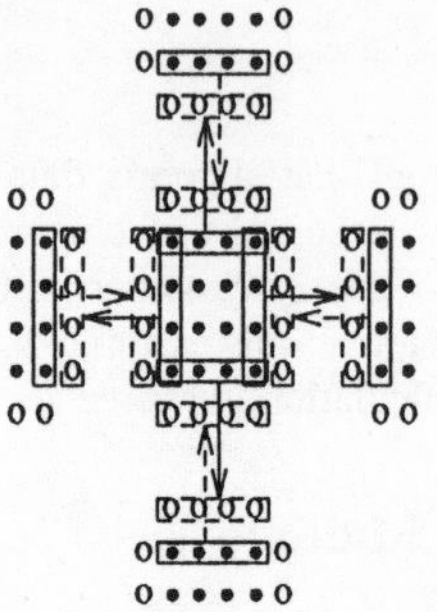

Figure 1. Data-Parallel Iteration Step on a Regular Mesh

We now compare the time required for calculation and communication in the envisaged applications [1]. For an Euler solver based on explicit methods on a two-dimensional logically rectangular mesh, about 400 flops are needed per gridpoint in each iteration step. For a 64x64 grid 0.8 Mflops/iteration are needed. On the iPSC/2 hypercube with 16 processors the calculation takes about 800 milliseconds/iteration. The unknowns at each gridpoint consist of 4 floating point numbers. Exchanging 4 messages, each containing data for 16 gridpoints, takes only 3.3 milliseconds. Discretizations with finer or three-dimensional meshes, the use of implicit time-stepping schemes, or the solution of the Navier-Stokes equations, lead to an even larger calculation to communication ratio.

1.2 Parallel Data Structures

To perform a calculation in a gridpoint - e.g. the Jacobi update in the previous paragraph - the data associated with several other gridpoints are needed. We call these points *neighbors*. These do not always coincide with the geometrically nearest gridpoints. In the case of classical iterative methods for the elliptic problems on a two-dimensional grid, a gridpoint has 4, 6 or more neighbors, depending on the discretization molecule. In the case of relaxation methods for systems obtained after upwind discretization of the Euler equations, the data-dependencies between gridpoints vary with the local sub- or supersonic nature of the flow.

We call the pieces into which the mesh is decomposed *units*. The neighboring relation between gridpoints induces a similar relation between units. This relation can be represented by a unidirectional interconnection graph. The data structure representing a mesh that is distributed among the processors, is a set of units. With each unit a list of neighbors is associated. As in the Jacobi relaxation example, each unit holds some information obtained from these neighboring units by data exchange. A unit can be subject to three types of operations. The *calculation* applies an arithmetic operation to each gridpoint in the unit. In a *data exchange* operation the duplicated information is sent or received. During load-balancing, as will be explained later, it can be useful to *move* the data of a unit to another processor.

1.3 Data Parallel Phases

An application consists of a sequence of calculations. We call each step in this sequence a *phase* [9]. The data-dependencies between gridpoints may vary from one phase to another. During a phase we apply the three basic operations to each unit in the following order :

data exchange to make duplicated data consistent
move when this reduces load imbalance
calculate for each gridpoint in the unit

In our approach a phase looks like :

define units
define operations (calculation, flush/move send/receive)
execute operations on units
update the table with the current position of all units

In order to identify units and to express their varying interconnections, we must be able to assign globally unique names to them. With each name we associate the physical location of the unit data : the couple (process number, address), which is sometimes called a *foreign pointer* [14] in the distributed memory address space. This mapping relation is stored in a *global name table*, a copy of which is present in each processor. At the end of the phase the locations of moved units have to be updated.

1.4 Load Balancing

The division of the data into units, and their distribution among the processors, is closely related to the *load-balancing* problem : how to distribute the work so that the load imbalance is reduced. *Static load balancing* techniques determine a fixed work distribution initially. *Dynamic load balancing* techniques allow the distribution to vary throughout the program. The load balancing model we propose is one of *iterative static load balancing*, rather than truly dynamic load balancing : we use a static load balancer at the beginning of each phase. Static load balancers are applied successfully to numerical problems (e.g. [4]). Iterative static load balancing is possible only when a priori load information is available. The application provides this information by assigning calculation and communication costs to units. These are used as input to some cost function. An optimal mapping of units to processors is obtained by minimizing this function.

There are two ways of decomposing a grid. A first technique consists of *decomposing the grid in significantly more units than there are processors*. Load is then redistributed by finding an optimal mapping of units to processors. Because of the large number of units, usually a good balance can be obtained. A disadvantage is that the units are relatively small, which might degrade both the quality and the efficiency of the calculation :

— The convergence properties of the numerical scheme can degrade with increasing number of units, as is the case with Block Jacobi point Gauss-Seidel iteration [1].
— As a consequence of the perimeter-effect, communication increases when introducing more units than strictly needed.

The second technique is *to consider all data in a processor as one unit*. In this case the optimal unit-to-processor mapping is simple : there is a one-to-one correspondence between them. A good load balance can be obtained when we construct units of equal sizes. When load imbalance is detected, data is split off from busy processors and joined with data in idle ones.

For irregular grids this can be done by moving work from large units to smaller neighboring units. To limit communication, the perimeter of the units should be kept small.

While in the first technique load balancing is obtained by intelligently mapping units to processors, in the second case the problem has been shifted to the construction of the units.

2. A General Tool for Load Balanced Applications

We have developed a tool that assists the programmer in writing data parallel applications. It is based on the concepts of unit and phase as introduced in the preceding section. This tool serves as a framework in which load balancing strategies can be incorporated.

During the execution of a data-parallel program we discern two tasks on each processor : the *application*, which requires calculations, data exchanges and moves, and a *controller task* that monitors the load distribution and plans the operations in a balanced way. This controller task consists of three subtasks : a *scheduler*, which schedules the operations on units so as to avoid idle time, a *minimizer*, which determines an optimal mapping, and a *communication subprocess* that handles the receipt of flush and move messages. These subtasks use the global name table, which is available all the time.

2.1 The Scheduler

The scheduler is responsible for planning the operations on units within one phase. Several limitations must be taken into account : before the calculation can be applied to a unit, the data exchange for that unit must have finished to ensure consistency of the information, and the minimizer must have decided that the calculation for this unit has to be executed on *this* processor. The scheduler tries to overlap communication and calculation whenever possible.

2.2 The Minimizer

The minimizer tries to find a mapping of units to processors that yields the minimal value of the cost function. We call the minimization *global* if information about all units in all processors is used in this optimization. If only information about units in a processor subset is used, it is called *local*. In the latter case, the load imbalance is partially reduced by rearranging the units in each subset. A global minimizer can find a better mapping than a local minimizer, but requires much more communication and calculation.

The minimization is called *exact* if it returns the exact minimum cost for the processor subset, and *approximate* otherwise. The latter is faster, but some imbalance remains. The trade-off between this imbalance and minimization time depends on the quality of the load estimates and of the cost function used, and the unit calculation workload as compared to the minimization time.

The minimization within one processor subset can be executed on one processor (*centralized minimization*), or it can be a distributed algorithm itself (*decentralized minimization*). In the second case the additional load caused by the minimization is distributed evenly among the participating processors.

In our current implementation minimization is global and centralized. We use a variant of the evolution algorithm, as applied to the general graph partitioning problem by Muhlenbein [8]. Sometimes a local minimum is found; the technique is therefore approximate [6].

2.3 *The Communication Subprocess*

The communication subprocess is responsible for receiving all flush and move messages. It has to make sure that flush information is transferred to the destination units, and, in case units are moved, it has to add arriving units to the local set of units.

When a flush message is received for a unit that was moved to another processor earlier in this phase, it must be forwarded to its final destination. This can be avoided when the scheduler imposes the additional restriction : move a unit only after all data exchanges have finished. A phase in which data is exchanged must end with a synchronization to avoid interference with messages of the following phase.

3. Irregular Grids

In this section we show how we applied our data-parallel programming tool to adaptive irregular grid generation and relaxation.

Discretization of the domain for PDE problems based on conservation laws is often done by considering control volumes or *cells*. A *grid* is a set of non-overlapping cells that together constitute the domain. A *multiple grid* is a set of grids defined on the same domain. In a multiple grid there exist several relations between cells. Cells within the same grid are *adjacent* if they have at least one edge in common. A cell is a *subcell* of a parent cell in another grid if its area is a subset of the area of the parent cell. A grid is called *regular* if each cell has the same number of edges, and thus the same number of adjacent cells; otherwise it is called *irregular*. A multiple grid is *regular* if each of its grids is regular and if each cell has the same number of subcells in the next finer grid.

Irregular grids have already been treated on distributed memory machines by several researchers. DIME [14] is an environment for using triangular meshes on distributed memory machines. The basic data unit used in DIME is a triangle with user-associated data. Communication is grouped to reduce the negative effect of the high communication startup time on some machines. Several load balancing strategies have been implemented in this environment. Parallel irregular multiple grids with nested polygonal cells are used by Lallemand and Dervieux [7]. They apply a triangulation on the finest level; on the coarser levels triangles from the fine level are grouped into irregularly shaped polygons. Load balancing is static. Our approach is close to this one, but we start with the coarse grid and we include load balancing after each refinement. We also allow general polygonal fine meshes.

3.1 *Multiple Grid Data Decomposition*

If we want to develop data parallel programs for multiple grids, we have to divide the grids on each level into pieces. In multiple grid algorithms there are two kinds of operations :

— operations treating cells on one level; data exchange then implies *intra-grid communication*
— operations involving cells on successive levels, requiring *inter-grid communication*

Intra-grid communication is limited if the perimeter-to-surface ratio of the pieces is low. Inter-grid communication is more costly : it is proportional to the surface of the pieces. We therefore try to keep cells and subcells in the same processor as much as possible. To this end, we defined two data structures : a *part* is a connected set of cells in a grid, and a *multipart* is a sequence of nested parts (i.e. all cells of a part in the sequence have their subcells in the next

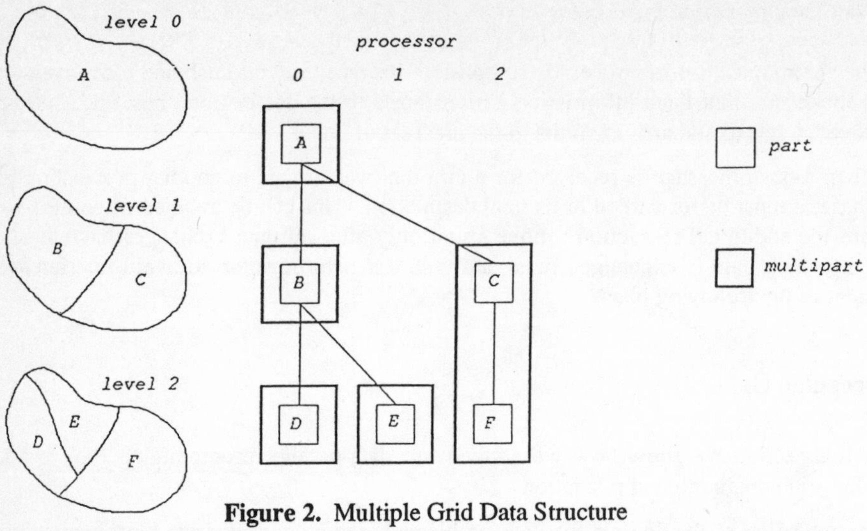

Figure 2. Multiple Grid Data Structure

part in the sequence). The parts are the units for intra-grid operations. The multiparts are used as units in the phases for inter-grid calculations. Multiparts also are the units used for moving. In this way we can keep cells and subcells in the same processor as much as possible.

The arithmetic load should bé balanced on the finest grid, where calculation is dominant. On coarser levels communication becomes important, and it might be advantageous to use less processors than available in order to reduce data exchanges. A discussion of this phenomenon for the case of regular grids can be found in [12].

As shown previously, the calculations in CFD are much more time-consuming than the intra-grid communication. Therefore our primary objectives are to achieve load balance and to limit inter-grid communication.

3.2 Multiple Grid Generation

It is our ultimate goal to implement an irregular multigrid Euler solver. Currently we have implemented the balancer tool, grid generation and relaxation. We now illustrate how our tool can be used for parallel irregular grid refinement. An irregular multiple grid can be built in parallel as follows (see figure 2) :

start with 1 multipart containing 1 part with convex cells (coarse grid)
for i = 0 .. #levels **do** {
  refine all parts of the grid at the current level
  split some of the multiparts in two
  allow moving of the new multiparts
  build the next gridlevel by duplicating each part
  relax the solution at this level
}

The basic parallel operations are initialization, grid refinement, grid duplication, and the splitting of parts. Additionally, routines are required to pack and unpack data structures to be able to move multiparts. For a detailed account of the implementation we refer to [6]. The algorithm creates a distributed data-structure, assigning work to each processor. As soon as this is done, load balancing can be achieved as discussed previously, either by reorganizing the multiparts using split and join operations, or by creating still more units and mapping them intelligently onto the processors. At this moment we only implemented the second technique.

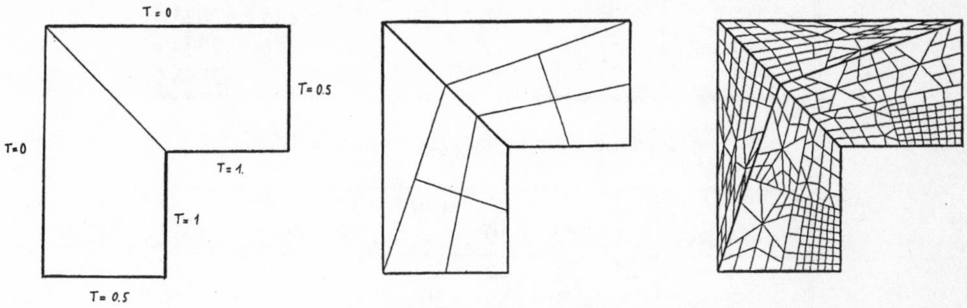

a. coarse mesh   b. after first refinement   c. after second refinement

Figure 3. Generated Mesh Sequence

We apply the algorithm given above to an L-shaped domain. The meshes shown in figure 3 have been obtained while solving the stationary heat equation :

$$\nabla^2 T = 0$$

with the Dirichlet boundary conditions indicated in the figure. We start with the initial grid shown in figure 3a. We then refine the mesh. The refinement is based on the triangle refinement algorithm of Rivara [10] and on the polygonal mesh refinement used in [11]. The refinement criterion is based on the heat flux. After the mesh refinement the part is split, and we obtain the situation of figure 3b. Bold lines represent the borders of the parts. Figure 3c shows the mesh after the next step.

3.3 Load Balanced Relaxation

The discrete system of finite volume equations on each level is solved by Jacobi relaxation. We generated balanced meshes with an increasing number of cells, with different average part sizes, and we performed some iteration steps. Let P denote the set of p processors, U the set of parts, U_j the set of parts in processor j, $t_j^{(phase)}$ the time needed by processor j to complete the phase, and $t_i^{(calc)}$ the calculation time for part i. For the case of a 4 processor iPSC/2 hypercube, we measured (table 1) :

— $t^{(phase)} := \sum_{j \in P} t_j^{(phase)}$: the total time needed by all processors to finish one iteration,

— $\lambda := (\sum_{i \in U} t_i^{(calc)}) \,/\, (p \,.\, \max_{j \in P} (\sum_{i \in U_j} t_i^{(calc)})$: the calculation load balance,

— $\alpha := (\sum_{i \in U} t_i^{(calc)}) \,/\, t^{(phase)}$ the fraction of time spent in the actual calculation.

The results for λ show that the combined action of the part splitting strategy and the mapping algorithm yields good calculation load balance, at least if the number of parts is sufficiently large. It is clear that $\alpha \leq \lambda$. The fraction $\lambda - \alpha$ is due to the overhead (including the

Nr of Parts	Nr of Cells 1	4	10	32	110	444	1788
1	13	24	56	176			
2		22	41	108	302		
4			57	138	189	620	
8				142	324	630	
16					301	845	2623
32						865	2909
64							2996

a. Total time for 1 phase (in milliseconds)

Nr of Parts	Nr of Cells 1	4	10	32	110	444	1788
1	25	25	25	25			
2		50	50	50	50		
4			63	50	95	97	
8				73	81	97	
16					76	83	83
32						82	86
64							82

b. Calculation load balance (in %)

Nr of Parts	Nr of Cells 1	4	10	32	110	444	1788
1	8	17	21	24			
2		14	32	39	42		
4			21	31	68	79	
8				29	39	77	
16					42	58	74
32						57	67
64							65

b. Percentage of time spent in calculation (in %)

Table 1. Timing Results for Jacobi Iteration on a 4 processor iPSC/2

communication for data exchange). A comparison of tables 1b and 1c shows how this overhead dcreases when the number of cells per part increases. Similarly table 1a shows that, for a fixed problem size, $t^{(phase)}$ remains approximately constant with increasing number of parts : although a larger number of parts allows to obtain a better load balance, more time will be spent in communication (the perimeter effect). For problems that are sufficiently computationally intensive, like the solution of the Euler equations, $\alpha \approx \lambda$. The overhead will then become relatively unimportant.

4. Conclusion

In this paper we applied *data-parallelism* to numerical applications characterized by irregular and varying problem topologies, and by a high computational load. A programming environment supporting this parallelization paradigm has been applied to irregular multiple grids. The load balancing problem has been reformulated as : *minimize the calculation imbalance and limit communication by putting restrictions on the data-structures.* The first results for Jacobi relaxation for the heat equation on an irregular grid show that the overhead encurred can be justified for sufficiently calculation intensive applications. In the future, comparisons between iterative static and truly dynamic load balancing strategies will be made.

Acknowledgement

This work has benefited greatly from discussions with Raf Van Driessche and Wouter Joosen. We also thank Stefan Vandewalle for his careful reading of this manuscript.

This research is supported by the Belgian Ministry Of Science ("Geconcerteerde Onderzoeksacties" and "Interuniversitaire Attractiepool nr. 17"), the Belgian Government (D.P.W.B. "Impulsprogramma Informatietechnologie") and Intel Scientific Computers U.S.A. ("University Partners in Computer Science Research Program").

References

[1] L. Beernaert, D. Roose, R. Struijs, and H. Deconinck, ''Implementation of a solver for the Euler equations on the iPSC/2 multiprocessor'' *Parallel Computing '89*, pp. 67-72, Elsevier (1990).

[2] G. Chesshire and A. Jameson, ''FLO87 on the iPSC/2 : A parallel multigrid solver for the Euler equations'' in *Proceedings of the Parallel CFD Conference '89*, Portland (May 1989).

[3] G.C. Fox, M.A. Johnson, G.A. Lyzenga, S.W. Otto, J.K. Salmon, and D.W. Walker, *Solving Problems on Concurrent Processors*, Prentice Hall (1988).

[4] W.D. Gropp and I.C. Ipsen, ''Recursive mesh refinement on hypercubes'' *BIT* (29) , pp. 186-211 (1989).

[5] P.W. Hemker and B. Koren, ''A non-linear multigrid method for the steady Euler equations'' pp. 175-196 in *Numerical Simulation of Compressible Euler Flows*, ed. A. Dervieux, B. Van Leer, J. Periaux, A. Rizzi, Friedr. Vieweg & Sohn, Braunschweig/Wiesbaden (1989).

[6] J. De Keyser, *Irregular Multiple Grid Generation on a Distributed Memory Machine*, Internal Report, Dept. of Computer Science, K.U.Leuven, (August 1990).

[7] M.-H. Lallemand, H. Steve, and A. Dervieux, *Unstructured multigridding by volume agglomeration*, Rapports de Recherche No. 1224, INRIA, Sophia Antipolis (May 1990).

[8] H. Muhlenbein, M. Gorges-Schleuter, and O. Kramer, ''Evolution Algorithms in Combinatorial Optimization'' *Parallel Computing* (7) , pp. 65-85, North-Holland (1988).

[9] D.M. Nicol and P.F. Reynolds, ''Optimal Dynamic Remapping of Data Parallel Computations'' *IEEE Trans. on Computers*, Vol.39 (2) (February 1990).

[10] M.-C. Rivara, ''Design and data structure of fully adaptive multigrid, finite-element software'' *ACM Trans. on Math. Software*, Vol.10 (242) (1984).

[11] R. Struijs, P. Van Keirsbilck, and H. Deconinck, *An adaptive grid polygonal finite volume method for the compressible flow equations*, AIAA CP 89-1959 (June 1989), paper presented at the AIAA 9th CFD Conference, Buffalo, NY.

[12] S. Vandewalle and R. Piessens, ''A Comparison of Parallel Multigrid Strategies'' pp. 65-79 in *Proceedings of the First European Workshop on Hypercube and Distributed Computers*, ed. F. Andre, North Holland, Amsterdam (1989).

[13] S. Vandewalle, J. De Keyser, and R. Piessens, ''The numerical solution of elliptic partial differential equations on a hypercube multiprocessor'' pp. 69-97 in *Scientific Computing on Supercomputers*, ed. J.T. Devreese and P.E. Van Camp, Plenum Press, New York (1989).

[14] R.D. Williams, ''Supersonic fluid flow in parallel with an unstructured mesh'' *Concurrency : Practice and Experience*, Vol.1 (1) , pp. 51-62 (September 1989).

AN OBJECT-ORIENTED INTERFACE FOR PARALLEL PROGRAMMING OF LOOSELY-COUPLED MULTIPROCESSOR SYSTEMS

Theo Ungerer and Lubomir Bic[1]

Institute of Mathematics
University of Augsburg
D-8900 Augsburg, Germany
ungerert@uniaug.de

Department of Information and Computer Science
University of California, Irvine
Irvine, CA 92717, USA
bic@ics.uci.edu

Abstract

This paper presents an object-oriented language interface as a basis for the programming of loosely-coupled multiprocessor systems and an algorithm for automatic translation into parallel programs. Starting with a sequential program written in a restricted subset of C++, the translator algorithm first generates a machine-independent communication graph and proceeds with the creation of the machine-specific parallel programs. The programmer uses object definitions and method invocations within a single sequential program instead of defining a set of parallel programs and programming explicitly with send/receive-primitives. The translator algorithm is demonstrated by the transformation of an example program into parallel programs for the Intel iPSC/2 hypercube and for transputer systems with HELIOS operating system.

1. Introduction

Multiprocessor systems that communicate by message passing like the Intel iPSC/2 [1, 2], the Ncube/10 [3], Caltech/JPL Mark II and Mark III [4], and transputer systems [5] are hard to program. In principle, separate programs have to be written for each processing node and for each process per processing node. For an Intel iPSC/2 hypercube with 128 nodes and up to 20 processes per node this amounts up to 2560 programs. Each message must be programmed explicitly by a send statement in the sending program, and a receive statement in the receiving program. This is especially hard to program and to debug if communication is high and irregular.

Consequently, in practically all application domains, parallel programs are constructed by loading the same program onto a set of processing nodes and by communicating in a very restricted and regular style. One example is farming [6], where a controller process distributes chunks of data to slave processes generated from a single program that is duplicated over many processing nodes. Such a restricted parallel programming style does not utilize the communication facilities of loosely-coupled multiprocessor systems.

Object-oriented programming is known for its superior structuring capabilities in developing large programs. Its potential for parallel processing has been promoted by providing specific concurrent object-oriented languages [7, 8, 9] or by augmenting existing sequential object-oriented languages with synchronization and parallel language features [10, 11, 12]. Our own approach promotes implicit parallelism by translating sequential programs written in a suitable subset of an existing object-oriented programming language, in our case C++ [13], into parallel programs. No new language features have to be introduced. The translator algorithm automatically generates separate programs for each processor and the necessary communication statements.

The paper is organized as follows. The language restrictions for the use of the proposed translator are discussed in Section 2. An example program is presented in Section 3. The concept of a

1 This work has been supported in part by NSF Grant CCR-8709817

communication graph, generated automatically from an object-oriented program and used as part of the translator algorithm for the construction of the node programs is introduced in Subsection 4.1. Subsection 4.2 gives the basic translator algorithm for the creation of the communication graph. Section 5 gives the algorithm for generating parallel programs for the Intel iPSC/2 (in Subsection 5.1) and for transputer systems with HELIOS operating system (in Subsection 5.2). Section 6 illustrates some experimental results and gives the conclusions.

2. Restrictions on C++

Object-oriented programs provide an abstract communication model: objects are defined to communicate with each other by message passing. If an object receives a message, a method of its defining class is invoked. This may change the internal state of the object or further messages may be generated. Such an abstract model of computation fits the message-passing capabilities of a loosely-coupled multiprocessor system. An object-oriented program consists of a set of objects communicating with each other by messages, while in a loosely-coupled multiprocessor system it is a set of node programs that communicate by message passing. Our approach is to transform each object into a node program, map it to a processing node of the multiprocessor, and transform the conceptual messages of the object-oriented program into actual messages exchanged between processing nodes.

We chose C++ as the object-oriented language to test our approach due to its popularity and general availability. However, since C++ is a superset of C it abounds with non object-oriented language features. For an automatic translation to be efficient, we have to restrict C++ to a subset of purely object-oriented language features that facilitate the construction of parallel programs. The programmer should obey two principal restrictions:

1. No global variables (that includes *STATIC* variables and *public data members* in class definitions), and no *functions*, except for the *main*-function, are allowed.
2. All user-defined objects and method invocations must be known at compile-time.

By enforcing these restrictions, a static communication graph can be derived. The first restriction affects the programming style only. The second restricts the class of possible applications. Relaxations of these restrictions are discussed in [14, 15, 16]. In this paper we concentrate on the basic algorithms.

```
class vec {    int v[2];
    public:    void put_value(int);
               int get_value(int);    };
void vec::put_value(int value)
         {     v[0] = v[1] = value;      }
int vec::get_value(int index)
         {     return v[index];          }
class element { int e;
    public:    void eval(vec, vec);    };
void element::eval(vec v1, vec v2)
         {     e=0;  for (int i=0; i<=1; i++)
                        e = e + v1.get_value(i) * v2.get_value(i);   }
main()   {     vec A[2], B[2]; int value = 1;
               for (int i=0; i<=1; i++)
               {  A[i].put_value(value);
                  B[i].put_value(value);
                  value++;  }
               element c[2][2];
               for (int m=0; m<=1; m++)
                 for (int n=0; n<=1; n++)
                   c[m][n].eval(A[m], B[n]);    }
```

Figure 1: A Sequential Object-Oriented C++ program

3. Example Program

A simple object-oriented C++ program that satisfies the above restrictions is shown in Fig.1. It multiplies two *2x2* matrices *A* and *B*. Each element *c[i][j]* of the resulting matrix *C* is the product of *A[i]* and *B[j]*, where *A[i]* is the ith row of matrix *A* and *B[j]* is the jth column of matrix *B*. Computations pertaining to each element *c[i][j]* are independent, and thus can be done in parallel. Conceptually, each row of matrix *A* and each column of matrix *B* is an object of class *vec*. Every element of the resulting matrix *C* is an object of class *element*. The first part of the program gives the definitions of these two classes. In the class *vec*, method *put_value* assigns values to objects of that class, i.e., to the 2-element vector *v*. To simplify the program the method *put_value* assigns the argument value to all components of the object of type *vec*. In the class *element*, the member function *eval* computes the inner product of a row of matrix *A* (*vector v1*) and a column of matrix *B* (*vector v2*). The main program declares two matrices *A* and *B*, then assigns values to these two matrices by repeatedly invoking the method *put_value*. Next, the *main* function declares the elements *c[i][j]* of the resulting matrix *C*. Then it computes the values of the resulting matrix *C* by invoking the method *eval* for every element of *C*.

4. Communication Graph

4.1 Structural Description of a Communication Graph

A communication graph describes the abstract communication model. It is an intermediate step in the translator algorithm and independent from the target machine and its configuration. A communication graph is a directed graph where nodes represent objects and named links represent messages sent between objects. One node that we will refer to as the *'Driver'* represents the *main* function of the C++ program. There are two kinds of links in the communication graph. Dashed links represent method invocation messages, which trigger the execution of methods. Solid links represent parameter messages, which carry the appropriate parameters to the involved method, and the returning values (if there are any) back to the caller. The communication graph is generated at compile-time, therefore all objects and method invocations have to be known at compile-time, as is guaranteed by the restrictions of Section 2.

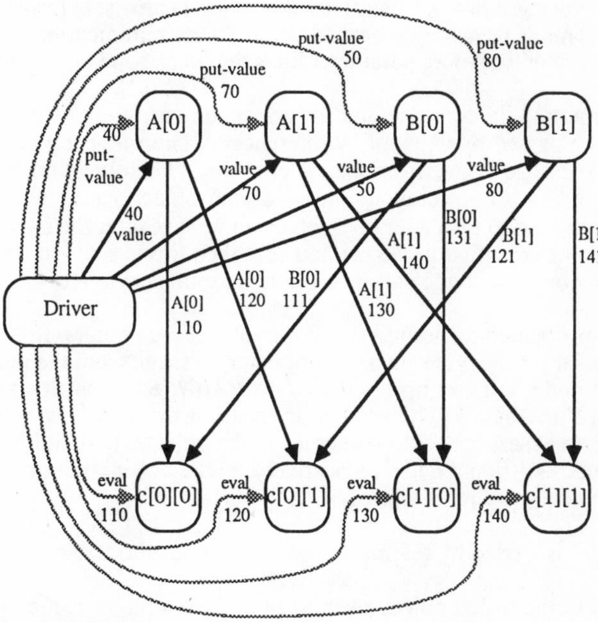

Figure 2: Communication Graph

The communication graph for the sample program of Fig.1 is shown in Fig.2. Four objects of class *vec* (*A[0], A[1], B[0], B[1]*) and four objects of class *element* (*c[0][0], c[0][1], c[1][0],* and *c[1][1]*) are included in this communication graph. The *main* function is represented in the communication graph as the *'Driver'* node. To illustrate the links in this graph consider for example, the statement *c[0][0].eval(A[0], B[0])* which means that the method *eval* in the object *c[0][0]* is invoked by the *main* function and objects *A[0]* and *B[0]* are passed to the member function as parameters. The caller is the *'Driver'* while the parameters are generated by the objects *A[0]* and *B[0]*. Because all objects reside on different processors, three separate messages are necessary; one for the method invocation and one for each of the two parameters *A[0]* and *B[0]*. Note, however, that additional synchronization is needed. The node *A[0]* has to send messages carrying the value of *A[0]* to *c[0][0]* and to *c[0][1]* after receiving the *value* message from the *'Driver'* and evaluating the *put_value* method. Otherwise a non-initialized data value would be sent. To solve the synchronization problem, we assign *precedence numbers* to the messages in the communication graph. The precedence numbers are derived from the statement numbers in the sequential program. The precedence numbers are shown in Fig.2 as simple integers. The exact meaning and derivation of the precedence numbers will be explained in the next Subsection.

4.2 The Translator Algorithm Part I - Generating the Communication Graph

Parallel programs are derived from the C++ program by first generating the communication graph and then the actual programs. There are five steps in generating the communication graph:

The first step verifies that the restrictions stated in Section 2 are satisfied. The second step unravels loops with object creations or method invocations in the loop body. Method invocations nested in statements are also unraveled. This makes the program easier to analyze and translate into parallel code. The third step creates all the object nodes by examining the object declaration statements in the program. For instance, *element c[2][2]* and *vec A[2], B[2]* result in the creation of the *c*, *A*, and *B* object nodes shown in Fig.2.

The fourth step creates message links by scanning through the *main* function derived in step 2, and generating one or more links in the communication graph for each method invocation. The first is the method invocation link which carries the method name sent from the caller node to the called object node. This is drawn by a dashed arc in the communication graph. If there are parameters, then there are one or more parameter links drawn as solid arcs in the graph.

A parameter for a method invocation could be a simple non-object parameter or an object parameter, and could be passed by value or by reference. All non-object parameters are combined into one parameter message drawn from the caller to the called object node. This is the case for both call-by-value and call-by-reference. In case of non-object parameters passed by reference the parameters are returned to the caller on a separate message after the execution of the method. If there is a return value specified in the method call, then this is sent back to the caller. This return value can be combined with the call-by-reference parameters to reduce message traffic.

Object parameters are treated differently from non-object parameters. If an object is passed by value, then a copy of this object is sent as a parameter message from the parameter object node to the called object node. For example, *c[0][0].eval(A[0], B[0])* has two parameters, both of which are call-by-value objects. The method invocation message *eval* is created as usual. In addition, two parameter messages bearing copies of the objects *A[0]* and *B[0]* are sent from the parameter object nodes *A[0]* and *B[0]*, respectively, to the destination object node *c[0][0]*. No return messages are necessary in this case.

If an object parameter is passed by reference, two different methods can be applied:

- the object is sent to the called object node, as in the case of a by-value object parameter, and returned to the parameter object node after execution of the method;

- the code of the called method is scanned, and each method invocation within the code is replaced by messages in the same way as described above. No copy of the parameter object is created.

The fifth step is the assigning of precedence numbers. The algorithm first sequentially numbers all statements in the *main* function and in each method of every class definition. The numbering is done in intervals of tens. It then scans the *main* program and, each time a method invocation is encountered, it's statement number is assigned as the precedence number to the corresponding method invocation link and, if there is only one, also to its parameter link.

If more than one parameter link exists, the following synchronization problems may arise:

- in the case of two or more parameter messages from different starting nodes but with the same callee node, the messages must be distinguishable by the callee node;
- in the case of a call-by-reference (non-object) parameter or a return value, the additional parameter message from the callee node back to the caller node must be sent after the receive of the parameters and the execution of the method by the callee node.

These problems are solved by the intervals of tens in the statement numbers. All parameter links that belong to a single method invocation are assigned intermediate numbers $x+0$ to $x+9$, where x is the statement number of the method invocation. The highest number is assigned to the return parameter link. This restricts the number of parameter links per method invocation to 10. To overcome this restriction when necessary, the statement numbering can be changed appropriately in specific cases when more parameter links are necessary.

Another case that has not yet been covered concerns object parameters passed by reference. According to the second method in step 4, messages are derived from method invocations within the code of the called method. These messages will be assigned precedence numbers of the form $n1.n2$, where $n1$ is the statement number of the original method invocation while $n2$ is the statement number of the method invocation in the method body. $n2$ is defined recursively by applying the same assignment algorithm to the statements of the method body. The same procedure is necessary if methods contain non-local method invocations.

The resulting precedence numbers capture the semantics of the sequential program. They are used when creating the individual node programs to ensure that messages are sent and received in the order prescribed by the sequential program. To illustrate this procedure, consider the original program in Fig.1. The program is first unraveled and each statement is assigned a unique number. Hence, statement *A[0].put_value(value)* has statement number *40*, statement *B[0].put_value(value)* has statement number *50*, and so on. As a result, the method invocation messages *put_value* and the parameters *value* have the numbers *40*, *50*, etc., as shown in Fig.2.

5. Creating Parallel Code

Here starts the machine-dependent part of the translator algorithm. This will be demonstrated for the Intel iPSC/2 (Subsection 5.1), and for transputer systems with HELIOS operating system (Subsection 5.2).

5.1 The Translator Algorithm Part II - Creating Parallel Code for the Intel iPSC/2 Hypercube

The target machine is an Intel iPSC/2 hypercube [1, 2] with up to 128 processor nodes and no common memory. All data exchanges between the processor nodes must be done by sending/receiving of messages. Although the nodes are physically connected in a hypercube topology, a dedicated routing hardware transports messages between arbitrary nodes in almost constant time. Thus, from a programmer's point of view, the machine can be viewed as fully connected. Each processor node executes its own program, loaded initially from a so-called host node. Four additional steps are necessary to generate code for each node of the hypercube machine:

The first step is to map object nodes from the communication graph onto processor nodes in the hypercube. In our approach, we have implemented a random mapping. With respect to communication, this simplification is justified, since the iPSC/2 architecture can be viewed as if it had a fully connected topology. With respect to objects, a better performance is likely to be achieved by attempting to distribute the load evenly over time. Each node in the communication graph is assigned to a separate node of the hypercube using one process per processor. Thus, for each object node and the *Driver* node, a process number and a processor number are assigned.

If there are more object nodes in the communication graph than processor nodes in the hypercube, we apply two different mapping strategies. First, the iPSC/2 hypercube allows 20 processes per node. Hence, we assign multiple objects to different processes of the same node. When the total number of processes is exceeded, or to reduce context switching overhead, a second strategy, which combines object nodes in the communication graph into one, may be applied. The messages within the combined object nodes are collapsed into ordinary method invocations, and the same algorithm, as defined below, can be applied to the combined object nodes. The code for mapping the example program is shown in the first part of Fig.3, where every node is assigned to a different processor number, but with the same process number.

The second step is to map precedence numbers onto message numbers. Only parameter links are transformed into actual hypercube messages, while method invocation links are used only for generating the code of the parallel programs. That is, all method invocations are explicitly embedded into the *main* functions of the target objects, as generated in the fourth step. For the iPSC/2 hypercube, message numbers, called *message types* of data type *long*, are assigned to the hypercube messages. We uniquely map precedence numbers onto positive numbers of data type *long* by using the lexicographic ordering of the precedence numbers.

The third step creates the '*Driver*' program, that plays the role of a central manager for the system of parallel node programs. It runs on the host node of the iPSC/2 hypercube. The first part of the '*Driver*' program always contains the load statements for the node programs, and other administration tasks necessary to run a iPSC/2 hypercube host program. This is followed by the code for the placement of objects onto nodes and processes as defined in step 1. The '*Driver*' program is created by scanning the modified *main* program (from step 2 of Subsection 4.2) and replacing all method invocations by send/receive statements. The structure and the *message types* of the send/receive statements are derived from the communication graph. Object declarations are omitted. Also all method invocations without parameters, and method invocations with only object parameters are omitted, as these do not need send/receive statements in the *Driver* program. All other code that is not related to method invocation remains unchanged. We illustrate this process using again the matrix multiplication example. The resulting *Driver* program is shown in Fig.3. Note that the *eval* statements are omitted because they only have object parameters; the corresponding parameter messages do not affect the *Driver* program.

```
// include load statements and placement statement
// mapping of objects to processor nodes and processes
node_Driver = 8, pid_Driver = 0;
node_A[0] = 0,    node_A[1] = 1,    node_B[0] = 2,    node_B[1] = 3;
pid_A[0] = 0,     pid_A[1] = 0,     pid_B[0] = 0,     pid_B[1] = 0;
node_c[0][0]=4,   node_c[0][1]=5,   node_c[1][0]=6,   node_c[1][1]=7;
pid_c[0][0]=0,    pid_c[0][1]=0,    pid_c[1][0]=0,    pid_c[1][1]=0;
main(){ int value = 1;
        csend(40,(char *)&value,sizeof(int),node_A[0],pid_A[0]);
        csend(50,(char *)&value,sizeof(int),node_B[0],pid_B[0]);
        value++;
        csend(70,(char *)&value,sizeof(int),node_A[1],pid_A[1]);
        csend(80,(char *)&value,sizeof(int),node_B[1],pid_B[1]);
        value++;  }
```

Figure 3: Parallel Code for the *Driver*

The fourth step creates the node programs. Each object node in the communication graph results in a separate node program. To deal with inheritance and *friend* declaration, all class definitions of the sequential C++ program are included in all node programs. For generating the node program, the communication graph is used. The general algorithm performs the following tasks for each object node in the communication graph: Select the arc(s) with the lowest precedence number. For each incoming parameter link, generate a receive statement. Next, if there is a method invocation link, generate the corresponding method invocation call. If there is an outgoing parameter link, generate a send statement. Repeat these steps for the arcs with the next lower precedence number until all have been processed. Parameter links in the communication graph may carry objects. However, messages between processor nodes in the iPSC/2 hypercube can only carry data of type character string. Hence, if a parameter link contains an object, the sending node program has to transfer it into a character string, and the receiving node program has to recreate the object. Two example node programs (one for object *A[0]*, and the other for object *c[0][0]*) are shown in Fig.4 and Fig.5.

```
// include all class definitions of the sequential C++ program
// include the mapping of objects to processor nodes and processes
main(){ vec A0; int value;
        crecv(30,(char *)&value,sizeof(int));
        A0.put_value(value);
        int buffer[2];
        buffer[0] = A0.get_value(0);
        buffer[1] = A0.get_value(1);
        csend(110,(char *)buffer,2*sizeof(int),node_c[0][0],pid_c[0][0]);
        csend(120,(char *)buffer,2*sizeof(int),node_c[0][1], pid_c[0][1]);}
```

Figure 4: Parallel code for Object *A[0]*

```
// include the class definitions for class vec and class element
// include the mapping of objects on processor nodes and processes
main(){ vec A,B; element c; int buffer[2];
        crecv(110,(char *)buffer,2*sizeof(int));
        A.put_value(buffer[0]);
        A.put_value(buffer[1]);
        crecv(111,(char *)buffer,2*sizeof(int));
        B.put_value(buffer[0]);
        B.put_value(buffer[1]);
        c.eval(A,B);  }
```

Figure 5: Parallel code for Object *c[0][0]*

5.2 The Translator Algorithm Part II - Creating Parallel Code for Transputer Systems

The target machine is a transputer system [5] with, in principle, an unlimited number of processor nodes, each equiped with up to 4 MBytes of local memory. There is no common memory. All data exchanges between the processor nodes are organized by the HELIOS operating system and must be specified by the programmer by *read/write*-statements, and by a so-called CDL-script. The CDL-script defines the resource and communication needs of the parallel programs and is written in a language called CDL (Component Distribution Language). The processors can be physically connected in any topology. Load distribution is done automatically by HELIOS at load-time. Likewise, intermediate processes, which are necessary if routing of a message is done via an intermediate transputer node, are generated and injected automatically by HELIOS. Each processor node executes its own program, loaded initially from a so-called host node.

Four additional steps are necessary to generate code for each node of the transputer system:

The first step creates a configuration graph which is a directed graph where nodes represent tasks (node programs) and links represent communication paths between tasks. Each link bears a unique name and two numbers, one for the sender and one for the receiver. The numbers are the so-called Posix numbers [6], which correspond with HELIOS communication channels. The numbers *0-2* are reserved, by convention, for *stdin*, *stdout*, and *stderr*; number *3* is not defined; otherwise, even numbers define receiver ports, and odd numbers define sender ports. Each node in the communication graph is assigned to a separate node in the configuration graph. All parameter links that share the same sender and the same receiver node in the communication graph are represented by a single link in the configuration graph. Method invocation links are omitted. Posix numbers are assigned to the links in ascending order, starting with number 4 for receiver ports and with number 5 for sender ports relative to each node. The link names are used as stream names when generating the CDL-script (next Subsection). The configuration graph for the example program is shown in Fig.6. The link names are shown in italic.

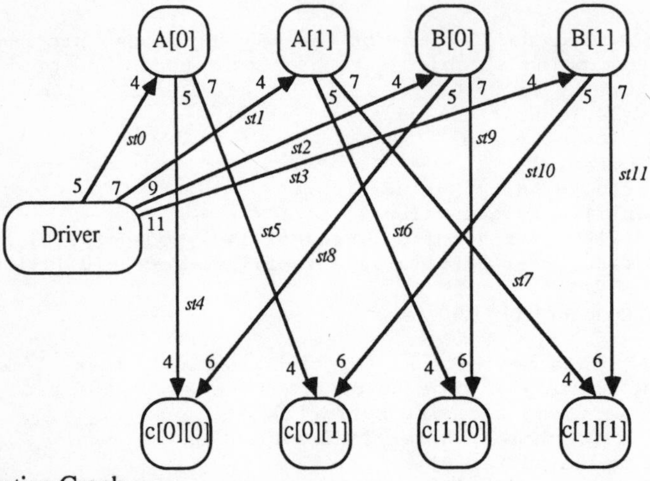

Figure 6: Configuration Graph

The second step creates a CDL-script [17], which specifies the communication paths of the parallel programs. A CDL-script consists of a *component*-description for each parallel program and a configuration string at the end. The component description consists of an object file name, various system configuration fields, and a *streams* field. The translator algorithm creates the configuration string in a uniform manner by connecting all component names with the CDL general parallel construct ^^, starting with the *Driver*. The actual communication paths are specified in the *streams* field of each *component*-description. The *stream* field consists of a number of entries, each separated by a comma. Each entry corresponds with a Posix number, and is either blank, if not defined in the CDL-script, or consists of a stream mode (>| means output, <| means input) and a stream name. The translator algorithm creates a *component*-description for each node in the configuration graph, and assigns the specific stream name together with the stream mode to each component. The CDL-script for the configuration graph in Fig.6 is shown in Fig.7.

```
component Driver {  code Driver; ...
                    streams ,,,,,>|st0,,>|st1,,>|st2,,>|st3; }
component A0     {  code A; ...
                    streams ,,,,<|st0,>|st4,,>|st5; }        ...
component c11    {  code c; ...
                    streams ,,,,<|st7,,<|st11; }
Driver ^^ A0 ^^ ... ^^ c11
```

Figure 7: A CDL-script.

As in the case of the iPSC/2, the third step creates the '*Driver*' program similar to Subsection 5.1, by scanning the modified *main* function and replacing all method invocations by *read/write* statements. The structure and the *Posix numbers* of the *read/write* statements are derived from the configuration graph. The resulting *Driver* program for our example is shown in Fig.8.

```
int main() {   int value = 1;
               write(5,(char *)&value,sizeof(int));
               write(9,(char *)&value,sizeof(int));
               value++;
               write(7,(char *)&value,sizeof(int));
               write(11,(char *)&value,sizeof(int));
               value++;    }
```

Figure 8: Parallel Code for the Driver

The fourth step creates the node programs, which is again performed as described in Subsection 5.1 except for the replacement of the iPSC/2-specific *csend*- and *crecv*-statements by the Posix-statements *write* and *read*, respectively. Likewise, a placement part is not necessary, because this is done automatically by HELIOS. Two example node programs (one that is duplicated for the *A*- and *B*-objects, and the other for the *c*-objects) are shown in Fig.9 and Fig.10.

```
// include the class definitions for class vec and class element
int main(){    vec A; int value;
               read(4,(char *)&value,sizeof(int));
               A.put_value(value);
               int buffer[2];
               buffer[0] = A.get_value(0);
               buffer[1] = A.get_value(1);
               write(5,(char *)buffer,2*sizeof(int);
               write(7,(char *)buffer,2*sizeof(int);   }
```

Figure 9: Parallel code for the *A*- and *B*-objects.

```
// include the class definitions for class vec and class element
int main(){    vec A,B; element c; int buffer[2];
               read(4,(char *)buffer,2*sizeof(int));
               A.put_value(buffer[0]);
               A.put_value(buffer[1]);
               read(6,(char *)buffer,2*sizeof(int));
               B.put_value(buffer[0]);
               B.put_value(buffer[1]);
               c.eval(A,B);   }
```

Figure 10: Parallel code for the *c*-objects.

6. Experimental Results and Conclusions

To study the performance of the resulting parallel matrix multiply programs we have varied the problem size by multiplying two *7xsize* matrices, *A* and *B*, producing a resulting *7x7* matrix *C*. As in the case of the sample *2x2* matrix multiplication of Fig.1, this larger example is transformed into a communication graph, where each element of the resulting matrix as well as each object of the class *vec* is a separate object (process) capable of running on one processor. Since there are more objects than processors, several processes are running on each processor. Using an *8*-node Intel iPSC/2 hypercube, we mapped *7* object nodes of type *element* onto each processor node, and mapped *2* object nodes of type *vec* (*A[i]* and *B[i]*) onto each processor node, thus running *7* processor nodes in parallel, each with *9* processes running in a multiprogramming fashion. This experiment showed a speedup of 3.15 over sequential execution of the matrix multiplication program (a slow-down by additional messages necessary for measurement included). Some additional optimizations have also been explored and the results of these experiments may be found in [14, 15]. The same programs, adapted to HELIOS-code, have also been running on a transputer system. However, our transputer system with only two transputers is too small to get comparable performance results.

In this paper, we presented our approach to parallel programming of loosely-coupled multiprocessors. The object-oriented programming language, C++, has been chosen as the vehicle for writing application programs, due to its message-oriented semantics. We believe that C++ is suitable for exposing high degrees of parallelism. Programmers should focus primarily on the tasks being solved at the application level and should not be bothered by explicit programming of send/receive statements. These should be taken care of by automatic tools. The tools we have described in this paper expect C++ programs written in a purely object-oriented style. For such programs, communication graphs can be derived automatically and mapped onto a given multiprocessor machine configuration. This mapping has been demonstrated for the iPSC/2 hypercube and for transputer systems with HELIOS operating system.

While the results of our experiments were quite encouraging by producing a significant improvement in performance even with the basic algorithm, we note that this is just the first step toward providing an automatic parallel programming environment. Our current research focuses on relaxing the restrictions on C++ programs as formulated in Section 2 and on developing more sophisticated mapping and object-combining strategies.

References

[1] R. Arlanskas: iPSC/2 System: A Second Generation Hypercube. Third Conference on Hypercube Concurrent Computers and Applications, Vol. 1, Pasadena, Jan. 1988.
[2] Intel Corporation: iPSC/2 User's Guide. Order# 311532-004, Intel Corp., Oct. 1989.
[3] S. Colley, J. Palmer, J. P. Hayes, T. Mudge, and Q. F. Stout: A Microprocessor-Based Hypercube Supercomputer. IEEE Micro, October 1986.
[4] J. Tuazon, J. Peterson, M. Pniel, D. Liberman: Caltech/JPL Mark II Hypercube Concurrent Processor. Proceedings 1985 International Conference on Parallel Processing.
[5] Inmos: Transputer Reference Manual. Prentice Hall 1988.
[6] Bill Noble, Rachel Ganz of Vardas, and Bart Veer: The HELIOS Parallel Programming Tutorial. Published by Distributed Software Limited, Bristol 1990.
[7] Henry Lieberman: Concurrent Object-Oriented Programming in Act 1. In: A. Yonezawa and M. Tokoro: Object-Oriented Concurrent Programming. The MIT Press, 1987.
[8] Pierre America: POOL-T: A Parallel Object-Oriented Language. In: A. Yonezawa and M. Tokoro: Object-Oriented Concurrent Programming. The MIT Press, 1987, pp. 199-220.
[9] Jan Van Den Bos, and Chris Laffra: PROCOL A Parallel Object Language with Protocols. OOPSLA '89 Proceedings, Oct. 1989, pp. 96-102.
[10] Yasuhiko Yokote and Mario Tokoro: Concurrent Programming in ConcurrentSmalltalk. In: A. Yonezawa and M. Tokoro: Object-Oriented Concurrent Programming. The MIT Press, 1987, pp. 129-158.
[11] Brian N. Bershad, Edward D. Lazowska, and Henry M. Levy: PRESTO: A System for Object-Oriented Parallel Programming. Software-Practice and Experience, Vol. 18, No. 8, August 1988, pp. 713-732.
[12] William J. Dally and Andrew A. Chien: Object-Oriented Concurrent Programming in CST. The Third Conference on Hypercube, Concurrent Computers and Applications, Vol. 1, Pasadena, CA., Jan. 1988, pp. 434-439.
[13] Stroustrup, Bjarne: The C++ Programming Language. Addison-Wesley 1987.
[14] Meng-Lai Yin, Lubomir Bic, and Theo Ungerer: Parallel C++ Programming on the Intel iPSC/2 Hypercube. 4th Ann. Symp. on Parallel Processing, Fullerton, Ca., April 1990.
[15] Meng-Lai Yin, Lubomir Bic, and Theo Ungerer: Parallelizing Static C++ Programs. TOOLS PACIFIC'90, Nov. 1990.
[16] Lubomir Bic: Distributing Object Arrays in C++. Tech.Rep. 90-35, ICS, UCI, Oct. 1990.
[17] Perhelion Software Limited: The CDL Guide. Distributed Software Limited, Bristol 1990.

On Automatic Loop Data-Mapping for Distributed-Memory Multiprocessors *

J. Torres, E. Ayguadé, J. Labarta, J. M. Llaberia and M.Valero

Departament d'Arquitectura de Computadors, Universitat Politècnica de Catalunya
c/ Sor Eulalia de Anzizu, Mòdul D4. 08034 - Barcelona. SPAIN
e_mail: torres@ac.upc.es

Abstract

In this paper we present a unified approach for compiling programs for Distributed-Memory Multiprocessors (DMM). Parallelization of sequential programs for DMM is much more difficult to achieve than for shared memory systems due to the exclusive local memory of each Virtual Processor (VP). The approach presented distributes computations among VPs of the system and maps data onto their private memories. It tries to obtain maximum parallelism out of DO loops while minimizing interprocessor communication.

The method presented, which is named **Graph Traverse Scheduling (GTS)**, is considered in this paper for single-nested loops including one or several recurrences. In the parallel code generated, dependences included in a hamiltonian recurrence that involves all the statements of the loop are enforced by the sequential execution of the computation assigned to each VP. Other dependences not included in the hamiltonian recurrence and involving data mapped onto different VPs will need explicit communication and synchronization.

1. INTRODUCTION

Parallelizing compilers exist today for high performance parallel computers in order to efficiently execute sequential programs written in conventional languages such as Fortran and C. These compilers mainly examine DO loops trying to obtain parallel code semantically equivalent to the original sequential one. DO loops offer a great amount of potential parallelism in numerical programs. Such parallelizing compilers perform the restructuring process based on dependence analysis for subscripted variables within the scope of each loop. Such dependences impose an execution order of the statements involved that must be preserved in the parallel code generated.

Most of the work on parallelizing compilers has been done for shared-memory multiprocessors [PGHL89, AlKe87]. On the other hand, few works have been presented in the literature for partitioning DO loops into computations well-suited for DMM systems [RaSa89]. In this case, it is necessary to automatically distribute computations and data among processors trying to maximize the parallelism obtained with a good load-balance over time while minimizing the amount of interprocessor communication required.

Other approaches try to extend a programming language with directives that control the mapping of variables to local memories [CaKe88, KeZi89, Tsen89]. The compiler automatically tries to perform a task partitioning assuming the data partitioning specified by the user. It also inserts all message-passing communication that is required to maintain the semantics of the original sequential program. Optimizing communication by message fussion is vital for obtaining efficient parallel programs [Gern90].

---

* *This work has been supported by the Ministry of Education of Spain (CICYT) in program TIC 299/89 and 392/89*

Another approach is to systematically map systolizable problems onto DMM [IbSo89, FLNV91]. The systolic algorithm derived from the specification of the problem is partitioned in order to adapt it to the size of the available DMM. The systolic algorithm is also increased in granularity in order to reduce communication overhead.

In this paper we describe GTS as a method for partitioning recurrences included in single-nested loops and generating code well-suited for DMM systems. The extension to the multiple-nested loop case can be found in [TALL90] and is not included in this paper for space reasons.

First GTS partitions the bounded statement per iteration space in threads in order to obtain maximum parallelism. Each thread consists of a set of points of the space linked by a dependence chain. Each thread will be executed as a task in a VP of the DMM system. The partitioning step assumes the existence of a hamiltonian recurrence in the dependence graph that generates the set of threads. Such hamiltonian recurrence involves all loop statements. If not present, one must be obtained by adding dummy dependences that do not limit the parallelism of the loop. The method proposed obtains a fully independent partition when a single hamiltonian recurrence appears in the dependence graph.

After that, referenced array elements are mapped onto private memories based on the distribution of computations between threads obtained in the previous step. In order to minimize interprocessor communication, all data computed or used in a thread are located in the private memory of the VP that executes this thread. Finally, dependences not included in the hamiltonian recurrence and involving data used on different VPs are satisfied by using the correct data communication and synchronization primitives.

This method was first presented in [ALTB89] and [ALTL90] as an approach for compiling single and multiple-nested loops for shared-memory multiprocessors, respectively. The outline of the remaining sections in this paper is as follows. In section 2 we describe the model of target machine for which GTS is presented. In section 3 we review some concepts and definitions on data dependences used along this paper. Section 4 presents GTS as a unified approach to task and data partitioning of single-nested loops derived from the original flow-dependence relations of the sequential program. Some comments to the multiple-nested case are given in section 5. The main concluding remarks and future work are given in section 6.

2. TARGET MACHINE AND PROGRAMMING STYLE

The architectural model that we consider in this paper is a fully-connected DMM system. In this model, processors do not have access to a shared memory. Each processor has only access to some amount of local private memory. In a fully-connected model, any processor of the DMM can exchange data with other processors through a direct link of the communication network. Routing switches provide this logically fully-connected network on DMM with a not fully-connected physical topology [iPSC88, Poun90]. In this case, it is assumed that end to end delay is not much larger than point to point delay. If load is high, congestion on the physical links will, of course, increase this delay.

The approach to processor communication is the message-passing model, where processors communicate through explicit messages by using send and receive like primitives. The statement *SEND (dest, var)* sends variable *var* from local memory to processor *dest*. The statement *RECEIVE (src, var)* receives a datum from processor *src* and stores it in variable *var*. We assume that *SEND* operations will complete without blocking while *RECEIVE* operations will block if there is no datum available.

Programming style is that a VP sends a new computed value as soon as possible if it is needed by another VP. The VP that needs this value performs a receive operation on the VP that computes it as late as possible.

3. DEFINITIONS

Restructuring compilers are based on the analysis of dependences among a collection of statements (S_1, S_2, ..., S_s) within the scope of a normalized loop. Dependence relations between statements reflect a given execution order that cannot be modified by the restructuring process.

As a result of the dependence analysis, a directed *dependence graph* G (V, E) is obtained, in which V is a set of nodes $V = \{S_1, \ldots, S_s\}$ representing statements in the loop body, and E is a set of arcs $E = \{d_{ij} | S_i, S_j \in V\}$ representing dependence relations between statements of the loop.

Between each pair of statements S_i and S_j, where S_i precedes S_j in the sequential execution of the loop, some *data dependences* are defined in the literature [KKPL81]. In our model only *flow-dependences* are of concern [ChCh87]. Statement S_j is flow-dependent on statement S_i if S_j uses a variable that S_i can modify. *Anti* and *output dependences* due to the reuse of variables can be removed by assigning different variable names to different versions of data.

Each arc $d_{ij} \in E$ involves two statements of the loop body (source and sink statement) and it has an associated *dependence distance* d_{ij} representing the number of iterations the dependence extends across. In this paper we only consider data dependences with constant dependences known at compile time.

A *chain* C_{ij} is an ordered set of arcs $C_{ij} = \{d_{ik}, d_{kl}, \ldots, d_{mj}\}$ between two statements S_i and S_j such that each node in the chain is visited only once. Given a chain C_{ij}, we define its *weight* $w(C_{ij})$ as

$$w_{ij} = \sum_{d_{lm} \in C_{ij}} d_{lm}$$

This weight $w(C_{ij})$ represents the number of iterations between any pair of instances of statements S_i and S_j.

A *recurrence* R is a cycle or closed chain in the dependence graph. A *Hamiltonian Recurrence* is a recurrence going through all nodes in the dependence graph.

Let $B = \{ R_1, R_2, \ldots, R_r \}$ be the set of recurrences in a given dependence graph G. This graph G is an *acyclic dependence graph* when $B=\emptyset$ and it is a *cyclic dependence graph* when $|B| \geq 1$. When at least one recurrence of B is hamiltonian, the graph is called *hamiltonian graph.*

The *iteration space* IS of a loop is the set of points defined by a vector index $I = \langle i_1, i_2, \ldots, i_n \rangle$ in a space with dimensionality equal to the depth of the nested-loop structure. Each point represents the execution of an iteration of the loop body. In the scope of this paper we will consider n=1. The *statement per iteration space* SIS of a loop is the set of points defined by the cartesian product IS × V, being V the set of nodes of the loop. Each point S_{rI} in this space represents the execution of a given iteration I of a given statement S_r

$$SIS = \{ S_{rI} | \ 1 \leq r \leq s, \ 1 \leq I \leq N \}$$

Dependence relations $d_{ij} \in E$ impose an execution order between any pair of points in SIS

$$S_{rI} \text{ and } S_{r\,(I+d_{ij})}$$

4. GRAPH TRAVERSE SCHEDULING

In this section we present GTS as a unified approach to task and data partitioning in an automatic restructuring environment for DMM. First GTS performs a partitioning of SIS in threads so that maximum parallelism is obtained. After that, data mapping is done so that interprocessor communication is minimized.

GTS is based on the knowledge of the average parallelism of the loop evaluated as described in [ALTL90]. This measure of parallelism can be defined as the average number of active processors executing iterations of the loop. Average parallelism can be evaluated as the quotient between the time to execute the sequential version and the time required to execute the longest path through SIS. The longest path is obtained by traversing the most restrictive recurrence of the dependence graph.

The partitioning strategy proposed covers the maximum number of possible dependences within the sequential execution of each VP. The algorithm is considered in sections 4.1 and 4.2 for single-recurrence hamiltonian graphs. If there is no such hamiltonian recurrence, one must be obtained by adding dummy dependences that do not limit the parallelism of the loop. Other flow-dependences involving data mapped on different VPs require explicit interprocessor communication introduced as described in section 4.3. Parallel code generation is briefly considered in section 4.4.

4.1 Thread Partitioning

GTS performs two basic operations: alignment of the loop body through a hamiltonian recurrence and an appropriate assignment of computations to VPs so that communication primitives can be easily introduced when needed.

Given a recurrence R, we define a *thread* as the set of points in SIS directly dependent through the recurrence. Let *Thread Set* TS be the minimum set of threads generated by a hamiltonian recurrence R that cover the whole SIS.

Each thread in TS can be characterized by the point in SIS which does not depend on any previous execution and from which the whole thread can be obtained by traversing recurrence R. Each arc d_{ij} in R determines those points of SIS associated to the sink statement S_j that can be initially executed. The set of initial dependence-free points can be expressed as

$$S_{jx} \mid 1 \leq x \leq d_{ij} .$$

Figure 1.b shows the threads generated by the hamiltonian recurrence for the loop and dependence graph of figure 1.a. Initial dependence-free points are shown with filled shapes.

GTS assigns each thread to a different VP of the DMM system. Dependences within the hamiltonian recurrence are embedded in the sequential execution of each thread. Observe that fully independent threads are obtained when dealing with single-recurrence hamiltonian graphs. Figure 1.c shows the assignment of threads to VPs proposed for the previous example. The assignment proposed fulfils that consecutive iterations of a given statement are executed in consecutive VPs. This characteristic will ease interprocessor communication described in section 4.3.

The scheduling of operations can be obtained by traversing the graph backwards and assigning to consecutive VPs all initial dependence-free iterations of each statement. In the assignment proposed, a point S_{jk} of the SIS is executed in virtual processor vp given by

$$vp = (k + w_{j1} - 1) \bmod w_R \qquad (1)$$

denoting by w_{j1} the weight of the chain C_{j1} through R and w_R its weight.

```
       DO i = 1, 98
S1:      A[i + 3] = B[i]
S2:      C[i + 2] = A[i] * D[i - 1]
S3:      B[i + 4] = C[i] / 3
       ENDO
```

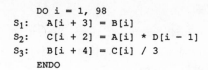

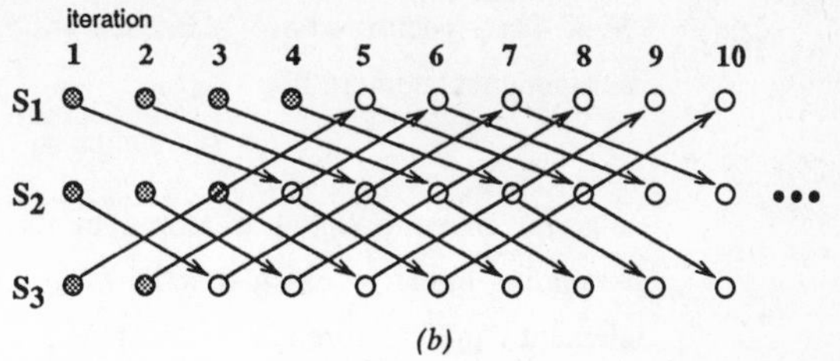

(b)

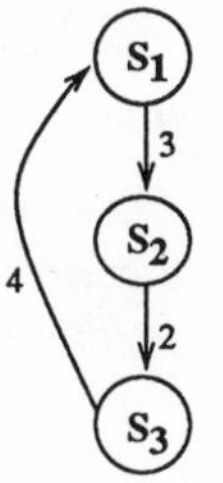

(a)

vp_0	vp_1	vp_2	vp_3	vp_4	vp_5	vp_6	vp_7	vp_8
S_{11}	S_{12}	S_{13}	S_{14}	S_{31}	S_{32}	S_{21}	S_{22}	S_{23}
S_{24}	S_{25}	S_{26}	S_{27}	S_{15}	S_{16}	S_{33}	S_{34}	S_{35}
S_{36}	S_{37}	S_{38}	S_{39}	S_{28}	S_{29}	S_{17}	S_{18}	S_{19}
$S_{1\ 10}$	$S_{1\ 11}$	$S_{1\ 12}$	$S_{1\ 13}$	$S_{3\ 10}$	$S_{3\ 11}$	$S_{2\ 10}$	$S_{2\ 11}$	$S_{2\ 12}$
⋮	⋮	⋮	⋮	⋮	⋮	⋮	⋮	⋮
$S_{1\ 91}$	$S_{1\ 92}$	$S_{1\ 93}$	$S_{1\ 94}$	$S_{3\ 91}$	$S_{3\ 92}$	$S_{2\ 91}$	$S_{2\ 92}$	$S_{2\ 93}$
$S_{2\ 94}$	$S_{2\ 95}$	$S_{2\ 96}$	$S_{2\ 97}$	$S_{1\ 95}$	$S_{1\ 96}$	$S_{3\ 93}$	$S_{3\ 94}$	$S_{3\ 95}$
$S_{3\ 96}$	$S_{3\ 97}$	$S_{3\ 98}$		$S_{2\ 98}$		$S_{1\ 97}$	$S_{1\ 98}$	

(c)

Figure 1: (a) Example of a single-recurrence hamiltonian dependence graph. (b) Statement per Iteration Space and threads. (c) Thread partitioning and assignment obtained by GTS.

4.2 Data Partitioning

Data partitioning is done by GTS so that the amount of communication between VPs is minimized. It considers the thread partitioning obtained as described in the previous section.

The basic idea is that each VP stores in its private local memory all array elements referenced by the assigned thread. In the case of single-recurrence hamiltonian graphs, these elements are computed and used in the same thread. In the case of multiple-recurrence graphs, a given vector element can be computed and used in threads assigned to different VPs. In this case, data is stored in the local memory of the VP that computes them. Communication primitives ensure the use of the correct value by the VP that uses them.

For each vector V in the original program, we generate a vector LV in each VP. Next we present the function that maps a given element of vector V onto the local vector LV of a VP:

* If V is a vector whose elements are computed in statement S_j, a given element V [f(i)] is stored in local memory of virtual processor

$$vp = (f(i) - a + w_{j1} - 1) \bmod w_R ,$$

assuming linear indexing functions $f(i) = i + a$ for the vector variable V.

The position of this element in the local vector LV is given by

$$(f(i) - a + w_{j1} - 1) / w_R$$

* If W is a vector whose elements are not computed within the loop but used in a assignment statement like

$$S_j:\ V[f(i)] = \ \ldots\ \ W[g(i)]$$

a given element W[g(i)] is stored in the same local memory as vector element V[f(i)]. Assuming linear indexing functions $f(i) = i + a$ and $g(i) = i + b$ for both vector variables, element W[g(i)] is stored in the local memory of virtual processor

$$vp = (\,(\,g(i) - a - b\,) + w_{j1} - 1\,) \bmod w_R$$

The position of this element in the local vector LW is given by

$$(\,g(i) - a - b + w_{j1} - 1\,) \,/\, w_R$$

As a result, there will be as many copies of a vector variable W as different uses in the loop.

With this distribution of data, only those elements of a vector used in the thread are stored in the local memory of the VP that executes it. For each vector V of size N, the size of the local vector LV is $\lceil N / w_R \rceil + 1$.

Figures 2.a through 2.c show the mapping of vector variables computed in each statement of the single-nested loop of figure 1.a. Only those shaded elements must be initially loaded in local memories. Other elements are computed during the execution of threads. Figure 2.d shows the mapping of variable D which is used but never computed within the loop. In this case all vector elements must be initially loaded in local memories.

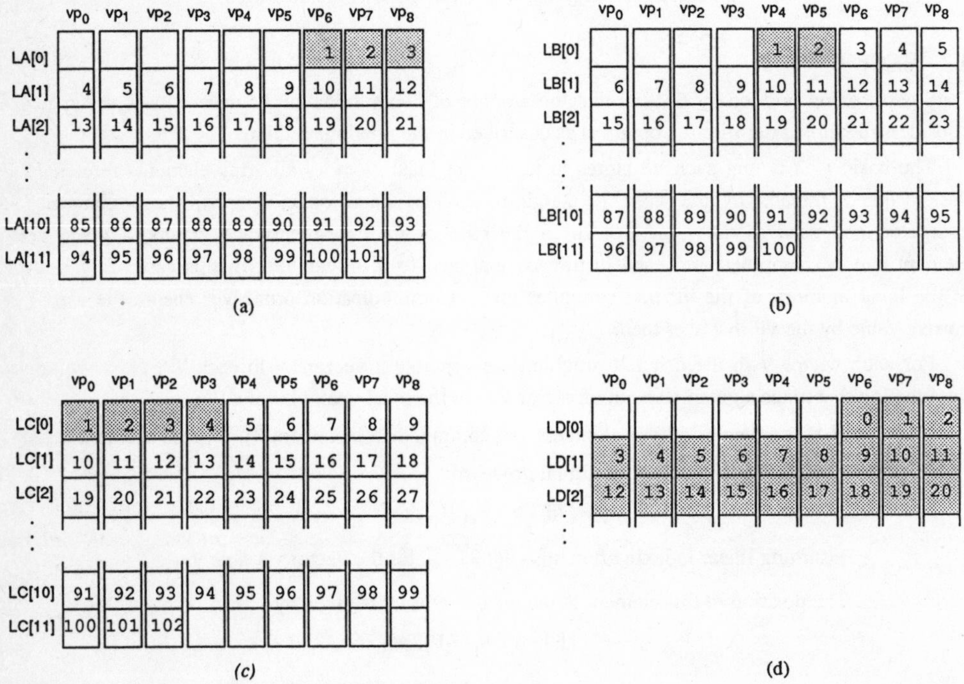

Figure 2: Mapping onto virtual processors of the elements of vector variables A, B, C and D of example 1.

4.3 Data Communication

In the case of a hamiltonian graph with more than one recurrence, the scheduling is performed by applying the same procedure described previously to a hamiltonian recurrence R_{sch} of the loop. Once R_{sch} has been obtained, dependences not included in R_{sch} and involving data mapped on different VPs require the use of communication primitives. On the other hand, dependences included in R_{sch} are embedded in the sequential execution of each thread.

Explicit communication must be introduced for any arc $d_{ij} \notin R_{sch}$ in the graph going from node S_i to node S_j. Detailed proofs of expressions given in this section can be found in [TALL90].

For each arc $d_{ij} \notin R_{sch}$, a *send* operation to virtual processor *vp'* must be executed in virtual processor *vp* after the source statement S_i. A *receive* operation from virtual processor *vp* must be executed in virtual processor *vp'* before the sink statement S_j. Due to the thread assignment proposed in the previous section, the relationship between both *vp* and *vp'* can be expressed as follows:

$$vp' = (vp + d_{ij} - w_{ij}) \bmod w_R \qquad \text{and} \qquad vp = (vp' - d_{ij} + w_{ij}) \bmod w_R \qquad (2)$$

Figure 3.b shows the thread partitioning obtained by GTS for the dependence graph of figure 3.a. Arrows represent data communication that must be introduced due to the flow-dependence d_{32}. Observe that virtual processors vp_5 and vp_6 need some elements of vector C not computed in virtual processors vp_1 and vp_2 respectively due to the actual bounded iteration space. These elements must be initially sent in order to allow the execution of threads that use them.

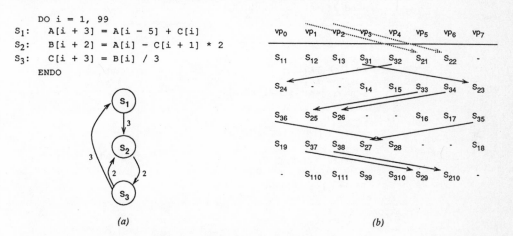

```
      DO i = 1, 99
S1:     A[i + 3] = A[i - 5] + C[i]
S2:     B[i + 2] = A[i] - C[i + 1] * 2
S3:     C[i + 3] = B[i] / 3
      ENDO
```

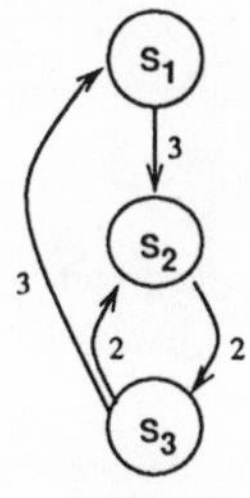

(a)

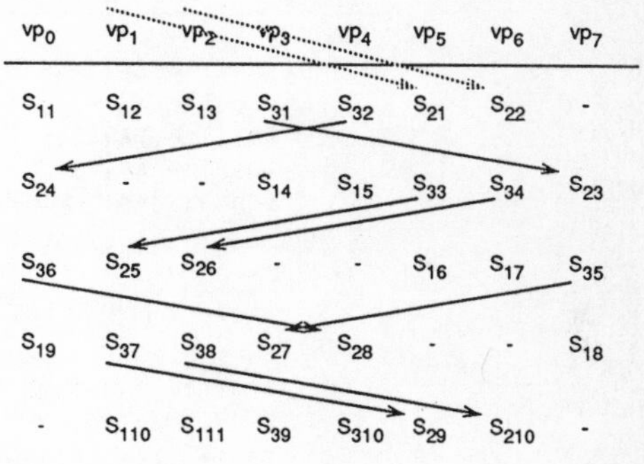

(b)

Figure 3: (a) Multiple-recurrence hamiltonian graph. (b) Thread partitioning and communication introduced by GTS.

Any dependence arc $d_{ij} \notin R_{sch}$ allows the execution of the first d_{ij} iterations of the sink statement S_j. In order to allow their execution, those elements of the vector variable that causes the dependence must be initially sent by the appropriate VPs. Taking into account where the free iterations of the sink statement are executed (1), each virtual processor *vp* will do the following number of initial sends

$$\lfloor d_{ij} / w_R \rfloor + 1 \qquad \text{if } (vp - w_{i1} + d_{ij}) \bmod w_R < d_{ij} \bmod w_R$$

$$\lfloor d_{ij} / w_R \rfloor \qquad \text{if } (vp - w_{i1} + d_{ij}) \bmod w_R \geq d_{ij} \bmod w_R$$

to virtual processors *vp'* given by (2).

Observe that if we consider a new dependence relation d_{11} in the graph of figure 3.a with an associated distance d_{11}=8, this dependence relation will not need explicit inter-processor communication because the element of vector A used in a given iteration of a thread has been computed in the previous iteration of the same thread.

4.4 Code generation

Finally, parallel code must be generated so that each processor of the DMM system executes a given thread and establishes communication with the appropriate processors. In the parallel code generated, all VP execute the same program on the variables allocated in their local address space. Explicit communication is automatically inserted to provide access to non-local data.

Figure 4 shows a possible version of the parallel code generated by GTS for the sequential loop of figure 3. In this case, it can be decomposed in three parts: *prolog, core and epilog.*

```
DOACROSS j= 0,7
  Δ=⌊(93-j)/8⌋
................................................................
  IF (j>=1 && j<=2)
       send ((j-4) mod 8, LC[0])
  ENDIF
  IF (j>=5)
       receive((j+4) mod 8, X)
       LB[0] = LA[0] - X * 2                          prolog part
 ENDIF
 IF (j>=3)
       LC[0] = LB[0] / 3
       send ((j-4) mod 8, LC[0])
 ENDIF
................................................................
 DO i = 1,1 + Δ
       LA[i] = LA[i-1] + LC[i-1]
       receive ((j+4) mod 8, X )
       LB[i] = LA[i] - X * 2                          core part
       LC[i] = LB[i] / 3
       send ((j-4) mod 8, LC[i])
 ENDDO
................................................................
 IF ((1 + Δ) * 8 + j < 99)
       LA[1 + Δ] = LA[Δ] + LC[Δ]
 ENDIF
 IF ((1+ Δ)*8 + j + 3) < 99)                          epilog part
       receive((j+4) mod 8, X)
       LB[1+ Δ] = LA[1+ Δ] - X * 2
 ENDIF
................................................................
ENDOACROSS
```

Figure 4: Parallel code generated for the example of figure 3.

In the prolog part, each processor executes the initial send primitives and some initial iterations of statements extracted from the inner sequential DO loop. This has been done in order to use the same code for all the processors. The epilog part executes the final part of the thread that can not be executed in a complete iteration of the core part. The general code structure is described in [TALL90].

5. SOME CONSIDERATIONS TO THE MULTIPLE-NESTED CASE

In this section we briefly outline some aspects on the extension of GTS to the multiple-nested loop case. Figure 5 shows a dependence graph and SIS for a possible double-nested loop. In this case we distinguish between *unbounded and bounded statement per iteration spaces.* The bounded SIS is the finite subset of the unbounded one determined by the actual loop iteration limits. Points outside the bounded SIS are drawn in dashed lines in figure 5.b. In this case, a thread is considered as the set of points of the bounded SIS linked by a dependence chain in the unbounded space. Figure 5.b shows some of the threads in the SIS generated by the hamiltonian recurrence of figure 5.a

The length of the threads generated is not constant so the load assigned to processors of the DMM will not be balanced if as many VPs as threads are allocated. A good load balancing can be obtained if we statically group threads without overcoming the execution time of the largest thread before grouping. It is important to guarantee that the grouping of threads is deadlock-free when dependences of the graph require explicit synchronization. In the example of figure 5, the two shortest threads can be executed in the same VP without overcoming the execution time of the longest thread generated before grouping.

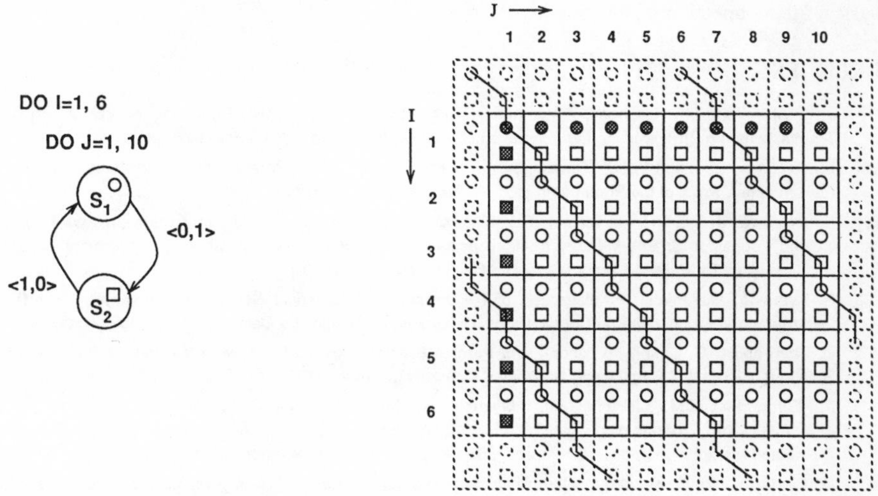

(a) *(b)*

Figure 5: (a) dependence graph for a double nested-loop and (b) associated SIS and threads generated.

As in the single-nested loop case, each matrix V is distributed among local memories of VPs and stored in one-dimesional local vectors LV. Each VP stores only those elements computed by the thread assigned and those used by it but not computed in the loop.

6. CONCLUSIONS AND FUTURE WORK

In this paper we have extended a previous work on loop parallelization for shared-memory machines to the distributed memory ones. In this case a unified approach to data and task partitioning has been considered in order to achieve maximum parallelism and minimum interprocessor communication.

Next we briefly comment some open questions left by the work presented in this paper. The partitioning method presented assumes the existence of a hamiltonian recurrence in the dependence graph. This is not the common case, so the problem must be taken into consideration [Aygu89]. A hamiltonian recurrence can be obtained by adding a set of dummy dependences E' such that the parallelism of the loop is not limited by the new set of recurrences that appear in the dependence graph. Many sets of dummy arcs E' can be used to obtain a hamiltonian recurrence. In this case, we will choose that solution which minimizes the number of threads generated and the cardinality of set E', in order to reduce the amount of synchronization required. Fast heuristics for obtaining good E' sets should be looked into if the size of the problem becomes large enough.

Dummy-arcs addition is a technique that can be also used to modify the number of processors for which parallel code is generated. In this case we avoid the overhead due to dynamic scheduling of processors in systems with less processors than parallelism of the loop.

In the case of a sequence of loops, the data must be reorganized between the end of one loop and the begin of the next [GaJG88]. It will be interesting to minimize data reorganization by using a similar dummy-arc addition technique by considering the whole loop sequence.

In the case of non fully-connected DMM, it would be interesting to reduce data routing through processing elements by performing a mapping of virtual to real processors, taking into consideration the physical interconnection topology.

REFERENCES

[AlKe87] J.R. Allen and K. Kennedy, "Automatic Translation of FORTRAN Programs to Vector Form", ACM Transactions on Programming Languages and Systems, Vol. 9, No. 4, October 1987.

[ALTB89] E. Ayguadé, J. Labarta, J. Torres and P. Borensztejn, "GTS: Parallelization and Vectorization of Tight Recurrences", Proc. of the Supercomputing'89, Reno-Nevada, November 1989.

[ALTL90] E. Ayguadé, J. Labarta, J. Torres, J.M. Llaberia and M. Valero, "Parallelism Evaluation and Partitioning of Nested Loops for Shared-Memory Multiprocessors", Proc. of the 3rd Workshop on Programming Languages and Compilers for Parallel Computing, Irvine-California, August 1990.

[Aygu89] E. Ayguadé, "Automatic Parallelization of Recurrences in Numerical Sequential Programs", Ph.D. Thesis, Departament d'Arquitectura do Computadors, Universitat Politècnica de Catalunya, Oct. 1989 (in spanish).

[ChCh87] Z. Chen and C-C. Chang, "Iteration-Level Parallel Execution of DO Loops with a Reduced Set of Dependence Relations", Journal of Parallel and Distributed Computing, No. 4, 1987.

[FLNV91] A. Fernandez, J.M. Llaberia, J.J. Navarro and M. Valero-Garcia, "Interleaving Partitions of Systolic Algorithms for Programming Distributed Memory Multiprocessors", Proceedings of the 2nd European Distributed Memory Computers Conference, Springer-Verlag (in this volume), 1991.

[CaKe88] D. Callahan and K. Kennedy, "Compiling Programs for Distributed-Memory Multiprocessors", The Journal of Supercomputing, No. 2, October 1988.

[GaJG88] K. Gallivan, W. Jalby and D. Gannon, "On the problem of Optimizing Data Transfers for Complex Memory Systems", Proceedings of the 1988 ACM International Conference on Supercomputing, St. Malo-France, 1988.

[Gern90] H.M. Gerndt, "Automatic Parallelization for Distributed Memory Multiprocessing Systems", Ph.D. dissertation, University of Bonn, Technical Report Series ACPC/TR 90-1, Austrian Center for Parallel Computation, 1990.

[IbSo89] O.H.Ibarra and S.M.Sohn, "On Mapping Systolic Algorithms onto the Hypercube", Proceedings of the 1989 International Conference on Parallel Processing, Vol. I, August 1989.

[iPSC88] iPSC/2, Intel Corporation, 1988. Order Number 280110-001.

[KeZi89] K. Kennedy and H.P. Zima, "Virtual Shared Memory for Distributed-Memory Machines", Proceedings of the 4th Hypercube Conference, Monterey-California, 1989.

[KKPL81] D.J. Kuck, R.H. Kuhn, D.A. Padua, B. Leasure and M. Wolfe, "Dependence Graphs and Compiler Optimizations", Proc. of the 8th ACM Symposium on Principles of Programming Languages Williamsburg, January 1981.

[PGHL89] C.D. Polychronopoulos, M. Girkar, M. R. Haghighat, C.L. Lee, B. Leung, D. Schouten, "Parafrase-2: An Environment for Parallelizing, Partitioning, Synchronizing and Scheduling Programs on Multiprocessors", Proceedings of the 1989 International Conference on Parallel Processing, Vol. II, August 1989.

[Poun90] D. Pountain, "Virtual Channels: The Next Generation of Transputers", BYTE, April 1990.

[RaSa89] J. Ramanujam and P. Sadayappan, "A Methodology for Parallelizing Programs for Multicomputers and Complex Memory Multiprocessors", Proceedings of the Supercomputing'89, Reno-Nevada, November 1989.

[TALL90] J. Torres, E. Ayguadé, J. Labarta, J.M. Llaberia and M. Valero, "A Technique for Data and Task Partitioning of Nested Loops for Distributed-Memory Parallel Computers", Departament d'Arquitectura de Computadors, Universitat Politècnica de Catalunya, UPC/DAC Research Report RR-90/13, June 1990.

[Tsen89] Ping-Sheng Tseng, "A Parallelizing Compiler for Distributed Memory Parallel Computers", Ph.D. Thesis, Carnegie Mellon University, CMU-CS-89-148, May 1989.

Efficient and Scalable Logical Busses for Message-Passing Interconnection Networks

H.Scheidig, M.F.Schneider, R.Spurk
University of Saarbrücken, Department of Computer Science

Abstract

Distributed-Memory, point-to-point connected MIMD-architectures (multicomputers) realize the communication between their constituent nodes by message-passing interconnection networks. The development of high-speed *cut-through-type routing modules* for interconnection networks has passed two generations: modules of the first generation offer distributed applications a pseudo-complete interconnection structure; modules of the second generation are enhanced by end-to-end functions which aim at the reduction of the software latency imposed on network nodes. This paper presents a third generation of cut-through routing, a 2-level cut-through routing method, and its utilization for the implementation of efficient, scalable *Logical Busses*. A Logical Bus represents an abstraction of a global interaction relationship between an arbitrary set of asynchronously operating nodes and allows their convenient coordination.

I. Cut-through-type routing for message-passing interconnection networks

The constituent nodes of multicomputers communicate by means of message-passing interconnection networks. Technological reasons and costs prevent the construction of interconnection networks with a complete graph structure. It is, therefore, an important goal of cut-through-type routing to equip distributed applications with adequate and dedicated interconnection structures and to hide the incomplete physical interconnection topology.

The cut-through routing technique. Cut-through routing propagates a message from a source node to a target node, pipelining it along a 1, 2, 4, ...-bit wide path of the physical topology Ψ. Three aspects of cut-through-type routing are of particular importance:

- To keep the overhead (that is, the number of processor/memory cycles "stolen" for message-passing purposes) on intermediate nodes at a minimum;
- to handle collisions which occur when two messages, arriving at the same time at a node via different input connections, have to leave through the same output connection;
- to reduce the software latency on a node which is typically caused by complex, higher-level software protocols, performed on the system- or application level.

Existing cut-through routing methods. At present, we recognize the following well-known cut-through routing methods:

a. The **virtual cut-through method**: It was introduced by Kleinrock [8] as a theoretical model. Conflicts are resolved by taking colliding packets from the network and storing them temporarily within intermediate nodes. If conflicts occur frequently, interconnection networks of this type behave as store-and-forward packet-switching networks.

b. The **worm hole method**: Conflicts are resolved by stopping the transfer of one of the colliding messages; the message is retained within the network (-queues). The Torus Routing Chip [1] as the first VLSI-implementation of this routing technique realizes deadlock-free cut-through routing for packets in k-ary n-cubes (Torus-networks).
The Direct-Connect-Routing (DCM)-module [2], manufactured by Intel and applied in their hypercube system, can already be viewed as a second generation cut-through-type routing module. A message is transferred by first constructing a path from the source to the target and then transmitting the message proper; flow control is performed on the operating system level.

c. The **Dynamic Circuit Switching** with emulation of a **Common Memory Interface (DCS/CMI)**: The Dynamic Circuit Switching method [6] works by connecting physical links by setting logical gates within the routers of the contributing nodes. A message is transferred by a synchronously operating pipeline of x-bit wide transfer units. The construction of the pipeline is controlled by the message header. This header consists of a sequence of incremental address elements every one of them causing the extension of the message's path by a further link.

II. The Dynamic Circuit Switching method (DCS/CMI)

The following section summarizes the important aspects of our DCS/CMI cut-through method and its implementation [6]. This method DCS/CMI is used as the lower routing level of the 2-level cut-through routing method introduced in section III.
We assume that a node of a multicomputer consists of two components: the *Execution Unit* (*EU*) contributes to a distributed application by performing some tasks delegated to it by the application; the *Communication Unit* (*CU*) enables its associate EU to communicate with other nodes. Abstracting from these technical details, we call such a node a *Computational Node* (abbreviated: *Cnode*).
The DCS/CMI-method [6] consists of

1. A **local switching mechanism**: it "reflects" an incoming message M into the required direction — without inspecting the remaining bits in any way. Conflicts are *resolved* by informing the sender by a hardware signal (*break signal*) about a conflict, causing it to abort the transmission and possibly retry it after a random time interval. For this purpose, every link of the physical topology Ψ is realized by a pair of hardware channels (see 3, below). The probability of conflicts is *reduced* below a certain limit by realizing every Ψ-link by a sufficient number of physical channel-pairs. An analytical model determines the appropriate channel number [5]. As topology Ψ, *2-Way Binary Digit Exchange* (*2WADE*) [3] is chosen [5, 6].
2. A **global message forwarding method**, called *Dynamic Circuit Switching*: it causes a message to construct on the fly a path from a source node S to a target node T, via intermediate nodes C_1, C_2, ..., C_n, where each Cnode C_i works as explained in 1.
3. The **emulation of a** *Common Memory Interface (CMI)* between any two communicating nodes S and T. Actually, this CMI consists of two physical channels:

- a *forward channel* which transfers a message M from S to T, and
- a *backward channel* which notifies S by a *break signal,* if the construction of CMI fails, or by a *consistency signal* about the arrival of state information. By means of these state information, DCS/CMI is able to perform flow control, realize elementary protection schemes, and to deliver to S some information about the execution state of T.

The main properties of the DCS/CMI-method can be summarized as follows: The component SW can be realized as a VLSI-chip [4] the typical performance of which can be characterized by the following figures:

a. Capacity of SW: SW typically offers 32 4-bit/8-bit wide channels.

b. Transfer rate: a channel will typically be driven with 10 MBit/sec (higher rates would principally be possible). Thus, the aggregate data rate of a 32-channel SW will be 32·4 (4-Bit wide) ·10 MBit/sec = 1.28 GBit/sec.

c. Latency: is given by a connection set-up of typically 200 ns (for 4-Bit wide 10 MBit-channels), and a synchronization delay of 100 ns (per bit). If we consider a 2WADE network of dimension 10 (10.240 nodes), this results in a maximum transfer latency of about 4 µs, i.e., 4 µs after the header of a message leaves some node, the data will start to enter the destination. Thus, the DCS/CMI-method makes message locality considerations unnecessary.

III. DS/DCS/CMI: a third generation cut-through-type routing module

Motivation. Programmers of parallel applications should think about control and domain decomposition in terms of problem-oriented structures rather than in terms of the topological structures of a given parallel computer. In consequence, environment tools, runtime support systems or even the parallel architecture itself has to perform the mapping of problem-oriented structures onto topological structures.

Unfortunately, multicomputers based on "low-latency" interconnection networks offer no adequate support for problem-oriented structures and complex communication relationships. As examples of those relationships we mention: symmetric communication patterns, multiparty communication patterns as e.g. one-to-many communication patterns, and dynamically varying communication patterns.

Thus, runtime systems have to be installed (as global software layers) and realized by the concurrency units of a given kernel operating system. However, the introduction of such layers leads to an increase in overhead, and thus to an increase in the grain size of parallelism. Furthermore, a complex communication relationship between different remote concurrency units has to be simulated by several invocations of unicast communication primitives. The consequence is that an application which comprises powerful interrelationships between its decomposition components is not a good candidate to effectively utilize the parallel potential of a multicomputer. It is therefore our main goal to attack and reduce the overhead imposed by global runtime support layers for applications.

For that purpose, we introduce a hardware facility on each node which allows us to handle an incoming message directly (in terms of application-oriented structures) and as early as possible.

Operational model. In the following, we present a message-passing communication method which is an incarnation of this operation principle. From a rather technical point of view, the proposed communication method is a 2-level cut-through routing method, extended by powerful routing control functions. The lower routing level is given by the DCS/CMI-method, described above, which achieves the node-to-node transfer. The higher routing level operates in a "symbolic" manner, using the location independence provided by the lower level. Routing functions are selected and executed by Cnodes in order to influence the routing process. They are called Decision Functions and Decision Commands, respectively.

1. "Decision-driven" routing on the logical level Λ. A *logical path* p, taken by a message M = (DS | DATA), is given by a path specification DS. DS = $dp_1\ dp_2 \dots dp_{n-1}$ consists of a sequence of *Decision Patterns* dp_i (cf. fig. 1).

Let now p be a path S = C_1 -> C_2 -> ... -> C_n = T. Every dp_i contributes to the construction of p by invoking a *Local Decision* LD(dp_i, DT). LD, executed on Cnode C_i, (i = 1, ..., n-1) compares dp_i against a sequence DT = (dt_1, dt_2, ..., dt_r, default) of *Decision Templates* dt_j, defined by C_i. The result of LD is the corresponding network address, $daddr_j$, which specifies the Ψ-connection of C_i to its Λ-successor C_{i+1}on path p; the default template ensures that there is always a match of dp_i with DT. A mask field [mf_j] selects a specific dt_j out of a class of templates (compare section 3). The following action is then taken: the leading Decision Pattern dp_i — consumed by the actual local Decision LD — is removed from M, and M is transferred to C_{i+1}.

Message M arrives at C via link dt_j; the match between dp_i and dt_r causes M to leave C via link dt_r.

2. Routing on the physical level Ψ. The network address, $daddr_j$, serves as input to a DCS/CMI-routing step which constructs a Ψ-connection from C_i to the target C_{i+1}. This Ψ-step works as explained above: it builds a CMI from C_i to C_{i+1}, extending an already existing CMI if i>1. Thus, the following holds: a CMI is constructed between S and T when S and T are interconnected by a logical path p.

Example. The following figure shows a binary "Decision Tree" T: the logical interconnection structure, defined and "seen" by the application, is a distributed, binary tree T; path p leads from the root T0 through the elements T00, T000 to T0000. The *Decision Area DA* of a Cnode comprises the *Decision Entries DE*, every Decision Entry specifying one Λ-interconnection of this Cnode.

Fig. 1: Symbolic routing.

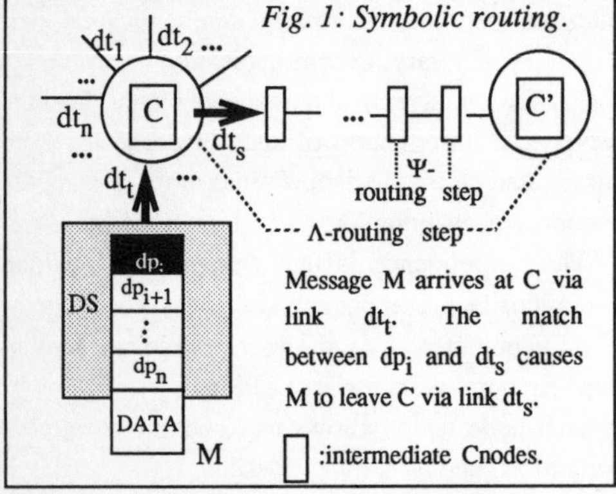

Fig. 2: a binary tree T as a Decision Tree.

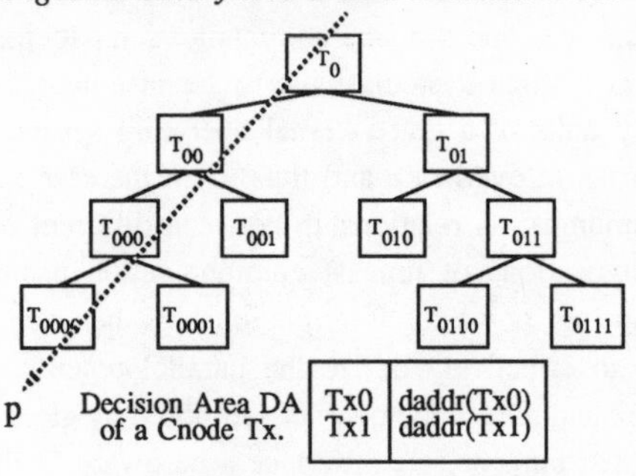

Path p is given by DS = "T0 T00 T000".

3. Decision Functions, Decision Commands. The description of Λ-routing above is simplified and has to be enhanced by the following two features:

a. A Decision Entry DE = (dt, df, daddr), specifying a Λ-connection, may contain the call of a Decision Function df. df is executed every time a message passes a Cnode via the link to which df is attached. We distinguish the following Decision Functions:

- **insert**(new_dp): inserts new_dp as the new leading Decision Pattern.
- **remove**(): removes the leading Decision Pattern.
- **break**: generates a break signal notifying the source that the construction of the Decision path is not possible (e.g. because the Cnode in question is currently inoperable).
- **terminate**: unconditionally terminates a message without generating a break signal; the message is handed over to the Execution Unit of the actual Cnode for further processing.
- **listen**(on/off): changes the listening-mode of a Cnode (with respect to p). If the mode is "listening on", then every message passing along p is copied and handed over to Cnode.EU.

b. Decision Commands are of no further relevance for this paper (details in [7]). We mention only that they are part of the Decision Patterns, allow to change the listening mode and to increment/decrement *message counters*. The use of message counters permits the formulation of elementary termination conditions.

We denote the sequence of Local Decisions, to be performed when constructing a DS-path, as a *Distributed Decision.*

Note the following important properties:

- A message passing along a DS-path from S to T constructs a Common Memory Interface, CMI, between these nodes by simply extending the CMI from S to every instance determined by a single Local Decision. Thus, Distributed Decisions allow a Cnode S to communicate with some other Cnode T. The path from S to T may depend on varying conditions evaluated by S, and possibly by other Cnodes contributing to this Decision.
- DS specifies a path through a Logical Network in an abstract manner. It codes that path by means of Decision Patterns/Templates, which are arbitrary identifications chosen by an application, or which may obey some generic principle, e.g. in order to construct regular structures.
- The Decision path actually constructed by executing a DS is completely independent from the underlying physical topology. Any node which performs a Local Decision LD(dp, DT), dp $\in$ DS, can be replaced by some arbitrary other node able to perform the same Local Decision.
- A *Logical Network* is a graph; its vertices are Cnodes, its edges are (parts of) DS-paths.

4. The Hardware Realization of Distributed Decisions. This section gives a brief description of the hardware architecture of a Cnode (cf. fig. 3) and sketches the tasks of the main components MTE and DP. A more detailed discussion can be found in [7].

The Message Transmission Engine MTE:

- accepts messages M from the network (SW), puts messages onto the network (DP).
- depending on M, the component (EU, DP) responsible for the further processing of an incoming message M is selected, and M is transferred to this component.
- organizes the Message Buffer Memory MBM: implements message input and output queues, buffers messages to allow non-immediate processing and/or retransmissions, and is smoothing out the data flow between synchronous and asynchronous channels.
- performs the end-to-end protocol by repeating a message in case of a break signal.

The At&T-chip [9] performs similar tasks for HDLC as communication method.

The Decision Processor DP:

DP uses a fully associative memory to perform local Decisions; the size of it is assumed to be small

(≤ 32 entries) in order to keep the costs down. However, by applying bit masks to the matching process, thereby extending the patterns to classes, the effective size of the area is much larger.

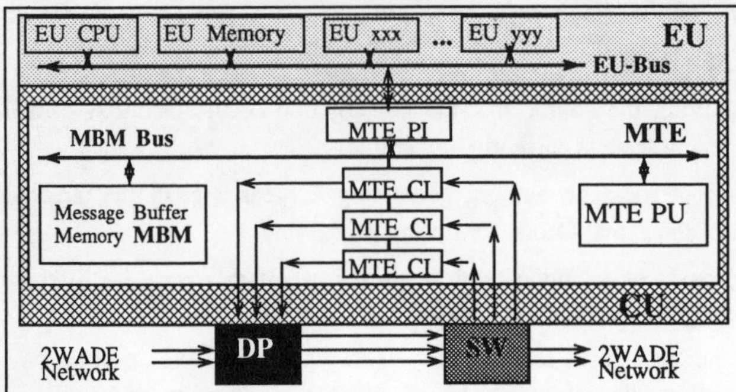

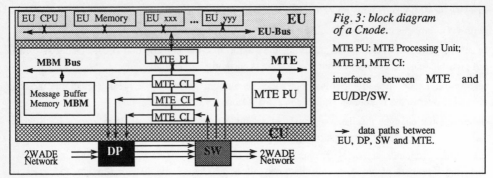

Fig. 3: block diagram of a Cnode.

MTE PU: MTE Processing Unit;
MTE PI, MTE CI:
interfaces between MTE and EU/DP/SW.

→ data paths between EU, DP, SW and MTE.

5. Performance Figures for Distributed Decisions. We have the following performance figures for hypercube nodes H_i and Cnodes C_i:

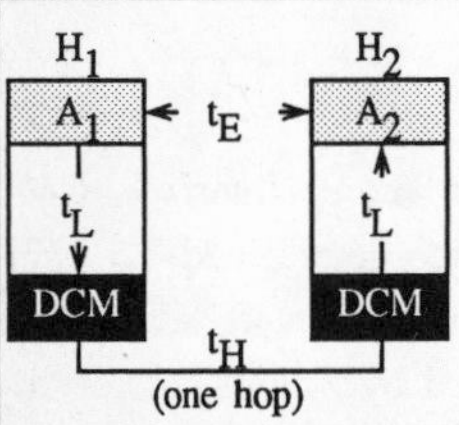

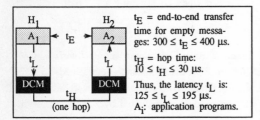

t_E = end-to-end transfer time for empty messages: $300 \leq t_E \leq 400$ µs.
t_H = hop time: $10 \leq t_H \leq 30$ µs.
Thus, the latency t_L is: $125 \leq t_L \leq 195$ µs.
A_i: application programs.

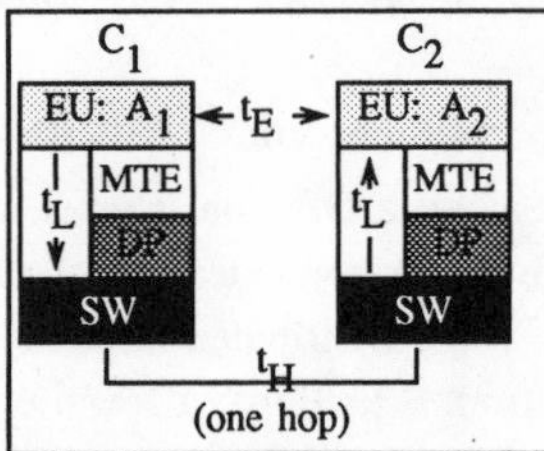

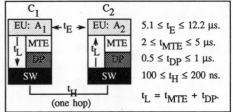

$5.1 \leq t_E \leq 12.2$ µs.
$2 \leq t_{MTE} \leq 5$ µs.
$0.5 \leq t_{DP} \leq 1$ µs.
$100 \leq t_H \leq 200$ ns.
$t_L = t_{MTE} + t_{DP}$.

In practice, the avarage t_E for hypercube nodes will be ≈ 1 ms. Note that the performance figures for Cnodes are estimated values; they may have to be increased if the application programs A_i require more (software) support than provided by the MTE-interface.

We see that a DS-path of length r (r Decisions) generally connects elements of $Z = \{C_1, C_2, ..., C_n\}$ with arbitrary physical locations of C_i. With other words, the distance between C_i and C_{i+1} will be k_i hops, where k_i depends on the Ψ-locations of the Z-elements and the DCS/CMI-routing strategy. Assuming that an "intelligent" *placement strategy* maps the logical structure Λ in an optimal manner onto the physical topology Ψ' — keeping $k_i = 1$ — then the overhead of the DS-layer is very small: a Local Decision will typically take a time t_{DP} between 0.5 µs and 1 µs. That means, a Bus B is scalable in the following sense: if B is extended by inserting one additional element, then the "Bus-cycle-time" of B is icreased by $t_{DP} + t_H$.

The attribute "intelligent" of the placement strategy stresses the necessity

- to separate the tasks of configurating and placing Logical Networks onto Ψ, from working with Logical Networks, that is, designing algorithms which operate on them, and
- to delegate the placement operation to specialists and/or to rely on appropriate tools, relieving thus the application programmer from the need to know details of the physical topology.

There are several possibilities for optimizations. It can, for example, be noted that a CMI (for a short message) has not to span the complete Bus if higher-level protocols provide the necessary end-to-end security. Furthermore, a short-cut around DP can be provided for messages not relying on the Λ-routing.

Existing prototype. There exists a small-scale, experimental version of a multicomputer based on the concepts described above: it consists of 24 + 8 (= 2WADE 3 + 2WADE 2) nodes, the hardware of which is simplified by implementing the MTE and DP by software. The present realization of the Switch SW yields 8 bitserial channels per node [4].

IV. Logical Busses

A *Logical Bus* B is a DS-path with the following properties:

1. A specific Decision Pattern β defines B on all Cnodes sharing B. A message M, passing B, carries a path specification DS which essentially consists of β; β will be reproduced on every Cnode by a call of **insert**(#) which reinserts the actual DS-Pattern (denoted by #); compare fig. 4 below.
2. B can dynamically be generated by creating a Decision Entry for β in every Cnode sharing B.
3. The DS-path B is a *cyclic* path.
4. In order to restrict the traffic load on B, the following condition has to be observed: every message M, passing through B, takes at most one round trip; if M is not "consumed" by a previously encountered node, then the sender C_{source} removes M after a complete cycle. The following figures illustrates this mode of operation.

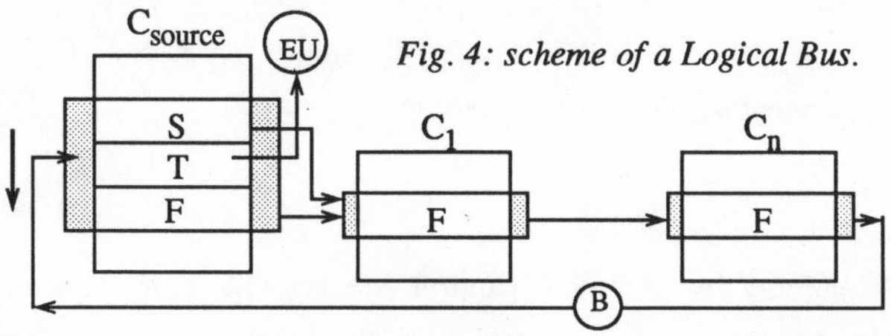

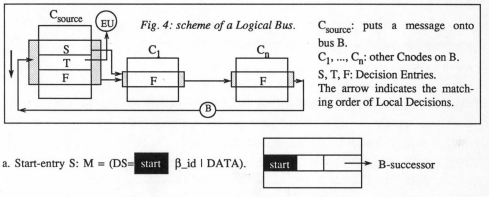

Fig. 4: scheme of a Logical Bus.

C_{source}: puts a message onto bus B.
$C_1, \ldots, C_n$: other Cnodes on B.
S, T, F: Decision Entries.
The arrow indicates the matching order of Local Decisions.

a. Start-entry S: M = (DS= start β_id | DATA).

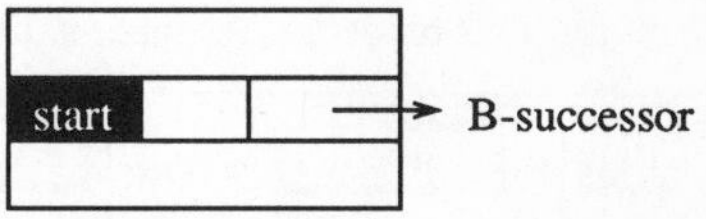

The match between the DS-Pattern "start" with the Template "start" causes M to be put onto B.

b. Forwarding-entry F: M = (DS= β_id | DATA).

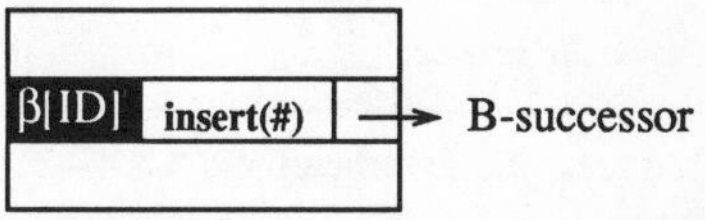

The Pattern β_id consists of the general "bus"-Pattern β concatenated with an individually chosen Pattern id. id distinguishes the different Cnodes uniquely. Every C_i matches the actual DS = β_id by masking out the part [ID] which contains the individual pattern id. **insert(#)** reinserts the actually consumed part of DS, that is, reproduces the state before the last Decision.

c. Termination-entry T: M = (DS= β_id | DATA).

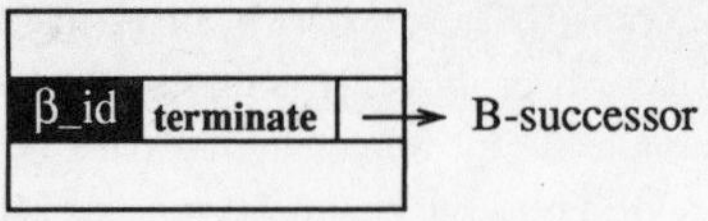

The termination-entry T causes a match with the full Pattern β_id; the message terminates. Note that the matching order guarantees that T is checked for a match with the DS-Pattern before R.
This scheme is "non-blocking" in the following sense: the termination of a certain message M in Csource does not affect (block) other messages.

Logical multicast. Let $Z = \{C_1, C_2, ..., C_n\}$ be the set of Cnodes sharing B, and let $C^* \in Z$ be a Cnode which wants to send a message M to all the elements of $Z \neq C^*$. C* will construct a Logical Bus B connecting all the elements of Z, put M onto B, and remove M after it arrives in C*. The reaction of the elements of Z upon the arrival of M can be defined in different ways by Bus protocols (see 3.2). If necessary, the CMI property can ensure that a multicast is an atomic action: either all the elements sharing the Bus get a message or none of them.

Bus protocols. The term "Bus protocol" comprises the rules which have to be obeyed by the Cnodes sharing the Bus. In the following, we describe some Bus protocols which model well-know hardware protocols.

a. Simple ACK-protocol

- $C^* \in Z$ puts an **Activation Message** M_a on Bus B. M_a initiates a certain activity on every Cnode $C_i \in Z$, $C_i \neq C^*$ ($\equiv$ multicast of M_a to Z).
- Every C_i, having completed its activity, sends a **Control Message** M_c with an ACK back to C*. The arrival of the last M_c signals C* the termination of the whole activity.

b. Daisy chaining

- An activity is started as described above, in a.
- C* determines the state of the whole activity by putting a Control Message M_c onto B: every Cnode C_i having not yet completed its local activity takes M_c from B and puts it back after termination of its activity. This process is repeated until M arrives again at C*.

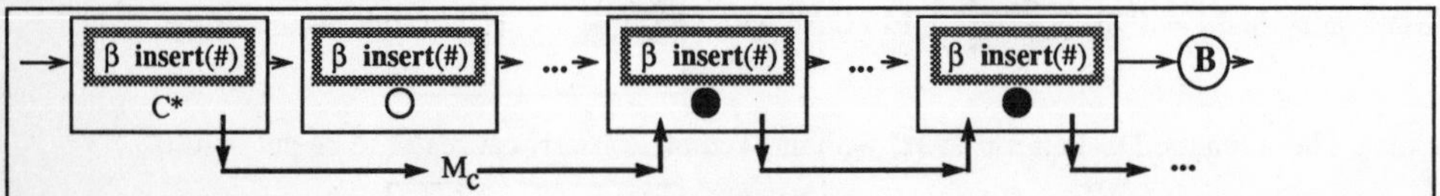

Fig. 5: Daisy chaining scheme: → daisy chaining path of M_c; ● Cnode has not yet completed its activity.

This mode reduces the overhead on C* — C* must not be prepared to be interrupted by asynchronously arriving ACKs — and allows a convenient handling of activities with different execution times on different Cnodes.

c. Token scheme

B can model a **Token Ring**: a Token-Message M_T is put onto B, providing the next requesting Cnode C with an exclusive access to B. After termination of its activity, C releases B by putting M_T back onto B. Under reasonable assumptions about the lengths of activity phases, critical situations (deadlock, starvation) can be omitted. Moreover, by using a multiple-linked path B, defect Cnodes (that is, Cnodes with only the DC/DCS/CMI-hardware functioning) can be detected and excluded from B — without a central monitoring instance.

d. Cascading Busses

We build groups (subgroups, subsubgroups, ...) G_i of elements and connect them by Busses, Subbusses, ... where Subbusses branch from the main Bus B.

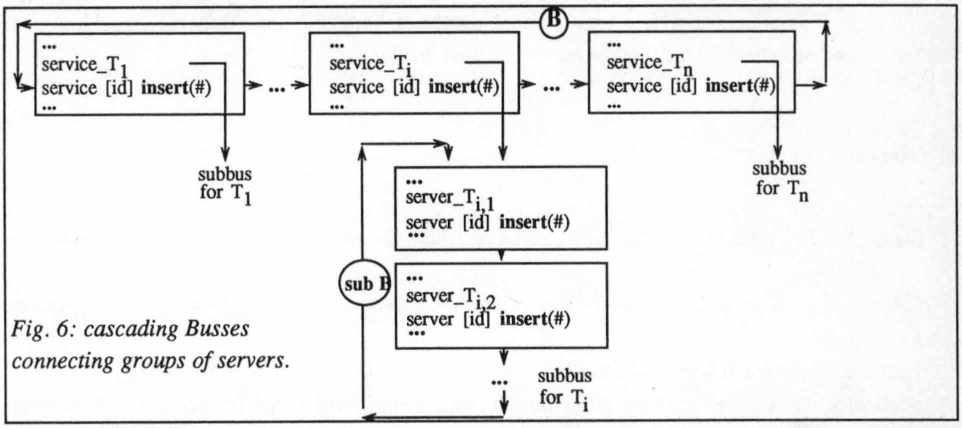

Fig. 6: cascading Busses connecting groups of servers.

In fig. 6, cascading Busses connect *services* service_T_1, service_T_2, ..., service_T_n of "type" T_i (e.g. $T_i \in$ {file, printer, directory, ...}) where every service consists of a group of *servers* ser-ver_$T_{i,1}$, server_$T_{i,2}$, ... A message M with DS = "start service_T_i server_$T_{i,j}$" will be delivered to server $T_{i,j}$. This example shows that standard tasks of a distributed operating system can be realized by Logical Busses in an efficient and elegant manner.

An example. Let us consider the Decision Tree T of fig. 2. Let us assume that every Cnode of T administrates a local domain D of objects o, providing an interface which consists of the following functions:

- search(x): determines whether $x \in D$, and
- execute(x): starts an activity depending on x.

We can then define the following operations of T:

- A leave T* of T generates a Logical Bus B, connecting all or some elements Z of T.
- T* initiates a parallel search for an object o, by invoking search(o) on all elements of Z.
- T* puts a Control Message Mc on B which determines whether and how many Cnodes contain x (the number of Cnodes can be delivered to T* by a message counter).
- Depending on some conditions — e.g. the uniqueness of the Cnode containing x — the function execute(x) is invoked on Z.

The edges of Logical Networks have thus some similarity with pointers of data structures. Note that a single Logical Bus may be replaced by several (e.g. hierarchically ordered) Busses.

In this way, we proceed from a Logical Network "Decision Tree" to a Tree-machine which operates in parallel on a distributed, global domain.

V. Conclusion

The described third generation cut-through-type routing module is very efficient and provides applications with Logical Networks which abstract from the physical topology, and in terms of which the user can "think" and design its algorithms. Moreover, Logical Busses allow the control and coordination of asynchronous activities with a minimum of overhead; they stimulate thus the transition from distributed, logical structures to parallel operating, abstract machines.

VI. References

[1] Dally, W. J., Seitz, C. L.: *The Torus Routing Chip*; Distributed Computing, Vol. 1, Springer-Verlag 1986.

[2] Nugent, S.F.: *The iPSC/2 Direct-Communication Technology*, ACM Proc. Third Hypercube Conf., 1988.

[3] Upfal, E.: *Efficient Schemes for Parallel Communication*, JACM, 31(3), 1984.

[4] Schneider, M. F.: *Entwicklung eines intelligenten Vermittlungsbausteins für 2WADE-Kommunikation in Polyknoten-Systemen*; Fachbereich Informatik der Universität des Saarlandes, Diplomarbeit, 1989.

[5] Malowaniec, K. T.: *Das dynamische Leitungsvermittlungsnetz für verteilte Systeme*; Fachbereich Informatik der Universität des Saarlandes, Dissertation, April 1990.

[6] Malowaniec, K. T., Scheidig, H., Schneider, M. F., Spurk, R.: *Efficient Communication in Polynode Systems*; Proc. of the 1st European Workshop on Hypercube and Distributed Computers, 4–6 October 1989, North Holland.

[7] Scheidig, H., Schneider, M.F., Schweizer, M., Spurk, R.: *Hardware support for Symbolic-Communication Multicomputers*, Technical Report, Dept. of Comp. Sci., University of Saarbrücken, Nov. 1990.

[8] Kermani, P., Kleinrock, L.: *Virtual Cut-Through: A New Computer Communication Switching Technique*; Computer Networks, 1979.

[9] AT&T: *T7110 SPYDER-S User Manual*; AT&T 1987.

[10] Scheidig, H., Schneider, M.F., Spurk, R.: *An Efficient Organization for Large, Network-Based Multicomputer Systems*; Proc. of the 5-th Jerusalem Conf. on Information Technology, Oct. 22 - 25, 1990.

Performance Benefits from Locally Adaptive Interval Routing in Dynamically Switched Interconnection Networks

H. Hofestädt, A. Klein, E. Reyzl
SIEMENS AG, Corporate Research and Development

Abstract Dynamically switched, sparse interconnection networks are the major element of scalable general purpose parallel computers. This paper presents different network structures and corresponding routing schemes based on a universal routing device. A locally adaptive enhancement to the basic deterministic routing mechanism is proposed and its impact on the network performance is proved by simulation results. This is done comparatively for different network topologies and with respect to network throughput and size scalability. Finally, the extension of the results to very large networks is demonstrated by analytical methods.

1. Introduction

A wide range of specialised parallel computer systems do already exist and have been successfully used in different application areas. Growing attention is currently given to *highly* parallel architectures for *universal* use. These targets impose certain conditions on the interconnection network: The (virtually) complete connectivity required for universal use must in sparse networks be realised through virtual channels (by multiplexing data packets on common physical channels) and dynamic routing of packets through intermediate nodes. For the expandability to very large networks, communication structures are needed where the effective throughput scales linearly with the network size.

Except for the transmission protocol which is often determined by constraints of communication model and implementation technology, the network topology and routing scheme are the elements which mainly affect the performance and the size scalability of a communication system. It was the goal of our investigations to identify such topologies and routing schemes which provide both, good universal performance (i.e. not relying on specific communication patterns known in advance) and good scaling properties.

Our starting point was a universal routing component for the construction of arbitrary networks. It is assumed to be a 32-way crossbar switch for dynamic packet routing with a versatile basic routing mechanism that can be programmed to fit a variety of network topologies. The *interval routing* technique [3] which we describe in some more detail in the following section, is an example for such a mechanism. A switching component of this kind is currently being developed by Inmos for their next generation of transputers ([4], [5]).

Based on such components we have specified a variety of network topologies and corresponding labelling schemes which satisfied the conditions to be deadlock-free, optimal and well-balanced (for random traffic). Our construction of the deterministic routing scheme with a static balance of the destination address space over equivalent links led us to the observation that the performance of the networks could be improved by the introduction of a natural, locally adaptive extension to the routing mechanism, which guarantees a dynamically balanced utilisation of equivalent links. The performance effects of such a mechanism have been explored by means of simulation for the different network topologies and they turned out to be significant in all cases, particularly for the multistage networks.

In section 2, we describe the universal routing mechanism by interval labelling and specify its application to certain important topology categories, before we motivate and define the proposed adaptive enhancement. In section 3, we introduce the network and load models used for the simulations and present and discuss simulation results which demonstrate the benefits achieved from the adaptive routing scheme.

Due to resource restrictions our simulations were limited to networks with less than thousand ports. In order to determine the scaling properties of the proposed networks and routing schemes beyond that limit, we have established analytical models incorporating certain fitting parameters derived from the simulation results. In section 4, we briefly present this approach and its major results.

The work reported in this paper has been carried out in the context of the cooperative project PUMA (P*arallel* U*niversal* M*essage-passing* A*rchitectures*) and has partly been funded under ESPRIT P2701.

2. Network Design Space

As a basic component for constructing networks we assume a single-sided 32-way crossbar switch; i.e. it has 32 bidirectional links capable of dynamic packet routing. Each packet carries a header containing the destination address. Routing decisions are taken according to the header, based on an interval routing scheme [3]. We start with a brief summary of interval routing.

The network *address space*, which is an integer interval, is defined by enumerating the terminal network links consecutively. An *integer interval* is denoted by [i, j) representing the set {i, ..., j–1}.

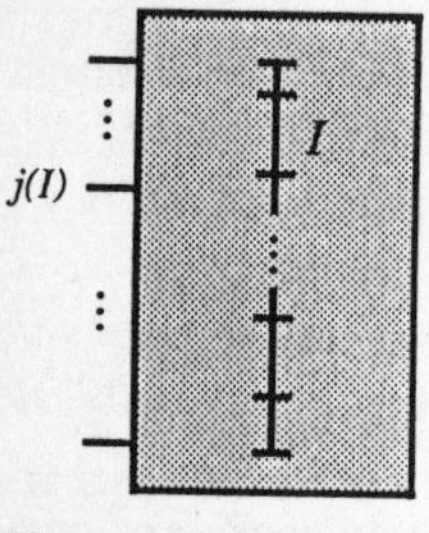

Figure 1: Interval routing mechanism.

On each routing chip in the network the global address space is represented by a partition of the global address space consisting of as many disjoint subsets as there are outgoing links (fig. 1). To each interval *I* exactly one outgoing link *j(I)* is associated.

If a packet enters a switch along an arbitrary link it is examined and decided into which subset *I* the packet header falls. The whole packet is then submitted along the associated outgoing link *j(I)*.

The boundary values between neighbouring subsets are called *labels*. A *labelling scheme* for the whole network is called *valid* if all packets are routed correctly. It is called *optimal* if each packet takes the shortest possible path through the network. Each valid labelling scheme defines a *deterministic routing algorithm.*

It is known that each network has a valid labelling scheme. There exists an algorithm which produces a valid labelling scheme by constructing a spanning tree of the network [3]. Generally, this algorithm will not produce optimal labelling schemes and it is therefore not used in this paper.

In order to guarantee that our labelling schemes are deadlock-free we have used the following sufficient condition. Essentially, we show that if an ordering relation on the set of network links can be found such that each routing path defines a strictly increasing link sequence then the routing algorithm is deadlock-free. With this result, for a given network it is sufficient to find such an ordering relation which is generally a much easier task compared to proving the absence of cycles in dependency graphs ([6], [7]).

For a number of relevant network topologies like, for example, grids and cubes valid, deadlock-free, and optimal labelling schemes can be derived. In addition, we have found a family of near-optimal schemes for Clos-like multistage networks. In case of three stages they are in fact optimal.

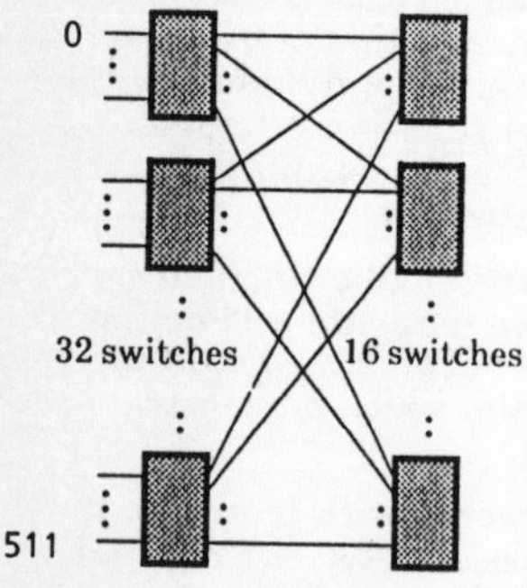

Figure 2: Three-stage network.

Consider for example the 3-stage network shown in fig. 2 which is built from 32×32 crossbar switches and has 512 terminal links. Its 48 switches are organized in two columns. Each crossbar of the left column is connected to every crossbar of the right column and vice versa. Stages one and three share the crossbars of the left column. Logically, each (two-way) left-side link is incoming link to stage one and outgoing link from stage three at the same time.

A possible valid, optimal, and deadlock-free *labelling scheme* is given by the following intervals $I_{k,c,i}$, associated with an output *link i* of *crossbar c* in stage k (i and c counted from top to bottom, and $d_c(i) := 16(c+1)+31i$):

$$I_{1,c,i} = [d_c(i), d_c(i+1)) \qquad i=0,..,15; \quad c=0,..,31,$$
$$I_{2,c,i} = [16i, (i+1)16) \qquad i=0,..,31; \quad c=0,..,15,$$
$$I_{3,c,i} = [16c+i, 16c+i+1) \qquad i=0,..,15; \quad c=0,..,31.$$

Smaller 3-stage networks (256, 128, 64 terminal links) are obtained by successively halving the number of switches in both columns. The 16 links, connecting each switch of stage one to stage two are grouped in *multiple links* of *width* 2, 4, 8 respectively. The number of crossbars in the left column is called the *size parameter n* of the network. In addition, the number of terminal links per crossbar, which is equal to 16 in fig. 2, can be varied between 1 and 31. This parameter is called the *cluster size a*. Each such network is called a three-stage *building block*.

5-stage networks are constructed from 3-stage building blocks and switches in a modular way by putting a column of switches in front of a column of building blocks similar to fig. 2. Building blocks are viewed as single (larger) switches. In a similar way general s-stage networks can be constructed recursively. Their *size N* (number of terminal links) is expressed in terms of the size and cluster size parameter by $N = n\,a$. Labelling schemes can be generalized to s-stage networks in a straight forward manner. For $1 \le k < (s+1)/2$, we found for example:

$$
\begin{array}{lll}
I_{s+1-k,c,i} = [a^{k-1}(ac+i), a^{k-1}(ac+i+1)) & i=0,..,a-1; & c=0,..,C_k-1 \\
I_{k,c,i} = [d_{k,c}(i), d_{k,c}(i+1)) & i=0,..,b-1; & c=0,..,C_k-1 \\
I_{(s+1)/2,c,i} = [ie, (i+1)e) & i=0,..,31; & c=0,..,C_{(s-1)/2}
\end{array}
$$

where $b := 32-a$, $d_{k,c}(i) := a^k(c+1) + \lfloor i(N-a^k)/b \rfloor$, and $e := n/(b/a+1)$. C_i is the number of crossbars in column i. Related labelling schemes are obtained by permuting the intervals associated with outgoing links of the first (s-1)/2 stages arbitrarily.

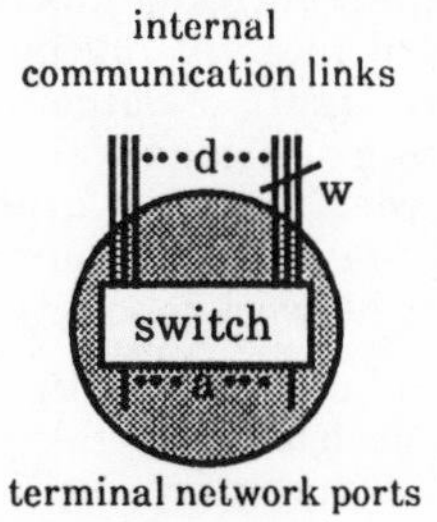

Figure 3: Node of a direct network.

Direct networks, represented by graphs, are obtained as follows. In our context each node (vertex) consists of a single crossbar along with a partitioning of its links into internal communication links and terminal network ports (fig. 3). The edges of the graph consist of one or several internal communication links depending on the *node degree d*. In the latter case the edge is called a multiple link of width $w = (32-a)/d$, were a is the number of terminal links per node, called *node (or cluster) size*. In the sequel we assume that all nodes of a network have the same node size.

Labelling schemes for direct networks are given in a *generic* form; i.e. each graph node is assumed to have only a single terminal link and each multiple link is replaced by a single link. An individual labelling scheme for a given direct network can be constructed easily from the generic labelling scheme by expanding all generic intervals by the node size; i.e. $[x, y) \rightarrow [ax, ay)$, and partitioning each interval associated with a multiple link into subsets of (possibly) equal size - one for each member.

As a first example we consider *n-dimensional open grids of width k* with no wrap around. At the boundary of the network, Internal communication links which are not connected to any other node are not used. Nodes are denoted by tuples $(j_0, j_1, \dots j_{n-1}) \in [0, k)^n$. They are enumerated using a node-ID function: $NID(j_0, j_1, \dots j_{n-1}) = \Sigma_{0 \le l < n} j_l k^l$.

The following generic labelling scheme for deterministic routing is valid, optimal, and deadlock-free. To each node $(j_0, j_1, \dots j_{n-1})$, $2n+1$ intervals are attached; two intervals $I^<_i$, and $I^>_i$ for each dimension $i \in [0, n)$ and a single one-element set I_{node} containing the node-ID:

$$
\begin{array}{ll}
I_{node}(j_0, j_1, \dots j_{n-1}) & = [\, NID(j_0, j_1, \dots j_{n-1}), NID(j_0, j_1, \dots j_{n-1}) + 1\,) \\
I^<_i(j_0, j_1, \dots j_{n-1}) & = [\, \Sigma_{i<l<n} j_l k^l, \Sigma_{i \le l < n} j_l k^l\,) \\
I^>_i(j_0, j_1, \dots j_{n-1}) & = [\, (\Sigma_{i<l<n} j_l k^l) + (j_i+1)k^i, \\
 & \quad (\Sigma_{i+1<l<n} j_l k^l) + (j_{i+1}+1)k^{i+1}\,)
\end{array}
$$

All calculations are to be performed modulo k^n. We set $j_n := 0$.

Our second example is the class of *n-dimensional binary cubes*. As usual, a node of a cube is denoted by $(j_0, j_1, \dots j_{n-1}) \in [0, 2)^n$. Graph nodes are enumerated using the standard node-ID function: $NID(j_0, j_1, \dots j_{n-1}) = \Sigma_{0 \le l < n} j_l 2^l$.

To each node $(j_0, j_1, \dots j_{n-1})$, $n+1$ generic intervals are attached; one interval I_i for each dimension $i \in [0, n)$ and a single one-element set I_{node} containing the node-ID. We have:

$$I_{node}(j_0, j_1, \dots j_{n-1}) = [\, NID(j_0, j_1, \dots j_{n-1}), NID(j_0, j_1, \dots j_{n-1}) + 1\,)$$
$$I_i(j_0, j_1, \dots j_{n-1}) = [\,(\Sigma_{i<l<n} j_l 2^l), (\Sigma_{i+1<l<n} j_l 2^l) + (j_{i+1}+1)2^{i+1}\,) - [\,(\Sigma_{i\leq l<n} j_l 2^l), (\Sigma_{i<l<n} j_l 2^l) + (j_i+1)2^i\,)$$

where "–" here denotes the difference operator for sets. All calculations are to be performed modulo 2^n. We set $j_n := 0$. The labelling scheme is valid, optimal, and deadlock-free.

Like all deterministic routing algorithms interval routing cannot take advantage of redundant paths in networks. Take for example the three-stage network of fig. 2. Its most striking feature is that from each crossbar of the center stage (right column) the packets can still reach any terminal network link. Thus, from the topology point of view, in stage one, it is not necessary to associate a single fixed outgoing link with an address interval because all links are equivalent. Any other link, leading to stage two would be equally well suited. Similar in case of direct networks. All members of a multiple link are completely equivalent to each other. There is no necessity of a static interval partitioning among its members.

With the following natural extension of interval routing exactly the above kind of redundancy in networks can be exploited optimally. Load will be distributed evenly among equivalent links.

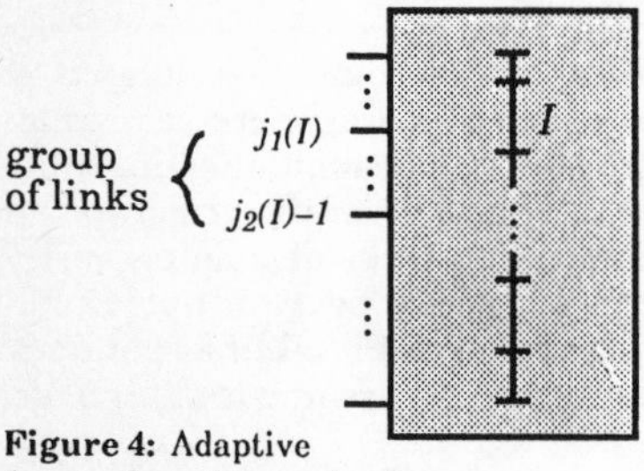

Figure 4: Adaptive interval routing mechanism.

Locally adaptive interval routing works as follows. Instead of mapping intervals onto a single outgoing link of a switch, as is the case in standard interval routing, they are mapped onto a group $[\, j_1(I), j_2(I))$ of outgoing links (fig. 4) among which the routing decision is taken adaptively; i.e. packets are forwarded along an arbitrary free link from the group, if available. Of course the grouping of links has to meet the network topology.

In case of direct networks the members of a multiple link define a group and routing decisions are taken adaptively among them. This leads to an optimal utilization of all links in a group. The necessary changes to the labelling scheme are as follows. Take the above generic labelling scheme for direct networks as a starting point. Instead of partitioning an interval associated with a multiple link, it is kept as a single interval and the link group defined by the multiple link is associated to it. Adaptive routing remains deadlock-free.

In the network given by fig. 2 all the 16 outgoing links of a switch c in stage one leading towards the central stage can be put into a single group. The corresponding interval for this group is the union of all intervals $I_{1,c,i}$, $i = 0, .., 15$. Thus, any packet entering a crossbar of stage one is either immediately routed to its final destination, if this is located at the same switch, or adaptively forwarded to stage two. In general s-stage networks, packets are routed adaptively in the first $(s+1)/2$ stages until the center stage is reached. In addition, if the three-stage building block contains multiple links, packets can be forwarded adaptively from the center stage to stage $(s+3)/2$ as discussed above for multiple links in direct networks. From here routing has to be performed deterministically. It is easy to see that adaptive routing remains deadlock-free in multistage networks, too.

For direct networks it is obvious that adaptive routing will perform better than deterministic routing in any load situation. Our performance evaluations, presented in the remaining two sections, show that adaptive routing improves performance significantly for direct as well as indirect networks.

3. Simulation Results

To investigate the interconnection networks and the routing mechanisms introduced in the previous chapter we applied the simulation and evaluation tool package PARSIVAL, which has already been successfully employed during earlier projects ([8],[9]). PARSIVAL supports investigations by modelling the interconnection network and the communication load in sufficient detail.

The network model consists of the network topology and a detailed functional description of the network building components: the processor communication hardware and the switching component. The component models include all essential communication mechanisms, e.g. the packet-acknowledge-protocol for messages, the local routing decision at the switching element and all dynamic effects caused by contentions and queue handling.

Focussing on the different routing mechanisms we had to apply communication patterns that reveal the impact of the routing strategy on the network performance. Obviously, this performance depends considerably on the communication pattern. In order to take full advantage of the network's capability, there are several common approaches to increase network performance by reducing message contentions. Techniques like application mapping or load balancing aim at avoiding contentions by locating or distributing application processes and the resulting communication load in an appropriate way. In general, however, those techniques cannot avoid all network internal bottlenecks caused by the underlying deterministic routing decision. The adaptive routing approach aims at resolving those bottlenecks dynamically by using all the network's possible connections. The communication patterns applied in our investigations proved to be very useful illustrating the benefits of adaptive routing. With respect to the occurrence of internal bottlenecks, the two communication models can be viewed as two extremes within the space of the communication patterns.

The first load model, called the random communication generator (RCG), creates a randomly determined, equally distributed communication pattern. Internal bottlenecks for deterministic routing occur occasionally according to statistical variations within the communication pattern. In this model, at each network port a certain number of transmission requests to random destinations is created. In order to investigate the network at saturation and at moderate load, the communication intensity can be determined by varying the input rate at the network ports. For the RCG pattern, we measured the network performance in terms of throughput and packet transmission time. In this context, the sustained throughput supported at saturation and the average packet transmission time at moderate load turned out to be the decisive characteristics.

In the second load model, the cluster-to-cluster permutation pattern (CPP), communication only takes place between pairs of clusters, i.e. each group of processors connected to the same switching element communicates with a single other group. In contrast to the RCG pattern, the CPP pattern defines a sustained internal bottleneck for the deterministic routing scheme. Although there are no destination conflicts due to the permutation pattern, this communication can be viewed to be a worst-case pattern for the deterministic routing. This is because all messages between two clusters have to share a small number of the network's possible connections. In contrast to this, the adaptive routing is able to resolve this bottleneck. Measuring throughput achieved per input port for the CPP pattern, we verified the capability of the adaptive routing to take full advantage of all physical connections between each pair of clusters.

In our investigations by simulation we focussed on network architectures that had been selected from the huge design space by applying analytical evaluations. The analytical approach is described in some more detail in the following section. For the different topologies there is an obvious trade-off between the architecture's cluster size and the achieved performance. Small clusters increase the number of switches necessary to connect the same number of network ports. Nevertheless, increasing the network's costs generally does not lead to a proportional increase of the network's performance. Applying the analytical model we determined cluster sizes that lead to the best cost/performance ratio for the different topologies. Independent of the network size the optimal cluster size turned out to be about 16 and 12 for the multistage and the direct networks, respectively.

For system sizes from 64 up to 512 network ports, we simulated multistage and direct networks of equal size applying deterministic and adaptive routing to RCG and CPP communication patterns, respectively. Based on the analytical results, we focussed on multistage networks built up with the optimal cluster size of 16. Equal costs for direct networks would lead to a cluster size of about 12. But due to architectural constraints arising from the equal size, we had to select direct networks with cluster sizes of 8 and 16. In order to compare architectures of different costs, we adjusted the measured throughput values according to the cost ratio with the corresponding multistage network.

The results for the RCG pattern are illustrated in fig. 5 (cost-adjusted throughput) and fig. 6 (packet transmission time). For the architectures we measured the maximum sustained throughput per input port. In general, the increase of the throughput for adaptive routing turned out to be 10-30%, i.e. adaptive routing serves a higher input rate by resolving internal bottlenecks occurring for deterministic routing. Further on, for the moderate input rate of 1 MByte/sec, reduced average packet transmission time can be observed with adaptive routing, too.

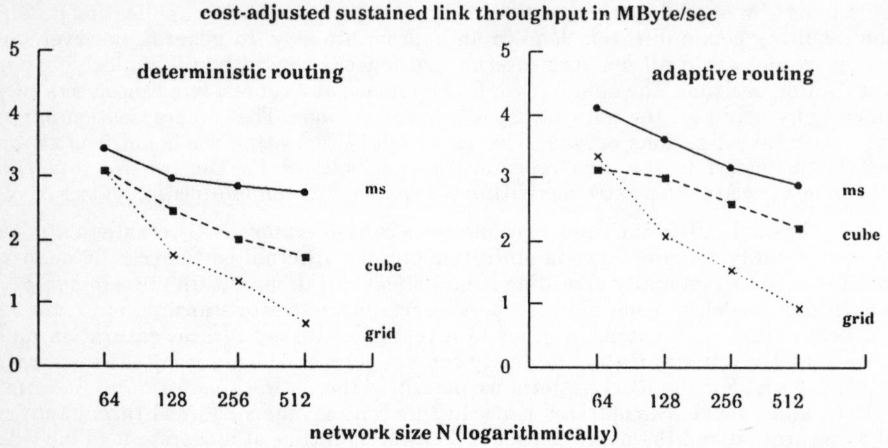

Figure 5: Cost-adjusted throughput per input port for random communication pattern (relative to multistage costs). For 3-stage, cube and 2d-grid networks, adaptive routing increases sustained throughput by 10-30%.

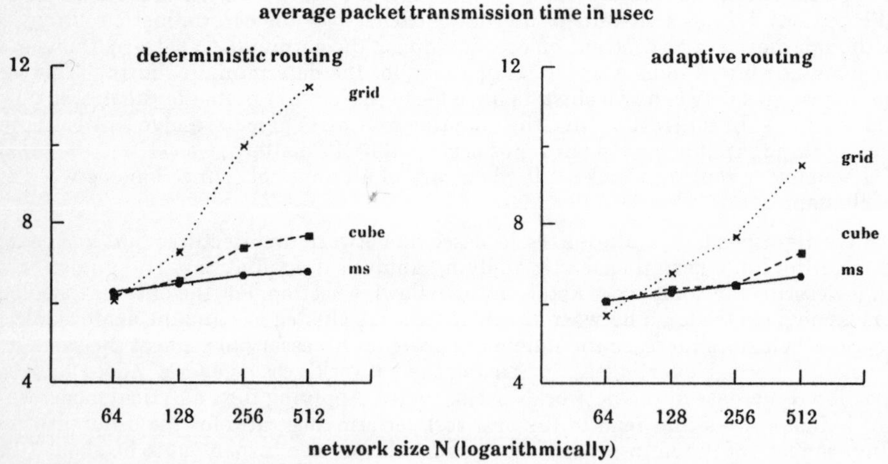

Figure 6: Average packet transmission time for moderate RCG load (input rate 1 MByte/sec). For 3-stage, cube and 2d-grid networks, adaptive routing reduces packet transmission time.

The benefits of adaptive routing are stressed applying the highly structured CPP communication pattern (fig. 7). For the deterministic routing the internal bottleneck becomes obvious. Even if there are several physical connections between the communicating clusters, only a small number of them is used by deterministic routing. The number of utilized links in this context depends on the actual cluster-to-cluster mapping and the labelling scheme. In

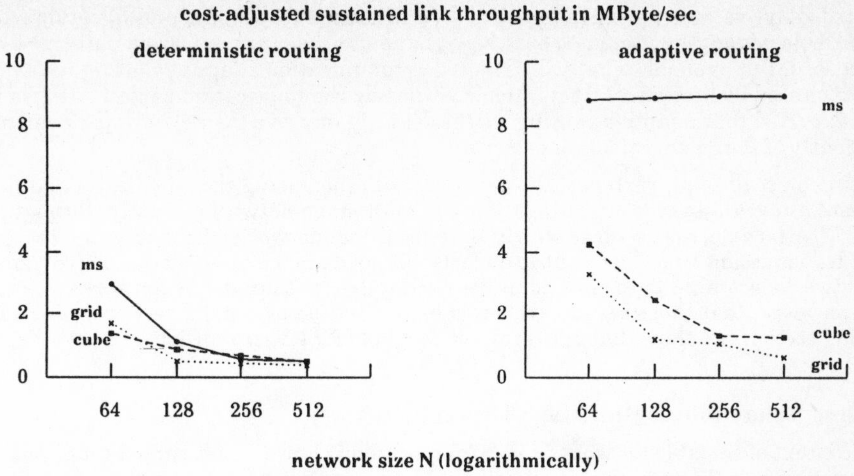

Figure 7: Cost-adjusted throughput per port for the cluster-to-cluster permutation (relative to multistage costs). For 3-stage, cube and 2d-grid networks, adaptive routing takes advantage of the network's connectivity and increases throughput. Substantial increase can be observed for multistage networks.

contrast to this, adaptive routing takes advantage of the physical connectivity and increases the throughput per network port, accordingly. Nearly independent of the network size, throughput is increased by a factor of two or three for grid and cube networks, respectively. For multistage networks throughput is 3 to 16 times higher compared with the deterministic routing. In the sequel, this outstanding result is discussed in detail.

For the multistage networks, adaptive routing reaches the maximal possible link throughput of 8.9 MByte/sec for non-blocking communication, which is determined by the nominal link bandwidth of 10 MByte/sec and the protocol overhead of the packet header and the acknowledge packet for every packet of user data. This is due to the specific nature of the cluster-to-cluster pattern. The adaptive mechanism distributes all packets starting from the same cluster (all of them having the same destination cluster) to different intermediate switches of the center stage. Due to the width of the multiple link, which corresponds to the number of packets arriving from the same sender cluster, no contention occurs at the center stage, and the packets are transmitted to the destination cluster. Thus, being a permutation, they are routed to their destination without any blocking. Therefore, adaptive routing takes full advantage of the network's connectivity.

In contrast to this, deterministic routing only uses a part of the possible connections. Depending on the system size the number of used connections decreases from 5 or 6 for a network size of 64 to 1 or 2 links for 512 ports. Table 1 illustrates the strong correlation between the measured throughput and the links used for the different routing mechanisms.

network size N	64	128	256	512
throughput ratio	2.97	7.58	15.08	16.79
ratio of used links	3.00	7.00	15.00	16.00

Table 1: The ratio between the 3-stage throughput for the adaptive and for the deterministic routing is strongly correlated to the ratio of the connections used by the routing mechanisms to transmit packets.

Summarizing our observations the following holds. In the case of internal bottlenecks occurring for deterministic routing, adaptive routing proves to be an adequate approach to resolve those bottlenecks dynamically taking advantage of the network's connectivity. Surely, the benefit of adaptive routing depends strongly on the structure of the communication pattern. Considerable advantage is achieved for highly unbalanced communication patterns like the CPP pattern. But even for equally distributed communication adaptive routing resolves bottlenecks caused by statistical fluctuations within the communication pattern. In general, it can be expected that adaptive routing will essentially improve the network performance independently of the communication pattern.

Focussing on scaling properties of the networks with increasing size, the illustrated simulation results reveal obvious advantages for the multistage networks: Firstly, throughput at the RCG pattern decreases more slowly than for direct networks. Secondly, the increase of packet transmission time turns out to be faster for grid and cube networks. Thirdly, multistage networks are able to exploit adaptive routing better than direct networks. It must be noted, however, that these results are based on evaluation of 3-stage networks, only. In the following section, we show that our results in fact hold for larger multistage networks, too.

4. Scaling Behaviour of Multistage Throughput

In the context of scalable networks a central question is how the network throughput scales with network size. To answer this question we have employed a combination of simulations and analytical techniques because of the resource constraints of our simulations.

We start from a probabilistic model introduced in [1] and [2]. Throughput is calculated statically for evenly distributed random traffic which essentially means that queuing effects are neglected. By comparing the calculated throughput values t_{cal} with simulated values t_{sim} for small and medium size networks (up to 512 network ports) we derived a suitable fitting parameter f; i.e. $t_{sim} = (1-f)\, t_{cal}$. It turned out that in fact f is a function f(a) of the cluster size parameter introduced in section 2. We found that the choice f(a) = a/47 reproduces the simulation values within 5-10% independent of network size. This fitting term f summarizes the impacts of queuing, acknowledge packets, and packet overhead on the network throughput. It shows the expected qualitative behaviour; i.e. it increases monotonically with the cluster size because there is significantly more queuing in networks of larger cluster size.

With this extended analytical model we are able to extrapolate simulation results to larger networks in a reliable way. In fig. 8 the sustained link throughput versus the network size N is presented for deterministic and adaptive routing for three different cluster sizes (a = 8, 16, 24).

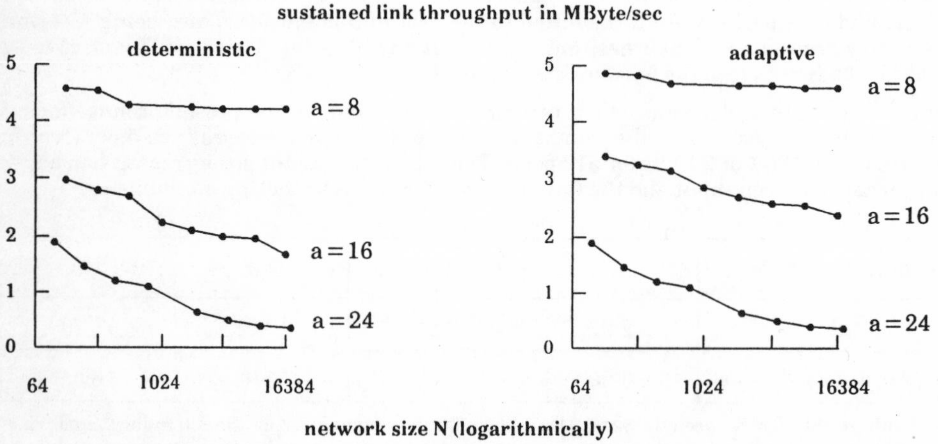

Figure 8: Scaling behaviour of sustained link throughput of multistage networks. Network size N is scaled by increasing the number of stages and varying the three-stage building blocks.

In the deterministic case, sustained link throughput drops by 8, 44, and 81% for a = 8, 16, and 24, respectively, increasing network size from roughly 100 to 16000 terminal links. The corresponding values for adaptive routing are 5, 31, and 81%, respectively.

From the network designer's point of view it is desirable to provide a constant sustained link throughput with increasing network size. In fact, for the a=8 network class this is approximately the case. The sustained link throughput remains close to the theoretical upper limit of 5.6 MByte/sec for random load (destination address conflicts, packet header overhead, and acknowledge protocol taken into account). Unfortunately, it is a very expensive class. Network costs in terms of crossbars grow quadratically with network size N. For the 16000-port network roughly 40000 switches are needed, for example. The network classes corresponding to a=16 and a=24 show an O(N log(N)), and O(N) cost behaviour, respectively. We found out that the optimal cost/performance ratio is obtained for a=16. Hence, constant link throughput and optimal cost/performance ratio cannot be achieved at the same time.

The adaptive mechanism improves sustained link throughput for a=8 by 6-10% compared to deterministic routing, increasing with network size. The corresponding values for a=16 are 14-40%. Moreover, the slope is significantly reduced for a=8 and a=16. For a=24 there is no measurable improvement. That is because we investigate networks under heavy load conditions (sustained link throughput) which implies that for a=24 all links are congested with high probability; i.e. adaption cannot help. For lower network load there is an improvement for these networks, too.

5. Summary and Conclusion

Assuming a realistic dynamic packet switching component with a versatile deterministic routing mechanism (such as interval routing) we have selected a range of regular, scalable network structures and specified corresponding routing schemes. These are deadlock-free, (near-)optimal and well-balanced for random load and hence, the best achievable as far as prevailing communication patterns are not known in advance.

We have proposed and specified an enhancement to the routing mechanism which maintains the versatility, but improves the balance of communication load between equivalent paths by an adaptive dynamic selection instead of a static mapping. Although the purely local view of the adaptive selection does not necessarily lead to the globally optimal balance, the mechanism is perfectly suited to the requirements of *universal* message-passing architectures where no pre-assumptions on the load patterns can be made and consequently, no optimal deterministic routing scheme exists (i.e. for any deterministic routing scheme there is a worst-case communication pattern which leads to massive contention).

The results of our simulations for random as well as extremely unbalanced traffic show a significant performance improvement of adaptive over deterministic routing in both, effective throughput and average packet delay. The extent of that improvement is mainly determined by the number of alternative paths for the adaptive selection which is highly topology-dependent. In general, it is much higher for the presented (Clos-) type of multistage networks, since in the direct networks the selection scheme is restricted to the link width which itself is limited by the node degree and cluster size of the topology variant. While in the random case performance is improved by roughly 10 - 30%, the worst case performance is improved dramatically, which helps to close the gap between average and worst case network response in applications as is desired for general purpose computing.

The synthetic load patterns used in our investigations are certainly not typical for any specific application. However, they are extremely useful to expose how the networks and routing schemes respond to the most important cases of internal contention: statistically or systematically generated. Another important source of network-internal contention are external hot-spots and these will be an important topic of further investigations.

With our scalability results for very large networks we were able not only to confirm the throughput increase by adaptive routing, but also to demonstrate improved scalability in case of adaptive routing, in particular for the more expensive multistage networks. This in addition motivates us to recommend the multistage topology in combination with the adaptive routing scheme as a very appropriate structure for universal, highly parallel computers.

References

[1] J.H. Patel: *Performance of Processor-Memory Interconnections for Multiprocessors*; IEEE Trans. Comput., vol. c-30, no 10; pp. 771-780; 1981

[2] C.P. Kruskal, M. Snir: *Performance of Multistage Interconnection Networks for Multiprocessors*; IEEE Trans. Comput., vol. c-32, no 12; pp. 1091-1098; 1983

[3] J. van Leeuwen, R.B. Tan; *Interval Routing*; The Computer Journal 30 (4): pp. 298-307; 1987

[4] D. Pountain; *Virtual Channels: The Next Generation of Transputers*; BYTE April 90, Europe&World: 3-12; April 1990

[5] D. May, P. Thompson; *Transputers and Routers: Components for Concurrent Machines*; Proc. of Japanese Occam User Group; 1990

[6] W.J. Dally, C.L. Seitz; *Deadlock-Free Message Routing in Multiprocessor Interconnection Networks*; IEEE Trans. Comput., vol. c-36, no 5; pp. 547-553; 1987

[7] P.A.J. Hilbers, J.J. Lukkien; *Deadlock-free message routing in multicomputer networks*; Distributed Computing 3; pp. 178-186; 1989

[8] E. Reyzl; *Comparative Evaluation of Message-Based Parallel Systems: Bus vs. Hypercube*; GI-PARS Mitteilungen Nr. 6; pp. 220-231; 1989

[9] E. Reyzl, H. Eckardt; *Performance Evaluation for High-Performance Interconnection Networks*; Tagungsband der 11. ITG/GI Fachtagung "Architektur von Rechensystemen"; pp. 275-287; 1990

An Optimal Structure that Accommodates Both a Ring and a Binary Tree

Xiaohong Xie
Computing Laboratory
Oxford University
Oxford OX1 3QD UK

Youmei Ge
Computer Science Department
Nanjing University
Nanjing, China

Abstract

A class of novel networks called *ringtree* network is presented in which any ringtree of n nodes can accommodate an n-node ring and an n-node complete binary tree. Ringtree is optimal in respect of the embeddability of ring and complete binary tree in the sense that it has the lowest degree and the minimum number of communication links and the embeddings have no dilation and expansion. Like a binary tree, it permits a simple and efficient layout which is important in VLSI design.

1 Introduction

The rapid advance in VLSI technology has provided a cost-effective means of increasing the computational power by linking many computing elements together through an interconnection network to form a powerful computing engine. Systems with a few to as many as thousands of computing elements can be built up using different network architectures to suit the needs of different applications. The interconnection network is thus one of the most important issues in parallel computing.

During the past decades, many interconnection networks have been put forward, for example, linear array, ring, toroidal meshes (2D, 3D), binary tree, X-tree, shuffle exchange network, hypercube, mesh of trees and pyramid. Some systems adopt complex structures such as hypercube or pyramid, others are in favour of the simpler ones like linear array [1], ring [17], or binary tree [21]. In this paper, we are mainly interested in the following structures: linear array, ring and binary tree.

Ring (and linear array) as a network topology for parallel computing has several advantages. First, it is very simple, therefore easier to programme and to implement in hardware. Second, it is powerful enough to support wide variety of applications in science and enginnering. Many efficient parallel algorithms have been designed on the ring or linear array structures, for example, numerical computation [13, 6, 18, 16], computational geometry [5], image processing [2], and relational database [15]. Indeed, as indicated in [11], the ring structure supports many important computational models such as pipelining, local computation, recursive computation, domain decomposition and multi-function pipelining. Third, since a ring can be embedded in many popular structures like hypercube, any algorithm designed on the ring or linear array structure can be easily ported into the machines with those network architectures. Besides, any mesh algorithm can be very easily mapped onto a ring structure. However, the ring and linear array structures is not favourable with a large class of algorithms, i.e. the divide-and-conquer based algorithms.

On the contrary, the binary tree structure is the natural choice for supporting the divide-and-conquer based parallel algorithms. It is also a fundamental structure in computer science and has been studied for many years as an interconnection network for parallel and distributed computing in application such as database machine [7] and knowledge machine [21]. Ullman enumerated some of the problems for which a tree of processors is especially suitable, e.g. select-and-rotate, broadcast, census functions (e.g. multiplication and addition, minimum and maximum functions), selection of an arbitrary number from a set of numbers and depth computation [22]. Jarosz *et al* showed that any problem belonging to the polynomial-time hierarchy which includes all NP-hard problems can be solved on a binary tree machine in polynomial time [10]. Therefore *ring+binary tree* constitutes a powerful tool for parallel and distributed computing. Moreover, in practice, it is often the case that most non-trivial problems consist more than one basic subproblem which may favour a ring as well as a binary tree structure.

Many existing networks can fulfill this requirement, for example, hypercube and X-tree. Some of these networks have the capacity of more than this, and in consequence, more complex and expensive. They may not be cost-effective in those applications where the network requirement is not necessarily more than ring and binary tree. Our aim is to find a network which can accommodate both ring and binary tree, and yet with the lowest possible cost which is characterised bellow.

Low degree: the maximal number of communication ports that can be implemented on a single silicon chip is highly limited due to many practical reasons. Currently four communication ports are implemented in most on-chip-computers, e.g. INMOS Transputers and Intel *i*Warp cells [4]. Since in many applications, extra ports may be occupied for input and output of data from outside the systems (see e.g. [2]), at most three ports are left for interprocessor communication. On the other hand, any ring-and-binary-tree-embeddable network must have degree not lower than than three, it is therefore necessary to have such a network that has the minimum possible degree.

Less communication links: generally speaking, dense interconnection is expensive and may have difficulty in VLSI layout.

Efficient use of all processors: when a network is used as a host network for embedding a ring and binary tree, it is hoped that the derived ring and binary tree are as large as possible so that no processor is to be wasted. Put it in another way, the expansion of the host graph should be kept minimum.

Short communication path: every direct links in a ring or binary tree should be implemented in a shortest possible paths in the host network, ideally, using direct links. In terms of graph embedding, the embeddings should have the minimum dilation.

Simple and efficient layout: this is especially important in VLSI design.

In this paper, we present a class of novel interconnection networks called *ringtree* in which both ring and a complete binary tree can be embedded. The main advantage of ringtree over the existing ring-and-binary-tree-embeddable networks such as hypercube, X-tree, Sneptree [14] or DeBruijn graph [20] is that it has the lowest degree (three), this is especially useful when the commonly available 4-port chips such as INMOS Transputers or Intel *i*Warp cells are used to construct networks. Indeed, we show that ringtree is optimal as a ring-and-binary-tree-embeddable network in the sense that, in addition to its lowest degree, it has the minimum number of communication links and the embeddings have no dilation and expansion. It has also a simple and efficient VLSI layout.

2 Embedding of a Linear Array and a Binary Tree

We follow the notation in [19]. Let G and H be simple undirected graphs. An *embedding* of G in H is a one-to-one association of nodes of G with the nodes of H, together with a specification of paths in H connecting the images of the endpoints of each edge of G. Here the graph H is referred to as the host of target graph G. The *dilation* of the embedding is the maximum length of any of these G-edge-routing paths. The *expansion* of the embedding is the ratio $| H | / | G |$, the number of nodes in H to the number of nodes in G. If there is an embedding of G in H with dilation 1, we say that H accommodates G.

Our target graph is a ring and a complete binary tree, both with n nodes. In this section, we will first present a host graph called *linear tree* that accommodates a linear array and a complete binary tree. It will then be used in the next section by linking the head and the tail of the linear array to form a ringtree.

Definition 1 *A k-linear tree ($k \geq 1$) is a graph obtained by adding to a complete binary tree of depth k some edges in the following way (these additional edges are called horizontal edges):*

- *if k is an odd number, beginning from the second leaf on the left or, if k is an even number, from the third leaf on the left, for each group of three consecutive leaves (if any), add an edge between the left and middle leaf and between middle and right leaf;*
- *if k is an even number, in addition, add an edge between the left most leaf and the second left most leaf, and between the second right most and the right most leaf of the binary tree.*

here k is called the depth of the linear tree. The leaves of the original binary tree are also called the leaves of the linear tree. □

It is obvious by the definition that a complete binary tree of depth k is a subgraph of a k-linear tree. In order to show that it can also accommodate a linear array of length $n = 2^{k+1} - 1$, it is sufficient to show that a k-linear tree contains a Hamilton path. We distinguish four types of edges for each node p in the graph:

- *leftson edge*: the edge linking the left son of p;
- *rightson edge*: the edge linking the right son of p;
- *father edge*: the edge linking the father of p;
- *horizontal edge*: the added edge linking the node p.

To find a Hamilton path in a k-linear array, we assign the following search priority to the edge of each node:

1. horizontal edge;
2. left son edge;
3. right son edge;
4. father edge.

For any complete binary linear tree, the following simple algorithm performs a traversal of the graph.

Algorithm 1 (Hamilton Path) *For any k-linear tree,*

1. *set count c to 0 and choose the left most leaf of the linear tree as the current node;*
2. *label the current node with c and then increase c by 1. If the current node has unlabelled neighbours, choose the one that is linked by an edge of the highest search priority and move to that node;*
3. *repeat the above procedure until the current node has no unlabelled neighbours.*

□

We now prove that a trip by the above algorithm does cover each node of the linear tree once and only once, i.e. the trip form a Hamilton path of the graph.

Theorem 1 *For any k-linear tree, the trip by Algorithm 1 forms its Hamilton path.*

Proof: First we notice that any complete binary linear tree is symmetric by Definition 1. We prove the theorem by induction on $k \geq 1$. It is trivial to check that the theorem is true for $k \leq 2$. Suppose that the theorem holds for all $k \leq s$, we prove it also holds for $k = s + 1$.

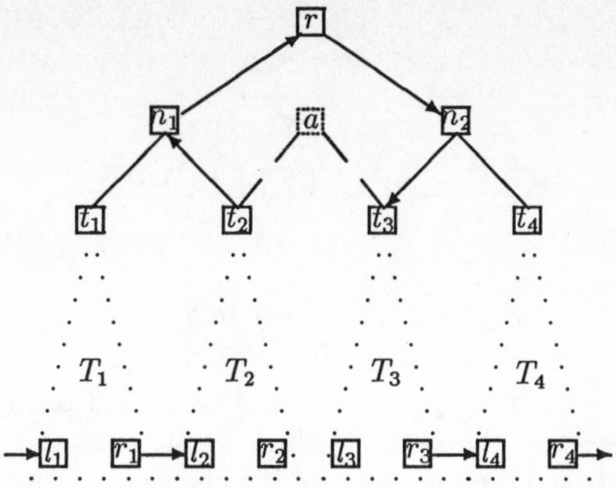

Figure 1: The subgraphs of an $(s+1)$-linear tree

Figure 1 shows that an (s+1)-linear tree can be divided into subgraphs which include T_1, T_2, T_3 and T_4. Because of the symmetry of the graph, there must not be horizontal edge between the node r_2 of T_2 and l_3 of T_3. Besides, T_1 is an $(s-1)$-linear tree from the way the $(s+1)$-linear tree was constructed and therefore there must exist an edge between r_1 of T_1 and l_2 of T_2, because otherwise the three right most leaves of T_1 would form a three-node-group, which in turn violated the symmetry of T_1. By the symmetry of the graph, T_4 is also an $(s-1)$-linear tree and has an edge (r_3, l_4) linked with T_3. By the inductive hypothesis, Algorithm 1 generates a Hamilton path in T_1 and T_4 respectively:

$$P_1 \; : \; l_1, \cdots, t_1, \cdots, r_1 \; \textit{in} \; T_1$$
$$P_4 \; : \; l_4, \cdots, t_4, \cdots, r_4 \; \textit{in} \; T_4$$

Now we break the edge (n_1, t_2) and (n_2, t_3), and add an auxiliary node a to form the root of T_2 and T_3, and call the graph formed by the subgraph T_2 and T_3 and the node a the graph T_a. It is not difficult to show that the newly formed graph T_a is also an linear tree of depth s. So from the inductive hypothesis, Algorithm 1 also generates a Hamilton path from l_2 to r_3 in T_a:

$$P_2 a P_3 = l_2, \cdots, t_2, a, t_3, \cdots, r_3$$

Since the node a is the only node that links T_2 with T_3, the subpath $P_2 = l_2, \cdots, t_2$ must be a Hamilton path for T_2 and the subpath $P_3 = t_3, \cdots, r_3$ must form a Hamilton path for T_3. Now we remove the auxiliary node a and recover the original graph. Starting from l_1, Algorithm 1 will generate the path P_1 ending at r_1 from which it visits l_2. Note the existence of edge (t_1, n_1) does not change the choice of the next node at t_1, because at t_1, there are at least 2 unvisited neighbours including n_1 who is linked with t_1 by an edge of the lowest priority. From l_2, the algorithm finds the path P_2 ending at t_2. From t_2, the algorithm will have to choose the following path leading to t_3:

$$P_5 : t_2, n_1, r, n_2, t_3$$

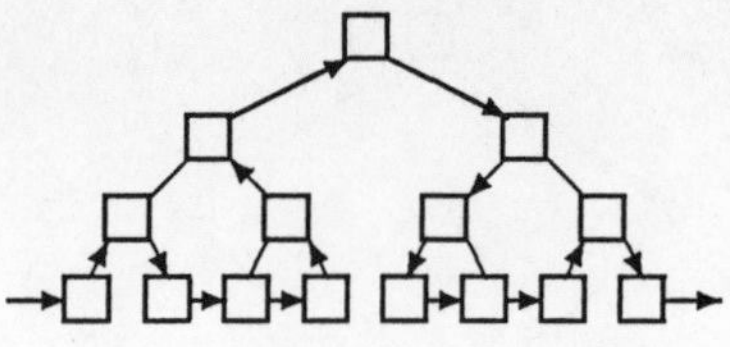

Figure 2: A 3-linear tree

and from t_3, the algorithm finds the path P_3 ending at r_3 and continue to go to l_4 and from l_4, the algorithm generates the path P_4 which finally ends at r_4. Also at the node t_4, the existence of edge (t_4, n_2) does not change the choice of the next node, because n_2 has already been visited. The path formed by the 5 subpaths

$$P = P_1P_2P_5P_3P_4$$

will cover all the nodes in the graph once and only once, hence form a Hamilton path starting at the left most leaf and ending at the right most leaf of the graph. Therefore the theorem is also true for $k = s + 1$. By induction, the theorem holds for all $k \geq 1$.□

Example 1 *Figure 2 is a linear tree of depth 3. The arrowed lines form a Hamilton path.* □

3 Ringtree

The following definition is about the construction of a ringtree from its respective linear tree.

Definition 2 *A k-ringtree is the graph obtained by rotating the left and right subtrees of the root of the k-linear tree at* 180° *and then linking the right most leaf of the resulting left subtree with the left most leaf of the resulting right subtree.*□

Lemma 1 *Every complete ringtree has at least one Hamilton cycle.*

Proof: From Theorem 1, Algorithm 1 generates a Hamilton path starting at the right most leaf of the left subtree to the left most leaf of the right subtree, by including the newly added edge to the path we obtain a Hamilton cycle of this k-ringtree.□

Example 2 *Figure 3 shows a 4-ringtree together with its Hamilton cycle in solid arrow lines.* □

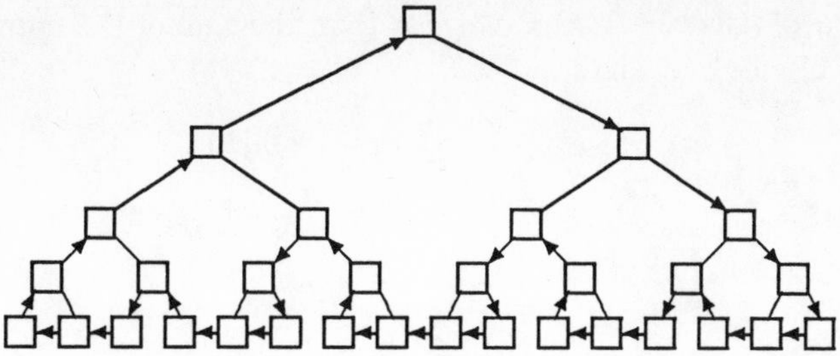

Figure 3: A 4-complete binary ring tree

We now show that any complete ringtree consists only of the minimum number of edges in respect of the embedding of ring and binary tree.

Theorem 2 (Minimum Number of Edges) *Let $n = 2^{k+1} - 1$ and $G(k) = (V, E)$ be any graph which accommodates a ring and a complete binary tree of n nodes and let the number of edges in a k-ringtree be $E(k)$, we have $E(k) \leq \mid E_{G(k)} \mid$.*

Proof: First there are 2^k leaves in a k-ringtree. According to Definition 1 and 2, there are total of $2\lfloor\frac{2^k}{3}\rfloor + 1$ added edges which equals $\lfloor\frac{2^{k+1}-2}{3}\rfloor + 1 = \lfloor\frac{n-1}{3}\rfloor + 1$. Therefore the number of edges in a k-ringtree is

$$E(k) = (n-1) + (\lfloor\frac{n-1}{3}\rfloor + 1) = n + \lfloor\frac{n-1}{3}\rfloor.$$

Now we are to look at the number of edges in $G(k)$. Let the ring and the complete binary tree in $G(k)$ be R and CBT respectively, and the set of edges in R be E_R. Then $\mid E_R \mid = n$. On the other hand, any internal node of CBT (degree three node) must have at least one of its associated edges not belonging to E_R. Such kind of edges is called *off-cycle edges.* Each node in depth $k-1$ of the CBT has at least one off-cycle edge, so do nodes in depth $k-3$, and henceforth until nodes in depth 1 if k is even or in depth 2 if k is odd. Moreover nodes on different depths (with difference in depth no less than two) do not share any edges. So the number $m(k)$ of off-cycle edges in CBT is:

if k is even,

$$\begin{aligned} m(k) &\geq 2^{k-1} + 2^{k-3} + \cdots + 2^1 \\ &= \frac{2^{k+1}-2}{3} = \frac{n-1}{3} = \lfloor\frac{n-1}{3}\rfloor \end{aligned}$$

or if k is odd,

$$\begin{aligned} m(k) &\geq 2^{k-1} + 2^{k-3} + \cdots + 2^2 \\ &= \frac{2^{k+1}-4}{3} = \frac{n-1}{3} - \frac{2}{3} = \lfloor\frac{n-1}{3}\rfloor. \end{aligned}$$

The total number of edges in $G(k)$ is not less than the sum of the number of edges in R and the number of off-cycle edges in CBT:

$$\begin{aligned} | E_{G(k)} | &\geq | E_R | + m(k) \\ &= n + \lfloor \frac{n-1}{3} \rfloor . \end{aligned}$$

Therefore we have

$$E(k) \leq | E_{G(k)} | .$$

□

Corollary 1 *There exists an embedding of binary tree of depth k in a k-linear tree as well as k-ringtree with dilation 1 and expansion 1; And there exists an embedding of a ring (linear array) of n nodes in a k-ringtree (k-linear tree) where* $n = 2^{k+1} - 1$. □

In many applications, the binary tree in use is usually incomplete. Such situation may due to the nature of the computations in the underlying problems, e.g. the parallel computational graph is not a complete binary tree, or due to the limitation of the available processors in a system. For example, the number of processors that are available for use may not be the power of 2 minus 1. It is therefore natural to ask how to obtain a Hamilton cycle in a given arbitrary binary tree by adding some additional edges on it such that the degree of the resulting graph is still kept minimum. We have proved that the above result can be extended to include any arbitrary binary tree as well. Due to the limitation of the size of the paper, this will be presented in a separate paper.

4 VLSI Layout

The VLSI layout of binary tree has been studied for many years [8, 23, 3]. Lerserson described a method for the layout of the completely linked binary tree (a complete binary tree in which all the neighbouring leaves are linked together)[12], Horowitz and Zorat presented another method to allow the efficient layout of a completely linked binary tree on a square and even took a further step to study the layout of an arbitrary binary tree [9]. As our (complete) ringtree is a subgraph of a completely linked tree, their results can be directly applied to our ringtree.

5 Conclusion

In this paper, we present a class of novel networks called ringtree in which a ring and a binary tree can be optimally embedded. This network should be useful in a wide area of applications. The advantage of ringtree over the existing ring-and-binary-tree-embeddable networks is its lower degree and lower cost as summarised in Table 1 which shows the number of nodes, the number of edges and the degree of the networks in which an n-node ring and an n-node complete binary tree can be embedded. Table 1 also shows the

network	*nodes*	*edges*	*degree*	*dilation*	*expansion*
hypercube	$n+1$	$\frac{1}{2}(n+1)\log(n+1)$	$\log(n+1)$	2	$\frac{n+1}{n}$
X-tree	n	$2n-\log(n+1)-1$	5	1	1
DeBruijn	$n+1$	$2n$	4	1	$\frac{n+1}{n}$
Sneptree	n	$2n$	4	1	1
completely linked tree	n	$\frac{3}{2}(n-1)$	3	1	$\frac{2n}{n+1}$
complete ringtree	n	$n+\lfloor\frac{n-1}{3}\rfloor$	3	1	1

Table 1: A Comparison of n-Node Ring and Binary Tree Embeddable Networks

dilation and expansion of the embedding in each network in which an n-node ring and an n-node complete binary tree can be embedded. (We assume $n = 2^{k+1} - 1$). Although the completely linked tree is a supergraph of the complete ringtree, to our knowledge, only the leaves of the completely linked tree have been used as a linear array, which account only half the number of nodes in the graph. From Table 1, the ringtree has the lowest cost as measured in terms of the number of nodes, the number of edges, degree of the network, the dilation and the expansion of the embedding as compared with other ring-and-binary-tree-embeddable networks.

Acknowledgement

The first authors is grateful to his supervisor Bill McColl and to Jesus College Oxford for providing a scholarship.

References

[1] M. Annaratone *et al.* The Warp computer: Architecture, implementation and performance. *IEEE Trans. on Comput.*, C-36(12), 1987.

[2] H. R. Arabnia and M. A. Oliver. A Transputer network for the arbitrary rotation of digitised images. *The Computer Journal*, 30(5):425-32, 1987.

[3] D. A. Bailey and J. E. Cuny. An efficient embedding of large trees in processor grids. In *Proc. of Int. Conf. on Parallel Processing*, pages 819-923, August 1986.

[4] S. Borkar *et al.* iWarp: An integrated solution to high-speed parallel computing. Tech. Rep. CMU-CS-89-104, Comput. Sci. Dept, CMU, January 1989.

[5] B. Chazelle. Computational geometry on a systolic chip. *IEEE Trans. on Computers*, C-33(9):774-85, 1984.

[6] M. Cosnard and Y. Robert. Systolic Givens factorization of dense rectangular matrices. *Int. J. Computer Math.*, 25:287-98, 1988.

[7] M. A. Bonncelli *et al.* A VLSI tree machine for relational databases. In *Proc. 10th Computer Architecture Symp.*, pages 67-73, June 1983.

[8] D. Gordon. Efficient embedding of binary trees in VLSI arrays. *IEEE Trans. on Computers*, C-36(9):1009-18, 1987.

[9] E. Horowitz and A. Zorat. The binary tree as an interconnection network: Applications to multiprocessor systems and VLSI. *IEEE Trans. on Comput.*, C-30(4), 1981.

[10] J. Jarosz and J. R. Jaworowski. Computer tree—The power of parallel computations. *The Computer Journal*, 29(2):103-8, 1986.

[11] H. T. Kung. The Warp computer: a cost-effective solution to supercomputing. *An Annual Report, Comput. Sci. Dept., CMU*, 1988.

[12] C. E. Lerserson. Systolic priority queues. In *Proc. Caltech Conf. on VLSI*, pages 199-214, January 1979.

[13] G. Li and T. F. Coleman. A new method for solving triangular systems on distributed-memory message-passing multiprocessors. *SIAM J. Sci. Stat. Comput.*, 10(2):382-96, 1989.

[14] P. P. Li and A. J. Martin. The Sneptree—A versatile interconnection network. In *Proc. of Int. Conf. on Parallel Processing*, pages 20-7, 1986.

[15] Y-C. Lin and F-C. Lin. A family of systolic arrays for relational database operation. In *Systolic Arrays*, W. Moore *et al* Eds., pages 191-200. Adam Hilger, 1987.

[16] R. Melhem. A systolic accelerator for iterative solution of sparse linear systems. *IEEE Trans. on Comput.*, 38(11):1591-5, 1989.

[17] C. Rieger *et al.* ZMOB: A. new computing engine for AI. In *Proc. 7th IJCAI-81*, pages 955-60, 1981.

[18] Y. Robert, B. Tourancheau, and G. Villard. Data allocation strategies for the Gauss and Jordan algorithms on a ring of processors. *Inf. Proc. Letters*, 31:21-9, 1989.

[19] A. L. Rosenberg. Graph embeddings 1988. *Lecture Notes in Computer Science*, pages 160-9, 1988.

[20] M. R. Samatham and D. K. Pradhan. The de bruijn multiprocessor network: A versatile parallel processing and sorting network for VLSI. *IEEE Trans. on Comput.*, 38(4):567-81, 1989.

[21] S. J. Stolfo and D. E. Shaw. DADO: A. tree-structured machine architecture for production systems. In *Proc. Nat. Conf. on AI AAAI-82*, pages 242-6, 1982.

[22] J. Ullman. *Computational aspects of VLSI.* Computer Science Press, Inc, 1984.

[23] H. Y. Youn and A. D. Singh. On implementing large binary tree architectures in VLSI and WSI. *IEEE Trans. on Comput.*, 38(4):526-37, 1989.

A Scalable Communication Processor Design supporting Systolic Communication

H. Corporaal J.G.E. Olk
Delft University of Technology
P.O. Box 5031
2600 GA Delft, The Netherlands
email: heco@duteca.et.tudelft.nl

Abstract

In getting a high performance computer we have the choice between expensive single processor systems and massive parallel computers. The latter are more difficult to program, but offer almost unlimited extensibility of computing power.

This paper describes a scalable and flexible communication processor for message passing in massive parallel processor systems. This communication processor is currently being implemented as a parameterized VLSI cell within a framework for automatic generation of application specific processors. It adds MIMD capabilities to this framework. In contrast to many existing designs, this design covers a large area within the communication processor design space.

Keywords high performance communication processor, fine-grain communication, virtual connections, routing, scalability of design, message compression

1 Introduction

The research into the field of high performance computing results both into very expensive single (or few) processor supercomputing systems and into the design of massive parallel processing systems, using many identical low cost nodes. The latter offer a far better cost-performance ratio at the expense of redesigning existing algorithms and applications. Shared memory parallel processing systems aim at reducing the software redesign costs. They support a similar programming model as used on classic Von Neumann sequential systems. However, the correct use of shared data requires proper synchronization. Incorrect locking of shared data leads to indeterministic results. These faults are very hard to debug. The use of shared data may also cause network and memory congestion. On the other hand, message passing systems offer easy synchronization by combining the synchronization and communication mechanism. These systems are easy extensible and naturally exploit the computation and communication locality available in many scientific applications.

Not every application is suitable for (massive) parallel computing, because of inherent serial algorithmic components which dominate the application. The success of sequential supercomputers is partly related to that. Fortunately, large classes of applications, and among them those which require processing power most, can easily be mapped on a regular network of processing nodes.

Massive parallelism inherently results into fine-grain computational tasks which show a high communication-computation bandwidth ratio. This requires high performance communication support between different nodes. Recently many communication processor proposals and designs are made, supporting message passing in massive parallel systems [S*85, Pou90, Dal87, Dal90, AvT87, RG87, Hil85, B*89, Moo89]. In [CO91] we explored the design space for building such processors. It turned out that many designs cover a very restricted area into this design space, and are therefore only suitable for very limited application areas. A possible exception is the DOOM-communication processor described in [AvT87], however this processor offers a rather low performance (long latency and low network bandwidth) and is by that unsuitable for massive parallelism.
This paper is oriented towards the design of a scalable communication processor which supports massive fine-grain parallelism. Especially the large class of systolic applications [Kun82] can be efficiently executed. These applications are characterized by a regular data flow between (near) neighbor nodes, requiring very high communication bandwidth on dedicated channels. The communication bandwidth has to be well balanced with the processing bandwidth. However because of the scalability and flexibility, the described design is also suitable for more general classes of computations.

In the computation of specific applications one has the choice between dedicated hardware (as used traditionally for systolic applications) and general purpose processor building blocks. The latter offer flexibility, quick design and prototyping, but offer substantial lower performance. Today, using automatic VLSI design compilation systems, the advantages of both approaches can be combined.

In this paper, first the desirable scalability and flexibility of communication processors is discussed. Next we describe a scalable communication processor which is currently under design, using the ASA[1] VLSI compilation system. This communication processor is part of the SCARCE[2] framework [M*89] for designing high performance application specific computers. It is being implemented as a parameterized standard VLSI cell which can be incorporated into the dataprocessor framework to obtain a MIMD building block. This way we are able to cover a range of interconnection topologies, change the number of virtual connections per node, and balance the needed communicational power with respect to the computational bandwidth.

2 Scalable and flexible design

Scalability and flexibility are essential to permit the adaptation of the communication processor (CP) design to specific applications, which is more cost effective than designing a completely new CP architecture for each application. Scalablility is applied at chip design time or board design time. At compile time and run time, flexibility of CP behavior is possible. Obviously, scalability offers more variation of CP characteristics than flexibility.

[1] ASA is a trademark of SAGANTEC
[2] SCalable ARChitecture Experiment

2.1 Scalability

Scalability is important to keep up with the increasing computing demands of existing and future applications. Also scalability allows balancing of communication and computation power required by the application.
For communication processors a distinction can be made between two ways of scalability: scalability of the network topology and scalability of performance.

Scalability of network topology
There is no network topology that performs well for all applications so scalability of the network topology is required to allow optimization towards a specific application. When, for performance reasons, we assume hardwired routing, i.e. no routing tables are used, scalability of network topology can be obtained by scaling of:

- **Degree:** Alteration of the degree, the number of links of a CP, allows the use of various different network topologies. The degree of a CP can be varied by:
  - The use of several separate, and independent, physical networks.
  - Changing the dimensionality of the network. For instance by using a 3-dimensional cube instead of a 2-dimensional mesh.
- **Number of nodes:** the maximum number of nodes in a network. This is achieved by changing the size of the address field of the message as far as allowed by the implemented routing algorithm.
- **Virtual networks:** Systolic algorithms mostly require multiple connections between DPs. This can be realized by mapping several connected or independent virtual networks[3] on one physical network.

Scalability of performance
Scalability of performance is important to meet the required communication bandwidth of an application and can be achieved by adjustment of:

- **Link bandwidth:** the implementation of the physical link between CPs allows to vary the bandwidth of the link, i.e. the number of bits that can be transferred over the link in a certain time. For instance, a serial or parallel communication protocol may be used. A parallel link implementation increases the bandwidth and at the same time reduces message latency. Further adaptation to the communication traffic pattern of a specific application is possible by using either unidirectional or bidirectional pins.
- **Internal CP datapath:** the internal bandwidth of the CP can be increased by expanding the internal datapath, i.e. the wordsize. The wordsize is usually a trade-off between the available chip area and the desired throughput.
- **Buffersize:** larger buffers smoothen the data transmissions over links and permit full utilization of the links. However, small buffers improve the hot-spot performance since messages are not buffered around the hot-spot. Due to the limited bufferspace around the hot-spot, messages block earlier and are more spread over

[3] Connected virtual networks allow intermediate node(s) routing.

<table>
<tr><td>core set</td><td rowspan="2">co-processor support</td><td rowspan="2">short instruction support</td><td rowspan="2">trap, emulation, interrupt support</td><td rowspan="2">virtual-memory support</td><td rowspan="2">VLIW support</td><td rowspan="2">MIMD support</td></tr>
<tr><td>function units</td></tr>
<tr><td colspan="7">base architecture</td></tr>
</table>

Figure 1: SCARCE architecture framework with additional MIMD support.

the network. So they may be routed around the hot-spot instead of through it, so the congestion is limited. It is clear that there is no general optimal buffer size and the ideal buffer size is application dependent. E.g. in systolic applications buffer size depends on the message delay required in communication paths.

- **Implementation technology:** higher performance may be accomplished by implementing the communication processor chip in a fast and lower density technology, e.g. GaAs, rather than a slow and dense one.

2.2 Flexibility

Flexibility of CP behavior at compile and run time is possible for:

- **Switching method:** wormhole switching, described in [S*85], allows emulation of packet and circuit switching methods.
- **Virtual topology:** although the physical topology can not be altered, the virtual topology can be changed however. For example by not using all links of the network. Combining circuit switching and virtual networks allows for fixed logical connections between neighboring nodes.
- **Routing:** the routing path taken by a message may be chosen, e.g. using intermediate node routing.
- **Message control:** the exchanging of messages between the data processor (DP) and the CP can be implemented in several ways. A CP may use Direct Memory Access (DMA) to deliver or send a message, but also the DP can be employed for message transfer.

3 Functional Communication Processor Design

This section discusses the generic CP architecture, with emphasis on the first implementation currently under design, for the SCARCE framework [M*89] and clarifies the implemented scalability and flexibility issues of the previous section. The SCARCE framework allows automatic generation of application specific processors and embedded controllers. The addition of a CP architecture to SCARCE gives the framework MIMD support and allows processor generation for a wider range of applications. The base architecture, with MIMD support, of the SCARCE framework is pictured in Figure 1.

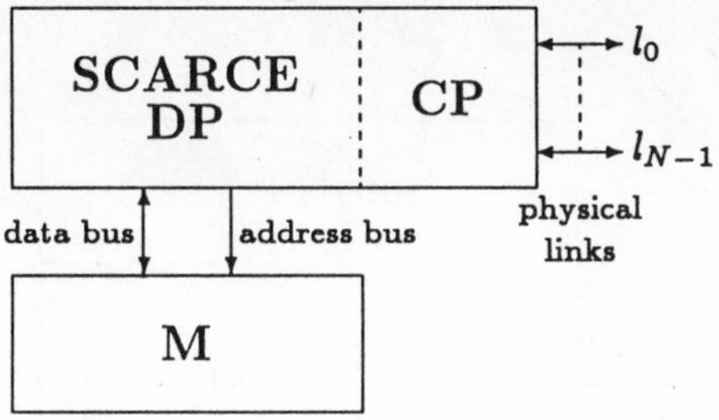

Figure 2: Architecture overview with SCARCE processor and CP.

This CP architecture defines a space of possible CP implementations and will be incorporated in SCARCE using a parametrized basic VLSI cell. So the resulting CP architecture is specified at chip design-time. A high-level overview of the architecture is shown in Figure 2. The CP, connected to neighboring CPs with N physical links ($l_0...l_{N-1}$), is fully integrated in the SCARCE processor, with its own (external) memory M, and resides on the same chip.

The design of the CP can be divided in three functional parts: the DP interfacing, the virtual networks and the actual physical network. The DP interfacing performs the injection and ejection of messages into or from the virtual networks. The virtual networks buffer and route, using wormhole switching, the messages over the physical links, which performs the actual transfer of data between neighboring CPs. The physical links may be shared between several virtual networks. The virtual networks may be interconnected with each other to allow messages to traverse from one network to another. A global view of the first CP architecture under implementation, which uses four prioritized virtual networks and four physical links (N, S, W, E), is shown in Figure 3.

The message structure, DP-CP interface, virtual networks and physical link implementation are examined in relation to the current, and first, realization. Finally an overview is given of the routing support and scalability of the CP architecture.

3.1 Message structure

The message structure, shown in Figure 4, consists of one or more address *field(s)*, containing a relative address, followed by one or more data *field(s)*. Both the data and the address part of the message are terminated by a trailing *field*.

The address part of the message supports routing over multi-dimensional networks and each *field* is associated with a different dimension of the network. The current implementation supports a two-dimensional grid and uses 32-bit *fields*[4], so the largest grid possible consists of 2^{64} nodes[5]. The choice for 32-bit *fields* is mainly influenced by the SCARCE DP processor which is a 32-bit RISC processor and can't handle smaller units,

[4] A fieldsize of 32-bit seems inefficient for small networks; each address *field* is 32-bit but only a small part of it is used. However, a data compression scheme is used when messages are transferred over the network. Since relative addressing is used and the achieved compression is best for small (signed) integers, the inefficiency of the 32-bit *fields* for small networks is reduced.

[5] Actually the grid may be larger, but the relative addressing only let a node reach 2^{64} nodes directly.

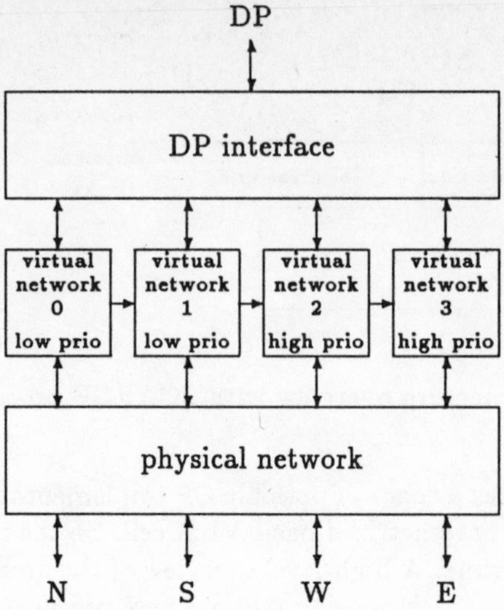

Figure 3: Architecture overview of first implemented CP.

address *field(s)*	trailing address *field*	data *field(s)*	trailing data *field*

Figure 4: Message structure.

e.g. 8-bit data elements, very well. So the 32-bit *field*size is chosen to fit the DP and to attain high speed DP-CP communication.

Each address *field* can be considered as a signed *dimension counter* and the absolute value of this counter indicates the number of hops the data has to take in the associated dimension. The address *field* is incremented or decremented for negative and positive values respectively. When the address *field* becomes zero, the message has completed its journey over the dimension and must be routed across the next dimension or must be delivered to the DP. Since the wormhole switching method and E-cube routing are used, this heading address *field* can then be chopped off the message and the next address *field*, if present, becomes the heading address *field*.

The CP resides on the same chip as the SCARCE processor and thus the available chip area is limited. Therefore, to minimize the amount of required hardware, the internal data path of the currently realized CP is only 4 bits wide and each *field* is divided in 4-bit *flits*. Of course, when higher density technologies become available and more chip area may be used, the internal data path width can be extended to, for instance, 32 bits which increases the internal bandwidth.

To reduce the consumed bandwidth of, among other things, the physical links, the first

field value	field control $flit^a$	data field $flit(s)$
$-2^3 - 2^3$-1	ct00	xxxx
$-2^7 - 2^7$-1	ct01	xxxx xxxx
$-2^{15} - 2^{15}$-1	ct10	xxxx xxxx xxxx xxxx
$-2^{31} - 2^{31}$-1	ct11	xxxx xxxx xxxx xxxx xxxx xxxx xxxx xxxx

[a]c = fieldtype control bit (0 = data field, 1 = address field), t = trailing tag bit (0 = not last field, 1 = trailing field)

Figure 5: Division of *field* in *flits*.

realization uses a simple data compression scheme[6]. The number of *flits* a *field* occupies varies and depends on the 32-bit signed value of the *field*, e.g. the values -8 to 7 only take a single *flit*. In addition, a control *flit* is added to the *flits* of a *field* consisting of a 2-bit *field*size value (4, 8, 16 or 32 bits) and a 2-bit control tag, indicating the type of *field* (data or address) and whether it is a trailing *field* or not. This division of a *field* in *flits* is illustrated in Figure 5.

3.2 DP-CP interface

The DP-CP interface is realized by the implementation of a Communication Processor Functional Unit (CPFU) and by a DP register interface which consumes several, one for each virtual network, of the 32 available registers of the DP. The sending and receiving of data is done via these registers, i.e. writing to a register will send data to the corresponding virtual network while data can be received from the virtual network by reading the register. Using a register interface for transferring data between CP and DP provides fast communication and allows to perform arithmetic operations directly on incoming data. For instance, just one (single cycle) instruction[7] is needed to receive two 32-bit words, perform an add operation and send the result back over the network.
The current implementation uses four virtual networks and thus four registers are mapped to four CP registers. The CPFU handles the message control and may issue an interrupt request on certain conditions, e.g. on incoming messages. The DP-CP interface is pictured in Figure 6.

3.3 Virtual networks

The network of the CP architecture consists of independent prioritized virtual networks (0–n). The virtual networks share the same physical network, using virtual links, and are not used to avoid deadlock[8] but to improve link utilization. So a blocking virtual link will not block the physical link, and one DP may have multiple virtual connections to other DP's which provides support for systolic communication.
The virtual networks are interconnected with each other and a message can go from one virtual network to another. Yet, to avoid deadlock, this is only possible in one

[6]Due to the simple data compression algorithm, no additional latency is introduced for compressing and decompressing the data on injection and ejection.

[7]ADD $R_{r1}, R_{r2} \rightarrow R_{s1}$

[8]Deadlock is avoided by using E-cube routing.

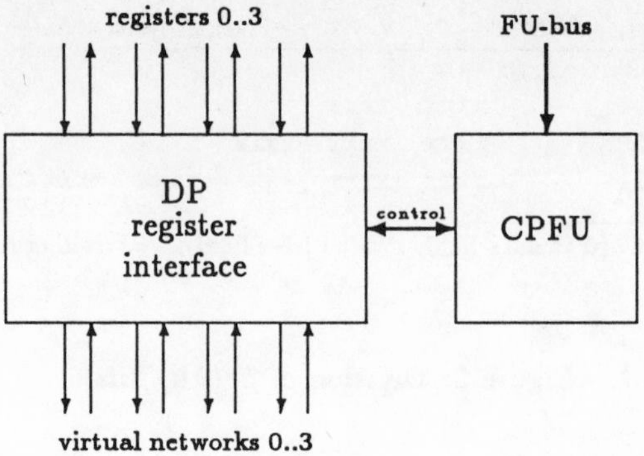

Figure 6: DP-CP interface.

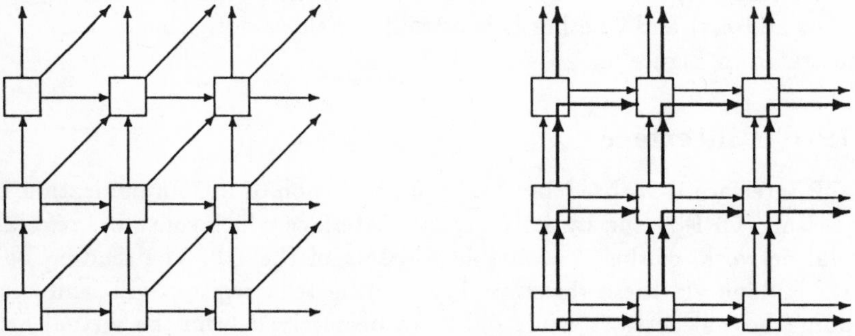

Typical systolic communication.

Systolic communication using virtual links.

Figure 7: Use of virtual links for systolic communication.

direction: from virtual network 0 towards n. The connected virtual networks are used to allow (random) intermediate node routing which is used to implement nondeterministic routing when still using a deterministic routing algorithm (E-cube). Figure 7 illustrates the use of virtual links for systolic communication.

In the currently implemented CP architecture, each of the four virtual networks can be seen as a two-dimensional grid network of CPs connected by virtual links. The priority of a virtual network is used for arbitration between two or more virtual links sharing the same physical link[9]. The data of the virtual link with the highest priority will be sent first over the physical link. So a virtual link with a low priority will only get permission to send data over the physical link when all virtual links with a higher priority are idle, i.e. don't need to send data. Between two virtual links with equal priority the available bandwidth of the physical link is fairly divided, i.e. when a virtual link has no data to send or it can't send data because the next virtual link is blocked, it will not consume any bandwidth and the full bandwidth is available to the other virtual links.

[9] The priority mechanism used here must not be confused with the class climbing of DOOM [AvT87] which is used to prevent deadlock.

type	control *flit*[a]	additional *flits*
idle	11xx	
field	01nn	field *flits* (control + data)
acknowledge	10nn	
reserved	00xx	

[a]nn=virtual link (0-3), x=don't care.

Figure 8: Possible data transfers over physical link.

The priority mechanism can be used to provide, for example, a fast communication network for acknowledge messages. The virtual networks 0 and 1 have an equal low priority and the virtual networks 2 and 3 are assigned the same high priority. It is not sensible to give just one network the highest priority since this network may then consume all bandwidth of the network and effectively block all other networks. Generally the low priority networks will be used to transfer the normal, possibly large, messages. The high priority networks are meant for short (emergency) messages.

3.4 Physical link

The transferring of data between neighboring CPs takes place over physical links. Each CP of the initial implemented architecture has four physical links (north, south, east, west), where a physical link consists of two 4-bit unidirectional links and thus has four input and four output pins. Control signals and data signals are time-multiplexed over these pins. So each physical link needs just eight chip pins and 32 pins are needed for the four physical links. Although the low pin count for the physical links limits the available bandwidth, the low pin count is important because the CP resides on the same chip as the SCARCE processor which also needs quite an amount of pins for the (32-bit) address, data and instruction busses.
The number of required pins is further reduced by the lack of handshake signals. The two CPs at each end of a physical link have the same clock, i.e. the data transfer over a physical link is synchronous. As shown in Figure 8, there are three types of transfers over the physical link: the link may be idle, a data transfer may take place, or an acknowledge can be sent.

3.5 Routing support

The CP architecture uses the deterministic E-cube routing algorithm on each virtual network, i.e. a message is first routed along the first dimension, then along the second dimension etc. So the path a message takes from its source to its destination is always known. However, it is possible for a message to transfer from one virtual network to the next. This allows implementation of intermediate node routing where a message is first routed to a, software determined, node and then routed to its actual destination over another virtual network. Intermediate node(s) routing can be used to avoid hot-spots of the network.

The routing support provided by the CP architecture is deadlock free since a deterministic routing algorithm is used for each virtual network and a message can only transfer to the next virtual network, not the previous. So there can never exist a cyclic dependency.

3.6 Scalability

The implemented scalability of the CP architecture supports, without significantly sacrificing performance, scalability and alteration of several properties such as:

- **Network topology:** different topologies are possible by variation of:
  - **Degree:** the varisized address field of a message allows support for topologies ranging from one-dimensional grids to n-dimensional grids. The size of a network may thus range from 2 to 2^{32n} nodes.
  - **Number of networks:** both the number of physical and virtual networks can easily be adapted. Each SCARCE processor can have a variable number of independent CPs by adding CPFUs to the base architecture. Alternatively, the number of virtual networks can be changed without influencing the physical topology.

- **Performance:** the available bandwidth is adjustable by choosing:
  - **Physical link implementation:** the current implementation uses two 4-bit unidirectional links but it is also possible to implement the physical link by using one 8-bit bidirectional link. A bidirectional link is advantageous for unidirectional network traffic, i.e. messages mainly travel from one side of the network to another but almost no messages travel in the opposite direction.

    Also the size of the physical link may be altered. Although expensive, most performance is achieved with two 32-bit unidirectional links.
  - **CP datapath width:** at the moment the width of the internal CP datapath is 4 bits in order to reduce the amount of required hardware, and thus chip area. In the future the width of the datapath may be increased to at most 32 bits.
  - **Virtual network to network connectivity:** current implementation only permits messages to go to the next virtual network. Additional hardware could increase the bandwidth between virtual networks and would allow communication from one virtual network to an arbitrary higher virtual network without visiting intermediate networks.
  - **Implementation technology:** the SCARCE framework allows processor generation for different technologies ranging from high-density technologies (e.g. CMOS) to low-density, but fast, technologies (e.g. GaAs).

4 Conclusions

In this paper we investigated the scalability and flexibility of communication processors for message passing distributed memory computers. The described scalable and flexible communication processor, currently being implemented at our laboratory as a

parametrized VLSI cell for the SCARCE framework, covers a wide subspace of the design space for communication processors.
This SCARCE communication processor supports multidimensional arrays and has a flexible routing strategy using intermediate node routing. Scalability in performance is achieved by freedom of physical link implementation, internal data path width, virtual network to network connectivity, and implementation technology. A data compression scheme is used to reduce bandwidth usage of small data values.

The scalable design of the SCARCE communication processor is highly oriented towards systolic communication and combines the speed of fully dedicated systolic hardware with the flexibility and quick prototyping of general purpose computing. It allows simple design of application specific massive parallel processor systems and makes the design process of such systems more a form of science than of art.

References

[AvT87] J. K. Annot and R. A. H. van Twist. A novel deadlock free and starvation free packet switching communication processor. In *Parallel Architectures and Languages Europe*, page 68, 1987.

[B*89] S. Borkar et al. Iwarp: an integrated solution to high-speed parallel computing. In *Proceedings of Supercomputing '88*, pages 330–339, ACM SIGARCH, January 1989.

[CO91] Henk Corporaal and Eddy Olk. Design and evaluation of communication processors supporting message passing in distributed memory systems. Submitted to 6th Distributed Memory Computing Conference (DMCC6), April 1991.

[Dal87] William J. Dally. *A VLSI Architecture for concurrent Data Structures*. Kluwer Academic Publishers, 1987.

[Dal90] William J. Dally. Performance analysis of k-ary n-cube interconnection networks. *IEEE Transactions on Computers*, 39(6):775–785, June 1990.

[Hil85] Daniel Hillis. *The Connection Machine*. MIT Press, 1985.

[Kun82] H.T. Kung. Why systolic architectures? *IEEE Computer*, 15(1):37–46, January 1982.

[M*89] J.M. Mulder et al. A framework for application-specific architecture design. In *Proceedings of the 14th International Symphosium on Computer Architecture*, May 1989.

[Moo89] W.G.P. Mooij. *Packet Switched Communication Networks for Multi-Processor Systems*. PhD thesis, University of Amsterdam, September 1989.

[Pou90] Dick Pountain. Virtual channels: the next generation of transputers. *BYTE Magazine (International Edition)*, 15(4):E&W 3–12, April 1990.

[RG87] Daniel A. Reed and Dirk C. Gronwald. The performance of multicomputer interconnection networks. *IEEE computer*, June 1987.

[S*85] Charles L. Seitz et al. *The Hypercube Communications Chip*. Technical Report, Dept. of Computer Science, California Institute of Technology, 1985.

Simulation Facility of Distributed Memory System with 'Mad Postman' Communication Network

V.S. Getov and C.R. Jesshope

Center for Informatics and Computer Technology
Bulgarian Academy of Sciences
Acad G Bonchev Bl 25A
SOFIA 1113, BULGARIA

Department of Electrical and Electronic Engineering
University of Surrey
Guildford, Surrey
GU2 5XH, UK

ABSTRACT

This paper presents a simulation facility developed for the 'mad-postman' packet routing communication network. Unlike previously published results for this network this facility and the results generated provide a complete simulation of the network, the network-processor interface and the application layer. The results are presented in terms of average message latency against network throughput for applications that generate randomly addressed packets at random intervals. The results show that if we measure message latency against throughput then at some stage latency increases rapidly with little increase in throughput. This point is independent of message length.

1. Introduction

The assertion that the communication networks development is one of the main sources of distributed memory systems performance advancement does not need any proof[BAI]. In the last ten years, several groups have advocated such an approach to parallel processing, based on large networks of interconnected microcomputers[DAL, KER and REE]. During this period communication networks for these architectures have been particularly developed and significant results have been obtained improving the ratio computation/communication time[MIL and REE]. These results extend the range of application areas for parallel computers and allow fine-grain parallel processing to be employed in distributed memory systems.

Among the communication networks for such kind of parallel computer architectures the 'mad postman' routing strategy[YAN] appears to offer minimal message latency through the network for a given wire cost; it performs eager routing of packets along the dimension in which a packet travels. Each packet comprises two or more address/control flits one for each dimension of the network in which the packet is to travel. The leading address flit is always the address in the dimension the packet is travelling, so that when eager routing gives message overun, it is only the redundant information which proceeds beyond the addressed node. Thus a message travelling in X will lose its X address at the node that that address is satisfied and only the remaining address(es) and data will 'junction' into the new network dimension.

Packets which adapt due to blockages in the dimension in which they are travelling will exchange the order of the address flits, incurring an address byte transmission latency per adaption. It should be noted that this is exactly the latency per node in a wormhole[DAL] or cut-through[KER] network. Any alternative would cause an indeterminate delay due to blockage.

A prerequisite for the 'mad-postman' routing strategy is a decomposition of the network into deadlock-free acyclic virtual networks. As well as providing deadlock-free routing this decomposition will ensure that no dead address flit (there will be one of these for each dimension each message travels) remains in the network indefinitely. If the dead address flit is blocked, it will be ignored, otherwise it will reach the edge of the network and dissappear. This decomposition also allows for adaptive routing and message sourcing after blockage, which also contributes to the robustnes of the results presented here.

Until now analysis of this routing strategy has been restricted to the 'mad postman' network itself, which has been examined as a closed system without any interface with the processing elements[MIL]. This approach is quite suitable for comparison with other types of communication networks, but the object of this and other research has been considered in conditions very different from the real ones.

The main purpose of the present study is to examine various architectures incorporating the 'mad postman' network as a whole from the communication performance point of view. Our aim is to find those elements of the architecture which exert a significant influence on both message latency and queue length. This information is absolutely essential to assess an optimum price/performance ratio of the projected systems.

2. Sources of Latency

2.1 Definitions

In this paper we shall be interested in the performance analysis of distributed memory computer system constructed with the 'mad postman' communication network (Fig.1); we are interested primarily in the communication subsystem, which comprises not only the network itself but also some elements of the rest of the system. The two main network performance indices are data throughput and message latency and our goal is to investigate the relationship between them. The message latency is defined as the delay from the message transmission request generation to the last bit of message arrival in the destination processor. Transmission request and arrival must be measured in terms of the application layer.

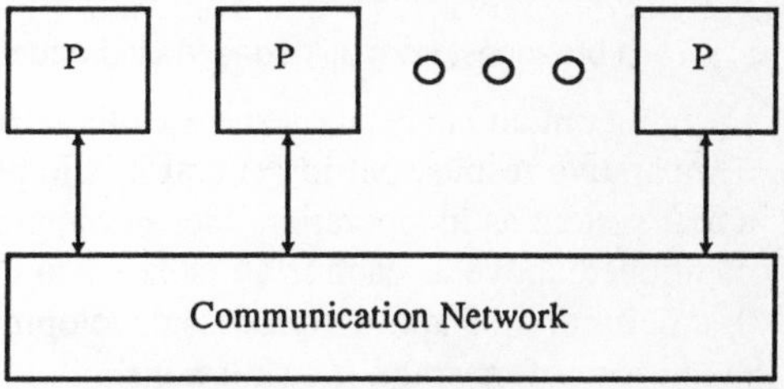

Figure 1. Distributed memory architecture

Obviously the latency depends directly on the each processor's communication traffic, the so called injection rate. (In our simulations, although the statistics may vary we are investigating the case of uniform load.) The latency for a given injection rate will of course be significantly effected by message length; at a given injection rate, the longer the message, the greater the latency. Thus we identify two experiments, to determine:

Latency = f(injection rate)

for a given message length, and

Latency = f(message length)

for a given injection rate.

The message format comprises two types of information, namely control and effective information (or data). The ratio of effective information/message length is called the communication network efficiency. Obviously the longer the message length, the greater the efficiency. The major question to be answered will be to achieve an appropriate compromise between latency and efficiency. To answer this one can find the definition of network throughput as an effective information per second quite useful. In such a way the throughput represents both efficiency and message length.

In a number of cases the aim is to obtain a throughput as high as possible, but in some applications however, the main goal is to assure high speed packet transmission within a definite period of time. In these cases we shall be ready to sacrifice throughput in order to achieve the restriction of a maximum packet delay through the network.

2.2 Communication operations

The network itself is not considered as a single resource. It has a number input and output channels for each node in the network, all of which may operate simultaneously. The communication operations which mark off the theoretical boundaries of the network behaviour are:

- a single message transfer;
- a single message broadcast;
- a message transmission from all nodes;
- a broadcast from all nodes (multibroadcasting).

Carrying out an analysis on some of these operational modes would be useful to reach comparative results, but in general it is impossible to approximate the network operation in a real system as its operation does not approach any of the communication operations mentioned above as each is an isolated and idealized case. Moreover the transmission begins in a definite time and the process development is analysed without taking into consideration the history of message transmissions.

In order to obtain adequate results, it is necessary to carry on the analysis in conditions close to those found in real world operation, where the transmission requests are generated by an application, probably randomly and at different times in different nodes. The generated communication traffic depends in intensity and operation types on the application and its granularity, as well as on the distribution of that application over the distributed memory system. Most commonly the real integrated traffic includes:

- randomly generated single messages;
- randomly generated multicast messages;
- randomly generated broadcast messages.

Obviously analytical methods are not suitable for carrying out the performance analysis of such a system. Therefore, a simulation which closely follows the behaviour of a real system must be performed. We present in this paper such results.

3. Node Architectures

This paper does not analyse either a detailed node architecture nor a computational model in use. Instead we are interested in those particular features of such an architecture which exert

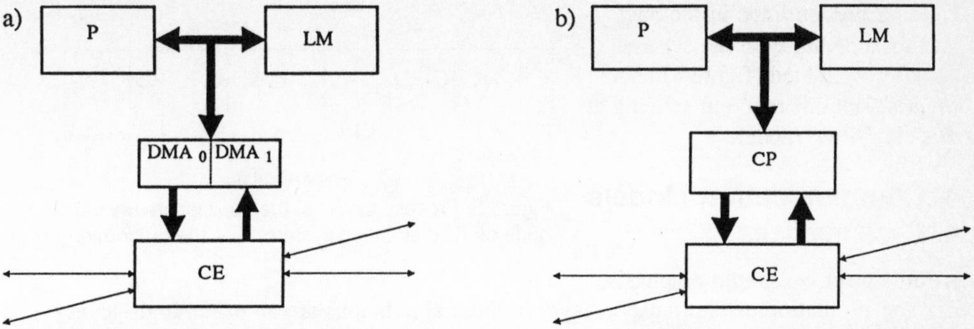

Figure 2. Two possible node architectures for a distributed memory system: a) CE interfaced by DMA channels; b) CE interfaced by communication co-processor (P - Processor, CE - Communication network element, LM - local memory.

a direct influence on communication and, more precisely, on packet latency. In the most popular view, each node in a distributed memory system contains some processor (P) with some local memory(LM), a communication element(CE) capable of routing messages, and a small number of connections to its nearest neighbours, see figure 2. It is also assumed that there is a network of processes running over the nodes and communicating between each other using asynchronous message passing. Every process may therefore send a message through the network when dictated by the application and then continue processing. The message arrives at a queue of incoming messages in the local memory of the processor to which it was addressed. The receiving process likewise reads from this queue as the applications dictates.

In the simplest case (figure 2a) the transfer between LM and CE is performed by two independent DMA channels, one for sending and the other one for receiving messages. The main disadvantage of this node architecture is that the communication drivers are implemented by the processor, adding additional delay and/or a buffering requirement to the process execution. The classical solution of this problem is to provide simultaneous execution of the communication drivers and the application process by employing a Communication Processor (CP) in the node architecture (figure 2b). In this case it will be mandatory to maintain a queue of outgoing messages in the LM of the sending node, as PE and CP are working fully asynchronously and independently of each other. A scheme suitable for modelling both of these two cases is shown in

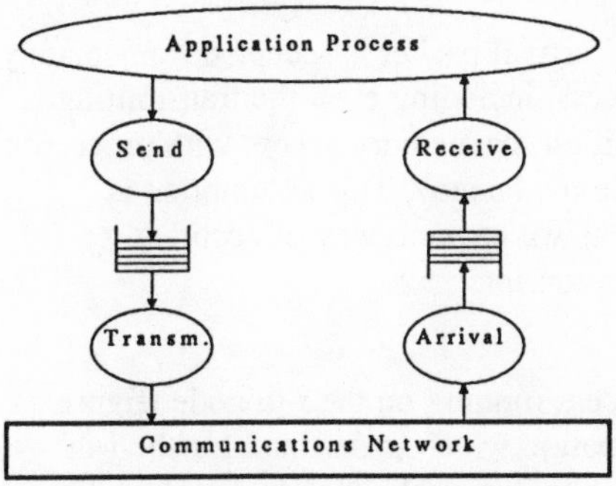

Figure 3. Process model of application running on a distributed memory system, ideal cas

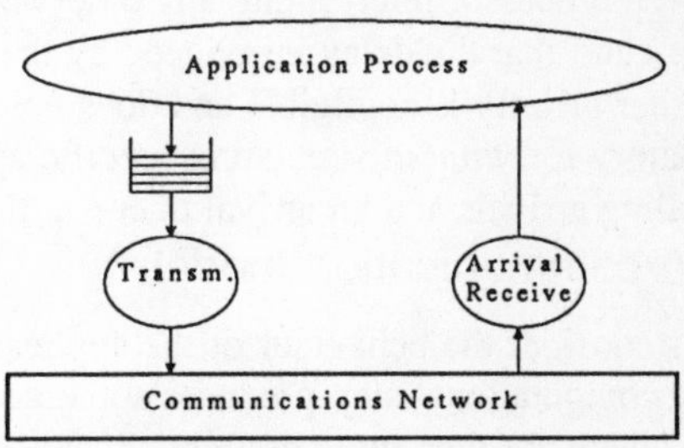

Figure 4. Process model of application running on a distributed memory system, as simulated.

figure 3 and outlined in the next section together with the scheme actually simulated (figure 4) and the assumptions made in arriving at this simplified model.

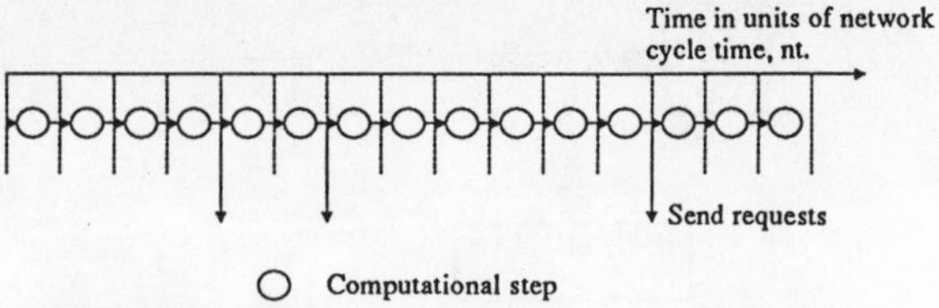

Figure 5. Process model of the application running on one node of the distributed system, note the random requests.

4. Communication Models

4.1 Assumptions

At the outset we should emphasise that the simulation of the transport layer in these simulations are an exact, logic-level simulation of an entire array of 1024 mad-postman network chips. However, the present study includes interface and application layers and is based on some assumptions which we believe will not significant influence the validity of the results presented, but which will of course considerably simplify the implementation. We assume that each computational process executes on its own processor being itself a sequence of computational steps. Every computational step takes equal execution time (T) and moreover that T is an integer multiple of the the communication network cycle time (t). In reality an asynchronous timing scheme is employed in the interface between the processor and CE. This application model is shown in figure 5, where we may assume T=t but that not every computational step produces a request to send in the network.

Furthermore, for a given T and t (depending on the price, technological level of the implementation and the processor architecture) one can establish reasonable bounds for the injection rate (for a given message length) which corresponds to the granularity of parallelism in use in the application. This assumption is in fact dictated by practicalities as in a real application, if the injection rate is so high that the network blocks and buffers become full, then the application will usually be suspended, degrading the efficiency of processor usage. To invert this argument our simulations may predict injection rate bounds for optimal processor efficiency.

We also assume that each message is transmitted through the network in one packet (with our current implementation plans this restricts message lengths to 32 bytes) and that the node architecture allows a half-duplex connection between LM and CE.

We also assumed that the distribution of the application is such that the destination address of a data packet is a random function with a uniform distribution (i <> j).

Perhaps our most restrictive assumption is that every arrival packet is accepted immediately from the processor interrupting any other active process, including even the transmitting process and that the delay introduced by the competition for memory access with processes of higher priority is negligible and does not influence the latency. This assumption is mandatory for without simulating specific applications we have no way of accurately modelling arrivals and an arrival queue at the application interface.

4.2 A communication model

Let us consider the behaviour of the application process running on the i-th node (figure 5). Every computational step produces some new information which is destined for the j-th node. There are then two possibilities, depending on how the application is distributed:

1. i = j . The information remains in LM and no request to send is generated; the process continues with the next computational step.
2. i <> j . The information has to be sent from LM to the j-th node through the network. A

request to send a message to node j is generated and the process continuation depends on the respective node architecture.

If we assume that either architecture uses a transmit queue, whether handled concurrently by P and CE or using internal concurrency on only P, then providing a sufficient large queue is used (or sensible injection rate bounds are used) we may use the following model.

When the application process running on P reaches a request to send, a command block to be read by the driver process for that message is written to a queue in LM. The CP or P empties the queue in a FIFO manner as the network interface becomes free. There then follows the network delay, which is fully modelled in our simulation and based on previously published work[MIL]. When the packet reaches the arrival buffer, a request is addressed to the driver process to receive a message, which is then transferred to LM for use by the application process. This may be realized in two ways:

- Asynchronous message passing. A queue is organized from the messages having arrived in LM, which are read and used by the application process, at any time, on its own initiative.
- Interrupt driven message passing. After the message is written to LM, an interrupt is sent to the application process to deal with the message.

In its most general form this model may be represented by figure 3, where the application process is modelled as in figure 5 and where the Send, Transmit, Arrival and Receive processes introduce deterministic delays and the two queues must be modelled in some manner due to their non-deterministic nature. However, in the light of the assumptions above, we assume that the Send delay is negligible and that the application is always able to receive the incoming message. The model simulated therefore is as shown in figure 4, where again the application process is modelled as in figure 5. The Transmit process represents the deterministic delay that the communication driver experiences in transferring the message to the communication network. In our simulations this is based on estimates of a two channel DMA transfer interface between a T800 transputer and the network. The Arrival/Receive process represents a similar delay for unloading the network. The justification for the application model is considered separately in the next section.

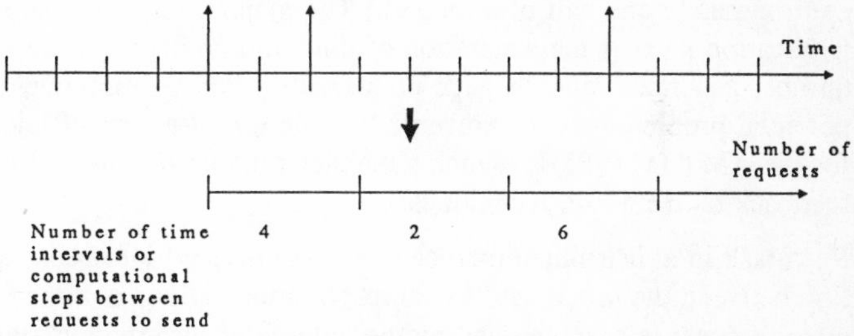

Figure 6. Requests to send plotted on two axes to support the justification of the proposition that requests have Poisson distribution.

4.3 Proposition

We propose that the requests to send generated by the above model has a Poisson distribution. This proposition defines the relation between (i = j) and (i <> j).

Let us examine once again the requests to send experienced within the application, figure 5. The distance between two subsequent send requests is defined by a random number of computational steps. This figure may be redrawn on the time axis as in figure 6, whose axis is measured in units of time t. Let us now represent this process on a new axis x, which is measured in units of the number of send requests. We can relate the two axes by annotating this x axis with the number of time intervals between requests. The set of time intervals is randomly distributed along x, which in turn defines the same number of time intervals between two subsequent send requests as is shown the time axis. The nature of the send request generation is such that the conditional probability to have n-time cycles in the interval between two subsequent send requests is independent of the number of time cycles in any other interval. Thus the set of time intervals is collectively random [FRY] and hence the conditions under which the Poison distribution is exactly applicable are satisfied and the probability to have x send requests after n time cycles is:

$$P(n,x) = (kx)^n e^{-kx}/n!.$$

5. Implementation

The simulations presented here are based on simulations of an implementation of a 2-dimensional array of 1024 nodes implementing the ‘mad-postman’ routing strategy[MIL]. The simulation of the communication network is based on the logic level implementation of a chip currently being designed its results are therefore exact; we assume 30MHz operation. The interface simulation is based on estimates of runtime for a software driver for a DMA channel interface also being designed for the T800 transputer and the ‘mad-postman’ network chip.

The simulation is implemented on an AMT DAP510, written in C and FORTRAN +. The results presented in this paper were made possible by modelling and implementing the applications layer, which generates random requests to send messages. The messages are sent to randomly addressed nodes with a uniform distribution, as outlined in section 4. The parameters which may be varied within this simulation are the average injection rate, its deviation and the message length. The average injection rate is uniform for all 1024 nodes in the system.

Although the simulation of the communication network is performed efficiently on the AMT DAP, we were concerned that the implementation layer should not dominate the iteration time for the network. (In the original network simulator one clock cycle was simulated in approximately one half of a second.) The major computational requirement for the application layer is the generation of random numbers and the AMT supplied random number generator routines gave poor results and was moreover inefficiently executed. This potential problem was circumvented by the use of a very efficient random number generator for the AMT DAP[SMI], which generates random numbers of excellent quality using linear feedback shift register techniques.

Each task in a distributed memory model is divided into process execution and communication between the processes. As far as communications in this simulation are concerned, every process is characterized by the volume of information which it has to transmit through the network to other application processes. This will change for the network under consideration according to the performance of the chosen processor or computation to communication ratio of the application. By varying this volume we can find the throughput limitations per single node of a communication network.

Ideally the information to be transferred through the network should be sent immediately after it has been generated, the exchanged messages length should be small, but the sending frequency will be high. This case is known as a fine grain parallelism. It is natural to aim to ensure such a mode of operation in a distributed memory system, but the use of brief communications may reduce the network throughput. It is for this reason that the simulation of Latency = f(Message length) for a given throughput is particularly important.

The degree of regularity of the injection requests in an application is roughly represented by means of the deviation parameter. The larger the changes in the injection requests through different periods of the application process execution, the higher the deviation. It is by means of deviation that the particularities of a given application are represented. The length of the queues (send and receive) depends on the deviation and on the working area chosen for the injection delay.

6. Simulation Results

Figure 7 shows the main simulation results for a four plane 'mad postman' network using 6, 16 and 32 byte messages. Each point on this graph represents the average of approximately 1 msec of network operation or the cumulative result of between 1 and 15 thousand messages injected per node, depending on message length and injection rate. Because we simulate a uniform network load, the total network throughput can be obtained by multiplying the injection rate by the number of nodes (1024 in this simulation). Moreover, because each message is addressed to a random location it will traverse a number of network nodes. Thus the average bandwidth for each network node may be obtained by multiplying the injection bandwidth by the average number of nodes traversed (21 nodes in this simulation).

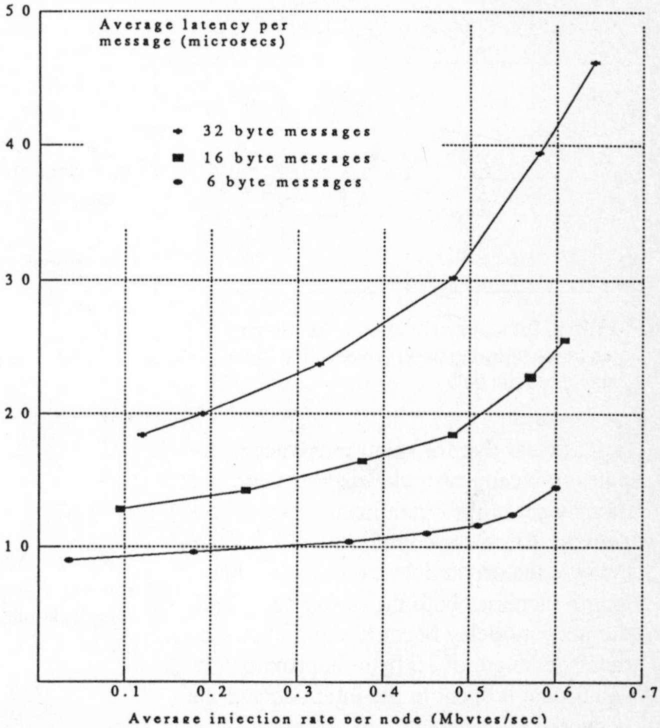

Figure 7. Results of the distributed memory simulation facility showing average message latency against average injection rate per node using the mad-postman network. The three curves show latency for 6, 16 and 32 byte messages.

The graph clearly shows that, as expected, latency increases with increased throughput. This increase is initially slow, especially for short messages, but as the network capacity is approached latency increases rapidly. In this simulation this occurs at an injection rate of approximately 0.6 Mbytes per second of data injected at each node, or a total network capacity of 600 Mbytes per second. This represents a node-bandwidth of approximately 100 out of the total possible bandwidth of 240 Mbits per second per node (30 Mbits per second for each of two channels in each of four planes).

Figures 8,9 and 10 show a breakdown of the delays involved in the latency shown in figure 7. The combined driver delay (injection and arrival) is a constant (6.7 microseconds) and in each case the lower curve shows the total interface delay, which comprises the combined driver delay and the queue delay, and the upper curve is the total latency as plotted in figure

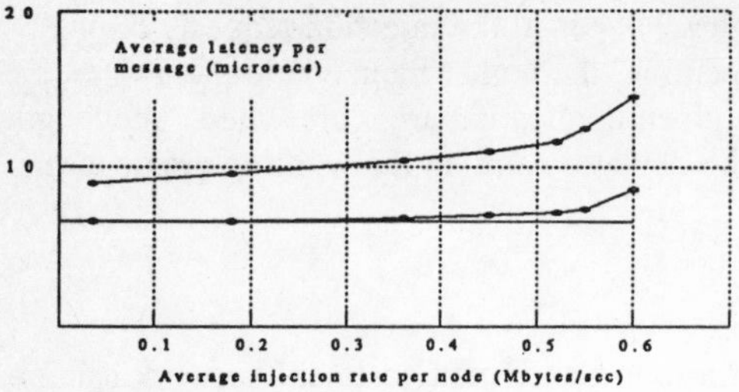

Figure 8. Breakdown of latency for 6 byte messages showing fixed driver delay, queue delay and total delay.

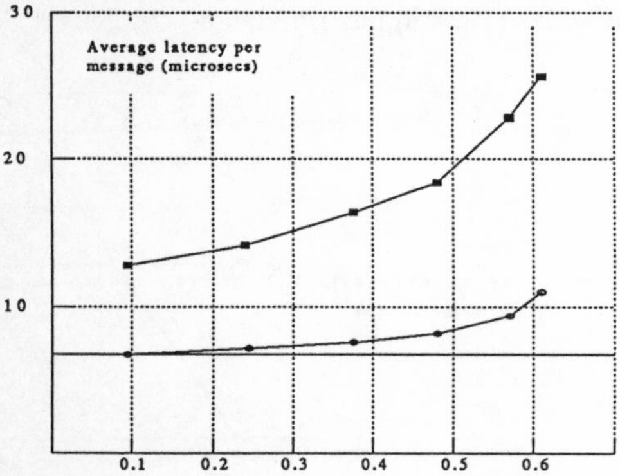

Figure 9. Breakdown of latency for 16 byte messages showing fixed driver delay, queue delay and total delay.

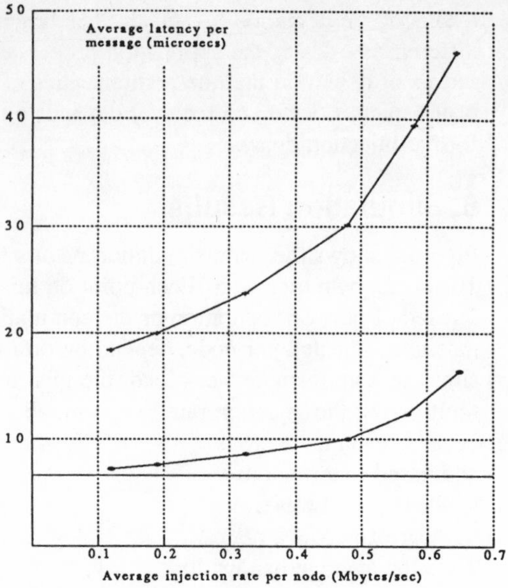

Figure 10. Breakdown of latency for 32 byte messages showing fixed driver delay, queue delay and total delay.

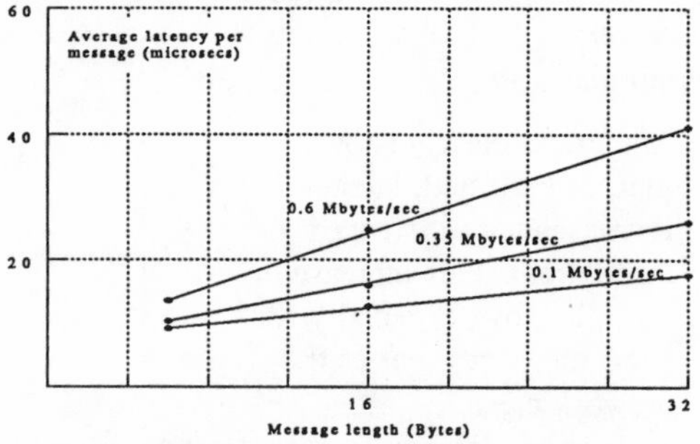

Figure 11. Average message latency against message length for three values of message length simulated.

7. It is clear that for small messages of 6 bytes (typically two address bytes and four data bytes) in the operational region of the network the major component of message delay is the driver delay, but that as message length increases both the queue delay and the network delay become significant. For a message length of 16 bytes approximately equal time is spent in the interface and the network.

Finally in figure 11 we show the average message latency against message length for different injection rates. It is interesting to note that in all cases there is an approximately linear dependence of latency against message length, but that as injection rate increases so does the slope of this relationship.

7. Conclusions

We have presented a simulation facility based on the 'mad-postman' network routing strategy which models not only the network operation but also the interface between the application running on the distributed memory system and the communication network. This facility has been used to present results of application message latency against network throughput. These results define an operational region for this network and application model where, in applications which address messages randomly to other nodes with uniform distribution, the upper bound of injection rate should be approximately 0.6 Mbyte per second per node. This corresponds to an average duty cycle of a little under 50% for each node in the network. Clearly if network size is decreases then the average injection rate defining the operational region of the network will increase linearly with the linear dimension of the network.

The dependence between average message latency and average injection rate is probably the most significant relationship in determining what is a well balanced distributed memory computer system. Supposing that the application is known, in particular the ratio of computation to communication and the degree of parallelism. As we are able to predict the message latency as a function of injection rate, then we may match an appropriate type of processor to accompany the mad-postman network chip, or alternatively determine the number of mad-postman network chips that should be interfaced to a given processor.

Thus a design strategy based on realistic simulation will allow system designers to squeeze the highest possible cost/performance from the triple: application, computation architecture, communication architecture.

8. Acknowledgements

We would like to acknowledge the work of Mr P Miller in the development of the mad-postman network simulator used as a basis for the facility described in this paper. We also acknowledge the SERC for the support of the design and implementation of the mad-postman communication chip and finally the Bulgarian Academy of Sciences for the support of Dr V Getov, during his sabbatical visit to Southampton University.

9. References

[BAI] Baillie C.F. Comparing Shared and Distributed Memory Computers. Parallel Computing 8, 1988, pp.101-110.

[DAL] Dally W.J., C.L. Seitz. Deadlock-Free Message Routing in Multiprocessor Interconnection Networks. IEEE Trans. Comput., vol.C-36, No. 5, May 1987, pp. 547-553.

[FRY] Fry T.C. Probability and Its Engineering Uses. D. van Nostrand Company, 1965.

[KER] Kermani P., L. Kleinrock. Virtual Cut-Through: A New Computer Communication Switching Technique. Computer Networks, No.3, 1979, pp. 267-286.

[MIL] Miller P.R., J.T. Yantchev. Developing Powerful Communication Mechanisms for Distributed Memory Computers from Simple and Efficient Message-Routing. Proceedings of DMCC5, Charleston, South Carolina, April 9-12, 1990.

[REE] Reed D., R. Fujimoto. Multicomputer Networks: Message-Based Parallel Processing. The MIT Press, 1987.

[SMI] Smith K.A., S.F. Reddaway, D.M. Scott. Very High Performance Pseudo-Random Number Generation on DAP. Computer Physics Communications 37 (1985) 239-244. North-Holland, Amsterdam.

[YAN] Yantchev J.T., C.R. Jesshope. Adaptive, Low-Latency, Deadlock-Free Packet-Routing for Networks of Processors. IEE Proc.E, vol.136, No.3, May 1989, pp. 178-186.

ON THE DESIGN OF DEADLOCK-FREE ADAPTIVE ROUTING ALGORITHMS FOR MULTICOMPUTERS: THEORETICAL ASPECTS

J. Duato
Facultad de Informática. Universidad Politécnica de Valencia
P.O.B. 22012. 46071 - Valencia, Spain

Abstract

Second generation multicomputers use wormhole routing, drastically reducing the dependency between network latency and internode distance. Deadlock-free routing strategies have been developed, allowing the implementation of fast hardware routers. Also, adaptive routing algorithms with deadlock-avoidance or deadlock-recovery techniques have been proposed for some topologies, being very effective and outperforming static strategies.

This paper develops the theoretical aspects for the design of deadlock-free adaptive routing algorithms. Some basic definitions and three theorems are proposed, developing conditions to verify that an adaptive algorithm is deadlock-free, even when there are cycles in the channel dependency graph. As an example, a new adaptive algorithm for 2D-meshes is presented.

1. Introduction

Multicomputers [1] rely on an interconnection network between processors to support the message-passing mechanism. The network latency [1] can be defined as the time from when the head of a message enters the network at the source until the tail emerges at the destination. In first generation multicomputers, a store-and-forward mechanism has been used to route messages. Each time a message reaches a node, it is buffered in local memory, and the processor interrupted to execute the routing algorithm. Accordingly, the network latency is proportional to the distance between the origin and the destination.

However, in second generation multicomputers, the message routing hardware uses a mechanism known as wormhole routing [9]. As messages are typically at least a few words long, each message is serialized into a sequence of parallel data units, referred to as flow control units, or flits [8]. The flit at the head of a message governs the route. As the header flit advances along the specified route, the remaining flits follow it in a pipeline fashion. If the header encounters a channel already in use, it is blocked until the channel is freed; the flow control within the network blocks the trailing flits.

This research is supported by CICYT grant number TIC 87-0655

This form of routing and flow control has two important advantages over the store-and-forward packet routing. Firstly, it avoids using storage bandwidth in the nodes through which messages are routed. Secondly, this routing technique makes the message latency largely insensitive to the distance in the message-passing network. Since the flits move through the network in a pipeline fashion, in the absence of channel contention, the network latency equals the sum of two terms:

- T_pD is the time associated with forming the path through the network, where T_p is the delay of the individual routing nodes found on the path, and D is the number of nodes traversed.

- L/B is the time required for a message of length L to pass through a channel of bandwidth B.

In second generation multicomputers, the network latency is dominated by the second term for all but very short messages.

Another improvement in message performance results from selecting the optimal topology for the implementation on printed circuit boards or VLSI chips. As message latency is dominated by the term L/B, more wirable network topologies will increase the bandwidth B at the expense of increasing the network diameter. An analysis [5,7] shows that, under the assumption of constant number of wires through the network bisection, a two dimensional network minimizes latency for typical message lengths for up to 1024 nodes. For larger sizes, a three dimensional network achieves better performance. Among these networks, meshes are preferred because they offer useful edge connectivity, which can be used for I/O controllers. Also, meshes partition into units that are still meshes, simplifying the design of routing algorithms that are independent of the network size, as well as the implementation of space-sharing techniques.

However, deadlocks may appear if the routing algorithms are not carefully designed. A deadlock in the interconnection network of a multicomputer occurs when no message can advance toward its destination because the queues of the message system are full. The size of the queues strongly influences the probability to reach a deadlocked configuration. First generation multicomputers buffer full messages or relatively large packets. By contrary, second generation machines buffer flits, being more deadlock-prone. So, the only practical way to avoid deadlock is to design deadlock-free routing algorithms.

Many deadlock-free routing algorithms have been developed for store-and-forward computer networks [11,13,19]. These algorithms are based on a structured buffer pool. However, with wormhole routing, buffer allocation cannot be restricted, because flits have no routing information. Once the header of a message has been accepted by a channel, the remaining flits must be accepted before the flits of any other message can be accepted. So, routing must be restricted to avoid deadlock.

Dally [9] has proposed a methodology to design static routing algorithms under general assumptions. He defines a channel dependency graph and establishes a total order among channels. Routing is restricted to visit channels in decreasing or increasing order to eliminate cycles in the channel dependency graph. This methodology has been applied to the design of routing chips for multicomputers [8] and multicomputer nodes with integrated communication support [2]. It has also been applied to systolic communication [18,2].

The restriction of routing, although avoids deadlock, can increase traffic jams, specially in heavily loaded networks with long messages. In order to avoid congested regions of the network, an adaptive routing algorithm can be used. Adaptive strategies have been shown to outperform static ones in store-and-forward routing [3] and in packet-switched communications [17,20]. In general, adaptive routing needs additional hardware support.

Several adaptive algorithms have been developed for wormhole routing. A deadlock-free adaptive algorithm for the hypercube is the Hyperswitch algorithm [4], which is based on backtracking and hardware modification of message headers to avoid congestion and cycles. Another deadlock-free adaptive algorithm has been proposed for the MEGA [12]. This algorithm always routes messages, sending them away from their destination if necessary, like the Connection Machine [14]. If a message arrives to a node without free output channels, deadlocks are avoided by storing the message and removing it from the network. In this respect, it is similar to virtual cut-through [16]. Jesshope [15] has proposed an algorithm for n dimensional meshes, by decomposing them into 2n virtual networks. Inside each virtual network, displacements along a given dimension are always made in the same direction, thus avoiding cycles and deadlock.

An alternative way consists of recovering from deadlock. Reeves et al. [21] have used an abort-and-retry technique to remove messages blocked for longer than a certain threshold from the network. Aborted messages are introduced again into the network after a random delay. In [21] three adaptive routing strategies have been proposed and evaluated for a binary 8-cube.

In a previous paper [10] we have proposed a very simple methodology to design deadlock-free adaptive routing algorithms for wormhole networks. The routing algorithms obtained from the application of that methodology to 2D and 3D-meshes have been evaluated by simulation.

This paper develops the theoretical aspects for the design of deadlock-free adaptive routing algorithms. Some basic definitions and three theorems are proposed, developing conditions to verify that an adaptive algorithm is deadlock-free, even when there are cycles in the channel dependency graph. As an example, a new adaptive algorithm for a 2D-mesh is presented.

2. Definitions and theorems

The basic assumptions are very similar to the ones proposed by Dally [9], except that adaptive routing is allowed. These assumptions are the following:

1) A node can generate messages destined for any other node at any rate.

2) A message arriving at its destination node is eventually consumed.

3) Wormhole routing is used. So, once a queue accepts the first flit of a message, it must accept the remainder of the message before accepting any flits from another message.

4) A node can generate messages of arbitrary length. Packets will generally be longer than a single flit.

5) An available queue may arbitrate between messages that request that queue, but may not choose among waiting messages.

6) The route taken by a message depends on its destination and the status of output channels (free or busy). At a given node, the routing function supplies a set of output channels based on the current and destination nodes. A selection from this set is made based on the status of output channels at the current node. So, *adaptive* routing will be considered (this will be the default when not explicitly stated).

Before to propose the theorems, some definitions are needed:

Definition 1: An *interconnection network* I is a strongly connected directed multigraph, I = G(N, C). The vertices of the multigraph N represent the set of processing nodes. The edges of the multigraph C represent the set of communication channels. More than a single channel is allowed to connect a given pair of nodes. Each channel c_i has an associated queue denoted queue(c_i) with capacity cap(c_i). The source and destination nodes of channel c_i are denoted s_i and d_i, respectively.

Definition 2: Let B be the set of valid *channel status*, B = {free, busy}. Let T: C →B be the status of the output channels in the network.

Definition 3: An *adaptive routing function* R: N x N → C^p supplies a set of p alternative channels to send a message from the current node n_c to the destination node n_d, $R(n_c, n_d) = \{c_1, c_2, \dots c_p\}$. In general, p will be less than the number of output channels per node to obtain deadlock-free algorithms. As a particular case, p = 1 defines a static routing function. Also, the channels in the set supplied by R are not necessarily different. So, p is the maximum number of choices. In particular, $R(n, n) = \emptyset, \quad \forall n \in N$.

Definition 4: A *selection function* S: C^p x B^p → C selects a free output channel from the set supplied by the routing function. From the definition, S takes into account the status of all the channels belonging to the set supplied by the routing function. The selection can be either random or based on static or dynamic priorities. It is even possible to take into account additional information, such as the time a message is waiting for free channels, thus extending the definition of the selection function. Also, in the same way the result of a static routing function may be a busy channel, if all the output channels are busy, any of them is selected. The decomposition of the adaptive routing into two functions (routing and selection) is critical, because only the routing function determines whether a routing algorithm is deadlock-free or not. The selection function only affects the performance. Its influence must be evaluated by simulation. A deeper study falls out of the scope of this paper.

Definition 5: A routing function R for a given interconnection network I is *connected* iff

$$\forall i, j \in N, \quad i \neq j, \quad \exists c_1, c_2, \dots c_k \in C \ni$$

$$c_1 \in R(i, j) \quad \wedge \quad c_{m+1} \in R(d_m, j) \quad \forall m \in \{1, k-1\} \quad \wedge \quad d_k = j$$

In other words, it is possible to establish a path between i and j using channels belonging to the sets supplied by R. Notice that the interconnection network is strongly connected, but it does not imply that the routing function must be connected.

Definition 6: A *routing subfunction* R_1 for a given routing function R and channel subset $C_1 \subseteq C$, is a routing function R_1: $N \times N \rightarrow C_1^q$, $0 < q \leq p \ni$

$$\forall i, j \in N \quad R_1(i, j) = R(i, j) \cap C_1$$

Definition 7: A *channel dependency graph* D for a given interconnection network I and routing function R, is a directed graph, D = G(C, E). The vertices of D are the channels of I. The edges of D are the pairs of channels $\ni$

$$E = \{ (c_i , c_j) \mid c_i \in R(s_i , n) \wedge c_j \in R(d_i , n) \quad \text{for some } n \in N \}$$

Notice that $n \neq d_i$. Also, there are no 1-cycles in D, because channels are unidirectional.

Definition 8: A *sink* for a given interconnection network I and routing function R is a channel $c_i \ni$

$$\forall j \in N, \quad c_i \in R(s_i , j) \quad \Rightarrow \quad j = d_i$$

In other words, all the flits that enter a sink channel reach their destination in a single hop. As a result, there are no outgoing arcs from a sink channel in the channel dependency graph D, as can be easily seen from the definitions.

Definition 9: A *configuration* is an assignment of a list of nodes to each queue. The number of flits in the queue for channel c_i will be denoted size(c_i). The destination of a flit j will be denoted dest(j). However, if the first flit in the queue for channel c_i is destined for node n_d, then head(c_i) = n_d. A configuration is *legal* iff

$$\forall c_i \in C, \quad \text{size}(c_i) \leq \text{cap}(c_i) \quad \wedge \quad c_i \in R(s_i , \text{dest}(j)) \quad \forall j \in \text{queue}(c_i)$$

that is, the queue capacity is not exceeded and all the flits stored in the queue have been sent there by the routing function.

Definition 10: A *deadlocked configuration* for a given interconnection network I and routing function R is a nonempty legal configuration $\ni$

$$\forall c_i \in C \mid \text{head}(c_i) \in N \quad \Rightarrow \quad \text{head}(c_i) \neq d_i \quad \wedge$$

$$\wedge \quad (\text{size}(c_j) = \text{cap}(c_j) \quad \forall c_j \in R(d_i , \text{head}(c_i)) \quad \vee \quad R(d_i , \text{head}(c_i)) = \emptyset)$$

In this configuration there is not any flit one hop from its destination. Flits cannot advance because the queues for all the alternative output channels supplied by the routing function are full. Alternatively (for disconnected routing functions), the routing function does not supply any output channel. The expression head(c_i) $\in$ N means that the queue associated to c_i is not empty. So, a deadlocked configuration does not imply that all the queues are full.

Definition 11: A routing function R for an interconnection network I is *deadlock-free* iff it does not exist any deadlocked configuration for that routing function on that network.

Taking into account the previous definitions, we propose the following theorems:

Theorem 1: A connected and adaptive routing function R for an interconnection network I is deadlock-free if there are no cycles in the channel dependency graph D.

There are some interesting considerations:

1) The theorem gives a sufficient but not necessary condition for an adaptive routing function to be deadlock-free. As will be seen later, the existence of cycles in the channel dependency graph does not imply the existence of deadlocked configurations.

2) For most networks and routing functions, even for static ones, only a partial ordering between channels can be defined, based on the set E. In general, there will be more than a single sink in D.

Theorem 2: A connected and adaptive routing function R for an interconnection network I is deadlock-free if it exists a subset of channels $C_1 \subseteq C$ that defines a routing subfunction R_1 which is connected and has no cycles in its channel dependency graph D_1 .

Again, there are some interesting considerations:

1) The basic idea behind theorem 2 is that one can have an adaptive routing function with cyclic dependencies between channels, provided that there are alternative paths without cyclic dependencies to send a given flit towards its destination.

2) If the routing function were defined as $R: C \times N \rightarrow C^p$, then the theorem would not be valid. Consider, for instance, two subsets of C, namely, C_1 and $C - C_1$, and a routing function defined in such a way that all the messages arriving to a given node through a channel belonging to $C - C_1$ are routed through a channel belonging to the same subset. Suppose that there are cyclic dependencies between the channels belonging to $C - C_1$ and that C_1 defines a routing subfunction which is connected and has no cycles in its channel dependency graph. That routing function is not deadlock-free.

3) The routing subfunction R_1 is not necessarily static. It can be adaptive.

Theorem 3: A connected and adaptive routing function R for an interconnection network I is deadlock-free if it exists a channel subset $C_1 \subseteq C$ that defines a deadlock-free routing subfunction R_1.

Once again, another consideration:

1) At first glance, this theorem seems useless. However, it will allow us to define more flexible design methodologies. One can think about a routing function which has a deadlock-free routing subfunction with cycles in its channel dependency graph, which in turn has a connected routing subfunction without cycles in its channel dependency graph.

The proofs of the theorems will be given in another paper.

3. Design example

The generation of static deadlock-free routing algorithms requires to restrict routing by removing edges from D to make it acyclic. If it is not possible to make D acyclic without disconnecting the routing function, edges can be added to D by splitting physical channels into a set of virtual channels, each one requiring its own buffer. This technique was introduced by Dally [9] to remove cycles from the channel dependency graph.

However, a physical channel can be split into more virtual channels than the ones strictly necessary to avoid deadlock [6,10]. In such a case, the router can choose among several channels to send a message, reducing channel contention and message delay. Alternatively, more physical channels can be added to each node, increasing the network bandwidth and allowing the design of adaptive routing algorithms.

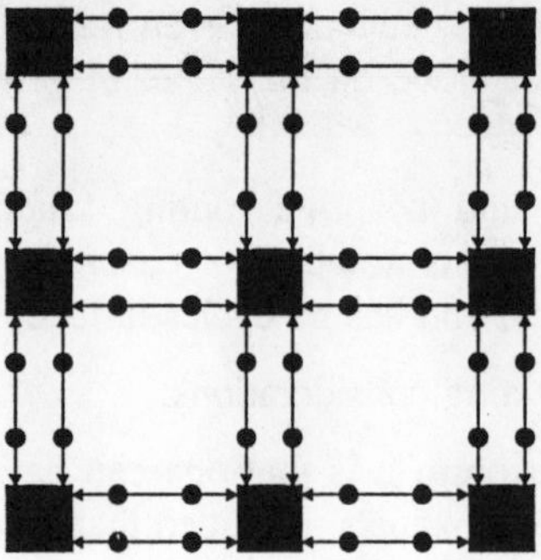

Figure 1. 3 x 3 mesh

Here we will present a design example based on the above proposed theorems. Consider a 2D-mesh in which each node (except the ones on the border) has two (physical or virtual) output channels in each direction (north, south, east and west). The channels in direction north are named east-north and west-north, channels in direction east are named north-east and south-east and so on. For a given message, the relative distance between the source and destination nodes will be decomposed into two terms, namely, ΔX and ΔY. The X and Y axes are considered positive in east and south direction, respectively.

The routing algorithm is somewhat long to describe, because there are several options:

If $\Delta X > 0$ and $\Delta Y > 0$ then use either south-east or east-south
If $\Delta X > 0$ and $\Delta Y < 0$ then use either north-east or east-north
If $\Delta X < 0$ and $\Delta Y > 0$ then use either south-west or west-south
If $\Delta X < 0$ and $\Delta Y < 0$ then use either north-west or west-north
If $\Delta X = 0$ and $\Delta Y > 0$ then use either east-south or west-south
If $\Delta X = 0$ and $\Delta Y < 0$ then use either east-north or west-north
If $\Delta X > 0$ and $\Delta Y = 0$ then use either south-east or north-east
If $\Delta X < 0$ and $\Delta Y = 0$ then use either south-west or north-west

Figure 1 shows a small 2D-mesh as described. Nodes are represented by squares. Channels are bidirectional. Each one has two small circles on it (one for each direction), indicating the position of the channels in the following figures. Figure 2 shows the channel dependency graph for the proposed algorithm and the network of figure 1. For the sake of clarity, some arrows have two arrowheads. If we remove some channels (for instance, west-south and west-north) from all the nodes, the resulting routing subfunction is still connected. Its channel dependency graph has no cycles, as can be seen in figure 3. So, applying theorem 2, the proposed routing algorithm is deadlock-free.

So far as we know, the above proposed algorithm has not been published elsewhere (there are some similarities between it and the one proposed by Jesshope [15], but our algorithm is more flexible because when a message has to move always in the same direction (e. g. when $\Delta Y = 0$), it supplies two alternative channels instead of one). Although we designed it some time ago, we could not prove that it was deadlock-free until the development of theorem 2.

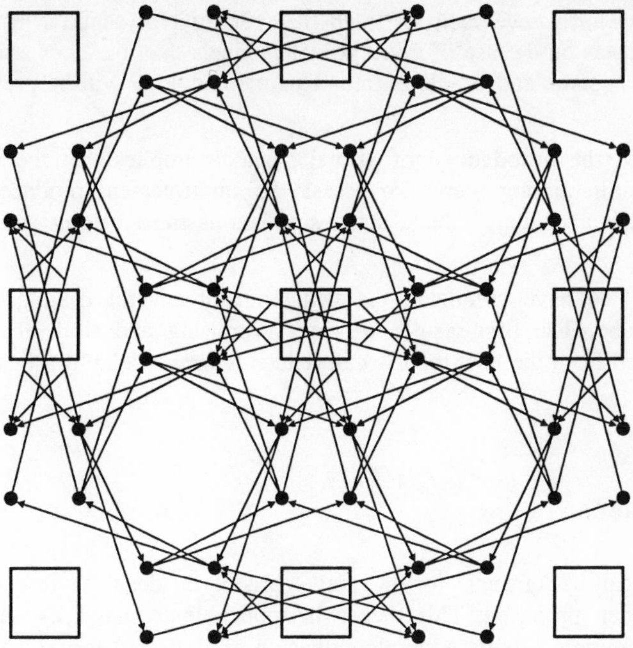

Figure 2. Channel dependency graph for R

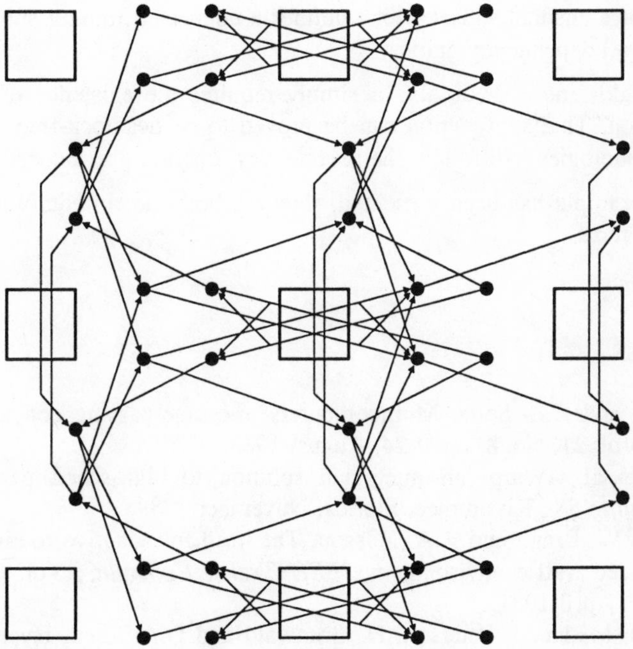

Figure 3. Channel dependency graph for R_1

Currently, we have developed a design methodology for adaptive routing algorithms, with special emphasis on the use of more virtual channels than the ones strictly necessary to make the algorithm static and deadlock-free. This methodology will be presented in another paper.

Unfortunately, the introduction of virtual channels implies that the physical channel shares its bandwidth among them. To assess the improvement produced by the above presented algorithm and many others, some simulations must be run under different load conditions.

Up to now, we have simulated the behaviour of several routing algorithms on a 256-node hypercube. The first results are very promising and show that some adaptive algorithms, derived from the new theory, can reduce message delay drastically, specially for short messages.

4. Conclusions

The theoretical background for the development of deadlock-free adaptive routing algorithms has been proposed. This theory is applicable to networks with any topology using wormhole routing. Firstly, a simple extension of Dally's theorem has been presented, allowing the design of adaptive algorithms. However, the absence of cycles in the channel dependency graph is too restrictive.

Theorem 2 gives a more flexible condition for the development of adaptive algorithms, by allowing the existence of cycles in the channel dependency graph. The only requirement is the existence of a channel subset which defines a connected routing subfunction with no cycles in its channel dependency graph.

Theorem 3 adds more flexibility. It simply requires the existence of a deadlock-free routing subfunction. That subfunction can be proved to be deadlock-free using theorem 2. The design methodologies will follow the reverse way, operating in a constructive manner.

Finally, an example has been presented, showing both the simplicity and the power of the proposed theorems.

References

[1] W.C. Athas and C.L. Seitz, Multicomputers: message-passing concurrent computers, *Computer*, Vol. 21, No. 8, pp. 9-24, August 1988.

[2] S. Borkar et al., iWarp: an integrated solution to high-speed parallel computing, *Supercomputing'88* , Kissimmee, Florida, November 1988.

[3] W. Chou, A.W. Bragg and A.A. Nilsson, The need for adaptive routing in the chaotic and unbalanced traffic environment, *IEEE Trans. Commun.*, Vol. COM-29, No. 4, pp. 481-490, April 1981.

[4] E. Chow, H. Madan, J. Peterson, D. Grunwald and D.A. Reed, Hyperswitch network for the hypercube computer, *Proc. 15th Int. Symp. Computer Architecture*, Honolulu, May-June 1988.

[5] W.J. Dally, *A VLSI architecture for concurrent data structures*, Kluwer Academic Publishers, 1987.

[6] W.J. Dally, Virtual-channel flow control, *Proc. 17th Int. Symp. Computer Architecture*, Seattle, Washington, May 1990.

[7] W.J. Dally, Performance analysis of k-ary n-cube interconnection networks, *IEEE Trans. Computers*, Vol. C-39, No. 6, pp. 775-785, June 1990.

[8] W.J. Dally and C.L. Seitz, The torus routing chip, *Distributed Computing*, Vol. 1, No. 3, pp. 187-196, October 1986.

[9] W.J. Dally and C.L. Seitz, Deadlock-free message routing in multiprocessor interconnection networks, *IEEE Trans. Computers*, Vol. C-36, No. 5, pp. 547-553, May 1987.

[10] J. Duato, Deadlock-free adaptive routing algorithms for multicomputers. Submitted to *Tech. et Sci. Informatique* .

[11] D. Gelernter, A DAG-based algorithm for prevention of store-and-forward deadlock in packet networks, *IEEE Trans. Computers*, Vol. C-30, pp. 709-715, October 1981.

[12] C. Germain-Renaud, Etude des mécanismes de communication pour une machine massivement parallèle: MEGA, Ph.D. dissertation, Université de Paris-Sud, Centre d'Orsay, 1989.

[13] K.D. Gunther, Prevention of deadlocks in packet-switched data transport systems, *IEEE Trans. Commun.*, Vol. COM-29, pp. 512-524, April 1981.

[14] W.D. Hillis, *The Connection Machine*, MIT Press, Cambridge, Mass., 1985.

[15] C.R. Jesshope, P.R. Miller and J.T. Yantchev, High performance communications in processor networks, *Proc. 16th Int. Symp. Computer Architecture*, Jerusalem, Israel, May-June 1989.

[16] P. Kermani and L. Kleinrock, Virtual cut-through: a new computer communication switching technique, *Computer Networks*, Vol. 3, pp. 267-286, 1979.

[17] C.K. Kim and D.A. Reed, Adaptive packet routing in a hypercube, *Proc. 3rd Conf. on Hypercube Concurrent Computers & Applications*, Pasadena, California, January 1988.

[18] H.T. Kung, Deadlock avoidance for systolic communication, *Proc. 15th Int. Symp. Computer Architecture*, Honolulu, May-June 1988.

[19] P.M. Merlin and P.J. Schweitzer, Deadlock avoidance in store-and-forward networks - I: Store-and-forward deadlock, *IEEE Trans. Commun.*, Vol. COM-28, pp. 345-354, March 1980.

[20] S. Ragupathy, M.R. Leutze and S.R. Schach, Message routing schemes in a hypercube machine, *Proc. 3rd Conf. on Hypercube Concurrent Computers & Applications*, Pasadena, California, January 1988.

[21] D.S. Reeves, E.F. Gehringer and A. Chandiramani, Adaptive routing and deadlock recovery: a simulation study, *Proc. 4th Conf. on Hypercube Concurrent Computers & Applications*, Monterey, California, March 1989.

Parallelization of Lee's Routing Algorithm on a Hypercube Multicomputer

Tahsin M. Kurç, Cevdet Aykanat, and **Fikret Erçal**
Faculty of Engineering & Science, Department of CIS
Bilkent University
06533, Bilkent, Ankara, TURKEY

Abstract

Lee's maze routing algorithm is parallelized and implemented on an Intel iPSC/2 hypercube multicomputer. Our contribution to the previous work in [2] is that we propose a new parallel *front wave expansion* scheme which performs two *front wave expansions* concurrently, one starting from the source cell and the other one starting from the target cell. The proposed scheme increases the processor utilization and decreases the total number of interprocessor communications. We experimentally show that our scheme outperforms the scheme given in [2]

1 Introduction

Lee's maze router[1] is a well known algorithm for global wire routing in VLSI. In global routing for gate arrays, a global grid like the one shown in Fig.1(a) will represent the wiring surface when one layer is used for net interconnections. Net terminals are located within the cells. The vertical and horizontal grid lines between neighbor cells represent the channels for wire routing. The overall objective is to realize all the net interconnections using shortest routes. Lee's maze router[1] is then applied to find the shortest interconnection route between individual net terminals in a predetermined order. As the interconnection paths between net terminals are constructed, some of the cells will be declared as *blocked.* Hence, an instance of the global wiring can be shown as shown in Fig. 1(a). Here, for the sake of simplicity, a cell is declared as *blocked* when it is used in a single wire path. In this figure, empty cells represent the *free* cells available for routing and the shaded cells represent the *blocked* cells which are not available for routing. There are two special empty cells as s (source) and t (target) cell. These cells designate the terminal locations of a two-pin net to be constructed at that instance of the global wiring algorithm. Only two pin nets are considered in this paper. Path for a net can go from a cell to a *free* neighbor cell by crossing either a common vertical or horizontal channel. Hence, moves from a cell are restricted to its four adjacent cells (*i.e.* the cells to its *North*, *East*, *South*, and *West* in the maze). Lee's maze routing algorithm consists of three phases, namely, *front wave expansion*, *path recovery*, and *sweeping* [2]. *Front wave expansion* phase is a *breadth-first* search strategy starting from the source cell s. The algorithm for the *front wave expansion* phase is given below.

A queue initially contains only the source cell s. A two dimensional NxN *Status* array holds the status for the cells of an NxN grid. All the *free* cells are initially *unlabeled.*

1. Remove a cell c from the queue.
2. Examine the four adjacent cells of the cell c using the current information in the *Status* array. Discard the *blocked* and already *labeled* adjacent cells. Update the status of the *unlabeled free* adjacent cells as *labeled* in the *Status* array and add those cells to the queue.
3. Go to step 1.

The labeling operation (at Step 2) of a *free* and *unlabeled* adjacent cell is performed such that, the label points to the cell c being expanded. The algorithm terminates successfully when the target cell t is labeled during Step 2 of the algorithm. The algorithm may also terminate when a remove operation from an empty queue is attempted. Such a termination condition indicates the non-existence of a wire-path from the source to the target. The Lee's maze routing algorithm is guaranteed to find the shortest wire path between the source and the target. Fig. 1(b) illustrates the first two cycles of the Lee's algorithm for the example grid shown in Fig. 1(a). Labeling process at Step 2 of the algorithm are illustrated by the following four labels, $\downarrow$, $\leftarrow$, $\uparrow$, and $\rightarrow$ in the figure. The *front wave expansion* phase is followed by the *path recovery* and *sweeping* phases. Fig. 1(c) illustrates the successful termination of the *front wave expansion* phase. Fig. 1(d) shows the final configuration after the *path recovery* and *sweeping* phases.

Since the grid size may be quite large for real VLSI problems, Lee's router algorithm is time consuming and it requires large amount of memory to hold the status of the grid cells. Hence, Lee's algorithm is a good candidate for parallelization on a distributed memory multiprocessor. In this paper, the parallelization of Lee's maze routing algorithm on a commercially available multicomputer implementing the hypercube topology is addressed. The parallelization of the *front wave expansion* phase of the Lee's algorithm and experimental results on an *NCUBE/7* hypercube multicomputer are presented and discussed in [2]. The implementations of the same algorithms proposed in [2] on an iPSC2/d3 are presented in Sections 2-5. Our main contribution to the previous work in [2] is that we propose a new parallel *front wave expansion* scheme which performs two *front wave expansions* concurrently, one starting from the source cell s and the other one starting from the target cell t. This proposed scheme is presented and discussed in Section 2.1. The scheme which is devised to overlap local communication with computation is discussed in Section 3. A different global synchronization scheme which avoids the use of a machine dependent parameter is proposed in Section 4. Section 5 includes the discussion for the asynchronous version of *Expansion Starting from Source and Target (S+T)* scheme. Finally, Section 6 presents the experimental results.

2 Parallel Implementation

The effective parallel implementation of the *front wave expansion* algorithm on a hypercube multicomputer requires the partitioning and mapping of the *expansion* computations and the *status* array. This partitioning and mapping should be performed in a manner that results in low interprocessor communication overhead and low processor idle time. The *atomic* operation can be considered as the *expansion* of a single cell in the current *front wave*. In this *atomic* process, the *north*, *east*, *south*, and *west* adjacent cells of the cell being expanded are examined. Hence, the nature of communication required in *front wave expansion* phase corresponds to a two dimensional mesh. That is, each processor needs to communicate only to its *north*, *east*, *south*, and *west* neighbors. It is well known that, a $2^{\lfloor d/2 \rfloor} \times 2^{\lceil d/2 \rceil}$ processor mesh can be embedded into a d-dimensional hypercube [3]. The trade-off between volume of interprocessor communication and processor utilization is resolved by following the scheme proposed in [2]. The NxN routing grid is first covered by hxw square (or rectangle) subblocks starting from the top left corner and proceeding left to right, top to bottom. Scattered mapping is then applied over the coarse

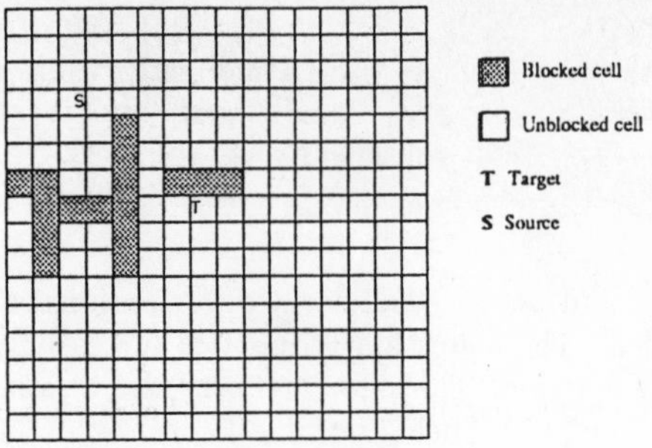

Fig.1.(a) Global Grid

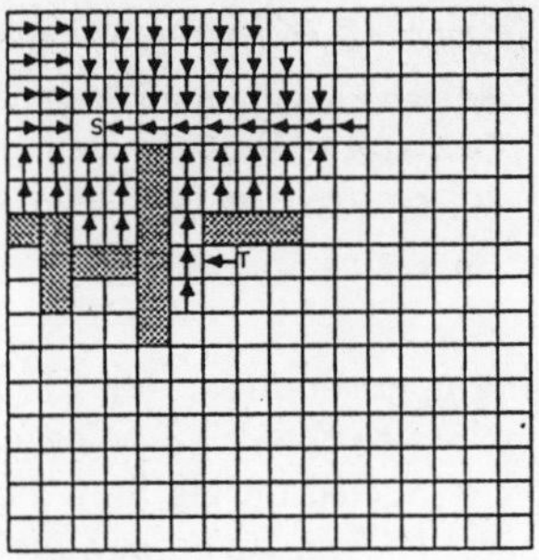

Fig.1.(c) Before path recovery

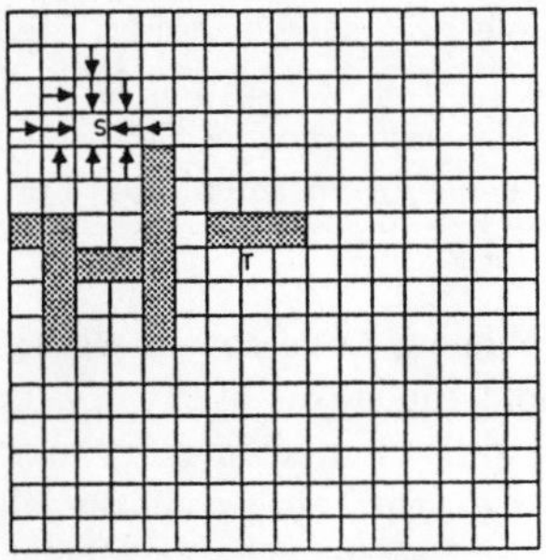

Fig.1.(b) Front Wave expansion

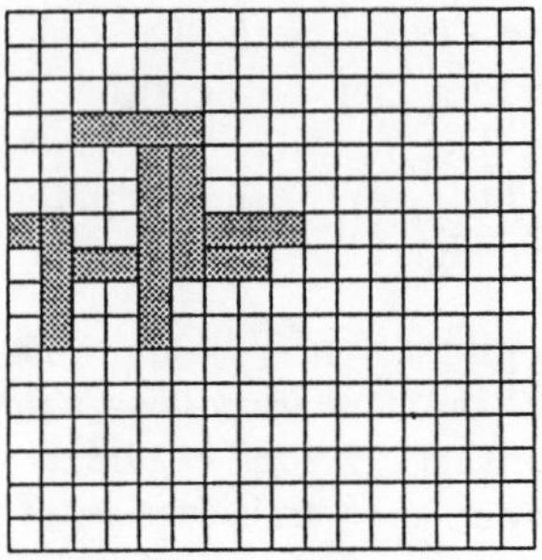

Fig.1.(d) After Sweeping phase

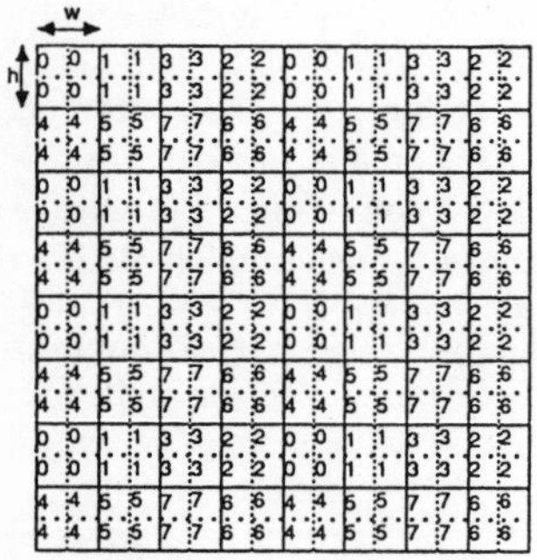

Fig.2.(a) h = w = 2 for 16 x 16 Grid

Fig .2.(b) h = 2w = 4 for 16 x 16 Grid

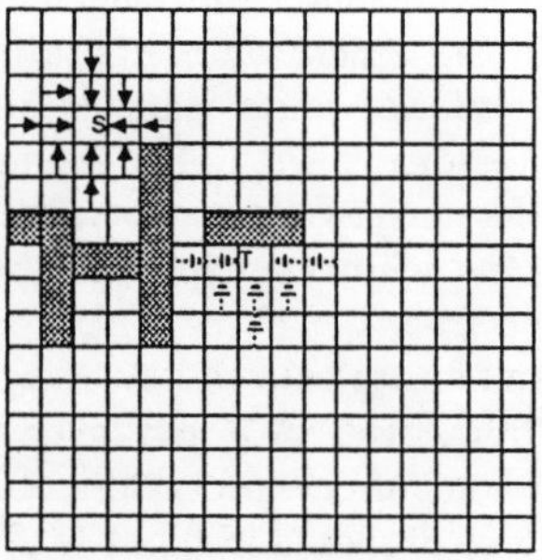

Fig.3.(a). Front Wave expansion
From Source + target. Initial two cycles.

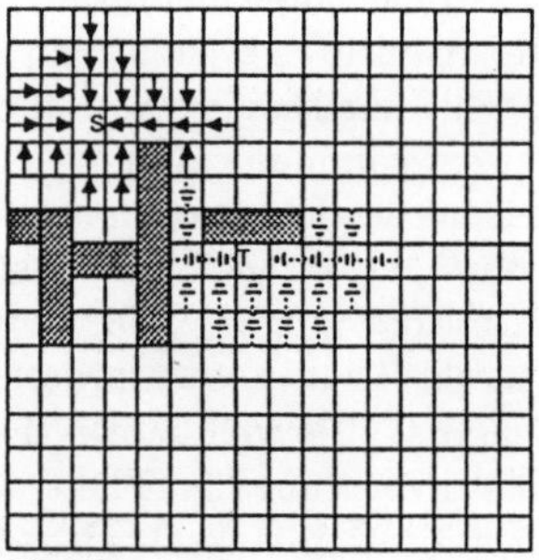

Fig.3.(b). Front wave expansion from
Source + Target.

grid consisting of contiguous *hxw* grid subblocks. Hence, adjacent grid subblocks are assigned to different but neighbor processors of the mesh. The following simplifications presented in [2], $N = 2^n$, both h and w are a power of two, $h = w$ or $h = 2w$, and $h \ll N$, are also maintained in this work. Fig. 2 shows the scattered mapping of 2x2 and 4x2 grid subblocks over a 16x16 routing grid to the processors of a 2x4 processor mesh embedded in a 3-dimensional hypercube.

The first parallel front wave expansion algorithm implemented in this work is very similar to the parallel algorithm given in [2]. This scheme is referred to as *Expansion Starting from Source Only (Sonly)* scheme here. This scheme initiates a *breadth first* search starting from the *source* cell as is indicated in Section 1. In spite of the given partitioning scheme, the *Sonly* scheme may result in low processor utilization for large h and w values. Some processors may still stay idle particularly during the initial and final *front wave expansion* cycles. This is due to the *expansion* of a single *front wave* beginning from the source cell. Note that, finding a routing path from source to target is equivalent to finding a path from target to source. Hence, two *front waves*, one beginning from the source (*source front wave*) and the other one beginning from the target (*target front wave*), can be *expanded* concurrently. If the source and the target cells are assigned to different processors, this scheme has a potential to increase the processor utilization.

2.1 Expansion Starting From Source and Target

This scheme initiates *breadth first* search starting from the *target* cell as well as starting from the *source* cell. Fig. 3(a) illustrates the initial two cycles of this scheme for the example grid shown in Fig. 1(a). The Fig. 3(b) illustrates the *collision* of two concurrent *front waves* initiated from the source cell s and the target cell t. Each processor stores and maintains a local *status* array. Each processor also maintains a local queue to process the *front wave expansion* for local cells, and four *send* and four *receive* queues for communicating with its four neighbor processors. The parallel algorithm is given below.

Initially, all local queues are empty and all local cycle counts are initialized to 1. The host processor broadcasts the coordinates of the *source* cell and the *target* cell to all processors. The processor which owns the source cell location adds the local coordinates of the *source* cell together with a source front wave *tag* to its local queue. Similarly, the processor which owns the *target* cell location adds the local coordinates of the *target* cell together with a *target* front wave *tag* to its local queue. Then each processor executes the following algorithm.

1. The cells in the local queue may belong either to the current *source front wave* or to the current *target front wave*. Each processor examines these cells accordingly for expansion in four directions. The local adjacent cells of the cells being expanded are examined for adding to the local queue for later expansion. The adjacent cells that are detected to belong to grid partitions assigned to neighbor processors are added to the corresponding *send* queues for later communication together with the *tag* of the cells being expanded.
2. Each processor transmits the information in its four *send* queues to their destination processors.
3. The adjacent cells in the four *receive* queues may belong either to the current *source front wave* or to the current *target front wave*. Each processor examines these cells accordingly for adding them to its local queue for later expansion.
4. Each processor, after incrementing its local cycle count by 1, checks whether it has received a message from the host. It proceeds to Step 1 if the message has not been received yet or if the message has been received with an upper bound value greater than or equal to the current value of the local cycle count. It terminates only if the local cycle count value is greater than the upper bound value received, and signal the host about its termination.

Three identifying parameters are needed for each cell in the local queues; its local x,y coordinates, and a *tag* to indicate the type of the *front wave* it belongs to. The cells that belong to the *source front wave* are identified with *positive* x,y coordinate values, whereas, the cells that belong to the *target front wave* are identified with *negative* x,y coordinate values. This *tagging* scheme is chosen in order to keep the local memory requirement due to local queues and the volume of communication low. Similarly, most significant bit of the low byte of each status word is reserved for *tagging* purposes. If a local cell has a *blocked* or *unlabeled* routing status, this bit conveys no information. If, however, a local cell has a *labeled* routing status, the value of this bit indicates whether the cell is *labeled* on the *target front wave*, or *labeled* on the *source front wave.*

During the expansion process at Step 1, the routing status of four adjacent cells of a cell being expanded are examined. If the current routing status of an adjacent cell is *unlabeled*, the local x,y coordinates of the adjacent cell are *tagged* accordingly (depending on the *tag* of the cell being expanded) and added to the local queue for later expansion. Then, the adjacent cell is labeled with the reverse expansion direction and *tagged* with the *tag* of the cell being expanded in the local *status* array. However, if the current routing status of an adjacent cell is *blocked* or *labeled* with the same *tag* of the cell being expanded, then the adjacent cell is discarded. Otherwise, if the adjacent cell is already *labeled* with a different *tag* compared to the *tag* of the cell being expanded, it shows the *collision* of two different *front waves.* The processor which detects the *collision* at Step 1, signals the host about the collision. It also includes the current value of the local cycle count and the local coordinates of the pair of adjacent cells in the message. At Step 3, the local cells stored in the *receive* buffers are examined in a similar way. However, a *collision* at this step will be detected concurrently by two neighbor processors. This situation corresponds to the mutual collision of two different type of *front waves* at two adjacent boundary cells in two adjacent grid partitions assigned to two neighbor processors. For example, if a processor detects a *collision* during the examination of a cell in its *east receive* queue, its *east* neighbor processor will concurrently detect the same *collision* during the examination of a cell in its *west receive* queue. In this case, those two neighbor processors will inform the host about the same *collision.*

The given parallel algorithm does not guarantee that all processors will be executing the same front wave expansion cycle at any instant of time. If a snapshot of the parallel system is taken, some of the processors may be found to be *leading* some others by a number of expansion cycles. A *leading* processor may be the first processor which detects a *collision.* Hence, if the host processor terminates the *front wave expansion* as soon as it receives a *collision* message, the path to be recovered may not be the shortest path from source to target. All *lagging* processors should be allowed to perform *expansion* until the cycle count of the *leading* processor which has detected the *collision* the first time. Those *lagging* processors have potential to detect collisions on earlier cycles. This is achieved by the scheme given at Step 4 of the algorithm. Any processor which detects a *collision* informs the host with the current value of its local cycle count. The host processor, after the receiving the first *collision* message, broadcasts the cycle count q in this message as an upper bound on the local cycle counts. The *leading* processors which have already performed the q-th *front wave expansion* cycle terminate and inform the processor about their termination. The *lagging* processors which have not yet performed the q-th *front wave expansion* cycle continue to execute the given algorithm until the q-th cycle. These processors also inform the host about their termination after executing the q-th cycle. Meanwhile, the host processor stores all the subsequent *collision* messages until it receives P termination messages. The host processor chooses the *collision* message with a minimum cycle count. Then it broadcasts the coordinates of the chosen pair of adjacent cells to signal the initiation of the *path recovery* phase.

In the proposed parallel algorithm, the number of *expansion* cycles to be performed in the *front wave expansion* phase is reduced by a factor of two compared to the original parallel algorithm. Hence, the total number of local communications is reduced by a factor of two, since the number of local communications per *expansion* cycle is fixed to four. The proposed algorithm is also expected to reduce the total number of expanded cells, on the average, almost by a factor of two. Assume a large grid with no blockages. If the original algorithm requires q *expansion* cycles to reach the *target* cell, the proposed algorithm will require only $q/2$ *expansion* cycles to reach the *collision* of two front waves. The total number of cells expanded in the original algorithm will be $1 + 2q(q + 1)$ compared to $2 + q(q + 2)$ in the proposed algorithm. The total number of expanded cells in both algorithms will of course vary when blockages exist in the grid. Unfortunately, the proposed algorithm increases the amount of computation required for the expansion of an individual cell. However, the computational overhead per cell expansion will decrease with increasing blockage percentage in the grid. As is discussed earlier, an unused bit in a local cell *status* word and unused bits in the cell coordinate information words are used for *tagging* purposes. In this way, the total memory requirement and communication volume requirement for an individual cell is not increased compared to the original algorithm. Hence, the proposed algorithm will also reduce the total volume of communication since the total number of expanded cells is reduced. Furthermore, the proposed parallel algorithm will increase the processor utilization, compared to the original algorithm, when source and target cells are assigned to different processors. The relative increase in the processor utilization will grow with increasing h,w parameters, and with increasing mesh distance between the two processors which own the source and the target cells.

3 Overlapping Communication and Computation

Blocking (synchronous) *send* and *receive* messages are issued at step 2 and step 3 , respectively, of the parallel algorithm given in Section 2.1. Each processor may stay idle waiting for data from its four neighbors after sending data to them. This idle time can be reduced by rearranging the algorithm for node processors as follows :

1. i. Issue four *non-blocking receives* to receive data into receive queues.
   ii . Issue four *non-blocking sends* for front wave cells (at depth q) to transmit send queues to corresponding processors.
2. Expand the front wave cells (of depth q) in local queue and insert their adjacent cells (of depth q+1) either into the local queue or into the corresponding send queues accordingly.
3. *Synchronize* on the *asynchronous receive* messages issued at step 1. Then, expand the front wave cells (of depth q) in the receive queues and add their adjacent cells either into the local queue or into the corresponding send queues accordingly.
4. Repeat the steps 1, 2, 3, 4 until the target cell is reached for *Sonly* scheme and same as step 4 (Section 2.1) for *S+T* scheme.

Note that, in the non-overlapped scheme given in Section 2.1, data in the send queues are transmitted after being constructed at the same expansion cycle. In the overlapped scheme, the transmission of data in the send queues constructed in the previous expansion cycle is initiated before the local expansion computation in the current cycle. Furthermore, the front wave cells in the receive queues are expanded in place instead of being added into the local queue for later expansion.

The node executive (NX/2) Of the iPSC/2 handles short messages ($\leq$ 100 bytes) and long messages (> 100 bytes) differently. Short incoming messages are always stored first in a buffer inside the *NX/2* area regardless of a pending *receive* for that message and then copied from the *NX/2* buffer to the user buffer. However, long incoming messages are directly copied into the user buffer if a *receive* is pending for that message. If not, the message is kept in the *NX/2* buffer until a receive is issued for that message. The local messages in the given algorithms are predicted and observed, in general, to be of long type messages. Hence, non-blocking receive messages are issued as early as possible at step 1, although the *receive queues* are to be processed at step 3, in each cycle to ensure that receives are already pending for the incoming long messages so that they can be directly copied into the *receive queues* instead of being copied into the *NX/2* area and then transferred into the indicated receive queues due to the late issued receives.

At step 1, the send operations for the send queues constructed at step 2 and 3 of the previous cycle are initiated. Then, each processor continues execution by expanding the front wave cells in the local queue as indicated at step 2. Hence, the set-up time and the transit time for the four send operations at step 1 are overlapped with the computations at step 2 and even at step 3 of the given algorithm. The set-up times for the send operations are overlapped on the cycle-stealing basis and the transit time of the messages are overlapped completely.

The non-blocking *send* messages issued at step 1 returns control back to the node program just after informing *NX/2* about the *send* requests. The expansion computations at steps 2 and 3 may contaminate the buffers allocated for the send queues by inserting new cells (to be transmitted on the following cycle). A *switching buffer* is used for each send queue in order to ensure the transmission of the correct data. A buffer of size 2M (Buffer[2M]) is allocated as a send queue, where M is the maximum number of front wave cells that can be transmitted between any two neighbor processors at any depth. The first half of the buffer (Buffer[0...M-1]) is transmitted, while expansion computations at steps 2 and 3 use the second half of the buffer (Buffer[M...2M-1]) in *even* expansion cycles and vice versa in *odd* expansion cycles. In this scheme, a buffer area is used for transmitting data on alternate expansion cycles. Hence, synchronization on an asynchronous send message issued at step 1 of an expansion cycle can be delayed until step 2 of the next expansion cycle, thus providing the maximum overlap between communication and computation.

4 Synchronization

The *synchronous (blocking) receive* messages at step 3 of the non-overlapped scheme (Section 2.1) and the *synchronization* on asynchronous receive messages at step 3 of the overlapped scheme (Section 3) constitute a local synchronization between neighbor processors of the mesh. That is, processors do not proceed to the next *front wave expansion* cycle before receiving messages from all four neighbors. Due to this local synchronization, both of the parallel algorithms are guaranteed to find the shortest path between the source and the target whenever a path from source to target exists. However, these parallel algorithms will not terminate if no path exists between the source and the target. The schemes to provide global termination detection for such cases are discussed in the following paragraphs.

In previous work [4], the *Global Synchronization* scheme is reported to give worse results than the *Counter Termination* scheme. Because, the *Global Synchronization* scheme involves $P + log_2(P)$ messages at each expansion cycle between host and node processors. Furthermore, it decreases the processor utilization since each processor has to be globally synchronized with all other processors (through host) before beginning the next *front wave expansion* cycle. Hence, only *Counter Termination* scheme is used for termination detection in this paper. The counter termination scheme proposed in [2], requires a Δ time parameter to account for the message transit time. This parameter is a characteristic of the multicomputer used [2]. In order to avoid the use of such a machine dependent parameter, a different counter termination scheme is used here. In addition to the previous work in [4], node processors start communication with host after manhattan cycles of frontwave expansion is done. In this scheme, host maintains a one dimensional array to keep a counter for each *front wave expansion* cycle. The host and node programs for this version of the counter termination scheme for a P processor hypercube are given below.

Host Program

1. $counter(q) = 0$ for all possible q
2. Enable *front wave expansion*
3. **If** a signal with label q received **then**
   i. $counter(q) = counter(q) + 1$
   ii. **If** $counter(q) = P$ **then** terminate
4. Go to Step 3

Node Program

1. $q = 0$
2. Wait for an enable signal from the host
3. $q = q + 1$
4. Perform steps 1, 2, and 3 of the given algorithm
5. **If** local queue empty **then**
   signal the host with the cycle count q
6. Perform step 4 of the given algorithm
7. Go to Step 3

The condition $counter(q) = P$ checked by the host indicates that all local queues are empty at the *q-th expansion* cycle. Hence, the given algorithm ensures the global termination detection when there is no path from source to target.

5 Asynchronous Scheme

The local synchronization being performed at step 3 of the non-overlapped and the overlapped schemes may be avoided as is indicated in [2]. The asynchronous algorithm presented in [2] is implemented with minor modifications here for the *Sonly* scheme. However, the asynchronous algorithm for *S+T* scheme needs some major modifications as shown below :

Host Program

1. last-path = empty,stpath = ∞.
2. Enable node processes.
3. Wait message from nodes.
4. **If** (new-depth < stpath) **then**
   i. last-path = new-path.
   ii. stpath = new-depth.
   iii. send stpath to nodes.
5. **If**(all processors empty) **then**
   terminate the program.
6. Goto 3.

Node Program

1. p-depth = ∞;s-depth = 0 , t-depth = 0;
2. Examine each cell c in local queue for expansion;
   if (c in target-front-wave) **then**
     expand c only if c-depth + t-depth < p-depth;
   else
     expand c only if c-depth + s-depth < p-depth;
   endif;
3. Send only non-empty send queue(s) to neighbor(s).
4. **If** there is/are pending incoming msg(s) from neighbors **then**
     add cells in the receive queue(s) into local queue;
   endif;
5. **If** there is a pending incoming msg from host **then**
     If (first received from host) **then**
       compute local min-s-depth and min-t-depth;
       exchange these min. values to find global mins;
       s-depth = global min. for min-s-depth;
       t-depth = global min. for min-t-depth;
     endif;
     p-depth = stpath (received from host);
   endif;
6. Inform the host about status.
7. Goto 2.

In *S+T* scheme, the counter termination scheme proposed in [2] is used. For that purpose, the host processor holds a counter to count the number of non-empty processors. However, unlike the *Sonly* scheme, the counter is set to 2, if the target and the source cells are in different processors, and set to 1 otherwise. An additional two byte word is associated with each status word of the local status array. If a local cell has a labeled routing status on the *source front wave* or *target front wave* then this word indicates the depth of the cell from the *source* cell and the *target* cell respectively. The expansion of a cell at step 2 of the node algorithm needs more explanation. If the current status of an *adjacent* cell is labeled with the same tag of the cell being expanded, then its depth is compared with the depth of the cell being expanded. If its depth is less than the depth of the cell being expanded plus one, then the adjacent cell is discarded. Otherwise, the adjacent cell is added to the front of the local queue (instead of adding it to the rear of the local queue) with its depth being one more than the depth of the cell being expanded. Hence, the local queue behaves as a LIFO instead of FIFO for such collisions. The LIFO scheme implemented for such collisions implicitly prevents the further expansion of the cells in the local queue which are expanded originating from the indicated adjacent cell. In fact, considerable performance increase is measured by using the LIFO scheme instead of the conventional FIFO scheme. Hence, the data for the conventional FIFO scheme is not included.

6 Experimental Results

All schemes for parallel maze routing has been coded in C language and run on an iPSC/2 hypercube multicomputer. Timing results are obtained and displayed graphically in Figures 4-6. The meanings of the abbreviations in the figures are; **M** : communication with host after Manhattan distance from source and target cells, **CT** : Counter termination, **S + T** : Expansion starting from source and target, **S** : Expansion starting from Source Only, **NO** : No overlapping of communication and computation, **O** : Overlapped scheme, **AS** : Asynchronous scheme. Figures 4-6 are constructed by using the averages of the timing results measured on 4 different grids with 40-45% randomly generated blockages and randomly generated nets.

The following conclusions are deduced from the timing results. As is seen in Figure 4, efficiency of all synchronous parallel algorithms increases with increasing w at the beginning due to the decrease in the volume of communication. However, efficiency begins to decrease after a turn over value for w in each scheme due to the increase in the processor idle time with increasing w. Figure 5 is obtained by running S+T,O,CT,M scheme on the hypercube for various grid sizes. Figure 5 illustrates that speed-up and efficiency increase with increasing grid size as is expected. Figure 6(a) illustrates that overlapped scheme gives better speed-up compared to the non-overlapped scheme as is expected. Figure 6 also illustrates that *S+T* scheme outperforms the *Sonly* scheme. The efficiency of the asynchronous scheme is rather low as is seen in Figure 6(b). A maximum speed-up of 4.75 is obtained on an 8 processor hypercube for h = 2w= 8 and $N = 1024$ with the *S+T* scheme using overlapped communication. As is seen in Figure 5(b), the efficiency of the S+T algorithm with overlapped communication scheme remains almost constant when both the number of processors and grid size are doubled.

7 Conclusion

A new parallel *breadth first* search algorithm to implement Lee's maze router on a hypercube multicomputer is proposed. Different partitioning and search strategies are discussed. We experimentally show that our algorithm which performs two *front wave expansions* concurrently, one starting from the source cell and the other one starting from the target cell gives better performance compared to the one proposed in [2] which uses the *source only* expansion scheme.

Fig. 4(a). h = w , dim =2 , N = 1024

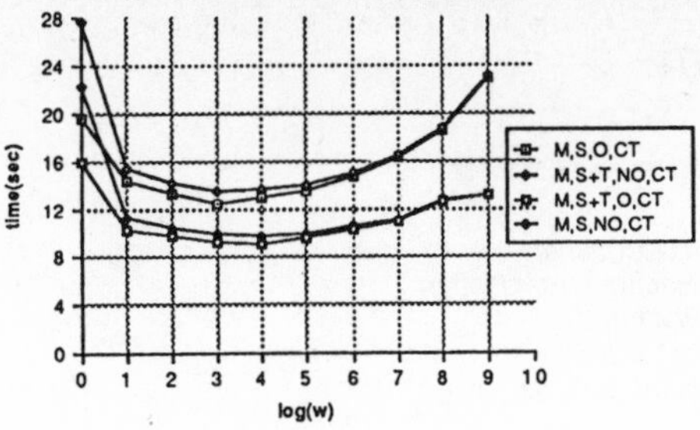

Fig. 4(b). h = 2w , dim =2 ,N = 1024

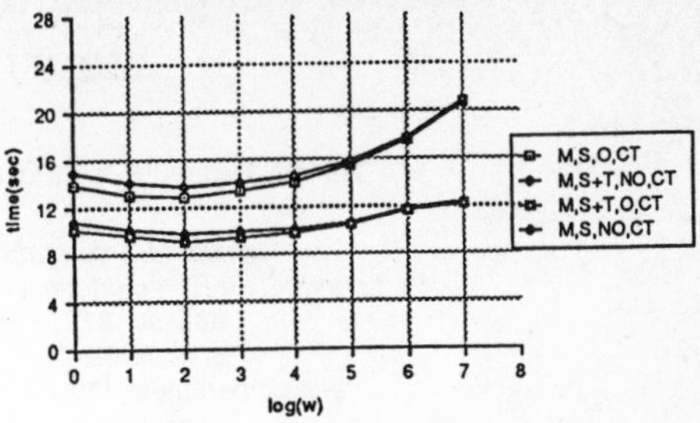

Fig. 5(a). Speed Up vs Grid Size

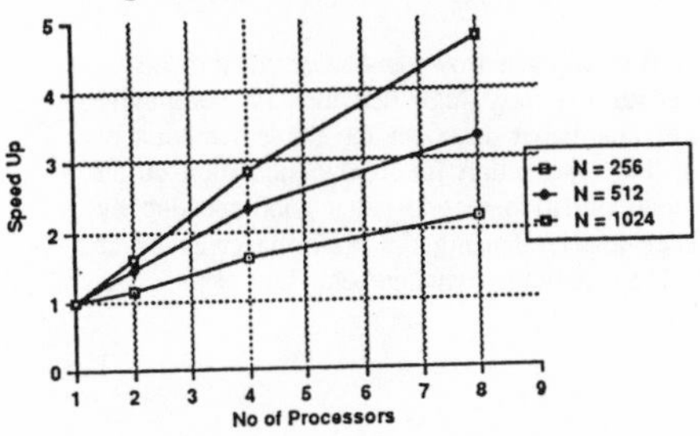

Fig. 5(b). Efficiency vs Grid Size

Fig. 6(a). Speed Up For N = 1024

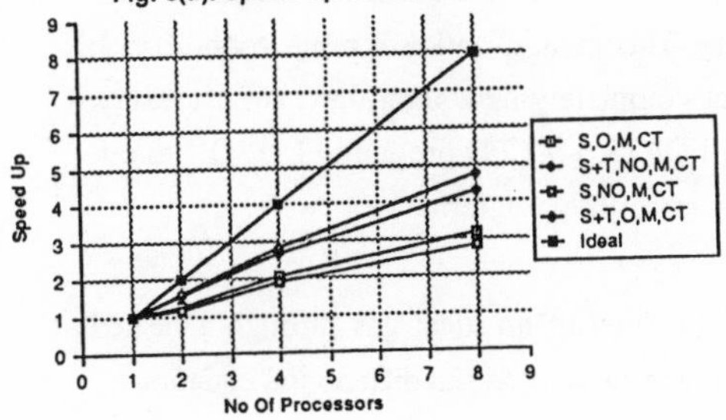

Fig. 6(b). Speed Up for Asynch. For N = 512

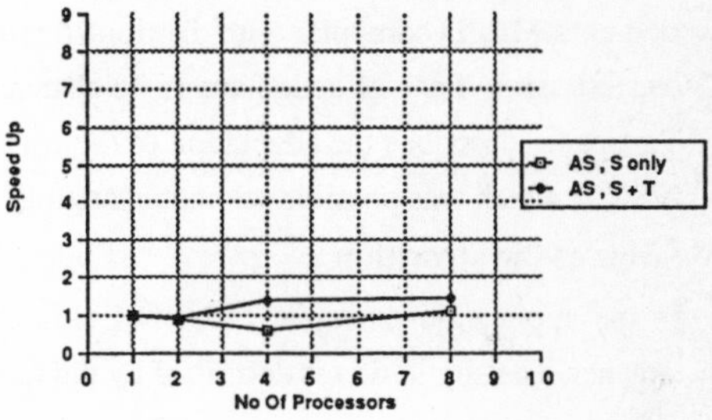

References

[1] C. Y. Lee, "An algorithm for path connections and its applications," *IRE Trans. Electronic Computers*, Vol. EC-10, pp. 346-365, Sept. 1961.

[2] Youngju Won and Sartaj Sahni, "Maze Routing On a Hypercube Multiprocessor Computer," *Proceedings of Intrl. Conf. on Parallel Processing*, St.Charles August 1987, pp. 630-637.

[3] Y. Saad and M. Schultz, "Topological properties of hypercubes," *Research Report, YALEU/DCS/RR-389, Computer Science Dept., Yale University*, Jun. 1985.

[4] T. M. Kurç , C. Aykanat ,and F. Erçal, "Maze Routing on an iPSC/2 Hypercube Multicomputer.", Proceedings of ISCIS V, Nevşehir, Turkey, Oct. 1990, pp. 327-336.

Experiences in parallelizing an existing CFD algorithm

Thomas Bemmerl[1], Udo Graf[2], Rainer Knödlseder[1]

[1] *Institut für Informatik der TU München*
Lehrstuhl für Rechnertechnik und Rechnerorganisation
Arcisstr. 21 D-8000 München 2
Tel.: +49-89-2105-8247 or -2382
e-mail: bemmerl@lan.informatik.tu-muenchen.de

[2] *Gesellschaft für Reaktorsicherheit (GRS)*
Forschungsgelände, D-8046 Garching

The numerical simulation of a 2- or 3-dimensional motion of viscous multiphase flow can be described by a system of partial differential equations. Because this simulation poses extremly high demands on computing capacity it is very well suited for calculation by a multiprocessor. This paper describes the implementation of FLUBOX, a two-dimensional fluid dynamics code developed at the Gesellschaft für Reaktorsicherheit on an iPSC/2 distributed memory multiprocessor. The main criterion for evaluation was to get a good speedup by changing only small parts of the program. The program has been analyzed using the performance analyzer PATOP developed in the TOPSYS project. In this way, we were able to study the dynamic behaviour of the algorithm.

1. Introduction

Today many problems can be simulated by numerical algorithms. As numerical simulations require large amounts of computing power, this kind of algorithm is a candidate for parallelization on a MIMD computer with distributed memory. This parallelization is often very difficult because many lines of code have to be changed, or completely new algorithms are necessary. This paper describes the adaptation of the existing FORTRAN CFD program FLUBOX to our iPSC/2, which was possible without changing big parts of the program.

Scope of the algorithm

In the application example, FLUBOX simulates the flow of an ideal gas through a heated channel. The simulation is described by the following system of partial differential equations:

$$\frac{\partial u}{\partial t} = L(u) + R(u), \quad \text{with } L(u) = \sum_{i=1}^{3} \left(G_i(u) \frac{\partial u}{\partial x_i} + K_i \frac{\partial^2 u}{\partial x_i^2} \right) \tag{1}$$

$$x = (x_1, x_2, x_3) \in V \subseteq R^3; \; t \in [t_0, t_1] \subseteq R; \; u = (u_1(x,t), \ldots, u_s(x,t))^T$$

The spatial semidiscretisation of these partial differential equations leads to initial value problems for ordinary differential equations (ODE) that are solved by FEBE (Forward Euler, Backward Euler) [Hof81]. For the implicit solution of these nonlinear equations the following discrete and linearized formula is considered:

$$\left(\frac{1}{\Delta t} - \frac{\partial f}{\partial u}\right)(u^{n+1} - u^n) = f(u^n, t_n) + \Delta t \, \frac{\partial f}{\partial t} \tag{2}$$

To be efficient and reliable, the step size Δt and the order of consistency $k \in \{1, 2, 3, 4, 6, 8, 12\}$ of the ODE-solver is adjusted to the behaviour of the local solution by an error control mechanism. For these purposes FEBE uses local extrapolation.

Partly funded by the Gesellschaft für Reaktorsicherheit and the German Science Foundation under contract number SFB 342 (project A1)

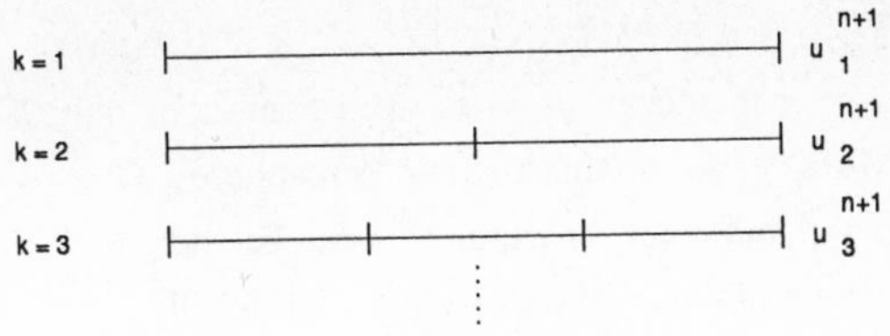

Figure 1: The extrapolation trableau of FEBE

As shown in figure 1, the basic step length Δt is divided into k subintervals of length $\frac{\Delta t}{k}$. On each subinterval the equation (2) is solved to yield the initial entries u_k^{n+1}, k = 1,2,.. for the construction of the extrapolation tableau. Because the different u_k^{n+1}, k = 1,2,.. are independent from each other, they can be calculated in parallel.

Since the linear system (2) of 2-dimensional problems consists of several thousands of unknowns, it is highly uneconomical to solve it directly. For its solution a fractional step method is used. The basic idea in fractional step methods is, that a multidimensional problem is split into successive 1-dimensional problems. In step one the rows and in step two the columns of the 1-dimensional problems are independent from each other and can be parallelized.

As described before, the Jacobian matrix is necessary in (2). The evaluations of the columns of the Jacobian matrix are independent from each other and can be done in parallel.

For more details of the algorithm see [GrW87], [Gra86].

2. The target machine and programming environment

The following sections describe the architecture and the programming environment that was available on the target machine.

2. 1. The iPSC/2 architecture

The iPSC/2 is a distributed memory MIMD parallel computer consisting of up to 128 nodes each containing an 80386 CPU and an 80387 arithmetic coprocessor. The nodes are physically connected in a hypercube topology. Message passing is done independently from the CPU by the Direct Connect Module, which performs circuit switching transmission of data without any store and forward. Thus, a CPU is not influenced by messages passing its node on their way from sender to receiver. Moreover, transmission delays are almost independent of the physical location of sender and receiver, so that the programmer can think of the iPSC/2 as a virtually fully connected system. For more details see [Sch90]

2. 2. The Multiprocessor Multitasking Kernel MMK

The Multiprocessor Multitasking Kernel MMK developed in our research group takes an object oriented approach to the program, and is based on parallel extensions of existing sequential programming languages (e.g. FORTRAN, C, C++). The programmer sees his program as a set of objects, that can be manipulated by predefined operations only. The following object types are offered by MMK: tasks, mailboxes and semaphores. Objects can be created and deleted dynamically. In a global object space objects can be addressed without regard to their present mapping onto the nodes (location transparency). [BeL90]

2. 3. Tools for programming and analyzing MMK applications

Because it is difficult to develop a program on a multiprocessor computer it is necessary to have good tools for program development. This is why in the TOPSYS (TOols for Parallel SYStems) project our group has developed an integrated tool environment for programming and analyzing parallel programs [Bem90]. This tool environment includes specification and mapping tools, a parallel debugger, a performance analyzer, a visualizer and dynamic load balancing tools. @BODY NO IDENT = With these tools an application's dynamic behaviour can be observed at various levels of abstraction. An integrated graphic interface supports interactive use of the tools. All tools operate in parallel to the running program. Data relating to the program's dynamic behaviour is collected by monitors and evaluated by the tools.

3. Parallelization concepts

The following section describes the concepts we used to parallelize FLUBOX on the iPSC/2.

3. 1. General aspects of parallelization

Our example consists of the calculation of the 2-dimensional flow of an ideal gas through a heated channel on a 16 * 14 grid. The program was parallelized by dividing it up into different MMK - tasks and letting these tasks communicate with each other by sending messages to specified mailboxes.

Because the iPSC/2 runs in a host target configuration the distribution of FLUBOX onto host and cube has to be done first. Since the host is also used by other users and communication between host and cube is much slower than communication on the cube itself, we decided to map only an IO server onto the host. Its work is to read the inputs from a file and to display the results on the screen.

The iPSC/2 we used has 16 nodes with 1 Mbyte of memory and another 16 nodes with 4 Mbyte of memory per node. On each node, some 600 kBytes are used by the operating system and some 300 kBytes are used by program code. Because FLUBOX uses large amounts of data, it was clear that the 1 MBytes nodes could not be used.

The main goal of our research was to parallelize the given program on our iPSC/2 by changing only small parts of the code. This design decision was made because many programmers believe, that adapting a software package to an MIMD machine means rewriting the program from scratch. So we decided to distribute the existing subroutines, shown in figure 2, onto different tasks. The resulting object graph of the parallelized version of

FLUBOX can be seen in figure 3. Each of the tasks shown can have several replications on different processors. A subroutine call of the sequential version (fig. 2) is replaced by sending the operands of the subroutine to the different tasks and waiting for the different results. No further changes were necessary for the parallelization.

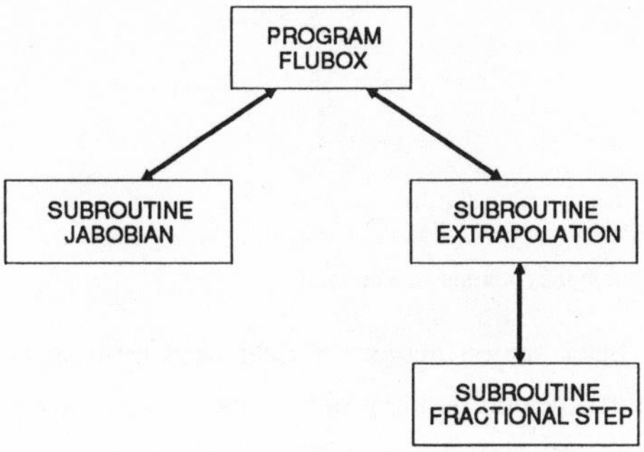

Figure 2: Structure of the sequential subroutines

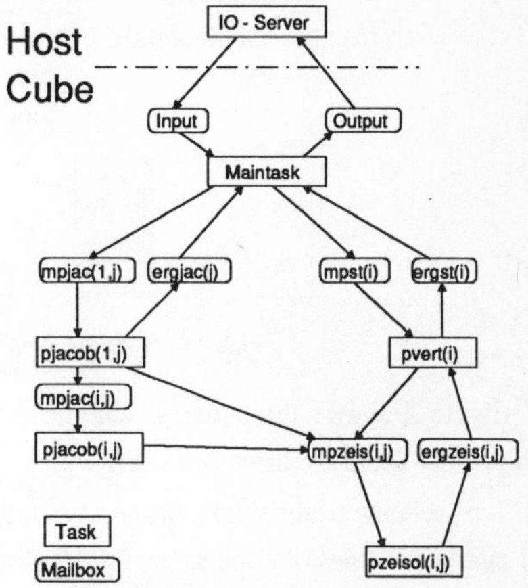

Figure 3: Processgraph of FLUBOX

3. 2. Parallelization of parts of the algorithm

To parallelize the different parts of FLUBOX, we had to determine the data used by the different replications of tasks, and which data are computed by them. This was very difficulty because of the big number of COMMON variables used in FLUBOX.

3. 2. 1. Parallelization of the construction of the extrapolation tableau

We will now describe the parallelization of the construction of the extrapolation tableau. As described before, the solution for different values of k can be calculated on separate processors.

The task, which computes the different parts of the extrapolation tableau is called *pvert*. Each replication of pvert receives a common set of operands and a set of values, indicating which part of the extrapolation tableau is to be calculated. After a whole step the different results of u_k^{n+1} are collected by *Maintask*.

3. 2. 2. Parallelization of the fractional step method

The following section describes the parallelization of the fractional step method. We have decided to parallelize only four routines, which consume 85% of the CPU - time at this level. This decision was made in order to reduce the time needed for parallelization. But we have also investigated the remaining parts of the fractional step method and learned that they could also be calculated in parallel. The calculation is done by several replications of the task *pzeisol.* To parallelize the four routines we had to handle two conflicting problems:

1. The size of the data exchanged between the tasks must be as small as possible to prevent a communication bottleneck, which would reduce the speedup.
2. The form of the data storage is not appropriate for parallelization on a distributed memory computer, because the data used by a processor is not stored at neighbouring memory locations.

Figure 4: Storage scheme used in the frational step method

Figure 4 shows this storage scheme. The black region marks the field used by a single processor. There are three solutions which address the conflicting problems mentioned above:

1. The scheme of the data storage is changed in the whole program. This would cause a huge number of lines of code to be modified which is in opposite to our fixed main goal.
2. The neighbouring parts of the data are transferred in individual parts. This would cause a huge overhead for the initialization of a high number of messages.
3. The solution we used, is that the data addressed by a single processor is copied to neighbouring memory locations. Because time wasted for copying data is very small, this solution is optimal in terms of speed and the number of lines of code changed is also very small.

In the parallel version of FLUBOX each replication of *pzeisol* receives different parts of the Jacobian matrix and one of the parts of a datastructure marked black in figure 4. Like before the results are sent to the calling task *pvert.* In contrast to the calculation of the extrapolation tableau the total amount of distributed data is independent from the number of processors used.

3. 2. 3. Parallelization of the Jacobian matrix

As described before the third routine running in parallel is the calculation of the Jacobian matrix used in (2). It is calculated by the task *pjacob.* Controlled by the error control mechanism of FLUBOX the Jacobian matrix is calculated only after 2 - 8 time steps.

The Jacobian matrix is used by the task *pzeisol* . Because the size of the Jacobian matrix is very large (702 kBytes) we have decided to calculate the parts of the Jacobian matrix on the same processor which uses it. The disadvantage of this solution is, that each part of the Jacobian matrix is calculated on several (2 or 3) processors (fig. 5). But the advantage of this solution is, that communication between processors is reduced. In this way the decrease in speedup is neutralized.

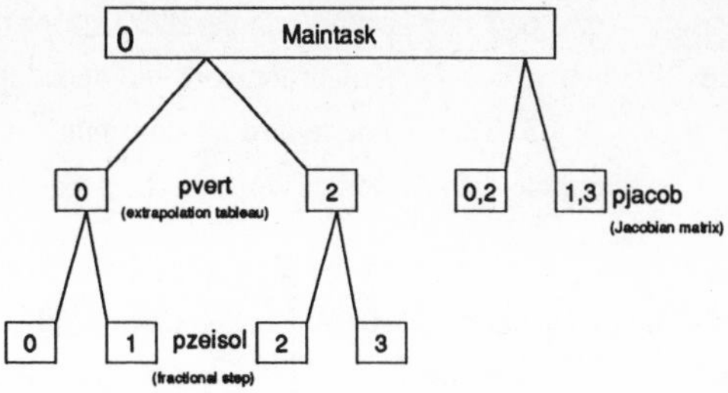

Figure 5: Mapping of the 2 - 2 configuration of FLUBOX

3. 3. Mapping

The mapping used for a configuration with 4 processors is shown in figure 5. Since the calling task has no work while a called task is working, it was profitable to map one replication of the called task onto the processor of the calling task.

4. Performance measurements and results

The following sections describe our measurements of speedup and dynamic behaviour of FLUBOX.

4. 1. Methods for measurement

Our measurements had two basic goals: To compute the speedup of FLUBOX for a number of different configurations of tasks and to find bottlenecks, caused by communication and by an unsuitable mapping of the tasks onto the processors. For this purpose we used two kinds of performance measurements:

1. Measuring the time which is spent in the parallel parts of FLUBOX using system calls. With these measurements we were able to compute the speedup.
2. Analyzing FLUBOX with the performance analyzer PATOP to explore the dynamic behaviour of the program and to find bottlenecks. For this, CPU idle times, communication rate between the processors and distribution of work on the task were measured.

We were also interested in finding out the highest number of tasks, which are able to work efficiently on the three levels of parallelization.

4. 2. Measurements of speedup of the parallel parts

4. 2. 1. The construction of the extrapolation tableau

With regard to the construction of the extrapolation tableau we have learned, that the speedup depends on the number of processors and also on the order k of the construction of the extrapolation tableau determined by the error control mechanism of FLUBOX.

We have learned, that it is not useful to parallelize this level on more than three processors. The separation of work for k = 12 can be seen in figure 6. As can be seen there is no remaining work for a fourth processor.

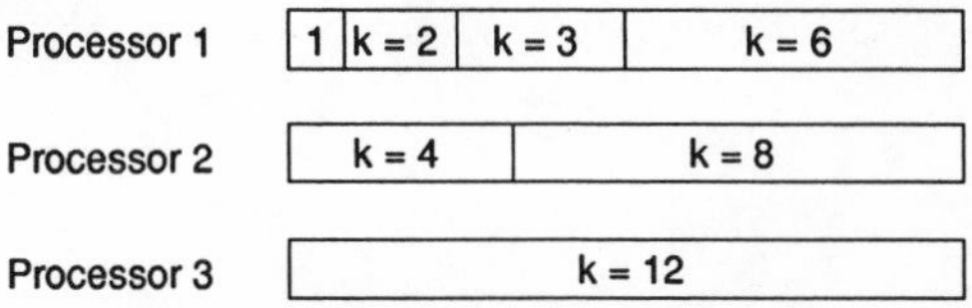

Figure 6: Distribution of work on 3 processors

The speedup we measured for 2 or 3 tasks running in parallel and for the different values of k can be seen in figure 7. Using n = 2 parallel processors the speedup is ideal. For n = 3 processors the speedup is only 2 - 3. This is not caused by communication delays but by the fact that for k = {3, 6, 8} no complete distribution of work on the processors can be achieved.

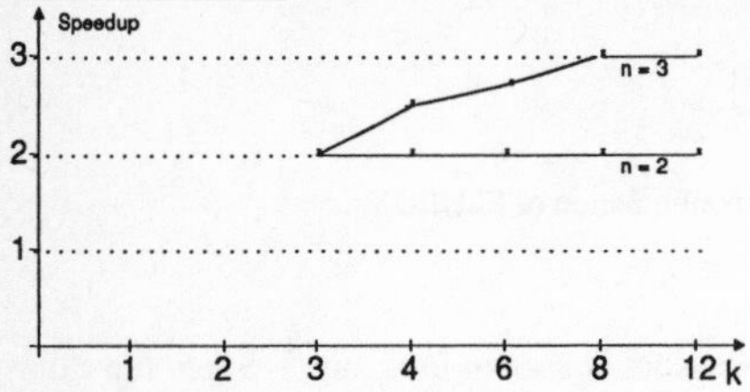

Figure 7: Speedup of the extrapolation tableau

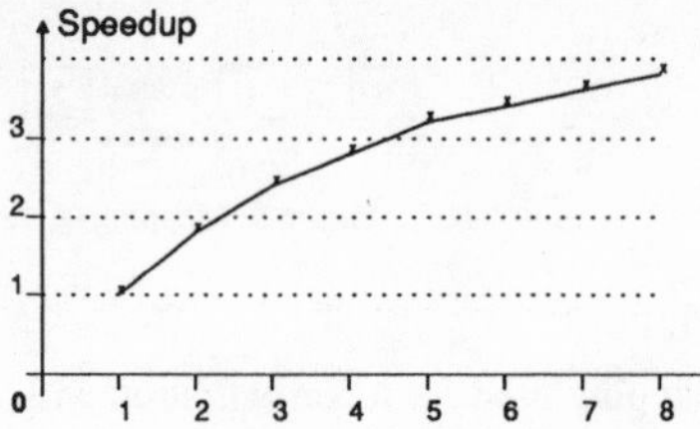

Figure 8: Speedup of the frational step method

4. 2. 2. The fractional step method

As mentioned above, most time of the algorithm is spent within the fractional step method. This means low speedup at this level would cause a low speedup of the complete algorithm.

The speedup of the fractional step method can be seen in figure 8. As can be seen, the speedup measured is only 45 - 80 % of the number of processors used and the difference gets larger if the number of processors increases. This difference is caused by three facts:

1. A communication delay which reduces the speedup by about 2 %
2. The grid size (here 16 * 14) can not be distributed in an ideal way onto the different processors.
3. Only 85 % of the fractional step method runs in parallel, which causes the main part of the difference described above.

To increase the speedup at this level the remaining sequential parts should be parallelized.

4. 2. 3. Parallelization of the Jacobian matrix

The speedup of the calculation of the Jacobian matrix has only little influence on the total speedup because its calculation is only done rarely and it needs only 40 seconds for a sequential calculation.

As mentioned above, each part of the Jacobian matrix is calculated on several processors. So the speedup of the calculation of the Jacobian matrix is the number of processors used divided by the number of parallel tasks used for the computation of the extrapolation tableau. It is only diminished by the rest of the division of the matrix size by the number of processors.

4. 3. Total speedup

As shown in figure 3 FLUBOX has a tree structure with two levels. So the speedup of the whole program is the product of the speedup of the construction of the extrapolation tableau and the speedup of the fractional step method. Our measurements of the whole program are shown in figure 9a for two parallel tasks at the construction of the extrapolation tableau and in figure 9b for three parallel tasks.

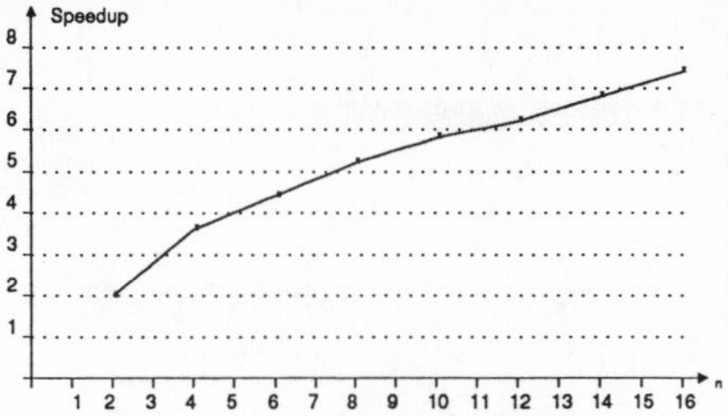

Figure 9a: Speedup for 2 tasks at the extrapolation tableau

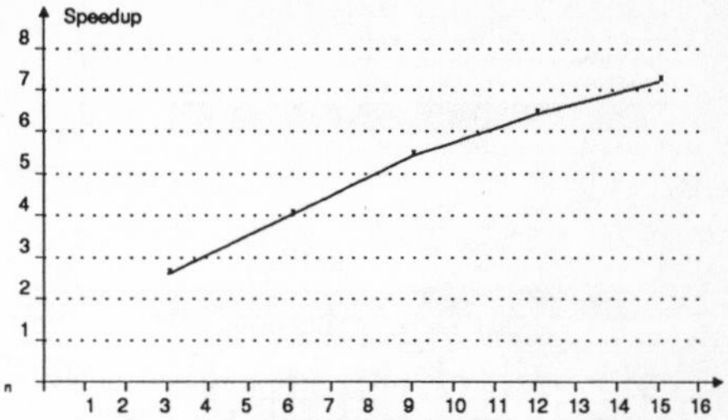

Figure 9b: Speedup for 3 tasks at the extrapolation tableau

As mentioned above, the limitation of speedup is caused by the remaining sequential parts of the code and not by communication delays. So there would be no further speedup on a shared memory computer.

4. 4. Measurements by PATOP

As mentioned above, we have also analyzed the dynamic behaviour of FLUBOX with the performance analyzer PATOP using the task configuration shown in figure 3.

Figure 10 shows the idle time of the different nodes. The idle time of node 1 and 3 has an average of 32%. This is caused by the sequential parts of the fractional step method and will be smaller, if the whole fractional step method runs in parallel.

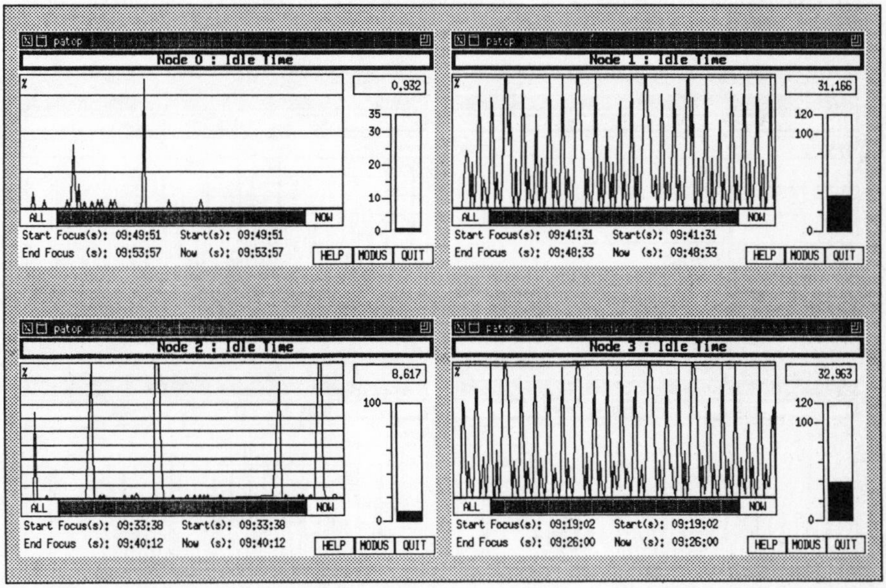

Figure 10: Idle times of the processors

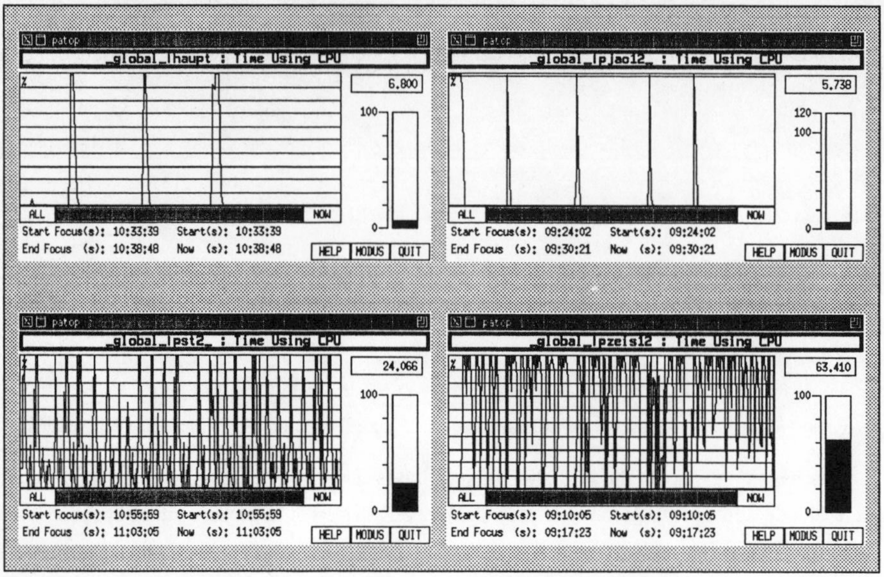

Figure 11: Distribution of work on the tasks of FLUBOX

In figure 11 the distribution of work among the different tasks is shown. As described above, most of the work is done by the fractional step method. The value of pvert(2) would decrease and the value of pzeisol(1,2) would increase if the fractional step method were parallelized completely.

The communication between the processors is shown in figure 12. The amount of data exchanged between the processors is small and does not cause any bottlenecks.

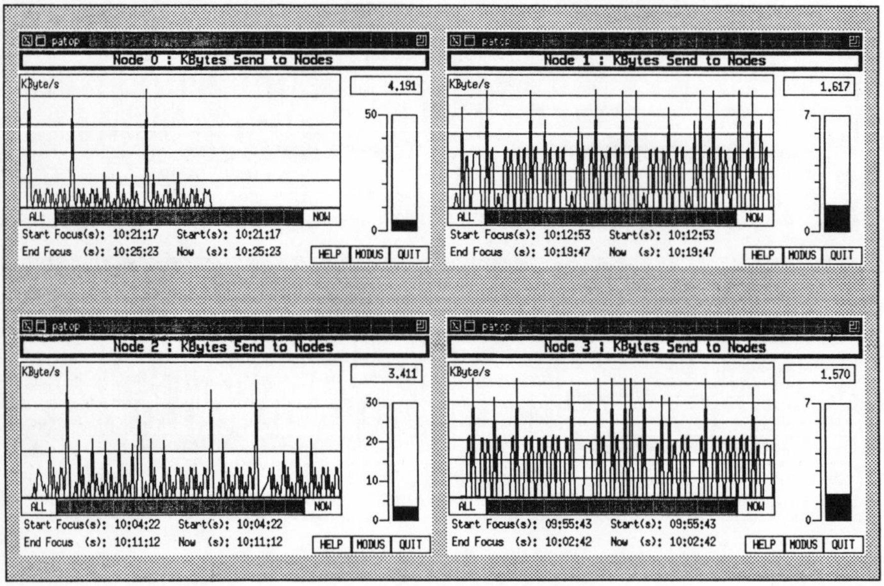

Figure 12: Communication between the processors

Summing up, the speedup of FLUBOX is limited by two main factors:

1. The fact that the distribution of work can not be done ideally as described before.
2. The parts of FLUBOX not running in parallel in this release of the program. We think we could get a speedup of 14 on 16 nodes, if the sequential parts were parallelized. The reason why a speedup of 16 will not be possible, is that for parallelization of the remaining parts of FLUBOX the communication rate is higher than before.

5. Conclusion

The computationally intensive existing simulation of the flow of an ideal gas through a heated channel has been implemented on an Intel iPSC/2 hypercube. The aim of our research was to get a high speedup while spending only little time on parallelization. Thus we had to find a solution where only small parts of the code were modified.

We have computed the speedup using system calls. In addition, the algorithm has been analyzed using the performance analyzer PATOP developed in our group's TOPSYS project.

The calculation of the extrapolation tableau shows good speedup for two or three processors. A higher number of processors does not make sense. But no limitation of speedup by communication between the tasks or of other bottlenecks of the implementation is visible.

In this implementation, 15% of the algorithm for the fractional step method are not parallelized. This decision was made in order to accelerate the time needed for parallelization. Consequently the speedup is only 3.7 on 8 processors. As shown above, the amount of communication is very low and causes no further limitation of speedup.

To get a better use of the resources of the iPSC/2 the parallelization of the remaining 15% of the fractional step method should be done. Our measurements support the hypothesis, that with this action the speedup would be linear.

In the future we intend to implement other examples of CFD algorithms on the iPSC/2. All these future implementations will be analyzed in more detail using the TOPSYS tools.

6. References

[Bem90] Bemmerl, T.: The TOPSYS Architecture; CONPAR 90 / VAPP IV, Sept. 1990, Zürich, Switzerland.

[BeL90] Bemmerl, T.; Ludwig, T.: MMK - A Distributed Operating SystemKernel with integrated dynamic loadbalancing; CONPAR 90 / VAPP IV, Sept. 1990, Zürich, Switzerland.

[BHL90] Bemmerl, T.; Hansen O.; Ludwig T.: PATOP for Performance Tuning of Parallel Programs; CONPAR 90 / VAPP IV, Sept. 1990, Zürich, Switzerland.

[Gra86] Graf, U.: Survey of a numerical procedure for the solution of hyperbolic systems of threedimensional fluid flow; Atomkernerengie - Kernenergie Vol. 49 (1986) pp.79 - 83

[GrW87] Graf, U.; Werner W.: Solution of 2- and 3-dimensional PDE problems: "An implicit time-integration method for parallel processing"; International topical meeting on advances in reactor physics, mathematics and computation, 27-30. April 1987, Paris.

[Hof81] Hofer, E.: An A(α) - stable variable order ODE-Solver and its applications as advancement procedure for simulations in Thermo- and Fluid - Dynamics. Proceedings of the international topical meeting on advances in mathematical methods for the solution of Nuclear Engineering Problems, April 1981, Munich.

[Sch90] Schuller, P.: Die Intel iPSC Systemfamilie; SUPERCOMPUTER 90, June 90, Mannheim

Simulation of the MC88000 Microprocessor System on a Transputer Network

Alexander R. Robertson & Roland N. Ibbett
Edinburgh Parallel Computing Centre & Department of Computer Science,
University of Edinburgh, The King's Buildings, Edinburgh EH9 3JZ

Abstract

This project investigated the feasibility of building a General Purpose Architecture Simulator on an MIMD transputer network. In the course of this study an Occam2 simulation of the 88100 Reduced Instruction Set micro-processor was developed on an MIMD T800 transputer Surface. A T414 graphics processor with gfx.library functions was configured to produce a visual presentation of the architecture's internal data flows, indicating, for example, the occurrence of read after write conflicts and providing useful information for performance analysis. Work Bench Test programs were written in 88000 assembly code including a convolution test program composed of load/store, integer and floating point arithmetic and conditional/unconditional control transfer instructions, which ran at an average throughput of 8 MIPS. The simulation program was distributed over a grid of transputers using the software harness **tiny** in an attempt to speedup the simulation runtime. Simulated performance was verified by a direct comparison with the Vax accerelator, an 88000 system (courtesy of SUPERCOSMOS, Edinburgh Royal Observatory), that could run a deblender sampling algorithm 10 times faster than a Vax machine, with an estimated performance of 8 to 9 MIPs. The inherent flexibility supported by Occam2 and the transputer enviroment was evaluated by attempting to alter the 88000 system architecture. Further performance improvement was achieved by developing a Front Panel Display to visualise internal data flow bottlenecks that were eliminated by optimising test program code.

1 Introduction

Logic and circuit simulators, [1][2][3][7] do not focus on performance bottlenecks nor do they provide a picture of an architecture's internal data flow. A performance tool for Computer Architects and Compiler writers is required to provide an enviroment for the optimisation of hardware and software interaction. This project explores the possibility of running a general purpose, architecture simulator with a Front Panel Display on the Multiple Instruction Multiple Data (MIMD) Meiko Computer Surface.

1.1 Objectives

The simulation has four objectives:-

- Examine the feasibility of building a general purpose simulator on an MIMD transputer network. Experiment by simulating the Motorola MC88100 microprocessor instruction set and running a series of Work Bench Test programs written in 88000 assembly.
- Record and analyse the simulation results from work bench test programs and study the performance effect of alterations to the architecture and assembly code optimisations.
- Distribute the simulator over a multi-transputer domain and attempt to reduce simulation run-time.
- Develop a Front Panel Display to provide run-time information concerning the loading of pipeline stages, together with the contents of general purpose and internal registers.

2 System Description

2.1 Motivation for Simulating the 88000 Architecture

One of the aims of this project was to evaluate how much parallelism an architecture simulator could utilise on an MIMD transputer system. The 88000 Reduced Instruction Set microprocessor has a high level of fine grain internal parallelism, including four independent pipelined execution units.

2.2 The External Architecture

There are three main types of instruction in the 88000 instruction set:

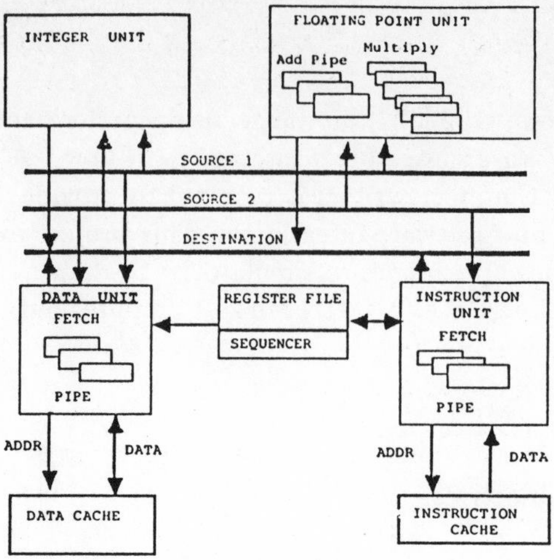

Figure 1: The 88000 Internal Architecture

- Data instructions, which load data into general purpose memory, store data to memory and exchange memory locations with general purpose registers.
- Flow instructions, which change the sequential flow of instructions.
- Register to Register instructions, which manipulate stored data in and out of General Purpose Registers.

2.3 Internal Architecture

The 88100 internal architecture, (see Figure 1) is similar to that of the CDC 6600 [5] which was also designed for scientific and engineering applications. The Sequencer determines which Functional Unit is master of the destination bus. There are three 32-bit busses, two busses for input operands and one bus for operation results. The right to control the destination bus is determined by a priority scheme. Integer Unit, logical and bit shift instructions have the highest priority because they only require one clock cycle. The lowest priority is given to division instructions. When a Functional Unit is denied access to the destination bus its pipeline must stop and the instruction unit is prevented from issuing new instructions to that unit.

Similar to the CDC 6600, scoreboarding [10] is provided by an internal scoreboard register that records the number of destination registers reserved by previously issued instructions, requiring more than one cycle for execution. After a blocked instruction has completed, the scoreboard entries are reset. The 88000's feedforwarding facility is comparable to the IBM System/360 Model 91's usage of a Common Data Bus. On aquiring a result from a Functional Unit, the Sequencer checks whether there is a Functional Unit awaiting operand values. Under these circumstances the result is sent directly to the appropriate source bus, thus eliminating the extra time involved in writing the result to the Register File. Excluding instructions executed in the Integer Unit, all operations complete in excess of one clock cycle. Each operation is therefore pipelined into discrete stages so that, assuming the pipelines are filled, an operation may complete every clock cycle.

3 Design of the Simulator

3.1 Model Structure

The model captures all essential performance determining characteristics. Performance is defined as the rate at which a system accomplishes work. Work is accomplished through the execution of activities, where an activity is defined as the smallest unit of work [3]. The simulator decomposes work into a logically related set of activities called processes.

The model adopts a process interaction approach because it emphasises the high degree of parallelism potentially available in the MC88000's internal architecture. Figure 2 illustrates the general structure of the simulator where the arcs represent channel communication. The 88000 instruction level simulation was abstracted to Register Transfer Level. The space resolution was determined by the instruction word and quantified as the smallest identifiable piece of information. The time resolution was the clock period, specified as the shortest interval of simulation time between two consecutive actions during the simulation runtime. The simulator uses **Barrier Synchronization** [6] to model the system clock.

4 Software Implementation

4.1 Simulating in Occam2

Occam2 is an ideal programming language for decomposing a system model into a collection of concurrent processes, communicating via channels; this is precisely the requirement for the abstract model described earlier. Occam2 is frequently used to simulate the behaviour of hardware devices because of its affinity for concurrent communication. The processes defined in the MC88100 model description were directly translated into concurrently running occam2 processes.

4.2 The Scheduler and Data Dependency Processes

The Scheduler (Figure 2) synchronises all peripheral processes in the process structure to the simulated clock. Peripheral processes must acknowledge the scheduler's *cycle event* before proceeding. The Scheduler also acts as an interface between the user and the simulator, providing the option of turning off Front Panel Display, switching on trace mode or displaying contents of scoreboard and/or contents of the Register File.

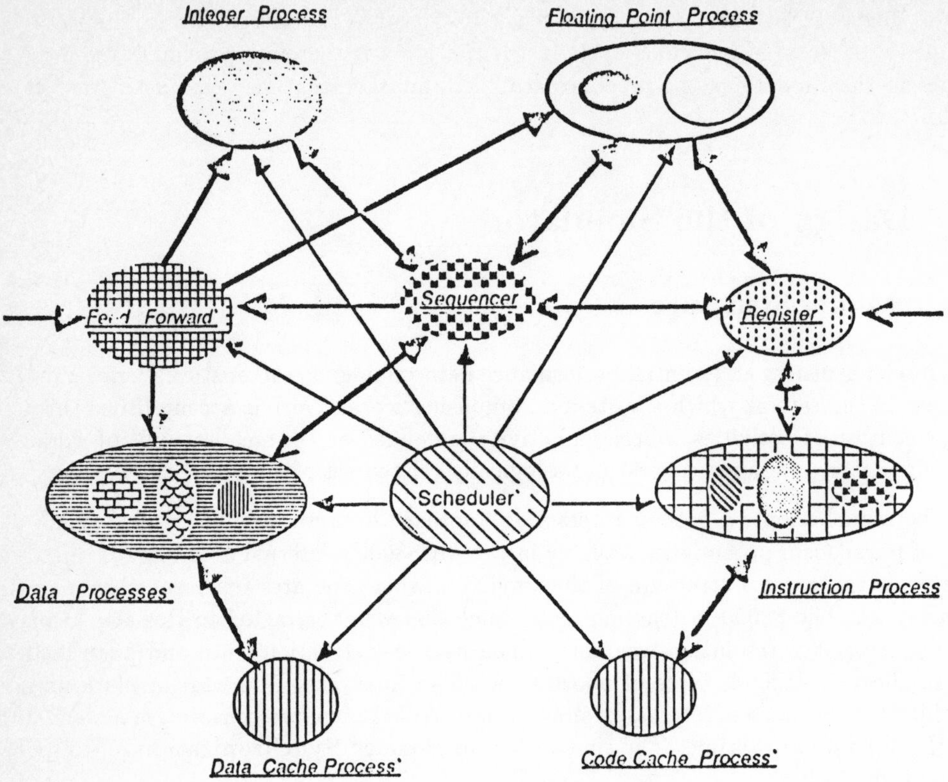

Figure 2: Model Structure

If an instruction has completed execution the Sequencer will allow the Functional Unit process singular access to the Register File. If there is more than one successful completion simultaneously, the Sequencer enforces a daisy chain priority scheme: the Integer Unit process has highest priority, division has lowest. After an uninterrupted simulation run, the Sequencer collects data from each Functional Unit, ie. number of instructions fetched, number of true and false writebacks for each Functional Unit and the frequency of 1st, 2nd and 3rd order conflicts. This information, including the estimated throughput of the architecture is displayed graphically.

A 1st order conflict occurs when a Functional Unit receives a false writeback from the Sequencer and stops. There is a pipeline halt channel from each Functional Unit to the Decode process. The Fetch process is blocked and the current state of the pipeline shadowed until the Functional Unit can write its result to the Register process, via the destination channel. A 2nd order conflict occurs when a source register is reserved by a previously issued instruction. If the source register has been set then the Register process synchronises with the Decode process to prevent further fetching from the code cache. The blocked instruction is written to the Feedforward Process where it is matched with the result collected from the Sequencer. If the destination register matches with the blocked operand then the missing operand is made available for execution. The simulation model is not affected by 3rd order conflicts. This is because a 2nd order conflict stops the Instruction Unit processes until the conflict has been resolved.

4.3 The Program

The Meiko Computing Surface is a network of 32-bit, 20MHz, INMOS T800 transputers. The user can select an arbitary number of transputers and connect them in a topology that will run a user's application most efficiently. The topology is limited by the four physical links on each transputer. The user can place any number of processes on each transputer provided the number of output/input channels is not greater than the number of physical links. This constraint is overcome by multiplexing the processes' occam channels onto a physical link. Another more recent approach uses the software harness **tiny** [4] which allows any process on any transputer to pass messages to any process on any other transputer in the network. The first simulator version ran on one transputer and operated the Front Panel Display by connecting it to a T414 Graphics processor.

5 Distributed Simulation

Since each of the simulation processes has in excess of eight input/output channels, a channel multiplexing method or software harness approach was necessary to configure a multi-transputer simulation. The latter technique was more flexible, because the number of transputers running the simulator can be varied by altering the placement definition. However, channel communication through **tiny** is asynchronous and because the simulator relied on **Barrier Synchronisation**, communication protocols were necessary. An input and output server Figure 3a ran in parallel with the simulator and **tiny**, sychronising channel communications to and from **tiny**.

The input server reads a synchronisation package from **tiny**. When synchronisation occurs, **tiny** is ready to receive. It synchronises with the simulator process and reads the data. The data is packaged and written to the **tiny** router. Similarly the output server writes a synchronisation message to the user process. When synchronisation has occurred the output server attempts to synchronise the **tiny** router. The server reads the package from tiny, unpacks it and writes it to the user process. Such a pair is required for every synchronising channel. Figure 3b illustrates how the simulation was distributed. There is a **tiny** router on each transputer connecting a sub-group of simulator processes. Each processor requires a table defining which channels and which process sources and destinations it must address.

6 Simulation Results

6.1 Test Programs and Assembly Code Optimisation

Test programs were written in simulation code which included Dot Product and Convolution algorithms. The simulation code resembled MC88000 machine code except that instruction fields were described in the test program file as a sequence of decimal numbers. The convolution program calculated the area of overlap at discrete delay intervals

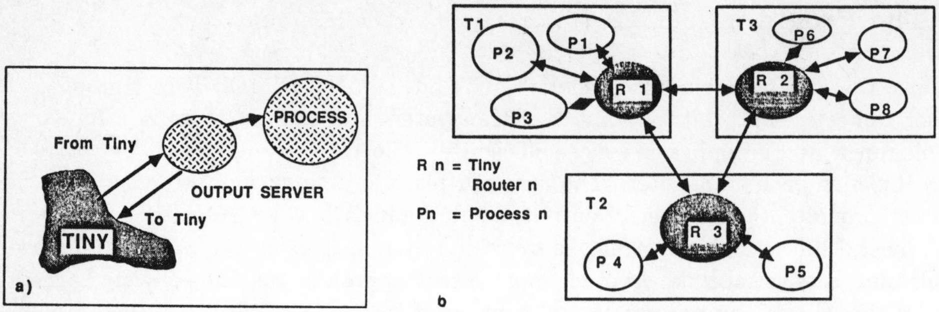

Figure 3: Distributed Simulation and Output Server

for two square impulse functions. The input vectors and the convoluted output vector were displayed graphically. Various versions of the convolution program were run on the simulator, and two plots of throughputs are given in Figure 4 and 5, illustrating unoptimised and optimised code respectively. Performance throughput for the Data, Floating Point and Integer Units increased from an average of under 10 Million Instructions per Second (MIPs) to an average of 15 MIPs after code optimisation. The former version has fewer conflicts than the latter and this is illustrated by the higher density of conflict fringes.

6.2 Simulation Time Speed Ups

Table 1a shows times to execute test programs, for a variable number of transputers. Table 1b gives the communication to computation ratio as defined by Fox [11], for a selection of processes. This information was obtained by using Occam2, timing processes that were placed before and after the communication and computation sections of each process.

7 Discussion

The Occam2 language was clearly a natural and convenient choice for supporting a processed based simulation and expressing the inherent parallelism of the 88000 microprocessor system on a transputer network. However, the direct mapping between Occam2 processes and 88000 Functional Units is responsible for the poor computation to communication ratios. When a 1st or 2nd Order Conflict occurred during the execution of floating point instructions the processes simulating the Instruction Unit and the floating

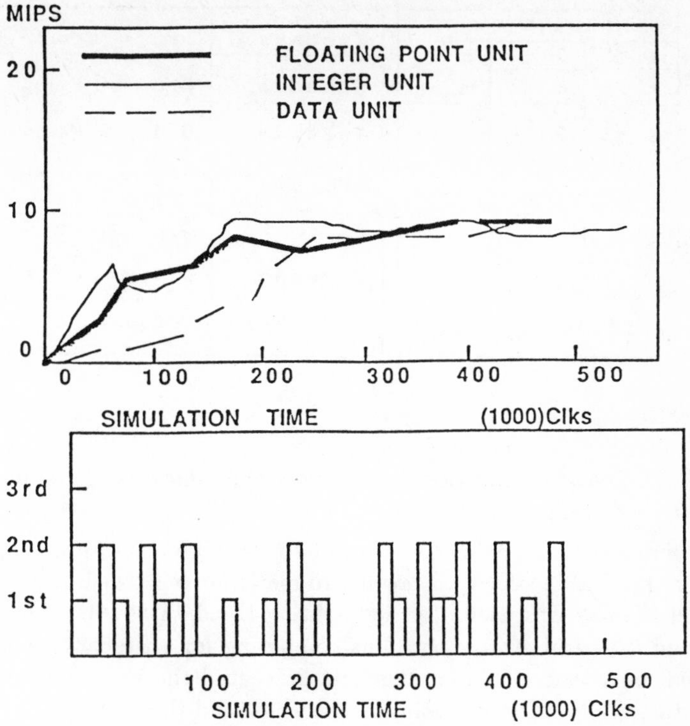

Figure 4: Unoptimised Convolution Test Program

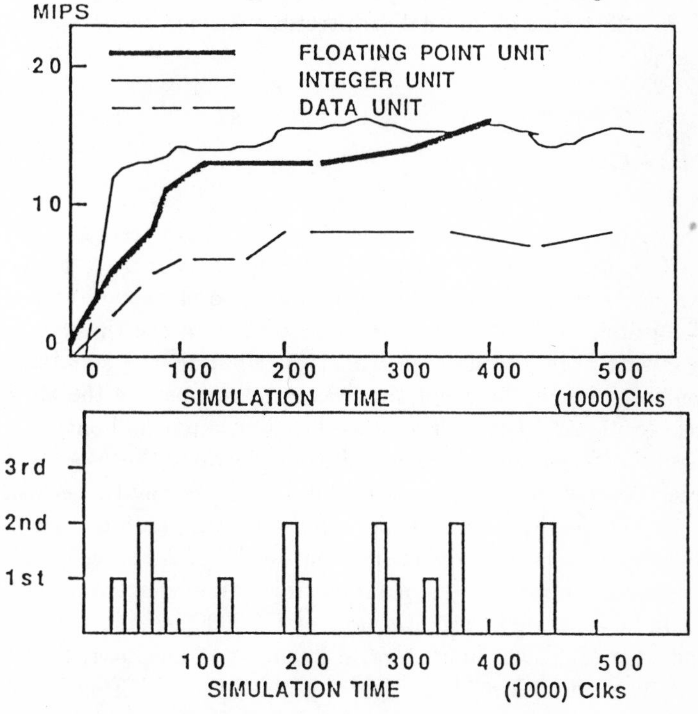

Figure 5: Optimised Convolution Test Program

TEST Code	PARALLELISM		
	1 T m s	3 T m s	5 T m s
Convol	3 15	3 48	4 27
Dot Prod	2 13	2 30	3 21
KEY:m = min s = sec T = T800 transputer			

a)

Process	Fc = Com / Cal
Schedul	0.5 <= Fc <= 0.7
Instruc	0.4 <= Fc <= 0.5
Integer	0.3 <= Fc <= 0.4
Float Pt	0.3 <= Fc <= 0.5
Sequenc	0.4 <= Fc <= 0.5
Feed For	0.6 <= Fc <= 0.8

b)

Table 1: Simulation Execution Times and Communication / Computation

point pipelines for example, would have to wait for the Sequencer process to allocate a true writeback or for the Feedforward process to match a result with a reserved register. The Front Panel Display was useful for highlighting the data flow bottleneck caused by floating point and load and store operations competing for writeback slots. Simulation experiments confirmed that 1st Order Conflicts prevented the Functional Unit pipelines from filling, particularly for floating point instructions, and that it was difficult to exploit the use of multiple Functional Units when only one writeback slot was allocated per clock cycle. Performance throughput was improved by optimising assembly code, but further improvement via alterations to internal architecture was non trivial due to the restrictive nature of Occam2.

8 Conclusion

A series of programs written in 88000 assembly code, were tested on an 88000 simulator written in Occam2 and running on a transputer network. A Front Panel Display identified bottlenecks in the flow of data through the architecture and emphasised how assembly code optimisations could be hand crafted to improve throughput performance. Two main problems were encountered whilst distributing the simulator over a multi-transputer domain. Firstly, the simulation was synchronous and the tiny harness which mapped process to physical channels was asychronous; input and output server processes were necessary to synchronise the communication between the user processors and the tiny harness for each of the 42 inter-process channels. Secondly, because the processes modelled the MC88000's Functional Units on a 1-1 basis, architecture bottlenecks prevented simulation processes from doing sufficient work. This reduced the computation to communication ratio and increased simulation time. More effective use of the transputer enviroment could be achieved in a multiprocessor MC88000 simulation, supported by running each duplicated MC88000 simulators on a separate transputer. Such a configuration could model an instruction level execution of a network of MC88000s, studying, for example, the effect of writethrough as opposed to copyback cache replacement [9] policies. Despite Occam2's affinity for expressing parallelism it did not support sufficient flexibility necessary for altering architecture features, that for example, reduce branch penalty [8].

Acknowledgement

The Meiko Computing Surface used for this project is a facility of the Edinburgh Parallel Computing Centre. The Centre is supported by major grants from the Department of Trade and Industry, the Computer Board and the Science and Engineering Research Council. In addition, thanks are due to the Meiko Computing Surface Support group and a special thanks to Brian Wylie, Lyndon Clark and Steve Booth, and to Magnus Patterson of the Edinburgh Royal Observatory.

References

[1] J. Djordjevic, R.N. Ibbett, M. R. Barbacci, *"Evaluation of Computer Architectures Using ISPS"* IEE PROC, Vol 127, No 4, July 1980

[2] D Beutty, K Brace, Randal E. Bryant *"COmpiled Simulator for MOS circuits"* Semiconductor Research Corporation, April 1989

[3] H. M. MacDougall *"Simulating Computer Systems Techniques and Tools"* The MIT Press, 1987

[4] Lyndon Clarke *"tiny documentation"* ECSP-UG-29 Tiny Version 2 (CS) Release 0 Occam Interface, Edinburgh Parallel Computing Centre

[5] R.N. Ibbett and N. P. Topham *"The Architecture of High Performance Computers"* Vol 1, Macmillan Educational Ltd, 1989

[6] T. Axelrod *"Effects of Synchronisation Barriers on Multiprocessor Performance "* Parallel Computing, No 3 pp 1-2-9-140, 1986

[7] Domenico Ferrari, *"Computer Systems Performance Evaluation"* Prentice-Hall, 1987

[8] D. J. Liljia *"Reducing the branch Penalty in Pipelined Processors"* IEEE Computer, July 1988

[9] A. J. Smith *"Cache Memories"* Computer Surveys, Vol 14, No 3, pp 473-530, 1982

[10] J. L. Hennessy and Patterson *"Computer Architecture:- A Quantative Approach"* Morgan Kaufmann Publishers, Inc. San Mateo, California 1990

[11] G. C. Fox *"Solving problems on concurrent processes"* Prentice-Hall, 1988

A DOMAIN DECOMPOSITION METHOD FOR SCATTERED DATA APPROXIMATION ON A DISTRIBUTED MEMORY MULTIPROCESSOR

L.Bacchelli Montefusco, C.Guerrini

Department of Mathematics University of Bologna, Italy

Abstract

łThe problem of reconstructing a function $f(x,y)$ from N experimental evaluations $(x_i, y_i, f_i), i = 1, \ldots, N$ irregularly distributed in the plane, has been considered for very large values of N. In this case the known local methods give the best sequential algorithms, but are not well suited for parallel implementation due to their excessively large arithmetic overhead. In this work we present a domain decomposition parallel method, especially studied for distributed memory multiprocessors which also achieves high efficiency as a sequential algorithm. In fact, it is based on the decomposition strategy already used in the local methods, but a particular decomposition in slightly overlapping regions and appropriate choice of the limited support weight functions has been realized in order to reduce arithmetic, communication and synchronization overheads. A good performance of the coarse grained parallel algorithm is then achieved by means of a dynamic arithmetic load- balance. Timings and efficiency results from a large experimentation carried out on a Hypercube iPSC/2 are given.

§1. Introduction

The problem of constructing smooth approximation based upon large sets of scattered data is encountered frequently in many areas of scientific applications. While a number of global and local methods have been proposed for solving the data-fitting problem, for large sets of data it is necessary to use local methods [1],[2]. The main idea of these methods is to decompose the domain of data D in subdomains D_k, construct on each subdomain a local approximation, $S_k(x,y)$, by solving a small data-fitting problem and obtain a smooth global approximation by suitably weighting these local approximations, making use of weight functions, w_k, having limited support. That is,

$$f(x,y) = \sum_k w_k(x,y) S_k(x,y) / \sum_k w_k(x,y) \tag{1}$$

In this work we have taken advantage of the inherent parallelism of local methods to realize a medium-grain asynchronous parallel algorithm for surface approximation, particularly suited for distributed memory multiprocessors. In the next sections we first describe the domain decomposition strategy chosen in order to achieve the greatest efficiency of the parallel algorithm, then we give the expression of the weight functions needed to obtain a global function of the desired smoothness and, finally, we discuss the dynamic work-load distribution realized to obtain good performance of the parallel algorithm giving also, some timings and efficiency results obtained by means of its implementation on a Hypercube iPSC/2 multiprocessor.

§2. Domain decomposition

Domain decomposition techniques have received much attention recently, as they are suited for parallel implementation. In fact the physical domain is divided into separate subdomains, each handled by a different processor. With the aim of eliminating the need for processors to communicate with one another in order to obtain the necessary smoothness of the global function on the interfaces of the subdomains, we have considered overlapping regions. On these regions each processor works independently and also weights the local approximation in order to obtain the global function of the smoothness desired . As this algorithm is specially studied for a message-passing distributed memory multiprocessor, this choice represents a powerful tool to reduce the synchronization and communication overhead. Moreover, in order to achieve the best performance of the parallel algorithm, a particular domain decomposition strategy has been studied. In fact a parallel algorithm performs better the better balanced is the arithmetic work-load among the processors. In the surface approximation problem the data are distributed irregularly on the domain and a uniform decomposition in equal-sized sub-regions would cause load imbalance as the execution times of the sequential part of the algorithm executed by each processor could be very different. This with consequent lost of efficiency, because the longest execution time determines the efficiency of the algorithm. In order to avoid load imbalance as much as possible the following domain decomposition has been carried out: given the even numbers ng1 and ng2 of grid-lines in the x and y directions, we have ordered sets $\{x_i\}$ and $\{y_i\}$ of the data and have realized the decompositions

$$D_1 = \{x_{min} = x_0 \leq x_1 \leq x_2 \leq \ldots \leq x_{ng1+1} = x_{ng1+1} = x_{max}\}$$

$$D_2 = \{y_{min} = y_0 \leq y_1 \leq y_2 \leq \ldots \leq y_{ng2+1} = y_{ng0+1} = y_{max}\}$$

so that each subinterval of two consecutive odd-odd and even-even grid-lines

$$[x_k, x_{k+2}], [x_{k-1}, x_{k+1}]; k = 1, \ldots, ng1 - 1$$

$$[y_j, y_{j+2}], [y_{j-1}, y_{j+1}]; j = 1, \ldots, ng2 - 1$$

contains 2N/(ng1-1) x_i points and 2N/(ng2-1) $y_i$points respectively. The relative position of the consecutive even-odd grid-lines x_k, x_{k+1}, and y_j, y_{j+1} k=2, …, $ng1 - 2$, $j = 2, \ldots, ng2 - 2$ is then determined according to the amount of overlap of neighboring intervals desired. This is automatically obtained acting on the number of points common to two neighboring odd-even intervals. In fact this number is given by $N/(ng1 - 1) * 1/(pd1)$ for decomposition D_1 and by $N/(ng2 - 1) * 1/(pd2)$ for decomposition D_2, thus by changing the values of parameters pd1 and pd2 it is possible to build up decompositions with different overlapping odd-even intervals. Finally, the subdomains where local approximations are executed, are given by the rectangles

$$R_{i,j} = [x_{in}, x_{if}][y_{jn}, y_{jf}]; i = 1, \ldots, n1; j = 1, \ldots, n2 \qquad (3)$$

$$with : n1 = ng1/2, n2 = ng2/2, in = 2i - 2, if = 2i + 1, jn = 2j - 2, if = 2j + 1$$

These regions, for not-very-poor point distributions, contain an approximately equal number of data points, with consequent work-load balance among processors. Figs. 1-2 show two decomposition for n=2000 data points obtained according to the data distribution and for different values of pd1 and pd2.

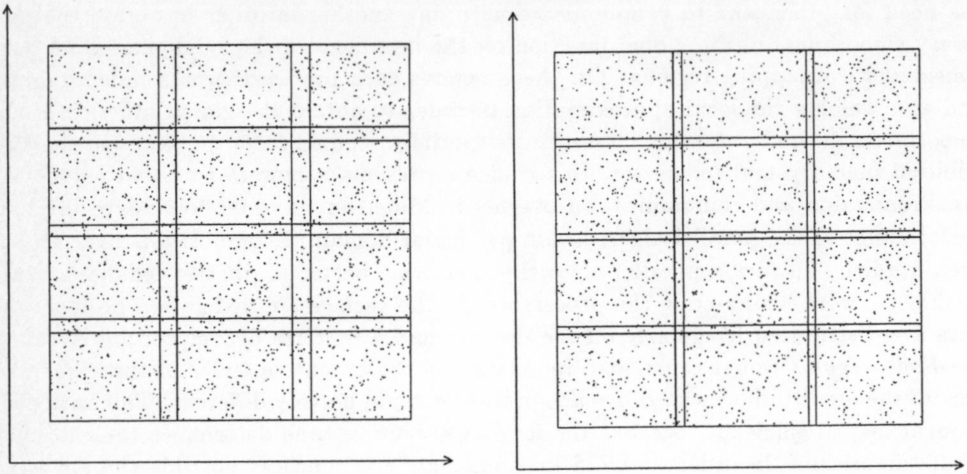

Fig.1-2 Example of decompositions:N=2000,n1=n2=4,pd1=pd2=8 (left), N=2000, n1=n2=4, pd1=pd2=8 (right)

§3. Weight functions

The rectangular regions $R_{i,j}$ defined in the previous section are of fundamental importance to construct the limited support weight functions necessary to smoothly join together the different approximations performed independently by each processor. In fact, with the aim of achieving good efficiency of the parallel algorithm, it is necessary to be able to govern the amount of overlap of the support of the weight functions so as to decrease the necessary joining computations as well as make evaluation of the weight functions easier. These computations represent the arithmetic overhead of the domain decomposition algorithm, and must therefore be kept as low as possible. A natural choice for the regions on which weight functions are non-zero is obviously given by rectangles $R_{i,j}$. In fact, acting on parameters pd1 and pd2 it is possible to opportunely decrease the overlap of neighboring rectangles; moreover for these regions it is possible to build up the bivariate functions $w_{i,j}(x,y)$ as products of the univariate functions $u_i(x)$and $v_j(y)$; these are defined by means of Hermite polynomials of prescribed degree according to the degree of smoothness of the local approximations. In fact the global function given by (1) is at least as smooth as the least smooth of functions w_k and s_k. In the present paper we have considered local approximations given by least-squares C^2 L-spline functions, thus we make use of the Hermite quintic

$$H_5(s) = 1 - s^3(6s^2 - 15s + 10)$$

satisfying

$$H_5(0) = 1,\ H_5'(0) = H"_5(0) = H_5(1) = H_5'(1) = H"_5(1) = 0$$

We then define functions $u_i(x)$ and $v_j(y)$ so that they are piecewise quintics with continuous second derivatives as follows:

$$u_i(x) = \begin{array}{lll} 0 & x \leq x_{in} & \\ 1 - H_5(s) & x_{in} \leq x \leq x_{in+1} & s = (x - x_{in})/(x_{in+1} - x_{in}) \\ 1 & x_{in+1} \leq x \leq x_{if-1} & \\ H_5(s) & x_{if-1} \leq x\ lex_{if} & s = (x - x_{if})/(x_{if} - x_{if-1} \\ 0 & x \leq x_{if} & \end{array}$$

$$i = 1, \ldots, n1; \tag{4}$$

the $v_j(y), j = 1, \ldots, n2$, being defined analogously. Then the weight functions with the support of rectangles $R_{i,j}$ are defined as

$$w_{i,j}(x,y) = u_i(x)v_j(y); i = 1, \ldots, n1; j = 1, \ldots, n2$$

It is easy to verify that they form a partition of the unity for the plane and that expression (1) for the global function is now

$$f(x,y) = \sum_{ij} w_{i,j}(x,y)S_{i,j}(x,y) \tag{5}$$

where, at most, four terms in the sum are non-zero. It is important to point out that, as the support of the weight functions coincides with subdomain $R_{i,j}$, each processor handling regions $R_{i,j}$ can independently calculate the local approximation and then weight it with the corresponding weight function.

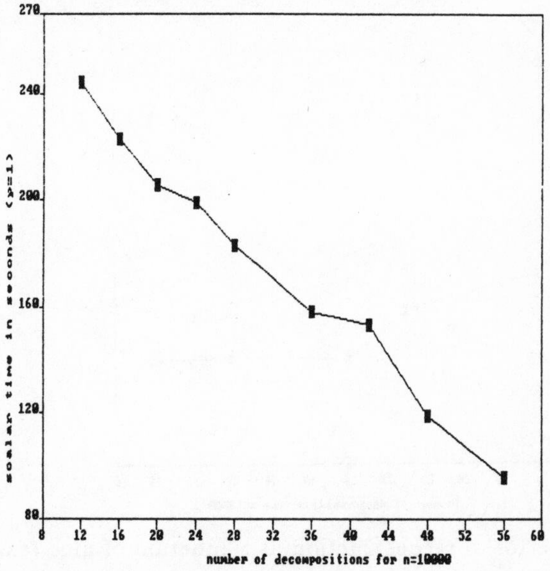

Fig.3 Sequential approximation time as a function of nloc

§4. Performance evaluation and numerical experiments

§The sequential algorithm

The algorithm presented in this paper, even if considered as a sequential algorithm, represents one of the most efficient methods to construct a smooth approximation of a large set of scattered data. In fact, as shown in fig.3 the time needed for evaluation of the global approximation $f(x,y)$ decreases as the number of local approximations increases, while the error of reconstruction, as a convex combination of the local approximation errors, is no worse than that of the poorest approximation $S_{i,j}$. As usual local approximation algorithms give better reconstruction than global ones, the overall approximation error of the presented domain decomposition method, even if strongly dependent on the local method used, seems to improve for coarse decompositions, then remains quite insensible to further refinement of the grid lines.

Fig.4 shows the behavior of the global error of the reconstructed function, (see fig.6), as a function of the number of local approximations ($nloc = n1 \times n2$) . These are given by bicubic natural spline least-squares approximations and the measured error is a mean square error with respect to the analytic function F(x,y), given in fig.5 whose values have been sampled at points $(x_i, y_i), i = 1, \ldots, N$, irregularly distributed in the plane, and perturbed with white noise with s=0.1. It is worth while to note that, when the number of experimental data is very large it is not possible to evaluate the error for the global approximation but we only consider the behaviour of the error beginning from a few local approximations to a large number of local ones.

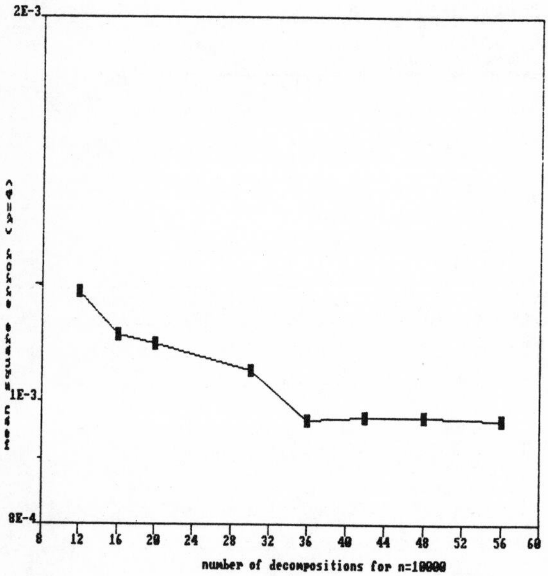

Fig.4 Mean square error of reconstruction as a function of nloc (example fig.6)

§The parallel algorithm

The parallel implementation of this approximation algorithm has been specially studied for a distributed memory message-passing multiprocessor. In such a machine the efficiency of a parallel algorithm is critically affected by the need for communication and synchronization and by the arithmetic load balance, which is usually determined in advance of the computations.

Therefore, in order to improve the performance of the algorithm, it is necessary to analyse the influence of the communication and synchronization time on the global one, as well as that needed by each processor for arithmetic computations.

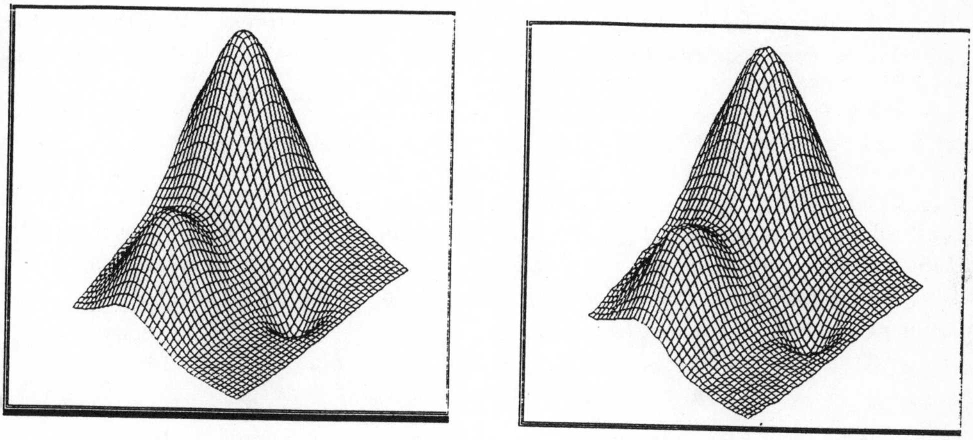

Fig.5-6 Analitic function (left); Global reconstruction ,nloc=56(right)

In our case, the time spent by a processor q performing nq weighted local approximations is given by

$$t_q = t_{aq} + n_q(t_{com} + t_{sync})$$

where t_{aq} is the arithmetic computation time required to execute nq weighted local approximations t_{com} is the communication time required by each local approximation t_{sync} is the synchronization time required by each local approximation

The parallel time for p processors is therefore given by

$$T(p) = \max_{1 \leq q \leq p} (t_{aq} + n_q(t_{com} + t_{sync})) \tag{6}$$

where $n_q \tilde{=} nloc/p$ is the number of local approximations executed approximately by each processor. On the contrary the sequential time T(1) is only given by

$$T(1) = \sum_{q=1}^{p} t_{aq}$$

Therefore, as the efficiency of the parallel algorithm is defined

$$E(p) = \frac{\frac{T(1)}{T(p)}}{p} \tag{7}$$

good efficiency is reached: (i) by minimizing the effect of t_{com} and t_{sync}; (ii) by optimizing the arithmetic load distribution so that

$$\max_q t_{aq} \tilde{=} \frac{T(1)}{p}$$

Aim (i) is reached by the use of the weight functions, which allows the processors to work independently and fully asynchronously (that is tsync=0) with only the communication cost required to send the weighted approximations to the host; that means

$$t_{com} = \beta + L\tau = \beta + \tau k/nloc$$

where β = start-up time; τ = the propagation time of a unitary number of data; L = length of the message, which is inversely proportional to nloc with proportionality constant k. Therefore the only overhead due to the parallel implementation of the domain decomposition algorithm (assuming perfect load-balance) is given by the total communication time

$$T_{com}(p) = n_q(\beta + \tau k/nloc) = nloc\beta/p + \tau k/p; \tag{8}$$

which is linearly increasing with nloc, but inverse proportional to the number of processors and represents a very small per cent of the total parallel time.

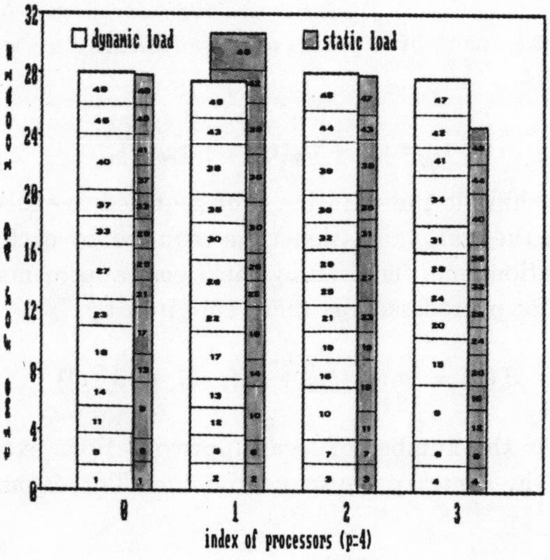

Fig.7 Dynamic and static work-load distribution.

To overtake aim (ii) we have studied the domain decomposition strategy given in 2. together with an efficient dynamic load repartition. In fact, we have not determined statically, in advance of the computation, the number of local problems that each processor has to solve, but the indices in, if, jn, jf, of a new local approximation is sent by the host to that processor from which it has just received a partial reconstruction. Fig.7 shows the total time repartition among the four processors of an hypercube iPSC/2 for an approximation problem with N=10000 and nloc=49, corresponding to the described dynamic work distribution, compared with the time repartition obtained with a static wrap-around work distribution [3]. It is clear that the dynamic arithmetic load repartition gives a more balanced work distribution with consequent better efficiency of the parallel algorithm.

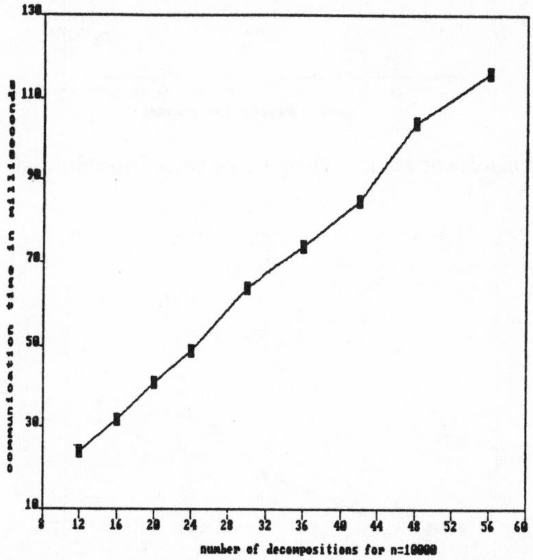

Fig.8 Communication time as a function of nloc

We can therefore conclude that the proposed parallel algorithm reachs good efficiency even with the increasing of the number of processors. Moreover its performance grows with the number of decomposition.

In fact, in spite of the linear increasing of the communication time with nloc (see fig.8), the parallel time show the same decreasing behaviour of the scalar time (fig.9) and the efficiency grows slightly due to the better balancing of the arithmetic work load (see fig.10). Obviously, using the least squares method as the local technique, there is a natural limit to the increase in the number of decompositions given by the feasibility of the local method .

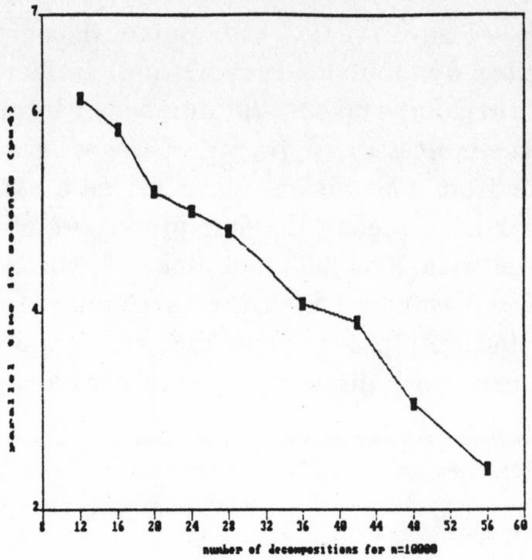

Fig.9 Parallel approximation time as a function of nloc

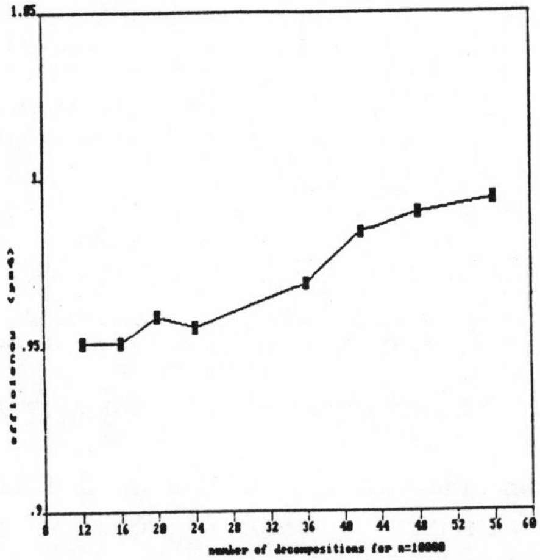

Fig.10 Efficiency as a function of nloc

§References

1. [1] R.Franke: "Smooth surface approximation by a local method of interpolation at scattered points",Report Naval Postgraduate School 27-78-008 (1978)
2. [2] L.Bacchelli Montefusco:"Ricostruzione di superfici mediante funzioni di forma locali ",Calcolo v.19,p.169-191(1982)
3. [3] G.A. Geist, M.T. Heath ," Matrix factorization on a Hypercubes Multiprocessors", Hypercube 1986,pp.161-180.

This work was conducted as part of the C.N.R. research contract n.90.00676.PF.69 "Sistemi informatici e Calcolo Parallelo"

Laura Bacchelli Montefusco, Carla Guerrini, Dipartimento di Matematica Piazza di porta San Donato 5, 40127 Bologna, Italy.

NONLINEAR ADAPTIVE FINITE ELEMENT SYSTEMS ON DISTRIBUTED MEMORY COMPUTERS

S. Nölting

Institute for Computer Applications, University of Stuttgart
Pfaffenwaldring 27, 7000 Stuttgart 80 (Germany)

The implementation of a large finite element program used for nonlinear industrial applications on an iPSC/2 Hypercube is described in this paper. Two strategies for the solution of the linearized system of equations are outlined and tested. A new method for the automatic spatial decomposition of the discretized finite element domain is presented and compared with other approaches. Finally, strategies for adaptive mesh refinement are discussed.

1. INTRODUCTION

The solution of nonlinear field problems on very large discretized domains by the finite element method is a common requirement today in a variety of fields such as aerodynamics, structural mechanics, weather forecasting, or plasma physics, among many others. The simulation of the flow around complete aircraft and the modelling of complex 3-dimensional forming problems, for example, are applications that often require computational resources well beyond the capabilities of today's fastest supercomputers. Parallel computers with distributed memory appear to be the most cost-effective and potentially most powerful approach to achieving the performance required for such problems. The implementation of finite element codes on such machines is therefore of great importance. Here some aspects of the implementation of an existing large finite element program, which has been used in industrial applications for a number of years, are presented.

2. FINITE ELEMENT PROCEDURES

The finite element programming system *FEPS* [1] is a modern development package for nonlinear, 3-dimensional problems that was written at the Institute for Computer Applications. Currently, applications include static and dynamic structural analysis, heat transfer, coupled problems, and a number of fluid dynamics applications ranging from incompressible viscous flow to compressible hypersonic flow with chemical reactions.

The module for the simulation of industrial forming problems will serve as a model application here and its parallel implementation will be described in chapter 3. A simplified flow diagram for the sequential algorithm is depicted in figure 1. After the initialization of the input data, an increment loop is executed a specified number of times until the simulation is completed. Within each increment, an initial estimate of new nodal point velocities and displacements (predictor) is improved iteratively (corrector-loop) until convergence yields the new nodal point values at the end of the current time step. Within the corrector-loop, a Newton-Raphson method is used to solve the nonlinear system of equations. First the relevant element matrices and vectors are constructed and assembled into the global system matrix and vector. These are then modified through a contact algorithm modelling rigid, moving contact surfaces representing dies, rollers, etc. in the forming process. The resulting system of equation is then solved using a direct solution method. Upon convergence, stresses are calculated at selected time steps. Adaptive modifications of the finite element mesh can then be carried out if geometric and/or physical error indicators imply a detrioration of the solution. This can be accomplished by either just moving nodal points and thus leaving the mesh topology unaltered, or, if that proves insufficient, by introducing new nodes and elements in regions of high error. For a more detailed discussion of the sequential algorithm, see [2].

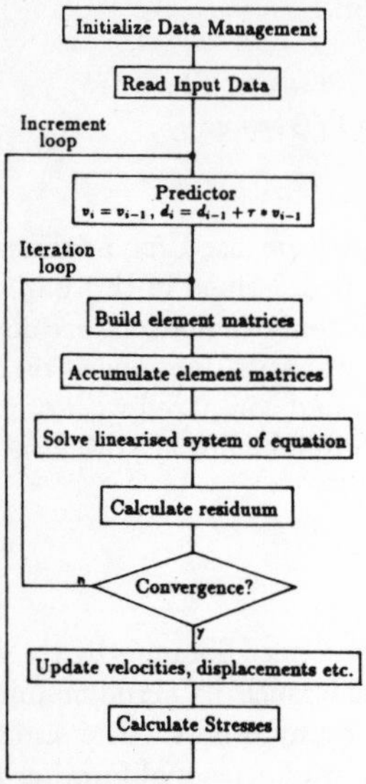

Fig 1. Sequential Algorithm

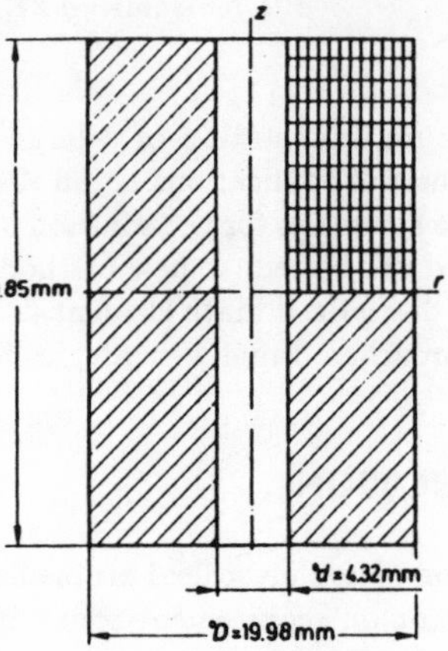

Fig 2. Example Problem and Discretization

3. PARALLELIZATION

Measuring the CPU-times corresponding to each phase of the algorithm indicates that the bulk of the time is spent inside the corrector-loop. As we move from smaller, two-dimensional problems to larger, three-dimensional ones, the solution phase becomes more and more dominant. The only other step that requires significant resources is the building of the element matrices and I will therefore focus the attention on these steps in the discussion of the parallel implementation.

3.1 Approaches to the Parallelisation of FE-Procedures

Parallelization of finite element procedures on distributed memory computers is most commonly achieved by spatial decomposition [3,4]. The discretized finite element domain is first automatically decomposed into a number of non-overlapping subdomains equal to the number of processors available. An optimal decomposition should obviously distribute the computational load evenly between the processors and keep communication to a minimum. The computational load per processor is determined by a variety of factors, most importantly the number of degrees of freedom and elements in each domain and by the number of internal boundary nodes, i.e., nodes that are common to at least two subdomains. Automatic domain decomposition will be discussed in more detail in the next chapter.

The major steps of the parallel finite element algorithm based on spatial decomposition are identical to those of the sequential algorithm shown in figure 1. Every processor performs the same computations, but on different data, which are specified in separate input files. These have the same format as those for sequential computations with some additional arrays identifying the boundary nodes. During the initialization and data input phases some data have to be exchanged between processors to determine the connectivity of the subdomains. This overhead is so small, however, that it does not discernibly reduce the efficiency.

The first major phase of the computations, the building of the element matrices and vectors, which has to be performed in every iteration of every increment, can now be accomplished entirely in parallel without any communication or sequential overhead. Sequential and parallel algorithms are identical in this phase. The major differences occur during the solution phase.

3.2 Parallel Solution Procedures

The linearized system of equations that has to be solved in every iteration step has the general form

$$\boldsymbol{A}\,\boldsymbol{v} = \boldsymbol{f}$$

where **A** is the n * n symmetric banded system matrix (here: viscosity matrix), **v** is the vector of unknown degrees of freedom (velocity increment), and **f** is the vector of external forces (residual forces).

Only direct solvers are considered here since iterative solvers, which in many respects lend themselves more easily to parallelisation, are not reliably enough yet to be used in industrial applications consistently. Two algorithms will be discussed here, a parallel Cholesky decomposition and a substructuring procedure.

3.2.1 *Parallel Cholesky Decomposition*

A general Cholesky decomposition is performed in three steps:

Factorization	$\boldsymbol{A} = \boldsymbol{L}\,\boldsymbol{L}^T$	
Forward substitution	$\boldsymbol{L}\boldsymbol{x} = \boldsymbol{f}$	$\rightarrow\ \boldsymbol{x}$
Backward substitution	$\boldsymbol{L}^T\,\boldsymbol{v} = \boldsymbol{x}$	$\rightarrow\ \boldsymbol{v}$

L is a lower triangular matrix and is stored in the same location as **A**.

In order to parallelize this algorithm the system matrix **A** has to be distributed among the processors. To ensure good load balancing during the factorization phase, this is best done in the column-wise fashion shown below. [5]

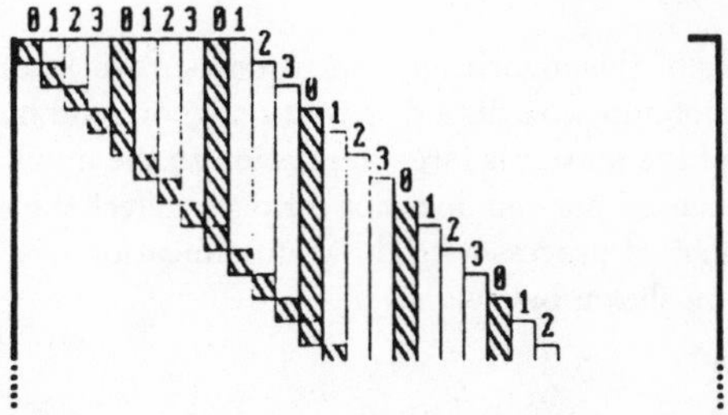

Figure 3 : Column-wise distribution of the system matrix

Since each element matrix is computed in one processor, there is some message passing necessary to achieve this distribution. To avoid excessive communication overheads, the element contributions to the system matrix that are to be stored in a different processor than they were computed in, are first stored in temporary buffers and sent only when these are full. In this way there are generally not more than 2-3 send operations per processor during the assembly phase.

The factorization and forward substitution can be performed at the same time to avoid spurious communication. **L** and **x** are computed in a row-wise fashion, whereby for each row first the diagonal element is computed in a sequential step by the processor storing it, and then the off-diagonal terms are processed in parallel. The algorithm can be described as follows:

FACTORIZATION AND FORWARD SUBSTITUTION

loop $i = 1,n$ — loop over n rows of **A**

processor storing column i of **A** :

$L_{ii} = (A_{ii} - \sum_{k=m}^{i-1} L_{ik})^{1/2}$ — m: row-index of the first non-zero element in column i of $\mathbf{L}^T$

$x_i = f_i / L_{ii}$

send $L_{ik,(k=m,i)}$ *and* x_i *to all other processors*

all processors :

receive L_{ik}

loop $j = i{+}1, i{+}ibnd{-}1$ — loop over off-diagonal elements row i, ibnd = bandwidth of **A**

$L_{ji} = (A_{ji} - \sum_{k=p}^{i+1} L_{ik} L_{jk}) / L_{ii}$ — p : row-index of first non-zero in column j of $\mathbf{L}^T$

$X_j = f_j - L_{ji} x_i$

end loop

end loop

BACKWARD SUBSTITUTION

loop $i = n,1,-1$ — backward loop over n rows of **A**

all processors :

$tmp = L_{ji} x_j \qquad j = i{+}1,\ i{+}ibnd{-}1$

send tmp tp the processor storing v_i

processor storing v_i :

$v_i = (x_i - tmp_j) / L_{ii} \qquad j = 1, nproc$

end loop

During the parallel parts of this algorithm, each processor works only on those elements it is storing and thus, due to the column-wise data distribution, good load balancing is achieved during this phase if the bandwidth of the matrix is large in relation to the number of processors. Likewise, it can be shown that the sequential portion does not seriously affect the efficiency if n is sufficiently large in relation to the number of processors. The communication overhead, however, can by no means be neglected, as will be shown below.

3.2.2 *Parallel Substructuring*

Substructuring is a technique that has been used in finite element applications for many years and that has attained new importance in the context of parallel computing. There are some conceptual differences, though, between the traditional applications and the parallel versions. Originally, the substructuring technique was intended to decompose a given large structure into a number of physically relevant components, either because the whole structure could not be analyzed at once, or to allow different teams to work on the various components at the same time. In parallel computations, on the other hand, the decomposition is done according to strictly computational guidelines and the individual subdomains need not have any physical meaning.

The idea behind substructuring is to reduce the $n * n$ system matrix to one comprising only degrees of freedom lying on the internal boundary between subdomains by eliminating all internal degrees of freedom. In parallel computations, this elimination process can be performed concurrently without any need for communication. The reduced system matrix is then solved with a conventional solution procedure, in this case the parallel Cholesky algorithm described above.

For the implementation of this algorithm, the interior and boundary d.o.f. have to be separated, so that the system of equations to be solved in each processor has the form:

$$\begin{bmatrix} \boldsymbol{A}_{ii} & \boldsymbol{A}_{ib} \\ \boldsymbol{A}_{bi} & \boldsymbol{A}_{bb} \end{bmatrix} \begin{bmatrix} \boldsymbol{v}_i \\ \boldsymbol{v}_i \end{bmatrix} = \begin{bmatrix} \boldsymbol{f}_i \\ \boldsymbol{f}_i \end{bmatrix}$$

Inserting the upper part of this equation into the lower yields :

$$\underbrace{[\boldsymbol{A}_{bb} - \boldsymbol{A}_{ib}\boldsymbol{A}_{ii}^{-1}\boldsymbol{A}_{bi}]}_{\boldsymbol{A}_{bb}^{\star}}\boldsymbol{v}_b = \underbrace{[\boldsymbol{f}_r - \boldsymbol{A}_{ib}\boldsymbol{A}_{ii}^{-1}]}_{\boldsymbol{f}_b^{\star}}$$

To compute $\boldsymbol{A}_{bb}^{\star}$ and $\boldsymbol{f}_b^{\star}$ the following steps have to be performed:

$$\boldsymbol{A}_{ii} = \boldsymbol{L}\boldsymbol{L}^T$$

$$\boldsymbol{L}\boldsymbol{M}_{ii} = \boldsymbol{A}_{ib} \rightarrow \boldsymbol{M}_{ii} \qquad \boldsymbol{L}^T\boldsymbol{x}_i = \boldsymbol{f}_i \,,\; \boldsymbol{L}g_i = \boldsymbol{x}_i$$

$$\boldsymbol{A}_{bb}^{\star} = \boldsymbol{A}_{bb} - \boldsymbol{M}_{ii}^T\boldsymbol{M}_{ii} \qquad \boldsymbol{f}_b^{\star} = \boldsymbol{f}_b - \boldsymbol{A}_{ib}^T\boldsymbol{g}_i$$

where $\boldsymbol{M}_{ii}$ is an intermediate array of dimension *(# of interior d.o.f.) ∗ (# of boundary d.o.f.).*

The individual matrices $\boldsymbol{A}_{bb}^{\star}$ from each processor are then assembled into the global boundary matrix $\boldsymbol{A}_{bb}$, which at the same time is distributed to all processors in a column-wise fashion to allow the subsequent parallel Cholesky solution. Finally, the solution vector $\boldsymbol{v}_i$ corresponding to the degrees of freedom in the interior of each subdomain is attained:

$$\boldsymbol{v}_i = \boldsymbol{A}_{ii}^{-1}(\boldsymbol{f}_i - \boldsymbol{A}_{bi}\boldsymbol{v}_b)$$

which can again be done in parallel by all processors.

3.3 Results

The parallel algorithms described above were implemented on an iPSC/2 hypercube with four nodes. They are also currently being tested on a 32-node transputer workstation, for which results were however not available yet at the time of publication.

Figure 2 shows the example forming problem that was used to illustrate the performance of the parallel procedures. A thick-walled cylinder is reduced to about 50% of its initial height during an upsetting process. Due to symmetry only one quarter of the structure is discretized. The simulation required 30 time steps with 4-5 iterations each for a convergent solution. Figure 4 shows the decompositions used for two and four processors and figures 5 and 6 summarize the performance on the iPSC/2. These results are based on the overall runtime of the simulation, including all steps of the algorithm (see fig. 1) except for data input and output of results. These were not taken into account because there was no parallel I/O-facility available, and I/O-performance was therefore dependent on a variety of factors not related to the algorithm.

Figure 5 shows the normalized runtimes for different numbers of processors with a constant size of the discretized domain (40∗40 elements) for parallel Cholesky solution and parallel substructuring. Figure 6 depicts the efficiency of the calculations on four processors with varying problem size.

Several points are notable:

- Parallel substructuring performs consistently better than parallel Cholesky.
- Both algorithms improve with increasing grain size (number of elements per subdomain).
- Effiencies decrease with increasing number of processors.

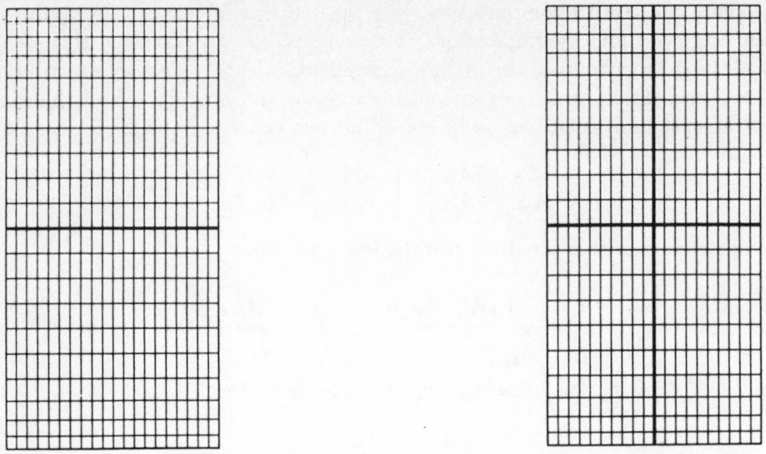

Figure 4: Decompositions of example problem for two and four processors

Parallel substructuring actually achieves efficiencies higher than 1.0, which is due to the fact that it is compared not to a sequential version of the substructuring algorithm (which is not available in ***FEPS***), but to an optimized band matrix solver usually used in sequential applications. To avoid any redundant computations, the parallel substructuring algorithm is optimized to a degree that could not be achieved for the sequential solver. Moreover, this algorithm requires very little communication, which almost exclusively occurs during the assembly and solution of the reduced system matrix.

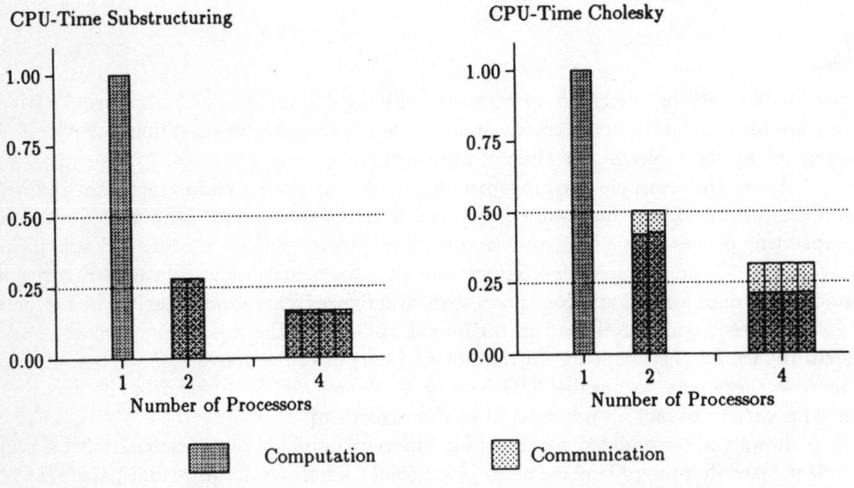

Figure 5: Overall runtime for 1, 2, and 4 processors

The parallel Cholesky solver, on the other hand, incurs a large number of message-passing steps. Even for large grain-sizes, communication accounts for over 30% of the overall runtime on four processors, a number that will increase even more if more processors are used.

The performance of the parallel substructuring algorithm also decreases when either the grain-size is reduced or the number of processors is increased, due in both cases to the lower ratio of number of interior nodes to number of boundary nodes. However, this ratio remains approximately constant above a certain number of processors if the overall problem size increases linearly with the number of processors. We therefore expect parallel substructuring to maintain high efficiencies as the number of processors increase *if the grain-size is kept constant.*

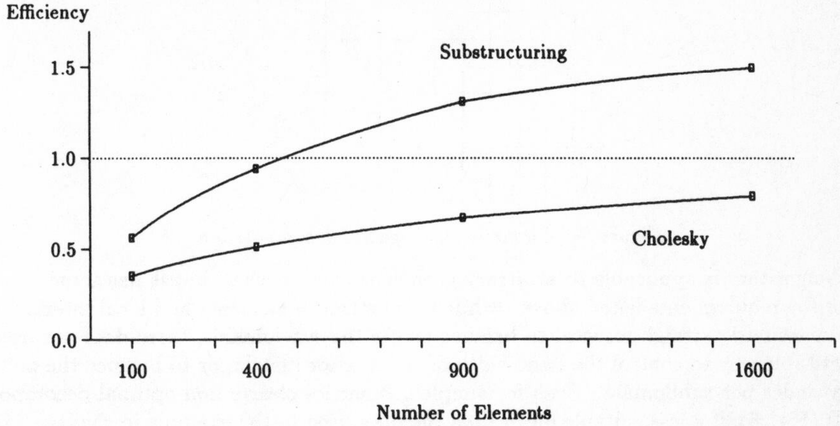

Figure 6: Efficiencies on four processors with varying problem size

4. AUTOMATIC SPATIAL DECOMPOSITION

In the previous chapter we have seen that good efficiencies can be achieved for complex finite element applications with a spatial decomposition approach. However, the usefulness of the presented algorithms depends on the availability of an automatic domain decomposer for arbitrary meshes and geometries. Besides this general applicability, the obvious requirement for a good decomposition algorithm is that it balances the computational load evenly among the processors without inducing excessive communication overhead. The major phases of the algorithm considered here (Fig. 1) determining the load are the building of the element matrices and the solution of the linearized system of equations. The computational requirement for the former is determined simply by the number of elements. If every subdomain contains the same number of elements (and if all elements are of the same type) then this step of the algorithm will be perfectly balanced.

The work load per processor during the solution phase, on the other hand, is controlled by a variety of parameters. If the parallel Cholesky algorithm is used, the domain is redistributed prior to the solution step as described above, and the initial decomposition does not influence the efficiency of the computations during this step. However, if the substructuring approach is used, the "right" decomposition is crucial for good performance. The load per processor in this case is determined by (a) the number of local interior degrees of freedom in each subdomain; (b) the bandwidth of the interior matrix A_{ii}; and (c) the number of boundary nodes bordering on other subdomains, which has a major influence on the steps performed during the reduction of the system matrix, and also determines the size of the reduced global matrix to be solved with the parallel Cholesky algorithm.

Experiments have shown that all three factors have to be taken into account in the a-priori determination of the load if a serious degradation of the performance is to be avoided.

A very general approach to automatic domain decomposition is to subdivide the mesh at the element level after the generation of the mesh [6]. Starting with an arbitrary or user-specified element, these schemes propagate through the finite element mesh by adding neighboring elements until the required number of elements or degrees of freedom for one subdomain is reached, and then proceed with the next subdomain in the same fashion.

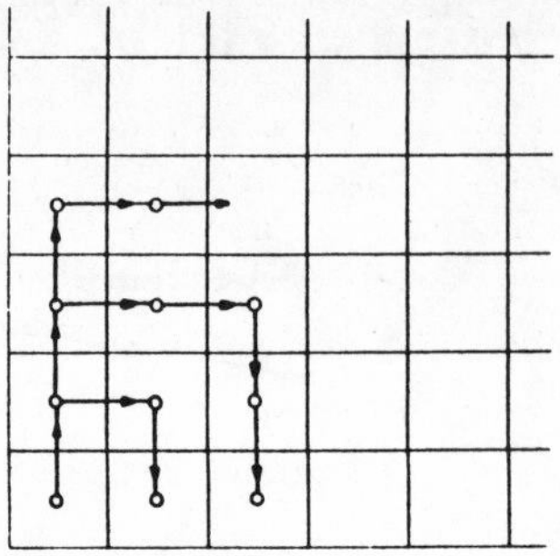

Figure 7 : Element-level spatial decomposition

This algorithm is applicable to arbitrary geometries and meshes, but it has some drawbacks in light of the requirements listed above. While the number of elements and local interior degrees of freedom are fairly straightforward to balance across the subdomains, there does not appear to be a practicable way to control the bandwidth of the interior matrix, or to balance the number of boundary nodes per subdomain. Even for simple geometries clearly non-optimal decompositions can result (Fig. 8), if a less suitable mesh than the ones used in the example in chapter 3 is used.

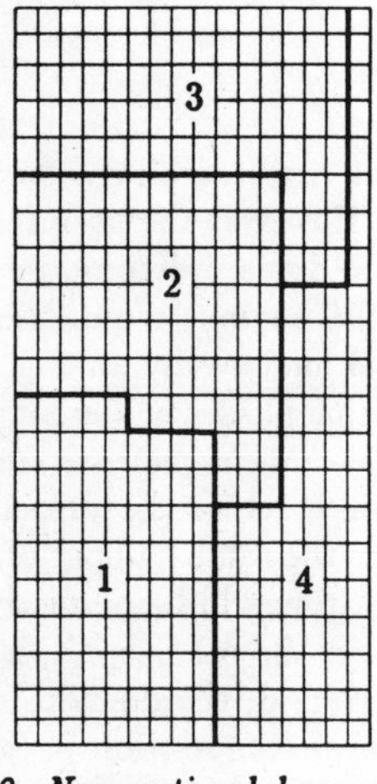

Fig. 8: Non-optimal decomposition for 4 nodes

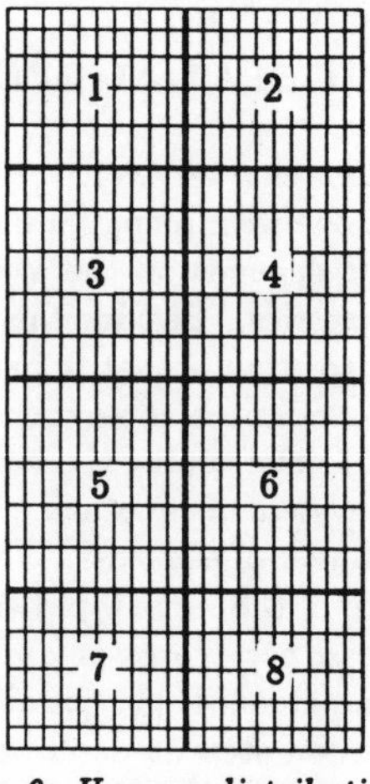

Fig 9: Uneven distribution of boundary nodes

Also, even for apparently good decompositions, an uneven distribution of boundary nodes can seriously degrade the performance. For the 8-processor example shown in Fig. 9, theoretical considerations show that the processors working on subdomains 3-6 need up to 30% more CPU-time than those working on subdomains 1,2,7, and 8 due to the higher number of boundary nodes. These problems become even more apparent if more complex geometries are decomposed.

An alternative approach to automatic spatial decomposition is therefore presented here. It is based on a structured multi-block mesh generator [7], depicted in Figure 10. First, the geometry of the structure to be discretized is subdivided into quadrilateral blocks, which currently has to be done manually. Local refinements can then be specified by the user and subblocks are created automatically to generate the refined regions. Finally, the number of elements on all edges of every block is computed and a regular mesh is generated on every block and subblock.

The decomposition of the mesh can now be accomplished on the level of the blocks instead of on the element level by assigning a number of blocks to every processor. The workload per block can be easily computed due to the regularity of the mesh and the resulting uniform bandwidth within each block. If there are more processors than blocks or if the blocks cannot be distributed evenly, individual blocks can be split into two or more subblocks. Even though the number of interior degrees of freedom, the number of boundary nodes, the bandwidth, etc. will usually vary on the different processors, a balanced distribution of the overall workload can be achieved with this method because the workload per block and thus the workload per processor can be determined exactly. This is true regardless of the complexity of the geometry because it is always split up into simple quadrilateral blocks.

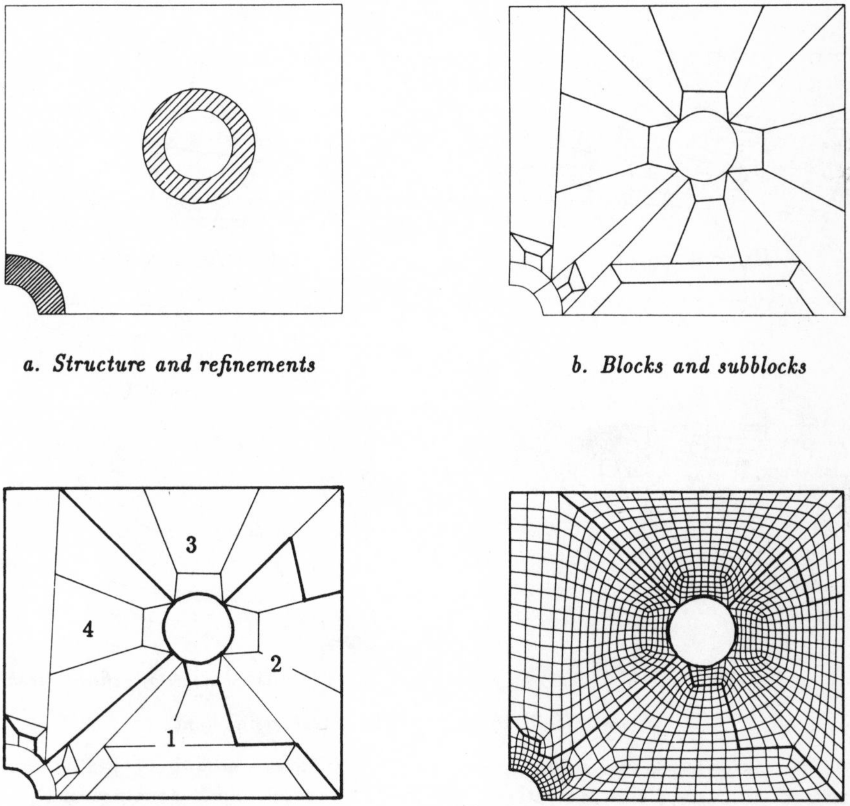

a. Structure and refinements

b. Blocks and subblocks

c. Decomposition

d. Finite element mesh

Figure 10: Block-level mesh generation and spatial decomposition

Another advantage of this approach is that the decomposition can be done prior to the actual generation of the mesh. This is by far the computationally most demanding phase of the overall mesh generation procedure and can now be accomplished in parallel.

5. ADAPTIVITY

Adaptive procedures, i.e., the refinement of a relatively course initial mesh in the course of the computations according to certain error indicators, are rapidly gaining importance in modern finite element applications. Refinement can be achieved by moving nodes without changing the topology of the mesh (r-method), by increasing the polynomial order of the approximation functions in selected elements (p-method), or by generating a new, finer mesh in areas of large error (h-method). While the r-method does not have any impact on parallel computations, both the p- and h-methods usually cause poor load balancing if the adaptive refinement is not uniform throughout the mesh. After a certain number of refinement steps a redefinition of the spatial decomposition can thus become necessary.

If the element level decomposition is used, the subdivision process has to be repeated entirely and a distribution completely different from the original one can result, making extensive inter-processor communication necessary. Moreover, the decomposition and the associated interpolation of the relevant field data from the old to the new mesh cannot be effectively parallelized.

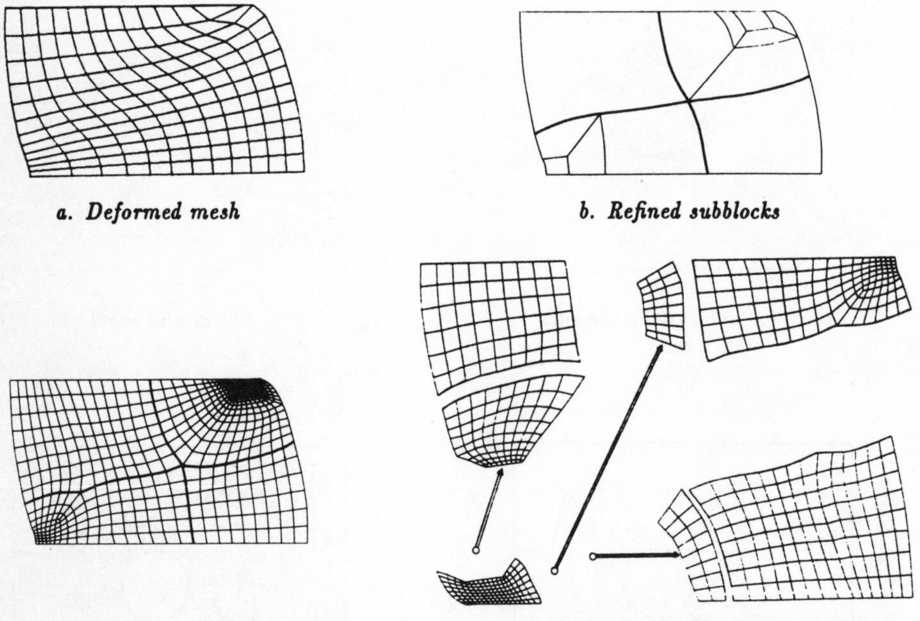

a. Deformed mesh *b. Refined subblocks*

c. Refined mesh *d. Redistribution of refined mesh*

Figure 11: Block level adaptive mesh refinement

The alternative block-level scheme presented above facilitates adaptivity. Refined regions can be generated with this algorithm without changing the overall block structure of the mesh by simply inserting new subblocks into already existing ones. The redistribution that is necessary to avoid poor load balancing can again be achieved more easily due to the fact that the decomposition is performed on the block level instead of the element level. Figure 11 illustrates the process for the example problem used in chapter 3. The original mesh comprised just a single block that was decomposed into 4 subblocks. Fig. 11a shows the deformed mesh after a certain number of time steps with error indicators suggesting the need for refinement in the circled regions. The necessary refinements are then enacted by creating new subblocks within the old ones (fig. 11b), generating the new mesh (Fig. 11c), and then interpolating the field data. Since the refinement does not influence the subdomains of other processors, these steps can be performed almost entirely in parallel.

To ensure good load balancing in the ensuing computations, parts of the refined meshes have to be sent to other processors working on unrefined subdomains. This can again be done on the block level as indicated in figure 10d.

The resulting communication overhead is very low in relation to the overall computation time, and the adaptive refinements in general do not cause a degradation of the efficiency of the subsequent continuation of the finite element simulation.

6. CONCLUSIONS

The results of the implementation of a large finite element system on an iPSC/2 Hypercube show that very good efficiencies can be achieved for the simulation of industrial problems. During the most important phase of the computations, i.e., the solution of the linearized system of equations, a parallel substructuring algorithm clearly outperforms a parallel version of the Cholesky decomposition, mainly due to the high communication requirements of the latter. We anticipate the substructuring algorithm to perform well also on larger numbers of processors.

A good automatic spatial decomposer is a crucial prerequisite if finite element procedures are to be generally useful on distributed memory machines. The block-level algorithm presented here has some advantages over the more commonly used element-level methods, and ensures good load balancing for arbitrary meshes. Moreover, adaptive procedures, which are an important element of modern finite element applications, can be effectively parallelized using this approach.

REFERENCES

[1] H. Wüstenberg, *FEPS3.3 Finite Element Programming System - User's Guide*, ICA-Report No.21, Stuttgart 1986.

[2] I.St. Doltsinis, J. Luginsland and S. Nölting, *Some developments in the numerical simulation of metal forming processes*, Eng. Comput., Vol. 4, Dec. 1987.

[3] C. Farhat and E. Wilson, *A New Finite Element Concurrent Computer Program Architecture*, Int. J. Num. Meth. in Eng., 24, 1771-92 (1987).

[4] J. Argyris, I.St. Doltsinis and S. Nölting, *Some Concepts for the Parallelisation of Finite Element Procedures*, Invited Lecture, NUMETA 90, Swansea, January 7–11, 1990.

[5] C. Farhat and E. Wilson, *A Parallel Active Column Equation Solver* Computers & Structures, 28, No. 2, 289-304 (1988).

[6] C. Farhat, *A Simple and Efficient Automatic Domain Decomposer*, Computers & Structures, 28, No. 5, 579-602 (1988).

[7] I.St. Doltsinis und S. Nölting, *Mesh Generation for the Numerical Simulation of Forming Problems*, Workshop "Numerische Methoden der Plastomechanik", Institut für Mechanik, Universität Hannover, July 1989.

PARALLEL ALGORITHMS FOR THE DIRECT SOLUTION OF FINITE ELEMENT EQUATIONS ON A DISTRIBUTED MEMORY COMPUTER

O. Zone[1], R. Keunings[1] and D. Roose[2]

[1]Division of Applied Mechanics, Université Catholique de Louvain, and [2]Department of Computer Science and Applied Mathematics, Katholiek Universiteit Leuven (Belgium)

1. Introduction

In the present paper, we focus on the generic problem of solving finite element equations on a distributed memory parallel computer by means of a direct frontal technique. For the sake of illustration, we consider the Galerkin/Finite Element solution of Poisson's equation [4]. Three different parallel algorithms based on a domain decomposition approach are proposed and implemented on the Intel iPSC/2 hypercube (16 processors). The first algorithm uses a very simple communication strategy that allocates the assembly and solution of the interface system to a single processor. The other two algorithms are similar to those developed in [3] for the solution of tridiagonal systems. For the one-dimensional case, we develop a model that predicts the efficiency of the proposed algorithms as a function of problem size, number of available processors and basic hardware characteristics. Agreement between model predictions and observed efficiencies is excellent. We find that the three algorithms behave similarly with up to 8 processors. Significant differences are seen, however, for larger numbers of processors. Close-to-optimal efficiencies are obtained with all three algorithms if the grain size is large. Finally, we discuss preliminary results obtained for the two-dimensional case.

2. Problem Description and Parallel Algorithms

Let us consider the generic problem of solving Poisson's equation by means of the Galerkin/Finite Element technique. In matrix form, the finite element equations read [4]

$$\mathbf{K}\,\mathbf{u} = \mathbf{f}, \qquad (1)$$

where **K** is the stiffness matrix, **f** is the load vector, and **u** is the vector of unknown nodal values. The stiffness matrix is usually very sparse. Available parallel algorithms for solving (1) are based on *iterative* methods [2]. Our purpose is to implement a *direct* frontal solution technique on a distributed memory parallel computer. The frontal technique [4] avoids the full assembly of the stiffness matrix. Each finite element is considered in turn. The element contribution to the stiffness matrix and load vector are first assembled in the so-called active matrix and active right-hand-side. Nodal variables that do not appear in subsequent elements are then eliminated from the active system by means of Gaussian elimination. The process is repeated for the next element. Once the last element has been processed, the nodal values are computed through a backsubstitution step.

The programming model used in this work is that of a set of $P=2^d$ interconnected, concurrent processors with local memory. At the beginning of the computation, the computational domain is divided evenly into P non-overlapping subdomains. Each processor is allocated the elements of a subdomain. In the algorithms described below, all processors perform the frontal method on their subdomain in parallel. At the end of this process, each processor holds an active system which corresponds to the nodes located at the interface with neighbor processors. A communication step is then needed to assemble the contributions of those interface variables. Once the set of equations for the interface variables has been solved, the processors compute their internal nodal values independently in a backsubstitution step. The three algorithms that we describe below for the one-dimensional case differ in the way the interface system is communicated, assembled, and solved.

Algorithm 1

It is the simplest of the three algorithms. Each processor communicates to a uniquely-specified processor its contribution to the interface system. This special processor assembles all these contributions, and solves the resulting algebraic system for the interface nodal values by means of Gaussian elimination. It then communicates to all processors the values of their interface variables (Fig.1). This simple approach clearly introduces a sequential bottleneck: all the other processors remain idle while the one devoted to the interface system is performing useful work.

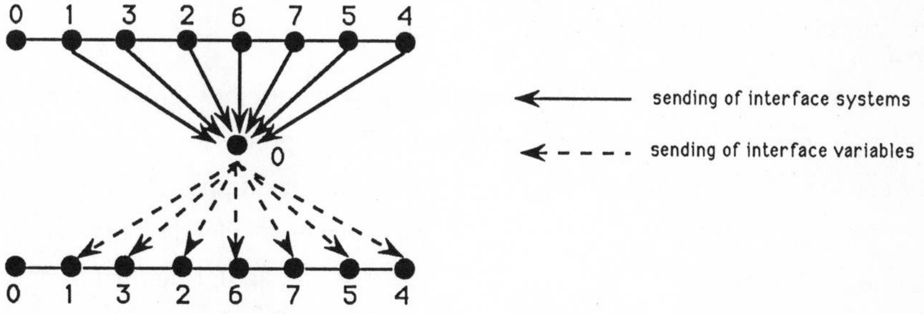

Fig.1 Schematic of Algorithm 1 for a hypercube of dimension 3.

Algorithms 2 and 3 are similar to those developed in [3] for the solution of tridiagonal systems on a hypercube architecture.

Algorithm 2

In this algorithm, the assembly and solution of the interface system are handled through a binary tree whose leaves are processors ordered according to the Gray code (Fig.2). A *first phase* involves traversal of the tree from the leaves to the root; it requires a number of communication steps equal to the dimension d of the hypercube. At each step, half of the active processors send in parallel their interface system to their neighbor processor, after which they become idle; the receiving processors assemble in parallel the contribution of their neighbor to their own, and eliminate the common variable by means of Gaussian elimination. The process is repeated until the root processor is reached. The *second phase* involves traversal of the tree from the root to the leaves. It consists in d steps involving communication of interface nodal values computed at the previous tree level together with a backsubstitution process in half of the processors at each tree level. A processor having performed the elimination of an interface variable in the first phase computes this variable through a backsubstitution step.

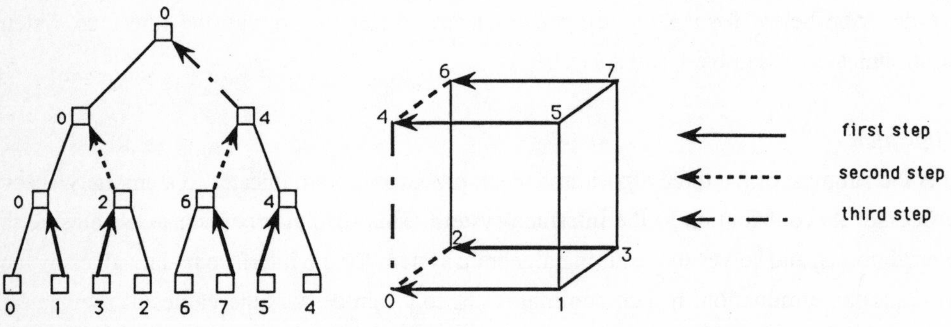

Fig.2 Schematic of Algorithm 2 for a hypercube of dimension 3.

Algorithm 3

The third algorithm uses bidirectional communications between neighbor processors. As shown in Fig.3, the algorithm consists of d steps. Each processor of the hypercube is physically connected to d neighbor processors, which defines d possible directions for the exchange of messages. At each step, all processors exchange in parallel their interface system to their neighbor in one of these directions. They assemble in parallel the incoming interface system to their own, and eliminate the common variable. The process is then repeated in another direction until all directions are covered. By the end of these d steps, all processors compute in parallel by backsubstitution the common interface variables that they have previously eliminated. No further communication is needed in this phase.

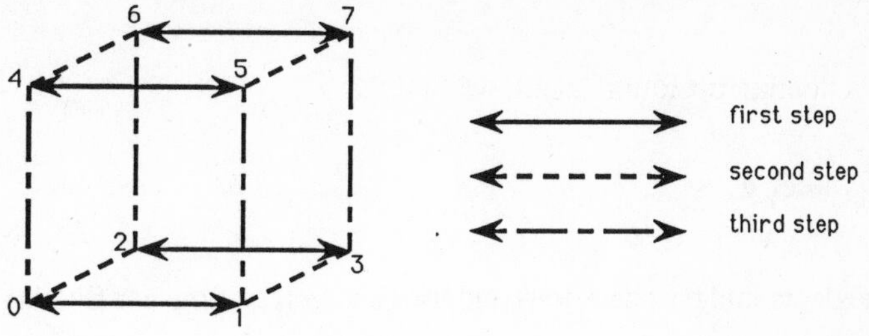

Fig.3 Schematic of Algorithm 3 for a hypercube of dimension 3.

3. Performance Model

We have developed a model for predicting in the one-dimensional case the efficiency of the proposed algorithms as a function of a number of parameters:

- the problem size, i.e. the number of finite elements N,
- the number of available processors $P = 2^d$, where d is the dimension of the hypercube,
- two basic hardware characteristics, i.e. the interprocessor communication bandwidth and the processors megaflop rate, characterized by t_{comm} and t_{calc} respectively [2].

We assume that the processors are synchronized and that the workload allocated to them is perfectly balanced. The grain size g is thus a constant given by

$$g = \frac{N}{P} . \tag{2}$$

The sources of overhead relative to the sequential algorithm are the communication steps needed to carry information on the interface variables, as well as the solution of the interface system.

Let us define

- T_{calc} : the CPU time spent by each processor in the processing of its internal variables (assembly, elimination, backsubstitution),
- $T_{overhead}$: the time spent in the communication of interface systems, as well as in their assembly and solution.

The efficiency ε of the parallel algorithm is thus given by

$$\varepsilon = \frac{1}{1 + \frac{T_{overhead}}{T_{calc}}} \quad . \tag{3}$$

On the basis of a floating operation count, we find that

$$T_{calc} = 116\, g\, t_{calc} = c_1\, g \, . \tag{4}$$

This estimate neglects integer operations and uses an average time per floating operation given by t_{calc}.

The overhead $T_{overhead}$ will depend on the actual algorithm used. On the basis of both communication and floating operation counts, we obtain the following estimates:

Algorithm 1

$$T_{overhead} = 2\,(P - 1)\, t_{comm} + (15\,P - 25)\, t_{calc} = c_2\, P + c_3 \;, \tag{5}$$

Algorithm 2

$$T_{overhead} = 2\,(\log_2 P)\, t_{comm} + [28\,(\log_2 P - 2) + 34]\, t_{calc} = c_4 \log_2 P + c_5 \;, \tag{6}$$

Algorithm 3

$$T_{overhead} = 2\,(\log_2 P)\, t_{comm} + [39\,(\log_2 P - 1) + 21]\, t_{calc} = c_6 \log_2 P + c_7 \;. \tag{7}$$

In these equations, t_{comm} stands for the communication time for short messages (i.e. under 100 bytes long); we take it as a constant corresponding to the start up time for communication [1]. The factors c_i appearing in (4-7) depend upon the hardware characteristics t_{calc} and t_{comm} only.

We shall exploit the above model in detail in the next section. An important conclusion can be drawn at this stage, however, without making reference to actual values for the hardware characteristics t_{calc} and t_{comm}. Indeed, equations (4-7) predict how the grain size g must evolve as the number of processors P increases in order to keep a constant value for the efficiency ε. For Algorithm 1, the grain size g must increase like P, while for both Algorithms 2 and 3, the grain size must increase like log_2P only. Algorithm 1 is thus expected to behave poorly relative to the other two algorithms as the number of processors increases.

4. Results for the One-Dimensional Case

We have implemented the above algorithms on an Intel hypercube iPSC/2 of dimension 4. Available communication benchmarks [1] give the following values for the hardware characteristics t_{calc} and t_{comm}:

$$t_{calc} = 5.95\ \mu sec/flop, \quad t_{comm} = 350\ \mu sec \text{ (startup time).} \tag{8}$$

On that basis, our model predicts (in milliseconds)

$$T_{calc} = 0.69\ g\ , \tag{9}$$

$$T_{overhead} = 0.79\ P - 0.85 \qquad \text{for Algorithm 1,}$$

$$T_{overhead} = 0.87\ \log_2 P - 0.13 \qquad \text{for Algorithm 2,}$$

$$T_{overhead} = 0.93\ \log_2 P - 0.11 \qquad \text{for Algorithm 3.} \tag{10}$$

As mentioned above, the actual values of the constants appearing in (9-10) are likely to be inaccurate since we have not taken *integer* operations into account in establishing the model. A least-square fit of the actual timings measured on the hypercube allows us to evaluate these few constants more accurately. In so doing, we obtain

$$T_{calc} = 0.89\ g\ , \tag{11}$$

$$T_{overhead} = 0.86\ P - 0.9 \qquad \text{for Algorithm 1,}$$

$$T_{overhead} = 1.49\ \log_2 P - 0.01 \qquad \text{for Algorithm 2,}$$

$$T_{overhead} = 1.45\ \log_2 P - 0.22 \qquad \text{for Algorithm 3,} \tag{12}$$

which is close to our estimates. We shall use (11-12) in our comparisons between predicted and observed efficiencies. Figure 4 illustrates the predicted and observed efficiencies for the three algorithms, as a function of the number of processors and the problem size. Agreement between the model and the experimental points (available for up to 16 processors) is excellent.

For a given number of processors, the efficiency increases as the problem size increases. This is an important result as far as large-scale applications are concerned.

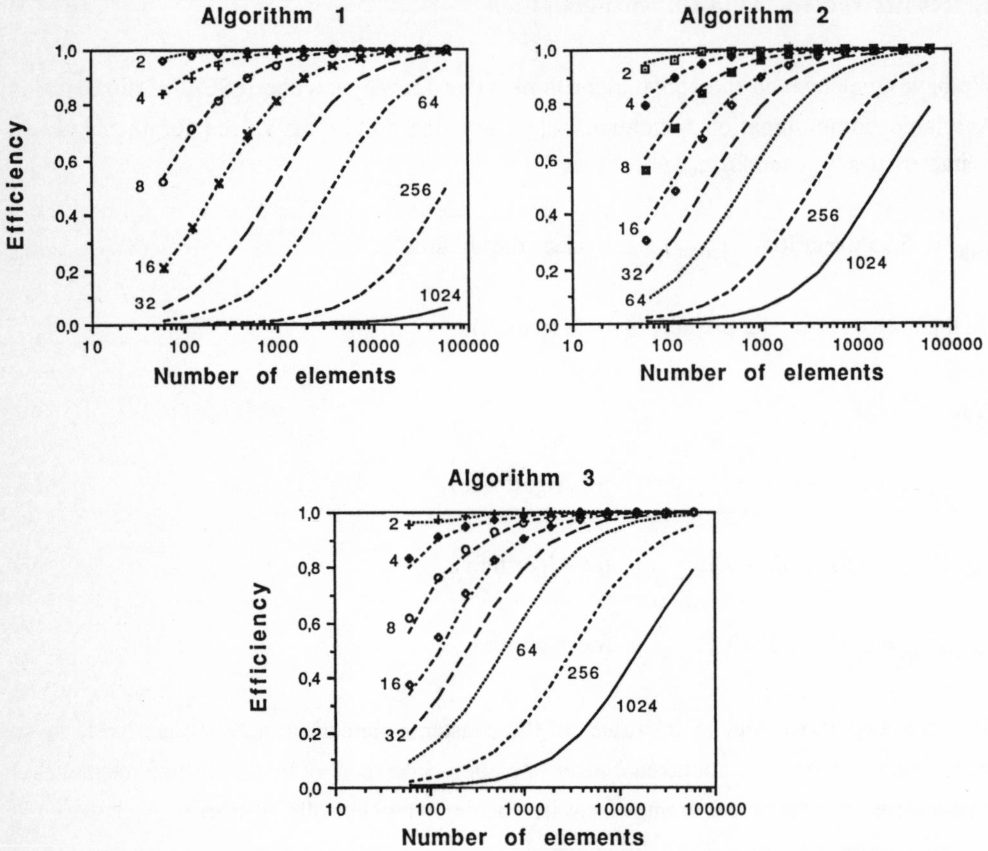

Fig.4 Efficiency as a function of problem size for various numbers of processors (from 2 to 1024). The points are the experimental timings on the iPSC/2 hypercube, while the curves are the predictions of the model equations (11-12).

A comparison of the three algorithms is given in Fig.5, where we show *predicted* efficiency curves. We find that all three algorithms behave very similarly with up to 8 processors. Algorithm 1 is indeed the most efficient with up to 4 processors, in view of the simplicity of its communication scheme. However, its efficiency deteriorates drastically relative to the other two algorithms as the number of processors increases. Algorithms 2 and 3 behave very similarly in all cases. The size of the messages is not large enough to exploit the bidirectionality of the communication scheme of Algorithm 3 to its full advantage.

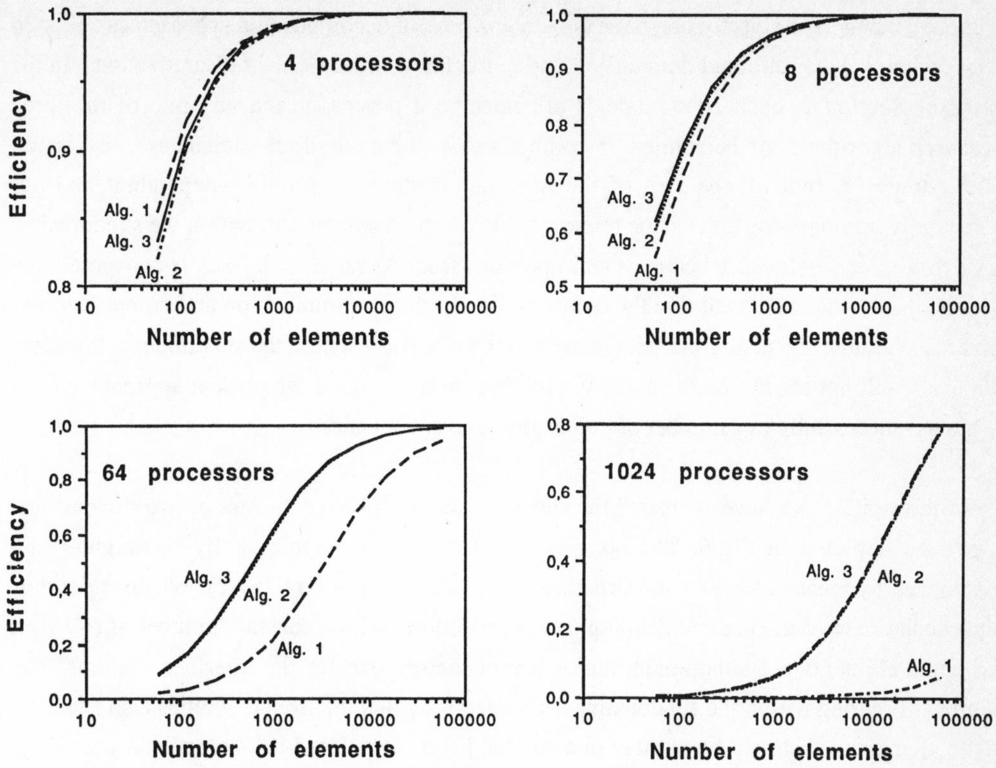

Fig.5 Predicted efficiency curves for an increasing number of processors.

5. Multi-dimensional case: Approach and Preliminary Results

Let us consider a multi-dimensional domain Ω of arbitrary shape. It is possible to exploit the algorithms described in Section 2 if the following general domain-decomposition approach is adopted :

- the computational domain Ω is divided into P non-overlapping subdomains Ω_i,
- the decomposition is organized topologically as a linear structure, i.e.

$$\Omega_i \cap \Omega_{i+1} = \Gamma_i \quad \text{for } i = 1, P\text{-}1 \; ; \qquad \Omega_i \cap \Omega_j = \varnothing \;\; \text{for } j \neq i\text{-}1, i\text{+}1 \tag{13}$$

- otherwise, the subdomains may have an arbitrary shape,
- each subdomain is discretized by means of a possibly non-structured finite element mesh, with continuity of the nodal values at the interfaces Γ_i.

Although being topologically one-dimensional, the present decomposition approach can be used with complex computational domains and non-structured finite element discretizations. In the spirit of Section 2, each subdomain is allocated to a processor and any one of the three proposed algorithms can be applied. In comparison with the one-dimensional case, new issues arise, however. Indeed, the size of the interface systems is problem-dependent and not necessarily homogeneous; the same remark holds for the frontal width within the subdomains. As a result, *load-balancing* becomes an important issue. As far as efficiency is concerned, the decomposition must be such that the overhead due to the communication and computation of interface variables be negligible with respect to the workload within the subdomains. It is clear that such will not always be the case. We believe, however, that the present approach can be exploited successfully in a number of practically-relevant situations.

As of this writing, we have evaluated the above procedure for the sub-class of two-dimensional problems depicted in Fig.6. The computational domain is topologically rectangular and discretized by means of a $N1$ x $N2$ structured finite element mesh ($N1>N2$). We consider thus a particular case of the general decomposition procedure, with a constant number of $(N1/P)$ x $N2$ finite elements per subdomain, and a homogeneous size for the interface systems. The elements ordering within the subdomains is selected such that the frontal width is also equal for all subdomains, whatever the number of available processors. Load-balancing is thus achieved automatically.

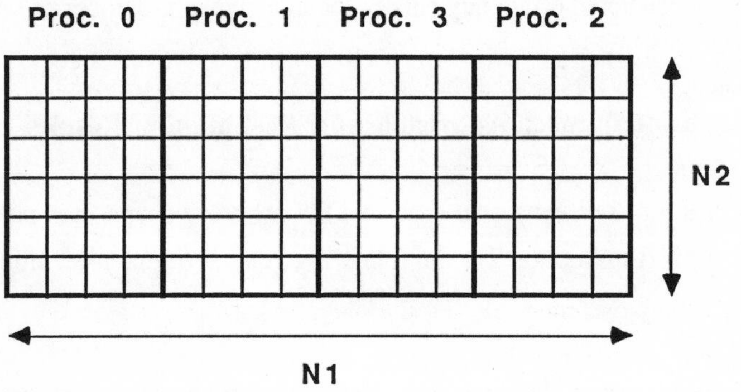

Fig.6 A sub-class of two-dimensional domain decomposition.

Figure 7 shows preliminary results obtained with Algorithm 2 and quadratic finite elements. We observe that the efficiency increases quite rapidly as the number of elements $N1$ increases. On the other hand, low efficiencies are obtained when $(N1/P)$ is not sufficiently larger than $N2$. The latter parameter determines the size of the interface systems. Clearly, Algorithm 2 behaves nicely for large problems such that the workload within each processor dominates that for the interface systems.

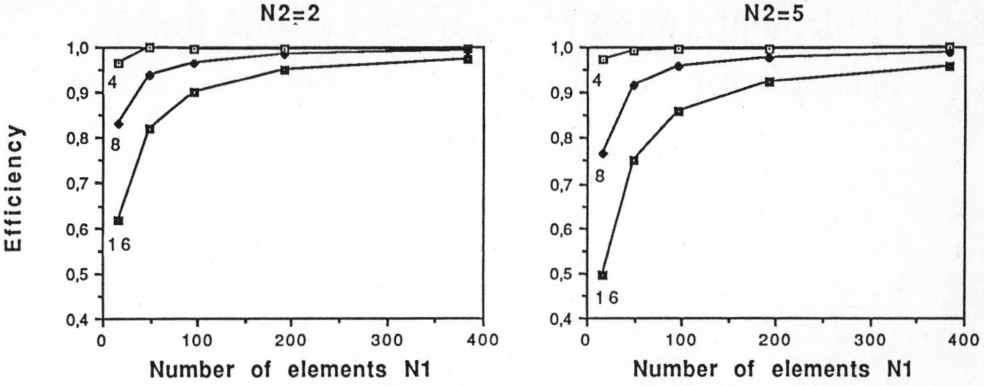

Fig.7 Efficiency as a function of number of processors and problem size (measured by the decomposition parameters *N1* and *N2*); experimental timings on the iPSC/2 hypercube.

6. Conclusions

This work constitutes the first phase of a long-term project, namely the efficient implementation of direct solution methods for complex finite element problems on distributed memory parallel computers. Although for the most part limited to the one-dimensional case, our results demonstrate the potential of parallel computing for this class of problems. It is found that the efficiency of the proposed algorithms increases as the problem size increases. We have shown that a performance model can be developed and used for predicting with good accuracy the behavior of the proposed algorithms. Finally, our preliminary results for the two-dimensional case are encouraging. Work is underway to further generalize the present approach to complex multi-dimensional problems.

Acknowledgments: The doctoral work of M. O. Zone is supported financially in the framework of the Programme FIRST of the Région Wallonne (Belgium).

7. References

[1] L. Bomans and D. Roose, *Benchmarking the iPSC/2 Hypercube Multiprocessor*, Concurrency, Practice and Experience, Vol.1, 3-18 (1989)

[2] G.C. Fox, M.A. Johnson, G.A. Lyzenga, S.W. Otto, J.K. Salmon, and D.W. Walker, Solving Problems on Concurrent Processors (Vol.1), Prentice Hall (1988)

[3] A. Krechel, H.J. Plum, and K. Stuben, *Parallel Solution of Tridiagonal Linear Systems*, Proc. of the 1st European Workshop on Hypercube and Distributed Computers, F. André and J.P. Verjus (eds), North Holland, 49-63 (1989)

[4] J.N. Reddy, Applied Functional Analysis and Variational Methods in Engineering, Mc Graw Hill (1986)

Implementation and evaluation of distributed synchronization on a distributed memory parallel machine

André COUVERT, René PEDRONO, Michel RAYNAL
IRISA
Campus de Beaulieu
F-35042 Rennes Cédex
FRANCE
raynal@irisa.fr

Abstract

Advent of distributed memory parallel machines make possible to study and analyze distributed algorithms in a real context. In this paper we are interested in a paradigm of distributed computing : the implementation of (binary and multiway) rendez-vous. This problem actually includes two subproblems encountered in several synchronization problems : how to realize a coordination (of the processes involved in the rendez-vous) and how to ensure some exclusion (between conflicting rendez-vous sharing some processes). Several algorithms implementing rendez-vous are presented. Implementations of these protocols on an hypercube are analyzed and compared according to a certain number of parameters ; an efficiency ratio is introduced in order to make these comparisons easier. In addition to the results exhibited, this paper suggests a way to conduct such experiments.

1 Introduction

Advent of distributed memory parallel machines make possible to study and analyze distributed algorithms in a real context. Such studies are interesting from two points of view. On the one hand they allow to compare distinct algorithms implementing the same function (or service) in terms of efficiency and computation time ; on the other hand they allow to gain knowledge about the mastering of these machines. This paper is concerned with these two aspects.

Here we are interested in a class of distributed synchronization algorithms : protocols implementing (so called binary or multiway) rendez-vous [HOA 78, CM 88, BUR 88, BAG 89b, C 87]. The problem is to allow a certain number of processes to synchronize in some points of their respective computations in such a way (C1) that all the processes involved in a rendez-vous are simultaneously at their meeting point and (C2) that a process is involved in at most one rendez-vous at any time. A rendez-vous can involve only 2 processes as in CSP[HOA 78] or OCCAM[BUR 88] (such rendez-vous are

called binary) or any number k of processes (multiway or k-ary rendez-vous also called committee coordination problem) [CM 88,BAG 89b]. The interest of the rendez-vous lies in its usefulness to solve practical problems [HOA 78, C 87, CM 88] as well as in the fact it grasps two important synchronization problems encountered in many situations : a rendez-vous implies a ***coordination*** between 2 (or k) processes (synchronism or mutual coincidence of the processes willing to participate in a same rendez-vous : C1) and a process can be involved at the same time in only one rendez-vous chosen in the set of rendez-vous it has announced to be non-deterministically interested in (***mutual exclusion*** between conflicting rendez-vous : C2). As such the rendez-vous is a paradigm of distributed systems control problems.
Two protocols (or distributed algorithms) implementing rendez-vous are studied. The first one is devoted to binary rendez-vous [BAG 89a] ; the second one to multiway rendez-vous [BAG 89b]. These algorithms are briefly described in the second part. The third part first gives the experimentation context : the underlying machine is a 64 processors Intel hypercube on which an implementation of the ISO programming language Estelle [ISO 86] has been developped [JJ 89] ; then the implementation choices concerning the two algorithms are presented. The parameters of the analysis and an efficiency ratio to allow comparisons are presented and explained in the fourth part. Part 5 presents and analyses the results of the experiments and the conclusion draws lessons from this experimentation.

2 Studied Algorithms

2.1 Binary rendez-vous

Each process of the distributed program (composed of n processes) is endowed with a manager. The set of managers has to establish rendez-vous described by rule (C1) without violating rule (C2). As an example let us consider the following ***rendez-vous graph*** between the processes P_0, P_1, P_2, P_3.

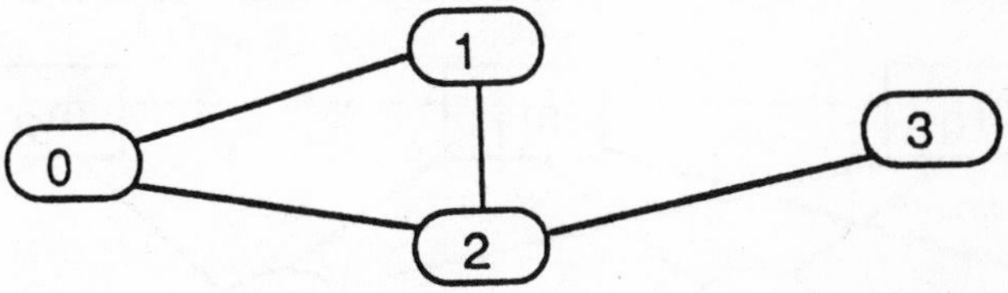

A possible rendez-vous between processes P_i and P_j is represented by the undirected edge *(i,j)* ; such a graph describes the possibilities of rendez-vous at a given time. In the example the process P_0 (resp. P_2) is willing to establish a rendez-vous non-deterministically either with process P_1 or with process P_2 (resp. P_0 or P_1 or P_3).
The algorithm [BAG 89a] associates a unique token to every possible rendez-vous; the token associated to *(i,j)* is noted *token(i,j)* and is initially owned by one of P_i or P_j. The manager associated to P_i tries to establish the rendez-vous *(i,j)* only if it has the corresponding token *token(i,j)* ; then it sends it to P_j's manager. If this one wants to establish the *(i,j)* rendez-vous it sends back the token to P_i's manager and they commit rendez-vous *(i,j)*. In the other case P_j's manager answer it with *no* and keeps the token

(it will have the initiative to request the next *(i,j)* rendez-vous) ; on receiving ***no***, P_i's manager will try to establish an other rendez-vous *(i,x)* it is interested in if it owns the associated token *token(i,x)*. Additionnal rules avoid deadlock situations (in wich rendez-vous are possible but none is established). The interested reader will report to [BAG 89a] for more details.
The association of a unique token to each potential rendez-vous is the basis of this algorithm ; the rules define how these tokens are managed. This algorithm is called *BIN* in the following. Other algorithms implementing binary rendez-vous are described in [RAY 88] (chapter 4).

2.2 Multiway (or k-ary) rendez-vous

In this case the algorithm [BAG 89b] considers *P* managers ($1 \leq P \leq n$) which have to cooperate in order to establish rendez-vous noted *(i,j,k,l,...)* (the size of this tuple defines the number of processes involved in the corresponding rendez-vous). These managers m_i are placed on an unidirectionnal ring ; and a valued token moves round on this ring. When a process P_i becomes passive waiting for some rendez-vous it sends the concerned managers the rendez-vous sets *(i,j1,j2,...)*, *(i,l1,l2,...)* it is interested in. When a manager owns the token it determines whether rendez-vous can be committed according to its own values and the values carried by the token ; if it is the case, it informs the involved processes. This algorithm will be called *GEN(k)* in the following ($k \geq 2$ being the biggest size of potential rendez-vous).
Uniqueness of the token ensures mutual exclusion between conflicting rendez-vous [RAY 86], and managers and token informations allow to enable and to commit some of the rendez-vous.
If we consider this algorithm with $k=2$, the preceding rendez-vous graph, and 3 managers, we can obtain the following structure (among a set of possible structures) in which an edge represents a link allowing a process and a manager to communicate ; the dotted line represents the ring.

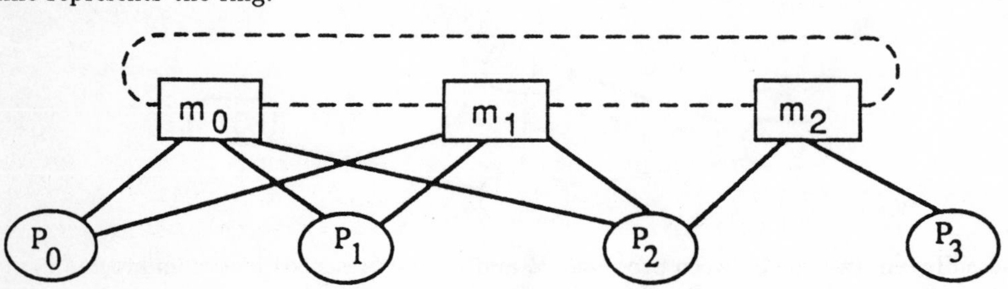

These 3 managers can, for example, manage the following rendez-vous :

m_0 manages *(0,1)* and *(0,2)*.
m_1 manages *(0,2)* and *(1,2)*.
m_2 manages *(2,3)*

Each rendez-vous is managed by at least one manager. In the preceding example other rendez-vous management assignments are of course possible. As one can see the number

P of managers is not related to the number n of processes. It is possible to have only one manager (and no token in this case) ; we get a centralized version of the algorithm. At the other extreme it is possible to have n managers each managing all the rendez-vous : in this case we obtain a very distributed version of the algorithm (distribution by duplication). All the intermediate implementation choices are possible. The interested reader will report to [BAG 89b] for more details.

3 Experiment context

3.1 Environment

The machine on which the experiments have been conducted is an Intel IPSC2 of diameter 6 (64 processors) [Intel 87]. The language in which the different algorithms have been programmed is Estelle [ISO 86, BUD 87], a language normalized by ISO, originally devoted to the specification and implementation of protocols. We have chosen this language as it is a high-level language, well suited to distributed system programming and an Estelle-to-C compiler for the IPSC2 [JJ 89] has been developped. The main feature of the language is the two-level programming : first the implementation of processes and managers by automata triggered by the arrivals of messages received through ports and second the separate specification of connections between input and output ports of these automata.

3.2 Studied implementation

As we aimed at studying efficiency of protocols implementing rendez-vous we consider that the application processes do not have proper activity but for rendez-vous requests. Processes are put on distinct processors of the hypercube.
The implementation of *BIN* corresponds to the description given in §2.1. [BAG 89a]. As we have noticed several implementation choices have to be done for the algorithm *GEN*. Two of then are particularly interesting as they are extreme according to the number of managers ; and they have been implemented :

- a unique manager (put on the same site as P_0). It manages all the rendez-vous. This algorithm is noted : *GEN(k)CENT*.
- n managers m_i ; m_i is put on the same site as P_i and manages all the rendez-vous P_i is involved in. This algorithm is noted *GEN(k)DIST*. (In this case the management of a size k rendez-vous is duplicated on k sites ; the set of managers being connected by a ring with an associated token).

3.3 Rendez-vous graphs

3.3.1 Binary rendez-vous

Processes are designed by $0,1,\ldots,n\text{-}1$. We have studied potential rendez-vous graphs presenting a regular structure, implemented on cubes of diameter d. Indeed irregular structures disallow simple interpretations and explanations of results. Studied rendez-vous graphs are defined by the following sets R_i associated to each process P_i.

$$R_i = \{processes\ among\ which\ P_i\ wants\ to\ establish\ non-deterministically\ a\ binary\ rendez-vous\}$$

- ring R :

$$R_i = \{i-1, i+1\} \quad (+;- : modulo\ n)$$

The corresponding algorithms will be named *BIN-R-n*, *GEN(2)CENT-R-n* and *GEN(2)DIST-R-n* (where n stands for the number of application processes).

- fully connected FC:

$$R_i = \{0, 1, 2, \ldots, n-1\} - \{i\}$$

These algorithms are named *BIN-FC-n*, *GEN(2)CENT-FC-n* and *GEN(2)DIST-FC-n* in the following.

- hypercube H :

$$R_i = \{i \textbf{ xor } 2^j : 0 \leq j \leq d-1\}$$

with the processes identities expressed in the binary notation.

- binary tree T: (**div** is the integer division operator)

$$R_0 = \{1\}$$
$$R_i = \{i \textbf{ div } 2, 2i, 2i+1\} 1 \leq i \leq (n-1) \textbf{ div } 2$$
$$R_i = \{i\ div\ 2\} \qquad 1 + (n-1) \textbf{ div } 2 \leq i \leq n-1$$

3.3.2 Multiway rendez-vous

The structure of potential rendez-vous is now an hypergraph. We have been interested in a regular structure generalizing in some sense the ring of the binary case. The set R_i^k of the set of processes with which P_i can be in k-rendez-vous is chosen of size k (the size of a rendez-vous is k and there are k choices of rendez-vous for P_i). For example for k=4 we get (*+,-* are *modulo n*) :

$$R_i^{k=4} = \{\{i-3, i-2, i-1\}, \{i-2, i-1, i+1\}, \{i-1, i+1, i+2\}, \{i+1, i+2, i+3\}\}$$

4 Experiment parameters and measures performed

4.1 Binary rendez-vous

4.1.1 Parameters

Each experiment we have realized is defined by the following parameters :

- a potential rendez-vous graph : *R/FC/H/T*.
- a number n of processes : *n=2,8,16,32,64*.
- a rendez-vous duration *RdvD* (once a rendez-vous is committed it lasts this duration). *RdvD* varies between 0 and *28* ms ; this duration is constant and the same for all the processes during an experiment.

- the duration *ExpD* of each experiment has been chosen to *60 s*. This value has been determined from several attemps (it allows to realize several tens of thousands of rendez-vous during each experiment).

4.1.2 Measures

The following measures have been done for the 3 algorithms *BIN-X-n*, *GEN(2)CENT-X-n* and *GEN(2)DIST-X-n* with *X=R/FC/H/T* and *n=8 to 64* :

- the average number of rendez-vous a process has committed : *nbrdv*
- the average duration spent by process within rendez-vous : *nbrdv*RdvD*

These values allow to compute the efficiency of an algorithm in some context (defined by -*X*-*n*) :

$$\text{efficiency ratio} \quad er = \frac{nbrdv * RdvD}{ExpD}$$

We have $0 \leq er \leq 1$. Moreover the value *1 - er* represents the average ratio of the time spent to establish rendez-vous, i.e. to realize control. The closer of 1 is its *er* value, the better is an algorithm.

4.2 Multiway rendez-vous

In addition to the preceding parameters an experiment requires a value of k (size of rendez-vous). Values of *k=2,4,8,16,32* with *n=32* have been experimented on the rendez-vous hypergraph "generalized ring" displayed in the §3.3.2.

5 Results and analyzes

5.1 Binary rendez-vous

In addition to the evolution of the efficiency ratio of a given algorithm for a rendez-vous graph we have been interested in comparing *BIN*, *GEN(2)CENT* and *GEN(2)DIST* in order to know if the specialized algorithm *BIN* has some advantage over the general ones with *k=2*.

5.1.1 Algorithms *BIN* and *GEN(2)CENT* :

Figure 1 represents for these two algorithms evolutions of efficiency ratios according to rendez-vous durations *RdvD* for a ring rendez-vous graph of 8 and 64 processes. Figure 2 shows this evolution when the rendez-vous graph is fully connected.
These results show :

- the efficiency ratio increases with the rendez-vous duration.
- for both algorithms the efficiency decreases with the number of processes (i.e. with the number of potential rendez-vous at a given time : n for a ring, *n(n-1)/2* for a fully connected network).

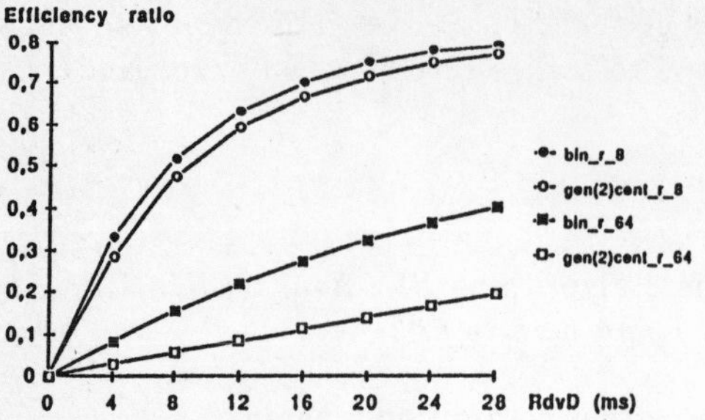

Figure 1 : The Rdv graph is a ring

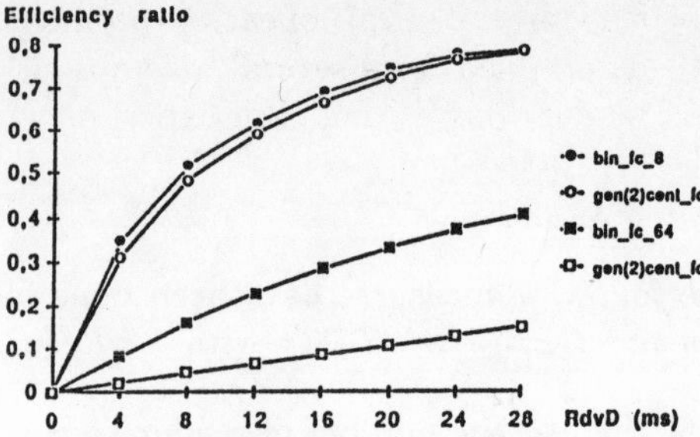

Figure 2 : The Rdv graph is fully connected

- the gap between *BIN* and *GEN(2)CENT* increases with the number of processes (this is due in part to the uniqueness of the manager).

The results obtained with hypercube and binary tree rendez-vous graphs are similar and strengthen this analysis.

5.1.2 Algorithms GEN(2)CENT and GEN(2)DIST

We now compare in the context of the binary rendez-vous the two extreme implementation strategies of the *GEN(k)* algorithm model.
Figures 3 and 4 are analogous to the preceding ones : they compare the efficiency ratios of both algorithms with ring and fully connected rendez-vous graphs of 8 and 64 processors. As previously these results are confirmed by the experiments done on hypercube and binary tree rendez-vous graphs.
The preceding analysis remains valid. The degradation according to n between *GEN(2)CENT* and *GEN(2)DIST* corresponds to the travelling and to the processing time of the token : indeed duplication introduced by the managers can allow to resist some faults but dont improve the parallelism as the token is unique.

5.1.3 Comparison according to the number of processes

Figure 5 gives efficiency ratios of *BIN-R-n*, *GEN(2)CENT-R-n* and *GEN(2)DIST-R-n* (i.e. for a ring rendez-vous graph) according to the total number of processes $n = 2^d$ $(2 \leq d \leq 6)$ and to a rendez-vous duration $RdvD = 20\ ms$.
For n=*2,4,8* (i.e. $d \leq 3$) the three algorithms have very close efficiency ratios ; for instance for n=*8* : *er(BIN-R-8)=0.71*, *er(GEN(2)CENT-R-8)=0.69* and *er(GEN(2)DIST-R-8)=0.66*. On the other hand for n=*16,32,64* (i.e. $4 \leq d \leq 6$) the specialized algorithm *BIN* proves to be the most efficient one ; the gap between the two others remains relatively stable ; for n=*64*, *er(BIN-R-64)=0.32*, *er(GEN(2)CENT-R-64)=0.14* and *er(GEN(2)DIST-R-64)=0.09*.

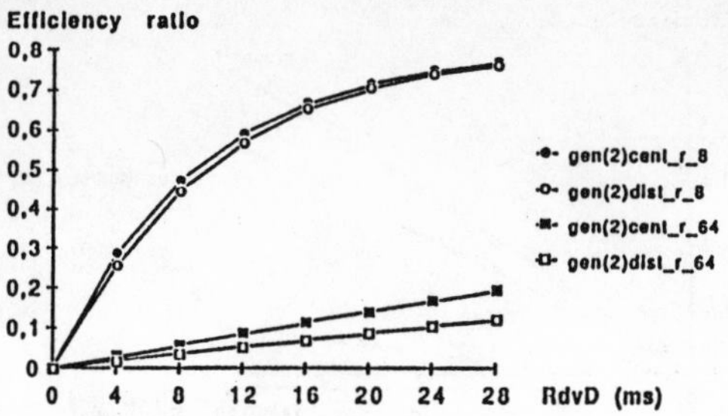

Figure 3 : The Rdv graph is a ring

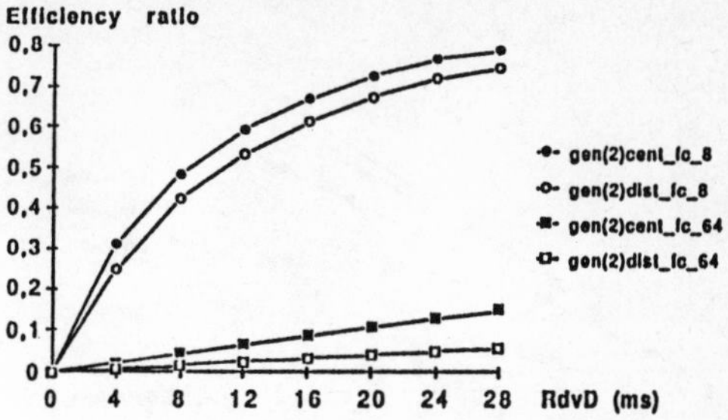

Figure 4 : The Rdv graph is fully connected

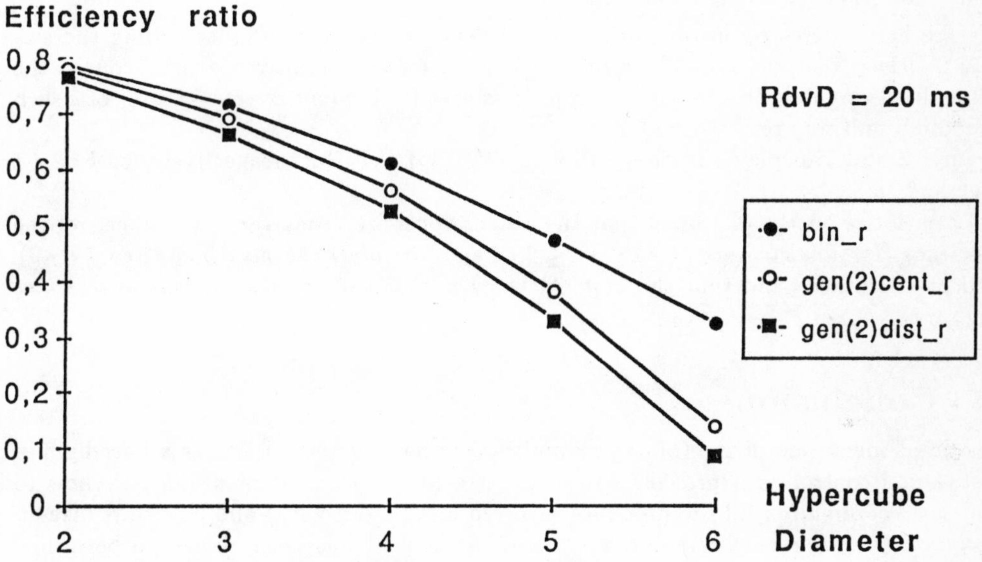

Figure 5 : The Rdv graph is a ring

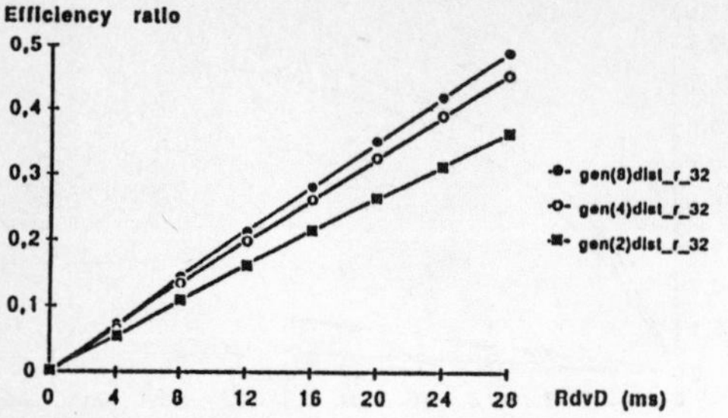

Figure 6 : The Rdv graph is a k-generalized ring

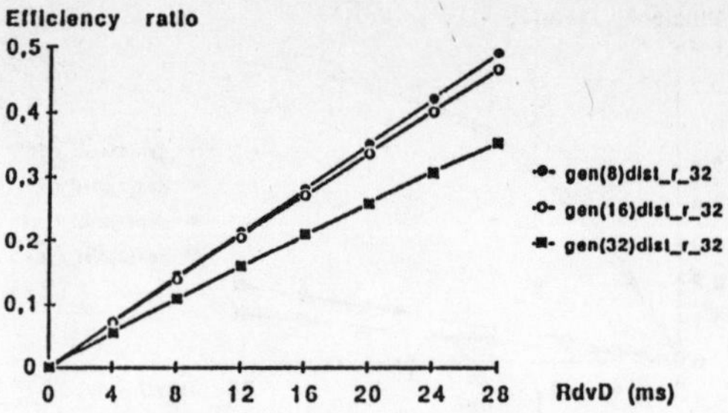

Figure 7 : The Rdv graph is a k-generalized ring

5.2 Multiway rendez-vous

We are here interested in measuring the efficiency of *GEN(k)DIST* according the size k of multiway rendez-vous. The structure studied for such multiway rendez-vous is the generalized ring described in §3.3.2. (a process asks for a k-rendez-vous in a set of k such potential multiway rendez-vous).

Figures 6 and 7 display efficiency ratios of *GEN(k)DIST-R-32* respectively for *k=2,4,8* and *k=8,16,32*.

On can notice on the one hand that the rendez-vous size k has very little effect on the efficiency (for *RdvD=8 ms* : $0.11 \leq er \leq 0.14$ and for *RdvD=28 ms* : $0.35 \leq er \leq 0.49$). and on the other hand that the best efficiency is obtained for rendez-vous of size *k=8* (figure 8).

6 Conclusion

The implementation of the (binary or multiway) rendez-vous constitutes a paradigm of distributed control as it presents two of the synchronization major problems : how to realize a *coordination* (of the processes involved in a rendez-vous) and how to realize an *exclusion* (between conflicting rendez-vous). As such it has been chosen to be implemented and evaluated on a distributed memory parallel machine.

Several conclusions can be drawn from these experiments. First for binary rendez-vous the specialized algorithm called *BIN* (based on the association of a unique token to each potential rendez-vous) reveals to be always more efficient than the algorithms *GEN(2)*. Then the comparison between *GEN(2)CENT* and *GEN(2)DIST* shows the first is the more efficient one : in other words a centralized control is better in this case. Finally algorithms *GEN(k)DIST* with a distributed control are interesting for rendez-vous of size $k > 2$, as they are relatively stable from an efficiency point of view.

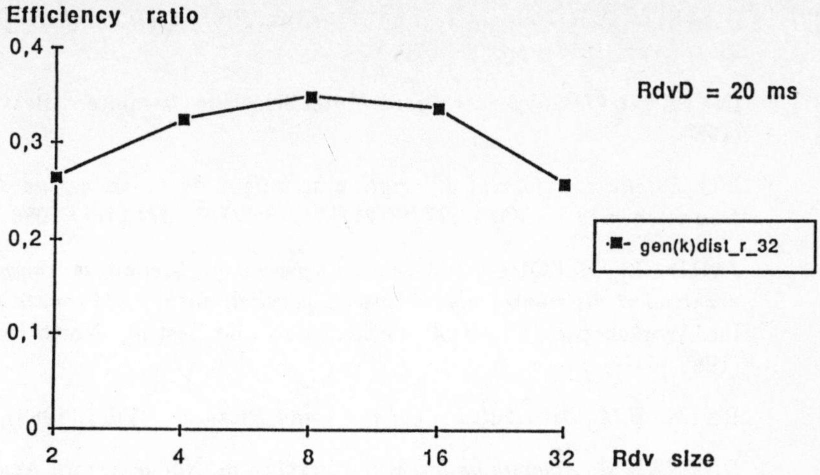

Figure 8 : The Rdv graph is a k-generalized ring

Moreover in addition to the results presented these experiments have allowed a better understanding of the hypercube and have proved the easiness a language such as Estelle provides to realize such an experimentation [A 88].

7 References

[A 88] ADAM M., INGELS Ph., JARD Cl., JEZEQUEL J.M., RAYNAL M.*Experimentation on parallel machines is helpful to analyze distributed algorithms.* Workshop Parallel and Distributed algorithms, North Holland, (1988), pp. 243-250

[BAG 89a] BAGRODIA R.L. *Synchronization of asynchronous processes in CSP.* ACM Toplas, vol. 11,4, (Oct. 1989), pp. 585-597

[BAG 89b] BAGRODIA R.L. *Process synchronization : design and performance evaluation of distributed algorithms.* IEEE Trans. on S.E., vol. 15,9, (Sept. 1989), pp. 1053-1065

[BUD 87] BUDKOWSKI S., DEMBINSKI P. *An introduction to Estelle : a specification language for distributed systems.* Computer Networks and ISDN Systems, vol. 14, (1987), pp. 3-23

[BUR 88] BURNS A. *Programming in OCCAM2* Addison-Wesley, (1988), 189 p.

[C 87] CHARLESWORTH A. *The multiway rendez-vous.* ACM Toplas, vol. 9,2, (July 1987), pp. 350-366

[CM 88] CHANDY K.M., MISRA J. *Parallel Program Design : a foundation* Addison-Wesley, (1988), 516 p.

[HOA 78] HOARE C.A.R. *Communicating Sequential Processes.* Comm. ACM, vol. 21,8, (Aug. 1978), pp. 666-670

[INTEL 87] INTEL *Intel IPSC/2 user's guide.* Intel Scientific Computers, Beaverton, (1987)

[ISO 86] ISO *Estelle : a formal description technique based on extended state transition model.* ISO/TC97/SC21/WG16.1/DP 9074,(July 1986)

[JJ 89] JARD Cl., JEZEQUEL J.M. *A multi-processor Estelle to C compiler to experiment distributed algorithms on parallel machines.* Proc. 9th IFIP Int. Workshop on Protocol Specifications and Testing, North-Holland, (1989),

[RAY 88] RAYNAL M. *Distributed Algorithms and Protocols.* Wiley,(1988),163 p.

[RAY 86] RAYNAL M. *Algorithms for Mutual exclusion.* North Oxford Academic and the MIT Press, (1986), 106 p.

EFFICIENT EXECUTION REPLAY TECHNIQUE FOR DISTRIBUTED MEMORY ARCHITECTURES

Eric Leu, André Schiper, Abdelwahab Zramdini
Ecole Polytechnique Fédérale de Lausanne
Département d'Informatique
CH - 1015 Lausanne, Switzerland
leu@eldi.epfl.ch

Abstract

Debugging parallel programs on MIMD machines is a difficult task because successive executions of the same program can lead to different behaviors. To solve this problem, a method called execution replay has been introduced, which guarantees the reexecution of a program to be equivalent to the initial execution. In this paper we present an execution replay technique in the context of distributed memory architectures. In contrary to all other proposed approaches, our technique can treat non-blocking message passing primitives, and can be adapted to any form of message passing communication. Since the technique is based on an events numbering, we show how to bound these numbers, and then analyse the influence of this bound on the amount of recorded information. The prototype implemented on an Intel iPSC/2 shows that the overhead due to the recording of control information is extremely low (about 1%).

1 Introduction

Use of efficient debugging tools for parallel MIMD machines should become more and more essential in the future. The reason is that we cannot hope for a wider use of parallel machines without the existence of powerful development tools, which include powerful debugging tools. Debugging parallel programs on MIMD machines is a more difficult task than debugging sequential ones because of their non-determinism: successive executions of the same program can lead to different behaviors.

To circumvent non-determinism a technique called execution replay has been suggested [2, 9]. The idea consists of first collecting a judicious execution trace during an initial execution of a given program. Using this trace, a new execution of the same program (called a replay) is then guided to an equivalent execution, meaning that each program component behaves identically, allowing for example breakpoints to be inserted without disturbing the execution. Various replay techniques have already been proposed, which can be classified in two categories. The first one, called "data driven replay", is based on the recording of all the information exchanged by the processes [2, 3, 7,11, 13, 14]. Techniques of this category are quite simple to implement but have the major drawback of perturbing too much the initial execution (because of the large amount of recorded information). The techniques of the second category, called "control driven replay" [4, 9, 12], are more sophisticated and more efficient. The amount of recorded information is reduced

Project funded by the "Fonds national suisse" under contract number 20-5495.88

by regenerating them during replay. The principles of this kind of replay has been introduced by [9] in the context of shared memory architectures. Our solution, which belongs to this second class, is presented in the context of distributed memory architectures, so we will restrict our purpose to message passing communication primitives. However, unlike other studies, we will not limit our purpose to blocking communication primitives. We will also consider non-blocking primitives, which allow to overlap computation and communication (see for example iPSC/2 primitives).

The paper is organized in the following way. In section 2 we present our technique in the context of distributed memory architectures, considering both blocking and non-blocking communication primitives. Since our technique is based on the numbering of events, we show in section 3 how to bound the event numbers. An analysis of the amount of recorded information is carried out in section 4. Finally we present in section 5 a prototype that has been implemented on an Intel iPSC/2.

2 General execution replay technique

2.1 Communication primitives

Our technique can be adapted to any form of communication as described in [10]. However, for sake of simplicity, we suppose in this paper that processes only communicate through message passing. As already explained, both blocking and non-blocking primitives will be considered.

a) **Blocking primitives**: in the context of message passing, the communication primitives we consider are the following:

(1) send(dest,m); (2) receive(m);

Send(dest,m) allows to send message "m" to process "dest". The process is blocked until the message has arrived at the destination site. Receive(m) allows to receive a message into "m" from any process. The process is blocked until a message has arrived.

b) **Non-blocking primitives**: such primitives are used more and more often in practice (as on the iPSC/2 for example) in order to overlap computation and communication. We consider here the following primitives:

(1) define_arrival_buffer (buffer); (2) message_arrived (buffer);
(3) define_departure_buffer (dest, buffer); (4) message_sent (buffer);

Primitives (1) and (2) are related to receptions, whereas primitives (3) and (4) are related to message sending. Primitive "define_arrival_buffer" gives a buffer (in the process space) to the operating system, into which a message can be stored. If a message is already available, it is immediately transferred from the system buffer into the process buffer. If not, the next incoming message for the process will be directly copied into the process buffer. "Message_arrived" returns true if and only if the process buffer contains a message. Primitive "define_departure_buffer" gives to the operating system the destination process and the buffer containing a message to send. Finally "message_sent" returns true if and only if the buffer can be reused (which is usually the case when the message has arrived at the destination site). The primitives are typically used as shown in figure 1.

```
Process 1                                        Process 2
...                                              ...
define_departure_buffer (Process 2, buf1);       define_arrival_buffer (buf2);
...                                              ...
if  message_sent (buf1) then                     if  message_arrived (buf2)  then
  "buf1 can be reused"                             "access to buf2"
else ...                                         else ...
```

Figure 1. Programming style with non-blocking primitives

2.2 Basic principle of the replay technique

Let us consider a parallel program composed of processes. What we want in a replay is that all processes behave identically as during initial execution, even if some breakpoints are placed in the program. In order to describe formally the notion of execution replay, let us consider each process independently. The execution of each process is characterized by the sequence of statements it executes. Some of these statements allow the process to communicate with its environment. The environment of a process consists of either other processes (communication through shared variables or message exchange) or the outside world (communication through I/O). It is (1) the **information received** by a process and (2) the **instants** when communication takes place that influence the process behavior. This leads us to model the execution of a process as a sequence of events, each event being related to communication. To be more precise, two kinds of event have to be considered:

- **explicit events**, which correspond to statements executed by the process, for example "send", "receive", "define_departure_buffer", "define_arrival_buffer", "message_arrived" or access to the buffer;
- **implicit events**, which correspond to events that modify the process state, but are not executed by the process itself (the implicit events are the result of explicit events executed by other processes). The arrival of a message, and the buffer release in the case of message sending are typical implicit events.

Consider for example the program of figure 2 composed of three processes P1, P2, and P3. One possible execution is given in figure 3. Note that a blocking send or receive is represented as two successive events: one explicit (the call to the communication primitive) and one implicit (buffer release or message arrival).

```
  P1                           P2                                       P3
                  define_arrival_buffer (buf1)
send(P2,m)        ...
                  if message_arrived (buf1) then
                    if "message in buf1 = some value" then
                      define_arrival_buffer (buf2)                 send(P2,m)
                    else
                      halt
                    end if;
                  else ...
```

Figure 2. Code of processes P1, P2 and P3.

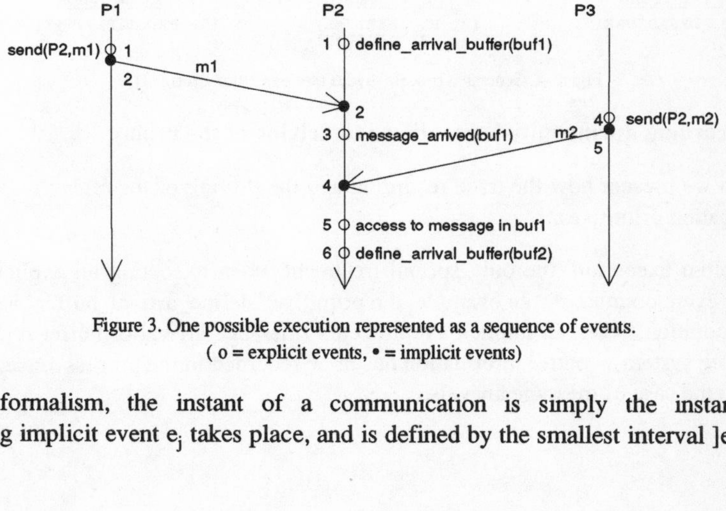

Figure 3. One possible execution represented as a sequence of events.
(o = explicit events, • = implicit events)

Using this formalism, the instant of a communication is simply the instant when the corresponding implicit event e_j takes place, and is defined by the smallest interval $]e_i,e_k[$ where e_i

and e_k are the parenthesizing events (preceding and following event e_j). In the case of figure 3 for example, the arrival of message m_1 (event 2) is defined by the interval]1,3[where 1 and 3 correspond to events "define_arrival_buffer" and "message_arrived". It is now easy to see that a replay reproducing for each process the events in the same order will be equivalent to the initial execution. We will show how to solve this event ordering problem, beginning with an informal presentation of the technique (which will be described more precisely in section 2.3). Communication channels are supposed to be FIFO.

The basic idea is to number the events of each process. In order to guarantee the correct sequencing of the different events during the replay, some control information has to be recorded in the execution trace during the initial execution. However only information concerning the implicit events has to be recorded in the trace. This information has two parts: the sequence number of the implicit event, and an identification of the event. To show that this is sufficient, notice first that during replay explicit events will always be executed in the same sequence by the process. Thus during the replay we only have to ensure that:

a) when executing an explicit event, all preceding implicit events have occurred;
b) an implicit event can take place only when all preceding (explicit and implicit) events have occurred.

Consider first a). By knowing from the trace the sequence number of the implicit events, explicit events can be delayed during the replay: an explicit event will only be executed once all preceding implicit events have occurred (i.e. when the event counter used during replay differs from the next implicit event number recorded in the process' trace, see 2.3). Concerning point b), consider a pair (E_ID, n) in the process' trace, where E_ID is the id of an implicit event E and n the corresponding event number. Event E will be allowed to take place during replay only when the replay event counter is equal to n, which guarantees that all preceding (explicit and implicit) events have occurred.

The problem is now to identify such implicit events. If the communication channels are FIFO, an implicit event corresponding to the arrival of a message can be identified by the pair (sender_prss, ARRIVAL); an implicit event corresponding to the departure of a message can be identified by the pair (destination_prss, DEPARTURE). In practice, the sender and destination process ids are generally associated to the messages, avoiding thus to carry any extra information along with the message for the purpose of execution replay. As an example, the process' traces produced by the execution depicted in figure 3 are shown in figure 4.

P1's Trace	P2's Trace	P3's Trace
(2, P2, DEPARTURE)	(2, P1, ARRIVAL) (4, P3, ARRIVAL)	(5, P2, DEPARTURE)

Figure 4. Generated process' traces (see execution on fig. 3).

2.3 Trace recording during initial execution and driving of the replay

In this section we present how the trace recording and the driving of the replay is integrated into the communication primitives.

During the initial execution, the only special treatment when executing an explicit event is to increment the event counter. As an example, the primitive "define_arrival_buffer" is illustrated in figure 5a. In addition, when an implicit event occurs (message arrival or buffer release, handled by the operating system), control information has to be recorded in the process' trace, as described in figure 5b in the case of message arrivals.

```
procedure define_arrival_buffer (var buf: buffer_type);
begin
  event_counter := event_counter + 1;
  " execute the primitive 'define_arrival_buffer(buf)' ";
end define_arrival_buffer;
```

a)

```
procedure message_arrival (sender_prss: process_type);
begin
  event_counter := event_counter + 1;
  SaveInEventFile(event_counter, sender_prss, ARRIVAL);
end message_arrival;
```

b)

Figure 5. Trace recording during the initial execution.

The first part of the control of the replay is done when executing explicit events: before executing a particular explicit event, we have to check if implicit events precede that event. If so, the process has to force these implicit events to occur in the correct sequence. Procedure Before_Explicit_Event of figure 6a is supposed to be called before each explicit event occurrence during the replay. As an example of an explicit event, the primitive "define_arrival_buffer" is given in figure 6b.

The second part of the control of the replay is done when a message arrives or an emission buffer could be released (implicit events). These events are allowed to take place (i.e. event counter incremented and trace consumed) only if they correspond to the next awaited event of the corresponding process. Otherwise the arrived message or the buffer release information are put in a temporary wait queue, to be handled later on.

```
procedure Before_Explicit_Event;
begin
  while "event_counter = next_recorded_event'NUMBER" do
    if "next_recorded_event'CLASS = DEPARTURE" then
      "wait for release of the buffer containing the
       message destinated to next_recorded_event'DEST_PRSS "
    else  /* next_recorded_event'CLASS = ARRIVAL */
      "wait for the message sent by next_recorded_event'SENDER_PRSS";
    end if;
    next_recorded_event := "next recorded event in the process' trace";
    event_counter:= event_counter+1;
  end while;
end Before_Explicit_Event;
```

a)

```
procedure define_arrival_buffer (var buf: buffer_type);
begin
  event_counter:= event_counter+1;
  Before_Explicit_Event;
  " execute the primitive 'define_arrival_buffer(buf)' ";
end define_arrival_buffer;
```

b)

Figure 6. Driving the replay when executing an explicit event.

3 Bounding the event numbers

Until now we have considered unbounded event numbers. This is however not acceptable for an implementation. It is possible to number the events modulo k if there are always less than k explicit events between two implicit events.

First let us show with an example that this condition is sufficient to correctly drive the replay. Suppose events are bounded modulo k=4. Consider figure 7 where process P2 receives two messages, m_1 from P1, and m_2 from P3.

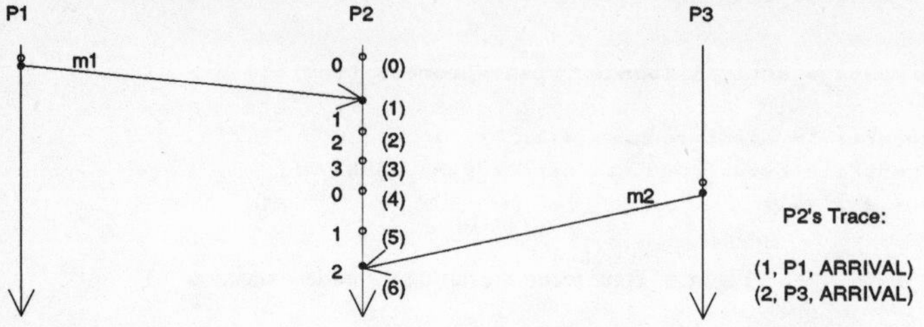

Figure 7. Events numbered modulo 4, and in brackets unbounded event numbers.

If events are bounded modulo 4, there will be a problem during the replay. As the condition mentionned above is not satisfied in figure 7, P2 will consume m_2 too early (as unbounded event number 2 rather than 6 as it should be). The condition is application dependent and nothing can apparently be done to enforce it. Apparently only, because we can add extra records to the trace. Suppose we have the following partial trace using the unbounded numbering of events (see fig. 7)

```
(1,P1,ARRIVAL), (2,P3,ARRIVAL), ...
```

and we want to number the events modulo 4 (events numbered from 0 to 3). This can be done by the following new trace

```
(1,P1,ARRIVAL), (1,,EXPLICIT), (2,P3,ARRIVAL), ...
```

An extra record is added to the process' trace during initial execution each time the difference between the last recorded event and the current event becomes greater than k, or in other words, each time an explicit event occurs and the event counter is equal to the last recorded event number. For example primitive "define_arrival_buffer" (fig. 5a) has to be modified as shown in figure 8.

```
procedure define_arrival_buffer (var buf: buffer_type);
begin
  event_counter := (event_counter + 1) mod k;
  if  event_counter = last_recorded_number  then
    SaveInEventFile(event_counter, EXPLICIT);
  end if;
  " execute the primitive 'define_arrival_buffer(buf)' ";
end define_arrival_buffer;
```

Figure 8. Trace recording with bounded event numbers.

During the replay, the trace is only consumed on implicit events, and also each time an extra record is encountered. Procedure Before_Explicit_Event (figure 6a) has then to be modified in the following way (figure 9).

```
procedure Before_Explicit_Event;
begin
  while "event_counter = next_recorded_event'NUMBER" do
   if  next_recorded_event'CLASS = EXPLICIT  then
    next_recorded_event := "next recorded event in the process' trace";
    event_counter := (event_counter + 1) mod k;
    exit;
   else
    if  "next_recorded_event'CLASS = DEPARTURE"  then
     "wait for release of the buffer containing the
```

```
        message destinated to next_recorded_event'DEST_PRSS "
      else  /* next_recorded_event'CLASS = ARRIVAL */
       "wait for the message sent by next_recorded_event'SENDER_PRSS";
      end if;
      next_recorded_event := "next recorded event in the process' trace";
      event_counter := (event_counter + 1) mod k;
    end if;
  end while;
end Before_Explicit_Event;
```

Figure 9. Driving the replay with bounded event numbers.

Note that the particular case k=1 (no more counter) is treated correctly: the occurrence of each explicit (and each implicit) event will be recorded in the trace. Figure 10 shows P2's trace in the case of the example of figure 7 when no counter is used.

```
(EXPLICIT)
(P1, ARRIVAL)  /* Implicit */
(EXPLICIT)
(EXPLICIT)
(EXPLICIT)
(EXPLICIT)
(P3, ARRIVAL)  /* Implicit */
...
```

Figure 10. P2's trace when no counter (k=1).

4 Amount of recorded information

The amount of recorded information is an important factor in an execution replay technique, because it is correlated to the perturbation of the initial execution. It is important to have a trace as small as possible, not because of disk space limitation, but mainly to reduce the perturbation of the initial execution due to the writing of the tràce. The goal of this section is to analyse the influence of the counter size on the trace size. We will however only consider hereafter counter sizes expressed in bytes.

Let us consider the execution of each process separately. Suppose that the execution of each process produced N events, among which N_i are implicit events. We start by considering the case of no counter which is simpler to analyse.

4.1 Case of no counter.

Let us compute the size of the process' trace. If no counter is used, we have seen (figure 10) that each event (implicit and explicit) has to be recorded in the process' trace. For each recorded event, we suppose that one byte is needed to record the class of the event (EXPLICIT, ARRIVAL, DEPARTURE). Furthermore, for each implicit event, the sender or destination process must be recorded. If the program has P processes, (1 + trunc($\log_{256}$ P)) bytes are necessary to record a process id, so the size of the process' trace is given by the following expression (Tot_x is the trace size in bytes, when a x bytes counter is used):

$$Tot_0 = N + N_i * (1 + trunc(\log_{256} P)) \quad (1)$$

4.2 Case of a b bytes counter (b>0)

We now suppose that a b bytes counter is used (events are numbered modulo $k=256^b$). We have seen in section 3 that explicit events had to be added to the process' trace each time the difference between the last recorded number and the current event number was greater than k. In the best case the difference between two implicit event numbers is never greater than k, meaning that only implicit events are recorded in the trace. Along the lines of the previous paragraph, the size of the process' trace is bounded by the following expression (lower bound):

$$Tot_b \geq N_i * (b + 1 + (1 + trunc(\log_{256} P))) \quad (2)$$

In the worst case, which is unrealistic, the greatest difference between two implicit events is $N-N_i$ (all implicit events are grouped at the beginning and/or at the end of the execution). So $(N-N_i)$ div 256^b explicit event numbers will have to be recorded. Under the pessimistic assumption that the same amount of space is used to record an explicit and an implicit event, we have the following upper bound:

$$Tot_b \leq (N_i + [(N-N_i) \text{ div } 256^b]) * (b + 1 + (1 + trunc(\log_{256} P))) \quad (3)$$

In order to compare Tot_b and Tot_0 in the next paragraph, it is realistic to consider the lower bound of Tot_b since in practice implicit events are always associated to explicit events (meaning that the difference between two implicit event numbers will seldom reach the modulo value):

$$Tot_b \approx N_i * (b + 1 + (1 + trunc(\log_{256} P))) \quad (4)$$

4.3 General discussion of the results

As expected, the trace size depends on the total number of events, the number of implicit events, and the total number of processes in the program. Once these parameters are given, the idea is to see if it is judicious to use a counter or not, and if it is better to use one, to determine the optimal size of the counter.

The comparison of expression (1) and (4) leads to the following result:

$$Tot_0 \geq Tot_b \quad \Longleftrightarrow \quad b \leq (N/N_i) - 1 \quad (5)$$

Consider first the special case of using only blocking primitives. In this case $N_i/N = 0.5$, because we have one explicit event (execution of the communication primitive) for each implicit event (arrival of the message or buffer release). Thus we obtain

$$Tot_0 = Tot_1$$
$$\text{and} \quad Tot_0 < Tot_b \quad \text{for } b>1.$$

Consider now non-blocking primitives. In practice we should have $N_i/N \leq 0.33$, because the implicit event corresponding to the message arrival or buffer release is associated with at least two explicit events: the execution of the communication primitive and one test of completion ("message_arrived", "message_sent"). Thus from (5) we obtain

$$\text{a)} \quad N_i/N=0.33: \quad \begin{cases} Tot_0 > Tot_1 \\ Tot_0 = Tot_2 \\ Tot_0 < Tot_b & \text{for } b>2 \end{cases}$$

$$\text{b)} \quad N_i/N<0.33: \quad Tot_0 > Tot_b \quad \text{for } b\leq 2$$

Let us consider an example. Suppose we have a program composed of less than 256 processes and 200'000 events (per process) were generated during the execution. Figure 11 shows the amount of recorded information for different values of N_i using expression (4). The upper bound of Tot_b from expression (3) is not represented on the graphic since hardly distinguishable from the lower bound (which justifies the approximation (4)).

These results show that in practice a one byte counter should be used. A larger counter could be justified only if the ratio N_i/N is very low (less than 2 %) and the total number of events is high.

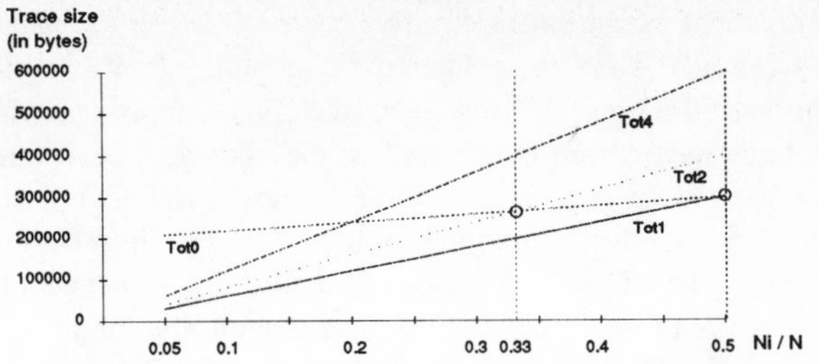

Figure 11. Amount of recorded information (for N=200'000).

5 Implementation on iPSC/2

Our execution replay technique has been implemented on an Intel iPSC/2 multiprocessor. The major part of the monitoring of the initial execution and the control of the replay is implemented by modifying the routines of the communication library. In order to track (initial execution) and control (execution replay) the arrivals of the messages and the buffer releases, an intervention at the operating system level was necessary (new system calls, modification of the receive interrupt routine). During replay, full use of Intel's symbolic DECON debugger is possible, allowing very efficient program development.

Our technique is evaluated by considering the execution overhead and the size of the traces produced during the initial execution for different sizes of the counter. In order to show the low overhead of our approach, we have chosen a problem (Knight's tour on a chessboard) which has voluntarily been inefficiently programmed to obtain an important execution trace (far too many communications). Moreover, we have been able to generate executions with different N_i/N ratios. Figure 12 shows the results with two different N_i/N ratios.

We first observe that the execution time overhead is proportional to the trace size and is very low (less than 2% with a one byte counter). Second, we observe that the trace sizes are in accordance to the theoretical predictions of section 4. A one byte counter seems to be the most efficient solution (only 870 bytes of extra information needed to bound the counter had to be recorded).

For real applications, the communication / computation time ratio should in general be low; as a consequence, the results we obtain with our technique are still better: 0.004% overhead for the Minimax algorithm [1], 0.04% overhead for a 500 x 500 matrix multiplication [5].

Counter size (Bytes)	Ni / N = 10 %, Execution time t without trace recording t = 66,27 s			Ni / N = 29 %, Execution time t without trace recording t = 170,18 s		
	Execution overhead (in %)	Trace size (KBytes)	N	Execution overhead (in %)	Trace size (KBytes)	N
0	5,8	771,23	695'629	3,5	1'220,02	957'022
1	1,9	233,21	781'521	1,3	885,240	1'009'652
2	2,9	278,20	705'391	2,2	1'066,996	967'092
4	3,4	432,91	777'995	4,9	1'570,620	920'792

Figure 12. Overhead due to trace recording and trace size obtained during the initial execution.

6 Conclusion

Debugging parallel programs on MIMD machines is a difficult task because successive executions of the same program can lead to different behaviors. The obvious way to get around this problem is to implement execution replay. We have shown in the paper how to implement execution replay on distributed memory architectures, including both blocking and non-blocking communication primitives (the non-blocking primitives, very important when programming for example the iPSC/2, have never been considered in the context of execution replay). We have also shown that a one byte event counter should be in most cases an optimal choice in order to minimize the amount of recorded information, i.e. indirectly to minimize the perturbation of the initial execution of the program. The overhead due to recording of the event trace has been shown to be less than 2%, even on an application programmed with a voluntarily high communication time / computation time ratio. The overhead should be in practice less than 1%, when considering "normal" applications, which are usually designed on a distributed memory architectures with a low communication time / computation time ratio.

When having implemented execution replay there are various extensions that could be done. One very easy extension could be to implement a P-causal replay, ensuring that each breakpoint in a given process P is a causal breakpoint [6]. Other extensions could consist of developing tools above the execution replay level, allowing a clever exploration of the program states (for example visualization tools). Execution replay allows in some sense to get rid of the non-determinism factor, and should for this reason be considered as a base on which various high-level debugging tools should be built.

Acknowledgment

We are particularly grateful to R. Simon for his numerous suggestions and remarks which substantially improved the presentation.

References

[1] M. Bramer, "Computer Game-Playing theory and practice", Ellis Horwood Series, Halsted Press, 1983.

[2] R. Curtis, L. Wittie, "BugNet: A Debugging System for Parallel Programming Environments", Proc. 3rd Int. Conf. on Distrib. Computing Syst. Hollywood, FL, Oct 1982.

[3] S. Feldmann, C. Brown, "IGOR: A System for Program Debugging via Reversible Execution", SIGPLAN Notices, Volume 24, Number 1, Jan. 1989.

[4] R. Fowler, T. Leblanc, "An Integrated Approach to Parallel Program Debugging and Performance Analysis on Large-Scale Multiprocessors", SIGPLAN Notices, Volume 24, Number 1, Jan. 1989.

[5] G. Fox, S. Otto, "Matrix algorithms on a hypercube I: Matrix multiplication", Parallel Computing, No 4, North-Holland, 1987.

[6] J. Fowler, W.Zwaenepoel, "Causal Distributed Breakpoints", Proc. 10th IEEE Int. Conf. on Distributed Computing Systems, Paris, May 90.

[7] S. Jones, "Bugnet: A Real-Time Distributed Debugging System", Proc. of 6th Internat. Symposium on Reliability in Distributed Sofware and DB Systems, Williamsburg, Va, March 1987.

[8] T. Leblanc, A. Robbins, "Event driven monitoring of distributed programs", Proc. 5th Int. Conf. Distrib. Comput. Syst., Denver, CO, May 1985.

[9] T. Leblanc, J. Mellor-Crummey, "Debugging Parallel Programs with Instant Replay", IEEE Transactions on Computers C-36(4), April 1987.

[10] E. Leu, A. Schiper, A. Zramdini, "Réexécution de programmes parallèles: une approche systématique", Technical Report 90-07, Ecole Polytechnique Fédérale de Lausanne, Département d'Informatique, Switzerland.

[11] D. Pan, M. Linton, "Supporting Reverse Execution for Parallel Programs", SIGPLAN Notices, Volume 24, Number 1, Jan. 1989.

[12] D. Peterson, H. Westphal, "An efficient Implementation of Instant Replay", Technical report, European Computer-Industry Research Centre, Muenchen, West Germany.

[13] D. Snowden, A. Wellings, "Debugging Distributed Real-Time Applications in ADA", University of York, UK, April 1988.

[14] W. Zhou, "PM: A System for Prototyping and Monitoring Remote Procedure Call Programs", ACM SIGSOFT Software Engineering Notes, Vol. 15, Number 1, Jan. 1990.

Distributed Heapmanagement using reference weights *

H. Corporaal
Delft University of Technology
P.O. Box 5031
2600 GA Delft, The Netherlands

Abstract

The progressive demand for computational power has stimulated the design of distributed memory multiprocessors. This in turn caused extensive research into efficient implementations of parallel functional, logic and object-based languages. Automatic heapmanagement using garbage collection is often an integrated part of those implementations. However, distributed garbage collectors can introduce a bottleneck for distributed processing. Both the number of communication messages and the processor idle time may increase untolerably. Independently, Bevan and Watson [Be87,Wa87] proposed a method which solves these problems at the cost of using pointer indirection cells. This introduces an unacceptable delay to every object access. In this paper an alternative is described which does not suffer from this access delay. Besides explaining our method and showing its additional advantages, it is demonstrated that within the framework of pipelined RISC architectures, efficient architectural support for this method is easily achievable.

Keywords: Distributed processing, garbage collection, reference counting, synchronization, real-time performance.

1 Introduction

Building massive parallel multiprocessing systems, especially when designed as distributed memory systems (DMS) is, at least in principle, not complicated. However making efficient use of them, without using low-level communication primitives explicitly, is very difficult. In order to alleviate programming DMSs, much effort is put into the design of efficient implementations of parallel object-based, functional and logic languages. Automatic heapmanagement, using distributed garbage collectors, forms an integral part of these implementations.
In the past garbage collection was considered expensive, restricting the usability of these languages. The development of new techniques like generation scavenging [Un84,Sh87] drastically reduce collection overhead. Parallel implementations of garbage collection however, introduce new efficiency bottlenecks. Ideally, one would require that every processor could perform collection of unused objects independently, without interference from other processors. In practice however, many parallel garbage collectors require lots of interprocessor communication. In addition they introduce new synchronization

*This research has been supported by IBM, as a part of a joint study agreement.

constraints between processors (e.g. between the different collection stages like marking and reclaiming of objects), which decreases processor utilization.
In [Be87] and [Wa87] Bevan and Watson introduced distributed reference counting. Although this method alleviates the above mentioned problems, it is not as efficient as it could be; all object accesses are delayed, due to the use of indirection cells. This paper presents an alternative, the *reference weight table method*, which is far more efficient. It avoids the use of indirection cells. The algorithm can be further improved by adding special architectural support.
In discussing this method we assume readers familiarity with standard reference counting. Section 2 recapitulates the distributed reference counting method, together with its (dis)advantages. In section 3 the principles of the reference weight table method are introduced, whereupon the algorithmic details are explained. An evaluation concludes this section. Section 4 shows how architectural support can improve the performance of the reference weight table method on RISC-based architectures by adding a few simple instructions. The final section summarizes the most important properties of the proposed method.

2 The Distributed Reference Counting Method

In standard reference counting each object keeps track of its incoming number of references by using one reference count (RC) per object. An object is collected if its RC drops to zero. The main advantage of this method is the distribution of garbage collection overhead over the reference creation, deletion and copying operations, which makes this method in principle suitable for interactive applications [1].
It is directly clear that the space and time overhead of standard reference counting is rather big. Besides, distributed implementation of this method gives extra problems. First, the counter update operations cause a lot of extra interprocessor communication. Second, RC can become zero while there are still RC-increment messages pending in the communication network.
The distributed reference counting method introduced by [Be87] and [Wa87] solves these problems. The next 2 subsections describe and evaluate their method.

2.1 The Distributed Reference Counting Algorithm

In the algorithm for the distributed reference counting method each object has a *reference count* (RC) and every reference has a *reference weight* (RW).
At any moment in time, the reference count of an object satisfies the following invariant:

$$RC = \sum_{References} RW, \tag{1}$$

where the summation of the reference weights is taken over all references to the object.

Reference counts are updated by sending a message to the corresponding object. In the following manner, invariant (1) is maintained:

[1] Reference counting in its standard appearance does not behave realtime. First, collecting an object may cause an avalanche effect of other objects to be collected. Second, reference counting does not collect circular structures.

1. Object creation. The RC of the object and the RW of its (single) reference are set to the same starting value, MAX.
2. Reference copying. The RW of the original reference is divided equally between the original reference and the copy. When MAX, the starting value, is a power of 2, a RW will always be divisible by 2 (or equal to 1).[2]
3. Reference deletion. The RW of the reference is subtracted from the RC of the object it referred to. This is achieved by sending a `Decrement_RC(RW)` message. If the object's RC becomes 0, the object is collected.
It is impossible to split a RW of 1 into two non-zero integers. This situation is called *weight underflow.* The solution suggested by [Be87] and [Wa87] is to create an extra object, called an *indirection cell* (Figure 1). The indirection cell consists of the reference that had to be copied and has a RC of MAX. The reference contained in the indirection cell implicitly has a RW of 1. The original reference is replaced by a reference, with a RW of MAX, to the indirection cell. Now the reference to the indirection cell is copied; its RW can be split.

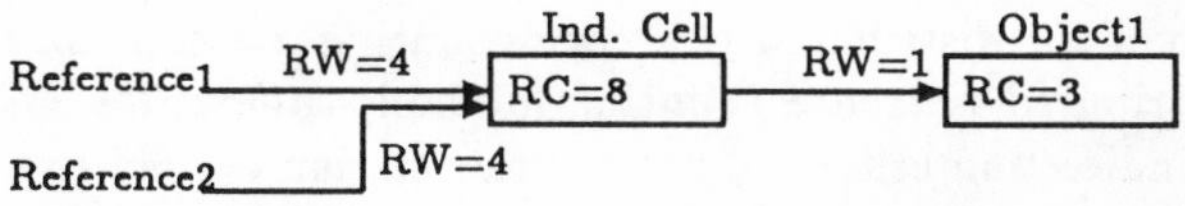

Figure 1: The indirection cell.

2.2 Evaluation of the Distributed Reference Counting Method

The time and space overhead of distributed reference counting is evaluated in comparison with standard reference counting.

Time Overhead

Regarding time overhead, the distributed reference counting method gives three *improvements* over the standard reference counting method. First, the *number of memory accesses is reduced,* since an object does not have to be accessed when a reference to it is copied. Second, using messages to update RC reduces the avalanche effect. Decrementing RC may cause new decrement messages, but they do not have to be processed immediately. Third, the distributed reference counting method does not require messages to be synchronized (there are no pending increment-RC messages), which makes this method more efficient than other garbage collection methods for DMSs.
A severe *disadvantage* is the unacceptable time overhead caused by the use of *indirection cells.* Although indirection cells do not occur often [3], *every time* an object is accessed a test has to be performed if the accessed location holds the actual object or an indirection cell. This will cause time overhead proportional to the number of LOAD instructions, which is a considerable amount. For example, about 25% of the instructions in LISP on a RISC are LOADs [St87]. When implemented without hardware support, the overhead

[2] Note that an object does not have to be accessed when a reference to it is copied.
[3] Measurements from [Be87] have shown that the mean number of indirection cells that has to be traversed to access an object, using two bits for RW, is 0.005.

created by indirection cells is 50%: in addition to every LOAD two instructions are needed to detect indirection cells. Even when supported by hardware, a LOAD instruction cannot be implemented without 1 extra cycle, which results in a 25% overall overhead. Therefore, the indirection cell should be abandoned in favor of a more efficient way to solve the weight underflow problem: the Reference Weight Table method, which is described in the next sections.

Storage Overhead

Compared with the standard reference counting method, the storage overhead of the distributed reference counting method is *small*. Since a RW is always a power of 2, it can be represented by its base 2 logarithm. Using b bits for the RW field, a RW from 1 to $2^{(2^b-1)}$ can be expressed. Since the ranges of RW and RC are the same, $2^b - 1$ bits are needed in the RC field. [4]

3 The Reference Weight Table Method

The Reference Weight Table (RWT) method solves weight underflow more efficiently and more effectively than the distributed reference counting method. The basis of the RWT method is the distributed reference counting method, *without the indirection cells*. Instead of creating indirection cells, it puts the information carried by indirection cells in a table. Before describing the RWT method, let us extract the *principles* on which the indirection cell (and the RWT) is based. When an indirection cell is created, the original RW (with value 1) is substituted by a *borrowed* RW (with a value of MAX). The indirection cell maintains invariant (1):

- the RC of the indirection cell compensates for the borrowed RW,
- the RW of the indirection cell replaces the lost, original, RW.

The principle of borrowing weight is valid; it is the *implementation* in indirection cells that makes it inefficient. The RWT method distinguishes a borrowed RW, called BW, from an ordinary RW. Furthermore, every processing entity (PE) has a Reference Weight Table (RWT). [5] Figure 2 shows how indirection cells are mapped into table entries. Every RWT entry consists of three fields:

- The BC (borrowed count) field corresponds to the RC of the indirection cell.
- The RW_T field corresponds to the RW of the indirection cell.
- The PF (PE field) field does not directly correspond to a part of the indirection cell. It is, however, necessary for this method, as is described in section 3.1.

Every reference has a weight field (WF), which contains either a RW or a BW. The RW and BW can only be powers of two, between 1 and 2^N and 2^M, respectively. When underflow occurs, a RWT entry is created. The BW is used analogously to a RW. When a reference with a BW is copied its BW is split. When a reference with a BW is deleted, the BW is subtracted from BC *in the* RWT. If this causes the BC to become 0, the RWT entry

[4] Three bits per object and two bits per reference are sufficient for adequate performance ([Be87]).

[5] The RWT can be implemented as a hash table, with its entries accessed by reference (= by object address).

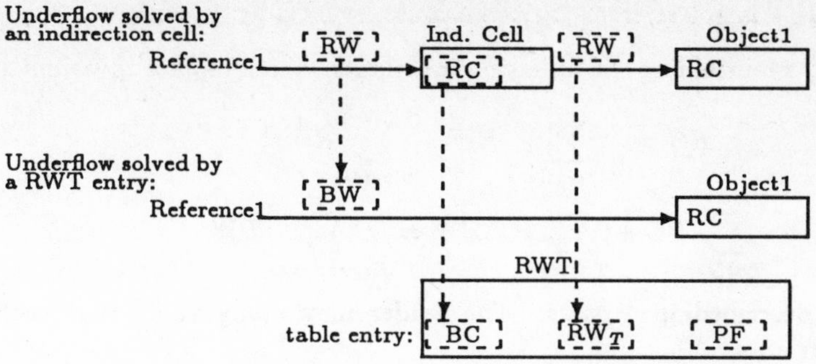

Figure 2: The indirection cell is mapped onto a RWT entry.

is 'reclaimed'; the value in the RW_T field is subtracted from the RC of the object and the entry is removed from the table. Figure 3 shows the lifecycle of a WF (every time a reference is copied, its WF changes one step in the direction of the arrows).

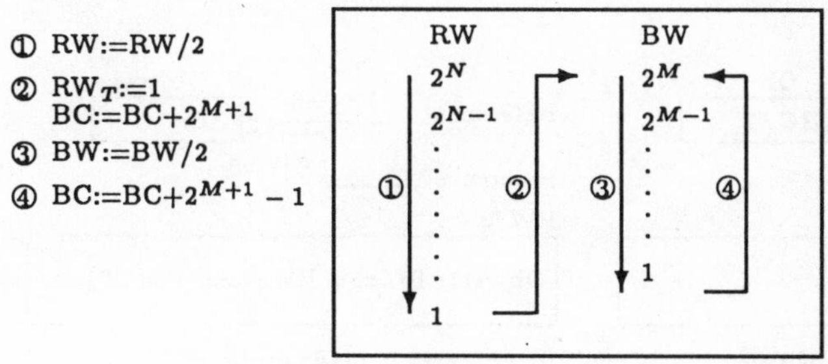

Figure 3: The lifecycle of the Weight Field.

So far, we have regarded the RWT as a functional *equivalent* to the indirection cell. Apart from not using indirection cells, the RWT exhibits an additional advantage: the BC and RW_T fields may be *as large as is desirable.* They are not bounded, like in indirection cells, by the size of the RWF or RCF. This means that in one RWT entry, ***multiple*** cases of underflow can be accounted for (more indirection cells can be mapped onto one RWT entry). The use of this fact is twofold:

- When a BW underflows, weight can be borrowed again. This is equivalent to creating two chained indirection cells.
- When underflow occurs, in the RWT method a weight of 2^{M+1} can be borrowed, by setting the BW of both the original reference and the the copy to 2^M. This is equivalent to creating two parallel indirection cells at once.

3.1 Algorithmic details of the Reference Weight Table method

In order to guarantee correct behavior, two conditions must be met at all times:

1. When an object is referenced, its RC must be greater than 0.

2. When an object is not referenced, its RC must, eventually, become 0.

This is achieved by maintaining the following invariants, which replace invariant 1.[6]

$$RC = \sum_{References} RW + \sum_{Tables} RW_T. \tag{2}$$

$$\sum_{Tables} BC + \sum_{Tables} PF.BW = \sum_{References} BW. \tag{3}$$

The algorithm is described in 4 parts. The reader may easily verify that each part maintains the invariants.

1. Object creation. Upon creation of an object, its RC is set to the starting value, 2^N. The weight WF of the reference to it is set to (RW, 2^N) [7].

2. Reference copying. When a reference is copied, its weight is split between itself and the copy. Underflow occurs when the weight value equals 1; the weight of 1 is lost, it is substituted by *two* BWs of 2^M (see Figure 4ab). The RWT entry is updated [8] to maintain invariants (2) and (3).

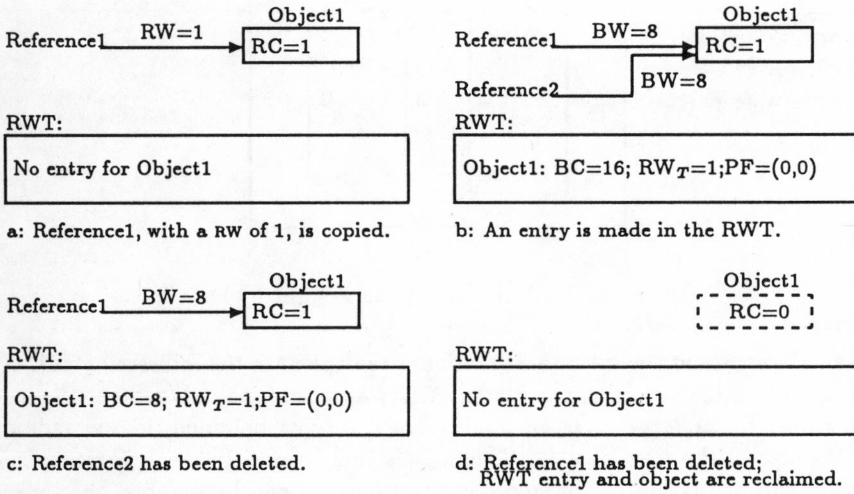

Figure 4: The Reference Weight Table method for M=3.

3. Reference deletion. When a reference with a RW is deleted, its RW is subtracted from the RC of the object. Deletion of a reference with a BW is handled analogously; the BW is subtracted from the BC in the RWT entry (Figure 4c).
If the RC of an object drops to 0, the object is reclaimed. When the BC of a table entry becomes 0, the entry is removed; its BC is subtracted from the object's RC (Figure 4d).

[6] The PF fields are only used in a special case of non-local reference moving (see rule 4). Usually, the PF.BW equals 0, to which it is initialized.

[7] The notation used for WF is (type, value), where type is either RW or BW.

[8] If no entry exists yet, one is created first.

4. Non-local reference moving. References can be moved from one PE to another in the message:

```
Move_Reference(Reference2, Source_PE_Id, Destination_PE_Id);
```

Figure 5 illustrates this. Reference1 on Source PE is copied to Reference2 on Destination PE, in two steps. First, a local copy is performed, as described in part 2 of the algorithm. Second, the copy is moved to Destination PE. When a PE receives a Move_Reference

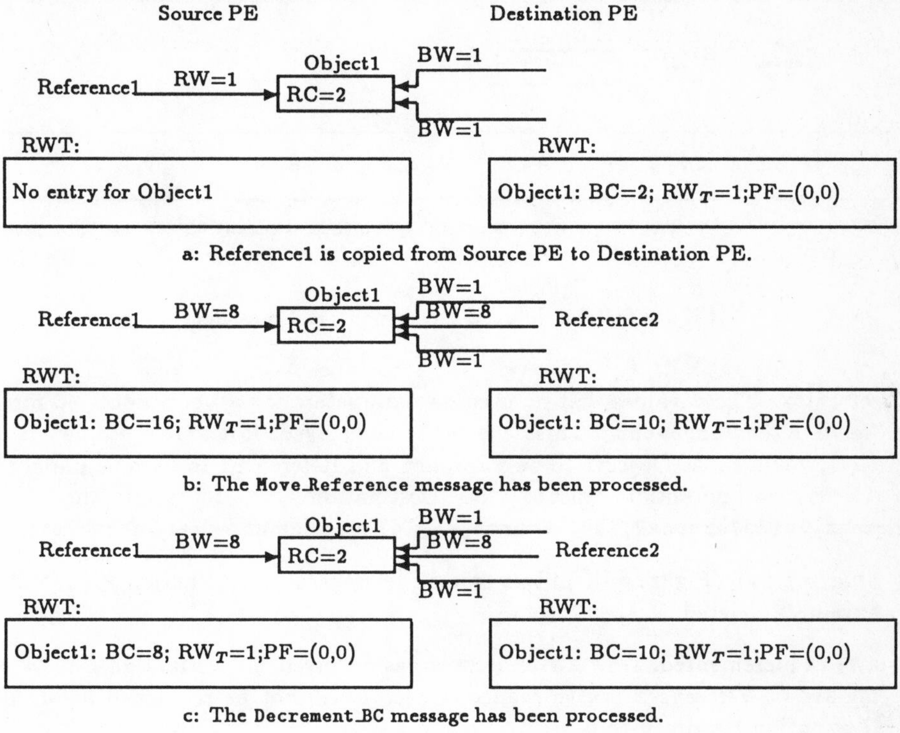

Figure 5: The non-local reference copy.

message, it inspects the WF of the contained reference. If the reference has a BW (instead of a RW), it has to be contained in the RWT. How this is done depends on the fact whether or not the RWT in Destination PE already contains an entry for Object1.

Figure 5 illustrates the former case, when underflow has occurred in Destination PE before reception of the message. The BC of the RWT entry is incremented by the BW of Reference2 (Figure 5b) (the BW is now accounted in both Source PE and Destination PE). After this, Destination PE sends a `Decrement_BC(Reference2, BW, Source_PE_Id)` message to Source PE. Reception of this message will cause the BC in Source PE to be decremented by BW (Figure 5c); Reference2 is now accounted only in Destination PE.

The latter case is depicted in Figure 6, where a reference with RW=1 has been copied and moved to the destination PE. No RWT entry for this reference existed in Destination PE. In this case, an entry is created, with its BC set to BW and its RW_T set to 0 (Figure 6a). The `BW` of Reference2 and the `PE_Id` of Source PE are stored in the PF (PE Field) of

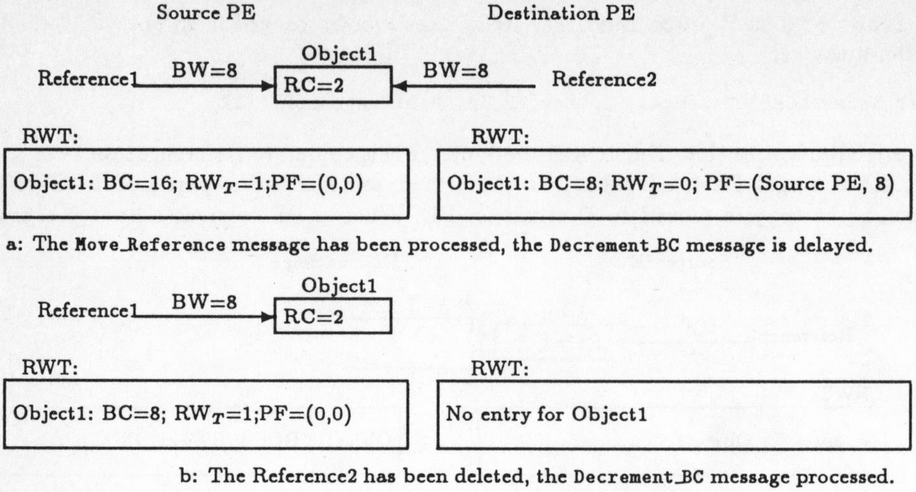

Figure 6: The delayed Decrement_BC message.

the RWT entry. These values will be used as parameters for a `Decrement_BC` message later. Sending the `Decrement_BC` message has to be delayed. If it were sent now, deleting Reference1 would cause Object1 to be reclaimed and Reference2 to become dangling. There are two potential reasons for Destination PE to send the delayed `Decrement_BC(Reference2, BW, Source_PE_Id)` message and clear the PF field:

1. BC drops to 0 (Figure 6b). In this case all references in Destination PE to Object1 have been deleted.

2. RW$_T$ is incremented. Now RW underflow has occurred in Destination PE, *to which the* BW *in Reference2 can be related.* Object1 will not be reclaimed before BC in Destination PE drops to 0.

3.2 Evaluation of the Reference Weight Table Method

The Reference Weight Table method for solving weight underflow is compared to the indirection cell method.

Time Overhead

The time overhead of the Reference Weight Table method is proportional to the amount of weight underflow. Storage access is not delayed by referential indirections as is the case with the indirection cell method. If the range of RW, 2^N, is chosen reasonably high, the frequency of underflow will be small; for N=3, only one out of two hundred references in a LISP system will have to be accounted for in a RWT ([Be87]). On top of that, the amount of repeated weight underflow in the RWT method is reduced; twice as much weight is borrowed per case of underflow than in the indirection cell method. To reduce the frequency of weight underflow even more, the Weight Increment method, which is described in [Co88], can be used. Furthermore, the RWT method can be effectively supported by hardware, as will be described in section 4.

Storage Overhead

The storage overhead of the Reference Weight Table method is of the same order as the storage overhead of the indirection cell method. Part of it is proportional to the amount of weight underflow. In the indirection cell method, it equals the storage occupied by an indirection cell for each case of underflow. In the RWT method, it consists of the storage occupied by a RWT entry, in each PE once for every object that is referenced by references with a BW.

Furthermore, the indirection cell needs an identification, which requires an extension of the tagspace. The RWT method needs a larger weight field than the distributed reference counting method, in order to have the same range for RW.

If b is the number of bits in a WF, then N and M are chosen so that $N + M = 2^b - 2$; they do not have to be equal. The optimal values for N and M will have to be determined by measurements.

WF	W
000	(BW, 1)
001	(BW, 2)
010	(BW, 4)
011	(BW, 8)
100	(RW, 1)
101	(RW, 2)
110	(RW, 4)
111	(RW, 8)

WF	W
000	(BW, 1)
001	(BW, 2)
010	(BW, 4)
011	(RW, 1)
100	(RW, 2)
101	(RW, 4)
110	(RW, 8)
111	(RW, 16)

Table 1: The WF; b=3, N=3 and 4, respectively.

4 Architectural Support

A storage manager can be implemented in any high-level language, on any general purpose architecture, as long as the performance is not too critical. To achieve optimal performance, however, storage management can profit from *architectural support*. In this section the possibilities for architectural support of the RWT method are discussed. This is done from a RISC point of view. The introduced instructions have to be simple, suited for single-cycle execution and must not introduce a critical path in the pipeline. In designing the instructions, MIPS/X [MI84] and SCARCE [9] [Mu89] have been used as guidelines.[10] It is demonstrated that these architectures can be extended to make the RWT method highly efficient.

For the sake of simplicity, we suppose that every memory word has space for a RWF and a RCF. There are three operations in the distributed reference counting method with RWT that can be given architectural support: Object creation, Reference copying and

[9] A VLSI implementation of this architecture has been developed at the Delft University of Technology.

[10] Mainly, this has three implications: Compare & Branch instructions with two delay slots are used. Branch instructions may be predictive to make maximal use of the delay slots possible. Register operations can have up to 2 read and 1 write operand.

Reference deletion. These three operations will be described in this section at machine level, using a hypothetic assembler language.

4.1 Object Creation

It is assumed that the architecture already supports a function that allocates storage for an object and returns the address of the object-to-be in register R1. Having executed this function, the system has to set the RCF and the RWF to the proper values. The word that has to be stored in the first word of the object is supposed to be in R2. The desired situation is to have a reference to the allocated object in R3. Without any special instructions the code would be:

```
OR      R2,START_COUNT          ;RC(R2):=START_COUNT
STORE   R2,(R1)                 ;(R1):=R2
OR      R1,START_WEIGHT         ;RW(R1):=START_WEIGHT
MOVE    R1,R3                   ;R3:=R1
```

To support object allocation the architecture could have two special instructions, MVREF and STREF. They combine the OR operation with a MOVE [11] and STORE, respectively. The code becomes:

```
STREF  R2,(R1),START_COUNT ;(R1):=R2, RC((R1)):=START_COUNT
MVREF  R1,R3,START_WEIGHT  ;R3:=R1, RW(R3):=START_WEIGHT
```

Comparing these two code examples shows that each new instruction saves 1 processor cycle.

4.2 Reference Copying

Consider a reference being copied from register R1 to register R2. Before the actual copy, the RW of the reference has to be divided by two. This comes down to extracting, decrementing and storing the RWF, as long as the RW is positive; the RW may never be negative. This yields a complicated operation, which should be implemented in hardware. A TRAP is performed if a RW of 0 is detected. The TRAP routine will cause the RWT to be updated. The architecture can support reference copying with the instruction HLFRW (halve RW).

```
HLFRW  R1               ;RW(R1):=RW(R1) DIV 2, if RW(R1)=0 then TRAP
MOVE   R1,R2            ;R2:=R1
```

Note that these 2 instructions can not be combined under the single destination operand assumption.

4.3 Reference Deletion

With reference deletion the referenced object has always to be accessed. Therefore a distinction has to be made between the deletion of local references and of non-local references.

[11] Often, a combination of OR and MOVE has been implemented already.

Local Reference Deletion

When a reference is being deleted, its RWF has to be extracted, the RCF of the referenced object has to be extracted, the RC has to be decremented by RW, and the RCF has to be stored, if greater than 0. If the RC has become 0, the object is collected. This has to be implemented in hardware for the sake of efficiency, and it can be supported by the instructions SUBRW and CPTGBR. The former extracts an RW and a RC value, subtracts the RW from the RC and stores the RC. The latter combines the extraction of a (RW or RC) field with a compare & branch instruction.
The code for overwriting (=deleting) the reference in R2 by the reference in R1 looks like this:

```
                 CPTGBR BW,ADJUST_TABLE,R2        ;if BW(R2) then ADJUST_TABLE
                 LOAD   (R2),R3                   ;else load object
                 SUBRW  R2,R3                     ;RC(R3):=RC(R3)-RW(R2)
                 CPTGBR RC,COLLECT_OBJECT,R3      ;if RC(R3)=0 then COLLECT_OBJECT
                 STORE  R3,(R2)                   ;else store object
                 BR     END_COPY                  ;done
ADJUST_TABLE:    .....                            ;code for adjusting the table
                 BR     END_COPY                  ;done
COLLECT_OBJECT:  .....                            ;code for collecting the object
END_COPY:        MOVE   R1,R2                     ;the reference is overwritten
```

Note that the delay slots of the CPTGBR instructions are filled successfully, assuming that these instructions are predictively non-taken. If the branches are taken the delay slots are squashed.

Non-local Reference Deletion

The difficulty with deletion of a non-local reference is that the object that is referred to by the reference cannot be accessed immediately. Instead of loading the object, the processor has to send a decrement-message to the heap holding the object. After receiving the message, the processor local to the object executes the code to decrement the object's RC. The code of the former example has to be divided into two parts. This is the part for the heap local to the reference:

```
                 CPTGBR BW,ADJUST_TABLE,R2        ;if RW(R2)=0 then ADJUST_TABLE
DECR_MESSAGE:    .....                            ;else send decrement-message
                 BR     END_COPY                  ;  done
ADJUST_TABLE:    .....                            ;code for adjusting the table
END_COPY:        MOVE   R1,R2                     ;the reference is overwritten
```

The other part of the code is executed in the heap local to the object (a copy of the deleted reference is sent in the decrement-message, and put into R2):

```
                 LOAD   (R2),R3                   ;load object
                 SUBRW  R2,R3                     ;RC(R3):=RC(R3)-RW(R2)
                 CPTGBR RC,COLLECT_OBJECT,R3      ;if RC(R3)=0 then COLLECT_OBJECT
                 STORE  R3,(R2)                   ;else store object
                 BR     END                       ;done
COLLECT_OBJECT:  .....                            ;code for collecting the object
END:                                              ;done
```

5 Conclusions

The distributed reference counting method described in [Be87] and [Wa87] is a real time garbage collector for distributed processing systems. It has several advantages over standard reference counting and other distributed garbage collectors, like independent collection by all processors, small space overhead, and no synchronization between garbage collection messages.
The use of indirection cells, however, causes *unacceptable time overhead* in object access. Depending on application and possible hardware support, this overhead may range from 25% till over 50%. The gains of the reference weight table method are:

- Object access is not delayed by indirection cells.
- The amount of weight underflow is reduced.
- Time overhead is proportional to the amount of weight underflow (which will be on the order of 1% or less for a three bits weight field representation).
- The reference weight table method can be supported easy and efficiently by RISC-like architectures.

The reference weight table method much improves the distributed reference counting method, without sacrificing its advantages above other garbage collection methods. It is therefore a likely candidate for future implementations on real time distributed memory systems, which require automatic heap management.

References

[Be87] D. I. Bevan. *Distributed Garbage Collection Using Reference Counting.* Proc. of Parallel Architectures and Languages Europe, June 1987.

[Co88] H. Corporaal, T. Veldman and A.J. van de Goor. *Reference Weight-based Garbage Collection for Distributed Systems.* Proc. of the SION Conference on Computing Science in the Netherlands, Utrecht, November 1988.

[MI84] Paul Chow. *MIPS/X Instruction Set and Programmer's Manual.* Computer Systems Laboratory Stanford University, November 1984.

[Mu89] J.M. Mulder e.a. *A framework for application-specific architecture design.* Proc. of the 14th symposium on computer architecture, May 1989.

[Sh87] Robert A. Shaw. *Improving Garbage Collector Performance in Virtual Memory* Stanford University, Tech. Rep. CSL-TR-87-323,March 1987.

[St87] Peter Steenkiste. *Lisp on a Reduced-instruction-set Processor: Characterization and Optimization* Stanford Univ, Computer Systems Lab, CSL-TR-87-324, March 1987.

[Un84] David Ungar. *Generation Scavenging: A Non Disruptive High Performance Storage Reclamation Algorithm.* ACM Sigplan notices, Vol. 19, 5, May 1984.

[Wa87] Paul Watson and Ian Watson. *An Efficient Garbage Collection Scheme For Parallel Computer Architectures.* Proc. of Parallel Architectures and Languages Europe, June 1987.

Code Generation for Data Parallel Programs on DMPCs

Jean-Louis Pazat
IRISA Campus de Beaulieu
F-35042 Rennes Cedex FRANCE
pazat@irisa.fr

Abstract

Programming Distributed Memory Parallel Computers (DMPCs) usually requires a lot of work both at the algorithmic level and at the programming level. We investigate here how to produce code for DMPCs from high level programming languages. We propose a language, a compiler and a run-time support which allow to program DMPCs with a sequential language including data distribution statements. The distribution statements allow the user to express data partitioning which will enforce code parallelization. One important feature of our approach is that data distribution does not modify the result of the program in any case, efficiency depends only on data distribution.

1 Introduction

DMPCs are mainly used for scientific codes which involve large data structures. A natural way to define a parallel algorithm is to partition the data among the distributed memory and to write one process devoted to each piece of data. This is what we call a *Data Parallel Program.* In some cases, synchronizations must be added to insure the coherence of data when some variables are duplicated. Distant accesses to variables are often needed because of the limited size of each local memory.

When the partitioning of data structures is defined, the work that remains to the programmer is the following:

1. to restrict the data domain accesses of each process to the exact part of data it works on,

2. to map the partitioned data among the local memories,

3. to implement local accesses to variables according to the local names of variables,

4. to implement distant accesses to variables using message passing procedures and a local temporary storage.

All this work needs to add many low level communication and synchronization constructs inside the parallel code. This task generates many errors and the final program is difficult to understand and to debug. Tools are needed to generate automatically this low level code from a higher level description of the data parallel algorithm.

In section 2 we present some of the current projects of compilers for high level languages. Our work on the PANDORE system is shown in section 3 and 4. We conclude with future work and open questions concerning the run-time associated to these high level languages.

2 Compilers for DMPCs

Parallelization tools have been studied and are available for parallel computers with a shared memory. All these tools achieve code parallelization through the analysis of the control flow of a program. Loops are analyzed in order to discover if they can be executed in parallel in some way (DOALL, DOACROSS) [1]. Here, the most important work of the compiler is to analyze (and sometime remove) dependencies between statements. These compilers do not take into account any data distribution in the parallelization process nor provide any hook to get informations for the mapping of data. A more promising approach is investigated in the specific field of DMPCs.

The MIMD model is the most commonly used for programming DMPCs. Many languages are built upon existing sequential languages (C or Fortran) and communication libraries. Some of them are more sophisticated and provide accesses to a global space as the tuple space of Linda [2]. More strongly defined languages provide process and synchronous (rendez-vous) communication as OCCAM based on CSP [3] or asynchronous (infinite FIFO queues) communication as in Estelle [4].

Other programming models are now being investigated in order to provide the user an easy way for programming DMPCs with a reasonable loss of efficiency.

In all cases the major issue is not to hide the distributed structure of the memory, but to allow the user to express local and distant accesses in the same way, without any message passing mechanism. That is why all projects of compilers for DMPCs, cited below, provide a global name space to the user. The transformation between global name and local names and the communication generation are done at compile-time or at run-time as it is the case in [5]. These approaches are different from implementing a virtual memory on a DMPC as described in [6] or using it in a specific algorithm [7]. In these approaches, the user is responsible for mapping its data which do not migrate from one processor to another during the program execution.

The models being investigated are not "exotic" but refer to well known programming methodologies as: Implicit parallelism (equational model, logic or functional models), Sequential model, SPMD model (Single Program Multiple Data), SIMD model .

The SIMD model is sometimes a more natural way to express algorithms for example in image processing. Hatcher et al [8] have implemented C* on an iPSC2 with a reasonable loss of efficiency by limiting synchronizations at communication points. Reeves et al. [9] are working on the implementation of an SIMD object oriented language including user specified data partioning.

The SPMD model without explicit communication between processes seems to be one of the most simple models to use and to implement on DMPCs. The DINO language [10] provides an easy way to write such programs. The language allows to access distant data through local copies without explicit message passing nor hand written synchronizations to insure coherence of copies. KALI [11] may be qualified as implicit SPMD as the language offers a special parallel construct (**forall**) for defining distributed iterations among a domain. In KALI, each iteration of a loop is executed on one processor specified by the user accordingly to the data distribution. Both KALI and DINO are based on user defined data partitioning.

The sequential model is well known to many programmers. Moreover, most of scientific codes are already written in some sequential language (most of them in Fortran). Superb [12], Parascope [13] and our project Pandore [14] are based on a sequential language with new constructs and statements to allow the user to express data distribution. Other projects in this field are Id-Nouveau [15],Aspar [16], Booster [17] and Oxygen [18].

Compiling implicit parallel languages for DMPCs is a much more difficult job because both execution scheme and data distribution must be discovered by the compiler. In the field of scientific programming the equational approach seems to be very interesting [19] and results for systolic architectures have been found [20]. Compiling equational languages for DMPCs is now only at the beginning stage of research.

3 The Pandore Language

3.1 Overview

We present here the source language of our prototype which is based on a restricted version of the C language. We plan to achieve further developments on a restricted Fortran as many scientific codes and benchmarks already exist in this language. Nevertheless, most of sequential languages can be "customized" for our purpose.

In a Pandore program data structures can be partitioned and distributed among *virtual distributed machines* (Vdm) in order to enforce code parallelization. In the actual prototype we consider only arrays as these structures are the most commonly used in scientific programming.

A Pandore program is divided into phases which are executed sequentially. Each phase can be sequential or parallelized as specified by the user.

A parallelized phase specified by `vdm my_vdm{...}` corresponds to: The distribution of the data to the Vdm, A parallelized block of code and the collection of the distributed data from the Vdm.

In a parallelized phase, the execution of a statement occurs on the processor of the Vdm where the data written by the statement is located, This implies that the data distribution induces the creation of processes (one process per "processor" of the Vdm). If there is a need of distant data, the compiler automatically generates the interprocess communication.

3.2 Data partitioning

An array which is declared to be a `distributed` array may be partitioned in sub-arrays by the statement `partition(A,f(i,j))` where `A` is the name of the array and `f(i,j,...)`

is a function which defines how sub-arrays are built from the original array. We provide a predefined function `Block(i,j)` which defines sub-arrays as blocks of size `i` × `j`. A function `Block_Overlap` is also implemented in order to allow boundary elements of blocks to reside on two different sub-arrays. This function is useful because local computations on a block of data often refer to boundary elements of a neighbor block (this is the case in the convolution algorithm). The Pandore language allows to partition an array more that once inside a program.

Sub-arrays are then distributed among the local memories of the DMPC which are represented by the Vdm. A Vdm is declared as an array of **processors** and the data distribution on the Vdm is implicitly defined from the partitioning function and the type and size of the Vdm.

If a variable is not distributed, it resides on the host processor (outside the Vdm). Scalar variables or unpartitioned arrays can be distributed. In this case they reside on one processor of the Vdm which is chosen by the compiler. This is different from what Parascope and Superb compilers do: they duplicate all these variables on each processor. Our compiler allows to create duplicated variables if they are defined inside a parallelized block. In this case each processor owns an independent copy of the variable (we call it a local variable).

In order to limit useless data migration, the data the user wants to distribute among a Vdm must be specified with a distribution type. Such a type tells the compiler if the code for sending the value to the Vdm (IN) at the beginning of a parallelized block or receiving it at the end of the parallelized block (OUT) has to be generated or not.

The mapping of the Vdm onto the real architecture is done at loading time. As the structures of the Vdms are very simple we will use a library of mappings rather than a general mapping algorithm. This is because the general problem is known to be NP-Complete and only heuristic algorithms can be used in practical cases.

An example of a simple Pandore program is shown in figure 1. Array `Win` and `Wout` are declared as "distributed" and are partioned at run-time into blocks of size `K`. For sake of efficiency, boundary elements of neighbor blocks are appended to each bloc of the array `Win`. This kind of partitioning avoids to access non-local data during the parallel execution because `Win[i]`, `Wout[i-1]` and `Win[i+1]` are located on the same procesor than `Wout[i]`.

4 Compilation and run-time support in Pandore

The Pandore compiler generates a SPMD program in an intermediate language which is independent of the target machine. Basically, the compiler replicates the original code on each virtual processor of the Vdm (one process for each processor). Each processor executes the same code but the data distribution induces a conditional execution for each statement as the execution scheme is based on local writes :

1. **Refresh phase** The compiler must manage remote accesses to variables. The execution of the fetch part of a statement depends on the data mapping : If the processor owns some data it sends it to the processor(s) needing it; if it needs some data, it waits for them, else it does nothing.

```
#define K 100
#define N 1000
...
distributed int Win[N] , Wout[N];
processor row[5];

main()
{
 ...
 /* parallelized phase */
  partition (Win, block_overlap(K,1,1));
  partition (Wout, block(K));
  vdm row ( (Win, IN), (Wout, OUT)) {
    int i ;
    for(i=1; i<N-1; i++) Wout[i]= A*Win[i-1] + B*Win[i] + C*Win[i+1];
  }
 ...
}
```

Figure 1: Convolution in C_Pandore

2. **Exec phase** The execution of a statement is effective on the processor(s) where the data written is mapped, elsewhere nothing happens.

This basic scheme is very similar to the one proposed in [13] and is defined more precisely in the following sections: The sets of data used in a statement are defined in 4.1, the semantics and implementation of the two phases (Refresh and Exec) are detailed in 4.2 and the compilation of assignments and control structures (If, While and For) are defined in 4.3. As there is always one process per processor of the Vdm we use the term *process* in the remaining of the paper.

4.1 Data sets

We call $\mathcal{V}$ the set of variables (data elements) of the program and $\mathcal{P}$ the set of processes of the Vdm.

Each statement of a program works on two data sets [21] :

- $IN(S)$: data read by the statement,
- $OUT(S)$ data written by the statement.

In the case of an array subscript overflow in the statement S, data read or written by S do not exist ($IN(S) \not\subset \mathcal{V}$ or $OUT(S) \not\subset \mathcal{V}$).

We also define :

- $Own(V) \subset \mathcal{P}$ as the set of processors where data in V are mapped.

- $Own(S) \subset \mathcal{P}$ as the set of processors where the statement S is executed.

For example in the case of an assignment $OWN(S) = Own(OUT(S))$.

In most cases $OUT(S)$ contains a unique element ; data needed to execute the statement S are in $IN(S)$ and data in $IN(S) - OUT(S)$ are remotely read from a distant process in the Refresh phase of a statement.

These sets are not always known at compile-time but when it is the case, the compiler may be able to improve the execution scheme presented in the next sections.

4.2 *Refresh* and *Exec* phases

The intermediate language possesses two special instructions $Refresh$ and $Exec$.

- $Refresh(V, P)$ updates each local copy of each variable in V on each process of the set P.
- $Exec(S, P)$ executes the statement S on the processes of the set P.

A straightforward (but naïve) run-time implementation of these function is shown bellow:

$$\begin{aligned} Refresh(V,P) \;\equiv\;& If\ myself\ in\ Own(V)\ Then\ send(P - Own(V), V) \\ & If\ myself\ in\ P - Own(V)\ Then\ recv(Own(V), V) \end{aligned}$$

$$Exec(S,P) \;\equiv\; If\ myself\ in\ P\ then\ S$$

Where

- $myself$ is the name of the current process,
- communication between processes is FIFO, no messages are lost
- $send(Q, W)$ sends the values of the variables in W to the processes in Q (this send is non–blocking: processes in $Own(W)$ do not wait for values in W to be received on Q.
- $recv(Q, W)$ waits for receiving values of variables in W from processes in Q.

In this model, it it possible for more than one value to be received for each variable. If it is the case, only one value is kept. As this is not very useful, we have introduced a function φ for choosing one process in the set $Own()$ when it is needed. In our actual implementation this case can only happen with the `Block_overlap` distribution: if some data in the overlap area is needed on another process than the ones where it is mapped.

$$\begin{aligned} Refresh(V,P) \;\equiv\;& If\ myself\ = \varphi(Own(V))\ Then\ send(P - Own(V), V) \\ & If\ myself\ in\ P - Own(V)\ Then\ recv(\varphi(Own(V)), V) \end{aligned}$$

$$Exec(S,P) \;\equiv\; If\ myself\ in\ P\ then\ S$$

The actual implementation of *Refresh* is tightly synchronous as:

- the asynchrony of a send is limited by the buffer size used in the system,
- the synchronous receive induces useless synchronizations between processes when a distant value is never written by its owner.

4.3 Compiling statements and control structures

Compiling a program into SPMD intermediate code can be described with the following compiling rules : for each statement or control structure we define :

- The set $IN(S)$ of data elements needed for its execution
- The set $Own(S)$ of processes that execute S
- the intermediate language statement generated ($\hat{S}$)

Assignment $X = Expr$

The transformation of an assignment is straightforward :

- $IN(X = Expr) = \{v \in Expr\}$ (set of data of the right hand side of the assignment)
- $Own(X = Expr) = Own(OUT(X = Expr))$ is the single data element written by the assignment.
- $$\widehat{X = Expr} = \begin{array}{l} Refresh(IN(X = Expr), Own(X = Expr)); \\ Exec(X = Expr, Own(X = Expr)) \end{array}$$

The definition of $OWN(S)$ induces a non trivial behavior in the case of subscript overflow when referencing arrays. When `T[i]=k` presents a subscript overflow in the array `int T[N]`, the statement is not executed in Pandore (no one owns T[i]). On the contrary `k=T[i]` will block indefinitely the process(es) which want to do the assignment since no process Owns T[i].

Sequence $S_1; S_2$

- $IN(S_1; S_2) = IN(S_1) \cup IN(S_2)$
- $Own(S_1; S_2) = Own(S_1) \cup Own(S_2)$
- $\widehat{S_1; S_2} = \hat{S}_1; \hat{S}_2$

Conditional Statement $if\ (Cond)\ S$

- $IN(If\ (Cond)\ S) = IN(S) \cup \{v \in Cond\}$
- Trivial implementation (Triv): $Own(If\ (Cond)\ S) = \mathcal{P}$
- Optimized implementation (Opt):$Own(If\ (Cond)\ S) = Own(S) \cup Own(IN(S))$
- $$\widehat{If\ (Cond)\ S} = \begin{array}{l} Refresh(IN(Cond), Own(If\ (Cond)\ S)); \\ Exec(If\ (Cond)\ \hat{S}\ , Own(If\ (Cond)\ S)) \end{array}$$

The optimized implementation is very simple if S is a single statement, but the conditional execution of a block of instructions needs to compute (probably at run-time) the set $OWN(S)$ which may be costly. So we have chosen the trivial implementation (Triv) when S is a block (each process tests for the conditional execution of the block S) and (Opt) when S is a single statement.

As the (Triv) scheme induces a broadcast of all data elements in $Cond$, our compiler uses an intermediate boolean variable for evaluating $Cond$ which is a distributed scalar mapped on an arbitrary process. Only this value is then implicitly broadcasted. An *If* statement is treated as the sequence :

$$bool = Cond;\ If\ (bool)\ S$$

While structure $While\ (Cond)\ S$

- $IN(While\ (Cond)\ S) = IN(S) \cup \{v \in Cond\}$
- $Own(While\ (Cond)\ S) = \mathcal{P}$
- $$\begin{aligned} While\ \widehat{(Cond)}\ S &= Refresh(IN(Cond), Own(If\ (Cond)\ S)); \\ & Exec(While\ (Cond)\ \hat{S};\ Refresh(IN(While\ (Cond)\ S), \end{aligned}$$

$IN(S)$ stands for the set of data elements read by all occurrences of the statement S in the $While$ loop. We use the same approach as in the previous case : The condition is evaluated in a boolean variable which is used in the modified while loop:

$$bool\ = Cond;\ While(bool)\ \{S;\ bool = Cond\}$$

For loops $for(i = I0; i < IN; i++)\ S$
is treated as the equivalent `While` loop:

$$i = I0;\ while(i < IN)\{S;\ i++\}$$

- If i is a distributed variable or a global variable, The iterations of the loop would be executed sequentially because of the assignment and tests on the control variable i,
- if a local variable is used for the loop control the $Refresh(i, \mathcal{P})$ generates nothing because all local copies are up-to-date. The implementation is consistent with this as $Own(i) = \mathcal{P}$ so that $Refresh(i, \mathcal{P})$ generates nothing. In this case, each iteration of a loop may be executed in parallel, depending of the data mapping.

This does not mean that parallelism is explicit in Pandore: if the loop needs to be executed sequentially because of data dependences, the Pandore run-time will execute the loop sequentially though a local control variable is used.

5 Conclusions

A prototype of the Pandore compiler is under test; in simple cases the compiler is able to remove useless Refresh and to limit the execution of the Exec phase to the local domain of each processor. A run-time for the iPSC/2 has been developped. As we are only at the first step of debugging and using the Pandore system, we have no experience of use in real cases.

The challenge is now to provide compilers in order to allow users to program DMPCs with high level languages. It seems that most of message passing MIMD languages does not meet the "high level" requirements. SPMD languages without message passing or sequential languages with data distribution directives are only a first step toward this goal. We think that the sequential programming model is the easiest to use though it requires clever compiling techniques to produce efficient code. Much work remains both in the field of compile-time analysis and in run-time support research. The main problem is to cope efficiently with remote data accesses and tests of locality of references.

We do not claim that data parallel programming is the only interesting approach of the problem, other techniques as shared virtual memories [6] might be more accurate for executing programs with irregular accesses to data elements (computations on sparse matrices for example). Nevertheless these two approaches have to be compared on real cases programs.

Acknowledgments

I want to thank Françoise André and Henry Thomas who are working on the Pandore project. Thanks to Thierry Priol and Claude Jard for their valuable comments on the draft of this paper.

References

[1] C. D. Polychronopoulos, M. Girkar, M. R. Haghighat, C. L. Lee, B. Leung, and D. Schouten. PARAPHRASE-2; an environment for parallelizing, partitioning, synchronizing, and scheduling programs on multiprocessors. *Int. Journal of High Speed Computing*, 1(1):45–72, 1989.

[2] N. Carriero, D. Gelernter, and J. Leichter. Distributed data structures in linda. In *Thirteenth Annual ACM Symposium on Principles of Programming Langages*, pages 236–242, 1986.

[3] C.A.R. Hoare. Communicating sequential processes. *Communications of the ACM*, 21(8):666–677, August 1978.

[4] *Estelle: A Formal Description Technique Based on a Extented State Transition Model.* ISO. ISO/TC97/SC21/WG1, IS9074.

[5] C. Koebel and P. Mehrotra. *Supporting Shared Data Structures on Distributed Memory Architectures.* Technical Report csd-tr 915, Department of Computer Science, Purdue University, 1990.

[6] K. Li and R. Schaefer. A hypercube shared virtual memory system. In *1989 International Conference on Parallel Processing*, pages 125–132, 1989.

[7] D. Badouel, K. Bouatouch, and T. Priol. Ray tracing on distributed memory parallel computers: strategies for distributing computations and data. In S. Whitman, editor,

Parallel Algorithms and architectures for 3D Image Generation, pages 185–198, ACM Siggraph'90 Course 28, Aout 1990.

[8] M. J. Quinn and P. J. Hatcher. Compiling SIMD programs for MIMD architectures. In *ACM Sigplan (PPEALS)*, 1990.

[9] A. P. Reeves. *The Paragon Programming Paradigm and Distributed Memory Multicomputers.* Technical Report EE-CEG-90-7, Cornell University, June 1990.

[10] M. Rosing, R. B. Schnabel, and R. P. Weaver. *The DINO Parallel Programming Language.* Technical Report CU-CS-457-90, University of Colorado at Boulder, 1990.

[11] C. Koelbel, P. Mehrotra, J. Saltz, and H. Berryman. Parallel loops on distributed machines. In *5' Int. Conf. on Distributed Memory Computing Conference*, April 1990.

[12] H. P. Zima, H.-J. Bast, and M. Gerndt. SUPERB: a tool for semi-automatic MIMD /SIMD parallelization. *Parallel Computing*, (6):1–18, 1988.

[13] D. Callahan and K. Kennedy. Compiling programs for distributed-memory multiprocessors. *Journal of Supercomputing*, 2:151–169, 1988.

[14] F. André, J.-L. Pazat, and H. Thomas. PANDORE: a system to manage data distribution. In *Int. Conf. on Supercomputing*, pages 380–388, June 1990.

[15] A. Rogers and K. Pingali. Process decomposition through locality of reference. In *Conference on Programming Language Design and Implementation*, pages 69–80, ACM,.June 21–23 1989.

[16] K. Ikudome, G. C. Fox, A. Kolawa, and J. W. Flower. An automatic and symbolic parallelization system for distributed memory parallel computers. In *5' Distributed Memory Computing Conference*, April 1990.

[17] E. M. Paalvast and A. J. Van Gemund. A method for parallel program generation with an application to the *Booster* language. In *Int. Conf. on Supercomputing*, pages 457–469, June 1990.

[18] R. Ruhl and M. Annaratone. Parallelization of FORTRAN Code on distributed memory parallel processors. In *Int. Conf. on Supercomputing*, pages 342–353, June 1990.

[19] G.-R. Perrin, P. Clauss, and S. Damy. Mappimg programs on regular distributed architectures. In F. Andre and J.-P. Verjus, editors, *1st Conference on Hypercube and Distributed Computers*, pages 175–188, INRIA, North Holland, October 1989.

[20] P. Quinton. Mapping recurrences on parallel architectures. In *3' nternational Conference on Supercomputing*, 1988.

[21] M. Wolfe. *Optimizing Supercompilers for Supercomputers. Research Monographs in Parallel and Distributed Computing*, Pitman, MIT press edition, 1989.

OAL: an Implementation of an Actor Language on a Massively Parallel Message-Passing Architecture

Jean-Louis Giavitto, Cécile Germain
LRI - Architecture et Conception des Circuits Intégrés
Bât 490 Université de Paris XI - 91405 Orsay cedex France
email: giavitto@lri.lri.fr
Julian Fowler
LFCS - University of Edinburgh

ABSTRACT

We study the implementation of an actor language, OAL, *on a massively parallel message-passing architecture:* MEGA. *Motivations and implementation constraints are exposed. A simulator has been built to investigate resource consumption. First results show the feasibility of the implementation but indicates serious problems in memory usage. Load-balancing strategies are presented which partially solve the memory problem. Actors adequacy as a model for exploiting massive parallelism is discussed in conclusion.*

I. Introduction

MEGA (Machines to Explore Giant Architectures) is a family of architectures dedicated to the exploration of message passing on massively parallel MIMD machines for Artificial Intelligence applications. Such computers attempt to achieve massive parallelism (more than 10^9 ips) using a very large number of processing elements and intensive communication between them [DAL88]. That implies the expression and the exploitation of a very fine-grained parallelism.

The Computer Architecture group of LRI has worked on several studies to investigate design key-points: the *processing element* [CAP90], the *network architecture* and the *packaging* [GER89] [BEC89], the *routing strategy* [GER90a] [GER90b] and the *execution model* [CAP91].

The last point is devoted to language implementation issues requested to exploit fine-grained parallelism and their repercussions on the architectural level. Actors languages have earned a reputation of being able to express the full parallelism of an application. The aim of this paper is to present motivations and considerations arising in the implementation of an actor language on MEGA.

The following section describes the MEGA underlying architecture, CPU and network. The second section presents briefly the actors concepts and our motivations in implementing them. Next we present the canonical actor language used in this study, **OAL**. The fourth section exposes the implementation of this language on MEGA and the simulator used to evaluate them. Finally we discuss the suitability of the actor paradigm to achieve massive parallelism.

II. A machine to explore giant architecture: MEGA

One of the most attractive architectural models for AI applications are message-passing architectures: they are characterized by an asynchronous MIMD control, distributed local memories and message-passing communications.

MEGA focus on fine grained parallelism relying on thousands of processing elements interconnected in a 3D grid. VLSI technological progress makes possible the integration of the entire network node, including CPU, memory and routing hardware, on a single chip [COR87] [ATH88] [GER89]. This modular approach minimizes the number of wiring interconnections making possible the structural feasibility of machines with up to 10^6 processing elements (PE).

II.1 The processing element

The CPU executes a reduced instruction set, *MegaTalk* [CAP90], designed to allow easy compilation and compact representation of a lexical LISP dialect (as for example based on Scheme [STEE75]). A detailed description of the CPU can be found in [CAP90]. The CPU access code and data are stored in on-chip memory. This feature severely constrains the memory size (between 4K and 64K following the actual technology) but drastically speeds up the memory accesses [STA86]. Thus, all instructions, including memory accesses, are performed in one clock cycle of less than 80ns with a standard 1.5 μm CMOS technology, achieving 8 Mips [BEC90].

II.2 Network and communication

The topology is a 3D grid

The monochip also includes a hardwired router dedicated to the routing management in a three-dimensional grid. The choice of a 3D-grid is not naive: in recent works on very large parallel machines, grids have been shown to be more efficient than hypercubes for very large networks. Roughly, this is due to the fact that they take into account technologically-limited resources such as wiring density [DAL87] or available pin number [REE87].

A hardwired mailing system

With very fine-grained parallelism, the average number of instructions executed between two message-passing operations tends to be small and therefore the network delay becomes a bottleneck for the whole system. If the message delivery time is too large, the processors have to wait for messages and they will stay idle. This constraint is known as the communication-calculus equilibrium [REE87]. Therefore, when massive parallelism is concerned, software message routing as in the Cosmic Cube [SEI85] and Intel iPSC/1 [INT86] is no longer possible, because it degrades the performance strongly [GRU87]. The routing tools must be embedded in hardware such as in iPSC/2 [NUG88]. Thus the main constraint on routing strategies relies on hardwired implementation feasibility.

A new routing algorithm, the *forced routing* [GER90a], is used in MEGA. It is a tradeoff between deterministic (e.g. *greedy* routing: geometrical dimensions of the network are ordered, and routing follows this order) and randomized routing [VAL82] [LEI88]. No buffering capacity is needed at the nodes and the algorithm is quite simple, thus well adapted to hardwired implementation [BEC90]. In non-conflicting case, messages are randomly spread on the paths of equal length insuring maximum efficiency in the use of network links. When a conflict for an output-link appears, all requesting messages are routed, possibly along directions moving them away from their destination. In this manner, when there is no contention, messages follow a shortest path and when contention increases, they are randomly spread in the network.

At programmer level, two kind of messages are offered by the hardware: ***direct*** and ***defered*** messages. A direct message embed the memory location where it must be stored. A deferred message has a fixed size and is stored at reception in a hardware managed queue. In case of overflow, the message is re-routed in the network and will come back later.

III. Actor languages

III.1 Actor concepts

Actors are a message passing based model of computation. An actor is a self-contained entity with its own processing power. The computation is performed by sending and processing messages in parallel between actors. The reception of a message triggers the execution of the current *behaviour* of the receiver. Processing a communication results possibly in:

- some simple computations (***arithmetic operations*** and the ***conditional*** control structure);
- the sending of messages to others actors (*send* command);
- the creation of new actors (*new* command);
- the specification of the ***behaviour*** which will govern the response to the next message (*become* command).

An ***unserialized*** actor, opposed to ***serialized*** actor, cannot change its internal state:. the same behaviour and the same *acquaintance list* (the actors with which an actor is able to communicate by sending messages) are used to respond to any message. So message processing can be done in parallel.

The concept of actor abstracts the notion of process, function or data structure. Patterns of passing messages represent various control structures; data structures and assignment are accomplished through the mechanisms of replacement behaviour and acquaintances list [HEW76]. (We will not enter more into details, the interested reader can find references in §III.3.)

III.2 Motivations

Among the available models of parallel execution, many features make actors very attractive to be implemented on a massive MIMD machine.

Abstracting the hardware

Actor communication is very close to that of MEGA. The assumptions underlying the mailing system are the same as provided by the hardwired routing of MEGA (guarantee of delivery but arrival non-determinism). Moreover, the granularity in an actor language like *Act1* or *Act2* (message size and number, task size and number) is well fitted to the number and power of available processing elements of MEGA. Therefore, an actor language can abstract a specific MEGA machine, hiding implementation details while staying a priori near enough, to enable a pertinent driving of the hardware resources.

Expressive power

Actor languages provide a natural expression of the parallelism and the distribution. These expression facilities are strengthened by theoretical results showing equivalence between actors and PRAM[1] [BVN91] [EPP88] [VAL89]. It means that problems efficiently solved in the PRAM framework are also efficiently solved by an actor program. A lot of research have been done on PRAM algorithm and interesting results exist (the set of problems efficiently solved by a PRAM algorithm is not an empty one).

Moreover, the expressive power of actor languages make them able to **emulate execution model** of other programming paradigms. For example, *continuation* can be used to implement the function call paradigm. Function call differs from actor message sending in that sending a message does not return a value. Continuation consist in putting an additional argument in the message, the receiver of the answer that will be elaborated in response to the message. So actors used together with continuation, realize a *demand-driven evaluation* scheme [BUR81] [TRE82] (evaluation of arguments of a function call is done in parallel).

Replacement behaviour is a cumbersome but powerful construct. It allows the implementation of more sophisticated communication schemes such as those required of *eager* and *lazy* evaluation. More elaborated communication primitives (e.g. *now* or *future* in ABCL [YON86a]) can be implemented using the basic primitives "become" and "send". Explicit translation, however, is obviously to hard to be done manually: the script of an actor must be broken in several parts linked by become commands (in addition, its acquaintance list must be copied through behaviour replacement).

Actor that does not change its script, acts like an object (the "become" command is just used to change acquaintances value). The part of the script dedicated to process a certain kind of messages correspond to a method. *Delegation* can be used to achieve inheritance: when a message is outside the domain of an actor, it is dispatched to a supply actor, the delegation, that can represent the "inherited part" of the object. See also works around POOL [AME88] about the combination of structuring mechanisms of object-oriented programming with the facilities for parallelism.

Finally, actor languages are not only able to process various functional evaluation scheme but also provide an effective support for *reactive systems* [PNU86] that is, systems that does not give an output for data in input (transformational systems) but that react at their environment stimuli.

So, an actor language must be seen as a *parallel assembly language*, the target for the compilation of more sophisticated languages :

Language hierachy on MEGA

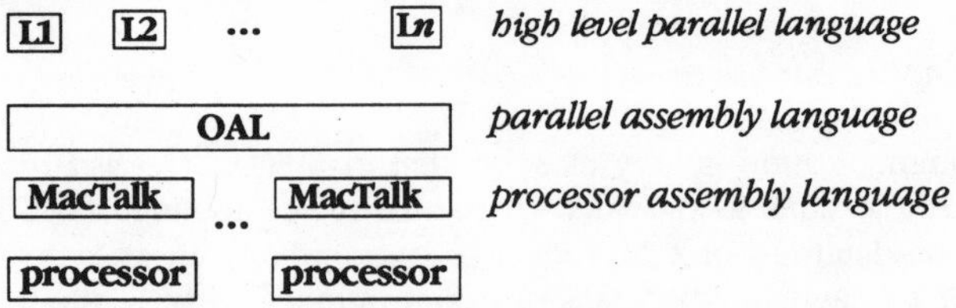

[1] More precisely, if a problem is solved by a CRCW-PRAM algorithm in time T(n) and in space S(n), then it exists an actor program solving the problem in time T(n)log(n) with high probability and in actor size complexity S(n) (cf. [BVN91]).

III.3 OAL in the actor languages family

PLASMA (Planner-like Language and System Model on Actor) is the ancestor of the family of actor languages [HEW75] and is purely sequential. Concurrence is introduced with the next generation, *PlasmaII*, and has motivated the development of the experimental language *Act1* [LIB81], a language focussed on message passing and behaviour mechanisms (the *PlasmaIII* and *Alog* [CAR84] descendents of PlasmaII are more aimed at the investigation of message filtering and logic in terms of actors). A denotational semantic of Act1 was given through the semantic of *Atolia* [CLIN81], a simplified form of Act1. Actor languages are usually seen as a kernel system to build more sophisticated languages. An example is given with *Omega* [ATT85] (a description and deduction system), and *Ether* [KOR79] (a reasoning system) built on top of Act1. They are aimed at knowledge representation and dedicated to ai-applications. Another example is *ABCL* [YON86b], an object-oriented computation model inheriting some concepts (message passing) from the actor computation model. The *Act2* [THE83] programming language blends kernel concepts from Act1, Omega and Ether to provide an extensible framework in which additional concepts (such as in the *Prelude* system) can be embedded. Act2 was effectively implemented in *Scrippter* a language running on a network of LispMachines emulating an actor-dedicated architecture: *Apiary* [HEW80]. *Act* and *Sal*, close to Act2, are used by [AGH85] to provide a transition-based semantics to actors. Sal is generally regarded as the minimal actor language and is also the basis of *OAL*.

OAL is a canonical actor language very close of *SAL* [AGH85] *TOONS* [ESP] or *SCRIPTS* [LIT90]. Some restrictions have been made in regard to SAL semantics for sake of simplicity and to respect staticity. The idea behind is to have a compiled language where most of the work (type checking, message dispatching, etc) can be done statically at compile-time.

The notable exception, with respect to the SAL semantic, is that the argument of a become command can only be a behaviour name (a new-expression in SAL terminology): in SAL, an actor can "become" another actor, meaning that all mail of the first is forwarded to the second. This can be done explicitly by hand in OAL but not implicitly. Implementation of such a "become" implies dynamic type checking.

We have to note the absence of *unserialized actors*: indeed, qualifying as unserialized an actor, as no influence on its implementation (message received by an unserialized actor are implicitly serialized for their processing, cf. §IV). A feature we have added in OAL, is actor *suicide*, for explicit release of resources owned by an actor. A more detailed description of OAL with its semantics can be found in [FOW90].

IV. Implementation issues

We describe here a possible implementation of OAL on the MEGA machine. Although OAL is not actually running on a MEGA machine, OAL programs can be processed and evaluated on a dedicated simulator. Several simulators of MEGA exist serving different purposes: *VLSI* simulation, evaluation of *MegaTalk* (the RISC instruction set), evaluation of the *forced routing* strategy, evaluation of the OAL implementation (see further).

IV.1 The actor representation

Each instance of an actor is represented by a data structure residing on a unique processor. This data structure contains the acquaintances of the actor, a link to the message input queue and to the current script. Because OAL "become" is static, we are able to determine at compile time the set of behaviours reachable from a given one and so we can compute the size needed to store the largest acquaintances list. So, acquaintances are accessed just as structure fields.

The current script consist of pieces of code glued together with a switch statement which makes the dispatch of the messages. Each case of the switch process a message type.

Each actor is referenced through an ***auid*** (actor unique identifier). The auid of an actor is composed at creation time and is the juxtaposition of a local number (an index in the actor table of the processor) and the processor address (3 bytes corresponding to its x,y,z coordinates). So the size of an auid is 5 bytes and more precisely for boundary alignment reasons, 3 words. It was considered to compact the processor address to gain 3 bits and to restrict the actors number in a processor to 512. With these assumptions, the size of a auid is lowered to 2 words. But the gain in memory resources is lost by the coding/decoding operations necessary to compact/uncompact the processor address when sending a message.

IV.2 The management of the CPU

The processing of a message by an actor creates a task. A task is managed through a *workspace*. The workspace is a structure 16 bytes long that contains the PSW (program status word of the task), the entry in the actor table referring to the actor responsible for the task, a reference to the acquaintance structure and a reference to the message. 8 additional bytes are used for temporary results computed during the processing of a message.

Tasks are scheduled following a simple ***reactive*** strategy as in the original operating system of the Cosmic Cube [SEI88]. Messages are processed in their order of arrivals. Because actor scripts are ensured to end in a bounded time, no preemptive mechanism is needed. The scheduler is part of a common *toolbox* resident on each processor (the toolbox summarizes the common routines needed to perform an OAL program). Actors resident on the processor are accessed by the toolbox through the actor table. Previous evaluation [GER90c] has showed that the size of the code of the scheduler (workspace management and scheduling) is about 0.5K.

IV.3 The mailing system

The purpose of the mailing system is to implement OAL messages on top of MEGA messages. The problem is not to split too long messages (cf. §IV.5) but to ensure the unlimited buffering assumption of the language.

The "send" statement in an OAL script submit the message to the mail service of a processor. Actions performed by the mail service take place between task scheduling. Each OAL message results in 3 MEGA messages managed by the toolbox.

When the toolbox has to send an OAL message, it first requests of the (toolbox of the) receiver the right to send its message. The response is delayed until the receiver has room enough to store the incoming message. The acknowledgement contains the remote memory address used to receive the OAL message and cause the final sending. Three messages have been exchanged: one "deferred" and two "direct" (see §II.2).

It appears more and more that the constraints ensured by the actor mailing system are very weak, making cumbersome even the coding of a trivial algorithm. Languages like ABCL or CANTOR [ATH87] assume a stronger constraint on message arrival: message order is preserved for messages sent from one actor to another one. This can be implemented adding a stamp field to each message. A table is linked with each actor, keeping track of number of messages sent to a given receiver. This count is used to give a value to the stamp field of the request message. The receiver delays its acknowledgement until it receives the previous communications.

IV.4 Load-balancing strategy

Load-balancing consist in spreading the work among the processors with the goal of maximizing task processing throughput (the overall throughput is considered as more important that the response time of an individual actor) [AMS84] [REE87]. As processors have very small memory resources, load-balancing is also crucial for MEGA not only to speed-up the program execution, but *to make possible* the processing of memory consuming application.

To reach these goals, we have to adjust two opposite effects: task processing throughput is increased and processor memory usage is reduced if the tasks are distributed among the available processors. But distributing the tasks also increases buffering and communication cost, slowing down task processing and using memory. So, a good load balancing must preserve *locality*.

Because OAL tasks are very small (few lines of code), the cost of migrating a task during its execution, is too expensive. Creating a task on another processor from where the concerned actor resides, implies at least to copy actor acquaintances and so are too much expensive too. The only solution is to keep the task on the same processor as the concerned actor. Thus, load-balancing is achieved through the distribution of actors.

Our current hypothesis is that an actor cannot migrate during its life from a processor to another for the following reasons. As a matter of fact, actor migration must be transparent to the programmer: actors are light weight dynamic entities and the user must be unaware of their physical positions. The decision to move an actor is thus done by the system. It is not possible to tell each actor concerned by the move because these actors are not explicitly known by the system (this is the inverse of the relationship maintained through the acquaintance lists). So when the system has to move an actor, it must leave a *forwarder* that ensures the mail delivery. And the benefit of moving the actor (reducing the task load of one processor) is lost by the increase of the network load and will not reduce memory usage.

After this consideration, it must be clear that, within our framework, only few solutions exist to control the load-balancing. The only parameter upon which we can act is the physical processor allocated to an actor at creation time (statement "new"). *Static load-balancing* is possible in OAL with the optional keyword "at" which explicitly gives the processor where to create the new actor. *Dynamic balancing* is done in absence of the previous keyword. It consist of the creation of the actor on a processor selected following some criteria (cf. §IV.6).

The creation of an actor on an another processor uses a communication protocol between toolboxes. For sake of simplicity, the simulator assumes that actor scripts are available on each processor. Protocol for code migration have not been considered.

IV.5 The management of the memory

Data structure and space limits

The expected average number of arguments in a message is 2.5 (cf. fig. 2) and we must add the auid of the receiver. That leads to a typical message not exceeding 20 bytes length: thus there is no problem to code an actor message in a MEGA message of maximum size of 64. Pathological messages resulting in overflow of this hard limit, are compile time errors.

The acquaintances list of an actor have an expected average length of 16 bytes (see the following table: the size of the OAL programs corpus is not significant enough so we consider the indication extrapolated from a large sized object-oriented application). The data structure representing an actor must be increased by the pointer to the current behaviour script. The average length of an actor also does not exceed 20 bytes. This implies a maximum of 200 actors resident on a small MEGA processor with 4Kb local memory and 3000 actors for a 62Kb local memory. Obviously, this estimation must be reduced taking into account the space occupied by the code, the space used for the input queues and the space used for the common services. With the hypothesis of 1000 actors per processor, a small cube of edge 10 may support one million actors and a full cube of edge 100 may support 10^9 actors.

	OAL examples library	object-oriented application (in C++)
acquaintances or slots in byte	**5.2** 223/127	**15.6** 97+126/33+33
arguments number	**2.4**	**2.4** 1051args/435methods

Static analysis of typical code providing evaluation of expected actor size and arguments message number. The ratio (223/127) for the OAL library refer to 223 acquaintance for 127 new statements. In the "object" column, 97+126 refer to 97 references to other objects and 126 slots of basic types. 33+33 stand for 33 root classes and 33 derivations. For transposition in the actor scheme, a reference is counted for 6 bytes and a reference is added for each derivation class (delegation). A basic type is coded in 2 bytes.

The Garbage Collector problem

Actor programs create a lot of short-lived actors (cf. to simulation results) and a *garbage collector* is needed to minimize the amount of memory used. The "suicide" OAL feature permits explicit deletion of resources used by an actor but is dangerous from a software engineering point of view: if a message arrives after the death of an actor, unpredictable results occur (dead actors are similar to pending reference in C). So, "suicide" can be only used to remove actors statically known as useless (for example, the programmer knows that some kind of actors have only two messages to process as arising in a dichotomic search). Therefore, an implicit system is necessary for garbage collecting distributed memory.

Here are the properties we expect from a good GC algorithm [COU89] [LIB83]: locality and minimization of communications, minimization of synchronisation needed, easy processing of the message on the way, earlier deletion of inacessible resources, independence from physical parameters (network size and topology) and cheap processing.

Mark-scan parallel garbage collection algorithm [HUD82] [HUG85] has several drawbacks. The first is certainly that they do not respond the important property of maximizing available memory: actors may be deleted long after they become inaccessible. In addition, synchronization constraints are needed between processors.

Reference counting methods [BEC86] [BEV87] [WAT87] answer to the previous objection and also solve the problem of "flying" references (actor referenced in a message on the way). But they have other shortcommings: actors part of a circular structure, are not deleted at all. Moreover, because actors are light entities, the cost of an additional counter is high.

A large amount of research are currently done in distributed garbage collection area. At this point, the garbage collector of OAL is an open question. Future work would be done to evaluate more precisely existing algorithms.

IV.6 Simulation

The simulator

The MEGA simulator used in this study consist of a set of *C*++ classes [STR87] modelling a MEGA machine: `processor`, `memory`, `message`, and `task`. Messages are similar to events in a discrete event simulation. An additional kind of object was defined, the basic `actor`, able to transform a message in a task.

The compilation of an OAL program results in a set of C++ classes inheriting from the classes `actor` and `message`. A new class inheriting of `actor` is defined for each ***head behaviour*** in an OAL program (a head behaviour corresponds to a behaviour appearing in a "new" statement). A derivation of `message` is produced for each kind of message recognized by a behaviour.

The C++ compilation of the translation of an OAL program is linked with the simulator itself to produce the final programme. Size, topology of the network and dynamic load-balancing strategy, are run-time parameters. The results of an execution are the messages received by the ***external*** actor `Output` and some statistics summarizing memory occupation, processor activity, network load, etc.

The adopted simulation scheme has several advantages. The compiled approach enables simulation of bigger size than possible through the direct interpretation of an OAL program (especially w.r.t. the number of processors). For example, one of our test program generates a binary tree of 32000 leafs and sorts it in parallel. This program mimics a realistic application, requiring more than 9.10^6 message exchanges. The simulation of this program on a 512-processors sized MEGA is possible and take less than 8 hours on a Sparc.

Moreover, the compiler allows a strict "type checking" (no run-time error of kind "unexpected message type") and furnishes interesting characteristics (actors size, average argument number, etc). At last but not least, the translation time is not annoying for the user (700 OAL lines/s) and the generated C++ is in a human readable form.

The simulations

The goal of the simulation was to quantify the execution of actors programs in term of resource consomption in order to compare with respect to efficiency the actor execution model against other paradigms.

Two main dynamic load-balancing strategies are under investigation. The first strategy consists in minimizing the number of actor residing on a processor (L1); the second one minimizes the number of current tasks on a processor (L2). These numbers are immediatly available on a processor. The following table shows the results for two applications (a ***beta-reduction*** [HIL86] of

4096 elements and a parallel bitonic sort [GIB 88] of 512 elements) and for various network size (this last parameters can correspond to a variable processor load). Each entry of the table gives the results for the *L1* and the L2 strategies. The L2 strategy is not always the best with respect to the throughput (the criterium "max processed task and max waiting task per processor") but minimizes maximum memory occupation.

L1 L2	1	512	1000	4096	8000	**network size**
Parallel summation of 4096 elements	*90K / 90K* 90K / 90K	*1 / 80* 6 / 40	*1 / 80* 3 / 40	*1 / 80* 0 / 40	*0 / 80* 0 / 40	**memory occupation** average / max
	0 / 0 0 / 0	*0 / 1* 0 / 1	*0 / 1* 0 / 1	*0 / 1* 0 / 1	*0 / 1* 0 / 1	**message path lenght** average / max
	16K / 4K 16K / 4K	*6K / 4* 1386 / 2	*6K / 4* 1386 / 2	*6K / 4* 1386 / 2	*6K / 4* 1386 / 2	**"througput"** max processed tasks / max waiting tasks
Parallel bitonic sort of 512 elements and array management	*21K / 21K* 21K / 21K	*49 / 12K* 138 / 11K	*25 / 12K* 79 / 4K	*6 / 12K* 25 / 12K	*3 / 12K* 13 / 12K	**memory occupation** average / max
	0 / 0 0 / 0	*0 / 10* 1 / 20	*0 / 10* 1 / 22	*0 / 10* 1 / 28	*0 / 10* 1 / 28	**message path lenght** average / max
	21K / 769 21K / 769	*12K / 512* 11K / 492	*12K / 512* 189 / 4K	*12K / 512* 513 / 12K	*12K / 512* 513 / 12K	**"througput"** max processed tasks / max waiting tasks

The most important remark about the previous results is that increasing the network size has very little effect to ***maximum caracteristics*** (memory occupation, waiting tasks...). That is, the load-balancing strategy is unable to spread the computation load homogeneously over the network. The reasons of this bottleneck will be discussed in the next section.

The simulation also help us to verify an important hypothesis about load-balancing. The previous simulation assumes that the load-balancing algorithm possesses complete knowledge of the global network state. In practice only limited information is available. However, it appears that state knowledge of nodes within a small distance suffices to approximate the result provided by the global knowledge hypothesis (the *event horizon* effect) [REE87] [LIN85]. The following table compares the two load-balancing strategies under the two hypothesis in case of extreme contention (small network, big job). The conclusion is that local hypothesis favours average characteristics a little bit but leads to more heterogeneous processing. This was predictable because if the event horizon is too large, the load charge reduction is offset by the increased cost of communication.

global local	L1	L2	
// bitonic sort of 32000 elements on 512 processors	*4 / 100* 3 / 786	*4 / 156* 3 / 710	/K **memory occupation** average / max
	10 / 21 1 / 16	*5 / 21* 1 / 21	**message path lenght** average / max
	5000 / 4 868 / 32	*59 / 6* 113 / 29	/K **max processed tasks/ max waiting tasks**

The previous programs create respectively 8K, 60K and 620K actors (i.e. more than the available processors). This stresses the idea of having an efficient garbage collector. Using the "suicide" feature in OAL, reduces the number of living actors to 1 at the end of the beta-reduction and to 3000 for the second application . But this technique is not always possible.

V. Conclusion

Actor implementation on MEGA

The simulation we are currently working with shows the feasibility of implementing actors on MEGA. The severe constraints on memory space can be managed through a relevant load-balancing strategy that minimizes processor memory occupation and load charge.

However, the test programs we have developed in OAL are space and time consuming in regards to other parallel language implementations (refer to [GER90c]), and this, even in the same functional programming style (there is for example no need for garbage-collecting processes in a demand-driven execution scheme). Consequently, the use of actors to achieve massive parallelism is questionable.

Actors and (massive) parallelism

To analyze the suitability or unsuitability of actors to massive computing, we first make a distinction between three kinds of parallelism usable to speed-up the execution of a program [SAN90]. ***Data-parallelism*** is the ability to process homogeneous set of data in an atomic operation. It is the parallelism exploited for example in *Lisp [HIL85] or ParalationLisp. ***Control-parallelism*** is the parallel processing of multiple threads of control. This parallelism is present in Occam, //Pascal, etc. The ***flow-parallelism*** is the one used through the multiple stages of a systolic architecture using a pipe-line effect.

The actor mechanisms are primitive enough to handle the various sources of parallelism in an application. Actors are able to express and to use the three sources of speed-up: one actor per "data element" correspond to the data-parallel paradigm, one actor per process correspond to the parallel control scheme while acquaintances list can be used to represent the fan-out of a pipe-line stage. However, this expressive power sacrifices the language efficiency on realistic computers. Indeed, opposite characteristics have to be joined to implement the actor paradigm. For example, data-parallel operations need dynamicity and accommodate well to synchronicity while control schemes are static and fitted to asynchronous execution model. Restricting also the actor programming to a given style, cannot gain against the more constrained assumptions made in one of the more specialized scheme. For example, the cost of doing an operation for each of ***n*** data-elements (***alpha-notation*** [HIL86]) is the cost of the scalar operation in a data-parallel language based on a SIMD model. To achieve the same result within the actor language, ***n*** messages must be exchanged.

In addition, resource management cannot be done in a fine manner: the usual resource management unit is the task, as being the resource consumer. But a task does not correspond to an actor, it correspond to the handling of a message by an actor. Actor management is a poor substitute to task management (some actors are the receiver of thousand messages while other are very ephemeral entities, waiting for just one message before dying). Also an actor cannot be viewed as cluster of tasks (no communication locality in this cluster, no control over CPU/network, memory/network tradeoff, ...).

In conclusion, the simulation we are currently working with, rules out the idea to use an actor language as a fine-grain parallel assembly language, a harness for more elaborated system. Although actors express very well distributed application and concurrency, they are not able to manage resource consumption in a fine way.

Acknowledgement

The MEGA project is developed within "Computer Architecture and VLSI Design" Research Group. The authors do thank the other members of this group: Dr D Etiemble and Dr J-P Sansonnet for their outstanding contribution to the project, F. Capello who worked on the architecture of the CPU and J-L Bechenec for VLSI development and many helpful discussions. We also thank the referees for their comments and helpful corrections. This work is currently supported by the french national research program on New Computer Architectures (PRC-ANM) and by DRET under grant #89342320047050. The stay of Mr. Fowler was possible thanks to the Erasmus EEC programs.

Bibliography

[AGH85] G. Agha, "*Actors: a model for concurrent computation in distributed systems*", AI tech. rep. 844, MIT, 1985.

[AME88] P. America, "*POOL-T: A Parallel Object-Oriented Language*", in Object-Oriented Concurrent Programming, eds. A. Yonezawa, M. Tokoro, MIT Press 1988.

[AMS87] J. Amsterdam, "*Load Balancing Strategies for the Apiary*", dissertation for the degree of Bachelor, Hardvard College, May 1984.

[ATH87] W.C. Athas, "*Fine Grain Concurrent Computations*", Tech. Rep 5242, Dep. of Computer Science, California Institue of Technology, May 1987.

[ATH88] W.C. Athas, C.L. Seitz, "Multicomputers : Message-Passing Concurrent Computers", IEEE Computer, vol. 21, n° 8, August 1988, pp 9-24

[ATT85] G. Attardi "*Building Expert Systems with Omega*", DELPHI, tech. rep. ESP/85/2, 1985.

[BEC86] M.J. Beckerle, K. Ekanadham, "*Distributed Garbage Collection with no Global Synchronisation*", IBM research report RC 11667 (#52377) january 1986.

[BEC89] J-L. Béchennec, "*MegaPack : a 3D Packaging for Massively Parallel Computers*", LRI-Archi TR 89-07-1989

[BEC90] J-L. Béchennec, C. Chanussot, V. Neri and D. Etiemble, "*VLSI Design of a 3-D Highly parallel message passing architecture*", International Workshop on VLSI design for Artificial Intelligence and Neural Networks, Septembre 90

[BEV87] D. I. Bevan, "*Distributed Garbage Collection Algorithm using Reference Counts*", ACM trans. on prog. lang. and syst., vol 2, n°3, july 87.

[BUR81] W.F. Burton, M.R. Sleep, "*Executing functional programms on a virtual tree of processors*", Proc. ACM Conference on Functionnal programming langages and computer Architecture - 1981 pp 187-194

[BVN91] F. Baude, G. Vidal-Naquet, "*Actors as a parallel programming model*", to appear in STACS91.

[CAR84] F. Carré, "*Alog: acteurs et programation en logique*" (Alog: actors and logic programming) Thèse de docteur ingénieur, juin 1984 (in french).

[CAP90] F. Cappello, J-L Bechennec, D. Etiemble "*A RISC Central Processing Unit for a Massively Parallel Architecture*", EUROMICRO 90, Amsterdam, August 90

[CAP91] F. Cappello, C. Germain, J-P. Sansonnet, "*Design of a reduced instruction set for massively parallel functional programming*", LRI-Archi TR 90-07, also submitted to publication.

[CLIN81] W.D. Clinger, "*Foundation of Actor Semantics*", PhD thesis, MIT May 1987 (ai-tr-633).

[COR87] R. Cornu-Emieux, G. Mazaré, P. Objois, "*A VLSI asynchronous cellular array to accelerate logical simulations*", proc. of the 30th. Midwest Internationnal Symposium on Circuit and Systems, 1987.

[COU89] A; Couvert, A. Maddi, R. Pédrono "*Object Sharing in Distributed Systems - Principles of garbage collection*", IRISA, INRIA report 963, January 1989 (in french)

[DAL87] W.J. Dally, "*Wire-Efficient VLSI Multiprocessor Communication Networks*", 1987 Stanford Conference on Advanced Research in VLSI, 1987, pp 391-415

[DAL88] W.J. Dally, "*Fine-Grain Message-Passing Concurrent Computers*", proc. of the Third Conference on Hypercubes Concurrent Computers and Applications, vol. 1, Pasadena, January 19-20, 1988

[EPP88] D. Eppstein, Z. Galil, "*Parallel algorithmic Technic for Combinatorial Computation*" Ann. rev. Compt. Sci., 3:233-283, 1988

[ESP89] Esprit Project P440, "*Final Report*", December 1989.

[FOW90] J. Fowler, "*Studies of algorithms adapted to a network of dynamic processes*", University of Edinburgh, M.Sc Report September 1990.

[GER89] C. Germain, J-L. Béchennec, D. Etiemble, J-P. Sansonnet, "*A New Communication Design for Massively Parallel Message-Passing Architectures*", IFIP Working Conf. on Decentralized Systems 1989, North-Holland ed.

[GER90a] C. Germain, J-L Béchennec, D. Etiemble, J-P. Sansonnet, "*An Interconnection Network and a Routing Scheme for a Massively Parallel Message-Passing Multicomputer*", Third Symp. on Frontiers 90 conference on Massively Parallel Computation, October 8-10 College Park, MD

[GER90b] C. Germain, J-L. Giavitto, "*A Comparaison of Two Routing strategy for Massively Parallel Computers*", 5th International Symposium on Computer and Information Science, Capadoccia, Nov. 90.

[GER90c] C. Germain, J-L. Giavitto, J-P. Sansonnet, "*Implementation d'un paradigme de programmation fonctionelle sur une machine massivement parallele*" (implementation of a paradigmatic functionnal programming style on a massively parallel computer), LRI-Archi TR 90-07, also submitted to publication (in french).

[GIB 88] A. Gibbons, W. Rytter, "*Efficient parallel algorithms*" Cambridge University Press - 1988, (chap. 5)

[GRU87] D.C.Grunwald, D.A. Reed, "*Benchmarking Hypercubes Hardware and Software*", Hypercube Multiprocessors 87, 1987, pp 169-177

[HEW75] C. Hewitt, B. Smith, "*A PLASMA Primer*", rough draft, 13:17 1975, MIT-AIL

[HEW76] Hewitt C., "*Viewing Control Structure as Patterns of Passing Messages*", MIT Artificial Intelligence Memo 410, December 1976

[HEW80] Hewitt C., "*Apiary multiprocessor architecture knowledge system*", prooc. of the joint SRC/Univ. of Newcastle upon Tyne Workshop on VLSI, Machine Architecture and Very High Level LAnguages, October 1980.

[HIL85] W.D. Hillis, "*The Connection Machine*", The MIT Press, 1985

[HIL86] W.D. Hillis, G.L. Steele, "*Data Parallel Algorithms*", CACM vol.29 n°12, December 1986.

[HUD82] P. Hudak, R.M. Keller, "*Garbage collection and task deletion in distributed applicative processing systems*", proc. ACM conference on Lisp and Functionnal Programming, 1982 pp 168-178.

[HUG85] J. Hughes, "*A Distributed Garbage Collection Algorithm*" proc. ACM conference on Functional Programming Languages and Computer Architecture, Nancy 1985, LNCS 201.

[INT86] INTEL Scientific Computers,"Intel iPSC System Overview", Order n° 310610-001, 1986

[KOR79] W. Kornfeld, "*Using Parallel Processing for Problem Solving*", AI Memo 561, MIT, december 1979.

[LEI88] F.T. Leighton, B. Maggs, S. Rao, "*Universal Packet Routing Algorithms*",29 st IEEE Symp. on Foudations of Computer Science,1988, pp 256-269

[LIB81] H. Lieberman, "*A preview of Act-1*", AI Memo 625, MIT AI Laboratory, 1981.

[LIB83] H. Lieberman, C. Hewitt, "*A real-time garbage collector based on the lifetimes of objects*", CACM vol. 26 n°6, pp 419-428 June 1983.

[LIN85] F.C.H. Lin, "*Load Balancing and Fault Tolerance in Applicative Systems*", Ph.D. Dissertation, Dep. of Computer Science, Univ. of Utah, 1985.

[LIT90] L. Litzler, M. Tréhel, "*The kernel of an actor language for a multi-transputer system*", ISMM Lugano, june 1990.

[NUG88] S.F. Nugent, "*The iPSC/2 Direct-Connect Communications Technology*", 3° Conf. on Hypercube Concurrent Computers and Applications, 1988

[PNU86] A. Pnueli, "*Application of temporal logic to the specification and verification of reactive systems : a survey of current trends*", LNCS, 1986.

[REE87] D.A. Reed, R.M. Fujimoto, "*Multicomputer Networks - Message-Based Parallel Processing*", The MIT Press, 1987

[SAN90] J.-P. Sansonnet, "*Concepts d'Architectures Avancées*", Tome 1, cours de DEA de l'Université d'Orsay, LRI 1990 (in french).

[SEI85] C.L. Seitz, "*The Cosmic Cube*", Com. ACM, vol. 28, n° 1, Jan. 1985, pp 22

[STA86] W. Stallings Ed., "*Reduced Instruction Set Computers Tutorial*", IEEE Computer Society Press - 1986

[STE75] G.L. Steele Jr., G. Sussman, "*Scheme : An interpreter for the extended lambda calculus*", MIT AI Lab memo 349 - 1975

[STR87] B. Stroustrup, "*The C++ Programming Language*" Addison-Weslay, 1987.

[THE83] D. G. Theriault, "*Issues in the design and implementation of Act2*", tech. rep. ai-tr èé!, MIT, June 1983.

[TRE82] P. Treleaven, D.R. Brownbridge, R.P. Hopkins, "*Data driven and Demand Driven Architectures*", ACM Computing survey Vol 14 n° 1 - 1982

[VAL82] L.G. Valiant, "*A scheme for fast parallel communication*", SIAM Jour. on Computing, vol. 11, n° 2, Mai 1982, pp 350-361

[VAL89] L.G. Valiant "*Bulk-synchronous parallel computers*" Prooc. of the A.I. and Message Passing Architecture Conference, p 15-22, London, 1989. J. Wiley.

[WAT87] P. Watson, I. Watson, "*An efficient garbage collection scheme for parallel computer*", proc. of PARLE II, LNCS 259.

[YON86a] A. Yonezawa, E. Shibayama, H. Matsuda, T. Takada, Y. Honda "*Modelling and Programming in an Object Oriented Concurent Language ABCL/1*", Research report C-75, Dept. of Information Science, Tokyo Institute of Technology, Nov. 86.

[YON86b] A. Yonezawa, H. Matsuda, E. Shibayama "*An Approach to Object Oriented Concurrent Programming: a language ABCL*", Proc. of the third Workshop on Object-Oriented Languages, Paris 1986.

Implementing Committed-Choice Logic Programming Languages on Distributed Memory Computers

Andy Cheese

Siemens AG, ZFE IS SOF 4,
Otto-Hahn-Ring 6, D-8000 Muenchen 83, West Germany

e-mail : unido!ztivax!venedig!abc

Abstract

Committed-choice logic programming languages provide the user with a paradigm to program declaratively in and at the same time allow the user to control and inform the implementation where parallelism might be exploited efficiently. The architecture which supports such programming languages is then outlined. The load balancing scheme for the architecture is then described followed by a method for recovering from deadlock due to there not being enough distributed memory available. Finally the results of the simulation of the distributed memory architecture are presented and discussed.

1. Introduction

Committed-choice logic programming languages [1] [2] [3] have foundations in first order predicate logic. The paradigm allows the programmer to express concepts of concurrency while endeavouring to remain within a declarative framework. Specifically these concepts are : concurrency, communication, indeterminacy, and synchronisation.

Concurrency is embodied by process interpretation of logic. A goal consists of a number of subgoals to prove correct. In the process interpretation each subgoal can be regarded as a process. A goal clause is then a system of concurrent processes. Subgoals that share variables are dependent upon each other. These dependent subgoals can be thought of as a process group in which the shared variables act as communication channels.

Each predicate consists of a number of clauses. When programming in the committed-choice style a predicate is written in such a way that no matter which clause is chosen if the clause fails then none of the others will give a correct answer. Thus the proof procedure commits to using a single clause out of the set that make up a predicates definition. The advantage of this programming style compared to that of parallel versions of Prolog [4] is that parts of the search tree are not shared between different processes. This is very important to a distributed memory implementation where communication plays a critical role.

It is possible in this programming paradigm to express the fact that one process should wait for another process to rendevouz with it before proceeding with its execution. This is done by expressing that a clause cannot be executed until its parameters are of a specific form. Thus a clause could specify that it cannot be executed until its first argument is bound to a term, its execution can proceed when some other process that shares this variable has performed the binding. There exist different mechanisms for expressing this in different committed-choice programming languages e.g in Parlog there are mode declarations and in Concurrent Prolog there is the read-only variable annotation.

In this paper we explore how such committed-choice logic programming languages can be implemented on loosely-coupled distributed memory machines. The results show that it is possible to obtain good speed-ups using multiple processors and at the same time good raw performance.

2. Abstract Machine

The search tree that results from a programs execution is explored by a set of workers. Each worker is a committed-choice logic programming language computer and represents the processing element of the simulated architecture. In the implementation this abstract machine is written in C and implemented as a separate Unix process. The abstract machine's memory is partitioned up into two memory spaces, the code space and the data space. This is to improve locality of reference and exploits the read-only property of the code since on a distributed memory machine copies of read-only pages can safely be duplicated because there will be no updates of these pages to propagate. In the implementation the code space contains a compiled image of the program to be executed.

The data space is considered as an array of words where each data object is made up of a set of words. There are several types of data object in the implementation. There are constants (integers, functors, atoms, and for efficiency reasons the nil list), lists, structures, and unbound variables. Each leading word of a set of words making up a data object is tagged to denote the data objects type.

For each active process in the system there is a process data structure. This contains a representation of a process when it is suspended or placed on a runnable process queue. The data structure contains several elements that represent the context of a process. There is the current program counter to be able to start or restart execution. There is a reference to its parent node so it can communicate the result of its execution back up the search tree. The current state of the process is also indicated to aid in the delayed removal of dead processes from any queues they may be on. In a distributed memory environment it is cheaper to mark a process on a shared queue as being dead than to access the remote pages containing the queues and update them. This would result in the worker "owning" the shared page for longer than is necessary. This can affect performance greatly since the shared pages containing the runnable process queues are updated very frequently.

To control the way the search tree is searched and coordinate the execution of the workers there are control nodes. There are two types, one for the And-parallel nodes of the search tree and one for the Or-parallel nodes of the search tree. Each of these nodes contains a reference to their child branches and their current status : active, suspended, or still dormant. These data structures are used to coordinate the clause commitment mechanism.

There are two queues of runnable processes that are manipulated by a worker. There is the local runnable process queue which contains process data structures for a branch of the tree for which it is known to be more efficient to execute locally. The pages which represent this queue are mapped private to the worker. The other type of queue is the global runnable process queue. On the global queue are placed process data structures for processes that are candidates for execution on any processor.

There is a reserved region of page frames per worker for the global runnable process queue. Each worker maps the pages for these areas from all the other workers into its own private virtual address space. This allows the workers to directly take work out of the queues. However, these pages are not scanned when a worker is idle and looking for work. This would entail page faults for those pages not resident and possibly not containing process data structures. The load balancing scheme described below is used as a more efficient alternative to that of scanning a set of page frames in the hope that one of them contains an item of work.

3. Load Balancing

Load balancing schemes can be very expensive. Because of this a simple algorithm is used. Each processing element (or worker) has a set of nearest neighbouring processing elements. This is a virtual neighbourhood system and need not reflect the physical topology of the architecture in any way. For each element of the set there is a busy/nonbusy indicator. If there is available work on a processing element's global runnable process queue, then each item of work is a candidate to be farmed out to another processing element. A nonbusy processing element is selected at random from the set of neighbouring workers indicated as being nonbusy. Its indicator is flipped to the busy state and the process is transferred. The only way the indicator can now revert to the nonbusy state is if the specified processing element asks for work.

The other situation to consider is when a processing element is idle. In this case, the processing element will inspect its indicator set looking for busy processors, and then request work from one of them. The chosen busy processing element sets the requesting processing element's indicator, in its processing element set, from busy to nonbusy indicating that the requesting processor is idle. If there is work available, it will be granted and farmed out. The whole conversation consists of busy processors asking idle processors if they want work, if they do not then they are ignored. At the same time idle processing elements are asking busy processing elements if they can have some work; if not then the idle processing elements go to sleep until they are once again asked if they want some work. In a more sophisticated implementation or physical architecture, it would be expected to multiplex several virtual workers on one single processing element; which would tend to reduce the amount of time processing elements spend idling. In the distributed memory machine, indicator sets are implemented as bit-vectors. This requires less communication and knowledge of global state than the case where idle workers search for work.

There is obviously a need for a decision algorithm for putting work on the local or global runnable process queues. In the current version of the emulator, all of a processing element's additional work, is put on its global runnable process queue. One optimisation would be to put work on the global queue only if it represents a call to a user-defined predicate but this assumes that system-defined predicates have been optimised into very fast sequential code. The next step would be to use abstract interpretation to identify the complexity of each predicate in terms roughly of how many logical inferences are associated with it. Using this, a compiler could annotate each relation and generate code appropriately.

When farming out work, the issue of binding environments has to be considered. An influencing factor on the strategy is that there can be a lot of short-lived processs. The situation must be avoided in which the whole environment of a process is transferred between processing elements, only to see the process quickly fail. As such, environment closing [5], where all arguments of a process are fully dereferenced and copied, is rejected as it would be too expensive. The attitude taken here, is to attempt to transfer as much information across processing elements, which will allow processes to decide whether they should fail or not, depending on the type of their arguments. In the majority of cases, clauses seem to be written so that their left hand sides are nonoverlapping, and there is a genuine non-deterministic choice to be made between those clauses that do have left hand sides with expected arguments of the same type.

Only enough of each argument is transferred to identify its type. Each word that is tagged as being a reference word is fully dereferenced and short-circuited before being transferred, in order to avoid chasing down chains of non-local references. Short-circuiting is a technique whereby if a chain of several references are followed and at the end of the chain is an item of data the original head of the reference chain is overwritten by the data item. Thus the next time the cell is accessed the data can be read directly. This is particularly important in a distributed memory implementation of a logic programming language. It is normal for such an implementation to create chains of reference words which could span many different memories in a physical architecture. All other tagged words are transferred as they stand. As a result, the environment management scheme is lazy, and values are only obtained when wanted. Two other possible additions to the information to be transferred are the principle functors of the subterms of a structure and the principle functor of the first element of a list. This is because the type checking performed on passed parameters by the system rarely exceeds the need to know more than the principal type of the argument being passed and not the type of the sub-arguments.

In every argument vector, the saved register set stored in the process data structure, many of the value cells may be unused and because of this, it is unnecessary to transfer the whole vector. The unit of information transferred is a minimalist argument vector simply called a minimal a-vector. In the emulator there is a maximum of sixteen argument registers. A bit-vector is used to denote which registers are in use. The integer representation of this bit-vector is constructed as an integer value cell and precedes any a-vector elements which are transferred. The integer value cell allows the receiver to reconstruct the original a-vector.

Thus, if only the first four shadowed argument registers are in use, then the bit-vector is `0000000000001111` and the corresponding integer is 15. The minimal a-vector would consist of an integer-tagged word containing a representation of 15 and the next four words would be copies of the first four argument registers.

4. Resource Exhaustion

An execution model for committed-choice logic programming languages must exploit And-parallelism. Processes suspend when encountering an unbound variable which they expect to be bound. In practice there is a limit to the number of processes present at any time. Thus it is possible to obtain a situation whereby an architecture can be full of suspended processes and there is not enough memory available to start other processes which might produce a binding to awaken any of the suspended processes. If this situation is reached the execution can never complete. However, if the search tree had been explored in a different manner the execution would never have blocked.

A solution proposed here is to destroy one of the suspended processes thus freeing memory. This is relatively expensive but cheaper than performing no computation at all. Destroying a process will involve interaction with both a suspended variable list, and a suspended process list. A process would then be chosen for extermination, its parent control node located, and the process's status reset to the unstarted (dormant) state. A dormant process has now to be chosen to be scheduled, in the hope that it will relieve the deadlock situation and bind some variable upon which a process is suspended. A search is made from the destroyed process, upwards in the tree, for a dormant process, whose control node has an a-vector which contains a reference to the variable which the (now killed) process was suspended on. The process located in this way may be a sibling process or a process associated with an ancestor but in either case this process is now activated.

5. Performance and Evaluation

The instruction timings and memory access times were based on performance figures obtained for that of the GRIP functional language architecture [6]. This is a machine similar to the envisaged hardware implementation of the distributed memory machine simulated here. The GRIP architecture contains several processor-memory cards which slot into a Futurebus cardcage. The processors themselves are from the 68000 family series. Thus the raw processor speed is comparable to that of many other conventional computer systems.

The results of three popular benchmarks are now reported and discussed. The first of them was quicksort of a list if six integers in reverse order which creates 110 processes.

Number of Processors	1	2	4	8	12
Microseconds	7965	4289	2539	1717	1604
KLIPS	13.8	25.6	43.3	64	68.6
Speedup	1	1.8	3.1	4.6	5

On this particular program, the architecture scales reasonably well up to 8 processing elements then very little is gained in performance by adding more processors. In fact performance tends to peak and then degrade suggesting that this particular program should only be run on a configuration of 8 processing elements. It is hypothesized that the performance degradation, if more than 8 processors are used, is probably due to the average number of active processes over time being 8, and that of the limited amount of parallelism present in the quicksort algorithm.

The second benchmark was the so-called Takeuchi benchmark [7] with the call `tak(18, 12, 6, X)`. The results are summarised below.

Number of Processors	1	2	4	8	12
Microseconds	1024830	528262	284791	163916	132597
KLIPS	6.2	12	22.3	38.8	48
Speedup	1	1.9	3.6	6.3	7.7

The results show good speedups up to eight processing elements. The performance from then on increases but at a declining rate. It is hypothesised that this is due to the large number of short lived processes that this benchmark produces. The overhead involved with accessing the shared runnable process queues and remote data being large compared to the amount of work performed by a process.

The last example benchmark was naive reverse of a list of thirty integers. The results are summarised in the following table.

Number of Processors	1	2	4	8	12
Microseconds	430110	225172	125680	74174	61272
KLIPS	18.7	35.8	64.1	108.7	131.5
Speedup	1	1.9	3.4	5.8	7

The speed-ups for naive reverse increase but the rate at which this happens decreases as the number of processors becomes larger. This is a common factor with all the experiments that were run. The overall speed was encouraging; it was possible to achieve 130 KLIPS with 12 processors.

6. Conclusions

In conclusion the speed-ups obtained on programs that exhibit parallelism are promising, though the rate at which the speed-up increases does decrease as the number of processors grows. The absolute speeds are encouraging with approximately 130 KLIPS achieved at one point. This shows that is possible to devise an efficient implementation of a parallel logic programming language allowing distributed memory machines to be programmed in a declarative way.

This research was sponsored by the SERC and was carried out whilst the author was at the University of Nottingham.

7. References

[1] Gregory S.
Parallel Logic Programming In Parlog : The Language And Its Implementation
Addison-Wesley Publishers Ltd., 1987

[2] Shapiro E.
Concurrent Prolog : A Progress Report
IEEE Computer, Vol 19, No 8, pp 44-58, August 1986

[3] Ueda K.
Guarded Horn Clauses
Thesis submitted to the Information Engineering Course of the University of Tokyo, Graduate School in partial fulfillment of the Requirements for the Degree of Doctor of Engineering, March 1986

[4] Westphal H. & Robert P. & Chassin J. & Syre J.-C.
The PEPSys Model : Combining Backtracking, AND- and OR-Parallelism
Proceedings 4th Symposium on Logic Programming, pp 436-448
September 1987

[5] Connery J.S.
Binding Environments for Parallel Logic Programs in Non-Shared Memory Multiprocessors
pp 457-467, Proceedings 1987 Symposium on Logic Programming
San Francisco, California, U.S.A., August 31 - September 4, 1987

[6] Peyton Jones S. L. & Clack C. & Salkild J. & Hardie M.
GRIP - A High Performance Architecture for Parallel Graph Reduction
Proceedings IFIP Conference on Functional Programming Languages and Computer Architecture, Portland, USA, pp 98-112, Springer Verlag Lecture Notes in Computer Science no. 274 (ed. Kahn G.), September 1987

[7] Crammond J.
Implementation of Committed Choice Logic Languages on Shared Memory Multiprocessors
Research Report PAR 88/4 and PhD Thesis
Department of Computing, Imperial College, October 1988

A Shared Environment Parallel Logic Programming System on Distributed Memory Architectures

Sergio A. Delgado-Rannauro, Michel Dorochevsky, Kees Schuerman, André Véron, Jiyang Xu

ECRC GmbH, Arabellastr. 17, D-8000 Munich 81, Germany.
email: elipsys@ecrc.de

Abstract

Current advances in Virtual Memory for Parallel Architectures have changed the idea that software architectures with global address spaces cannot execute well on Distributed Memory Message Passing (DMMP) architectures. This paper presents a parallel logic programming platform for complex applications based on a shared binding environment. The software architecture of this platform has been designed taking into account a range of parallel architectures, including DMMP machines. Preliminary results of the simulation of the software architecture on the EDS architecture, an Esprit II development of a DMMP machine, are also discussed.

1 Introduction

Parallelism in Horn-clause logic programming has been the subject of a considerable amount of research during the last decade. The sources of parallelism are now well known, and a variety of different parallel languages and computational models have been proposed. In recent years, the research effort has mainly concentrated on implementation techniques for these languages and models [7].

Our contribution to this area is the development of a parallel logic programming platform for complex applications. This platform, *ElipSys* [3], integrates mechanisms for solving constraint satisfaction problems [13], exploiting OR-parallelism and supporting a tightly coupled very large KBMS [5]. ElipSys is being developed as part of Esprit II Project 2025 EDS [2], which has as partners ECRC and its three shareholders Bull, ICL and Siemens.

In this paper we describe the ElipSys execution model: a shared environment OR-parallel execution model. We pay special attention to the design decisions taken to make this model particularly suitable for a range of parallel architectures. The software structure of ElipSys combines message passing abstractions for scheduling and control purposes and a shared address space for the representation of the binding environments.

In addition, we also describe and discuss how the shared address space can be implemented efficiently on a Distributed Memory Message Passing (DMMP) architecture. This implementation takes into account the new developments in Distributed Shared Virtual Memory in the next generation of operating systems.

This paper is structured as follows. Section 2 describes Shared Binding Environments for Logic Programming. Section 3 outlines the ElipSys Execution Model (EEM) of ElipSys. Section 4 presents Distributed Shared Virtual Memory support required for the EEM. Section 5 presents preliminary results from a simulator. Section 6 gives the conclusions and the directions for future research.

2 Shared Binding Environments

ElipSys uses OR-parallelism as the source of parallel evaluation; OR-parallel evaluation leads to independent computations which rarely need to communicate. The representation of the search space is by an OR-tree. In this OR-tree, there are opportunities for parallel evaluation. The amount of effective parallelism in ElipSys is restricted by user annotations (e.g. parallel declarations).

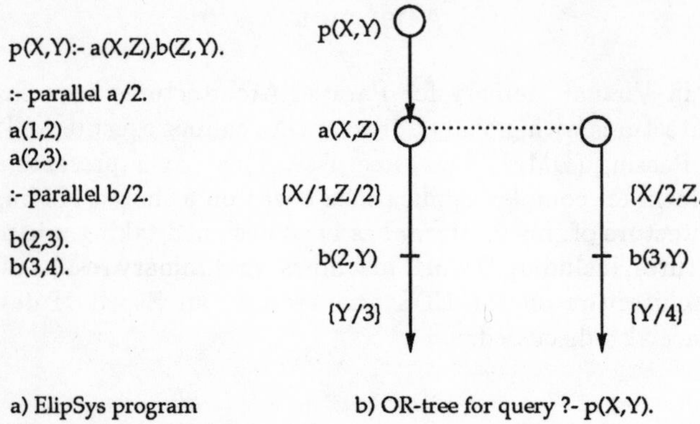

Fig. 1. An ElipSys program and its execution tree for query ?- p(X,Y).

The OR-parallel evaluation of logic programs needs a binding mechanism capable of recognising the scope of a *shared* variable. A variable is shared whenever it exists in multiple resolvents of the same derivation step. That is, all the successive derivations of the different resolvents may generate a binding to such a shared variable. Shared variables represent an implementation problem. The logic programming system must isolate the binding made to a shared variable in each refutation of the refutation procedure.

Fig. 1 shows an ElipSys program and its related OR-tree for the query ?- p(X,Y). Note in this example that variables *X*, *Y* and *Z* are *shared*, they require different bindings for the two proofs represented in the OR-tree, e.g. the shared variable X is bound to {X/1} and {X/2}.

There are several ways of representing the binding environments for a logic programming system based on OR-parallelism. In [7], three different methods are identified: (1) shared environments, (2) non-shared environments and (3) copied environments. The different environment schemes also assume different execution models. In this paper, we only concentrate on shared binding environment schemes (please refer to [7] for a discussion on the other two schemes).

A binding environment is *shared* whenever a descendent OR-node inherits the environment of all its antecedent OR-nodes. The representation of the binding environments in the shared scheme associates a unique name with every shared variable. At each OR-node the shared environment can be seen as a virtual copy of the inherited parent environment. The virtual copy must be unique to that path, so that bindings made to any shared variable are only local to every path. There are a number of different implementations of this virtual copy of the inherited environment, these are described in [7].

The shared environment scheme has been chosen to represent bindings in ElipSys because of (a) its flexibility to use the same abstraction in different execution models, (b) its development from well known techniques in sequential logic programming systems, and (c) the recent development of flexible virtual memory management for parallel architectures.

Currently we have a number of ElipSys prototypes each employing a different binding scheme based on the shared binding environment. The binding schemes that are under investigation are extensions to the binding array and hash windows models. These extensions are described in full in [8, 14]. We are carefully analysing them with respect to the following criteria: (a) simplicity to represent multiple bindings of variables, (b) their relative efficiency when compared to sequential implementations, and (c) the degree of scheduling freedom for different parallel architectures.

3 ElipSys Execution Model (EEM)

ElipSys has a hybrid execution model that combines message passing for scheduling and control purposes and a distributed shared virtual address space for the implementation of the shared binding environments. In this section, we describe first the abstract execution model to define the terminology used in later paragraphs. Then we define more precisely the software structure of the EEM.

3.1 Abstract Execution Model

In ElipSys, the OR-tree represents only non-deterministic OR-nodes. These can be sequential or parallel (it depends on the user annotation of a predicate). Choice-points are sequential non-deterministic OR-nodes. Branch-points are parallel OR-nodes.

Parallel computation in ElipSys may be created by the concurrent execution of the alternatives at the branch-points. The concurrent execution can be seen as a tree of *el-threads*, and the whole search space (OR-tree) as an *el-task*. Fig. 2.a shows the representation of an ElipSys OR-tree.

To solve an ElipSys query, an el-task, initially with a single el-thread, is created. In addition, a set of workers is assigned to the el-task at el-task initialisation. A worker consists of a scheduler and an engine. The computation starts after an engine is allocated by a scheduler to the initial el-thread.

Chronological backtracking within an el-thread is the means of local non-deterministic computation; this evaluation is strictly sequential and follows a depth-first ordering. During the execution of the el-thread, choice-points and branch-points are created.

The branch-points are made public according to a work publishing strategy. The publication of a branch-point involves the creation of el-thread(s), one for each alternative. The el-threads are placed in the work pool, the scheduler is the agent responsible for giving available work to requesting engines or schedulers. This involves the scheduler selecting an appropriate piece of work, updating the work pool, then either initialising a new el-thread corresponding to the piece of work, and finally allocating the ready engine to the ready el-thread, or sending the ready el-thread to another worker (through its scheduler).

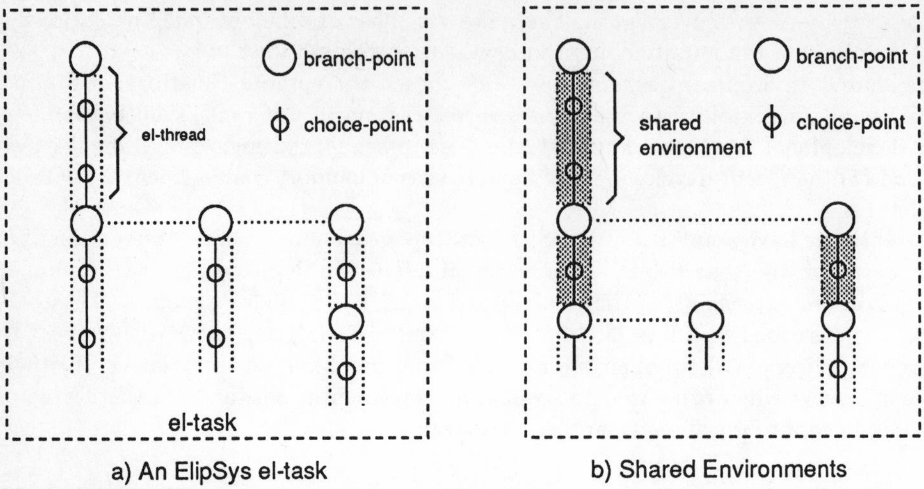

Fig. 2. ElipSys OR-trees

Depending on the work publishing strategy the processing of an el-thread may have to be suspended when it creates a branch-point. This is because the processing of an el-thread must suspend until all its child el-threads have been completed. Only then can the el-thread be considered ready for further processing and be allocated to a ready engine by the scheduler. Fig. 2.b shows an ElipSys control-tree with 6 el-threads, of which 3 are suspended and 3 are active. The suspended el-threads have a read-only shared binding environment.

Once the processing of an el-thread is completed it dies and ceases to exist any more. Therefore eventually all el-threads will die. The complete computation terminates when the initial el-thread dies. At this point, the el-task and its associated resources also cease to exist.

3.2 A Message Driven Execution Model

From the description of the abstract execution model it is clear that in ElipSys the scheduling and control issues can be separated from the binding environment issues. Most of the other implementations known to us [7] have made these two issues interdependent. Our motivation in ElipSys is to have a clear separation of them, which will allow us to have:

- well defined scheduler to engine and scheduler to scheduler interfaces.
- implementation independence for different parallel architectures.

Fig. 3 shows the current ElipSys software architecture. Note the decoupling of the control tree, i.e. the published part of the OR-tree, from the shared binding environment tree (Fig. 2.b). The control tree is managed in a completely distributed manner by the schedulers. Each scheduler has only a partial view of the control tree, the information that is currently local to each worker. The partial information of the control tree only corresponds to the currently existing published nodes.

Communication between schedulers is via a global message system. Communication between an engine and its corresponding scheduler is via local messages. In the current

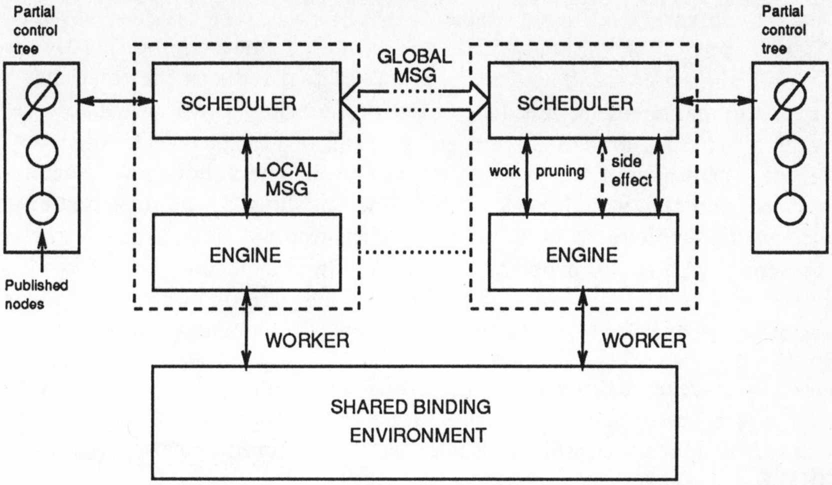

Fig. 3. ElipSys software architecture

message driven execution model the engine and the scheduler can each generate local messages to gain knowledge of the state of the other. For example the engine can decide not to publish more work, because the load factor in the machine is above a threshold limit. Details of the scheduling algorithm and the execution model can be found in [10].

The communication between an engine and its scheduler relates to three different aspects:

1. The work aspect involves the engine asking for work, the engine publishing work, the scheduler requesting load information from the engine and requesting work to be published.
2. The pruning aspect requires an interaction between the engine and the scheduler. An engine may find a commit action while working on an el-thread, this may involve pruning parts of the control tree.
3. The side-effects aspect involves synchronisation for the printing of the variable bindings in proofs, and for meta-control predicates which violate the principle of the shared binding environment tree, e.g. bagof, setof, findall.

The three aspects mentioned above may also require global communication (between schedulers) whenever the message refers to an el-thread in a part of the control tree which is not local to the worker.

4 Distributed Shared Virtual Memory (DSVM)

In recent years there have been a number of proposals for Parallel Operating System (POS) kernels [9, 12, 1]. One of the areas advanced by these new POS kernels is virtual memory management. This advance includes: sparse virtual memory maps, incremental creation of virtual memory maps and improvements in shared virtual memory (e.g. lazy evaluation and copy-on-write techniques). The latter benefit to an efficient implementation of distributed shared virtual memory systems like the one of the EDS machine [6].

In this section we state the requirements ElipSys places on distributed shared virtual memory. A feature of the shared binding environment method permits the realisation of a read only shared space. This feature is an asset, it reduces the coherency problems required for the management of a distributed shared virtual memory space.

Coherency schemes for DSVM are either weak or strong. Weak coherency has not been considered because it implies uncertainty about the validity of the shared virtual address space, and this would cause the constant flushing of the inherited environment in situations where coherency is unlikely to be ensured.

Strong coherency is the property of a DSVM which ensures that a read operation returns the value of the last write that occured. The strong coherency concept is also known as atomic, consistent or intuitive coherency. Strong coherence can be classified as:

- *Eager strong coherency* by default provides a strongly coherent view of the shared virtual space. Every memory access triggers the coherency handling mechanisms, which can produce a considerable increase in the communication requirements of a distributed system.
- *Lazy strong coherency* by default does not perform the operations to ensure a coherent shared space. These operations are triggered by synchronization points made explicit in the code of the application.

Lazy strong coherency is more suitable for the shared binding environment scheme used in ElipSys. Since, the need for invalidation only arises whenever the environment is overwritten. This situation occurs when the environment is again made local, that is an el-thread has changed state from suspended to active, e.g. no more active child el-threads.

5 Preliminary Results

ElipSys is the parallel logic programming subsystem of the European Declarative System (EDS) [2]. The EDS machine has a DMMP architecture with a multi-stage interconnection network of the delta type built from 8x8 switching elements.

A naive implementation of ElipSys on such a machine involves two messages for every access to the remote part of the shared binding environment. Such an implementation leads to a very high number of messages, a high number of implied context switches, and a relatively low system performance [11]. However, the number of messages can be reduced by using a sector copy mechanism (see below).

The ElipSys execution model and shared binding environment mechanism described have been run on an EDS machine simulator. The simulation assumptions are as follows:

- An address space divided into pages and sectors. A page comprises a fixed number of equal sized sectors.
- A lazy coherency DSVM scheme. A lazy inheritance of sectors and no inheritance of sector and page tables. Memory fault handling done on a sector basis, i.e. on a sector fault a sector is copied from a remote node. Copied sectors are cached and therefore only copied once.
- Messages consisting of a 16 bytes header, several bytes of data (optional), and 2 bytes CRC. A *sector_copy_request* message and a *sector_copy_reply* message comprise therefore 18 bytes and (18 + *sector_size*) bytes, respectively.

- A simple help-children scheduling policy, i.e. engines working on the same branch of the OR-tree help each other computing the alternatives of an OR-node low in the tree, thereby making available coarse grain pieces of work higher up in the tree.
- A single ElipSys worker per processor, i.e. ElipSys workers do not share any physical pages and sectors.

In ElipSys the access pattern to the shared environment can be highly irregular and of small quantities. Therefore, we have used the concept of sector-copy-on-access rather than page-copy-on-access. The preliminary results of this section analyse the relative number of memory faults and messages due to access to the shared binding environment, for various sector sizes. The figures shown below are measures relative to the naive implementation of the distributed shared environment, i.e. no environment caching.

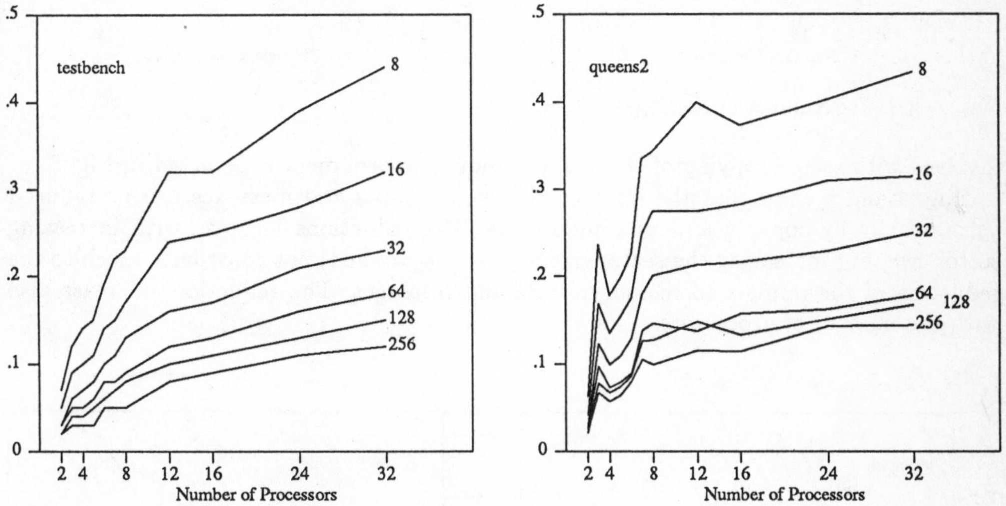

Fig. 4. Relative Number of Memory Faults

We have run a testbench of the following relatively small parallel ElipSys programs: *farmer*, *queens1* (8-queens), *queens2* (6-queens), *houses*, *mandel*, *map*, and *sam* [4]. Due to space limitations, only results averaged over the testbench and the results of the program *queens2* are presented. The *queens* programs solve the problem of placing N queens on an NxN chessboard withouth attacking each other.

Fig. 4 shows the relative number of memory faults as a function of the number of processors for various sector sizes. The numbers on the right-hand ends of the graphs correspond to the associated sector sizes measured in bytes. The minimum sector size is an ElipSys word, i.e. 8 bytes.

On a sector fault (i.e. a memory fault) the corresponding sector is to be copied from the environment of an ancestor worker residing on a remote processor. A *sector_copy_request* message is sent to the parent worker. If the parent worker does not have (a copy of) the requested sector, it forwards the *sector_copy_request* message to its parent worker. Otherwise, it sends a *sector_copy_reply* message containing the sector data to the worker which initially requested for the sector. The relative number of messages

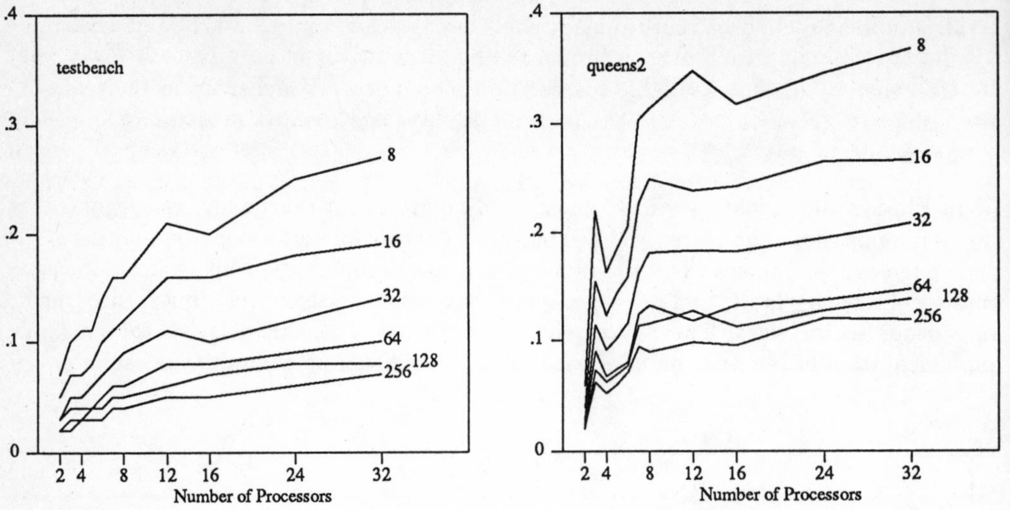

Fig. 5. Relative Number of Messages

involved with sector copying of the shared binding environment is depicted in Fig. 5.

Fig. 4 and 5 show that the number of memory faults and messages can be reduced substantially by copying and caching sectors. The reductions increase with increasing sector size, but increasing the sector size above 64 bytes does not contribute much to the reduction of the number of memory faults and messages. The reductions increase also with the number of processors.

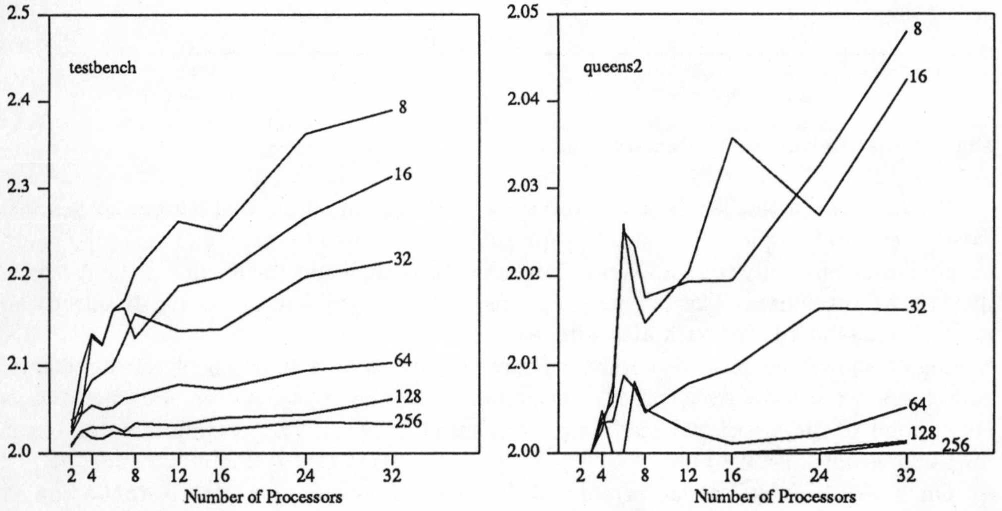

Fig. 6. Average Number of Messages Per Sector Fault

It can be observed that above 8 to 10 processors a stabilisation of the reduction is taking place. This can be explained by the fact that the simple scheduler used for the simulations does not incorporate any granularity control. A high number of processors implies therefore fine grain pieces of work and a minimum locality of reference. Note, that the absolute minimum is a single ElipSys word per copied sector. This absolute minimum will not be reached, since there is some natural clustering of ElipSys words (e.g. in run-time data structures) which is not affected by the granularity of computation.

The program *queens2* can easily be split up into 6 coarse grain pieces of work. Using more than 6 processor leads to fine grain computation and the effect described above (see Fig. 4 and 5).

The average number of messages per sector fault is depicted in Fig. 6. A sector copy involves two messages (i.e. a *sector_copy_request* and a *sector_copy_reply* message) if the requested sector resides in the parent worker. Otherwise, more messages are required. Fig. 6 shows that on average with a sector size of 64 bytes 90 % of the sector requests can be fulfilled by the parent worker. For the program *queens2* with the same sector size this is even higher than 99 %.

The number of memory faults and messages can be further reduced by (lazy) inheritence of page and sector tables. However, Fig. 6 shows that for sector sizes larger than 64 bytes no much more improvement can be achieved.

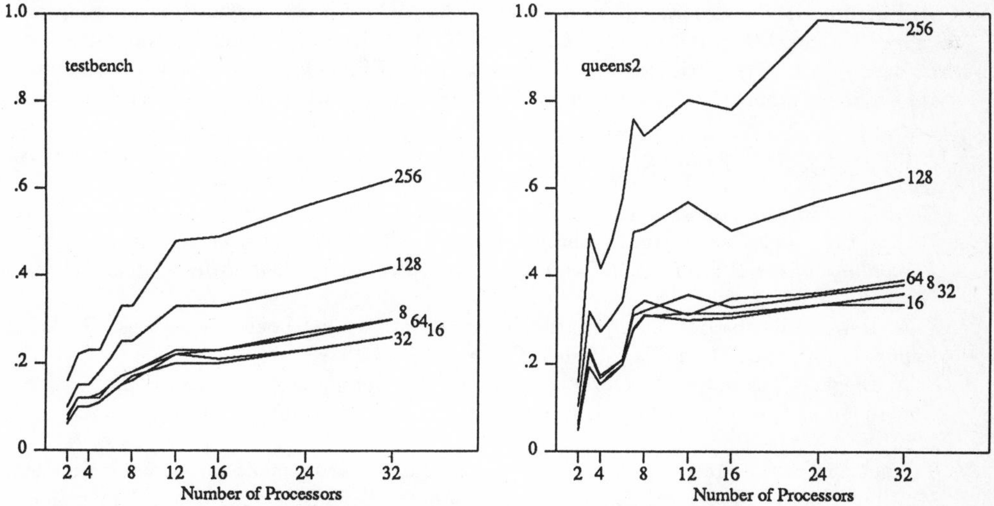

Fig. 7. Relative Network Bandwidth Requirements

The relative network bandwidth requirements are presented in Fig. 7. These requirements are determined by the number of *sector_copy_request* messages and the number and the size of *sector_copy_reply* messages. The average number of *sector_copy_request* messages per per sector fault decreases with increasing sector size (Fig. 6). Fig. 7 shows that network bandwidth requirements are minimal for sector sizes of 64 bytes and less.

A sector size of 64 bytes is a good choice for systems where network bandwidth and number of messages is of equal importance. The EDS machine has a high bandwidth interconnection network (20 Mbytes/s per channel) which led to the decision for a sector size of 128 bytes. Preference is therefore given to the reduction of the number of messages and related number of context switches.

6 Conclusions and Future Research

The ElipSys execution model gives a clear separation of the scheduling and control issues from the binding environment issues. The software structure of ElipSys aims for portability to different parallel architectures.

Lazy strong coherency in Distributed Shared Virtual Memory suits the shared binding mechanism of ElipSys. Preliminary results have been presented to show the suitability of our approach.

Future work will concentrate on the analysis of the memory reference behaviour of ElipSys with respect to the constraint satisfaction part, and a more flexible and adaptable scheduling algorithm.

References

1. V. Abrossimov and M. Rozier. Generic Virtual Memory Management for Operating System Kernels. In *Symposium on Operating Systems Principles*, pages 123–126, December 1989.
2. F. Anceau et. al. The European Declarative System. In *Esprit Information Processing Systems: Results and Progress of Selected Projects in 1990*, pages 32–44. November 1990.
3. U. Baron, S. A. Delgado-Rannauro, M. Dorochevsky, P. Heuzé, M. B. Ibañez Espiga, M. Ratcliffe, K. Schuerman, A. Véron, and J. Xu. The ElipSys Logic Programming Language. Technical Report DPS-81, ECRC GmbH, DPS Group, Munich, Germany, Dec 1990.
4. U. Baron, B. Ing, M. Ratcliffe, and P. Robert. The PEPSys Simulation Project Intermediate Progress Report. Technical Report CA-30, ECRC GmbH, Munich, Germany, February 1988.
5. J. Bocca. Compilation of Logic Programs to Implement Very Large Knowledge Base Systems - A Case Study: Educe * -. In IEEE Computer Society Press, editor, *Sixth Int. Conference in Data Engineering*, Los Angeles, CA, U.S.A, Feb 1990.
6. Lothar Bohrmann. A virtually shared memory model with customized coherency. In *Proceedings of the 11th ITG/GI-Conference - Architecture of Computing Systems*, Munich, Germany, March 1990.
7. S. A. Delgado-Rannauro. Computational Models of Parallel Logic Languages. Technical Report CA-46, ECRC GmbH, Munich, Germany, May 1989.
8. S. A. Delgado-Rannauro, M. Dorochevsky, K. Schuerman, A. Véron, and J. Xu. ElipSys Experimental System. Technical Report DPS-87, ECRC GmbH, Munich, Germany, Dec 1990.
9. T.J Leblanc, B. D. Marsh, and M. L. Scott. Memory Management for Large-Scale Numa Multiprocessors. Technical Report 311, Computer Science Department, University of Rochester, Rochester, New York, March 1989.
10. K. Schuerman. The ElipSys Scheduler. Technical Report DPS-84, ECRC GmbH, Munich, Germany, December 1990.
11. K. Schuerman and H. Benker. ElipSys on the EDS Machine: A Performance Estimation. Technical Report CA-50, ECRC GmbH, Munich, Germany, December 1989.
12. A. Tevanian Jr. *Architecture-Independent Virtual Memory Management for Parallel and Distributed Environments: The Mach Approach.* PhD thesis, Dept. of Computer Science, Carnegie Mellon University, December 1987.
13. P. Van Hentenryck. *Constraint Satisfaction in Logic Programming.* The MIT Press, Cambridge, Mass, 1989.
14. A. Véron, J. Xu, S. A. Delgado-Rannauro, and K. Schuerman. Virtual Memory Support for Parallel Logic Programming Systems. Technical Report DPS-83, ECRC GmbH, Munich, Germany, Dec 1990.

On the Design of Parallel Programs for Machines with Distributed Memory *

Dominik Gomm, Michael Heckner, Klaus-Jörn Lange, Gerhard Riedle
Technische Universität München, Institut für Informatik, Arcisstr. 21, D-8000 München 2

1 Introduction

The efficient and faultless use of parallel systems, in particular problems concerning the programming of parallel computers belong to the most important issues of computer science. These problems may be classified into two main categories: "*Distributed Parallelism*" deals with mastering concurrency and "*Speed-up Parallelism*" tries to improve on computation time by employing many processors to solve one task. Whereas the former treats questions of correctness, the latter — which is what we are concerned with — is determined by matters of efficiency. Problems of both areas are even becoming more difficult by the desire for an easy and clear way of programming parallel systems — if possible, similar to conventional programming.

These needs are fulfilled more easily on shared memory systems, where "synchronous" programming with a global clock yields both simplicity and good efficiency. On parallel systems with distributed memory (like the iPSC/2 Hypercube, Transputer Systems and others) both aims have at least to be reached independently or may even be considered as conflicting aspects. Programming distributed systems usually leads to rather coarse grained parallelism as the complexity of synchronization and communication prohibits a more fine grained implementation. Although this coarse grain approach is supposed to lead all the way back to conventional programming, we are then left with severe synchronization and consistency problems. In addition, this approach seems to work with algorithms that are characterized by a minor communication load, only. But, increasing the number of processors in a parallel system leads to a situation where technological constraints forbid "clocked" systems with a shared memory (e.g. [Vit86]).

The aim of this paper is to indicate a procedure for a convenient and machine-independent design of efficient programs for a large class of algorithms. This will be accomplished by hiding problems concerning concurrency and restrictions due to the communication topology of the underlying machine as far as possible. We want to point out that we do not think of an efficient implementation of a "universal" PRAM, but of developing and studying classes of problems or algorithms. These classes can be implemented in an efficient and convenient way. The expectation that these classes will nevertheless contain very relevant problems is supported by the fact that at present most computation-intensive "numerical" algorithms are of very regular structures allowing efficient partitionings.

2 Shared Memory Programming and its Desynchronization

In parallel complexity theory, one of the best known models describing parallel algorithms is the PRAM — the parallel random access machine. (See [Coo85] for an overview.) A PRAM can be thought of as a collection of processors (each of which having local memory) working in a synchronous way controlled by a global clock and communicating via *global memory*. There is a variety

*This work was carried out within the scope of DFG-SFB 342 by subprojects A3 and A4

of PRAM-models depending on how memory-conflicts are resolved. While the most general model, the *concurrent read concurrent write* CRCW-PRAM is a system with shared memory, each global memory cell of a *owner read owner write* OROW-PRAM is the conception of a directed communication channel. Hence, an OROW-PRAM is a (clocked) network of processors with distributed memory (see [Ros90]). We decided to consider the intermediate model, the CROW-PRAM, which already has some of the features of a real distributed memory computer.

As indicated above, it is relatively simple to design efficient algorithms on a synchronous parallel system with shared memory (i.e. the speed-up is proportional to the number of processors involved) and it is relatively simple to show their correctness. However, the PRAM-model makes some drastic and totally unrealistic assumptions: (A1) PRAMs work synchronously, i.e. the processors execute statements of unit length in a clock-controlled way. (A2) Processors have unbounded communication, i.e. each pair of processors can transfer data in unit time via a *global* (shared) memory. Thus, there is no difference in the time delay between local and remote communication. (A3) PRAM-algorithms use an unbounded amount of hardware, i.e. the number of processors involved in a PRAM computation is not fixed but depends (polynomially) on the length of the input.

Since the number n of virtual processors required by an PRAM-algorithm is usually much bigger than the number k of real processors of any existing parallel computer, there is the need to execute many virtual steps on one real node. This implies however that there is an ideal "PRAM-atmosphere" for these combined PRAM-processors in that there is no synchronization problem and no difference between local and remote communication, i.e. assumptions A1 and A2 are trivially fulfilled for PRAM-processors laid onto the same physical node. The problem is, of course, how to handle communications between PRAM-processors which are laid on different real nodes.

There seem to be two major ways to cope with this inhomogenity. According to one conception, all of the n virtual PRAM steps, which are to be executed in parallel, are distributed over the k real processors in a randomized way hoping for an equal load of all remote communications. Then each processor performs sequentially $\frac{n}{k}$ steps that were assigned to it. Each remote–step is handled by a communication–unit, such that (in the average) no processor has to wait for the execution of a remote–step, but instead can begin to execute the next of its $\frac{n}{k}$ steps [Val90]. This approach ends up in a flooding of the underlying network with a huge amount of small messages and in addition seems to pay off only if the ratio of remote to local communication time is not too far beyond 1. The other approach uses the fact that in most systems with distributed (nonuniform) memory the high cost (in terms of time) for a remote communication consists of a comparatively high *startup time* added to the usual transmission cost, which is linear in the length of the transmitted information and roughly corresponds to the cost of a local communication. Furthermore, it is possible to save in the cost of the startup time by *building blocks of communication.* Thus, it is very important within this approach to arrange and cut the n virtual steps in a way, that both the number of such blocks of communication and their sizes are balanced and equally shaped for all k processors. This is only possible if the communication structure of a parallel program is determined before run–time, i.e. we can consider algorithms with *data–independent communication structure* only. Thus, this second approach differs from the first one by providing very efficient programs for only a certain subclass of algorithms and by involving the user in the procedure. This is the most essential step of partitioning w.r.t. efficiency. The task is presumably unsolvable in an asynchronous environment.

This is why we treat the design of parallel programs in two major steps, *partitioning* and *desynchronizing*; this has to be done in this order. At first, in the *partitioning step* an appropriate PRAM algorithm is laid out on a synchronous PRAM with a small (i.e. realistic) number of processors in a way that the cost of inter-processor communication is reduced to a minimum. In order to avoid confusions we will call this machine in subsequent sections of this paper a *synchronous superstep machine* (SSM). Then, in the *desynchronizing step* the synchronous program is to be transferred onto an *asynchronous distributed memory machine* (ADMM) with the same number of processors using message passing mechanisms. As the global clock-pulse is missing in a distributed system we have to find means and ways to replace it. It turns out, that even in the case of complete information about how to build communication blocks optimally, this results in inefficient programs, unless we restrict ourselves to a small class of parallel algorithms with a very restricted communication structure. We intend to solve this inefficiency problem by allowing the user to give information concerning the asynchronous behaviour of certain parameters of his program. The succeeding *desynchronizing transformation* desynchronizes correctly and as efficiently as possible according to the given information the program resulting from the partitioning step. (In a certain way, data–independency of communication structure is just one example of this kind of information). These two steps shall now be presented in more detail.

2.1 Partitioning

Partitioning consists of three substeps: *cutting*, *building blocks of communication* and introducing *subbroadcasts*. The basic assumptions of the target machine, the SSM, that have to be met are: (S1) All processors work synchronously, (S2) global memory is still assumed but the OROW quality now required actually gives it the character of distributed memory and (S3) finally, the number of processors is restricted to a small (compared to n) value of k with respect to existing parallel architectures. Given this SSM architecture, we now want to present the three substeps that will carry PRAM programs onto SSM "hardware".

2.1.1 Cutting — Building Blocks of RAMs

Naturally, the partitioning starts with a reduction in parallelism. However, this goal is not achieved by some sort of multitasking of a certain amount of RAM programs on each SSM processor. [Val90]. Our basic idea is to cut the whole PRAM program (usually consisting of an enormous amount of n RAM programs) into parts in a way that each SSM processor obtains one program simulating the work of many RAMs. We want to stress that many RAM programs are merged in one program for each SSM processor. Consequently, within each piece of the original program there is still the ideal PRAM atmosphere as described in assumptions A1, A2 and A3. Only the connections crossing the frontiers of SSM processors will cause severe problems with respect to that model, i.e. communication and synchronization. We leave synchronization problems essentially to the second major phase, the desynchronizing step. Hence, the following criteria are of primary concern to achieve an efficient cutting: a) Equal loads for all SSM processors have to be produced and b) the pattern of communication, that is the algorithm's characteristic communication structure (which is practically never a fully interconnected one!) has to be considered in order to minimize external communication.

With this substep we introduce the concept of a superstep. A superstep in the program of a SSM processor comprises the execution of exactly one computational step of each of the RAMs that it has to simulate.

Having selected one cut of the PRAM algorithm a suitable sequential order of simulation has to be found. This is the second task that has to be solved within the substep cutting. Again, it may have considerable influence on the feasibility of building blocks of communication. (See convolution example).

A third task to be tackled by the cutting substep is the correct handling of non-monotonous algorithms. The following statement is a typical element of non-monotonous parallel algorithms: "a :=: b". Sequentializing this parallel statement correctly, entails that additional variables are introduced that protect variables a and b from being overwritten too early. However, given monotonous programs, the cutting could support a more efficient sequentializing of the PRAM algorithm due to some declaration given by the user indicating monotony.

2.1.2 Building Blocks of Communication

the second substep deals with the analysis of external communication. Within each superstep communication with external sources should be analyzed. This is aimed at finding a number of elementary (i.e. derived from single RAMs) read statements that access the same source SSM processor (but possibly different RAMs within that SSM program). This allows for reading these values within one communication setup before the execution of that superstep actually begins. Obviously, a clumsy cutting prohibits a successful building of blocks of communication. Therefore, it is realistic to conceive the cutting and the building of blocks as the two constituents of a feedback cycle.

This substep can be seen as a kind of local optimizing. For each SSM processor its read access to other, i.e. external SSM processors has to be optimized. It is the aim to give each SSM program the most efficient provision with external data (i.e. in blocks of messages).

2.1.3 Subbroadcasts

In contrast to the previous substep the subbroadcast step deals with the global aspect of communication. As we started with CROW PRAMs and, until now, did not resolve the concurrent reads, a certain, although reduced, amount of concurrent reads among the SSM processors is retained. To get in control of this concurrent access, the concept of subbroadcasts is introduced. To put it clear, the user does not resolve the concurrency. He simply "marks" it by using the subbroadcast statement. The actual resolution is done within a library function that is called by the subbroadcast statement.

Before having a more detailed look at subbroadcasts, we have to elaborate on the idea of a decomposition topology. [Fea88]

Keeping in mind the presumptions of hardware-independent programming on the one hand and the restricted interconnection topology typical of all large-scale parallel systems on the other hand, we propose standard decomposition topologies. Already indicated by the name this aid offers standard communication topologies for our decomposed PRAM algorithm, i.e. the algorithm after cutting and building blocks of communication. These topologies should guarantee the best mapping from this decomposition topology into any communication topology of real hardware systems. During the partitioning stage the user can select any of the decomposition topologies given in some sort of a library suitable for his algorithm. We think especially of grids, hexagonal meshes, hypercubes and trees. For example, matrix computations usually will be well represented on grids.

A subbroadcast enhances the expressive power of decomposition topologies as follows. Instead of restricting communication to the direct neighbours within the topology, communication is always possible in well-formed, distinguished subsets of the topology, e.g. within a 2-dimensional grid it is possible to address all members of a row or a column — the "dimensions" of the topology. The communication pattern of the algorithm has to fit into the expressiveness of subbroadcasts on the selected decomposition topology.

Resuming the discussion of concurrent reads, this third substep of partitioning finds all concurrent reads (that is all one-to-many communication links) and embeds them in subbroadcasts. Please note, that in our understanding the term subbroadcast does not imply any assumption about the direction of information flow, i.e. one sender, many receivers. It simply denotes the pattern of communication.

2.1.4 Comments on the Substeps of Partitioning

Considering the sequential order of substeps it is obvious that the partitioning stage has to start with cutting. But why is the building of blocks prior to subbroadcast treatment? The inverse order would not only inflict a concurrency of $O(n)$ to be dealt with where n is the enormous number of RAMs instead of $O(k)$, the small number of SSM processors but also prohibit a successful building of blocks of communication in some cases.

All substeps are supposed to be executed prior to any compilation and especially prior to execution of the program.

It is evident that no data-dependent algorithm such as any kind of pointer jumping will render this approach useless. There is no basis on which a sound building of blocks could rely. Furthermore, restriction to subbroadcasts cannot possibly be efficient as communication connections are unpredictable.

2.1.5 Examples

Partitioning will be described by two examples. Not every detail mentioned above will be demonstrated. The two examples differ in the time-dependence of their communication pattern. The first example, convolution, is marked by an invariable pattern as time passes on.

Convolution

```
Pi: repeat g(t) times
      ⌈ ≪ step ≫
        processorswitch i
           case 1    : A1 := f(0, A1, Ai+1)
           case n    : An := f(Ai-1, Ai, 0)
           default   : Ai := f(Ai-1, Ai, Ai+1)
        endswitch
      ⌊ ≪ endstep ≫
```

Figure 1: PRAM Convolution Algorithm (for any PRAM i)

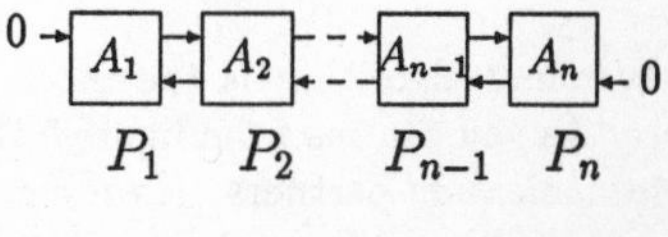

Figure 2: Communication Structure of the PRAM Convolution Algorithm

```
topology grid( dim 1, proc k)
Qj: repeat g(t) times
     ⌈ ≪ superstep ≫
       Al := subbroadcast ( row , sender ∀i ∈ row Qi, receiver Qi-1, value An/k)
       Ar := subbroadcast ( row , sender ∀i ∈ row Qi, receiver Qi+1, value A1)
       for i = 1(1)n/k do
          switch i
             case 1   : if j = 1 then A'1 := f(0, A1, A2) else A'1 := f(Al, A1, A2)
             case n/k : if j = k then A'n/k := f(An/k-1, An/k, 0) else A'n/k := f(An/k-1, An/k, Ar)
             default  : A'i := f(Ai-1, Ai, Ai+1)
          endswitch
       end
       for i = 1(1)n/k do  Ai := A'i
       end
     ⌊ ≪ endsuperstep ≫
```

Figure 3: Obvious Partitioning of the Convolution Algorithm

Let us assume that we have n RAMs and only k SSM processors (nodes), where $n \gg k$. There is one obvious way to cut this algorithm. It simply combines $\frac{n}{k}$ neighbouring RAM programs in one SSM processor program, thus giving us the k programs needed for the SSM. The result of this simple cutting can be seen in figure 3. Each node simulates the $\frac{n}{k}$ RAMs laid onto it from left to right within each superstep. Obviously, there are no elementary read access statements within each SSM processor Q_j that could become blocks because they address the same source SSM processor.
It seems worth mentioning that the change in sequential order of the simulation of RAMs would yield a possibility of blocking:
Choosing **snakelike** execution means that each node first simulates the $\frac{n}{k}$ RAMs within a superstep from left to right, followed by a superstep reversed in order. Thus the bordering memory location at the right or left end, respectively is updated twice in two successive computation steps. Both values are retained and combined in one block of communication. Thus computation only takes place after each "megastep" comprising to supersteps. This change in the sequential order of events cuts communication frequency in halves and doubles the length of each communication block which will make up to a considerable performance increase.

The **overlap** idea is based on redundancy. An overlap of o can be explained as follows: Each node starts with simulating not only its own $\frac{n}{k}$ RAMs but also a certain number of RAMs , precisely $2o$ RAMs, that belong to its right and left neighbouring nodes — o of them to each. Thus we can execute o succeeding computation steps without any communication by simulating a decreasing number of overlapping RAMs. Therefore we create a "megastep" on each node comprising o computational steps on $\frac{n}{k}$ RAMs plus the additional computation necessary for the overlapping RAMs. The message length is increased from 1 element to o elements, message frequency however is curbed drastically by factor of o.

In fact, the standard partitioning proposed above is a special case of overlapping: $o = 1$.

Warshall

The Warshall algorithm is the most popular algorithm for solving the problem of the transitive closure. As you can see from figure 5 the Warshall algorithm is characterized by a permanent change of communication partners. However, the communicating pairs of processors can be anticipated — they can be derived from the number of the computation step.

P_{ij}: **for** $r = 1(1)n$ **do**
⌈ ≪ step ≫
$A_{ij} := A_{ij} \vee (P_{ir}.A_{ir} \wedge P_{rj}.A_{rj})$
⌊ ≪ endstep ≫
end

Figure 4: PRAM Algorithm

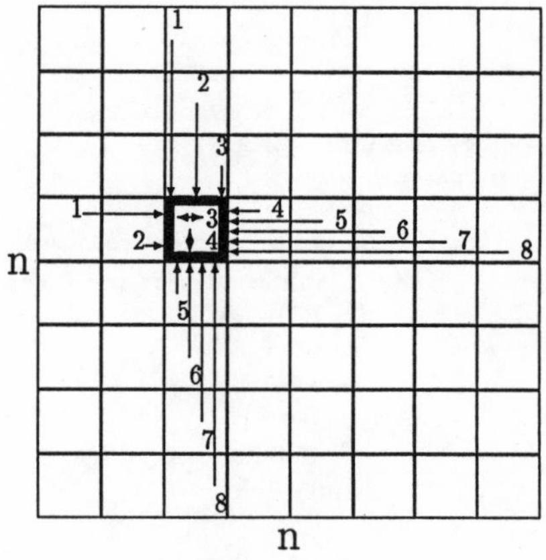

Figure 5: Warshall's Algorithm on an 8 × 8 Matrix (on RAM P_{43})

We will present two possible cuttings that can be ranked by the ability to build blocks of messages. For the time being, we will assume that we have n^2 RAMs but only k nodes. In the PRAM case every matrix cell has got a RAM doing the n computation steps necessary to determine the resulting value of this cell.

Partitioning the matrix by the **row**

$\frac{n}{k}$ rows of n RAMs each are merged in one node program. Since each superstep needs the values of one distinct row of the matrix these values can be transferred in one block and thus increase communication efficiency.

Note that the case of partitioning by the column is symmetric.

Partitioning the matrix by the **tile**

One node simulates a square of $\frac{n}{k'} \times \frac{n}{k'}$ neighbouring RAMs where $k'^2 = k$ nodes. This time each superstep operates on two message blocks: successive values of one section of a row and successive values of one section of a column. The section size equals the length of a tile. Note that this way of partitioning reflects the basic structure of the Warshall algorithm. The result is shown in figure 6.

It will turn out that this partitioning by tile results in an even more efficient SSM-algorithm with respect to communication than the partitioning by the row. (c.f. table 1). The total amount of information that has to be exchanged is smaller.

topology grid(dim 2, **proc** k)
Q_{rs}: **for** $t = 1(1)k'$ **do**
  for $u = 1(1)\frac{n}{k'}$ **do**
    ⌈ ≪ superstep ≫
      $(A_{in_{row}}1, \ldots, A_{in_{row}\frac{n}{k'}})$:= **subbroadcast** (**row** , **sender** $Q_{\mathbf{row}\ t}$,
        receiver $\forall_{i \in \mathbf{row}}\ Q_{\mathbf{row}\ i}$, **value** $A_{1u}, \ldots, A_{\frac{n}{k'}u}$)
      $(A_{in_{col}}1, \ldots, A_{in_{col}\frac{n}{k'}})$:= **subbroadcast** (**col** , **sender** $Q_{t\mathbf{col}}$,
        receiver $\forall_{i \in \mathbf{col}}\ Q_{i\mathbf{col}}$, **value** $A_{u1}, \ldots, A_{u\frac{n}{k'}}$)
      for $v = 1(1)\frac{n}{k'}$ **do**
        for $w = 1(1)\frac{n}{k'}$ **do** $A_{vw} := A_{vw} \vee (A_{in_{row}v} \wedge A_{in_{col}v})$
    ⌊ ≪ endsuperstep ≫
end

Figure 6: Partitioning by the Tile

Partitioning	messages		
	amount of messages	length	information total
by the tile	$2kn = 2k'^2n$	$\frac{n}{\sqrt{k}} = \frac{n}{k'}$	$2\sqrt{k}n^2 = 2k'n^2$
by the line	$kn = k'^2n$	n	$kn^2 = k'^2n^2$

Table 1: Comparison

2.2 Desynchronizing

In the second major step of transformation, called **desynchronization**, programs from the synchronous SSM stage are transferred onto an asynchronous distributed memory machine ADMM. Thereby, all access to global memory has to be replaced by message passing mechanisms. Read and write operations in a SSM superstep are replaced by **asynchronous send and receive operations** on the ADMM level.

As the ADMM is a model of a distributed system we can no longer rely on a global clock signal. Therefore, we have to use suitable synchronization mechanisms to simulate the missing global clock pulse such that every node operates on the correct data in each computation step.

The result should always be an efficient program where nodes can perform their local steps as independently as possible. Therefore, we are not interested in solutions like barrier–style synchronization [Val90] where a node can only start a new step if all nodes have performed their corresponding steps, which in addition requires an enormous overhead of synchronization messages on a distributed machine. Waiting for input values should be the only acceptable delay. This can be realized generally but inefficiently if each node stores each computed value of each step in a local list and sends such a value to another node whenever it receives a corresponding request. Desynchronization should yield more efficient distributed programs in the case of a more restricted communication structure of the synchronous program. If the communication structure does not depend on input data, it is predictable, such that requests for values and local lists can be omitted. Simple submission of values which must be indicated by the step they are computed at is sufficient to guarantee that all nodes are working on the correct data. Furthermore, if the communication structure is constant in time, i.e. the same in every step, indication can be omitted if we assume FIFO buffers.

Besides cheaper synchronization mechanisms, faster message passing system calls can be used to increase efficiency. In the case of a **cyclic** or even **symmetric** communication structure, the algorithm itself has enough inherent synchronization to make precise assumptions about worst case buffer sizes. Knowing this, we can always find implementations which rely on more efficient plain system calls than the ones usually provided, because free buffer space can be guaranteed – thus excluding the sender of having to wait.

We will use *Petri nets* to analyze *runs* of non–clock–controlled systems to find correct transformations using minimal synchronization mechanisms. Petri nets are adequate for the modelling and analysis of distributed systems. They can be nicely represented as bipartite graphs of passive (*conditions* which hold iff they are marked — drawn as circles), and active elements (*events* which may happen, thereby changing conditions they are related to — drawn as boxes), and by the notion of the runs of a net system they have a well-defined partial order semantics. Due to the lack of space we refer to [Rei85] for all technical details.

Convolution

In the case of the systolic convolution algorithm it can be shown that no additional synchronization mechanisms are necessary for a correct transformation because variables are accessed **symmetrically**: Each inner node has two communication partners that never change. In each superstep there is a send and receive operation — thus forming two communication cycles of minimal length (i.e., of symmetric shape). The convolution algorithm based on message passing can be modelled as a Petri net consisting of the behaviour of the k nodes and buffers — drawn as conditions — for communication as follows:

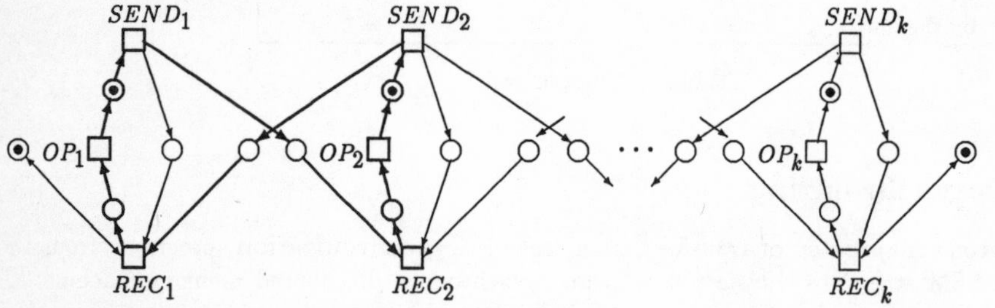

Figure 7: Petri Net Representation of the Partitioned Convolution Algorithm

In doing so, Petri net analysis methods can be applied. The thicker lines in Figure 7 form a *place invariant* over the buffers of two neighbouring nodes. The number of tokens on all these conditions remains constantly 2 under each reachable marking M of the system. Thus, in any system state there will never be more than two values in any buffer, such that a buffer capacity of 2 is sufficient. To guarantee correctness (each node operates always on the correct data) it is necessary that these buffers are having FIFO property. We will show the realization of FIFO-buffers of capacity 2 between two neighbouring nodes as a Petri net in Figure 8.

The basic idea is to model buffers consisting of two conditions. If all the buffer conditions are *complemented* we can now find place invariants for all conditions p in the channel, e.g. A_1 and its complement $\overline{A_1}$, such that $M(p) \leq 1$ which implies FIFO property.

To show the correctness of the system with buffers of capacity 2 we are going to have a look at the runs of the system, which are acyclic Petri nets: conditions and events are partially ordered. Here, we will determine on which value — received from neighbour $i+1$ — the node i is operating on in superstep t.

Figure 9 shows the unique minimal run of the system in which each node computes at least one value, i.e. an event "op" occurs at least once in both nodes. This run ends in the state it started

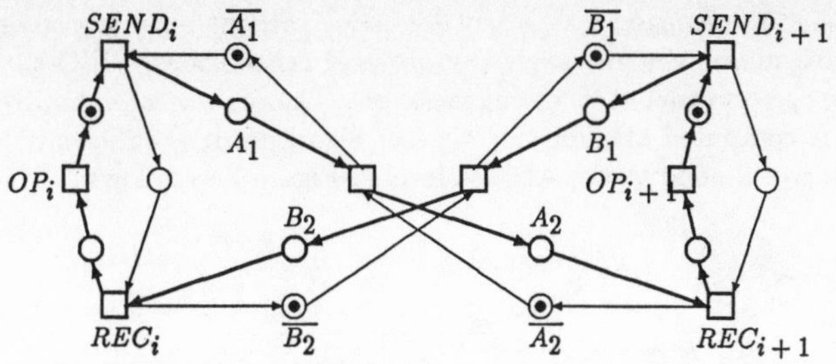

Figure 8: FIFO Buffers with Capacity 2 between two Neighbouring Nodes i and $i+1$

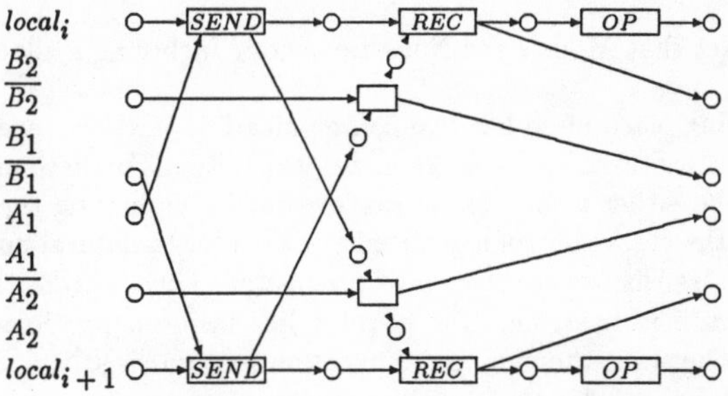

Figure 9: Run of the System Depicted in Figure 8

with. The one and only maximal run of the system is never-ending. This means that no deadlock will occur. Within clockcycle t node i computes a new value including the value of the neighbouring node $i+1$ from clockcycle $t-1$. The following relations between events hold:

1. $\mathrm{OP}_{i+1}^{t-1} < \mathrm{SEND}_{i+1}^{t}$ due to the cyclical order of local events
2. $\mathrm{SEND}_{i+1}^{t} < \mathrm{REC}_{i}^{t}$ due to the causality in the run of the system
3. $\mathrm{REC}_{i}^{t} < \mathrm{OP}_{i}^{t}$ due to the order of local events within each superstep
4. OP_{i}^{t} and OP_{i+1}^{t} may occur concurrently, as they are not causally ordered within the run of the system

It follows from 1 – 3 that $\mathrm{OP}_{i+1}^{t-1} < \mathrm{OP}_{i}^{t}$ and from 4 that $\mathrm{OP}_{i+1}^{t} \not< \mathrm{OP}_{i}^{t}$, guaranteeing that node i computes its tth value by using the $t-1^{st}$ value of neighbour $i+1$.
This desynchronizing step is optimal with respect to efficiency because we do not need any additional synchronizing mechanisms. The clock pulse is simulated solely by the values that have to be exchanged. This idea can be extended to systolic algorithms with **cyclic** access to variables: The maximal amount of values in a buffer equals the length of the shortest circle the buffer is located at. Being aware of that, the implementation of big enough buffers allows the usage of cheaper plain system calls for message passing. In the case of an implementation with one incoming buffer per node, messages from two senders will be merged which requires indication of the values by their senders' names for correct identification.

Warshall

If we consider the Warshall algorithm, access to variables is weaker synchronized. Although the communication behaviour changes dynamically in time, it is nevertheless predictable, i.e. does not depend on the input data. So, messages can be sent by nodes without receiving any requests. But because a node can receive subsequent messages from several other nodes, FIFO channels are not sufficient to guarantee the correct order of incoming messages. Therefore, each submitted value needs indication of the step it is computed at. For this class of algorithm it is sufficient to enhance the basic model for a superstep of a node at the ADMM level in Figure 7 as follows:

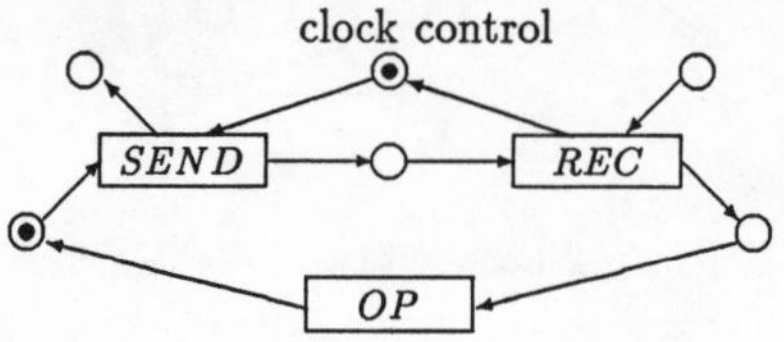

Figure 10: Petri Net that Models the Node Behaviour Including a Clock-Control

In the case of tile partitioning, each node has two communication partners: one within its line and one within its column. Both partners may change in any superstep. Furthermore each of these two communication events can be either a send or a receive event depending on the superstep number, but never both. Therefore, the clock control is realized as a counter (a natural number, initially 1) in Figure 11. Send and receive transitions are refined by predicates. Thus, a transition is only activated if the corresponding predicate is true, i.e. the counter lies inside a previously defined interval. Depending on x the *conflict* between the four communication patterns is solved deterministically, i.e. for any x exactly one of the four predicates is evaluated to true.

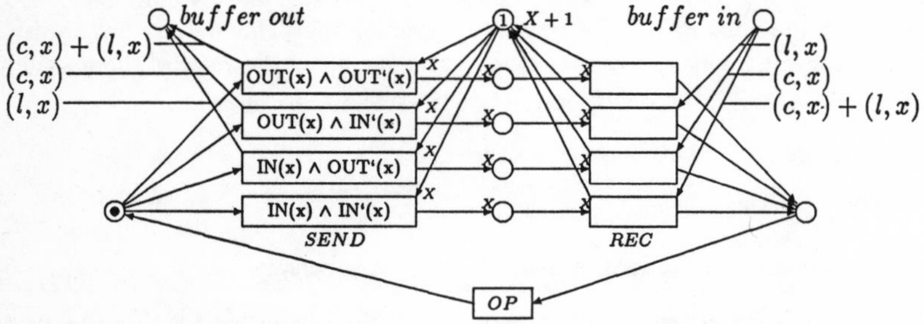

x: representing the superstep counter
c: representing the values of the column
l: representing the values of the line

For a node Q_{rs} it holds that:
- $\mathrm{OUT}(x) = \mathrm{true} \Leftrightarrow x \in \{(r-1)\cdot\frac{n}{k}+1 \ldots r\cdot\frac{n}{k}\}$
- $\mathrm{OUT}'(x) = \mathrm{true} \Leftrightarrow x \in \{(s-1)\cdot\frac{n}{k}+1 \ldots s\cdot\frac{n}{k}\}$
- $\mathrm{IN}(x) = \mathrm{true} \Leftrightarrow \mathrm{OUT}(x) = \mathrm{false}$
- $\mathrm{IN}'(x) = \mathrm{true} \Leftrightarrow \mathrm{OUT}'(x) = \mathrm{false}$

Figure 11: Communication of the Warshall Algorithm Partitioned by the Tile

Each time a section l of a line (or a section c of column) is sent, it is indicated by the corresponding superstep number x. The message l (or c) is **broadcasted** in the column (or line, respectively) of the sender. Indication guarantees that the receiver will operate on these values in the correct order. After each communication event the local counter is increased by 1.

Analogously to Figure 9 the runs of the system can be analyzed to show that the clock pulse is simulated correctly.

The capacity of the buffers has to be $n - \frac{n}{k}$ in the worst case, because during performance of the algorithm values are sent only from upper to lower tiles and from left to right, respectively. In particular there is no cycle synchronizing the algorithm by itself. Summarizing, again cheaper plain system calls for message passing can be used, but only if buffers with their size depending on n are implemented. In this case, indication of submitted values with the step number is sufficient for correct desynchronization.

Worst case buffer size needed for plain system calls can be decreased for the price of additional synchronization. After computation of some values, bottom and right nodes may send reply messages to upper and left nodes in the matrix, thereby constructing cycles of the desired length. So, buffer size and explicit synchronization messages can be regarded as two parameters which can be tuned reciprocally to yield an optimal result for the implementation.

3 Discussion

Our approach simplifies the design of programs for highly parallel, asynchronous computers by providing a synchronous view of the system. This is achieved by separating the relevant problems in two steps — partitioning and desynchronizing. This procedure is only applicable to a certain class of algorithms. Hence, a classification of algorithms is indispensable. At present parallel complexity theory does not meet this requirement satisfactorily i.e. the following question is not answered adequately: Is there an efficient parallel solution for a given problem w.r.t. to the restrictions of real parallel computers? Within the scope of SFB 342 which funded this work the subproject A4 tries to develop a new complexity theory. This new theory should take into consideration the desynchronizing types (e.g. periodic, cyclic, symmetric, etc.) and especially characterize data–independent communications. Based on this model the construction of a stable notion of reducibility which preserves the characteristic features mentioned above is a primary aim. In a later stage, these reductions could eventually provide transformations on the synchronous level useful in the partitioning stage.

It is not yet well understood up to which extent partitioning can be automatically supported. Obvious standard problem structures could lead to a fully automated partitioning. If this is not the case there should be at least some assessment information provided by the system evaluating partitioning proposals of the user (e.g. table 1). These questions will determine our future work.

References

[Coo85] Stephen A. Cook. A taxonomy of problems with fast parallel algorithms. *Information and Control*, 64:2–22, 1985.

[Fea88] G. Fox et al. *Solving problems on concurrent processors, Vol. I: General Techniques and Regular Problems.* Prentice Hall, 1988.

[Rei85] Wolfgang Reisig. *Petri Nets*, volume 4 of *EATCS Monographs on Theoretical Computer Science.* Springer, 1985.

[Ros90] Peter Rossmanith. The owner concept for PRAMs. Technical Report TUM-I9028, SFB-Bericht Nr.342/15/90 A, TU München, 8 1990. To appear in STACS 91.

[Val90] Leslie G. Valiant. A bridging model for parallel computation. *Communications of the ACM*, 33:103–111, 8 1990.

[Vit86] Paul M.B. Vitányi. Nonsequential computation and laws of nature. In *VLSI Algorithms and Architectures*, pages 108–120, 7 1986.

ADAM — An Abstract Dataflow Machine and Its Transputer Implementation

Wolfgang Schreiner
Research Institute for Symbolic Computation (RISC-Linz)
Johannes Kepler University, Linz, Austria

Abstract

This paper describes the design of the ADAM Abstract Dataflow Machine. This abstract machine has a hybrid distributed-memory architecture combining features from conventional register machines and from dataflow computers. The ADAM processor has a conventional instruction set augmented by primitives for the creation and synchronization of parallel tasks. Memory units on each ADAM module are responsible for the management of non-strict data structures. A prototype implementation of the concept on a multi-transputer system shows promising speed-ups.

1 Introduction

In the last decade, there has been much international research on how to efficiently exploit the fine-grained parallelism inherent in all algorithms. Non-von Neumann architectures have been designed in order to effectively utilize this parallelism by hardware primitives that minimize the overhead for the creation and synchronization of large numbers of parallel tasks. Dataflow architectures seem to be among the most promising of these approaches. Several dataflow computers have already been realized in hardware, e.g. the *Manchester Dataflow Computer* [1], the *ETL SIGMA-1* at the Japanese Electrotechnical Laboratory [2] and the *ETS Explicit Token Store "Monsoon"* at the MIT [4].

In spite of these efforts, commercially available dataflow systems have not yet come into existence. One of the main reasons for this disappointing fact is the enormous amount of knowledge gathered on the design and use of conventional processors, as well from the hardware engineer's as from the software engineer's point of view. Recently, there have therefore been several attempts to combine the benefits of both worlds, of data-driven and of control-driven architectures [3].

In this paper, the main results of the author's diploma thesis [5] are presented dealing with the design and the implementation of a dataflow simulator on conventional parallel distributed memory hardware (i.e. on a multi-transputer system). The dataflow style

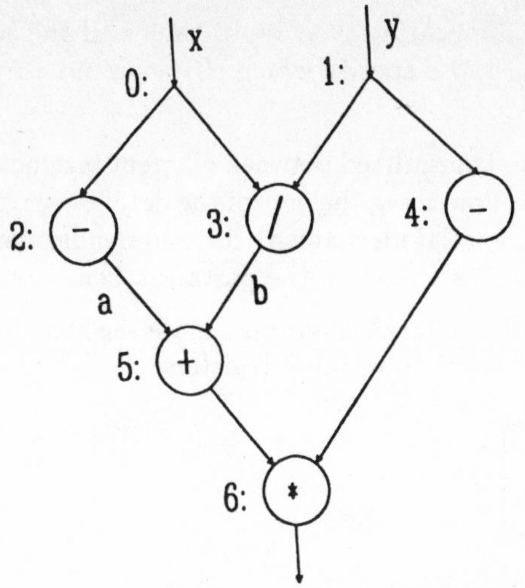

Figure 1: A Dataflow Graph

of programming shows essential benefits that have no counterpart in classical parallel programming. Our work is intended to show that this paradigma can also be based on conventional control-driven hardware. This is achieved by the ADAM Abstract Dataflow Machine that simulates dataflow behaviour by control-driven program execution.

2 Basic Idea

The basic idea of our approach is as follows. We take a mathematical expression, e.g.

$(a + b) * (-y)$ **where**
$a = -x$
$b = x/y$

This expression can be viewed as the body of a function $f(x, y)$ with formal parameters x and y and is translated in a dataflow graph as depicted in Fig. 1.

In dataflow machines, this graph is represented by a program similiar to the following one where each instruction consists of an operation code and the address of its successor:

```
0:  copy 2 3.l
1:  copy 3.r 4
2:  neg 5.l
3:  div 5.r
4:  neg 6
5:  add 6
6:  mul 7
```

Each node of the graph is translated into one instruction of the program where the arcs of the graph are represented by the instructions' successor addresses. Branches are translated into explicit copy instructions duplicating their input values. If the successor is a binary instruction, the predecessor must also specify which of the "input ports" of the successor is referenced.

In dataflow machines, values are transmitted between different instructions by pieces of information, called "tokens", that flow along the arcs of the dataflow graph. For instructions with more than one input arcs, special mechanisms have to handle the synchronization of the input tokens, i.e. a "rendezvous" between the partner tokens has to be organized.

In the ADAM model, the arcs of the dataflow graph denote registers and the nodes represent two-address instructions operating on these registers:

0:	copy	$x_1, x_2, 2$
1:	copy	$y_1, y_2, 4$
2:	split	3, 6
3:	neg	$x_1, x_1, 8$
4:	split	5, 6
5:	neg	$y_2, y_2, 10$
6:	wait	$e_0, 7$
7:	div	$x_2, y_1, 8$
8:	wait	$e_1, 9$
9:	add	$x_1, x_2, 10$
10:	wait	$e_2, 11$
11:	div	$x_1, y_2, 12$

Each instruction operates on two registers where the first one receives the result value. After an instruction has been executed, control flow is routed by the address field to its successor. `split` instructions fork the actual thread of control into two parallel threads starting at the specified successors. In above program, two threads enter the code block at addresses 0 and 1. The execution of each thread may be unhinderedly continued as long as no `wait` instruction is encountered.

Each `wait` guards a binary *event* encoded in the first field of this instruction. Each event may have one of the values "occurred" or "not occurred", initially no event has occurred. If execution reaches a `wait` whose event has not yet occurred, the actual thread of control is interrupted and the referred event is set to "occurred". The next time, this event is tested, the actual thread may unhinderedly pass the `wait`.

`split` and `wait` control the generation of parallel processes and the synchronization between them, they are the only instructions related to parallelism. However, they suffice to control the program execution in such a way that dataflow semantics is simulated.

We want to emphasize the essential difference between the pure dataflow model and our approach: In dataflow architectures, all data physically "flow" between instructions and, by this, control the computation. In the ADAM processor, threads of instructions are executed without any data flowing between them. Communication between different instructions is done via shared registers, synchronization between parallel threads are explicitely handled by `wait` statements.

This approach has two essential advantages:

1. In dataflow machines, all data referenced by more than one instruction have to be **explicitly duplicated** and sent to the required instructions, even if they belong to the same activation of a function and reside on the same processor. In our model, parallel program paths may **share data** held in common registers, an explicit duplication can be avoided in most cases.

2. In dataflow architectures, the synchronization model is fixed in hardware. Parallel program paths have to be generated and finally synchronized even if parallelism is not really utilized. This is especially the case if only whole function activations are placed on new processors i.e. parallel paths within an activation are always executed on the same processor. In our approach, a compiler is able to detect in which cases parallel paths may be safely (i.e. without changes to the dataflow semantics) executed in sequential and **serialize the code**[1].

Using both optimizations, we may rewrite the above program as follows:

0:	wait	e_0, 1
1:	copy	x_2, x_1, 2
2:	div	x_2, y_1, 3
3:	neg	x_1, x_1, 4
4:	add	x_1, x_2, 5
5:	neg	y_1, y_1, 6
6:	mult	x_1, y_1, 7

Assuming that there are two parallel tasks delivering their arguments in registers x_1 and y_1, there is only one `wait` instruction required to synchronizes these tasks. All other instructions may be sequentially executed requiring only one additional register x_2. Hence, the efficiency of the function body drastically increases, while the overall dataflow-like behaviour of a program consisting of a set of such functions remains unchanged.

3 Global Architecture

The ADAM architecture consists of several equally constructed worker modules that are connected by a network of unbuffered uni-directional channels. One special module, the *master*, is connected to the peripheral devices for input and ouput. The master handles all interactions with the outside world, in particular, it is responsible for loading and distributing the program to be executed, for triggering the execution of the program and for delivering the result values of the computation.

Each worker module of the ADAM consists of three components illustrated in Fig. 2:

- **The Arbiter** is the only unit with an interface to the neighbour modules. It receives messages from the other local units and from the neighbour modules and routes them to their correct places of destination.

[1]Sequentialization is not allowed in the case of non-strict functions, i.e. functions that may return values even if not all arguments have yet arrived. In general, a process called *strictness analysis* has to decide this question.

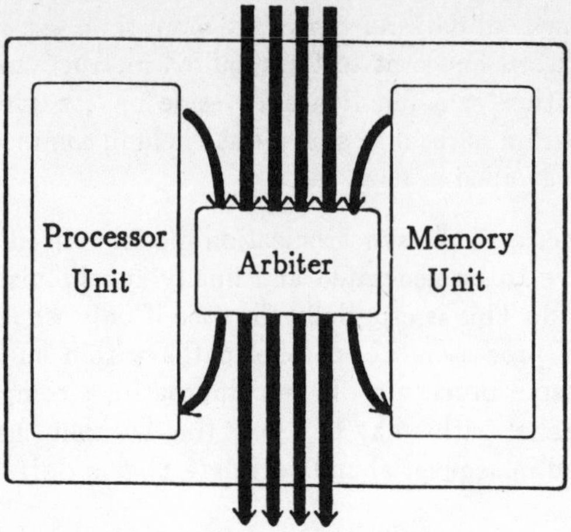

Figure 2: An ADAM Worker Module

- **The Processor Unit** executes the given program and, thereby, performs the actual computation. It receives messages (basically arguments for the local function activations) from and sends messages (basically results of local function activations) to other processors in the network.

- **The Memory Unit** contains a heap-organized store holding tuples, i.e. data structures of fixed size. Tuples may be allocated and referenced by a (local or distinct) processor via messages to the memory unit. Result values (either atomic values or tuple references) are sent as messages back to the callers.

Each worker module has only a restricted view of the network. It knows about the addresses and certain state parameters of its neighbours but has in general no global information about the network. The only exception is the arbiter that holds a network routing table in order to forward incoming messages to their correct destination.

4 The Processor Unit

The ADAM processor is basically a conventional control-driven processor with several extensions that allow the efficient simulation of dataflow behaviour. It consists of the following components (depicted in Fig. 3):

- **The Execution Unit** performs the arithmetical/logical computations.

- **The Program Store** holds a sequence of *code blocks* each of which corresponds to one user-defined function. Every processor holds the whole program code and may therefore execute any function of the program.

- **The Frame Store** is a heap-organized store holding a set of *activation frames* each of which corresponds to one particular function activation. Each frame represents

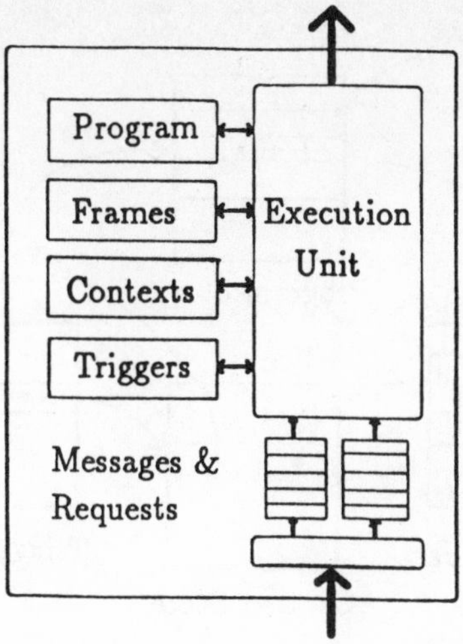

Figure 3: The ADAM Processor

the actual state of its activation by describing the contents of the registers and the state of the events.

- **The Context Store** is a table of activation descriptors called *contexts*. Each context uniquely describes one function activation on the processor by the base addresses of the activation's code block and of its register frame.

- **The Trigger Store** contains a set of *instruction triggers*, each of which is the description of a thread that may be started but has not yet been. When a `split` instruction is executed, a trigger for one branch is put into this store.

- **The Message Store** and **the Request Store** buffer all messages received. The first store holds arguments for local function activations and result values of parallel activations. The second store holds requests to activate new function instances.

The interaction between these components is illustrated in Fig. 4: When the execution of a new thread is started, the description of the actual activation (i.e. the base addresses of code block and register frame) is stored in two registers. Any register number encoded in an instruction is actually an offset to the frame pointer. Hence, every function activation has its private set of registers. All event numbers referenced by `wait` instructions are actually *negative* offsets to the frame base address. Hence, every activation has its private sets of events each of which is represented by a bit in the frame.

If a `split` instruction is executed, the start address of one of the parallel branches is pushed on the trigger store while the other one is continued by the current thread.

If a `wait` instruction fails, the actual thread is terminated. In this case, an instruction trigger is popped from the trigger store and a new thread (in the current activation) is started. Only if the trigger store is empty, a context switch has to be made and a new activation is executed. This may be triggered by one of two events:

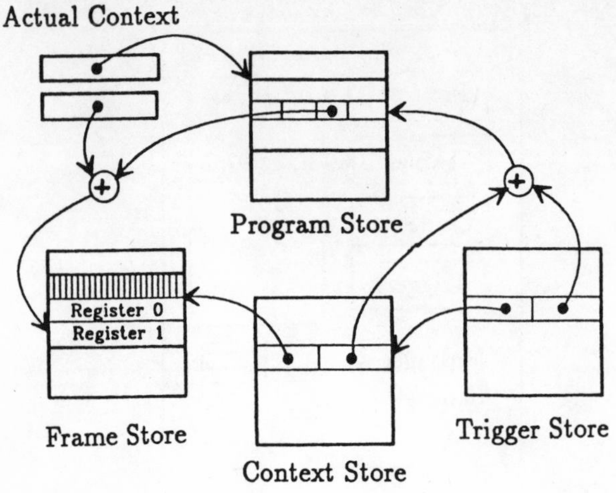

Figure 4: Interaction between Processor Components

1. A **message** is received from the message store. In this case, a new thread is started beginning with the instruction that represents the destination of the message. Such a message may either hold the argument for a function activation or it may hold the result value delivered by some activation or it may also hold the result of a memory request (see the next section).

2. An **activation request** is received from the request store. In this case, some neighbour processor has sent a request to activate a new instance of some particular function. If the processor decides to fulfill this request, a new activation frame and a new context descriptor are allocated and a reference to the context descriptor is sent back to the caller.

The decision between these two possibilities depends on the actual load of the processor. If it is heavily loaded, argument messages will be preferred, if the load is low, more activation requests will be fulfilled. This alternative is (besides the decision to which processor to send activation requests to) the basic tool for load balancing.

5 The Memory Unit

Since processor units are only able to handle atomic (integer) data, the management of compound data structures has been shifted to separate memory units. Each worker module contains one memory unit that is constructed as follows (see Fig. 5):

- **The Heap** holds a set of tuples, i.e. data structures of arbitrary but fixed size. Each field of a tuple is either empty or holds an integer atom or a tuple reference. All heaps on all network modules represent a global store, i.e. all references denote unique tuples within the network.

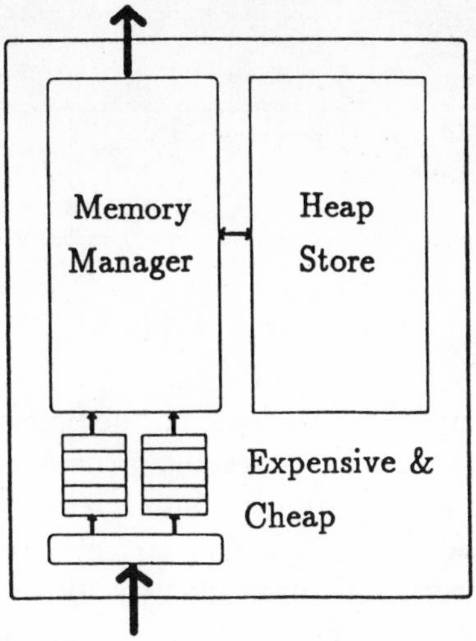

Figure 5: The ADAM Memory Unit

- **The Memory Manager** handles incoming requests to allocate a new tuple (`alloc`), to write a value into some tuple field (`write`) or to return the contents of some tuple field (`read`).
- **The "Expensive" Store** and **the "Cheap" Store** hold all incoming requests classified according to the fact whether fulfilling the request may require the allocation of heap memory ("expensive") or not ("cheap").

All tuples are **non-strict** i.e. references to them may be used even if (some or all of) their fields do not yet contain valid data. As a consequence, one process may allocate a tuple and send the tuple reference to another process *before* it has written any value into the fields of the tuple! However, in order to preserve determinism of program execution, special synchronization tools have been introduced:

Every field of a tuple has associated a **full/empty bit** indicating if a value has yet been written into this field or not. When a new tuple is allocated, all fields are marked as empty. If a read request arrives for a field that has not yet been defined, this request is put into a waiting queue and a reference to this queue is stored in the field. If then a write request for this field arrives, all waiting read requests are dequeued and the desired values are returned to the senders. However, if an attempt is made to overwrite an already defined tuple field, an error is reported. Hence, all tuples obey the **single-assignment rule** which is essential for non-strict data structures in parallel systems.

From the point of view of the ADAM instruction set, the allocation instruction `alloc` and the read instruction `read` are non-blocking: they immediately return their results, i.e. a reference to a new tuple and the contents of some tuple field, respectively. However, `read` and `write` are actually **split-phase operations**: Having submitted the memory requests, the processor immediately breaks the execution of the actual thread and starts another one. The interrupted thread is only continued at the arrival of the desired value.

Program	Input	1T / 2W Ring	2T / 2W Ring	4T / 4W Full	8T / 8W Chordal Ring	16T / 16W Torus
FIBO	20	54(1.0)	28(1.9)	16(3.3)	10(5.4)	7(7.7)
PRIMES0	2000	302(1.0)	163(1.8)	93(3.2)	59(5.1)	41(7.4)
PRIMES1	10000	237(1.0)	127(1.9)	88(2.7)	65(3.7)	51(4.6)

Figure 6: Several ADAM Benchmarks

This feature has a very important consequence on the performance of the system: since the processor does *not* have to wait for the result of a memory operation, the architecture is able to **tolerate extremely long memory latencies**. This is especially important in a distributed memory architecture, since any pointer may reference a tuple that is sited on another (even non-neighbour!) module of the network.

The ADAM architecture uses for garbage collection a **weighted reference counting algorithm**: Every tuple reference has associated a weight and every tuple has stored the sum of the weights of all pointers referencing the tuple. If this sum decreases to zero, the tuple may be reclaimed. The essential advantage of a reference counting method in contrast to other garbage collection algorithms is its suitability for distributed memory systems: garbage collection is done **during the normal computation**, all unreferenced cells are immediately reclaimed and no separate collection phase (eventually involving the whole network) is necessary.

The use of *weighted* references has the additional advantage that inter-processor communication is minimized: If a pointer is copied, both copies get half of the original weight, hence, no message to the involved tuple is necessary. Only if the weight decreases to zero, a memory request for a new reference is to be sent. In this case, the reference count of the tuple is increased (up to some upper bound considered as "infinity") and a pointer with the new weight is returned. With an eight bit reference count field and a two bit reference weight (storing the binary logarithm of the weight), the overall overhead for garbage collection is neglectible.

6 Implementation

Our work on the ADAM architecture is part of the project "ADAM & EVE" dealing with the prototype implementation of the non-strict functional programming language EVE on conventional parallel hardware using principles of dataflow architectures. The target hardware consists of a multiprocessor containing 16 INMOS T800 transputers that may be dynamically configured to the desired topology. At present, we have implemented the runtime system interpreting ADAM machine code (each transputer usually simulates one ADAM module) and a PC-based ADAM assembler generating this code.

Using this assembler, several test programs have been hand-coded and show rather promising speedups. Some of the results are listed in Fig. 6. Each column of the table represents one particular processor configuration with the number of transputers (T) used, the number of worker modules (W) simulated and the topology of the transputer network listed above. Each item in the table denotes the elapsed time in seconds, the values in parentheses denote the relative speedups achieved.

The performance of the implementation has been tested with the benchmark programs FIBO (a doubly recursive fibonacci number generator), PRIMES0 (a prime number generator using auxiliary lists) and PRIMES1 (a prime number generator making use of difference lists). The efficiency (speedup/processor ratio) ranges in both of the first test programs from more than 90 % to about 45 %. We are not yet able to estimate the influence of the processor topology on the results. The third test program shows significantly lower speedups, which is a consequence a not yet satisfactory load balancing.

7 Future Work

In the future, we will exhaustively test the ADAM architecture using various processor configurations in order to learn more about the dynamical behaviour of the machine. We will investigate several methods for load balancing and will try to improve the performance of the system by removing several bottlenecks. Simultaneously, we will work on the implementation of a compiler for the functional language EVE and experiment with several parallelelization and synchronization strategies. The overall goal of our work is to show the interrelationship between the paradigms controlflow and dataflow and to investigate how one model can be used to simulate the other one.

References

[1] J. R. Gurd, C. C. Kirkham, and I. Watson. The Manchester Prototype Dataflow Computer. *Communications of the ACM*, 28(1):34–52, January 1985.

[2] Kei Hiraki, Toshio Shimada, and Kenji Nishida. A Hardware Design of the SIGMA-1, a Data Flow Computer for Scientific Computations. In *Proceedings of the 1984 International Conference on Parallel Processing*, pages 524–531. IEEE Computer Society, August 1984.

[3] Robert Alan Iannucci. A Dataflow/von Neumann Hybrid Architecture. Technical Report MIT/LCS/TR-418, Laboratory for Computer Science, Massachusetts Institute of Technology, Cambridge, MA, May 1988.

[4] Gregory Michael Papadopoulos. *Implementation of a General Purpose Dataflow Multiprocessor*. PhD thesis, Department of Electrical Engineering and Computer Science, Massachusetts Institute of Technology, Cambridge, MA, August 1988.

[5] Wolfgang Schreiner. ADAM & EVE — An Abstract Dataflow Machine and Its Programming Language. Master's thesis, Johannes Kepler University, Linz, Austria, September 1990. Also: RISC-Linz Technical Report 90-42.

MAPPING SYSTOLIC ALGORITHMS ON DISTRIBUTED MEMORY COMPUTERS

Philippe Clauss
Laboratoire d'Informatique, Université de Franche-Comté
F - 25030 Besançon cédex

INTRODUCTION

Prefiguring the architecture evolutions, as parallel architectures, the formal presentation of *Uniform Recurrence Equations* by Karp, Miller and Winograd [8] defines a very important frame, in which the notions of data dependency, and its geometrical interpretation, of time scheduling, and its potential parallelism, are introduced. More generally, the expression of problems in terms of linear recurrence equation systems is powerful and used for vector or matrix problems in linear algebra, differential equations in discrete functional analysis.

Later on, the concept of systolic algorithms proposed by H.T. Kung [9] has been widely studied : besides the many proposals of systolic solutions for particular problems ([18], [10], [17], [5], etc.), many researchers have worked on methodologies for the design of systolic algorithms from a problem specification ([11], [15], [4], [13], [12], [6], [14], [19], [16], etc.). Because of their strict properties (identical elementary processes, local dependencies, strong synchronism) systolic algorithms offer a good framework for synthesis methods.

At the same time many parallel architectures have been developped. Among them, the Distributed Memory Parallel Computers (DMPC in the following) seem to be very promizing. These architectures are composed of nodes locally and regularly connected. The programmation and the efficient implementation on such computers have not yet received a full answer.

The general objective of all the methods of parallel solution design, in particular the systolic design methods, consist in a transformation of the equations defining the *variables* on *domains*, by mapping the domains on a cartesian product *processing space* × *timing* [2]. This mapping indicates for each point of the domains on which processor of the target architecture and at which instant it will be executed.

The aim of this paper is to give a contribution to these problems. We argue that because of their regularity and locality, processor arrays are closed to systolic solutions. So, formal tools to apply relevant synthesis techniques and to map systolic algorithms on these architectures, in a way suggested in Figure 1, are of a great interest.

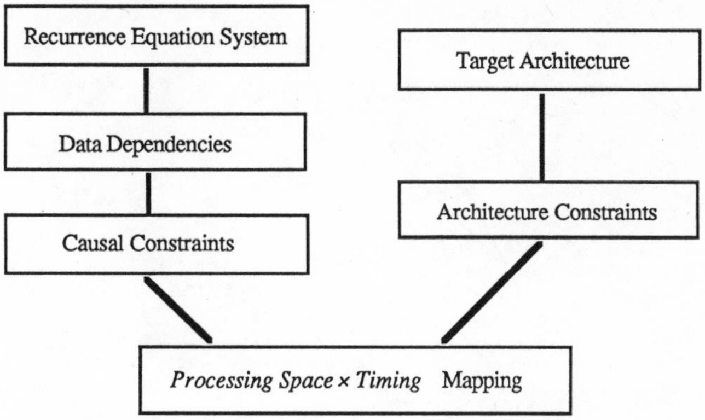

Figure 1. *Mapping recurrence equations*

Our objective is to present these tools and illustrate them on a classical example. Both first and second sections are devoted to the definition of convenient geometrical tools to synthetize systolic algorithms and map them on DMPC. These tools are used in section 3 to introduce our space-optimal mappings technique. In section 4 this technique is applied on the Gaussian elimination algorithm for which a space-optimal mapping is obtained.

1. GEOMETRICAL TOOLS TO SYNTHETIZE SYSTOLIC ALGORITHMS

The convex bounded occurrence domain $\mathcal{D}$ associated with a system of linear recurrence equations is represented in the affine space $\mathbb{Z}^p$. The points depending on the same occurrence for the associated calculations define a convex sub-polyhedron of $\mathcal{D}$. A basis of the hyperplane containing this polyhedron is composed by vectors called the *generating vectors*. Moreover this polyhedron is attached with the used occurence by a set of vectors called *inductive vectors*. These vectors define a cone which expresses the *causal constraints* of the problem. This cone can be partitionned in a set of *angular sectors*. Associated with the generating vectors, they define the *routing* of data in the solution array.

A *timing* is defined by a linear function t of the occurrences. Any timing has to satisfy a few necessary conditions induced by the causal constraints : an occurrence can be used only after its calculation. These conditions are expressed by a set of inequations : $\vec{\Psi}_x . \vec{\theta} > 0$, for any inductive vector $\vec{\Psi}_x$ associated with a variable x ($\vec{\theta}$ is a vector associated with the timing function such that for any occurrence z, $t(z) = \vec{Oz}.\vec{\theta} + \delta$, $\delta \in \mathbb{Z}$). To validate these properties some transformations of the equations or of the domain definition can be applied.

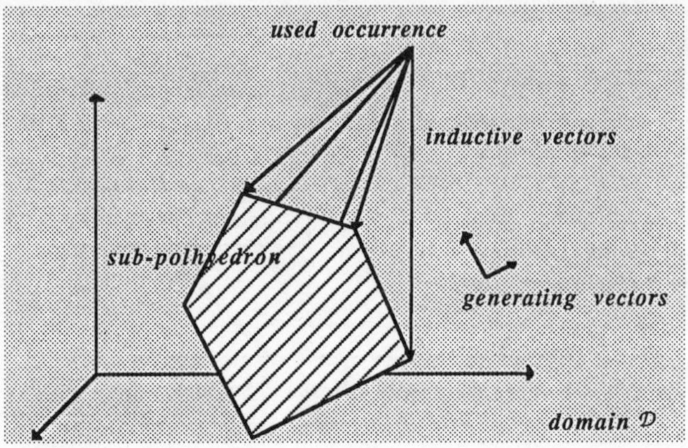

Figure 2. *geometrical modelling of dependencies*

Architecture constraints can be defined. For example, no data broadcast to define systolic algorithms, neither control stream nor programmable cells :
- the first condition is expressed by a property of the generating vectors : $\vec{\Phi}_x . \vec{\theta} \neq 0$,
- the second one may be satisfied by choosing a suitable *allocation direction.*

2. GEOMETRICAL TOOLS TO MAP ALGORITHMS ON PROCESSOR ARRAYS

The *potential parallelism* of an algorithm is the maximal number of simultaneous calculations allowed by a given timing. We are interested in mapping algorithms on processor arrays, specially in a space-optimal way, for which we present some results. Such optimal mappings use a number of processors equal to the potential parallelism. It is based on the following geometrical model of computations.

From a geometrical point of view, any linear allocation decomposes the convex bounded domain $\mathcal{D}$ into a set of lines parallel to the allocation direction $\vec{\xi}$. These lines project the domain on the systolic array surface. According to convex polyhedra properties, these parallel lines crossing $\mathcal{D}$ intersect with at least two faces of the polyhedron.

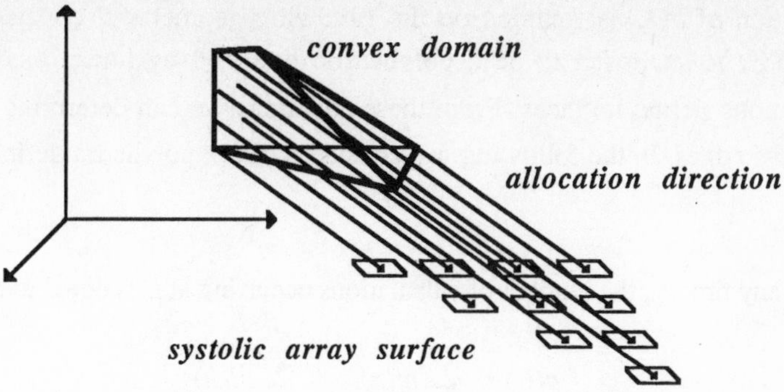

Figure 3. *geometrical modelling of a linear allocation*

With any timing function we can associate τ successive cutting planes of the convex polyhedron $\mathcal{D}$, orthogonal to the vector $\vec{\theta}$. All the points belonging to the same cutting plane are points having the same time component. Therefore, for this timing function, and for any line generated by an allocation direction $\vec{\xi}$, two intersection points define respectively the first activation time, and the last one, of the allocated processor. We call respectively *first face*, and *last face*, any hyperplane containing such points.

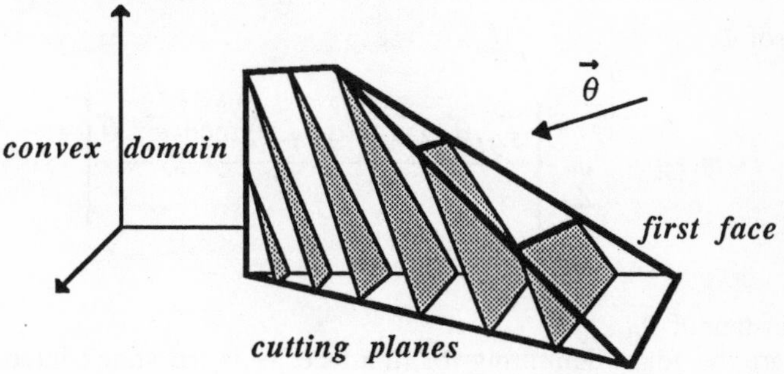

Figure 4. *geometrical modelling of the timing function*

Note that if the allocation defines one and only one first or last face, and if the intersection of this face with some cutting plane is the face itself, the deduced systolic array is space-optimal. In the other cases the following tools have to be introduced. These tools are presented for an allocation direction $\vec{\xi}$ whose time component is equal to 1. They can be generalized for any vector $\vec{\xi}$ [3].

For any timing function t and for any time t_0 we define the number of simultaneous calculations $p(t_0)$. The potential parallelism p is then defined by $p = max_{1 \leq t_0 \leq \tau}\, p(t_0)$.

The definition of $p(t_0)$ is founded on the following geometrical considerations. The convex domain $\mathcal{D}$ is supposed to be a polyhedron bounded by linear inequalities. The associated equations define its faces. From these equations we can determine *edge vectors* which generate its edges. In the following, we consider convex polyhedra defined from these vectors e_q.

Property. - For any time t_0, the number of calculations occurring at t_0 is equal to :

$$p(t_0) = \sum_{h=1}^{t_0} nf(h) - \sum_{h=1}^{t_0-1} nl(h)$$

where for any h in $1..\tau$, $nf(h)$ and $nl(h)$ are defined as following :

$$nf(h) = Card\,\{z \in \mathcal{D} \,/\, t(z) = h \text{ and } \vec{\mathcal{F}}.\vec{Oz} + f = 0\}$$
$$nl(h) = Card\,\{z \in \mathcal{D} \,/\, t(z) = h \text{ and } \vec{\mathcal{L}}.\vec{Oz} + l = 0\}$$

where $\vec{\mathcal{F}}.\vec{Oz} + f = 0$ (respectively $\vec{\mathcal{L}}.\vec{Oz} + l = 0$) is the equation of the plane generated by the edge vectors of the first (respectively last) face. We note $\vec{\mathcal{F}_s}$ and $\vec{\mathcal{L}_s}$ the vectors that generate the simultaneously active points in these faces.

These values $nf(h)$ and $nl(h)$ are defined at intervals $D_{ij} \subset [1..\tau]$ where D_{ij} is the time interval whose extremities are the intersection of a line generated by $\vec{\mathcal{F}_s}$ (respectively $\vec{\mathcal{L}_s}$) and the edges ed_i, ed_j of $\mathcal{D}$.

$$nf(t_0) = \sum_{q=0}^{\left\lfloor \frac{v_{ij0}}{\vec{e_i}.\vec{\theta}} \right\rfloor} \left\lfloor \frac{\vec{e_j}.\vec{\theta} - (\vec{v}_{ij0} - q\,\vec{e_i}.\vec{\theta}) \bmod \vec{e_j}.\vec{\theta}}{\vec{e_j}.\vec{\theta}} \right\rfloor$$

where
- t_0 is any given instant of D_{ij}.
- if ed_i and ed_j are the edges delimiting the first face, v_{ij} is the vertex intersection of these edges. We note $v_{ij0} = |\, t_0 - t(v_{ij})\,|$.
- $\vec{e_i}$ and $\vec{e_j}$ are the edge vectors generating ed_i and ed_j.

Note that in this value, i and j may be exchanged. Note also that the function *nl* is characterized in the same way. The demonstration of this property is given in [3].

3. SPACE-OPTIMAL MAPPINGS ON DISTRIBUTED MEMORY COMPUTERS

By projecting both vectors $\vec{\mathcal{F}_s}$ and $\vec{\mathcal{L}_s}$, along any allocation direction $\vec{\xi}$ we can represent them at the level of the systolic architecture associated with $\vec{\xi}$. For any time t_0 we call $\mathcal{L}t_0$ the line generated by $\vec{\mathcal{L}_s}$, at t_0, and $\mathcal{F}t_{0+\vec{\xi}.\vec{\theta}}$ the line generated by $\vec{\mathcal{F}_s}$ at $t_0 + \vec{\xi}.\vec{\theta}$. These lines characterize a cone containing the active calculations at t_0. The top of this cone is a virtual calculation point whose duration is negative.

A *folding mapping* allocates the calculations of $\mathcal{L}t_0$ and the calculations of $\mathcal{F}t_{0+}\vec{\xi}.\vec{\theta}$ to the same processor of the array. We note *np* the number of processors needed for this mapping. We prove the following theorem in [3] :

Theorem. - for any allocation direction $\vec{\xi}$ whose time component is 1, $np = p$, i.e. this mapping is space-optimal.

In the general case where the time component of $\vec{\xi}$ is > 1, this mapping is completed with a *coalescing* of non simultaneous calculations on the same processor. Such a mapping is determined by defining a set of allocation direction sequences of the form $\{\vec{\xi_1}, \vec{\xi_2}, ..., \vec{\xi_q}\}$ such that :

$$- \; q = \vec{\xi}.\vec{\theta}$$

$$- \; |\vec{\xi_m}.\vec{\theta}| = 1 \qquad \forall m \in 1..q$$

$$- \sum_{m=1}^{q} \vec{\xi_m} = \vec{\xi}$$

4. EXAMPLE : THE GAUSSIAN ELIMINATION ALGORITHM

The problem is to solve the linear system $Ax = b$ where A is a n×n matrix and b a n vector. In order to solve it, the Gaussian elimination algorithm first transforms A into an equivalent triangulate matrix and then solves the triangular system. We are only concerned here by the triangularization of A. Since the transformation affects vector b, we consider that A is a n×n+1 matrix whose last column is b. The elements of the resulting triangular matrix are defined as the final recurrence step $a(i,j,n-1)$ of the following system of recurrence equations :

$$a(i,j,0) = \begin{cases} a_{ij} & \text{if } j < n+1 \\ b_i & \text{if } j = n+1 \end{cases} \qquad 1 \le i \le n,\ 1 \le j \le n+1$$

$$a(i,j,k) = a(i,j,k-1) - c(i,k,k) \times a(k,j,k-1) \qquad 1 \le k \le n-1,\ k+1 \le i \le n,\ k+1 \le j \le n+1$$

$$c(i,k,k) = a(i,k,k-1) \,/\, a(k,k,k-1) \qquad 1 \le k \le n-1,\ k+1 \le i \le n$$

An optimal pure systolic timing is defined by the linear function $t(i,j,k) = i+j+k-3$. By projecting points relatively to the direction $\vec{\xi} = (1,1,1)$ we obtain the systolic array in Figure 5.

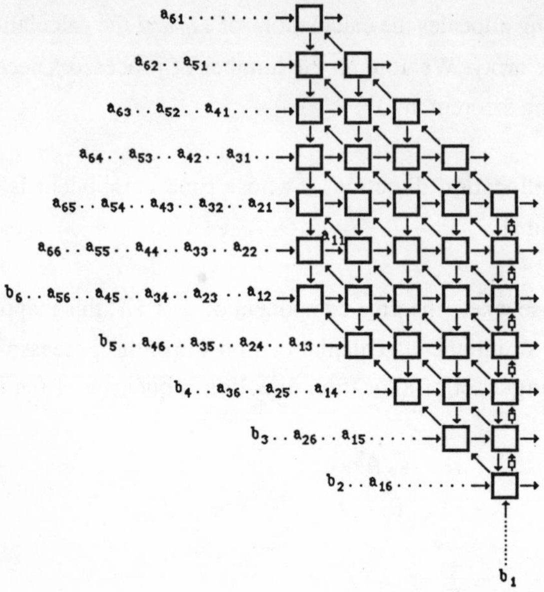

Figure 5. *A systolic solution the Gaussian elimination problem.*

The convex polyhedron of $\mathbb{Z}^3$ associated with this problem is defined from the following edge vectors :

$\vec{e_1} = (0,1,0)$ $\quad\vec{e_4} = (1,0,1)$ $\quad\vec{e_7} = (0,0,1)$

$\vec{e_2} = (1,0,0)$ $\quad\vec{e_5} = (1,0,0)$ $\quad\vec{e_8} = (0,1,1)$

$\vec{e_3} = (1,1,1)$ $\quad\vec{e_6} = (0,1,0)$ $\quad\vec{e_9} = (0,1,0)$

For the allocation direction $\vec{\xi} = (1,1,1)$, the orthogonal vector of the first face is $\vec{\mathcal{F}} = (0,0,1)$ and the orthogonal vectors of the last faces are $\vec{\mathcal{L}_1} = (1,0,0)$ and $\vec{\mathcal{L}_2} = (0,1,0)$. The unimodular vectors $\vec{\mathcal{F}_s}$, $\vec{\mathcal{L}_{1s}}$ and $\vec{\mathcal{L}_{2s}}$ are :

$\vec{\mathcal{F}_s} = (1,-1,0)$ $\quad\vec{\mathcal{L}_{1s}} = (0,-1,1)$ $\quad\vec{\mathcal{L}_{2s}} = (-1,0,1)$

The potential parallelism can be determined from the expressions of $nf(t_0)$ and $nl(t_0)$. These expressions are defined at intervals as following :

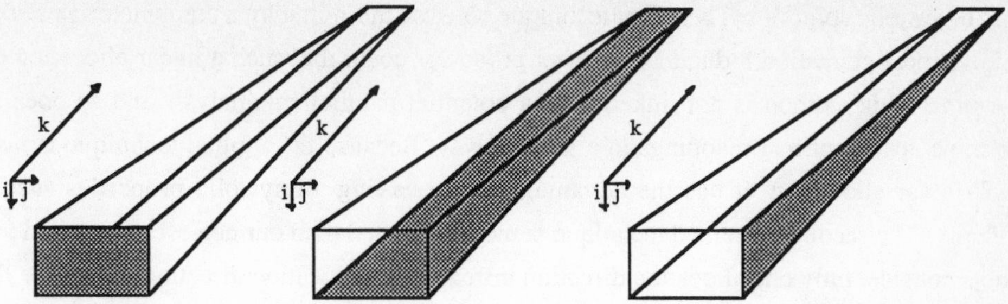

Figure 6. *First face and last faces for the Gaussian elimination algorithm and* $\vec{\xi} = (1,1,1)$.

First activations :

$$\forall\, t_0 \in [1..3n\text{-}5],\ nf(t_0) = \sum_{q=0}^{\left\lfloor \frac{3n-5-t_0}{2} \right\rfloor} \left\lfloor \frac{3 - (3n-5-t_0-2q) \bmod 3}{3} \right\rfloor$$

$$\forall\, t_0 \in [3n\text{-}4..3n\text{-}3],\ nf(t_0) = 0$$

Last activations :

$$\forall\, t_0 \in [1..n],\ nl(t_0) = 0$$

$$\forall\, t_0 \in [n+1..3n\text{-}3],\ nl(t_0) = \left\lfloor \frac{3n-3-t_0}{2} \right\rfloor + 1$$

For example, it is equal to $p = 10$ for $n = 6$.

The time component of the systolic allocation direction is $\vec{\xi}.\vec{\theta} = 3$. Then, a *folding mapping* can be deduced from the two cones $[\mathcal{L}1t_0 , \mathcal{F}t_0{+}3]$ and $[\mathcal{L}2t_0 , \mathcal{F}t_0{+}3]$ for any $t_0 \in [1..3n\text{-}3]$. To complete the mapping we apply a *coalescing* technique according to these two decompositions of the vector $\vec{\xi}$ (see Figure 7) :

$$\vec{\xi}_1 = (0,1,0),\quad \vec{\xi}_2 = (0,1,0),\quad \vec{\xi}_3 = (1,-1,1)$$
$$\vec{\xi}_1 = (0,0,1),\quad \vec{\xi}_2 = (0,0,1),\quad \vec{\xi}_3 = (1,1,-1)$$

which determines a space-optimal array.

CONCLUSION

In the literature a few works are developped about optimal mapping of systolic algorithms. In [20] Wong and Delosme present two allocation techniques allowing to reduce the processor count of systolic solutions. Their first technique consists in finding by a combinatorial method the best linear allocation inducing the lower processor count that such a linear allocation can determine. This method is not linked with a potential parallelism analysis and so does not determine space-optimal mappings in a general way. Because the applied technique is just a "best" linear allocation, it has the advantage of preserving all systolic properties such as regularity. The second presented technique is more restricted than our coalescing method : the authors consider only one allocation direction instead of an allocation direction sequence. This restriction induces the lack of possible and interesting systolic cells groupings. They also consider always the same cells grouping for a given systolic solution, which is not sufficient to get the lowest number of processors allowed by this method. Moreover, an explicit definition of the minimum number of processors reached by this method (see [3]) allows to conclude for any given systolic algorithm that only one of the presented mapping methods or both are needed to reach the space-optimality.

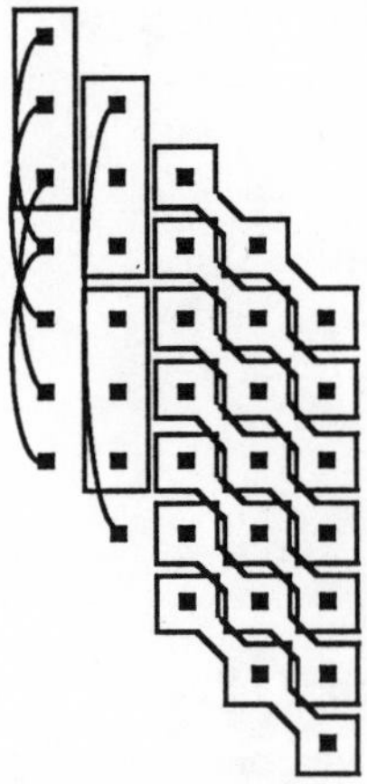

Figure 7. *Coalescing and folding techniques for a space-optimal mapping.*

The folding method gives space-optimal architectures. The price to pay can be the lost of scalability. Some existing algorithms dealing with planarity tests [7] and plane graphs drawings [1] can be an answer to this problem. Moreover, our results can be extended to restrict the class of solutions to regular ones, to aim *asymptotic* optimality.

Last a few works are developped about optimal mappings of systolic algorithms for given examples. This paper shows that a method can be proposed, free of any given example and that any systolic solution induces space-optimal mappings. The geometrical tools and the two mapping methods are powerful enough to be used in a general way, assuming that the problem can be expressed in terms of recurrence equations whose recurrence steps can be linearly time ordered.

Therefore, our calculus of space-optimal mappings should be easily implemented as an extension of existing tools as *Systol*. This would be the starting point for mapping algorithms on array processors, by determining the most efficient linear timings associated with a potential parallelism equal to the number of processors of some given architecture.

BIBLIOGRAPHY

[1] N. Chiba, K. Onoguchi and T. Nishizeki, *Drawing plane graphs nicely,* Acta Informatica 22, pages 187-201, 1985.

[2] Choo Y., Chen M.C., *A theory of program optimization,* TR-608, Yale Univ., 1988.

[3] Clauss Ph., *Synthèse d'algorithmes systoliques et implantation optimale en place sur réseaux de processeurs synchrones,* Thèse Univ. Franche-Comté (France), 1990.

[4] Delosme J.M., Ipsen I.C.F., *An illustration of a methodology for the construction of efficient systolic architectures in VLSI,* Int. Symp. on VLSI Technology, Taipei, 1985.

[5] Delosme J.M., *A parallel algorithm for the algebraic path problem,* Int. Workshop on Parallel and distributed Algorithms, North-Holland, 1988.

[6] Fortes J.A.B., Fu K.S., Wah B.W., *Systematic approaches to the design of algorithmically specified systolic arrays,* Int. Conf. on Acoustics, 1987.

[7] J. Hopcroft and R. Tarjan, *Efficient planarity testing,* JACM, Vol 21, 4, October 74, pages 549-568.

[8] Karp R.M., Miller R.E., Winograd S., *The organization of computations for uniform recurrence equations,* JACM, 14, 3, 1967.

[9] Kung H.T., *Why systolic architectures?,* Computer, 15, 1, 1982.

[10] Kung S.Y., Lo S.C., Lewis P.S., *Optimal systolic design for the transitive closure and the shortest path problem,* IEEE Trans. Computers, C-36, 5, 1987.

[11] Moldovan D.I, *On the design of algorithms for VLSI systolic arrays,* IEEE, 71, 1, 1983.

[12] Moldovan D.I., Fortes J.A.B., *Partitioning and mapping algorithms into fixed size systolic arrays,* IEEE Trans. on Computers, 35, 1, 1986.

[13] Mongenet C., *Une méthode de conception d'algorithmes systoliques,* Thèse INPL, Nancy (France), 1985.

[14] Mongenet C., Perrin G.R., *Synthesis of systolic arrays for inductive problems,* PARLE, Lect. Notes in Comp. Sc., 259, 1987.

[15] Quinton P., *Automatic syntheses of systolic arrays from uniform recurrence equations,* IEEE Symp. on Computer Architectures, 1984.

[16] Quinton P., Van Dongen V., *The mapping of linear recurrence equations on regular arrays,* Journal of VLSI Signal processing, 1, 1989.

[17] Robert Y., Trystram D., *Systolic solution of the algebraic path problem, Int. Workshop on systolic arrays,* Oxford, Adam-Hilger, 1987.

[18] Rote G., *A systolic array algorithm for the algebraic path problem,* Computing, 34, 1985.

[19] Yaacobi Y., Cappello P.R., *Scheduling a system of affine recurrence equations onto a systolic array,* Int. Conf. on systolic arrays, San Diego, 1988.

[20] Y. Wong and J.-M. Delosme, *Optimization of processor count for systolic arrays,* research report YALEU/DCS/RR-697, May 1989.

A COMPILER FOR A DISTRIBUTED INFERENCE MODEL

C. Percebois, N. Signès, P. Agnoletto

Institut de Recherche en Informatique de Toulouse
Université Paul Sabatier
118, route de Narbonne
31062 Toulouse Cedex - France

Abstract

This paper summarizes the main features of the CIAM Virtual Machine designed to efficiently compile and run large logic programs. The CIAM instruction set is closely tied to the COALA architecture, a Message-Based Multiprocessor whose aim is to bring to bear the parallelism inherent to PROLOG programs i.e. without any programmer's direct intervention.

1. THE AND/OR CONNECTION GRAPH MODEL

COALA (An Actor-Oriented Computer for Logic Programming and its Applications) uses R. Kowalski's connection graph [KOW79] and its proof procedure as parallel inference model [PER87, PER88]. Given a set of clauses, the associated connection graph contains an arc for each pair of matching literals on the opposite side of the implication arrow. The basic operation of the connection graph proof procedure is the selection of an arc and the incorporation of the associated resolvent into the connection graph.

1.1. Parallelism in the AND/OR Connection Graph

An arc is a set of bindings <variable,term> and links towards other arcs. A top-down strategy orientates the arcs of the graph from the conditions to the conclusions. So, an arc connects two parent clauses, called in the COALA terminology, the *Origin Clause* and the *Extremity Clause*. In our implementation, a set of bindings is split up into two subsets : the *Origin Environment* (OE) holds the variables of the origin clause and the *Extremity Environment* (EE) holds the variables of the extremity clause. Associated with the literals of the origin and extremity clauses are the *List of Brothers* (LB) and the *List of Sons* (LS) ; such lists contain, for each literal, the sublist of the arcs descending from that literal. In addition, a *Dependency Table* (DT) memorizes, for each variable, the list of literals in which the variable occurs.

To build the resolvent of an arc, unifications between its environment and the environment of the arcs descending from the parent clauses are attempted. Only the arcs descending from the parent clauses can produce the arcs of the resolvent. Each success builds a new arc. If arc Aj is chosen for the resolution, we note by Ai o Aj an arc produced by an arc Ai descending from the extremity clause (son arc) and by Ai x Aj an arc produced by an arc Ai descending from the origin clause (brother arc). Note that arcs Ai x Aj and Ai o Aj are built with the same algorihm, without identifying them as son or brother arcs.

1.2. Parallel resolution with the AND/OR Connection Graph

At the end of a precompilation step, arcs of the connection graph are distributed among a large number of interconnected computing nodes that asynchronously cooperate via message passing. The main messages of the COALA parallel model are :

- RESOLVE-REQ : construction of the resolvent of an arc,
- UNIFY-REQ : unification of environments,
- UNIFY-ACK : acknowledgement of a successful unification,
- UNIFY-NACK : acknowledgement of a unsuccessful unification,
- DESTROY-REQ : deletion of a resolvent.

1.2.1. Resolution

The resolution chooses the leftmost literal of a resolvent. Each arc descending from that literal receives a RESOLVE-REQ request, containing the identification of all brother arcs of the chosen literal. An arc receiving a RESOLVE-REQ request sends its unification environment to each of its sons and brothers in UNIFY-REQ requests. The answer to a UNIFY-REQ request is a UNIFY-ACK message in case of success, and a UNIFY-NACK message in case of failure. When a success has occured when building the resolvent, the resolution goes on with the choice of a new literal to resolve. The resolution of an arc having neither brother nor son corresponds to the generation of the empty clause. Such an arc contains a solution of the initial goal.

1.2.2. Unification

An arc receiving a UNIFY-REQ request unifies its environment against the environment of the request. New bindings can appear in the new arc. If the unification succeeds, a new arc is created in the same local memory of the old arc and a UNIFY-ACK answer is sent back ; otherwise, a UNIFY-NACK answer is sent back.

1.2.3. Garbage collection

Throughout the resolution of a goal, the graph is dynamically modified. New arcs are added and old ones are deleted. The location in the memory associated with a deleted arc can be garbage collected. Two messages of the model ensure the complete garbage collection of the graph.

2. OVERVIEW OF THE CIAM VIRTUAL MACHINE

CIAM (Coala Inference Abstract Machine) was motivated by a compiled implementation of the COALA model, as for the compiled implementation of the Prolog language [CLO85, DOB84, WAR77, WAR83]. The main idea is to translate an arc and its behaviour into a sequence of CIAM instructions associated with the basic operations of the parallel connection graph proof procedure : resolution, unification and garbage collection. As a result, CIAM is not an extension of the WAM architecture [WAR83], like ANLWAM (an OR-Parallel Prolog Architecture) [BUT86] and RAP-WAM (a Restricted AND-Parallel Prolog Architecture) [HER86] which rely upon the classical AND/OR resolution tree and introduce several management rules between parent and child processes, are.

Most of these parallel model implementations are based on the Abstract Machine proposed by Warren. As an example, the RAP-WAM Machine [HER86] applies similar techniques to those bought by Warren. In addition, a "Goal Stack" and the inclusion of "Parcall Frames" in the Local Stack of the WAM are proposed. The WAM instruction set is extended by special instructions for AND-Parallelism such as check instructions, goal scheduling instructions and control instructions. In our approach, as the connection graph and its proof procedure are used, no similar techniques can't be performed.

2.1. The CIAM storage model

The CIAM storage model is composed of four main areas : the *message FIFO queue* for incoming and outcoming messages, the *arc FIFO queue* holding the frames of the arcs, the *heap* holding the environments of the arcs and the *code space*, a static area holding the CIAM instructions. Binding a variable to a new structure is implemented by creating the structure on the heap and referencing the structure from the frame associated with the arc.

Besides these areas, the CIAM virtual machine has a number of special locations called registers. Some registers are used to hold the data of an arc : OE (Origin Environment pointer), EE (Extremity Environment pointer), LS (List of Sons pointer), LB (List of Brothers pointer), STS (Status : resolving, unifying or deleting), RCT (Reference Counter). These six registers, initialized by an *enter* instruction, define the context of an arc during the resolution and unification processes.

2.2. The CIAM actor blocks

The object-code produced by the compilation of the AND/OR connection graph is composed of independent blocks called *actor blocks*. An actor block is a script, which specifies the action that the actor will take when it receives a message, and data, which specify the particular instructions used by the script [HEW77]. Actor blocks are scenarios of their intented use. For the CIAM virtual machine, they correspond to the three behaviours of an arc : resolving, unifying or garbage collecting. In this section, we present resolution and unification blocks.

2.2.1. Resolution blocks

Related to the resolution messages are the resolution blocks RESOLVE-REQ, UNIFY-ACK and UNIFY-NACK.

i) The RESOLVE-REQ block

When receiving a RESOLVE-REQ message, one must send UNIFY-REQ requests to son and brother arcs with the unification environment of the arc, and waits the UNIFY-ACK and UNIFY-NACK answers.

First, the arc duplicates the list of sons and the list of brothers in order to build independent resolvents. Duplication is performed by the *duplicate_list_of_sons* and *duplicate_list_of_brothers* instructions, using registers LS and LB. The extremity environment is sent to son arcs owing to the *send_unify_req_to_sons* instruction and the origin one is sent to brother arcs owing to the *send_unify_req_to_brothers* instruction. Specific parts of the RESOLVE-REQ block are the transfer instructions which copy the parameters of a message from the heap to the message FIFO queue. These instructions depend on the context provided by the register EE for the extremity environment and by the register OE for the origin environment. They are selected owing to the *switch_on_extremity_variable* and *switch_on_origin_variable* instructions which indicate the location of the transfer instructions.

The script of the RESOLVE-REQ block is described by the Figure 1.

```
RESOLVE-REQ :    reallocate_arc
                 duplicate_list_of_sons
                 duplicate_list_of_brothers

L1 :             switch_on_extremity_variable  Si, n
                 send_unify_req_to_sons
                 continue L1

L2 :             switch_on_origin_variable  Bi, m
                 send_unify_req_to_brothers
                 continue L2
                 return
```

Figure 1 : Script of the RESOLVE-REQ block

As the resolvent is a list, we need iterative instructions to send a UNIFY-REQ message to each component of the list. We use the *continue L* instruction to return to a switch instruction that require invoking a transfer action and cause a branch to occur. This instruction acts as a *repeat ... until ...* instruction in procedural languages and needs a special register, NB, associated with the length of a list. When the value of the register NB is set to zero, execution continues with the next instruction of the script.

Labels Si and Bi point to switch tables used as guides to the transfer instructions *put_constant*, *put_variable* and *put_structure*. The second parameter of a switch instruction is the size of the environment. A switch table component is merely a pair <instructions counter,first instruction label> where the first argument indicates the number of transfer instructions executed for an origin or extremity variable and the second argument indicates the beginning of the object-code for that variable. The *put_structure* instruction copies the function symbol of the referenced structure in the message FIFO queue ; terms of the structure are processed by the execution of the *put_constant* and *put_variable* instructions immediately following the *put_structure* instruction. Execution of the *put_constant* instruction copies the constant in the message FIFO queue ; execution of the *put_variable* instruction causes the dereferenced value of the variable to be copied.

Variables of a clause are numbered from zero upwards ; this index is used to directly access code and so increase efficiency. Such an organization to find the code for a variable results from the undefined order of arrivals of variables to be unified against the environment of an arc.

ii) The UNIFY-ACK and UNIFY-NACK blocks

When receiving a UNIFY-ACK or a UNIFY-NACK answer, an arc updates its list of sons and brothers. It replaces the address of the old arc by the newly created arc in case of UNIFY-ACK answer, or, suppresses the arc from the list in case of UNIFY-NACK answer. These are performed by the *modify_son_or_brother L1,L2,L3* and *delete_son_or_brother L1,L2,L3* instructions.

A reference counter associated with an arc is used to count answers, causing a branch to label L3, when its value is not equal to zero. Otherwise, if at least the resolvent has an unlinked literal, a branch to label L2 occurs. This situation arises when all the arcs of a sublist of sons or brothers answer UNIFY-NACK. In this case, the status of the arc is set to deleting.

If the resolvent has been built with success, a branch to the label L1 occurs when only one arc has been created for the leftmost literal of the resolvent ; otherwise, execution continues to the next instruction of the script. The label L1 appears in a garbage collecting block, not described in this paper.

The scripts of the UNIFY-ACK and UNIFY-NACK blocks are described by the Figure 2.

```
UNIFY-ACK :      modify_son_or_brother L1,L2,L3
L :              send_incr_nb_resolvents_req
L3 :             return

UNIFY-NACK :     delete_son_or_brother L1,L2,L3
                 jump L

L2 :             send_destroy_resolvent_req
                 destroy_arc
                 return
```

Figure 2 : Scripts of the UNIFY-ACK and UNIFY-NACK blocks

The *destroy_arc* instruction sets the mark field of the arc as an inaccessible arc. If the arc is at the same location as the top of the arc FIFO queue, it will be automatically garbaged. Memory space is then recovered and the next arc in the FIFO queue is examined to be garbaged, and so on until the garbage collection process finds an accessible arc.

2.2.2. Unification blocks

Unification of the environment of an arc against the received environment in a UNIFY-REQ request is the most important operation of the parallel model and is taken into account by the UNIFY-REQ block. As for the RESOLVE-REQ block, this block uses a switch table for unifying the variables of an arc. Instructions executed are the *unify_constant*, *unify_variable*, *unify_structure*, *get_constant*, *get_variable* and *assign_extremity_variable* instructions.

In case of success, a new frame arc is allocated in the arc FIFO queue by the *allocate* instructions and a UNIFY-ACK message is sent to the caller arc owing to the *send_unify_ack* instruction ; otherwise, a *send_unify_nack* instruction is produced.

The script of the UNIFY-REQ block is described by the Figure 3.

```
UNIFY-REQ :       switch_on_variable Ti, n
SUCCESS :         allocate_new_arc
                  allocate_origin_variables
                  allocate_extremity_variables
                  send_unify_ack
L :               deallocate_arc
                  return

FAIL :            send_unify_nack
                  jump L
```

Figure 3 : Script of the UNIFY-REQ block

The *unify* and *get* instructions access the dereferenced value of the variable designated by the *switch_on_variable* instruction and unify the term received in the message against this dereferenced value. If the unification fails, a branch to the label *fail* occurs ; otherwise, the execution returns to the *switch_on_variable* instruction for unifying the next variable of the UNIFY-REQ message. This process occurs again until there is no variable in the received environment. Two special registers, N and PS, are used by the *switch_on_variable* instruction to execute this repeating process. N is the number of variables received in the UNIFY-REQ request and PS maintains the address of the *switch_on_variable* instruction to restore the PC program counter when the unification succeeds.

Note that the newly created arc is allocated in the arc queue only when a unification is successfully completed. When the value of the register N is set to zero, execution continues with the instruction specified by the label *success* in order to execute the *allocate* instructions.

Each variable of the origin and extremity environments of an arc is split up into two data : the index, stored in the arc queue, and the binding, stored in the heap. When unifying an unbound variable, structure sharing for a non-reference construct and structure copying for a reference construct are used. In particular, new bindings can be created by reusing existing structures. This prevents a large amount copying static parts of a binding. However, when unifying an unbound variable against a reference construct and because an arc is an autonomous entity, copying dynamic parts of a construct is necessary. Distinction between static and dynamic parts is implemented by a reference counter associated with the term in the heap.

Another interesting point of the unification process is the *assign_extremity_variable n* instruction. Execution of this instruction causes a new binding to be set for the extremity variable *n*. Assign an extremity variable is necessary to catch the value of an origin variable, as only the origin environment of an arc is directly concerned by the unification process. This instruction ensures communication between the two environments of an arc : values of the origin environment will be sent to son arcs later on, owing to the extremity environment.

Unification of a subterm of a structure is processed by the execution of the *get_constant* and *get_variable* instructions. The *get_constant* instruction is produced when the binding of the subterm in the initial AND/OR connection graph is a constant ; otherwise, the compiler produces a *get_variable* instruction.

3. FIRST EXPERIMENTAL RESULTS

A first version of the CIAM Abstract Machine is now available on a message passing communication based computer using Transputers. Table 1 shows times and speedups for different numbers of processors up to 36. Benchmarks considered are *ibm-40* (a database about IBM personal computers), *map* (a program for colouring several countries) and *cousin* (a family tree).

Programme	MPROLOG Sun3/50	CIAM (4)	CIAM (8)	CIAM (16)	CIAM (36)
ibm-40	300 ms	562 ms	345 ms	270 ms	200 ms
map	920 ms	870 ms	614 ms	543 ms	544 ms
cousin	360 ms	699 ms	447 ms	383 ms	323 ms

Table 1 : Times ans speedups

As indicated by this table, the performance results are encouraging. On one processor, CIAM is about 2.5 times slower than MProlog (one a fasted commercial systems) on a Sun 3/50 : for the *map* colouring problem, we obtained 920 ms with MProlog and 2097 ms with CIAM. On 4 processors, the duration of the execution is similar to the sequential implementation one and absolute performances are obtained while increasing the number of processors. These performance results demonstrate the feasibility of the COALA model and can be compared to others prototypes like Aurora [LUS88] and PEPSys [BAR88].

CONCLUSION

CIAM is an implementation of the AND/OR connection graph proof procedure. Both AND- and OR-parallelism are supported by arcs connecting two parent clauses. Each arc is an actor composed of an unification environment and links towards other distant arcs.

Associated with the behaviours of an arc are the actor blocks. Scripts of an arc specify the action that the arc will take when it receives a message. Because scripts are common to all arcs of the AND/OR graph, they can be shared within the code area.

All the CIAM virtual machine areas are FIFO queues, reducing the garbage collection process implementation. Garbage collection of memory blocks is based on reference counters, allowing a real-time algorithm.

The first version of the CIAM virtual machine is available on a message passing communication based computer. First experimental results are encouraging and demonstrate the basic feasibility of the COALA model.

ACKNOWLEDGEMENTS

This work has been realized within Professor R. Beaufils's team in the "Institut de Recherche en Informatique de Toulouse" Laboratory, at the University Paul Sabatier in Toulouse, France. It is supported by the "Gréco de Programmation du CNRS", France.

REFERENCES

[BAR88] U. Baron, J. Chassin de Kergommeaux, M. Hailperin, M. Ratcliffe, P. Robert, J.-C. Syre, H. Westphal - The Parallel ECRC Prolog System PEPSys : an Overview and Evaluation Results, Proceedings of the International Conference on Fifth Generation Computer Systems 1988, Tokyo, Japan, november 28-december 2, 1988, pp. 841-850.

[BUT86] R. Butler, E.L. Lusk, R.Olson, R.A. Overbeek. ANLWAM : A Parallel Implementation of the Warren Abstract Machine. Argonne National Laboratory, Argonne, IL 60439, 1986.

[CLO85] W.F. Clocksin. Design and Simulation of a Sequential Prolog Machine. New Generation Computing, Vol. 3, n° 1, 1985, pp. 101-120.

[DOB84] T. Dobry, Tep. A Prolog Machine Architecture. Technical Note, Computer Science Division, University of California, Berkeley, 1984.

[HER86] M.V. Hermenegildo. An Abstract Machine for the Restricted AND-Parallel Execution of Logic Programs. Third International Conference on Logic Programming, Imperial College, 1986, pp. 25-39.

[HEW77] C. Hewitt. Viewing Control Structures as Patterns of Passing Messages. Artificial Intelligence (8), pp. 323-364, 1977.

[KOW79] R. Kowalski. Logic for Problem Solving, Computer Science Library, Elsevier, 1979.

[LUS88] E. Lusk, R. Butler, T. Disz, R. Olson, R. Overbeek, R. Stevens, D.H.D. Warren, A. Calderwood, P. Szeredi, S. Haridi, P. Brand, M. Carlsson, A. Ciepielewski, B. Hausman - The Aurora OR-Parallel Prolog System, Proceedings of the International Conference on Fifth Generation Computer Systems 1988, Tokyo, Japan, november 28-december 2, 1988, pp. 819-830.

[PER87] C. Percebois, I. Futo, I. Durand, C. Simon, B. Bonhoure. Simulation Results of a Multiprocessor PROLOG Architecture based on a Distributed AND/OR Graph. International Joint Conference on Theory and Practice of Software Development, TAPSOFT'87, pp. 126-139, Pisa, Italy, 1987.

[PER88] C. Percebois, I. Durand, I. Futo. Parallel Execution of Independent Subgoals. International Symposium on Distributed Systems, Methods and Applications, IFAC-DIS'88, Varna, Bulgaria, 1988.

[WAR77] D.H.D. Warren. Implementing Prolog - Compiling Predicate Logic Programs. D.A.I. Research Reports n° 39 and 40, University of Edinburgh, 1977.

[WAR83] D.H.D. Warren. An Abstract Prolog Instruction Set. Technical Report 309, Artificial Intelligence Center, SRI International, 1983.

Making PEACE a Dynamic Alterable System*

Henning Schmidt

GMD FIRST
Hardenbergplatz 2, 1000 Berlin 12, FRG

ABSTRACT

The PEACE distributed operating system makes massively parallel systems fit for use. This paper describes the PEACE incremental loading scheme, encompassing two aspects. First, it provides capabilities for starting and initializing distributed or parallel applications and application-oriented operating systems. For systems consisting of many hundreds to thousands of nodes this is a problem which up to now is generally not solved satisfactory. Second, incremental loading supports dynamic alterations, taking advantage of the transparency supplied by a distributed symbolic naming system.

1. Introduction

Massively parallel systems like SUPRENUM [Giloi 1988] and GENESIS [Giloi 1989] are multiprocessor systems, consisting of many hundreds to thousands of autonomous nodes interconnected by a very high speed network. The nodes are equipped only with local memory and, hence, constitute a distributed memory architecture. System-wide message passing then ensures remote memory access as well as inter-node cooperation. The immense number of nodes makes system set up and initialization a time-critical procedure. PEACE [Schroeder 1990], the distributed operating system for SUPRENUM and GENESIS, approaches this problem profiting by its constitution of a multitude of system servers.

Modern distributed operating systems, matching in their concepts the problems of parallel systems too [Schroeder, Gien 1989], are process structured like e.g. V [Cheriton 1984], AMOEBA [Mullender, Tanenbaum 1986], MACH [Young et al. 1987], and CHORUS [Rozier et al. 1988]. A process providing dedicated system services forms a system server. Under this aspect system restructuring means the termination and creation of system server objects, concerning software scalability, and the booting and rebooting of single nodes, concerning hardware scalability.

For efficiency reasons, bootstrapping a complete operating system at each node is not acceptable. Moreover, in a massively parallel system it is not necessary, because it is sufficient to bootstrap only the nodes actually needed by the distributed (parallel) application. Since not every application utilizes each node, especially during initialization, *incremental loading* results in reduction of set up costs. The same consideration applies to servers constituting the distributed operating system. A

* This work was supported by the European Commission under the Esprit-2 program, grant no. P 2702, and by the Ministry of Research and Technology (BMFT) of the German Federal Government, grant no. ITR 9002 2.

system server has to be present and available at the time some process needs its functionality. With regard to this idea, PEACE realizes the construction of operating system families, following the concepts of program families [Parnas 1975]. Selecting only the servers that are going to be used by the application presumes a corresponding description containing the relations between application and operating system. A predefinition of the needed functionalities is not always possible for an application. Therefore, the straight forward approach is to load a system server exactly when it is going to be used the first time. On this basis one can specify a minimal subset of system services which are required for this *on-demand* load feature to get system servers running. This minimal subset has to be bootstrapped, i.e. *instantaneously loaded.* Exactly this feature distinguishes PEACE from most of todays distributed operating systems and is a novel for making massively parallel systems work.

On-demand loading of a server involves the problem server addressing. A server is required to be identifiable for communication. In PEACE, identification is done by a symbolic naming scheme, realized by distributed name servers, together constituting a structured name space. For being identifiable by the demanding process, a server needs to be registered properly in the name space. One of the most important tasks for managing dynamic restructuring is the reorganization of the name space after a new server has been loaded on demand. Therefore, this paper first gives a short survey of the PEACE naming system. Subsequently requirements for the on-demand loading are inspected, followed by a PEACE case study presentation.

2. Naming System Aspects

Above all PEACE is a process execution and communication environment. Extending the ideas of FAMOS [Habermann et al. 1976] and DAS [Isle et al. 1977] into a distributed environment, one of the aims was to support dynamic alterable operating system architectures on the basis of distribution and process structuring. An important role plays the distributed symbolic name service, influenced by hardware requirements of massively parallel systems and by some preconditions given by PEACE. Before discussing the naming service itself in the next chapter, the influences given by software as well as hardware are presented in the following.

Similar to THOTH [Cheriton 1979] in PEACE each unit of execution (*thread*) is member of a *team*, the unit of distribution. Different threads (*lightweighted processes*) together constitute a team (*heavyweighted process*) and are settled in the same address space. The basic communication service is realized by the *nucleus*, more exactly by a nucleus family [Schroeder 1990b]. The different nuclei all provide the same interface, i.e. they are abstract data types [Liskov, Zilles 1974]. They differ in the degree of multi-tasking they offer and in the communication performance they can achieve. Dependent on the application's performance requirements the choice of a single-tasking nucleus may become appropriate.

The first versions of PEACE were developed for SUPRENUM, a MIMD (multiple instruction, multiple data) supercomputer consisting of up to 320 nodes. Constituting a distributed memory architecture, SUPRENUM nodes are organized in 16 *clusters*. Although PEACE today is not restricted to be used for SUPRENUM only (see GENESIS), the architecture of this computer has significantly influenced the naming system at least in two aspects. First, there is the necessity of replicated services. For example cluster related services appear at each cluster. Replicated services, however, provided by replicated servers lead to the possibility of name clashes. Second, each thread at a cluster has to be capable of identifying the cluster related services with the aid of the naming system. Other services may be local to a node or global to the entire system. Hence, services respectively their names have a proper scope. In the example of SUPRENUM the scope's spectrum comprises three possibilities. To achieve location transparency this spectrum requires a corresponding structure from the naming system. Additionally, a name scope has to be configurable, because it can change under certain conditions when considering the scalability of the system.

3. Naming in PEACE

In contrast to naming systems as described e.g. in [Peterson 1988] or [Schwartz 1987], which work on top of a complete operating system, naming in PEACE is one of the most basic functionalities. Utilization of most PEACE operating system services is only enabled with the aid of the naming scheme. Particularly designed to make distributed operating systems work, it is also usable for distributed application programs.

3.1. The PEACE Structured Name Space

As outlined above each thread in PEACE and thus each server is addressed by a system wide unique identifier. Basis for all service invocation in PEACE are *remote procedure calls* [Nelson 1982]. They are the main utilization of the naming system with the aim to get the system wide unique identifier of the communication partner. The naming system is implemented by distributed name servers and by dedicated system libraries. Each name server administrates mappings from names to user definable values, which are not interpreted by a name server itself. The remote procedure call level defines these values as the system wide unique identifier of the service providing process and a server relative identifier designating a dedicated function. Within a *name plane*, managed by one name server, names are unique.

Using the remote procedure call basis, name server services are invoked in the same fashion as other services. Obviously, it is not possible to achieve the identification in the same way, i.e. by means of symbolic names. Therefore, a name server is identified by using a *domain identifier* associated with each team. Domain identifiers are managed by the kernel. Different teams may have either the same or different domain identifiers, being an important precondition for configuration. For example, teams being mapped onto the same node may share a domain identifier, and thus a name server, whereas the teams at a different node share a separate name server. In this manner each process is able to identify the node relative services of its home node.

Registering and resolving of names take place dynamically. During its initialization a server usually associates service names with its own unique identifier and a proper service code. It then requests from a name server the creation of its service names.

Further steps are necessary in order to identify global servers rather than local, e.g. node-relative servers. Global services are managed by separate name servers. Thereby, the identification of a global service is reduced to the identification of the name server managing the corresponding name. Since the PEACE kernel associates only one domain identifier with a team, from the team's viewpoint a name server chain has to be defined. The name server identifier maintained by the kernel serves as the head of the chain. Additional name servers are referenced respectively by a *domain link* in the preceding name server. A domain link is represented by a symbolic name. After name resolution has failed, domain link resolution is performed to get to know a new name server. In this way, distributed name servers together form a tree structure. Figure 1 illustrates this approach. See [Sander et al. 1989] for a more detailed explanation of naming in PEACE.

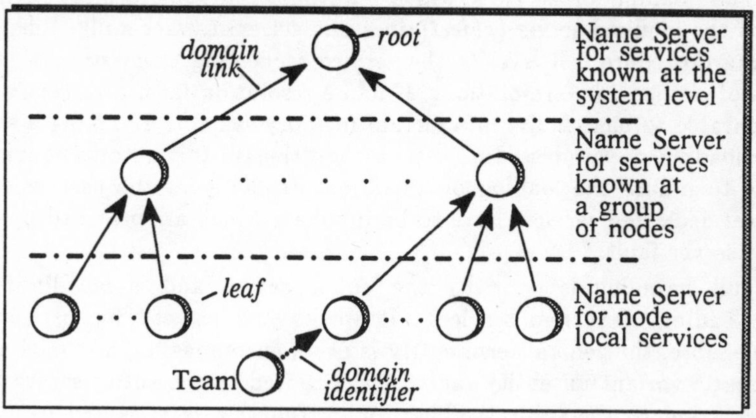

Figure 1: The PEACE structured name space

3.2. Name Space Configuration

One of the most important preconditions for the identification of communication partners by means of name servers is the name registration in the proper name server. Each service is associated with a scope implemented by a name server. Thus, before registration a server has to determine its scope in the actual environment. Scope management is provided by a dedicated system service, the *scope service*. In order to get knowledge of its scope a server has to disclose its identity to the scope service in the form of a symbolic name, called *temper*. The scope service manages a user definable table which maps tempers onto name server names, *scopes*. Upon request, a scope is returned to the server which is then resolved in the same way as usual service names. Resolving the scope means to identify the correct name server for name registration. The user definable mapping table is edited by a *third party configuration facility*. This way, flexible dynamic scope reconfiguration is achieved, transparently to servers and scope service.

The PEACE naming scheme provides so much transparency that integrating a new server object into an existing system is reduced to two main tasks. First, the correct domain identifier has to be set for a new server object. Second, the new server object must be prepared to identify its scope.

4. Incremental Loading

Neither system nor application need thousands of nodes equipped with a complete operating system. What is needed is that services are available at the time they are used. This is comparable to the *trap-on-use* property of Multics [Organick 1972].

The classical order of presence of application and operating system is, at least partially, reversed this way. The exception from the reversion is defined by the "traphandling" routines, i.e. the minimal subset of operating system facilities, needed to manage incremental loading of system services.

4.1. Server Faults

On demand loading of services will be automatically performed during service invocation, if the required server (*object*) does not yet exist. Generally, this is detected by the remote procedure call level of the service requesting client process (*subject*) in the progress of service name resolution. If name resolution fails, a *server fault* will be raised, comparable to page faults in a virtual memory system. Handling a server fault leads to the loading of the missed object. In addition to this automatic loading, it is also possible to induce the loading of an object explicitly at the user level. For all these purposes dedicated services have to be invoked, which are provided by the server handling the server fault.

Server fault handling is done by the *entity server* and is not limited to the incremental loading of system services. It works just as well for user application services. Therefore, the general term entity is used, encompassing all kinds of services. In the automatic variant an entity fault is propagated to the entity server by library functions belonging to the subject. The library function is activated by the remote procedure call level and blocks the subject until subsequent loading of the object is finished. Controlled by the entity server, unblocking will be performed when the new object has successfully announced service name registration.

Before loading can be carried out, the entity server has to decide which object provides the expected service. An object is controlled by a team image, which is stored in a file. For each load request the entity server has to select the right file. This is done on basis of configuration tables described in the next chapter.

4.2. Name Server Faults

In PEACE name servers play a distinctive role. This concerns both identification and incremental loading. Nevertheless, the idea of a minimal subset can also be applied for name servers. Initially, it is not necessary to establish the whole structured name space by starting all the constituting name servers. Unlike usual entity faults the occasion to start a name server appears in another way. Whereas a usual server will be started if any of its services is needed, a name server is loaded if its register service is required. Only if at least one name is registered by a name server, its existence will make sense. Therefore, a *name server fault* will be raised only, if a server detects the absence of the name server specified as its export scope. For example, in case of SUPRENUM the cluster name server will be needed if the first server providing cluster relative services is started.

A server invokes the scope service before registering its service names. A scope service query returns a name server name. This name may designate a still inactive (i.e. not yet loaded) name server. In this case a name server fault occurs. The *name usher*, a dedicated system server, handles name server faults by editing the name space. The name usher's work is based on a name space specification, which describes the maximal number of name servers building the name space as well as the global name server structure. Besides, it knows about the actual name server structure produced by previous name server faults and by instantaneous loading. Handling a name server fault means to start a new name server object and to arrange it into the actual name server structure, meaning to dynamically restructure an existing name space. For this purpose *domain links* have to be created and/or replugged. Where to arrange the new name server is determined by the name space specification.

5. Fundamental Requirements

Incremental loading and dynamic restructuring by means of handling entity faults and name server faults require some support for the entity server and the name usher. As suggested above some basic services are used to perform object loading and some fundamental specifications are indispensable. The entity server together with the basic services it uses build the minimal subset of services needed in PEACE to perform incremental loading. Note that the name usher is beyond this subset, because it is loadable as a result of an entity fault. However, in the following the loading of the name usher is anticipated. For a simple representation the minimal subset of services covers only a single node, the *radical node*, which serves as the source of all. The radical node is the only node that indeed has to be instantaneously loaded.

5.1. The Radical Node

The minimal subset of services is shown in figure 2, in which arrows reveal the uses relation. Since incremental loading considers processes, the nucleus is omitted. A name server, *name*, is necessary for every service invocation in PEACE. At the beginning this single name server encompasses the whole name space. Later, the name usher will expand the name space. The name server administrates service names created by the participating servers.

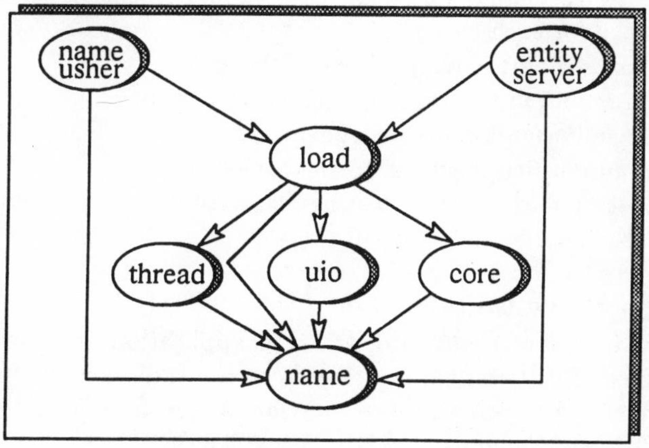

Figure 2: The radical node

The next hierarchy level is given by *thread*, *core*, and *uio*. The kernel server *thread* provides basic functionalities for the creation of team objects and thread objects. Free memory is supervised by *core*, whose services are memory allocation and deallocation, whereas *uio* provides uniform **i/o**-services. In this context the variant of a disk i/o-server is required to read the files containing the team images.

The load server *load* uses these three servers to start new teams. At the target node a team object and at least one thread object have to be created, memory is needed to store the team image and finally the team image has to be read from disk. Additionally, the load server is able to relocate the image. This capability is useful for multi-tasking target nodes without a memory management unit, which performs address translation.

Thread, *core*, *uio*, and *load* are emphatically designed to be utmost fundamental. Each provides only basic mechanisms. A dedicated process model, e.g. underlying the *fork()* call, is not assumed by *thread*. Strategies, which exceed the basic mechanisms, are implemented by more sophisticated servers loadable on demand. Similar considerations apply to *core*, *uio*, and *load*.

5.2. Configurations

For instantaneous loading as well as for incremental loading of a distributed application several data bases are interpreted, which contain *configuration specifications* [Kramer, Magee 1985]. They can be obtained by the compilation of a corresponding *configuration description* written in the PEACE system configuration language AIDA [Schmidt 1990]. The entity server and the name usher input their part of the specification upon startup.

AIDA provides language constructs to produce *logical* and *physical* specifications. A physical specification describes the actual hardware architecture and scaling extent of the underlying machine. Updates, e.g. caused by node failures are performed automatically. The physical description influences the initial mapping (i.e. static loadbalancing) of application entities onto a set of nodes.

In contrast to that the logical specification contains entity-dependent data. The name usher employes the name space structure and the entity server manages the following informations for each entity:

- a *file name* containing the team image of the entity;
- an *export configuration* to direct the name registration;
- a *target node definition* for site-dependent entities;
- *environment data* which is passed to the entity;
- *entity attributes* for example to distinguish entities for single-tasking or multi-tasking nodes.

6. Setting Up System and Application

In the following it is shown how a distributed application and the system services it requires is set up and distributed, starting from the radical node. The target node is assumed of having been bootstrapped previously. A first initial entity, *subject*, must be active. It then demands a service provided by *object*. Without confining generality the initial entity is placed for simplification reasons at the radical node. One step of initialization is anticipated in the following: a second name server, *global*, is loaded to manage the global service names. The name usher and the entity server have registered their service names in *global* to be identifiable also for processes, which will reside at remote nodes.

Assume *subject* will call the procedure *o_proc*. The remote procedure call level is entered, which tries to identify the server providing *o_proc*. For that purpose the name space is queried for the name *o_proc*. Since the name is not found, server identification fails. Therefore, a server fault is raised to the entity server. The entity server itself is identified in the usual way by querying the name space. Based on the configuration specification, the entity server decides which server object has to be loaded. An appropriate target node is selected, in this example the radical node. The entity server triggers the load server and keeps *subject* blocked by omitting the remote procedure call termination. Subsequently the entity server is ready to receive a new request. The new system formation is shown in figure 3.

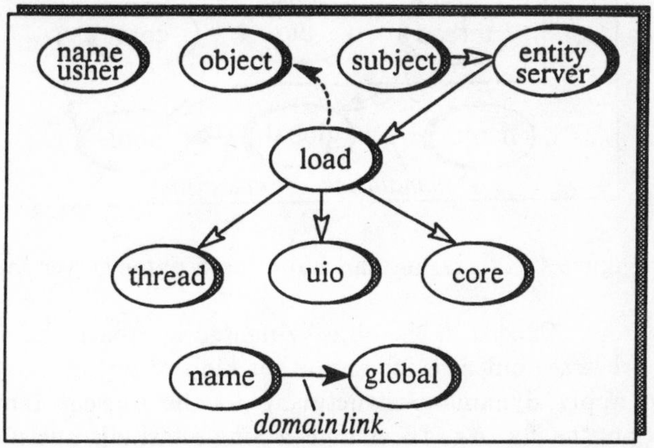

Figure 3: Triggering and handling a server fault

In order to register its service names, *object* asks the entity server for its scope. Assuming that the returned scope can't be resolved in the name space, *object* has to raise a name server fault. If the presence of the name usher hadn't been anticipated, it would be loaded now. In this case the name server fault would involve a server fault. Handling the name server fault by the name usher first of all means to start a new name server, *appl*. Depending on its name space specification the name usher arranges the new name server into the name space. In this example the arrangement encompasses two steps. First, a domain link in *global* is created, referring to *appl*. Second, the name of *appl*, i.e. the scope *object* is looking for, has to be created in *appl*. Now, the PEACE name space has got a new structure, shown in figure 4.

After the name server fault was handled successfully, *object* is able to perform its service name registration. By this means, *object* creates at least the name *o_proc* of the procedure it provides in the name server *appl*. Having registered its service names, *object* notifies its readiness to work to the entity server, which unblocks *subject*, by completing its remote procedure call. Further processes, which meanwhile had required the loading of *object* are unblocked likewise. *Subject* restarts the name resolution by querying an extended name space. The resolution now succeeds, i.e. the server providing *o_proc* can be identified and *o_proc* can be executed.

7. Concluding Remarks

This paper describes the PEACE incremental loading scheme, developed in consequence of the experiences made with the PEACE implementations for SUPRENUM, particularly in the bootstrapping field. The implementation of these concepts is

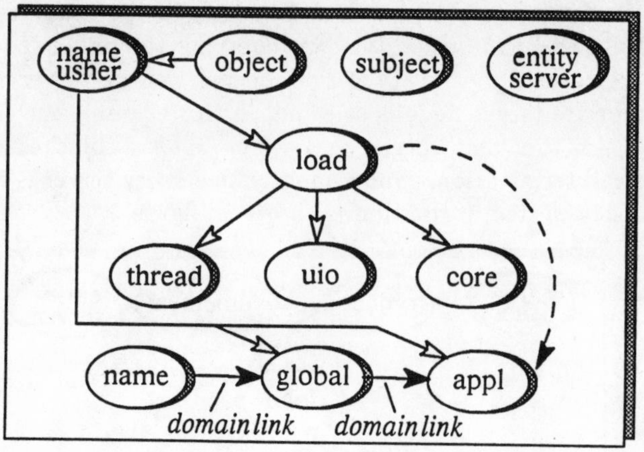

Figure 4: Triggering and handling a name server fault

currently in progress. Caused in the object-oriented approach the mechanisms are not only usable for processes but also for any other kind of object. One of the next steps in PEACE is to apply dynamic restructuring to the nucleus family. To exchange nucleus entities on the fly, e.g. to change a single-tasking nucleus against a multi-tasking nucleus, makes PEACE a completely dynamic alterable system.

The quality of incremental loading depends on the quality of the configuration specification. Practicable specifications need language support. The programming language at least is urged to provide modularity. Former PEACE versions were written in Modula-2 and C, whereas today the implementation language is C++. Likewise, an interface definition language plays an important role. The PEACE interface definition language PRECISE [Nolte 1990] ascertains the automatic production of stub modules which then capsules the entire service invocation sequence. Additionally, some object-oriented addressing schemes are available which direct deviating name resolution strategies. Finally, AIDA the PEACE configuration language provides high level language constructs to the user to describe distributed applications.

Last but not least, the PEACE project showed that massively parallel systems call for properly tailored distributing operating systems differing from most of the systems which are currently under development and/or usage [Lennon 1969].

Acknowledgments

The author want to express his gratitude to all members of the PEACE project. Especially to Jörg Nolte and Wolfgang Schröder-Preikschat for discussions on the incremental loading concepts and for careful reading the manuscript of the paper.

References

[Cheriton 1979] D. R. Cheriton: **Multi-Process Structuring and the Thoth Operating System**, Dissertation, Univ. of Waterloo, UBC Tech. Rep. 79-5, 1979

[Cheriton 1984] D. R. Cheriton: **The V Kernel: A Software Base for Distributed Systems**, IEEE Software 1, 2, 19-43, 1984

[Giloi 1988] W. K. Giloi: **The SUPRENUM Architecture**, CONPAR 88, Manchester, UK., 12th-16th September, 1988

[Giloi 1989] W. K. Giloi: **GENESIS: The Architecture and its Rationale**, ESPRIT Project No. 2447, Report of the GENESIS General Architecture Working Group, W. K. Giloi (Ed.), GMD FIRST, Berlin, FRG, 1989

[Habermann et al. 1976] A. N. Habermann, L. Flon, L. Cooprider: **Modularization and Hierarchy in a Family of Operating Systems**, CACM, 19, 5,, 1976

[Isle et al. 1977] R. Isle, H. Goullon, K.-P. Löhr: **Dynamic Restructuring in an Experimental Operating System**, Tech. Rep. 77-27, TU Berlin, 1977

[Kramer, Magee 1985] J. Kramer, J. Magee: **Dynamic Configuration for Distributed Systems**, IEEE Trans. on Softw. Eng., Vol. SE-11, 4, April, 1985

[Lennon 1969] J. Lennon: **"Give PEACE a Chance"**, The Plastic Ono Band - Live PEACE in Toronto, Apple Records, December, 1969

[Liskov, Zilles 1974] B. H. Liskov, S. Zilles: **Programming with Abstract Data Types**, SIGPLAN Notices, 9, 4, 1974

[Mullender, Tanenbaum 1986] S. J. Mullender, A. S. Tanenbaum: **The Design of a Capability-Based Distributed Operating System**, Comp. Journ., 29, 4, 1986

[Nelson 1982] B. J. Nelson: **Remote Procedure Call**, Carnegie-Mellon University, Report CMU-CS-81-119, 1982

[Nolte 1990] J. Nolte: **PRECISE – The PEACE Interface Definition Language**, GMD FIRST, 1990

[Organick 1972] E. Organick: **The Multics System: An Examination of its Structure**, MIT Press, 1972

[Parnas 1975] D. L. Parnas: **On the Design and Development of Program Families**, Forschungsbericht BS I 75/2, TH Darmstadt, 1975

[Peterson 1988] L. L. Peterson: **The Profile Naming Service**, ACM Transactions on Computer Systems, 6, 4, 341-364, 1988

[Rozier et al. 1988] M. Rozier, V. Abrossimov, F. Armand, I. Boule, M. Gien, M. Guillemont, F. Herrman, C. Kaiser, S. Langlois, P. Leonard, W. Neuhauser: **CHORUS Distributed Operating Systems**, Computing Systems Journal, Vol. 1, No. 4, University of California Press & Usenix Association, 1988

[Sander et al. 1989] M. Sander, H. Schmidt, W. Schröder-Preikschat: **Naming in the PEACE Distributed Operating System**, Proceedings of the International Workshop on "Communication Networks and Distributed Operating Systems within the Space Environment", Noordwijk, The Netherlands, Oct. 24 – 26, 1989

[Schmidt 1990] H.Schmidt: **AIDA – The PEACE Configuration Language**, to be provided, 1990

[Schroeder 1990] W. Schröder-Preikschat: **PEACE – A Distributed Operating System for High-Performance Multicomputer Systems**, Lecture Notes in Computer Science, Vol. 433, Springer-Verlag, 1990

[Schroeder 1990b] W. Schröder-Preikschat: **Overcoming the Startup Time Problem in Distributed Memory Architectures**, paper submitted for publication to HICSS24, 1990

[Schroeder, Gien 1989] W. Schröder-Preikschat, M. Gien: **Architecture and Rationale of the GENESIS Family of Distributed Operating Systems**, ESPRIT Project No. 2447, Technical Report, GMD FIRST, Berlin, FRG, 1989

[Schwartz 1987] M. F. Schwartz: **Naming in Large, Heterogeneous Systems**, Dissertation, Technical Report 87-08-01, University of Washington, Seattle, 1987

[Young et al. 1987] M. Young, A. Tevanian, R. Rashid, D. Golub, J. Eppinger, J. Chew, W. Bolosky, D. Black, R. Baron: **The Duality of Memory and Communication in the Implementation of a Multiprocessor Operating System**, ACM Operating Systems Review, 21, 5, 1987

Managing the recursive Generation of Tasks in a Transputer Network

Serge NICOLLE - Pascal LEGRAND - Jean-Pierre DERUTIN

Electronic Laboratory, URA 830 of the CNRS
Blaise PASCAL University F 63177 AUBIERE CEDEX

Keywords: Parallel architectures - Processors Farm - Transputers - Recursive algorithms.

Abstract

Computational constraints in image processing and image analysis, take advantage of a parallel implementation performed on a distributed memory parallel architecture; the following one is based on tranputers.This paper proposes a parallel implementation based on the "processors farm" method, of the splitting step of Kd-tree algorithms (split & merge); it is computationally expensive, but involves a large number of independant tasks. The project sets out to implement it on a on-board real time system.
The dynamic comportment of the network is formalized; both master and slave processes are described. A communication strategy is performed which stops the deadlock happening in the return communication network.
The recursive generation of sub-tasks may create some starvation points. When new sub-tasks are created, they have to be to idle workers.Two approaches are proposed :

- firstly, when a starvation point appears, a total starvation is created;
- secondly, the master does not stop its "farming", but manages the network temporal comportment and "farm" new sub-tasks to idle workers.

In the end, some experimentals results, performed on several networks composed from 2 till 12 transputers, are presented.

Introduction [1][2]

Hierarchical data structures are becoming increasingly important representation techniques in the domains of computer graphics, image processing, computational geometry, geographic information systems, and robotics. They are based on the principle of recursive decomposition. They are also known as quadtree, or more generaly speaking Kd-tree methods. In image processing, they may be used for image segmentation. The hierarchical segmentation may be performed according to three methods :

- The splitting method, where the image is successively subdivided until homogeneous blocks of data, according to a criterion, are obtained.
- The merging method, where at first the image is divided into a large number of small homogeneous regions. Merging two regions is allowed on condition it gives a larger homogeneous region.
- The third method proposes to devise a mixed split-and-merge scheme [2]. It begins with an arbitrary partition; the splitting method is applied on each region until all the sub-regions are homogeneous. Then, the merging method is applied on this group of homogeneous regions. This step is useful to re-create the real geometry of the homogeneous parts of the image, which have been arbitrary separated at the beginning and during the splitting step.

The algorithms which use the splitting method are computationally expensive, but have two main properties :

- Tasks are non-communating and can be computed in any order,
- It is quite feasible that the task recursively generates sub-tasks.

These both properties help us to define a parallelization scheme implemented on a transputer network [3]. At first, the dynamic comportment of the network is formalized; then, some parallel implementation problems, like deadlock, or distributing new tasks to idle processes, are resolved.

-1- Concept of parallelism

-1.1- Data parallelism [4]

DEW considers an application algorithm as a function F, mapping an input data set I, to an output data set O. Both in image processing and image analysis, the input data set are 2D images, while the output data set may be 2D images, a set of blocks of data, a set of connected components, etc.

Definition

The function F is said to be amenable to data parallelism if there exists a partitioning that can decompose the output data set O into m disjoint partitions
$\{O_i : i=1...m$ and $\cup O_i = O\}$ such that $\{f_i(I_i) :$ where $O_i = f_i(I_i)$, $i = 1...m\}$
where I_i is the subset of I sufficient to compute O_i.

- The input partition $\{I_i\}$ can overlap.
- In many cases the function f_i is independant of the input and output sets (i.e $f_i = F$).
- Data parallelism is also referred to as spatial or geometrical parallelism depending on the application. This a subset of the more general task queue model.

In the task queue model, tasks are generated (normally from a task dependency graph), sent to a computational engine (e.g a pool of processors) for processing and returned to the tasks consumer. The tasks generation and consumption processes are under the control of a task manager.

-1.2- "Processors farm" method [5]

It is a redefinition of the task queue model which has been first introduced by May and Shephard. In this method, both the "task consumer" and the "task manager" lie within the same process named "Master process" or "farmer". This process farms out the tasks to the pool of executing processes named "slave processes" or "workers", until all tasks have been allocated.

-1.3- Initial constraints [3][6]

The project sets out to parallelize such hierarchical data algorithms on a transputer network which belongs to the MIMD distributed memory architectures. The final result aims at the implementation on a on board real time system. Such a parallel scheme emphasizes the communication problems and the tasks allocation on a transputer network. We focus our attention on deadlock problems and the way to distribute new tasks to idle workers. In order to respect the implementation constraints, we define three initial constraints :

- *Using a static network,*
- *Not completely connected topology ,*
- *Every slave keeps in memory all the raw data .*

The third one makes possible to communicate only the parameters of a block of data. So, only small and constant size messages are transfered. A material architecture has been studied in order to improve the data transfer to slaves at the initialization step. All the raw data are transfered via a video bus; this bus is connected to some particular transputers named "video nodes" [18].

-1.4- The parallelization method

A recursive algorithm manages a dynamic set of tasks which cannot be predicted at the initialization step. So, implementing it on a SISD machine or on a MIMD one requires a dynamic allocation of the memory. One of the transputer properties is its static allocation memory performed at the compilation step. So, the recursivity cannot be easily implemented on a transputer network. Our parallelization scheme regards every task or sub-task as a single task without dependency.

The parallelization scheme uses the "processors farm" method; so, the farmer has in charge to subdivide a raw image according to a hierarchical structure based on the Kd-tree. The concurrency appears with the simultaneous studies of several parts of the image, by a number of workers. These workers must send back to the master their result pointing out on the homogeneity of the regions they are processed. When a worker Ei which has sent its result pointing out on a region B, it receives another new region, without knowing whether it is a sub-region (perhaps of B). When receiving a result, the farmer decides whether to split again the corres-ponding region. The tasks allocation is performed until all the regions are homogeneous.

-2- Formalizing the architecture [7]

-2.1- The slave process

The dynamic tasks allocation performed by the master, follows a "one-to-all" communication way; on the contrary, the Slave->Master communication network follows a "all-to-one" communication way. The taking into account of the initial constraints, results in several slaves passing some messages through. So, a slave process is subdivided into two processes :

- *The execution process (fig 2.1)*
- *The communication process (see § 3.31).*

These two processes exchange data via an internal channel. The communication process (it is in a high priority order) interfaces the execution one with its environment; it does not depend on the application algorithm. The execution process has in charge the analysing of the homogeneity of the region. So, it depends on the application algorithm (hierarchical structure, criterion).

-2.11- Instance of the slave process [7]

-2.111- Transputer network scheme

The transputer network may be described as a graph G=[X,U], where each vertex is associated with a transputer, and each edge with a transputer link [8][9]. In order to quantifiy the increasing of the computational charge due to the position of a slave process inside the network, let us call Ci, the set of workers for which the worker Ei belongs to their Master-Slave communication graph; we can say that :

(2) $Ci = \{Ej \in \mathcal{N} / d(Ej,M)=d(Ej,Ei)+d(Ei,M) \; ; \; d(M,Ej)=d(M,Ei)+d(Ei,Ej)\}$

$\mathcal{N}$: set of workers; $Card(\mathcal{N}) = N$: M: label of the master.

The Master-Slave communication graph may be described as a set of D communication layers numbered from 1 to D (D : network diameter). Every process of the same communication layer verifies d(Ei,M) = βdu = d(M,Ei). In such a description, each worker is labelled according to its communication layer and noted E^{α}_{i}; where i refers to the network processor order, which implements this slave process (i=[1..N]); the exponent α refers to the communication layer. It is omitted when not necessary.

Thus, the problem is reduced to a set problem and the topology viewed as a set of N+1 processors (1 master and N workers). This description is useful because of its geometric parameters abstraction of the further topology; so, it makes the generalization of the study easier.

-2.112- The communication time

The viewing of the transputer network as a graph, and the use of the previous scheme, permit us to define the communication time between a slave process and the master as [3]:

(3) $t(E^{\alpha}_{i},M) = \alpha(a+bNo+t_p+\tau) + t^{\alpha}_{i,M} = t_u(i) + t^{\alpha}_{i,M}$

$t_u(i)$: least communication time between Ei and the master M.

where *a* : *set up time of the communication channel*
b : *data rate transfer on a transputer link*
No : *number of bytes in a message*
k : *number of intermediary communication workers*
tp : *computational time of the communication process*
τ: *set up time of a high priority process interruption on a low priority process.*
$t^{\alpha}_{i,M}$: Global random waiting between the communicating processes.

-2.113- Slave execution process computational time

When a worker has to pass some messages through, its execution process is interrupted (during its computational time ti,s) every time a message is detected by the communication process. The global interruption time of the worker Ei is:

(4) $t_{fi,s} = M_{i,s} \cdot (t_p+a+\tau)$

Mi,s : number of messages to pass through when Ei processes a region size Ts
tp+a+τ : necessary time spent to process a communication.

The time $t_{fi,s}$ corresponds to an artificially computational time increasing and has to be minimized. In this way, Mi,s is studied and we are going to define some constraints on the further topology [10].

So, the computational time of the slave execution process is defined as :

(5) $ti,s = t_{Ts} + t_{fi,s}$

where t_{Ts} = computational time for a region Ts without interruption.

Determining the computational time of the execution process permits us to define the slave process efficiency as the ratio between this time,ti,s, and the global one (it includes the necessary time to transfer the region parameters). This global time depends on the way data are exchanged. We define two ways, according to the master, which waits for, or manages, the whole network communications. We name these ways : communication modes.

-2.2- Master-Slave communication modes

-2.21- Mode 1

The master communication process waits for communications. After it completes its computation, the worker Ei, sends its result to the master. After receiving the message, the master sends back a new block of data. This mode is subdivided into two modes according to the execution process, which is busy (mode 1.2) or not (mode 1.1) during the exchange of data with the master. It turns out that, in order to keep the execution process busy during this exchange, the worker has to buffer an extra item of work [5]

-2.22- Mode 2

The master process manages the whole communication frequencies with the network. When it estimates that a worker Ei is about to complete its computation, the master sends it a new block of data. In this paper, only the communication mode 1 is studied.

-2.23- Slave process efficiency

We show that [10], the efficiency in the mode 1.2 is better than in the mode 1.1. But, keeping in memory an extra item of work (mode 1.2) greatly increases the risk starvation points arise compared to mode 1.1(the master cannot send news tasks to idle workers whereas all tasks have not been effectively processed). So, the mode 1.2 is not suitable for processing images leading at each step to such a number of blocks Nz<2N (N : number of slaves). Another problem is that we cannot estimate this number at the start of an application. However, we show in §3 that the mode 1.2 allows a distribution of tasks to idle workers before waiting for a total network starvation . On the contrary, we cannot do this in the mode 1.1.

-2.3- The master process

The results which point out to the homogeneity studied by a slave process are divided into two parts :

(I): they point out that the block of data is homogeneous according to the criterion.

(II): they point out that the block of data is not homogeneous; so it has to be subdivided into K sub-blocks.

In order to complete its computation and communicate with its all workers, the master process is composed of two independant processes which communicate via an internal channel; a *communication process* and an *execution process*. These two processes use two dynamically partitionned ressources (PIP & HBA) [11]. These both processes may use a shareable memory, just because they own to the same processor.

-2.31- The Master Communication Process (fig 3.42)

This process has to manage the Master->Slave communications. Its algorithm depends on the communication mode (a high priority order is given to this process). The master waits for messages from its workers. In the usual case, when receiving a message from a worker Ei, the communication process stores parameters in the "*Homogeneity to Be Analyzed*" FIFO (HBA). Then, a new block of data is sent back to Ei; if it is possible to do this.

-2.32- The Master Execution Process (fig 2.32)

This process has in charge the studying of the hierarchical decomposition of the raw image in a partition of homogeneous regions verifying the application criterion. When the master receives a message from Ei, the corresponding parameters are analysed, in order to decide whether the region has to be sub-divided. In this case, K sub-blocks are generated and their parameters stocked into the *"Part of Image to be Process"* FIFO (PIP). But, when the region is said to be homogeneous, its parameters are stocked in the *"Homogeneous block"* stack (HOB). The main difference between modes 1.1 and 1.2 lies in the initialization step where in mode 1.2, the *"Idle WOrkers"* LIFO (IWO) is 2N long (every slave waits for two blocks).

-2.33- Computational time of the Master Execution Process

As for the worker, every communication process interruption artificially increases the computational time of the execution process : t_{eM}. In order to describe this increasing, we use a similar formula like (4).

$$(6) \quad t_{eM} = t_{\iota,M} + t_{f,M} = t_M$$

t_M : *symbolizes the overall master computational time*

$t_{\iota,M}$: *symbolizes the computational time when the execution process is not interrupted; it is not block size depending, with :*

$$(7) \quad t_{f,M} = \sum_{x=1}^{N_1} \sum_{h=1}^{m_x} m_h \cdot (a+\tau+t_{c,M})$$

$t_{c,M}$: *symbolizes the computational time of the communication process.*

m_h : *symbolizes the total number of messages that the worker E_x sends or passes through when the master execution process is busy.*

N_1 : *points out that only workers of the first layer are concerned.*

When the execution process is not interrupted we obtain :

$$(8) \quad t_{eM} = t_{\iota,M} \quad \text{and} \quad t_M = t_{eM} + t_{c,M}$$

The expression (7), points out that the more the master execution process is interrupted, the more its computational time is artificially increased; the master may become a bottleneck. So, in order to not interrupt the execution process, each message has to be processed before the following arrival (see § 3.13). In the next section, we show that, the "upper limit" is inversely proportional to t_M.

-2.4- Predicting the Theorical Upper Limit : Nmax

We define this upper limit as the maximum number of slaves which can be efficiently managed by the master; this last one must not become the bottleneck of the network; this condition has to be verified whatever the topology, and whatever the region size. For these reasons, we put ourselves into the most critical situation :

- every slave is directly connected to the master ($E^d_i = E^1_i$, $\forall$ i),
- no slave is interrupted,
- every slave works on the smallest region.

Nmax is defined as :

$$N_{max} = \frac{t\alpha_{i,m}}{\max(t_M)}$$

$t\alpha_{i,m}$: *global computational time of a slave working on the smallest region; it depends on the communication which is used.*

$\max(t_M)$: *maximum master overall computational time according to this mode.*

At first, $t_{fi,m}$ is said nil; it allows us to determine a raw value of Nmax; taking into account this value, we can estimate the time $t_{fi,m}$ and perhaps reduce the value of Nmax. In exemple, let us see the value of Nmax, when using the communication mode 1.2.

$$N_{max}(1.2) = \frac{2(a+t_p)+\tau+t_{esc}}{t_{M.1}} \quad \text{with } d_{max} < \frac{t_{esc}}{2(a+bNo+t_p)+\tau}$$

t_{esc} : *smallest slave execution process computational time*

The number dmax symbolizes the maximum diameter of the topology. Indeed, the return Master-Slave communication time has to be smaller than the slave execution process computational one; otherwise we fall down into the mode 1.1. Nmax is not the optimal value, because the topology is not taken into account (we consider a star topology). It does not give the best parallelization efficiency (ratio between the sequential time and, the parallel one multiplied by the number of processors). Indeed, it may be better to increase the number of slaves over Nmax, aiming to speed up the processing of the large regions, even if the slaves would have to be slowed down when processing small regions.

-2.5- Conclusion

This formalization permits us to define the dynamic comportment of a transputer network implementing the "processors farm" method. Master and slave processes have been described, and communication modes have been defined, without knowing anything on the further topology. Nmax gives a reference number of slaves to be managed without getting to a bottleneck. Nevertheless, the random variables $t^{\alpha}_{i,M}$ and $t^{\alpha}_{M,i}$ cannot be determine with accuracy. In the next section, we develop a communication rhythm which aims to minimize, until cancellation, all the random variables. The interlacing of M<->S messages makes deadlock situtations to appear; we also develop a strategy which stop its happening.

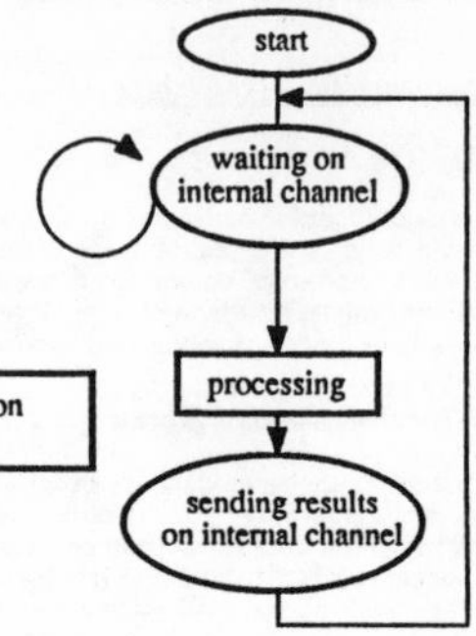

Slave execution process

figure 2.1

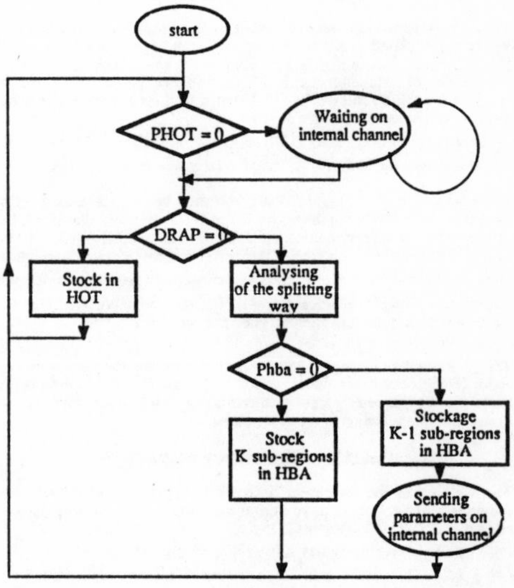

Figure 2.32 Execution process : communication mode n°1

-3- Communication strategy

-3.1- Giving a rhythm to the emission of messages

When doing this, we aim to minimize the variables $t^{\alpha}_{i,M}$ and $t^{\alpha}_{M,i}$ (waiting times due to the rendezvous between the intermediary processes during a Master-Slave communication), and the time $t_{f,M}$ too. In the next sections, the communication mode 1.2 is mainly used.

-3.11- Slave process Computational time according to Ts

The slave computational time is the time separating two successive emissions of messages from a slave to the master. We can say that :

$ta_{i,s} = t_{Ts} + t_{fi,s} + 2(a+t_p) + \tau$ and $ta_{i,s+1} = t_{Ts+1} + t_{fi,s+1} + 2(a+tp) + \tau$

Let us note that in the mode 1.1, the communication time is sequential to the computational one of the execution process; so, the time $t_u(i)$ (see §2.112) has to be taking into account in the previous formula.

In order to make the following factorization easier, at first, we consider that the time $t_{fi,s}$ remains quite constant whatever the size Ts. It may be justified on condition $t_{fi,s}$ is insignifiant compared to $ta_{i,m}$.

In the end, we can say

$$t_{a_{i,s+1}} \approx \frac{t_{a_{i,s}}}{K} + (1 - \frac{1}{K})\left[2(a+t_p)+\tau + t_{f_{i,s}}\right] \approx \frac{t_{a_{i,s}}}{K}$$

On condition that : $ta_{i,m} \gg 2a + \tau \approx 3\mu s$ (INMOS data) and $ta_{i,m} \gg t_p + t_{fi,s}$

$ta_{i,m}$ is the minimum computational time of the slave process.

We show that, minimizing $t_{fi,s}$ involves :

- CardCi is small, whatever i
- Every Ci element works on the same size region

Having a coarse grained architecture involves that $t_p \ll ta_{i,m}$; so it is a more general constraint, and not only related to this section.

Stating the previous constraints, the slave computational time is directly proportional to the current region size (i.e Ts). Once more, it may be considered as independant of the slave spatial position inside the network. By this way, the master can easily predict the instance of the slaves processes, without the use of its internal clock to manage the time; this property is useful to develop a starvation strategy (see §3.42). In mode 1.1, we have to verify : $ta_{i,m} \gg t_u(D)$; D is the network diameter. When giving a rhythm to the M->S communication, we put off the start of every slave execution process; in the next section we analyse the response timing of the slaves, knowing that no one of them start its processing at the same time.

-3.12- Master-Slave communication comportment

At first, we suppose that :

-1- There is no starvation point,

-2- The emission and the reception of messages are not interlaced; it amounts to pretend that after sending tasks to slaves, a starvation point appears; the master does not send back a task to a slave when this one has processed its current one.

-3- The emission order is inverse compared to label one

Both hypothesis 1 and 2, enable us to put ourselves into a simple case; the more general case is studied in the section 3.3.

Let us assume that the master starts its emission of messages at $t_0 = 0$:

Ei receives the message at : $t_{ei} = H(N-i) + t^{\alpha}_{M,i} + t_u(i)$

H(N-i) : time when the N-i following message is sent.

The master receives Ei 's response at : $t_{ri} = t_{ei} + t_{Ts} + t_{fi,s} + t_u(i) + t^{\alpha}_{i,M}$

The time interval between two receptions of messages coming from E^{α}_i and E^{γ}_j is : $\Delta t_r = \Delta H + (t^{\alpha}_{M,i} - t^{\gamma}_{M,j}) + (t^{\alpha}_{i,M} - t^{\gamma}_{j,M}) + (t_{fi,s} - t_{fj,s}) + 2(t_u(i) - t_u(j))$

At this moment, we assume that both instances of processes Ei and Ej are such that they seem to process both the same size regions, and the process Ej follows Ei in the emission order. One may consider that, according to the master, both emission and reception frequencies are the same on conditions that :

$$(1)\ t^{\gamma}_{M,j} \approx t^{\alpha}_{M,i}\ ;\ (2)\ t^{\gamma}_{j,M} \approx t^{\alpha}_{i,M}\ ;\ (3)\ t_{fj,s} \approx t_{fi,s}\ ;\ (4)\ t_u(j) \approx t_u(i)$$

Giving a rhythm to the emission of messages, results in the spreading out of the slaves processing start, thus causing the sending back of messages. By this way, every communication slave process has only one message per time to manage; Thus, the waiting time due to the rendezvous between processes tends towards nil. So, both constraints (1) and (2) are verified.

The constraint (3) involves a quite smooth communication charge throughout the network; the number of interruptions during its processing has to be the same for every slave. On condition the time $t_{fi,s}$ is insignifiant compared to $ta_{i,m}$, the constraint (3) may be passed over.

The constraint (4) links together the temporal order of the emission of messages and the spatial one. Indeed, two following slaves in the emission order have to be connected via a transputer link. Or, the clock rate ΔH has to be significantly greater than tu, so that the increasing of tu remains insignificant compared to ΔH.

Stating conditions from 1 to 4, the Slave->Master clock rate transfer follows the Master->Slave one.

-3.13- Determining the clock rate transfer

<u>*According to the time*</u> $ta_{i,m}$

Giving a rhythm puts off the overall emission time. But, it is necessary that every slave has received a computational task before the first slave completes its current one, and sends back its result; so :

$2N\Delta H < [ta_{i,m} + t_u(N) - t_u(1)]$ *ΔH : clock rate transfer ;*

$t_u(N)$: unitary communication time of E_N ; $t_u(1)$: the same with E_1

As a rhythm is given, the variables $t^{\alpha}_{i,M}$ and $t^{\alpha}_{M,i}$ tend towards nil, and are omitted.

<u>*According to the master computational time*</u> t_M

Because the master must not become the bottleneck when receiving messages, the parameters of a message have to be processed before the next message arrival; i.e :

$$\Delta H > t_M$$

The clock rate transfer has to verify :

$$t_M < \Delta H < [ta_{i,m} + t_u(N) - t_u(1)]/2N$$

In the next section, we see that the strategy brings a new constraint on the clock rate transfert.

-3.14- Conclusion

Giving a rhythm to the emission of messages, results in the fact that the network is not locally overloaded; By this way, random variables tends towards nil. Once more, stating that constraints on the master computational time are respected, the master execution process is never interrupted; so $t_{f,M}$ is nil. Thus, we perfectly control the master computational time, and the estimation of N_{max} is better. However, the deadlock problem which results from the interlacing of the M->S messages and S->M messages subsits. In the next section, we focus our attention on it.

-3.2- Deadlock in a transputer network

Processes normally manipulate some form of data, but they may also, read from, write to, input-output devices. The generic term for things which may be manipulated by processes is *resource*.

-3.21- Deadlock conditions [11]

When a number of processes compete for a limited number of resources, situations can arise where two or more processes cannot proceed since each required resource is already claimed by another blocked process. This is known as deadlock [12]. Deadlock can only occur if the following four conditions hold simultaneously :

- A circular wait, including several processes, is involved
- At least one process is waiting to acquire additional resources whilst holding at least one other resource.
- At least, one of the involved resources is non-shareable.
- The pre-emption is not allowed, that is, resources are retained by a process until it has finished with them.

-3.22- OCCAM2 deadlock situation including two processes

The OCCAM2 language allows several concurrent processes to be implemented within the same processor or, on several processors. Both processes exchange data via a communication channel. The used communication scheme is based on the rendezvous which involves a sychronization between two communicating processes.If the process Pi intends to communicate with the process Pj, these both processes have to be synchronized with each other; so that the receiver is ready to receive, and the sender is ready to send. Because Pi requests the communication, it is regarded as an inactive process by the scheduler, until Pj acceptes its communication. After this, data are exchanged [13].

The communication between two processes may be explained using the resources notion. So, two linked processes have a pair of non-shareable resources : the "sending" resource and the "receiving" one. The communication starts when the sender process has the "sending" resource and the receiver process, the "receiving" one. The exchange of data is symbolized by the exchange of these resources.

We show [10] that *"if both processes Pi and Pj intend to communicate one to each other"* the four deadlock conditions are verified. It would be the same when considering a ring topology; we just put ourselves into the situation where all the processes want to communicate with their following neighbour.

We must pay attention to the fact that the OCCAM constructor ALT permits to recover a deadlock situation involving two processes which are waiting to receive a message from each other. Let us see the next OCCAM source :

```
ALT
  channel ? message
  clock ? AFTER start_wait PLUS delay
```

We use the "watchdog" notion, that is, when the waiting on "channel" overlaps the "delay", the internal timer "clock", which is regarded as an internal channel, permits to get out to the ALT loop. Unsuccessfully, the same constructor adpated to the emission of messages does not exist.

There are two different strategies for dealing with deadlock :

- to stop its happening,
- to recover when it has happened

In OCCAM2, when a process is waiting to communicate, it is scheduled out. So, when the communication consists in sending a message, there is no solution to artificially schedule it again. In this case, the deadlock cannot be recovered. It obliges us to stop its happening.

-3.3- Master<->Slave communication: a strategy is needed

On stated conditions of the section 3.13, the clock rate transfer of the S->M messages, follows the M->S one. Since the master sends back a new task when it receives a result from a worker, the previous deadlock situation may occur. The communication strategy avoids two linked processes to send a message to each other, at the same time.

-3.31- The communication strategy

At first, when Ei has to pass a Ej->M message through, it does this, and puts itself into a waiting situation of the message coming from the master and intended to Ej. From this time, a S->M message having Ei to pass through, is stopped by Ei until it has received the message intended to Ej (this message comes from a slave process Ek, such that $Ek \in Ci$, but $Ek \notin Cj$, otherwise it would be stopped by Ej). Ei restores its normal communication mode after all the intended messages have been received. If two S->M messages are transfered at the same time on two different master communication links, the master process them one after each other. The flow chart in fig 3.31, describes the slave communication process, taking into account this strategy.

-3.32- Condition on the clock rate transfer

Only one transfer of message throughout the network is allowed when using the communication strategy. So, it is necessary that the return Master-Slave communication time and the master computational one remain smaller than the clock rate transfer; i.e :

$$\Delta H > t_M + 2t_u(N) \qquad \textit{both } t^{\alpha}_{i,M} \textit{ and } t^{\alpha}_{M,i} \textit{ are considered as nil}$$

-3.33- Starvation points in the network

The previous communication strategy involves that every slave which sends a message to the master has to receive a "response" from the master, in order to allow another blocked communication. But, when a starvation point arises, the master cannot send new task to the waiting workers. Therefore, a deadlock situation arises too, because the waiting workers block some other messages and so on. In order to stop its happening, the master must send back a "response"; even if it is a "starvation response". Thus, the master handles two sorts of messages :

- *messages including the parameters of a raw region,*
- *"nil messages" referring to a starvation point.*

The previous communication strategy may be use both in the communication mode 1.1 and 1.2. However, it is specially useful when using the mode 1.1. It is due to the temporal sliding which increases at every processing pass, when workers do not processed the same region sizes. In a result, several workers may finish their processing at the same time and send their results. The communication strategy is also useful when all the temporal constraints cannot be respected. Otherwise, in mode 1.2, only one message is sent through at a given time in the Ei-M communication way.

On the contrary, the current strategy cannot manage the allocation of new tasks after the arising of a starvation point. Indeed, in mode 1, the master does not manage the communication frequencies; so, it cannot determine the suitable moments to allocate tasks to idle workers, unless it creates a deadlock situation between two workers which would send a message to each other, at the same time.

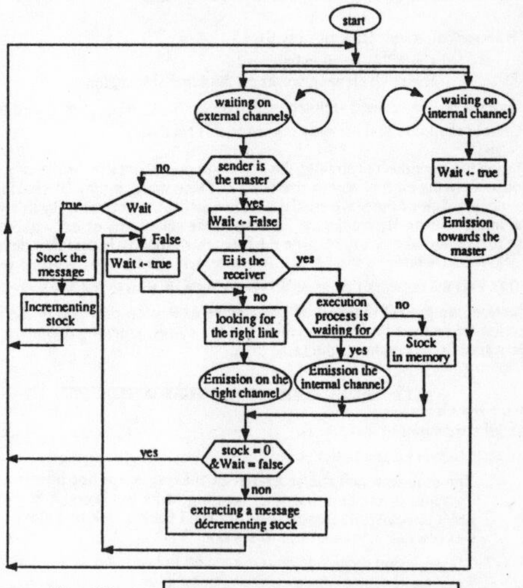

Figure 3.31 Slave communicating process including the strategy

-3.4- Allocating new tasks to idle workers

We put ourselves into the situation where we state temporal constraints pointing out the clock rate transfer. We suppose that a starvation point arises; then new tasks are generated. They have to be allocated to idle workers. There are two different strategies which permit to distribute new tasks after the arising of a starvation situation :

- Firstly [14], the master waits for a total starvation ; then new tasks are allocated as in the initialization step. This strategy is the only one which can be used with mode 1.1, because the master cannot determine the suitable moment to allocate new tasks to idle workers.

- Secondly, let us note that, in mode 1.2, the temporal sliding can be regarded as insignificant. So, we are able to determine the moments when all the active workers still processed their current task (named "busy moments"), and when they may send their results. The "busy moments" are useed to allocate new tasks to idle workers.

-3.41- Temporal comportment of the network

If the master sends a message to the slave Ei at time $t_0=0$, it receives its response at time : $t_{ri} = t_{ei} + t_{Ts} + t_{fi,s} + t_u(i) + t^{\alpha}_{i,M}$.

Let us state all the temporal constraints; one can say that :

$$t_{ei} = H(N-i)+t_u(i) \qquad t^{\alpha}_{i,M} \approx 0$$

$$t_{ri} = H(N-i) + t_{fi,s} + 2t_u(i) + t_{Ts}$$

$$2t_u(i) + t_{tM} < \Delta H \quad \text{and} \quad t_{a_{i,m}} > 2N\Delta H$$

We put ourselves into the situation where $t_{fi,s}$ is insgnificant compared to $t_{a_{i,m}}$. We can say that :

-a- The temporal difference between Ei and Ej is less than 2NΔH

It amounts to regard both Ei and Ej instances, as it seems they processed the same region size and Ej follows Ei in the emission order (It may be true);

So : $\Delta t_r = t_{ri} - t_{rj} \approx \alpha\Delta H + (t_{fi,s} - t_{fi+1,s}) + 2(t_u(i) - t_u(i+1))$

where α =temporal difference between Ei and Ej

$\underbrace{(t_{fi,s} - t_{fi+1,s}) + 2(t_u(i) - t_u(i+1))}_{<\Delta H}$

$$\Delta tr \leq (2N+1)\,\Delta H$$

-b- The temporal difference between Ei and Ej is greater than NΔH

It amounts to regard both Ei and Ej instances, as they processed both different size regions; So, the difference size is at least equal to $t_{a_{i,m}}$.

Once more, $t_{a_{i,m}}$ is assumed to be greater that 2NΔH; so :

$$t_{a_{i,m}} = 2N\Delta H + \beta\Delta H \quad \text{where} \quad \beta \geq 2\Delta H$$

Thus :

$$|t_{ri} - t_{rj}| \geq 2N\Delta H + \beta\Delta H \quad \text{that is} \; : \Delta t_r - 2N\Delta H \geq 2\Delta H$$

Outcoming

When the master receives a message from a slave Ei (which has processed a region size Ts), at time $t_{ri} = t_{si} + \varepsilon$ ($t_{s,i}$ corresponds to the time when no interruption appears; i.e $H(N-i)+t_{Ts}$), two different situations may occur :

-a- The instance of the following slave Ej results in the receiving of its message by the master at : $t_{si}+\Delta H \leq t_{rj} \leq t_{si}+ (2N+1)\Delta H$

-b- The instance of the following slave Ej results in the receiving of its message by the master at : $t_{rj} > t_{si} + (2N+2)\Delta H$

In the situation -b-, the master cannot receive a message from any slave before (2N+2) clock rates. So, it may send back its response to Ei at time $t = t_si + \Delta H$; then it takes advantage of the "busy moments" to allocate new tasks (if they exist) to idle workers; no one deadlock situation may arise.

-3.42- Managing the starvation points

On the arising of a starvation point, the master sends to idle workers a "starvation message". As soon as new tasks are generated, they are allocated to idle workers during the "busy moments". In order to determine these "busy moments", it simply manages a pool of pair of registers corresponding to the region size and to the temporal order of the workers. These registers are updated at every message arrival. Therefore, we can easily determine the "busy moments".The flow chart of the figure 3.42 corresponds to the master communication process in mode 1.2 when the second starvation strategy is implemented.

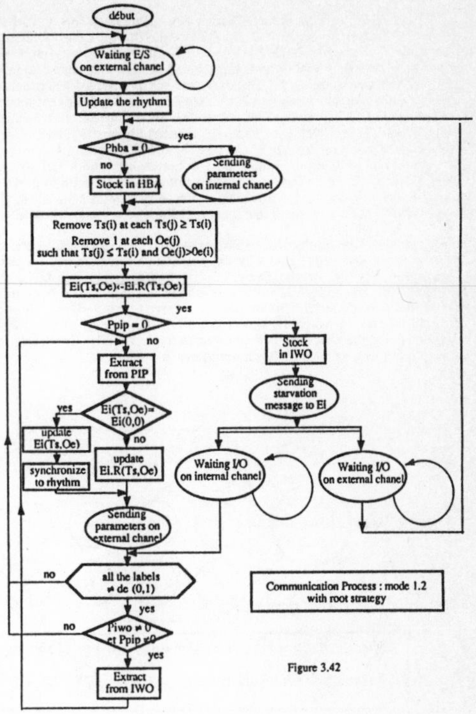

Figure 3.42

-4- Experimental results

This parallelization method has been employed for the parallel implementation of the splitting step of a spatio-temporal algorithm with a motion criterion [16][17]. In this section, we intend to emphasize the administration overhead when using the communication modes 1.1 and 1.2, with the fisrt starvation strategy (see § 2.23 and § 3.4). To do this, we determine :

$$\text{The speed up} : \sigma = \frac{t_{seq}}{t_{par}}$$

$$\text{and the parallelization efficiency} : Eff = \frac{\sigma}{N}$$

t_{seq} *: Sequential time ;* t_{par} *: parallel time ; N : number of slaves.*

In the two following situations, we use a synthesis image; we simulate a diagonal moving of one pixel, and the image is partitionned according to the situation in which we intend to put ourselves (fig 4.0). We choose a multi-linear chain topology [15].

Firstly, we put ourselves in the situation where a great number of tasks has to be processed, and no point starvation appears (fig 4.1); so the image is partitionned in 256 regions (each region size is 8x8 pixels). We emphasize the acceleration of the slave commputational time due to the extra item work in mode 1.2. This global acceleration is due to all the local ones compare to the wasted return communication time between slaves and master in mode 1.1. The parallelization efficiency always grows up from 67% (1 master, 2 slaves) till 90% (1master, 12 slaves). It is due to the larger the number of processors, the less the master contribution in calculating the efficiency (its computational contribution in processing tasks is quite insignificant).To show this, we do not take into account the master process, and determine the slave parallelization efficiency.

Secondly, we put ourselves in the situation where there is a few number of tasks and starvation points appear (fig 4.2); so the image is partitionned in 16 regions (each size region is 32x32 pixels). The root strategy increases their arizing, because a total starvation is created as soon as a starvation point appears. Once more in mode 1.2 this starvation points is arized when a slave process cannot keep in memory an extra item of work. So, this experimental case emphasizes the drawback of mode 1.2 for the artificial starvation points. When using 9 workers (3 fathers, 6 sons), the artificial starvation point is arized when processing 32x32 size regions (16 regions, whereas 18 are required), outcoming the important gap between the both efficiencies (mode 1.1 and 1.2). When using 12 slaves this starvation point appears at the same size region, for both modes. After a first total starvation, the number of new tasks is so small that there are all the time some idle workers.

Thirdly, we show the results of the splitting step applied to a road sequences when moving is detected (figure 4.3); the image is partitionned in 16 regions (size region 32x32). As the camera is on board, many sub-tasks are generated. But in mode 1.2, starvation points appears at the beginning because only 16 regions 32x32 are created whereas with 9 slaves, 18 ones are required and 24, when 12 slaves are used. Because of this artificial starvation point, the efficiency is lower than in mode 1.1. The first starvation strategy is not well adapted to the communication mode 1.2.

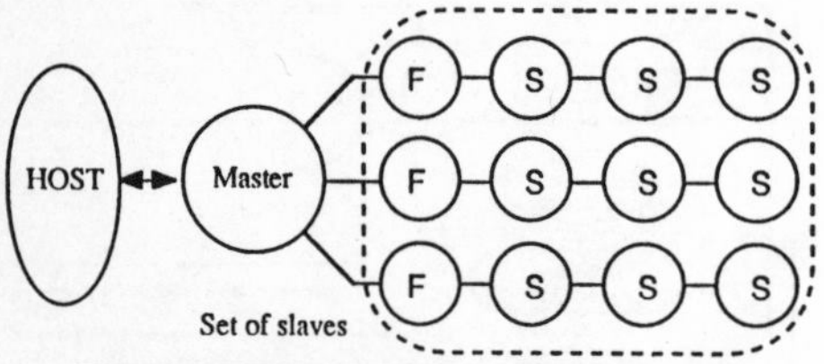

Experimental topology : 1 master with from 1 to 12 slaves

The transputer Network is composed of INMOS T800 -20

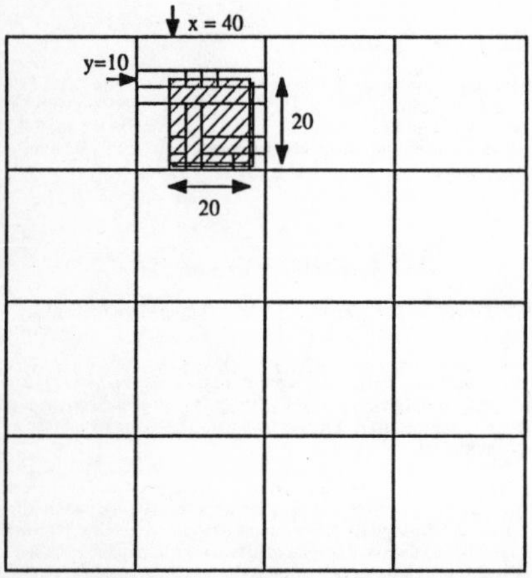

Figure 4.0 Synthesis image 128x128 : 1 pixel diagonal moving

Figure 4.1

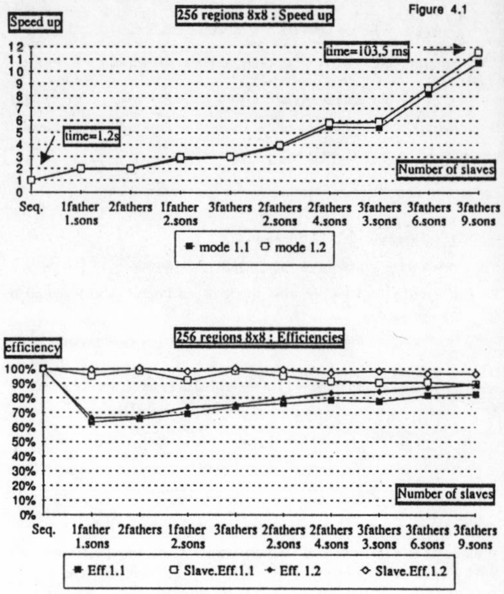

Figure 4.2

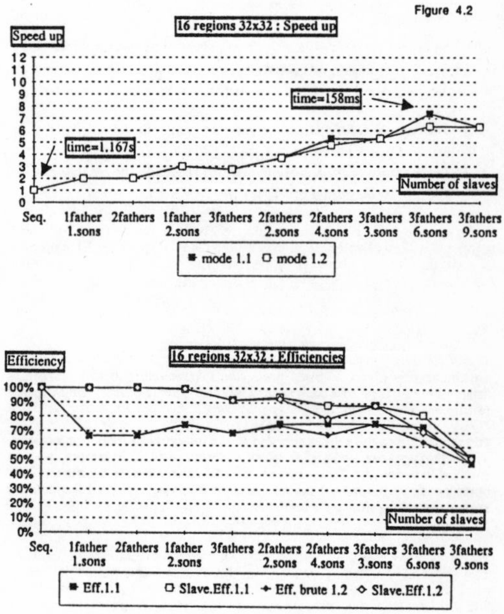

Road scene at time t

Road scene at time t+dt

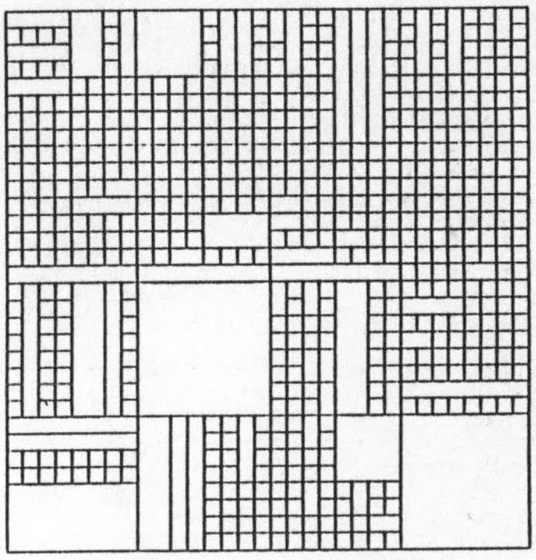

Spatio-tempral segmentation

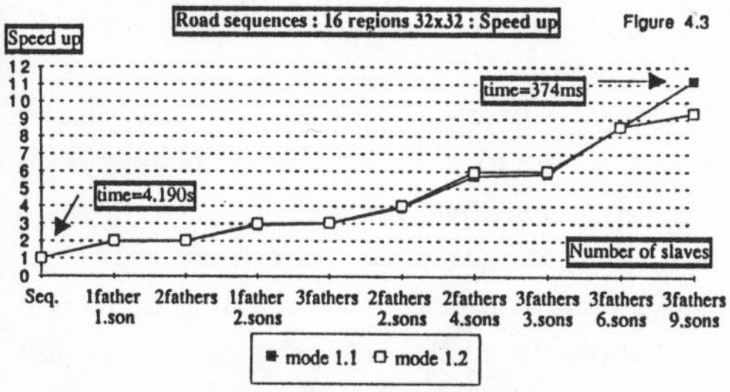

Figure 4.3

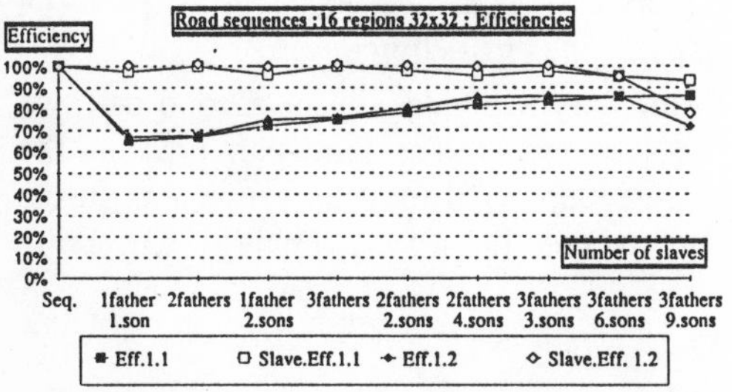

-5- Conclusion

In this paper, a parallel implementation of an algorithm using the Kd-tree method is developed. The formalization scheme allows to develop this implementation, making abstraction of the topology; once more, some constraints on the topology have been determined.

Still making abstraction of the topology, we show that to give a rhythm to the emission of messages permits to optimize the workers efficiency because no one local saturation point arises. We develop a simple strategy, which prevents all the deadlock from happening, and allows to allocate new tasks to idle workers, before waiting for the total network starvation. The greater the number of different starvation points, the greater the speeding up.

We are working to improve the strategy, in order to allow to pass over some state temporal constraints; in particular, at the mode 1.2 initialization step; i.e when the master has to send a pair of tasks to all the workers, before the first one finishes its current task. It would permits us to increase the number of slaves. Once more, we are now focusing our attention on the parallel implementation of the merging step, in order to complete the parallelization of a Kd-tree algorithm on a transputer network.

References

[1] *H.SAMET*
"The Quadtree and related hierarchical data structures"
Computer surveys, Vol.16, n°2, June 1984, p.187-260

[2] *L.HOROWITZ, T.PAVLIDIS*
"Picture segmentation by a directed split-and-merge procedure", 1974

[3] *INMOS limited*
"The transputer data book" ; Second edition INMOS, 1989[3]

[4] *P.M DEW, HAN WANG*
"Data parallelism and the processor farm model for image processing and synthesis on a transputer array" 1988
Proc SPIE Int. Soc. Opt. Eng. Vol 977

[5] *D.MAY, R.SHEPHERD, C.KEANE*
"Communicating process architecture: Transputer and OCCAM"
INMOS limited, 1987

[6] *P.VINCENT*
"Nouvelles architectures d'ordinateurs" ; Edition test Chap 6

[7] *S.NICOLLE, F.CHANTEMARGHUE, J.P.DERUTIN, P.BONTON*
"Formalizing Architecture Based on the "Processors Farm" Method, For implementation of Kd-tree Algorithms"
IASTED, June 18-21, 1990, Lugano, SWITZERLAND; p31-35

[8] *M.GONDRAN, M.MINOUX*
"Graphes et algorithmes" ; Edit EYROLLES, 1979

[9] *D.A.NICOLE, E.K.LLYOD, J.S.WARD*
"Switching networks for transputer links", 1987

[10] *S.NICOLLE*
"Formalisation d'une architecture utilisant la méthode ferme de processeurs: parallélisation d'algorithmes de vision de type Kd-tree".
Internal report 1990

[11] *R.D DOWSING*
"Introduction to concurrency using OCCAM"
Van Nostrand Reinhold (International) 1988

[12] *R.C.HOLT*
"Some deadlock properties of computer system"
ACM computer Surveys 1972, 4, 179-96

[13] *D.TRYSTAN, F.VINCENT*
"Programmation avancée du transputer", Lettre du transputer, 2, 1989.

[14] *P.LEGRAND, S.NICOLLE, J.P.DERUTIN*
"Parallélisation de la phase de division d'un algorithme de type division-fusion selon la méthode ferme de processeurs"
Internal report June 90

[15] *D.J.PRITCHARD*
"Mathematical models of distributed compilation"
7th OPPT, Sept 14-16, 1987, Ed Traian MUNTEAN

[16] *P.BOUTHEMY, J.SANTILLANA RIVERO*
"Region segmentation according to motion-based criteria"
Rapport de recherche INRIA n°629, February 1987.

[17] *F.CHANTEMARGUE, S.NICOLLE, P.BONTON, J.P.DERUTIN*
"Parallelization of the splitting step of a quadtree algorithm"
IASTED, June 18-21, 1990, Lugano, SWITZERLAND; p183-188

[18] *J.P DERUTIN, B.BESSERER*
"Transvision : an heterogeneous machine for real time image processing", Internal report 90.

Multicomputers UNIX based on CHORUS

Bénédicte Herrmann (Université de Franche-Comté - ONERA)
Laurent Philippe (Université de Franche-Comté - Chorus systèmes)
Chorus systèmes, 6, avenue Gustave Eiffel
F–78182, Saint-Quentin-en-Yvelines (France)
E-mail: lau@chorus.fr

1. Introduction

Today users require more and more computational leverage to speed up their applications. In their attempt to provide its machine architectures have become more complicated because traditional architectures were too limited. Different approaches have been taken, for instance shared memory multiprocessors, distributed memory multiprocessors, etc. We focus on distributed memory machines that we call multicomputers. But on this kind of machine there is a general lack of "ease of use" in the program development cycle. To provide a program development environment that facilitates the design, implementation, and debugging of parallel and distributed programs, we implemented a UNIX® system using the CHORUS®[Rozi88] technology on multicomputers. Our work is conducted on iNTEL's iPSC/2.
In the first part we justify our choice of distributed memory machines. In the second part, we describe the CHORUS technology based on the CHORUS kernel. The third part presents the architecture of a UNIX subsystem[Herr88] based on CHORUS, suited for multicomputers. In the fourth part we outline the steps required to port CHORUS onto the iPSC/2. Finally we describe our future work.

2. Multiprocessors and their environment

As the need for computing power increases, the conventional monoprocesor computer architecture becomes insufficient. To gain computational power, new multiprocessor architectures have been designed, which are based on a set of processors interconnected via a bus or a network.

2.1 Multiprocessor architectures

A distinction can be made between different basic classes of multiprocessors; this list is not exhaustive:

- symmetric multiprocessors, which are shared memory machines. The symmetric multiprocessor communication network is generally the system bus;
- distributed memory machines, which may be seen as a set of computers. Distributed memory machines require a scalable network;

® UNIX is a registered trademark of UNIX System Laboratories, Inc. in the U.S.A. and other countries.

® CHORUS is a registered trademark of Chorus systèmes.

2.1.1 Shared memory machines

There are different types of shared memory multiprocessors. The classical view of this architecture is the symmetric multiprocessor: a set of processors access all the memory space and devices of the computer with the same priority .

Generally, the architecture is transparent to the user: the operating system balances the load on the processors without user knowledge. This is easily possible because the operating system kernel data can be shared by all the processors. Operating systems such as UNIX have been extended in order to exploit these architectures (ex: Mach[Acce86, Boykin89])

However such architectures are known to have scalability problems when the number of processors exceeds a few dozen.

2.1.2 Distributed memory multiprocessors

We will call a totally distributed memory multiprocessor machine, a **multicomputer.** We define a **node** as a processor and its supporting environment. So a multicomputer is a set of nodes interconnected via a uniform scalable network. We will call the interconnection network of the multicomputers an **internal network** (inet) and the network used to connect the multicomputer to other machines (eg: Ethernet for workstations) an **external network** (enet).

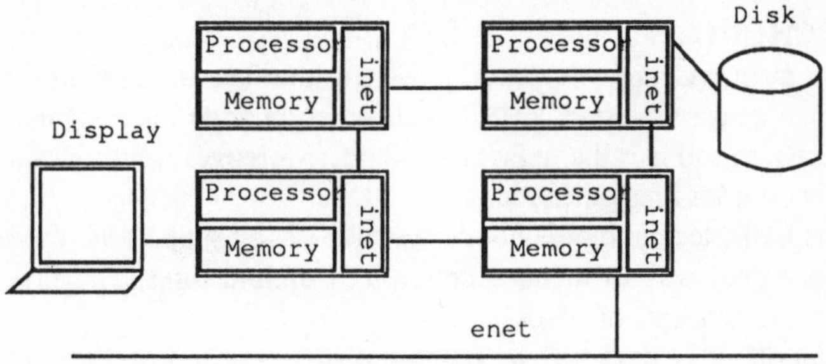

Multicomputer

In a multicomputer, there are two models of nodes. A **basic node** includes one processor with its own memory and a connection to the internal network. A **specialized node** consists of a basic node plus some devices. In multicomputers, each node has a private memory area which may be accessed only by the owner processor.

Each processor has its own interrupt control, which means that an interrupt occurring on one node cannot be managed by the processor of another node. An interrupt is always managed by the same processor.

The processors may only communicate by exchange of messages which means that the hardware of a node must support this functionality. Furthermore, messages are the only way of interacting between two nodes.

Operating systems are difficult to build for this type of architecture. Today, existing operating systems are very simple (ex: NX[Intel86] on iPSC/2, Helios[Garn87] on transputers, etc).

2.2 Software Environment for Multicomputers

Multicomputers are often used only as specialized coprocessor for a host computer. Users develop their code in a workstation environment (because of the ease of use) and download binary programs to the multicomputer. Generally, there are only a few facilities on the multicomputer to manage the needs of these applications such as input and output. As the use of multicomputers becomes more widespread, the lack of tools and environments for debugging and program development will become a more serious problem.

Tomorrow's goal will be to provide a program environment which facilitates the design, implementation, and debugging of parallel and distributed programs using multicomputers. These requirements must be taken into account by the operating system developers.
Moreover it is very important for the user to find the same interface on the multicomputer as on his workstation.

2.2.1 Operating systems requirements

We consider the following operating system requirements to be crucial for effective use of multicomputers:

- manage the devices attached to the specialized nodes.
- provide uniform access to the information or resources available on one node by the other nodes.
- provide debugging tools. On multicomputers the applications may be distributed so the programs cannot be debugged with standard tools. These new tools to be implemented represent a new class of problem.
- provide a uniform, standard operating system interface to support a large number of existing tools (eg: databases, graphic interfaces, etc).

2.2.2 UNIX and CHORUS:

Since UNIX is the most widespread operating system interface used on workstations, it seems to be a good choice as user interface. UNIX will satisfy a wide range of users because it is a general purpose system and it is the defacto standard. Moreover it provides a large number of tools, because it is used for many different applications.
Unfortunately, the UNIX technology is not designed to easily support the multicomputer architecture. Its primary goal was to manage centralized architectures, and distribution was not integrated in the basic concepts of UNIX.
The CHORUS technology is designed to support distributed architectures by integrating the communication concept at kernel level and in implementing a distributed virtual memory.
CHORUS also enables the implementation of a UNIX interface as a subsystem based on client/server model. This provides general and network-transparent access to resources at the UNIX level such as uniform file and device access. Its modular architecture allows the UNIX subsystem to be scaled. Servers are loaded only on the nodes where they are needed.

3. The CHORUS Architecture

3.1 Overall Organization

A CHORUS System is composed of a small-sized **Nucleus** and a number of **System Servers.** Those servers cooperate in the context of **Subsystems** (e.g., UNIX) to provide a coherent set of services and interfaces to their "users".
The CHORUS Nucleus plays a double role:

1. Local services:

   It manages, at the lowest level, the local physical computing resources of a "computer", called a *site* by means of three clearly identified components:

   - allocation of local processor(s) is controlled by a *real-time multi-tasking executive.* This executive provides fine grain synchronization and priority-based preemptive scheduling,
   - local memory is managed by a *virtual memory manager*,
   - external events – interrupts, traps, exceptions – are dispatched by a *supervisor*.

2. Global services:
   An *IPC Manager* provides the communication service, delivering messages regardless of the location of their destination within a CHORUS distributed system. It may rely on external system servers to operate all kinds of network protocols.

3.2 The CHORUS Nucleus basic abstractions

The physical support for a CHORUS system is composed of a set of *sites* (''computers'', or ''nodes''), interconnected by a communication *network* (i.e., a external network or internal network). A **site** is a tightly coupled grouping of physical resources: one or more processors, memory, and attached I/O devices. There is one CHORUS Nucleus per site.

The **actor** is the logical unit of distribution and of collection of resources in a CHORUS system. An actor defines a protected address space supporting the execution of one or more *threads* (lightweight processes) that share the address space of the actor.

Any given actor is tied to a site, and its threads are executed on that site. A given site may support many simultaneous actors. Since each has its own ''user'' address space, actors define protected *virtual machines*.

The **thread** is the unit of execution in a CHORUS system and is characterized by an execution context corresponding to the state of the processor (registers, program counter, stack pointer, privilege level, etc.). A thread is always tied to one and only one actor. These threads share the resources of that actor and no other actor. Threads are scheduled by the Nucleus as independent entities. In particular, threads of an actor may run in parallel on the many processors of a *multiprocessor* site.

Besides the shared memory provided by the actor address space, CHORUS offers message-based facilities (referred to as *IPC*) which allow any thread to communicate and synchronize with any other thread, on any site. The CHORUS IPC permits threads to exchange messages either *asynchronously* or by *demand/response*, also called *Remote Procedure Call* (*RPC*). Its main characteristic is its transparency with respect to the location of threads: the communication interface is uniform, regardless of whether it is between threads in a single actor, between threads in different actors on the same site, or between threads in different actors on different sites.

A **message** is composed of a (optional) *message body* and a (optional) *message annex.* Both are untyped string of bytes. Message passing is tightly coupled with the virtual memory mechanism to enable data transmission without copy.

Messages are not addressed directly to threads, but to intermediate entities called *ports.*

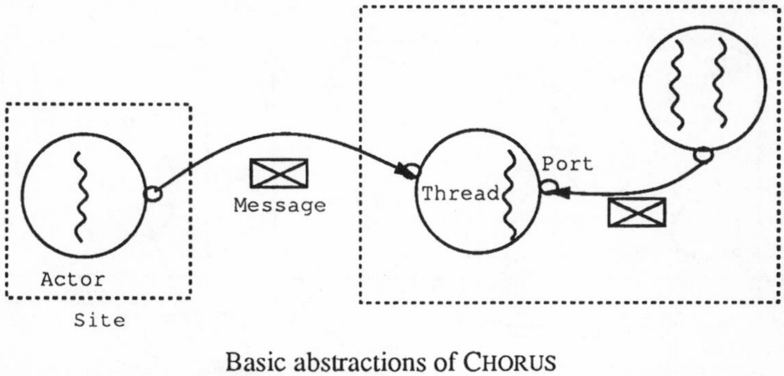

Basic abstractions of CHORUS

A **port** is an address to which messages can be sent, and a queue holding the messages received but not yet consumed by the threads. A port can only be attached to a single actor at a time, but can be attached to different actors successively, effectively *migrating* the port from one actor to another.

The notion of a port provides the basis for *dynamic reconfiguration*: this extra level of indirection between communicating threads, enables a given *service* to be supplied independently of a given actor. The servicing actor can be changed at any time, by changing the attachment of the port from the actor holding the initial thread to the actor holding the new one.

A **group** of ports connects those ports to a *multicast* facility: it allows one thread to communicate directly with an *entire group of threads* (via a group of ports); it provides also *"functional"* access to a service by selecting a server from a group of (equivalent) servers. A group is built by dynamically inserting ports into, and removing them from, the group.

Ports are globally designated with *Unique Identifiers* (UI's). A **UI** is unique in a CHORUS system. The CHORUS Nucleus implements a localization service, allowing threads to use these names without any knowledge of the location of the designated entities. UI's may be freely exchanged between actors.

Global names for other types of objects are based on UI's, but hold more information, such as protection information.

The CHORUS memory management service[Abro89, Abro89a] provides separate address spaces (if the hardware gives adequate support), associated to actors, called **contexts**, and efficient and versatile mechanisms for data transfer between contexts, and between secondary storage and a context. The mechanisms are adapted to various needs, such as IPC, file read/write or mapping, memory sharing between contexts, and context duplication.

CHORUS memory management considers the data of a context to be a set of non-overlapping **regions**, which form the valid portions of the context.

Regions are mapped (generally) to secondary storage objects, called **segments**. Segments are managed outside of the Nucleus, by external servers called segment **mappers**. These manage the implementation of the segments, as well as the protection and naming of segments.

4. CHORUS/MiX

4.1 Overall structure

UNIX facilities may logically be partitioned into several classes of services according to the different types of resources managed: processes, files, devices, pipes, sockets. The design of the structure of the UNIX Subsystem in CHORUS, called CHORUS/MiX, puts emphasis on a clean definition of the interactions between these different classes of services in order to provide a true modular structure.

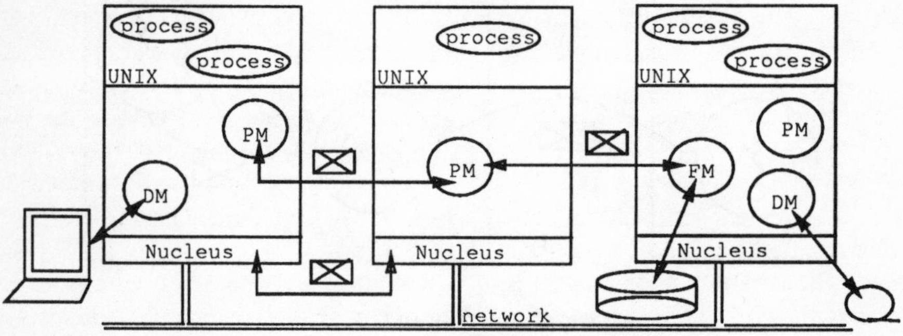

CHORUS architecture

The UNIX Subsystem has been implemented as a set of System Servers, running on top of the CHORUS Nucleus. Each type of system resource (process, file, etc.) is isolated and managed by a dedicated system server. Interactions between these servers are based on the CHORUS IPC which enforces clean interface definitions.

Several types of servers may be distinguished within a typical UNIX Subsystem:

- **The Process Manager (PM)** executes services directly related to UNIX process management (creation and destruction of processes, signals, etc.).
- **The File Manager (FM)** performs file management services. The current version is compatible with SYSTEM V3.2 services and physical disk layout.
- **The Device Managers (DM)** manage asynchronous lines, bit-map displays, ***pseudo-ttys***, etc. and implement the UNIX *line disciplines*.
- **The Socket Manager** (SM) implements BSD 4.3 socket services, providing access to TCP/IP protocols.

The CHORUS implementation of UNIX is especially suited to multicomputers because of its modularity and scalability. We will have the following mapping on a node:

CHORUS scalability	
one node	one process manager
one disk	one file manager
one device	one server

4.2 Functional extensions

CHORUS also provides extensions to the UNIX interface to take benefit of the distributed nature of the system and of the underlying CHORUS Nucleus services. Such access is not provided by directly invoking the Nucleus but rather through the UNIX Process Manager, in order to eliminate inconsistencies.

- File System extension : the naming facilities provided by the UNIX file system have been extended, to permit the designation of services accessed via Ports. This is used to interconnect file systems and provide a global name space.
- Process Management extensions : the basic extension to process management is to enable remote creation or execution of processes. A "creation site" information has been added to the system context of UNIX processes.
- Virtual Memory services : UNIX processes can use the Virtual Memory services of the CHORUS Nucleus to create regions, map segments within a region, share regions, etc. They can thus gain access to the physical memory (e.g., for mapping bitmap memory).
- Inter Process Communication : UNIX processes can create ports, insert ports into groups, and send and receive messages. They can migrate ports from one process to another. CHORUS IPC mechanisms allow them to communicate transparently over the network. Applications can therefore be tested on a single machine, and then distributed throughout the network, without any modification necessary to adapt to a new configuration. Using port migration or group facilities provides a sound basis for doing dynamic reconfiguration and developing fault-tolerant applications.
- Multi-threaded UNIX Processes : Multiprogramming within a UNIX process is possible with **u_threads.** A u_thread can be considered as a lightweight process within a standard UNIX process. It shares all the process resources and in particular its virtual address space and open files. Each u-thread represents a different locus of control.

This UNIX interface allows the user to execute parallel applications, and is therefore suited to take advantage of a multicomputer architecture.

5. UNIX on iPSC/2

The current CHORUS implementation runs on sets of workstations interconnected via a local area network. The first stage of our project will provide the same view of the CHORUS/MiX subsystem on a hypercube as on a a set of interconnected workstations. In a second step of the project, which is not yet implemented, we will provide a UNIX interface taking into account multicomputer user needs.
To validate all the CHORUS concepts on multicomputers we ported the CHORUS kernel and the UNIX subsystem onto an Intel iPSC/2 as independently as possible of its architecture. We present the current state of the project and our porting work.

5.1 Overview of the iPSC/2

The iPSC/2[Close88] is a hypercube architecture marketed commercially by Intel Scientific Computer. Our configuration is a 32 node hypercube, but the architecture supports up to 128 processors. Each node is a board plugged into a cabinet. Below is a brief overview of the composition of one basic node :

- The processor is an Intel 386.
- The board has 4 Mbytes of RAM, wich can be expanded to 16 Mbytes.
- In addition to the central processor, a coprocessor which can be either a WEITEK or an i387. Our cube uses WEITEKs.
- There is a DCM (Direct Connect Module) communication module, reachable by the CPU via advanced DMA. This communication module allows connection with up to seven nodes.
- There is a direct line, controlled by an UART, called USM (Unit Service Module).
- An SCSI interface, supports disks, network (Ethernet) or devices.

The nodes can communicate with each other via the DCM. Routing between any two nodes is automatic and does not requires CPU intervention. There is a host station (PC/AT) which is used to download the programs to the nodes and centralize the information coming from the nodes. For the moment we have a very centralized implementation of the hypercube because all the applications must pass through the host to reach the hypercube.

5.2 Downloading CHORUS on the iPSC/2

It was necessary to develop tools to load CHORUS onto the nodes because the host facilities were not sufficient.
To ensure the modularity of the CHORUS system, each server is implemented as an independent program. The binaries generated include a COFF (Common Object File Format) header. This header contains information on the binary file structure. To load the set of binaries onto the nodes we must group them in a boot archive which is the concatenation of all the binaries. For instance, at test time the boot archive includes the boot, the kernel and some test actors. We had to develop a tool to automatically prepare this boot archive.
The structure of the CHORUS archive is stored in a LOAD table, in the boot's data area. The data and code sizes, entry point, etc. (found in the COFF header) of each binairy are store in this LOAD table so that, the kernel knows which actors it must run at run time.
The binary image is then loaded to every node , via the direct line (USM).

5.3 Porting CHORUS

Porting of the kernel was thus reduced, although it was still necessary to update the boot and architecture dependent parts of the kernel.

5.3.1 The boot

In this part we initialize all the hardware structures necessary to prepare execution of the CHORUS kernel (ie: mmu tables, interrupt tables, descriptors, etc) and the hardware components of the node. In particular, we must initialize the DCMs. As the DCMs exchange data synchronously between two nodes, their initialization must be synchronized. This is done using the USM line. Each step the nodes wait for a message from the host on the USM. They all read the message at the same time when the host sends and start their initialization synchronously. When they are finished, the nodes send an acknowledgement to the host. When all the nodes are finished, the host sends the next message.

5.3.2 The kernel

The portable parts of the kernel, of course, do not cause any problems Most of the kernel code has been reused. We only changed some machine dependent parts of the kernel: interrupt management, site number, etc. The currently implemented version of the CHORUS kernel is version 3.3. This version takes into account heterogeneous networks. It also implements a new virtual memory management providing mapped file facilities and allows the integration of an external mapper providing virtual shared memory on the network.

5.3.3 The communication

The communication part of the kernel is independent of the network. It implements only local communications. When a message must be sent to a distant port, the CHORUS kernel locates the destination site and gives the message to the corresponding protocol server. After adding the necessary headers to the message, the protocol server calls the network driver.

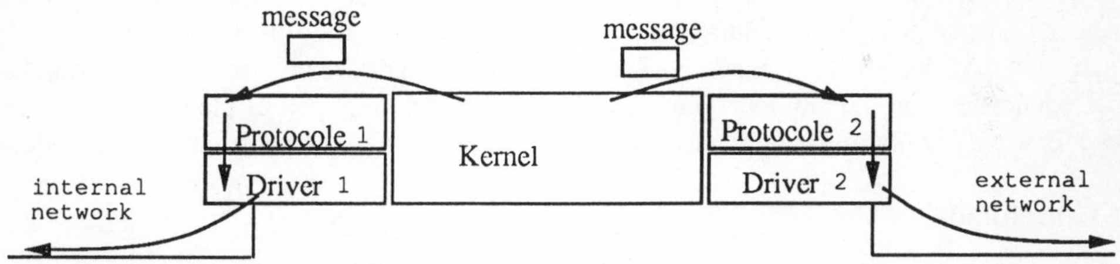

CHORUS communcation protocole

This communication scheme is not particular to the iPSC/2 network. We can implement different protocols when we want to access other communication mediums. For instance, Intel provides nodes with Ethernet boards. Thus it is possible to access sites on an external network. We have implemented a communication protocol dedicated to the iPSC/2 network. To optimize the exchange of messages we avoid copying data, using the hardware features and the memory management services of the CHORUS kernel.

5.3.4 The debug

The main problem encountered during porting was the lack of debugging facilities. There is no display on the nodes, so we have to use other means to obtain traces. Traces are necessary to follow the execution of the kernel (register values, parameters, contents of a memory address, etc).

Our first debugging tool was an optic link. We used it to display traces on a console by displaying them on a led (the bits of the ASCII value of each character are sent on the led and interpreted by the console).

When the first steps of the boot had been debugged, we developed a driver for the serial line and we established a protocol using this driver between the host and the nodes. This protocol was integrated to use the kernel debugger. The nodes may be chosen dynamically with the traces kept in a buffer on the other nodes. This debugging environment allows a user to work from a remote workstation.

Driving the USM line was also useful to implement the `printf` and `scanf` routines used by the kernel.

5.4 Porting the CHORUS/MiX subsystem

As CHORUS/MiX is modular, we proceeded by steps to port the UNIX servers. We first loaded a process manager on each node to provide the UNIX interface and to allow the execution of processes. The processes were loaded in the boot archive as we cannot dynamically access them without a file manager. These processes did not perform file accesses.

To use UNIX we must have access to files (data or binary). Generally this is provided either by accessing a local disk or by remote disk access (NFS, RFS, etc). Unfortunately we do not yet have Ethernet boards on our iPSC/2 and our disks are not in a standard UNIX file system format. The only way to dynamically load files is to use the connection between node 0 and the host. As CHORUS/MiX is modular, it was really easy to replace the existing File Manager with a simple one on node 0 which sends the file requests to a process on the host. On the host side, this process performs normal UNIX file accesses.

Processes running on nodes other than node 0 transparently access their files by communicating with this simple File Manager, by construction of CHORUS/MiX. This illustrates the power of CHORUS/MiX: MiX servers are located where the resources are. Processes then access their services transparently. In the future, File Managers will be located in the specialized nodes provided with disks. Socket Managers will only be present in nodes provided with external network connection. On the multicomputer, each node runs only that part of the operating system which is strictly necessary to implement the UNIX abstractions and to control the local devices.

6. Conclusion

For the moment the UNIX interface provided is similar to the UNIX interface on a set of workstations interconnected via a network. So our future work will be:

— to validate the portability of our CHORUS implementation on other multicomputers;

— to adapt the UNIX interface to the needs of the multicomputer users.

6.1 Requirements to port CHORUS to others multicomputers

As we have said before, we have attempted to port CHORUS as independently as possible of the iPSC/2 architecture. As a result, it will be easier to port it to other kinds of multicomputers. Below is a short description of what will have to be updated to port the CHORUS kernel to other machines, with respect to the model we have chosen.

— The processor: most of the CHORUS supervisor is portable, but the lower layers must be updated for a given processor.

— The memory: to implement the CHORUS/MiX subsystem with all its functionality we need an mmu (memory management unit). As a result, the lower parts of the virtual memory must be updated. If there is no mmu, we can not implement all the functionalities on the UNIX interface, so there will be some restrictions to the UNIX interface.

— The network: the CHORUS communication part of the kernel is independent of the network. We must update the protocol used (if it is not currently implemented in CHORUS) and develop a new driver. CHORUS provides facilities to integrate new network drivers (in the NDM: network device manager) and protocols.

From this, it can be conclude that the kernel is very portable and its concepts are well suited to multicomputers.

6.2 Requirements to adapt UNIX to multicomputers

CHORUS/MIX 3.2 extends the use of UNIX to a set of computers interconnected via a network. This UNIX interface allows the user to take the distribution of his programs into account, while providing general and network transparent access to resources such as uniform file device access. In our view, however these facilities are not sufficient to provide a comfortable programming environment. Programmers may use multicomputers to gain computing power but do not care about the best possible mapping of their applications on the set of processors. For these users we have to provide distribution facilities which will hide the underlying architecture. They will see the multicomputer as a single machine running UNIX. This means that we must provide transparent access at system level to all the devices and tools to control placement on multicomputers while maintaining the ability to manage it.

Our future work includes the study and implementation of these new facilities. In addition, the development of a distributed debugger is in progress.

7. References

[Abro89a] Vadim Abrossimov, Marc Rozier, and Michel Gien, "Virtual Memory Management in Chorus," in *Lecture Notes in Computer Sciences*, Springer-Verlag, Berlin, Germany, (18-19 April 1989), p. 20.

[Acce86] Mike Accetta, Robert Baron, William Bolosky, etc., "Mach: A New Kernel Foundation for UNIX Development," in *Proc. of USENIX Summer'86 Conference*, Atlanta, GA, (9-13 June 1986), pp. 93-112.

[Boykin89] Alan Langerman, "The Parallelization of Mach/4.3BSD," in *Proceedings of Workshop on Experiences with Distributed and Multiprocessor Systems* , Usenix Association, Fort Lauderdale, FL, (October 5-6, 1989), pp. 105-126.

[Close88] Paul Close, "The iPSC/2 Node architecture," in *Technical Report*, Intel Scientific Computers, Portland, OR, (88/06), pp. 43-50.

[Garn87] N. H. Garnett, "HELIOS - An Operating System for the Transputer," in *Proc. of OUG-7, 7th occam User Group Technical Meeting*, Traian Muntean ed., IOS, Grenoble, France, (14-16 September 1987), pp. 411-419.

[Herr88] Frédéric Herrmann, François Armand, Marc Rozier, Michel Gien, etc., "CHORUS, a New Technology for Building UNIX Systems," in *Proc. of EUUG Autumn'88 Conference*, EUUG, Cascais, Portugal, (3-7 October 1988), pp. 1-18.

[Intel87] Intel, "iPSC/2 System," in *Product and Market Information*, Intel Scientific Computers, Portland, OR, (87/08), pp. 23.

[Rozi88] Marc Rozier, Vadim Abrossimov, François Armand, Ivan Boule, Michel Gien, etc., "CHORUS Distributed Operating Systems," *Computing Systems Journal*, vol. 1, no. 4, The Usenix Association, (December 1988), pp. 305-370.

The Architecture of the European MIMD Supercomputer GENESIS*

U. Bruening, W.K. Giloi, and W. Schroeder-Preikschat

GMD Research Center for Innovative Computer Systems and Technology
at the Technical University of Berlin
Hardenbergplatz 2, D-1000 Berlin 12, e-mail: giloi@gmdtub.uucp

Abstract

GENESIS is a European supercomputer development project funded by the European Commission within the ESPRIT-II program. The aim of the GENESIS project is to render a contribution to the world-wide efforts concerning the development of the next generation of scalable parallel computers of the highest possible performance and cost-effectiveness. Scalability means that the whole spectrum of parallel computers, ranging from super workstations with several hundred MFLOPS to supercomputers with several hundred GFLOPS, can be realized with the same hardware and software components. This requirement leads to a distributed memory architecture. The performance requirement calls for a peak performance of the single node of at least 100 MFLOPS. The performance of the interconnect through which the nodes communicate must match the node performance. In order to obtain competitive products, the specific cost should not exceed $200/MFLOPS in the next couple of years and $100/MFLOPS in the mid-nineties. The paper discusses the technological and architectural measures by which these goals can be accomplished. Based on the rationale presented, the design decisions concerning the node architecture, the interconnection network, the protocol structure, and the operating system structure and functionality are discussed. The paper also addresses the issues of application software models and supporting tools. Finally, the Virtual Shared Memory Architecture approach is briefly outlined. This approach reconciles the advantages of the distributed memory architecture with a conventional programming style.

1. INTRODUCTION

Since the mid seventies supercomputers were synonymous with vector machines. The ability of the pipelined vector processor to execute with every clock tick one or even two or three (chained) floating point operations, in combination with an extremely high clock frequency, accounted for a peak performance of several hundred MFLOPS at a time when the largest mainframes delivered less than 10 MIPS per (scalar) processor.

In the meantime, the more cost-effective alternative to the vector machine has become the MIMD architecture consisting of a large number (some hundreds to thousands) of nodes. First attempts in this direction have been the iSPC2 of Intel Scientific [1] with up to 128 nodes and a vector peak performance of 10 MFLOPS per node, or the SUPRENUM [2] with up to 256 nodes and a vector peak performance of 20 MFLOPS (double precision) per node. The 256-node SUPRENUM has a peak performance of 5 GFLOPS and, thus, outperforms both the CRAY-Y MP and the CRAY-2.

A large number of nodes rules out memory sharing as the means of communication between the nodes, because the shared memory would create untolerable 'hot spots' of memory access conflicts. To avoid that problem, large MIMD architectures must be *distributed memory architectures*, i.e., systems which have no global memory but only the local node memories. In a distributed memory architecture each node executes a number of cooperating processes that communicate through message-passing with each other,

* This work was partly sponsored by the European Commission, ESPRIT grant no. P2702

as well as with processes in other nodes. To this end, the nodes are interconnected by an *interconnection network*, and an appropriate protocol hierarchy must exist to ensure an efficient and yet secure message passing.

Unlike shared memory architectures, distributed memory architectures are highly scalable. Scalability means that with the same hardware and system software one can arbitrarily configure small, medium size, or large systems; thus, the entire range from super workstations to supercomputers of the highest performance may be covered. Table 1 characterizes three product classes and the peak performance which they may be expected to have. The lower performance figures pertain to about 1992 and the higher one to the situation around 1995. Of course, the supercomputer may have a smaller size than the 4096 nodes listed, which we consider the practical upper limit.

Table 1 Product classes and their performance

Product Class	Number of Nodes	Peak Performance (GFLOPS d.p.)	Packaging
personal supercomputer	1	0.1 to 0.4	single board
engineering superworkstation	4 to 16	0.4 to 6.4	single cabinet
highest performance supercomputer	4096	400 to 1600	many cabinets

The nodes of a highly parallel MIMD architecture are realized in low-power VLSI technology, i.e., CMOS or BiCMOS. This allows a complete node, including many Mbytes of memory, to be accommodated on a single circuit board and cooled by forced air (e.g.: the 20 MFLOPS SUPRENUM node with 8 Mbytes of EDC-DRAM and 128 Kbytes of SRAM vector memory is a 19"x10" board that consumes only 60 watts [3]). Consequently, the cost of packaging and cooling and, thus, the specific cost (dollars per MEGAFLOPS) are relatively low. For example, the specific cost of the SUPRENUM is only one third of that of the CRAY-Y MP. For future designs, however, even this is much too high. For a system that is under design now and scheduled to be marketed in the 1991/92 time frame, the specific cost should be brought down to about $200/MFLOPS, in order to be competitive. For the mid-nineties we anticipate specific cost around $100/MFLOPS. In a scientific "number cruncher," MFLOPS pertains to IEEE standard double precision.

Until 1989, the only way to obtain an acceptable peak performance from a node computer was to *vectorize* it by supplementing its CPU by a (pipelined) *vector processor*. Consequently, the architecture of such a node is quite similar -- at a much smaller scale -- to that of a vector machine. The current state of the art for off-the-shelf floating-point processor components is a clock frequency of 33 MHz, resulting in 66 MFLOPS of peak performance for two chained operations (double precision). New devices have been announced that will run at a clock speed of up to 100 MHz; hence offering a peak performance of 200 MFLOPS.

However, *superscalar processors* have recently evolved that are equally powerful. An example is the Intel processor i870 (alias N11), whose 50 MHz version will offer a double-precision peak performance of 100 MFLOPS for two chained operations. Table 2 gives a forecast of the peak performance of superscalar processors that can be expected to be reached over this decade [4].

Compared to node vectorization, the scalar solution is considerably cheaper and requires much less development efforts. On the other hand, this new brand of superscalar processor mandate highly "intelligent," optimizing compilers which go way beyond the global optimizations performed by the best compilers presently existing. The first existing compiler for the i860, for instance, leads to a *Linpack benchmark* of about 3 MFLOPS (double precision, 33 MHz version). On the other hand, the same processor can perform the hand-coded inner product algorithms at a rate of 27 MFLOPS. In a hand-coded ray tracing algorithm [5], 50 MFLOPS of single precision have been reached.

Table 2 Performance forecast of superscalar processors

Processor	Clock MHz	Tech-nology	CPUs	MIPS	FP-units	MFLOPS (d.p. peak)	Year
N11 (i870)	50	CMOS	1	50	2	100	1990
N12	50	CMOS	2	100	2	100	1991
???	100	BiCMOS	2	200	2	200	1993
???	200	BiCMOS	2	400	2	400	1996
i80786*	250	BiCMOS	4	800	8	2000	1999
* there will be 4 processors of the i870-type on a chip							

There exists an important difference between vector processors and superscalar processors. Pipelining is natural in the processing of vectors, for the uninterrupted stream of data needed to feed the pipeline is given by the vector elements, and the operations performed on them are data-independent. In contrast, for the superscalar processor it becomes the task of the compiler to generate the stream of instructions and data needed to fill the pipeline. This requires a highly optimizing compiler which, based on a data dependence analysis, re-schedules the instructions of the (scalar) program so that the stream of executable scalar operations needed to fill the pipeline is obtained. Consequently, a parallel architecture is as good or as bad as its compiler. The price for a good compiler is its high complexity, which increases with the complexity of the architecture.

Compilers for the i860 or i870 that would generate code nearly as good as assembler code are still some years away. Currently, this problem is overcome by a makeshift measure: In a first step, the code is vectorized, either directly by writing the code in Fortran-90 or indirectly by applying a vectorizer to a FORTRAN-77 program. In a second step, the thus obtained vector constructs are then mapped through appropriate assembler routines onto the superscalar processor. However, the final solution will be the highly optimzing compiler that will directly generate the streams of executable operations needed to keep the pipeline of the superscalar processor filled. A theoretical basis for such compilers has been laid in the form of the *Perfect Pipeline* principle [6].

The highly parallel MIMD systems which we envision as the future supercomputer architecture will exhibit a high degree of hardware and software standardization, enforced by the wide-spread use of a new generation of very high performance 64-bit processors, as well as the system software (operating system, compilers) that comes with it. Therefore, products of that type of different vendors will differ not so much in the node architecture but in such areas as specific communication hardware in the node, interconnection network architecture, software tools for program development, and application software packages.

The adequate granularity of programming distributed memory architectures is given by *communicating processes*. To this end, an application program must be partitioned into at least as many processes as the system has nodes. Currently this must be done by the programmer, who may be assisted by some interactive software tools. It is expected that fully automated "parallelizers" [7] will still take a long time to evolve.

The cooperating processes in the system communicate on the basis of an appropriate *inter process communication* (IPC) protocol. Communication is either explicitly programmed by the application programmer, in which case the programming language must offer the appropriate constructs, or it is provided by preprogrammed communication routines available from a library. Data objects are encapsulated into the processes that own them. Hence, we recognize one of the constituent features of *object-oriented programming*. However, the prevailing programming languages such as Fortran, Lisp, Ada, or C require the view of a global address space. The conventional programming style expressed by those languages thus requires the shared memory.

This paper presents an overview of the GENESIS design which is based upon the above considerations. GENESIS can be viewed as the European equivalent of the *Touchstone* Project in the USA. The GENESIS design aims at providing an optimal solution in terms of absolute performance, cost-effectiveness, and ease of use. To obtain a high cost-effectiveness, GENESIS will be realized in low-power VLSI technology, using the least expensive, high density packaging available and as many off-the-shelf components as possible.

In Section 2 we shall outline the GENESIS node design and its rationale. Prototypes of that node are up and running. Section 3 deals with the GENESIS interconnection structure whose underlying concepts are discussed. Section 4 describes the construction principles and the functionality of the node operating system, PEACE. Special emphasis is put on the issues of scalability and communication efficiency. Section 5 deals briefly with the issues of the GENESIS programming models and parallelization, as well as programming tools and environments. It also shows to what extent a Virtual Shared Memory approach will be supported by the GENESIS architecture.

2. THE GENESIS NODE ARCHITECTURE

2.1 The GENESIS Node Version.1

In the first phase of the GENESIS development, we designed and realized a scalar node, the block diagram of which is shown in Figure 1 [8]. We recognize that the GENESIS node has two processors: The node CPU proper, called *Application Processor* (AP), is supplemented by a dedicated *Communication Processor* (CP) [9]. In addition, there is a local communication interface (LCI), connecting AP and CP, and a network link interface (NLI) connecting the node with the interconnection network. The node is used as the basic building block for a highly scalable distributed memory system. Therefore, the node design comprises innovative concepts to speed up message passing.

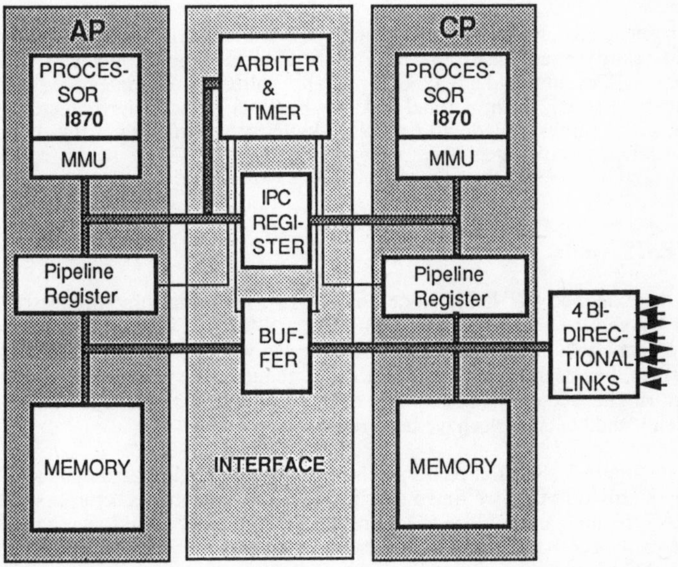

Figure 1 GENESIS Node Version.1 -- Block diagram

The realization of the AP is based upon the use of the most powerful existing microprocessor, the Intel i870 (N11). The i870 will feature a peak performance of 50 MIPS and 100 MFLOPS, respectively, and a memory transfer rate of 320 Mbytes per second. The memory interface consists of a 3-stage pipeline, the main memory consists of 4 banks of DRAM with 8 Mbytes each.

The CP works with the i870 processor too. It communicates with the AP via the LCI for the purpose of instruction issuing and synchronization. Furthermore, it shares the node memory with the AP. The CP controls the NLI, transports messages, and implements the message-passing protocol. Specifically, the CP meets the following requirements:

- it has the same logical view of memory as the AP, i.e., the same MMU functions and main memory access modes.;

- it performs the high speed data transport by performing the address computations needed and controlling the appropriate devices;

- it supports the high-level language implementation of the protocols.

Thus, the dedicated CP enhances the efficiency of the AP greatly [9]. All the AP must do when it encounters a *send* command is to put a *send message* into the send queue. The CP, which is polling that queue, executes the send operation, while the AP can go on with its work. Conversely, when the CP receives a *receive message* from the CP of another node, it puts it into the *receive queue*. The AP, on executing a *receive* command, goes to that queue and looks for the corresponding message. This has the following advantages:

- o AP and CP work concurrently;
- o in a single task environment, the AP works without interrupts;
- o in a multi task environment, the AP works without interrupts or environment switches.

Thus, the communication startup time can be reduced by an order of magnitude [9]. Furthermore, in a virtual shared memory architecture (see below) the CP will also perform the functions of the *page manager* and *concurrency controller* of the node. In all these cases, the AP is freed to concentrate its work on doing the computations, i.e., producing MEGAFLOPS.

The LCI has been designed for maximum efficiency of communication between AP and CP. The LCI transfers message passing instructions from the AP to the CP and acknowledgements back from the CP to the AP. Its hardware will eventually be realized by an application specific integrated circuit (ASIC). The NLI provides four byte-serial, bi-directional links with a data rate of approximately 100 Mbytes per second for each link. The links include all necessary logic for wormhole routing. Its hardware will be realized by an application specific integrated circuit (ASIC).

2.2 The GENESIS Node Version.2

Figure 2 depicts the extended GENESIS node design [10], featuring three processors: the node CPU (i870), the CP (i870), and the vector processor. The GENESIS Node Version.1 described above realizes part of this design, namely the CPU and the CP. Adding the vector processor, including the high-speed vector memory banks, has been planned so far for the second phase of the GENESIS development. A prototype version of the vector processor has been built, using the BIT B2110/20 floating-point processors (33 MHz), and benchmarks have been run on it.

As demonstrated by Figure 3, the LINPACK benchmarks for this single-board node are excellent. With a peak performance of only 66 MHz, we find a sustained performance that is better than SUPRENUM, the i860, and the CRAY-1S and comes close to that of the CRAY-Y MP. The Lawrence Livermoore Loop benchmarks are equally good and better than those of the CRAY-1S. The excellent sustained-to-peak performance ratio is obtained by the innovative memory architecture shown in Figure 2, consisting of four independent memory banks interconnected with the pipeline processor via a 4x4 crossbar. Each memory bank has its own address generator (AG). That is, at the machine language level the memories are not addressed by location addresses but by descriptors. This *descriptor referenced autonomous memory access* (DRAMA) principle [11] allows data structure objects to be accessed in any desired fashion [12]. Consequently, two operand streams and one result stream can flow from and to the memory simultaneously. In parallel, one of the three streams may be written into the fourth memory bank, to be in the right place for the next access. The memory is videoRAM that can be simultaneously read at the serial output and written into the random input.

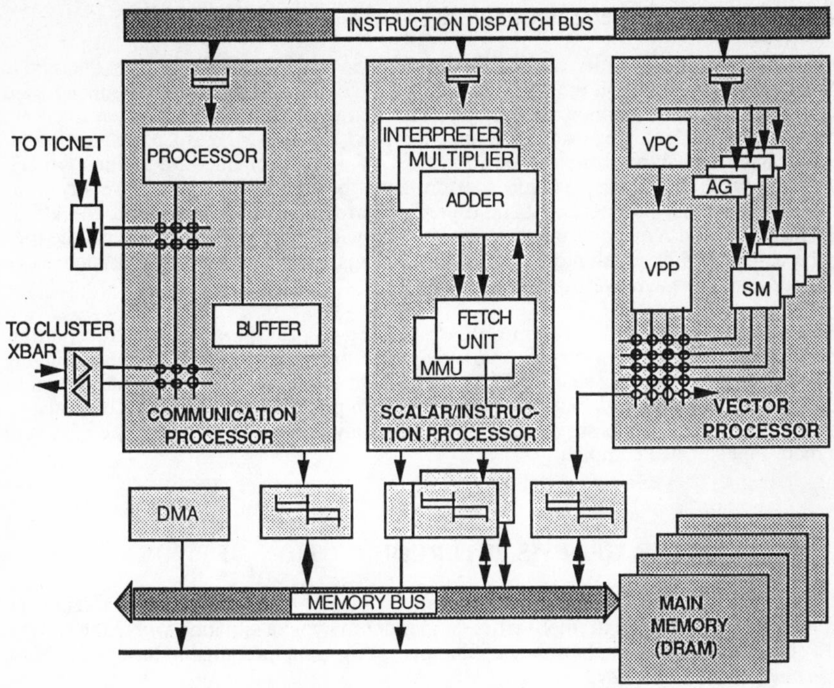

Figure 2 GENESIS Node Version.2 -- block diagram

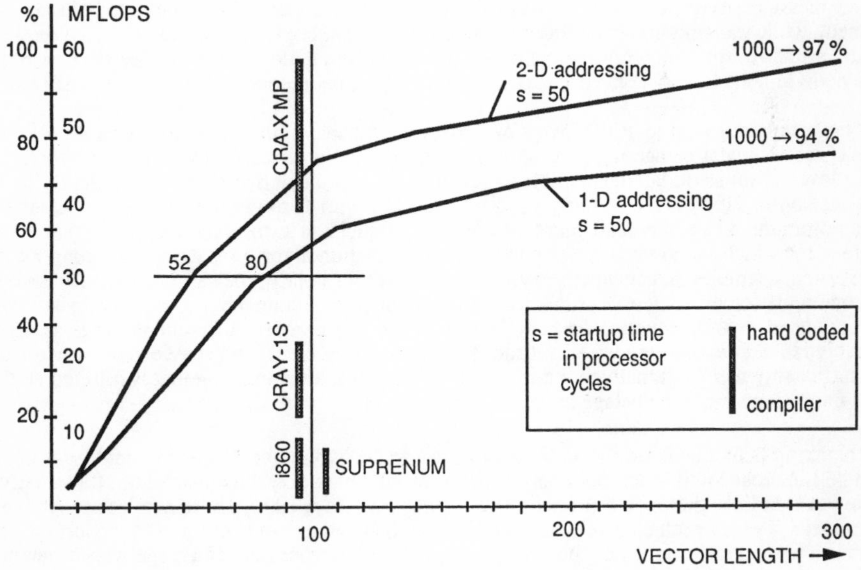

Figure 3 LINPACK benchmarks of the vector processor in comparison to other machines

2.3 Does it Still Pay to Vectorize the Node ?

Regardless of these excellent results, the question has arisen whether it still is the right decision to add the vector processor to the node. On the one hand, a new ECL chip set recently announced by a leading manufacturer would allow us to build a vector processor that would bring the peak performance up to 200 MFLOPS (at 100 MHz clock frequency). On the other hand, the 100-MHz BiCMOS version of the i870 processor will have a peak performance of 200 MFLOPS for two chained operations too. The vector processor would provide a better sustained performance for vectorized code; however, at the cost of doubling the hardware development cost and time. Furthermore, a vector processor with 200 MFLOPS peak performance would require thrice the memory bandwidth, a requirement that can be met only by replacing the videoRAM by much more costly SRAM. Thus, for the cost and real estate needed for one vectorized node one may have two superscalar nodes.

Hence, the vectorized node will still win on the sustained-to-peak performance front, at the risk of missing the market window with respect to development time and cost-effectiveness. Having several application processors in the node sharing the common node memory will be a cheaper way of increasing the node performance further. Last but not least, a very high performance machine with scalar nodes will find a much broader application spectrum. The price to pay for this approach is the efforts needed to develop a more sophisticated compiler.

3. THE GENESIS INTERCONNECTION NETWORK

The crucial issue of distributed memory architectures is *communication overhead.* Great care must be taken to make communication extremely efficient in order to avoid a situation where the communication overhead would consume too much of the parallel processing gain, measured in terms of MFLOP wasted because of *communication latency.*

Communication latency stems from two sources: (1) the latency of the interconnection network and (2) the time it takes the operating system to start a communication. The network latency is primarily a function of its transmission bandwidth, whereas the startup time depends on the protocols employed and the degree of hardware support provided to the operating system. It does not suffice to minimize one or the other of the two factors. However, the factors may have different weights depending on the message size. Short, fixed size messages require a very short startup time and a favorable blocking behavior of the interconnect, while transmission bandwidth is hardly of concern. High volume data transfer, on the other hand, calls primarily for a high communication bandwidth. Simulations have yielded the rule of thumb that each node-to-node link must have at least as many Mbytes per second as the node has MFLOPS [8].

With current technology up to 100 Mbytes of transmission bandwidth are readily feasible. Within that limit, the choice of installed bandwidth is a matter of economy. In connection with the *wormhole routing* strategy a low transmission latency can be achieved as long as the network has a sufficiently favorable blocking behavior. However, economy requirements also call for cost-optimization. Therefore, the tolarable communication overhead must be identified which, in turn, depends on the nature of the applications for which the system is designed. If the application algorithms exhibit a strong locality of communication, a simpler and cheaper network, e.g., the 2D-mesh [13], may suffice. If there is no strong locality, one must resourt to networks that have a higher degree of connectivity, e.g., the *hypercube* [14] or the *multi-level crossbar networks* [15]. An important area where different network types differ considerably is the *blocking behavior.* In order to obtain a good blocking behavior, the network should provide sufficiently many alternative, non-interfering data paths, a requirement that is fulfilled neither the 2D-mesh nor by the simple multistage interconnection network.

A good blocking behavior is provided by the hypercube. A hypercube of dimensionality N allows 2^N nodes to be interconnected. Each node has N links into the network, thus providing N alternative data paths. However, a link, that is, a bi-directional channel with, say, 100 MHz transmission bandwidth, is quite expensive. Twelve such channels, as needed for a 12-cube interconnect for 4096 nodes, may readily cost more money and real estate than the node proper with all its processors and megabytes of memory.

Since a node can send or receive through only one channels at a time, it is more economical to have only a minimal number of channels and provide the multiplicity of alternative data paths by virtue of complex multi-way switches in the network. Such multi-way switches can be provided by crossbars. The ideal topology would be the one-level crossbar network, since it provides total connectivity. However, such a network is practically feasible only for at most 32 nodes [8]. To interconnect a larger number of nodes must employ multi-level crossbar switches [16]. Building hierarchies of crossbars allows the use of relatively small crossbar networks (e.g., 16x16) that fit readily into a single ASIC. This allows one to form a basic cluster with N nodes interconnected by an NxN crossbar. To interconnect N clusters a second tier of N crossbars is needed. This principle can be recursively applied to obtain systems with N, N^2, N^3, N^4, ... nodes.

Figure 4 illustrates the two-level crossbar network called 2D-TICNET [15]. Such a network does not provide the total connectivity of the single-level crossbar. However, simulations have shown that the blocking behavior of the two-level hierarchical crossbar topology is as good as that of the hypercube, while the diameter and the number of links needed is much smaller. For a crossbar hierarchy with L levels only L links are needed [15].

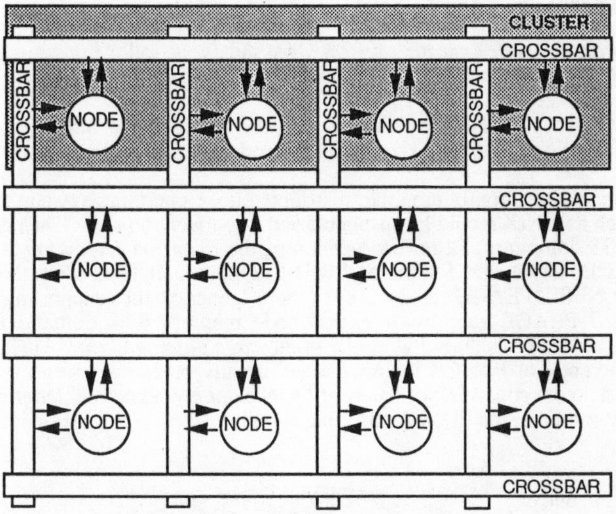

Figure 4 Illustration of the two-level hierarchy of crossbars

The simulation is based on a statistical model in which a significant number C of logical connection requests per time unit are generated with random occurrence and random destination addresses among 1024 nodes. By selecting the frequency distribution of the distance the message has to travel, any degree of locality from strictly nearest-neighbor to a uniform distance distribution may be considered. Based on this model, a number of significant parameters are estimated. The most important parameter is the number of successfull/blocked connections as a function of C. The traffic density at which the number of blocked connections reaches the number of successful connection is considered the *saturation point* of the network; it does not make sense to increase traffic beyond that point. Table 3 lists the saturation point for 2D-mesh, the hypercube, and the 2D-TICNET [15].

Table 3 Saturation points of major network topologies

Topology	2D-mesh	Hypercube	2D-TICNET
Saturation point	82	340	316
Number of links	4	10	2

We recognize that both hypercube and 2D-TICNET, which in the example stands for a two-level hierarchy of crossbars, exhibit approximately the same favorable blocking behavior. However, the 2D-TICNET needs only 2 links whereas the hypercube needs 10 links. Moreover, the hypercube is not scalable while the hierarchical crossbar topology (TICNET) is scalable. Compared to the TICNET, the 2D-mesh needs more links, yet has a very poor blocking behavior. When considering the cost of a link, it is not so much the logic (FIFOs, multiplexors, transceivers, etc.) that counts but the cables and connectors.

4. THE NODE OPERATING SYSTEM

It is a characteristic feature of the distributed memory architecture that each node must have its own operating system kernel, to perform the following tasks:

- manage the resources (processes, memory, etc.) of the node;
- carry out inter process communication (IPC) with other nodes.

Furthermore, an appropriate *node operating system* must satisfy the following requirements:

- message-passing must be carried out with minimal startup time;
- scalability must be supported by providing the view of an abstract machine;
- an arbitrary distribution of global services over the nodes must be allowed.

These requirements call for a highly modular, distributed node operating system; therefore, a standard operating system such as UNIX would be unsuitable and also much too slow. The node operating system used in the GENESIS computer is a refined version of the *Program Execution And Communication Environment* (PEACE) developed for the SUPRENUM computer [16]. Compared to SUPRENUM PEACE, the new GENESIS PEACE version is even more "generic," thus supporting ultimate scalability. Moreover, GENESIS PEACE supports a virtual node memory with demand paging. The notion underlying the PEACE design is that of a *familiy of message passing kernels* [17]. Despite its extreme modularity, the efficiency of PEACE is unsurpassed by any other operating system. This has been accomplished by a structure consisting of *teams of lightweight processes* and *leagues of teams*. Figure 5 illustrates the process model of the PEACE operating system.

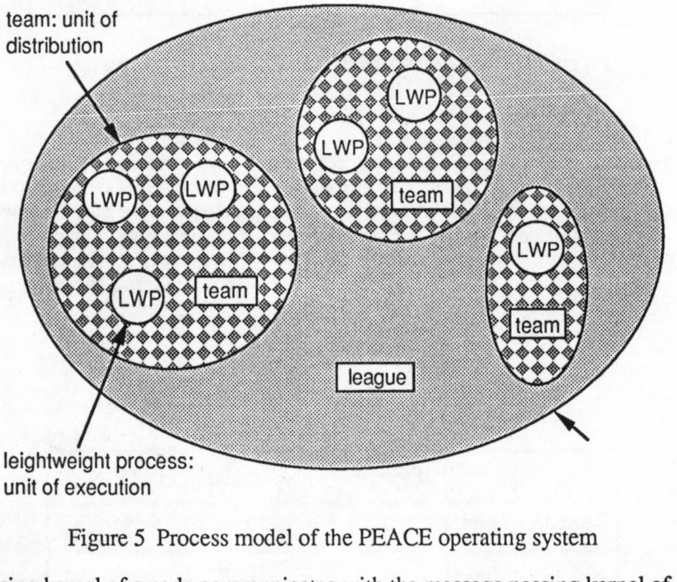

Figure 5 Process model of the PEACE operating system

The message passing kernel of a node communicates with the message passing kernel of another node by a *non-buffered synchronous IPC mechanism* based on *send-receive-reply sequences*. This is the fastest possible form of communication [18]. Short messages between teams are exchanged with very low overhead through *signal-await* sequences. System services can be invoked anywhere in the system by *remote procedure calls* (RPC). While this mechanism takes care of the high speed message exchange needed for the purpose of system organization and synchronization, data objects of application programs are transferred by a mechanism called *high volume data transfer* (HVDT) as described below. In case the programming model calls for *asynchronous communication*, this is readily provided by an appropriate lightweight process that works "on top" of the basic synchronous communication mechanism. In this scheme, the light-weight process sends the message, while the original sender process, after having started the lightweight process, continues with program execution.

Figure 6 illustrates the HVDT mechanism. Sender process and receiver process both communicate with a PEACE server called *Network Independent Communication Executive* (NICE). NICE is the interface to the *Communication System* (COSY) of the node. Each COSY includes a *DMA address generator* that can be set-up to address the elements of data structure objects (e.g., arrays) in the desired order. The first step of a HVDT is to establish a *rendezvous* between the COSY of the sender node and the receiver node, respectively. This ensures the receiver's readiness, i.e., provides the *end-to-end significance* required for a secure communication. It also initializes the address generators. Subsequently, a data object of arbitrary size and structure can be copied directly from the address space of the sender process into the address space of the receiver process. In GENESIS, the COSY has its own, dedicated processor, viz. the CP.

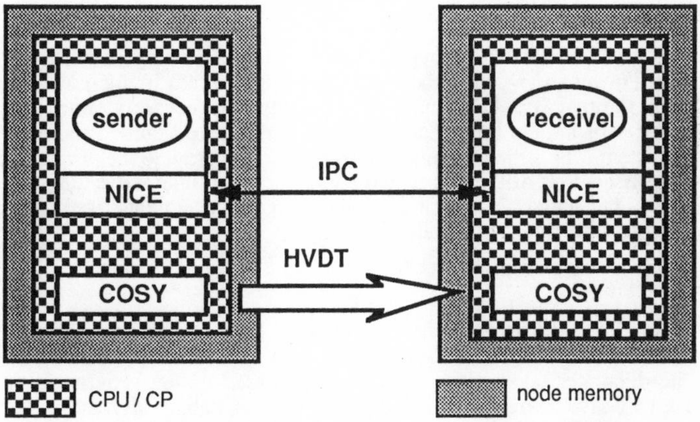

Figure 6 Illustration of the high volume data transfer mechanism

5. GENESIS SOFTWARE DEVELOPMENT

5.1 Programming Distributed Memory Architectures

First attempts have been made to develop automatic parallelizers [7] for distributed memory architectures, yet practically usable result may still be some years away. Therefore, in the present state-of-the-art the user must explicitly partition the application program into cooperating tasks, distribute the tasks over the nodes of the system, and put the necessary IPC constructs in the right places. In all grid problems with regular solution spaces, the partitioning of the program can readily be performed by dividing the solution space into as many equal slices as there are nodes in the system and assigning a slice to each node.

In regular grid problems, grid generators, communication routines, and standard algorithms may be preprogrammed for a parameterized solution space and made available to the application programmer in the form of library routines. For example, SUPRENUM offers such a library for linear algebra computations as well as a multigrid PDE solver package. Whenever the user wants to solve a problem of one of the classes for which a library exists, all he has to do is to bind the library into his application program and call the appropriate routines.

If the solution space is not regular or if the application is not a grid problem in the first place, program partitioning may be a more complicated task. In general, a good partitioning may be found only by a trial-

and-error procedure. In this case the user does a partitioning, runs the program, and corrects the partitioning, if the first attempt has not led to a satisfactory node utilization. Furthermore, the user will have to program the inter process communication explicitly. In this endeavor the user may be supported by performance evaluation and visualization tools.

5.2 GENESIS Program Development and Execution Environment

In the following we describe several tools considered of vital importance for the program development in a distributed memory architecture such as GENESIS [8]. These tools are being developed by various partners as part of the GENESIS project.

5.2.1 GENESIS-fortran Compiler

GENESIS-fortran is a fortran-90 type language, i.e., it comprises vector datatypes. In addition, the language must encompass a process concept as well as the necessary IPC constructs. The code generator of the compiler must produce optimized code for the i870 processor. Such a compiler is under development.

5.2.2 Simulator

Program development and verification is supported by simulators running on other conventional UNIX machines. No changes occur in switching between testing a program in a simulator environment and running a program on the real GENESIS machine. Invoking preprocessors rather than the GENESIS-fortran compiler itself will handle the specific MIMD features and embed the user program into a simulation runtime system. The simulator has various options, to provide the programmer with detailed information about the behaviour of the distributed application. An interactive simulation interface will allow the user to control the actual run of a simulation package. The simulator must be fast enough to run simulations even of large problems in reasonable time.

5.2.3 Parallel Debugger

The Parallel Debugger allows the user to debug a distributed fortran program on the GENESIS machine. It is based on the abstract machine view and can be used interactively or on a post mortem dump. Interaction with the debugger takes place via a window-based dialog program running on the host computer. Each task will have its own subwindow attached; thus, debug information can be received and displayed asynchronously. Graphical symbols are used to indicate the state of the processes currently represented on the screen.

5.2.4 Performance Analysis and Visualization Tools

During program development and tuning, there will be a need for detailed performance data as well as an understanding of the behaviour of the individual tasks of the application program. The Performance Analysis and Process Visualization Tools provide insight into the behaviour of a distributed application at the cost of execution speed. The tools can be used on either the real machine or the simulator. Information about the executing tasks will be displayed in graphic form at three levels:

- animated replay of task activities;
- time protocol;
- statistical data on processor utilization and inter process communication

5.2.5 Execution Environment

The user controls the execution of a program by issuing appropriate UNIX system commands, which then are executed by specific servers. The collection of all servers is called the GENESIS Execution Environment . A multitude of requests for the execution of user tasks may occur at the same time. These tasks must be scheduled with the aim to maximize the total system throughput. This is performed by the GENESIS Job Manager. The GENESIS Job Manager maintains a table of active (frozen) jobs as well as a queue of waiting jobs.

File handling is performed by the GENESIS File Manager on each node that has a disk. The user sees one logical file system into which the distributed file systems are integrated. A dedicated, uniform access path syntax will be common to all file server components.

5.3 Virtual Shared Memory Architecture (VSMA)

As is pointed out in the introduction, the Virtual Shared Memory Architecture (VSMA) is the attempt to free the programmer from the task of having to partition his program into cooperating processes, distribute the processes over the nodes, and program the necessary IPC. This will allow the user to use conventional languages that require the view of a global address space. We anticipate at least the smaller systems listed in Table 1 to be eventually of the VSMA type.

A program written for a VSMA must be partitioned by a *parallelizing compiler* into a number of concurrent *threads of control* (TOC), which are then distributed over the nodes. The TOCs may share data entities which they may read or write, depending on the access capability they possess for them. In compliance with the data dependencies in the program, the data accesses must be synchronized by critical regions. It is advantageous to choose the pages of a virtual memory with demand paging as the sharable entities; such an approach is called *Shared Virtual Memory* [19].

Locking and unlocking critical regions requires indivisible semaphor operations. Implementing a lock by agreement between N sharing nodes of a distributed system requires 2*(N-1) messages [20]. Therefore, when executed by software, the data access synchronization through critical regions in the VSMA program induces a considerable overhead that may readily exceed the IPC protocol overhead in distributed memory architectures. Consequently, specific architectural support must be provided to make a VSMA efficient. Here, the most important single measure is minimization of the message passing overhead.

For efficiency reasons, the nodes of a VSMA operate on their own copies of a shared *primary page*. This raises the problem of ensuring the consistency of the primary page and its copies. That is, the main problem of a VSMA is to maintain the *coherence* of the virtual shared memory. Data coherence may be maintained all the time, in which case it is called *strong coherence*, or only at certain synchronization points, in which case it is called *weak coherence*. Adding weak coherence enhances the efficiency of the VSMA. Both kinds of coherence can be achieved in an efficient manner by a capability-based mechanism [22].The CP in the GENESIS node will strongly support our VSMA mechanisms. For details please refer to [21].

REFERENCES

[1] Rosenberg R.: *Supercube*, Electronics, Feb. 11, 1985, 15-17

[2] Giloi W.K.: *The SUPRENUM Architecture*, in (Jesshope C.R., Reinartz K.D.(eds.): CONPAR 88, Cambridge University Press 1989, 10-17

[3] Behr P., Montenegro S.: *The SUPRENUM Node Computer*, in (Jesshope C.R., Reinartz K.D.(eds.): CONPAR 88, Cambridge University Press 1989, 18-26

[4] Lewis P.H.: *Chips for the Year 2000*, New York Times, June 19, 1990

[5] Giloi W.K.: *Development of Future Supercomputer Architecture -- The Challenge of the Nineties*, Proc. 6th German-Japanese Technology Forum, Berlin 1990

[6] Aiken A., Nicolau A.: *Perfect Pipelining, a New Loop Parallelization Technique*, In: European Symposium on Programming, Springer-Verlag, LNCS no. 300 (June 1988), 221-235

[7] Zima H.P., Bast H.J., Gerndt H.M.: SUPERB: *A Tool for Semi-Automatic MIMD/SIMD Parallelization*, Parallel Computing 6 (1988), 1-18

[8] Giloi W.K.: *GENESIS - The Architecture and Its Rationale*, ESPRIT Project P2702, Internal Tech. Report June 1989

[9] Giloi W.K., Schroeder W.: *Very High-Speed Communication in Large MIMD Supercomputers*, Proc. ICS '89, ACM Order No. 415891, 313-321

[10] Bruening U., Giloi W.K.: *Architecture of a Functionally Parallelized Processor With Hardware Synchronization and Communication*, Proc. ICS 89, Internat. Supercomputing Institute 1989, 248-252

[11] Giloi W.K.: *The DRAMA Principle and Data Type Architectures*, in Niedereichholz J.(ed.): Datenbanktechnologien, Teubner-Verlag, Stuttgart 1979

[12] Bi Hua: *Exploiting Two-Dimensional Explicit Parallelism On Vector Architectures*, Ph.D.Thesis, Technical University of Berlin, FB Informatik 1991

[13] Feng T.Y.: *A Survey on Interconnection Networks*, COMPUTER 14,12 (1981)

[14] Dally W.D., Seitz C.L.: *Deadlock-Free Message Routing in Multiprocessor Interconnection Networks*, IEEE TRANS. ON COMPUTERS, C-36,5 (May 1987), 547-553

[15] Giloi. W.K., Montenegro S.: *High Bandwidth Interconnects for Highly Parallel MIMD Supercomputers*, Proc. 24th Hawaii Internat. Conf. on System Sciences, IEEE Publication, Jan. 1991

[16] Schroeder W.: *The PEACE Operating System and Its Suitability for MIMD Message Passing Systems*, CONPAR 88, Cambridge University Press 1988, 27-34

[17] Schroeder-Preikschat W.: *Overcoming the Startup Time Problem in Distributed Memory Architectures*, Proc. 24th Hawaii Internat. Conf. on System Sciences, IEEE Publication, Jan. 1991

[18] Behr P.M., Giloi W.K., Schroeder W.: *Synchronous versus Asynchronous Communication in High Performance Multicomputer Systems*, in Wright M.(ed.): Proc. IFIP WG 2.5 Working Conf. on Aspects of Computation and Asynchronous Parallel Processors, North-Holland, Amsterdam 1989, 239-248

[19] Li K.: *Shared Virtual Memory on Loosely Coupled Multiprocessors*, P.D. Thesis, Yale University 1986

[20] Ricart G., Agrawala A.K.: An Optimal Algorithm for Mutual Exclusion in Computer Networks, CACM 24 (Jan. 1981), 9-17

[21] Giloi W.K. et al.: *A Distributed Implementation of Shared Virtual Memory with Strong and Weak Coherence*, in these proceedings

Fault-tolerant gossiping on hypercube multicomputers

Pierre FRAIGNIAUD*

Laboratoire de l'Informatique du Parallélisme — IMAG
Ecole Normale Supérieure de Lyon
46, Allée d'Italie
69364 LYON CEDEX 07, France

Abstract : Various algorithms for reliable *gossiping* in faulty n dimensional hypercube multicomputers are described and analyzed. The goal is that each processor receives complete information from all the other processors even in the presence of faults. One of the main characteristic of the algorithms is that no information on the identity of the faulty nodes/links is required. The exchange between any two processors is realized such that the data moves through *disjoint* paths. We propose solutions designed for systems which use *store and forward* models of communication. The proposed algorithms are parametrized by the maximum number of faults that they can take into account. In all cases, they approach the minimum time complexity.

Keywords : Gossiping, Total Exchange, fault tolerance, hypercube, time complexity

1. Introduction

Broadcasting and *Gossiping* are two problems of communication for a distributed memory multicomputer. In broadcasting, one processor (or node) has a message which needs to be communicated to everyone else. In gossiping every processor in the network has a message which needs to be communicated to everyone else. Loading a program code from a front end to all the processing elements is a typical example of broadcasting, while a total exchange of data corresponds to gossiping.

In recent papers, C.T. Ho and S.L. Johnsson [10], Y. Saad and M. Schultz [17] and Q.F. Stout and B. Wagar [19] investigate communication in common multicomputers topologies. They give optimal algorithms, within a small constant factor, for a fault free situation. But, as claimed by many computer scientists dealing with distributed computation, the interconnection of more and more processors will be efficient only if the implemented algorithms possess fault tolerance properties. Communication among the processors is the basis for all applications running on parallel computers. Thus, the study of fault tolerant communicating algorithms is very current in the field of parallel computation [1, 2, 4, 12, 13].

* This work is supported by the Research program C3 of the CNRS and MEN, and by the Direction des Recherches et Etudes Techniques (DGA).

In [14], P.Ramanathan and K.G.Shin propose a reliable *broadcasting* algorithm which completes in any n dimensional hypercube, even when as many as $n-1$ faults of links or nodes occur. In their approach, fault tolerance is achieved by sending multiple copies of a message through *disjoint* paths. Another approach is based on the identification of the faulty processors/links "on line". In this case, each node keeps information about the status of the processors and the links in the system, and the fault tolerant routing is achieved by going around the faulty nodes/links. But, the overhead of identifying these faulty elements could be quite severe (see [8]). P. Ramanathan and K.G. Shin note that this approach is not suitable for many time critical applications. Moreover, the messages may be corrupted, and then using disjoint paths permits the identification of the original message from the received copies by using simple majority voting. Indeed, simple hand shaking cannot be used in case of byzantine modification of the message. The problem of quorum establishment is studied in [14]. In the following, in order to simplify the analysis, we do not consider alterations of the messages and we refer to [14] for discussions in case of corruption. In this paper we build algorithms based on the same approach as Ramanathan and Shin, that is disjoint paths, to achieve reliable *gossiping* in hypercubes.

Thus our algorithms are based on *simultaneously using disjoint paths between any pair of processors of an hypercube.* This is quite easy, but there is a constraint. The load of each communication link (i.e. the total amount of information passing through each link) must be as small as possible. Otherwise, the time to perform the total exchange of the data will increase more than proportionally to the length of the messages.

This paper is organized as follows. Section 2 describes the problem, the communication model and the hypercube. Then, in section 3, lower bounds of fault tolerant gossiping algorithms are studied. In section 4, a class of reliable gossiping algorithms is described assuming that the processors are able to simultaneously communicate through all their ports. In section 5, similar reliable algorithms are described, assuming that only one port can be used by a processor at a given time. Finally section 6 concludes the paper.

2. Statement of the problem

In this section, we present the communication model used and the relations between reliable communication and disjoint paths. We recall the definition and the basic properties of the hypercube.

2.1. Communication scheme

There is a straightforward relation between graphs $G(V,E)$ of order N and networks of N processors. Each vertex of V corresponds to a processor which is a node of the network, and each edge of E corresponds to a communication link. If there exists an edge $(x,y) \in E$, then the corresponding processor x can send a message directly to y. If not, the message from x must pass through other processors to reach its destination.

In this paper, we assume that the communications are based on message passing procedures. Moreover, we assume that the messages are sent in *store and forward* or *packet-switched* mode (as opposed to *circuit-switched* mode). Indeed, in case of intensive communications like gossiping, the *circuit-switched* scheme does not offer significative advantages over the *store and forward* scheme (see [18]). The time T to send a message of length L between two neighbor processors is usually assumed to be the sum of a start up β_c with a propagation time $L\tau_c$ proportional to the message length ($\frac{1}{\tau_c}$ is the bandwidth) [10, 17, 19]:

$$T = \beta_c + L\tau_c \tag{1}$$

Generally, $\beta_c \gg \tau_c$ holds [3], but the propagation time will be not neglected in the following due to the length of the exchanged messages. Indeed, assuming that all messages are of the same length, each processor has to receive global information of total length $(N-1)L$. Thus, the propagation times and the start-up times are often of the same order. This model corresponds to common coarse grain architectures, but there exist other models, such as those assuming that $T = 1$ by using transmission systems where the communication time is not depending on the message length [9], or those assuming that the bandwidth and the start-up time can depend on the number of communication links used [6].

Typically, links are bidirectional and can be used in *half duplex* or in *full duplex* mode. In half duplex, only one message can pass through a link (x, y) at a given time, either from x to y, or from y to x. In full duplex, two messages can simultaneously pass through a link in opposite directions. In the following, we use the full duplex mode of transmission.

We mainly consider the case where a processor is able to simultaneously communicate through all its ports. We call this mode *shouting* (this corresponds to the *link bound* mode [19], or the n–ports mode [10]). Indeed, in most of the existing multicomputers, processors can simultaneously communicate with all their neighbors. This communication pattern may not be realistic if the degree of the nodes is large, so we will briefly consider gossiping under the *whispering* mode of communication, that is when each processor can only use one port at a given time (this corresponds to the *processor bound* mode [19], or the 1–ports mode [10]). Note that there exist other communication modes, such as the *DMA bound* communication mode [11], but we do not consider them in this paper.

2.2. Disjoint paths and fault-resistance

The existence of disjoint paths between any two nodes and the fault-resistance of a network are closely related notions. The connectivity of the graph gives an estimate of its fault-resistance. We define here some terms used in the following.

Definition 2.1 Two distinct paths between the vertices x and y will be said to be *disjoint* if and only if they do not possess any common vertex except x and y.

Definition 2.2 A link is *faulty* if it cannot transmit any message.

Note that we assume that a link does not corrupt messages. A faulty link correctly transmits messages or does not transmit any messages at all.

Definition 2.3 An algorithm for gossiping in a graph $G(V, E)$ is f_n-resistant if and only if, assuming that E has at most f_n faulty links, then each node surely receives all the messages sent by all the other nodes.

2.3. The hypercubes

Selecting a graph for interconnecting a network is usually based on three criteria. First the network must be as regular as possible insuring the possibility of doing inducting reasonings, including practical subtopologies (multi-dimensional grids), etc. Another criterion is a small degree insuring the feasibility of the network. Finally, the diameter must be small insuring fast communications. Thus among the new architectures, multiprocessors based on the hypercube topology have become increasingly popular for parallel computations.

An n dimensional hypercube (n cube), denoted H_n, is defined by Saad and Schultz [15] as a graph with $N = 2^n$ vertices labeled by the binary numbers from 0 to $2^n - 1$ such that there is an undirected edge between any two vertices if and only if the binary representation of their labels differs by one and only one bit. Thus there are $n2^{n-1}$ undirected edges. In this paper, we call a general purpose multiprocessor, whose processors are connected through a network having a hypercube topology, an "hypercube multicomputer". Moreover, we assume that the processors run with a *Multiple Instructions Multiple Data* scheme of computation. There is a one to one correspondence between an undirected edge and a bidirectional link.

Let x be a vertex of the n cube. For $0 \leq d < n$, $\oplus_d(x)$ will denote the vertex adjacent to x such that x and $\oplus_d(x)$ differ by the dth bit (written x_d). The edge $(x, \oplus_d(x))$ is referred as an edge through dimension d. Each vertex has n neighbors respectively through dimensions $0, \ldots, n-1$. The two opposite subcubes in dimension d are the two $(n-1)$ cubes respectively composed of the vertices labeled $(x_{n-1}, \ldots, x_{d+1}, 0, x_{d-1}, \ldots, x_0)$ and $(x_{n-1}, \ldots, x_{d+1}, 1, x_{d-1}, \ldots, x_0)$ with $x_i \in \{0, 1\}$, $i = 0, \ldots, n-1$, $i \neq d$.

Let J be a subset of $\{0, \ldots, n-1\}$ and x be a vertex of H_n. $H_n^J(x) \subset H_n$ is the subcube composed of the vertices labeled $(y_{n-1}, \ldots, y_0)$ where $y_i \in \{0, 1\}$ for $i \in J$, and $y_i = x_i$ for $i \notin J$. For instance $\forall x \in H_n$, $H_n^{\{0,\ldots,n-1\}}(x) = H_n$, $H_n^{\emptyset}(x) = x$, and $H_n^{\{0,\ldots,n-1\}-\{d\}}(0)$ and $H_n^{\{0,\ldots,n-1\}-\{d\}}(2^d)$ are the two opposite subcubes in dimension d.

For any two vertices x and y of the n cube, we call $d(x, y)$ the Hamming distance between x and y (x and y differ by $d(x, y)$ bits). The algorithms presented in this paper are mainly based on the following property.

Theorem 2.4 [15] *Let x and y be two vertices of the n cube. There exist n disjoint paths between x and y such that*
1) $d(x,y)$ of the paths are of length $d(x,y)$
2) the $n - d(x,y)$ others are of length $d(x,y)+2$. □

3. Complexity of fault resistant gossiping

In this section, we give lower bounds on the time needed to perform reliable gossiping in H_n.

Proposition 3.5 *The propagation time complexity of f_n-resistant gossiping, $f_n < n$, is at least $\frac{f_n+1}{n}(N-1)L\tau_c$ using the shouting mode of communication, and $(f_n+1)(N-1)L\tau_c$ using the whispering mode of communication.*

Proof: Let x and y be two distinct nodes of H_n. Let $M_{x,y}$ be the message of x destined for y. Each byte of $M_{x,y}$ must be duplicated at least f_n+1 times in order to reach y through at least f_n+1 input links since f_n communication channels of y may be faulty. The unitary propagation time is τ_c for each channel. Each message received by y being replicated at least f_n+1 times, the time of y to complete the gossiping is at least $(f_n+1)(N-1)L\tau_c$ using whispering and $\frac{f_n+1}{n}(N-1)L\tau_c$ using shouting. □

Proposition 3.6 *A lower bound of the total start up time to perform f_n-resistant gossiping, $f_n < n$, is* $\begin{cases} T_{inf}(f_n) = n\beta_c & \text{if } f_n < n-1 \\ T_{inf}(n-1) = (n+1)\beta_c & \text{otherwise} \end{cases}$.

Proof: Clearly, n start up times are at least necessary due to the diameter of H_n. Moreover, if $f_n = n-1$, let x and y be two distinct nodes of H_n such that $d(x,y) = n-1$. Following the same kinds of arguments as in the proof of proposition 3.5, each byte of $M_{x,y}$ must pass through n edge disjoint paths. Now, it is impossible to build n edge disjoint paths of length $\leq n-1$ between x and y, thus one of them is of length $n+1$.□

Note that we do not add the minimum start up time and the minimum propagation time (see [7, 19]), but a global lower bound can be obtained taking the maximum of these two values:

$$T_{min}^{f_n\text{-resistant gossiping}} \geq \max(\text{min propagation time}\ ,\ \text{min start up time}) \qquad (2)$$

In the case $f_n \geq n$, it is difficult to give general results on the complexity of gossiping. Indeed, the n output links of a processor x may be faulty and, in this case, the other nodes will not receive the data from x. Our most reliable gossiping uses n disjoint paths between any couple of processors. So, it will fail only if there exists a couple of nodes such that one link (or more) of each of the n corresponding paths becomes faulty. However, note that the probability that such a situation occurs is less than the probability that n links become faulty. Hence, our $(n-1)$-resistant algorithm often resists more than $n-1$ faults.

4. Reliable gossiping under the shouting mode

We describe in this section f_n-resistant gossiping algorithms, $f_n < n$, whose time complexities are asymptotically optimal when the length of the messages or the size of the hypercubes is increasing. These algorithms are parametrized by the maximum number of faults that they can take into account.

First, a formal description of $(n-1)$-resistant gossiping is given below. This algorithm is based on the n *Edges-disjoint Spanning Binomial Tree* defined by Ho and Johnsson in [10]. Note that we do not use the *Rotated Spanning Binomial Tree* (see [10]) nor the *Alternate Direction Exchange* algorithm of Saad and Schultz (see [16]); indeed, these algorithms can only be modified to produce 1–resistant gossiping (see [5]). Our algorithm is next modified to insure a good compromise between the time complexity and the fault resistance. The different algorithms could be the codes of programs executed simultaneously by all the processors of the hypercube.

4.1. An $(n-1)$-resistant gossiping algorithm

We use the following notation:

1. The label of each processor is stored in x.
2. M_x is the message of processor x, $x = 0, \ldots, 2^n - 1$.
3. K_x^k, $x = 0, \ldots, 2^n - 1$, $k = 0, \ldots, n-1$, are sets of messages received by x.

The algorithm is decomposed into two stages:

During the first stage, each processor x sends its message M_x to its n neighbors $\oplus_k(x)$, $k = 0, \ldots, n-1$. During the second stage, all the M_x, $x = 0, \ldots; 2^n - 1$ are simultaneously broadcasted respectively from all the $\oplus_k(x)$, $k = 0, \ldots, n-1$, each using successively dimensions $k+1, \ldots, n-1, 0, \ldots, k$. Of course, M_x is not returned from $\oplus_k(x)$ to x (see figure 1).

Algorithm: **Resistant Gossiping**
Begin
1. Send simultaneously M_x through all the dimensions $k = 0, \ldots, n-1$;
   Receive simultaneously $M_{\oplus_k(x)}$ through all the dimensions $k = 0, \ldots, n-1$;
   For $k = 0, \ldots, n-1$, $K_x^k \leftarrow M_{\oplus_k(x)}$;
2. For $j = 0$ to $n-1$ do
   If $j = n-1$ then For $k = 0$ to $n-1$ do $K_x^k \leftarrow K_x^k \setminus M_{\oplus_k(x)}$;
   Send simultaneously K_x^k, $k = 0, \ldots, n-1$, respectively through the dimension $(k+j+1) \bmod n$;
   Receive simultaneously $K^k_{\oplus_{(k+j+1) \bmod n}(x)}$, $k = 0, \ldots, n-1$ respectively through the dimension $(k+j+1) \bmod n$;
   For $k = 0, \ldots, n-1$, $K_x^k \leftarrow K_x^k \cup K^k_{\oplus_{(k+j+1) \bmod n}(x)}$;
   EndFor
End.

For instance, figure 1 shows the trajectory of M_{000} beginning with the edge (000, 001) (i.e. $k = 0$), in the 3–cube. At the end of stage 1, $M_{000} \in K^0_{\oplus_0(000)} = K^0_{001}$. Now, during stage 2, at step $j = 0$, K^0_{001} is sent through the dimension 1 from 001 to 011, and $K^0_{\oplus_1(011)} = K^0_{001} \ni M_{000}$ is added to K^0_{011}, thus $M_{000} \in K^0_{001} \cap K^0_{011}$. At step $j = 1$, K^0_{001} and K^0_{011} are sent through dimension 2 respectively from 001 to 101, and from 011 to 111, and thus M_{000} is included in K^0_{101} and K^0_{111}. Finally, at step $j = 2$, M_{000} is removed from K^0_{001}, and the four sets $K^0_{x_2x_11}$ are sent through dimension 0, from (x_2x_11) to (x_2x_10), $\forall x_i \in \{0, 1\}$, $i = 1, 2$.

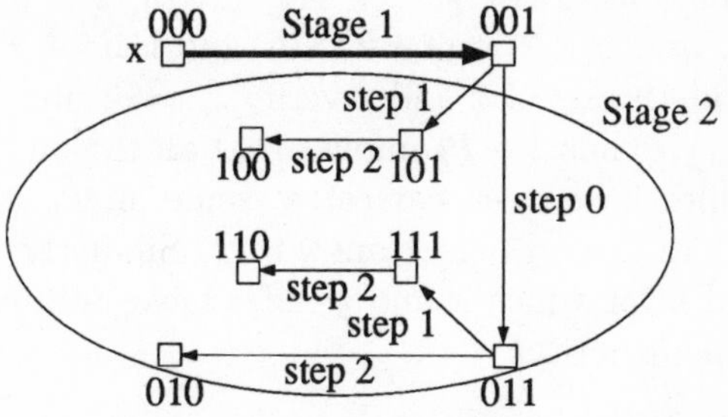

Figure 1 A trajectory of the message M_{000} in a 3–cube.

Sending and receiving are assumed to be done in parallel. We prove now that this algorithm achieves $(n-1)$-resistant gossiping.

Proposition 4.7 *In the absence of faults,*
a) each processor receives n identical copies of each message sent by all the other processors.
b) the distinct copies of any particular message arrive through n disjoint paths.

This is proved using the two following lemmas:

Lemma 4.8 *In the absence of faults, at the end of Resistant Gossiping:*
$\forall x, y \in \{0, \ldots, 2^n - 1\}$, $x \neq y, M_x \in K^k_y$, *for all* $k \in \{0, \ldots, n-1\}$.

Proof: Let x be a node of H_n, and $k \in \{0, \ldots, n-1\}$. At the end of the instruction 1, $M_x \in K^k_{\oplus_k(x)}$ thus $M_x \in K^k_y$, $\forall y \in H^{\varnothing}_n(\oplus_k(x)) = \{\oplus_k(x)\}$. Assume that, at the beginning of step j of instruction 2, $M_x \in K^k_y$, $\forall y \in H^{\{k+1,\ldots,k+j\}}_n(\oplus_k(x))$ where the summations are taken modulo n and $\{k+1, \ldots, k+j\} = \varnothing$ if $j = 0$. During step j, the packet K^k_x is sent through dimension $(k+j+1) \bmod n$. Then, at the end of step j, $M_x \in K^k_y$, $\forall y \in H^{\{k+1,\ldots,k+j+1\}}_n(\oplus_k(x))$. Thus, at the end of step $n-1$ of instruction 2 (end of the algorithm), $M_x \in K^k_y$, $\forall y \in H^{\{k+1,\ldots,k+n\}}_n(\oplus_k(x)) = H^{\{0,\ldots,n-1\}}_n(\oplus_k(x)) = H_n$ (In fact, the test in the loop of instruction 2 insures that M_x is not sent back to x during the last step). $\square$

Lemma 4.9 $\forall x, y \in H_n$, $x \neq y$, *the n copies of* $M_x \in K^k_y$, $k = 0, \ldots, n-1$ *reach y through n disjoint paths.*

Proof: In this proof, all the summations are taken modulo n. Following the proof of lemma 4.8, M_x reaches y passing through $\oplus_k(x)$, $k = 0, \ldots, n-1$. From $\oplus_k(x)$, M_x moves through, successively, the dimensions $k+j+1$, $j = 0, \ldots, n-1$, from the nodes of $H_n^{\{k+1,\ldots,k+j\}}(\oplus_k(x))$ to the nodes of $H_n^{\{k+1,\ldots,k+j+1\}}(\oplus_k(x))$. This procedure, builds a shortest path between $\oplus_k(x)$ and y, correcting successively the bits from which they differ in order $k+1, \ldots, n-1, 0, \ldots, k$. Hence, the algorithm builds n paths from x to y, called P_k, $k = 0, \ldots, n-1$, (P_k begins through the edge $x \rightarrowtail \oplus_k(x)$). Hence, P_k consists in modifying a bit k, and next correcting the bits from which $\oplus_k(x)$ and y differ, successively from $k+1$ to $n-1$, and next from 0 to k. These paths are disjoint. Otherwise let $z \in H_n$, $z \neq x$, $z \neq y$ be a common vertex of two paths, called P_k and $P_{k'}$. Assume $k' > k$, and let $z \in P_k \cap P_{k'}$. This implies that the k–th and the k'–th bits of x and z verify $z_k = \overline{x}_k$ and $z_{k'} = \overline{x}_{k'}$, where $\overline{x}_k$ is the bit complement of x_k. Thus $z \in P_k$ implies that all the bits between $k+1$ and k' from which x and y differ have been corrected, since, in P_k, the bits are corrected successively from $k+1$ to n, and next from 0 to k. Similarly, since $z \in P_{k'}$, all the bits between $k'+1$ and k for which x and y differ have been corrected. Thus $z = y$ which contradicts the hypothesis.□

Proof of proposition 4.7: Point a) directly follows lemma 4.8, and lemma 4.9 proves point b).□

Proposition 4.7 insures that, even in case of $n-1$ faults, at least one copy of each message M_x, $x = 0, \ldots, 2^n - 1$ reaches each processor y, $y = 0, \ldots, 2^n - 1$. Thus *Resistant Gossiping* is $(n-1)$-resistant.

4.2. Complexity of "Resistant Gossiping"

The first stage of *Resistant Gossiping* has a cost of $\beta_c + L\tau_c$. It is straightforward that, at the beginning of steps j, $0 \leq j \leq n-1$ during stage 2, $length(K_x^k) = 2^j L$, $\forall x \in \{0, \ldots, 2^n - 1\}$, $\forall k \in \{0, \ldots, n-1\}$ except for the $(n-1)^{st}$ step where $length(K_x^k) = (2^{n-1} - 1)L$, $\forall x \in \{0, \ldots, 2^n - 1\}$, $\forall k \in \{0, \ldots, n-1\}$. Thus step 2 has a total cost of

$$n\beta_c + \left(\sum_{j=0}^{n-2} 2^j + \left(2^{n-1} - 1\right)\right) L\tau_c = n\beta_c + (2^n - 2)L\tau_c \tag{3}$$

Hence the global complexity of *Resistant Gossiping* is

$$T_{ResistantGossiping} = (n+1)\beta_c + (N-1)L\tau_c \tag{4}$$

Thus, comparing 4 with 2 (and propositions 3.5 and 3.6), the complexity of *Resistant Gossiping* is optimal within a small constant factor since it is the sum of two terms instead of the maximum of these two terms.

4.3. f_n-resistant gossiping

In this section, we briefly describe how to modify *Resistant Gossiping* to obtain f_n–resistant gossiping for $f_n < n-1$.

Each message M_x, $x = 0,\ldots,N-1$, is cut in n blocks, $B_x^0,\ldots,B_x^{n-1}$. We group f_n+1 copies of these blocks into n packets as follows. The packet k, $0 \le k \le n-1$ is composed of blocks $B_x^k \cup B_x^{(k+1) \bmod n} \cup \ldots \cup B_x^{(k+f_n) \bmod n}$. Now we modify stage 1 of *Resistant Gossiping* by replacing the send of M_x through all dimensions with the send of packet k through dimension k, $k = 0,\ldots,n-1$. Then, at the end of stage 1, $K_x^k = B_{\oplus_k(x)}^k \cup B_{\oplus_k(x)}^{(k+1) \bmod n} \cup \ldots \cup B_{\oplus_k(x)}^{(k+f_n) \bmod n}$. The only modification of stage 2 is that in the test $K_x^k \leftarrow K_x^k \setminus M_{\oplus_k(x)}$ is replaced by $K_x^k \leftarrow K_x^k \setminus \left(B_{\oplus_k(x)}^k \cup B_{\oplus_k(x)}^{(k+1) \bmod n} \cup \ldots \cup B_{\oplus_k(x)}^{(k+f_n) \bmod n}\right)$. For each processor x, each block B_x^k is contained in f_n+1 initial packets. Then, following lemmas 4.8 and 4.9, each block reaches each of the other processors passing through f_n+1 disjoint paths.

The complexity of this f_n–resistant gossiping is now of $\beta_c + \frac{f_n+1}{n} L\tau_c$ for the first stage, and $n\beta_c + (2^n-2)\frac{f_n+1}{n} L\tau_c$ for the second stage. Hence, the global cost is

$$(n+1)\beta_c + (N-1)\frac{f_n+1}{n} L\tau_c \qquad (5)$$

Thus, comparing 5 with 2, the complexity is optimal within a small constant factor since it is the sum of two terms instead of the maximum of these two terms.

5. A few comments on reliable gossiping under the whispering mode

Our (n–1)-resistant gossiping algorithm and the reliable broadcasting algorithm of Ramanathan and Shin in [14] are both based on the *n Edges-disjoint Spanning Binomial Tree* (*nESBT*) described by Ho and Johnsson in [10]. Moreover, Ho and Johnsson define a labeling of the *nESBT* in order to construct a 1–port gossiping. Being careless of the memory control costs, their algorithm performs in time $2n\beta_c + (N-1)L\tau_c$. Each message is cut into n packets of size $\frac{L}{n}$, and each packet is broadcasted through disjoint paths. Hence, if instead of cutting the messages, we replicate them in order to route the distinct versions through disjoint paths, we obtain an (n–1)-resistant gossiping performing in $2n\beta_c + n(N-1)L\tau_c$ and thus asymptotically reaching the lower bound given in proposition 3.5. However, note that a formal description of the algorithm is difficult to give due to the problem of grouping the messages. Ho and Johnsson propose that if the node address is included in the message, then a node upon receipt of a message makes use of a *children* function to determine on what ports the received message should be retransmitted. We refer to [10] for more details.

6. Conclusion

This paper has proposed reliable gossiping algorithms for the class of hypercube multicomputers. We study here the *store and forward* routing. Algorithms are described which resists f_n link faults, for $0 \le f_n \le n-1$. They are based on the construction of disjoint paths, and their complexities are optimal within a small constant factor. These algorithms can also resist processor faults. In this case, the time complexity is slightly changed, but it is easy to modify *Resistant Gossiping* in order to reach the optimal propagation time [5].

Acknowledgments: We are grateful to prof. J.Peters of Simon Fraser University for many helpful discussions and remarks.

Bibliography

[1] M. Alam and R. Melhem. How to use an incomplete binary hypercube for fault tolerance. In F. Andre and J. Verjus, editors, Hypercube and Distributed Computers, pages 329–341. North-Holland, 1989.

[2] M. Chen and K. Shin. Depth-first search approach for fault-tolerant routing in hypercube multicomputers. IEEE Trans on Parallel and Distributed Systems, 1(2):152–159, 1990.

[3] M. Cosnard and P. Fraigniaud. Finding the roots of a polynomial on an MIMD multicomputer. Parallel Computing, 15:75–85, 1990.

[4] A.-H. Esfahanian. Generalized measures of fault tolerance with application to n-cube networks. IEEE TC, 58(11):1586–1591, 1989.

[5] P. Fraigniaud. Asymptotically optimal broadcasting and total exchange algorithms in faulty hypercube multicomputers. Research report 89-05, LIP-IMAG, ENS Lyon, France, 1989.

[6] P. Fraigniaud. Performance analysis of broadcasting in hypercubes. In F. Andre and J. verjus, editors, Hypercubes and Distributed Computers, pages 311–328. North-Holland, 1989.

[7] P. Fraigniaud. Performance analysis of broadcasting in hypercubes with restricted communication capabilities. Research report 90-16, LIP-IMAG, ENS Lyon, France, 1990.

[8] A. Ghafoor and P. Sole. Performance of fault-tolerant diagnostics in the hypercube systems. IEEE Trans. on Comp., 38(8):1164–1172, 1989.

[9] S. Hedetniemi, S. Hedetniemi, and A. Liestman. A survey of gossiping and broadcasting in communication networks. Networks, 18:319–349, 1986.

[10] S. Johnsson and C.-T. Ho. Optimum broadcasting and personalized communication in hypercubes. IEEE Trans. Comp., 38(9):1249–1268, 1989.

[11] E. Lazard. Broadcasting in DMA-bound bounded degree graphs. Research report (to appear in Disc. Appl. Math.), LRI, Orsay, France, 1990.

[12] C. Li and W. Fuchs. Graceful degradation on hypercube multiprocessors using data redistribution. Proceedings of DMCC5, Charleston, SC, April 8-12, 1990.

[13] R. McLeod and J. Schellenberg. Percolation and anomalous transport as tools in analyzing parallel processing interconnection networks. JPDC, 8:376–387, 1990.

[14] P. Ramanathan and K. Shin. Reliable broadcast in hypercube multicomputers. IEEE Transactions on Computers, 37(12):1654–1657, 1988.

[15] Y. Saad and M. Schultz. Topological properties of hypercubes. IEEE Transaction on Computers, 37(7):867–871, 1988.

[16] Y. Saad and M. Schultz. Data communication in hypercubes. JJPD, 6:115–135, 1989.

[17] Y. Saad and M. Schultz. Data communication in parallel architectures. Parallel Computing, 11:131–150, 1989.

[18] S. Seidel. Circuit-switched vs. store and forward solutions to symmetric communication problems. HCCA 4, 1989.

[19] Q. Stout and B. Wagar. Intensive hypercube communication, prearranged communication in link-bound machines. JPDC, 10:167–181, 1990.

Architecture, Implementation, and System Software of K2

M. ANNARATONE, G. ZUR BONSEN, M. FILLO,
M. HALBHERR, R. RÜHL, P. STEINER, AND M. VIREDAZ

*Integrated Systems Laboratory, Swiss Federal Institute of Technology
Gloriastrasse 35, 8092 Zurich, Switzerland*

Abstract

The K2 project started in 1988 with the goal of designing and implementing a distributed memory parallel processor with an architecture efficiently supporting a time-sharing, multi-user, multi-tasking operating system and an automatically parallelizing Fortran compiler. This paper introduces the architecture of the machine, its hardware implementation, the parallelizing compiler, and an overview of the operating system.

1 Introduction

The design space of a distributed memory parallel processor (DMPP) should be constrained by considerations on the efficient execution of important classes of applications *and* by the requirements of the system software. DMPPs' designers have so far largely ignored the latter aspect. This disregard for system issues could be justified on the basis that optimizing the execution of single, compute-intensive jobs was the overall goal (batch-mode utilization of the machine, cumbersome programming and debugging environment, and lack of code portability being the unfortunate consequences). Eventually such strategy does not pay off, and in fact DMPPs do not seem to increase their market share.

Our goal is to design a DMPP that exploits the benefits of this class of machines, but appears to the user—and can be programmed and debugged—much like a conventional uniprocessor. To accomplish this, a DMPP shall feature a time-sharing, multi-user, multi-tasking operating system, and automatically parallelizing compilers (APCs). The paper presents an overview of the K2 project, spanning from the architecture and hardware implementation of the machine to the parallelizing compiler and operating system, and it is organized as follows. First, the architecture of K2 is introduced and discussed, followed by a description of the hardware implementation. Second, the APC is presented, followed by the operating system. Finally, the status and evolution of the project is outlined.

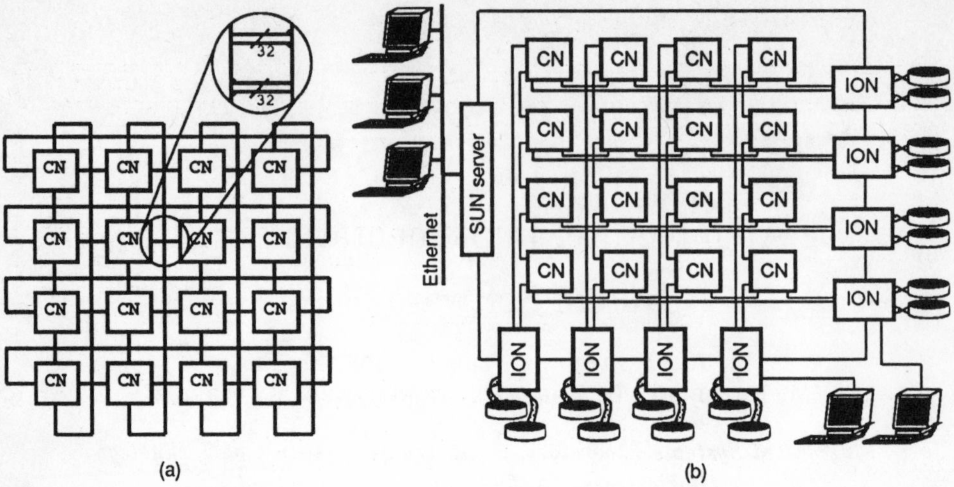

Figure 1: *The K2 user-level machine abstraction (a) and the K2 system-level machine abstraction (b).*

2 Overview of the K2 architecture

DMPPs are commonly designed as "attached processors," i.e., with a host computer between the user and the DMPP. This approach dates back to the Solomon [1] and ILLIAC IV [2] DMPPs. On such machines jobs run on the attached processor (i.e., the DMPP) in batch-mode. Batch processing makes it unrealistic to run interactive programs, and tends to favor post-mortem debugging. Interactive use and debugging is possible on some DMPPs only by locking the machine; this results in an increase of the cost per job, and decreases the performance/price advantage that DMPPs have over vector supercomputers. Abandoning the attached processor design style is hence a necessary—albeit not sufficient—condition to achieve true multiprogrammability.

A multi-user, multi-tasking, time-sharing operating system is another necessary condition: this implies that interprocessor communication activities in K2 shall take place at two levels, that is *user* and *system*. User level communications include all data transfers occurring during program execution (programs can be manually parallelized or parallelized automatically by the compiler). System level communications include all those data transfers under the control of the operating system, such as I/O, pages, server calls, synchronization messages, queries, scheduling information, etc.

K2 provides a programming environment and a user interface similar to that of conventional uniprocessors. K2's time-sharing, multi-user, multi-tasking operating system will ease interactive debugging, and decrease the cost per job. To support this, the machine shall have (1) a disk subsystem with enough bandwidth to support paging activities, process swapping, and large files transfers, through parallelism of the mass storage; (2) an I/O architecture matching the performance of the parallel disks, and exploiting the interconnection topology and communication mechanism *at the system level*; (3) large

Table 1: *Characteristics of the user channels and the system channels.*

PARAMETER	USER CHANNELS	SYSTEM CHANNELS
Info carried	Application	System
Communication mechanism	Raw data, blocking and non-blocking	Message passing, non-blocking
Routing done by	PE	SNIK
Medium	Parallel wires	Coax and optical fibers
Throughput per channel (peak)	$400 Mb/s$	$100 Mb/s$
CN to CN latency	$200 ns$	$1.5 \mu s$

local storage to decrease the load on the interprocessor communication channels [3], and to accommodate the working sets of several large-sized processes; and (4) virtual memory support and memory protection on each node. Moreover, efficient support of compiler-generated parallel programs is required, and calls for a careful design of the interprocessor communication mechanism *at the user level.*

While there is a large body of literature on efficient DMPP topologies and communication mechanisms for parallel applications, architectural requirements imposed by system software are relatively unknown. As far as application software is concerned, previous works demonstrated that low-dimensionality topologies benefit significantly from fast neighbor communication, and do not require the flexibility of message-passing with its larger set-up times [4, 5].

Let us define the processing element (PE) communication/computation ratio q as $q = \frac{t_{io}}{t_c}$, where t_{io} is the time for a PE to send or receive a double-precision quantity to or from a neighbor processor, and t_c is the time to perform a double-precision multiply-add operation as in DAXPY [6]. Our studies have shown that code parallelized by an APC is more sensitive to q than manually parallelized code [7]. Specifically, a severe performance degradation (i.e., lower speedup) occurs for values of q greater than about four. Architectures with $q < 4$ typically employ systolic communication (as opposed to memory communication [8], i.e., message passing), and only two DMPPs of this kind are commercially available, that is Warp [4] and iWarp [9].

Figure 1(a) shows the K2 *user-level machine abstraction*, which consists of a torus of computation nodes (CNs). CNs are interconnected by point-to-point (32-bit wide) pairs of unidirectional channels, hereafter referred to as *user channels.* The K2 *system-level machine abstraction* is shown in figure 1(b). Each row (or column) of CNs is connected to an input/output node (ION) to which terminals and disks are attached. The connection between each ION and a row (or column) of CNs is a serial token-ring, referred to as *system channel.* On each CN or ION a dedicated serial network interface controller (SNIK) manages the two system channels. An identical token-ring serves all IONs and connects them to an Ethernet gateway. The characteristics of both user and system channels are summarized in table 1.

A global pathway controlled by "torus synchronization units" (TSUs) located on the CNs connects all CNs together. (The TSU is not shown in figure reffigK2architecture(b) to keep the latter readable.) The TSU allows the operating system to coordinate critical operations like context switching on all CNs within some microseconds. Namely, it allows a node to initiate any kind of cluster switch operation (a cluster being a subset of CNs) and to wait until all CNs have performed it.

Parallel jobs execute on the torus of CNs, while users login on the IONs and run on them ordinary processes such as editing, sending mail, etc. In addition, the IONs are used as file servers and disk caches.

3 Hardware implementation

K2 consists of two basic building blocks, i.e., a computation node (CN) and an input/output node (ION). They are shown in figure 2(a) and 2(b), respectively.

A CN includes a processing element (PE), four outgoing and four incoming 32-bit wide user channels (Queues), and a serial network interface controller (SNIK), managing the communication through the system channels. The PE consists of an AMD Am29000 microprocessor with AMD Am29027 floating-point co-processor (FPC), separate instruction (2 Mbyte) and data memories (8 Mbyte) with error detection and correction, and the already mentioned TSU. The SNIK communicates with the PE through a dual-port RAM, and utilizes a Motorola MC68030 microprocessor, with its own local boot ROM and program/data memory. The physical connection to the system channels is implemented through two pairs of AMD "TAXI" chips, which perform the parallel (8-bit) to serial conversion on transmission and vice versa on reception. These chips communicate either on balanced coaxial cables or—by simply plugging the AMD "FOXY" chips in place of the TAXI chips—on optical fibers. The SNIK MC 68030 is in charge of packet routing and "corner turning" (i.e., hopping from a horizontal ring to a vertical ring or vice versa), checksum calculation and test, and packet acknowledgement. FIFOs between the 68030 and the TAXI chips smooth packet flow. A large finite-state machine (FSM) (one per ring) interprets the address of the incoming packets and buffers them if they are destined for the local PE or if a corner-turning is required. Otherwise, cut-through occurs. The FSM also implements the token-passing protocol and various error detection mechanisms.

The ION includes a PE, a SNIK, a mass storage controller (MSC), and terminal interfaces, but no user channels. The PE of the ION is identical to that of the CN, except that its local storage is four times larger (40 Mbyte vs. 10 Mbyte), since the IONs are intended to implement an intelligent disk cache mechanism to increase the performance of the paging and I/O system. The MSC interfaces directly to the PE through a dual-port memory and provides a peripheral SCSI interface with a peak throughput of about 4 Mbyte/s. In fact, interfacing each ION to an industry standard bus such as VME, and utilizing commercial disk controller cards was ruled out on performance grounds. First, the PE burst mode bandwidth requires a bus system much faster than any industry standard bus. Second, no DMA is available for the 29000 processor. The MSC hardware is based on a 68030 CPU which supervises, without direct involvement, the flow of data between the SCSI controller and the PE through a dual-port memory, and manages all the SCSI generated interrupts. The MSC software implements an aggressive management strategy interleaving two disks to boost the mass storage throughput.

Four basic units were designed, i.e., the PE, the user channels, the SNIK, and the MSC. The machine being implemented is that shown in figure 1(b). Finally, the choice of the local microprocessor, the design of the memory architecture and of the user channels has been presented and justified elsewhere [10].

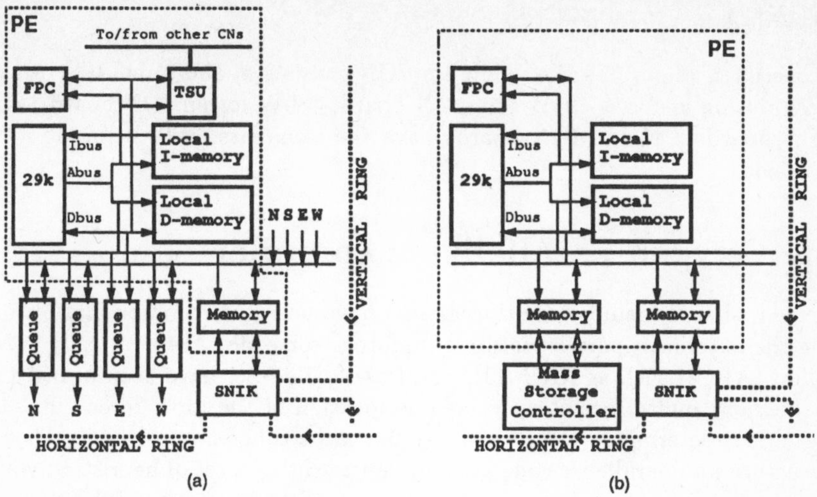

Figure 2: *Block-diagram of CN (a) and ION (b).*

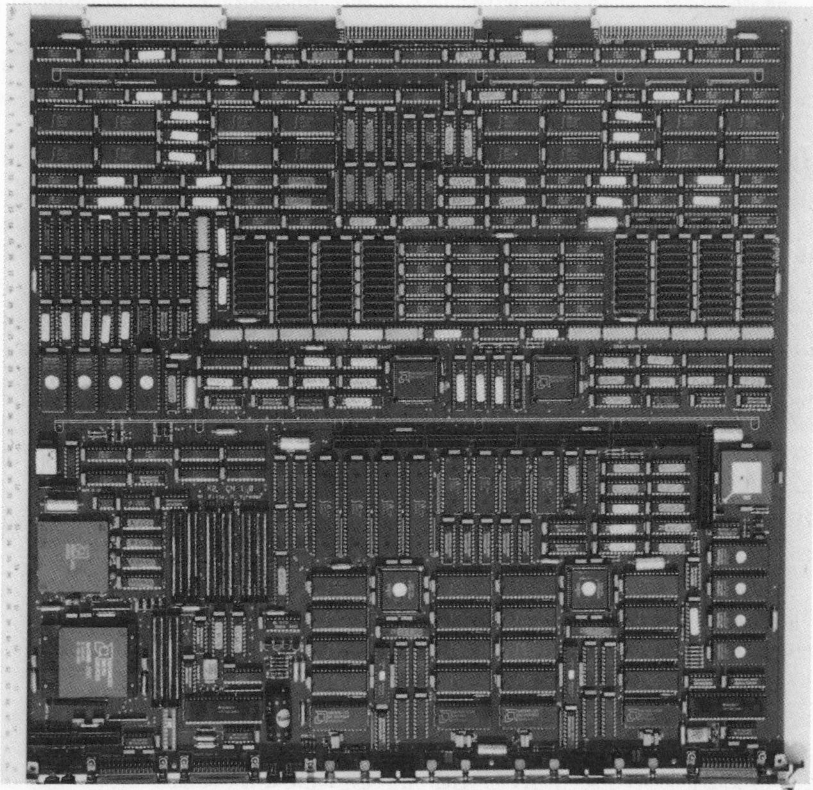

Figure 3: *The CN board. The prototype K2 consists of 16 boards identical to the one shown here, plus 8 ION boards that are of similar complexity. The entire machine is housed in three cabinets containing the 24 boards, power supplies, fans, and the mass storage (16 hard disks). Each cabinet is 175cm tall, 60cm (19in) wide, and 80cm deep.*

3.1 Metrics

The CN consists of about 380 ICs, while the ION consists of about 340 ICs. Maximum power consumption is about 195W for a CN board, 180W for an ION board. Figure 3 shows a CN board. CN and ION boards have the same size, each being about 50*cm* (19*in*) on a side.

4 The Oxygen parallelizing compiler

Bus-connected, shared memory multiprocessors have been the common platform for investigating the automatic parallelization of uniprocessor code. Automatically parallelizing compilers (APCs) such as KAP [11], Parafrase-2 [12], etc. have been in fact tailored to shared memory multiprocessors, where the location of the most recent update of a shared variable is determined *in hardware* by the cache coherency protocol. These compilers restructure and parallelize code at compile-time using a set of heuristics; while this approach does not introduce extra run-time overhead, compile-time heuristics cannot detect all possible data dependencies.

When implementing an APC for DMPPs, a different set of constraints comes into place, and the designer has to cope with (1) the decomposition of the problem's domain and the allocation of the subdomains to the local memories of the processing elements, (2) the nonuniformity of memory accesses, (3) the management of the interprocessor communication, and (4) the enforcement of data consistency across the various local memories.

By "data consistency analysis" we mean the process of determining the location of the most recent update of a shared variable in the local memories in a DMPP. Data consistency analysis, in the sense of determining which cache memory contains the most recent update of a shared variable, is carried out in shared memory multiprocessors as well. However, such procedure is implemented in hardware and it is therefore transparent to the APC designer. On DMPPs, data consistency analysis becomes part of the APC responsibilities, and requires that run-time activities be performed in the general case. As an example, let us consider the matrix-vector product part of a conjugate gradients algorithm for unsymmetric matrices stored in a YSMP data structure [13, 14]:

```
          DO 20 I = 1, N
             DO 10 K = JA(I), JA(I + 1) - 1
                J = JA(K)
                Y(I) = Y(I) + A(K + ETA) * X(J)
                Y(J) = Y(J) + A(K) * X(I)
    10       CONTINUE
    20    CONTINUE
```

On shared memory multiprocessors both loops can be parallelized regardless of the values of JA (and ETA), with the location of the (cached) elements of A and JA determined by the hardware. On DMPPs, an APC without run-time data consistency analysis could

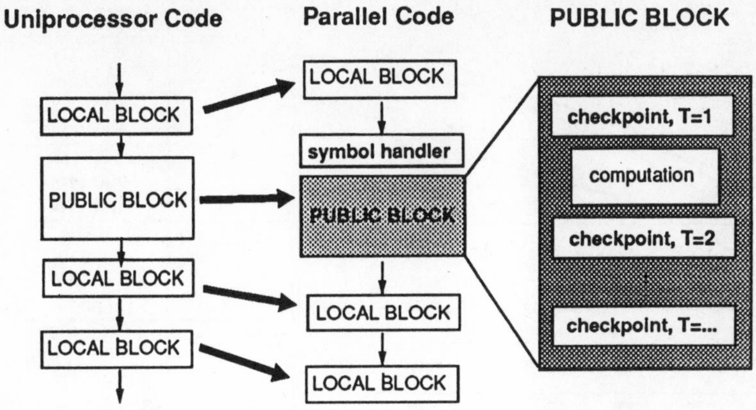

Figure 4: *The model of uniprocessor code embedded in Oxygen.*

not even compile the loop (unless in the uninteresting case when all data are completely allocated into one local memory).

Examples like the one presented above, and the lack of any hardware mechanism to resolve memory access conflict and sequencing in DMPPs lead us to the design specifications of Oxygen, which makes extensive use of run-time data consistency analysis.

4.1 Design philosophy

The development of Oxygen proceeds through two steps: first, a version with compiler directives is developed. Second, a preprocessor which automatically generates the compiler directives is implemented. The first internal release of Oxygen is with compiler directives, and this is the version this section refers to.

Oxygen assumes that any Fortran program can be decomposed into a sequence of *code blocks.* Code blocks may belong to either one of two classes:

- **Local blocks**. Local blocks do not require interprocessor communication. They may be decomposed and parallelized on more than one PE, but they perform locally on each of them.

- **Public blocks**. Public blocks, called P_BLOCKS from now on, run in parallel on more than one PE and require interprocessor communication because they operate on data structures allocated across processor boundaries.

The model of uniprocessor code embedded in Oxygen is shown in figure 4. The leftmost column in the figure shows how the uniprocessor code is decomposed, via compiler directives, onto the various blocks. The second column shows the source code, common to all PEs, generated by Oxygen. Before every P_BLOCK there is some extra code, referred to as "symbol handler," which is inserted by Oxygen during compilation. The symbol handler runs on every PE, resolves data access conflicts, and constructs data structures

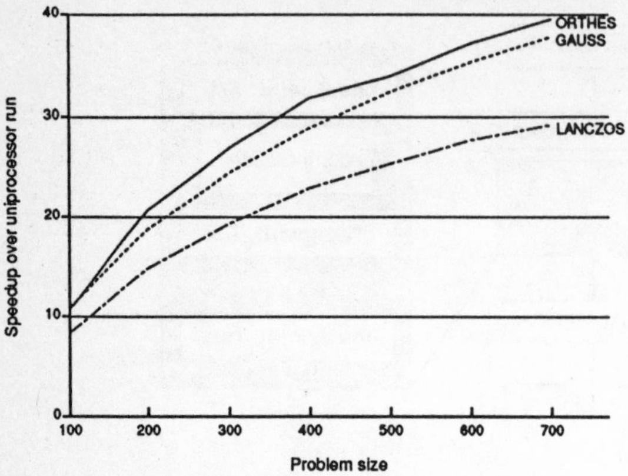

(a)

Algorithm	*Problem size*	*Speedup*
SVD	100×100	9.5
	200×200	15.9
	300×300	21.4
	400×400	25.2
FLUID	100×50	13.9
	200×100	23.8
	400×200	36.6
GFFT	10000	11.3
	20000	12.6
	40000	16.3
	80000	17.0
CG	80000 (600)	9.5
	160000 (800)	13.1
	240000 (1000)	15.1
	320000 (1100)	17.4

(b)

Figure 5: *Speedup results for* GAUSS, ORTHES, *and* LANCZOS *for different problem sizes on an* 8×8 *processor torus (a). Speedups for the EISPACK* SVD *routine, the generalized FFT (*GFFT*), the fluid dynamics application (*FLUID*), and conjugate gradients (*CG*)(b).*

that will be used by each PE to generate and execute interprocessor communication primitives at specific "communication checkpoints." This is shown in the rightmost column of figure 4, where a P_BLOCK has been expanded; the P_BLOCK consists of a sequence of computation phases intermixed with interprocessor communication phases (i.e., the aforementioned communication checkpoints).

The model shows that data-consistency is ensured at run-time by the execution of the symbol handlers. Run-time data-consistency check can also be used to analyze data dependences dynamically as we discuss elsewhere [15].

4.2 Oxygen benchmarks

We present here seven test programs, namely (1) Gaussian elimination with partial pivoting (GAUSS), (2) similarity transformation of an unsymmetric matrix to Hessenberg form (ORTHES), (3) the Lanczos iteration for unsymmetric matrices (LANCZOS), (4) the EISPACK SVD routine (SVD), (5) the generalized FFT (GFFT), (6) the solution of a two-dimensional, steady-state transonic small disturbance equation for fluid dynamics applications (FLUID), and (7) conjugate gradients on YSMP data structures [13, 14] (CG).

The benchmarks have been executed on a general-purpose architectural simulator for DMPPs, which has been developed at the Laboratory [16].

Speedup results for the first three test programs are shown in figure 5(a) for different problem sizes, while speedups for SVD, GFFT, FLUID, and CG are tabulated in figure 5(b).

5 The Chagori operating system

Chagori is a virtual memory, multi-user, multi-tasking operating system with demand paging. Because of time-sharing, several users can run (and debug) interactively large parallel programs at the same time. Furthermore, Chagori supports parallel I/O through a distributed file system which implements file-striping across the IONs on multiple disks. While the user's motivation to use a DMPP is that of raw computational power, the operating system should increase resource sharing and utilization by overlapping computation and communication and by exploiting locality using virtual memory.

5.1 Parallel process clusters

From the operating system point of view, the architecture of K2 consists of two units, i.e., the computing unit (CU) which is the collection of CNs and user channels, and the I/O unit (IOU) which is the collection of IONs and system channels. The CU supports parallel computation, while the IOU allows for parallel I/O.

Chagori multiplexes the CU (or parts of it) between several parallel programs running on the system. However, the operating system cannot be involved in the fine grain communication through the user channels of a running parallel program, because the communication latency of the user channels is as fast as an ordinary memory access. While Chagori does not exploit the idle times of PEs blocking on user channels, it must nevertheless isolate the various parallel programs from each other in time and space, since the user channels do not maintain multiple contexts.

Besides traditional processes and multiple threads within processes, Chagori supports an additional mechanism of execution of parallel programs. We call this *parallel process cluster*, and it is an abstraction representing a virtual CU. A parallel process cluster consists of a set of processes, with each process running on a different CN. The operating system activates the processes of a cluster simultaneously in order to allow the processes to communicate with their neighbors. Similarly, Chagori disactivates the processes of a cluster simultaneously to completely isolate different clusters from each other in time and space with respect to their access to user channels.

5.2 Clustered memory agents

The low-level file system supports striped files of fixed-size blocks that are maintained by distributed servers running on the IONs. Parallel high-level I/O must ensure atomicity of logical records that are arbitrarily mapped into low-level file blocks. To avoid the overhead of a general coherency protocol of a distributed record management system, Chagori extends the concept of memory agents [17, 18] to clusters. This can be accomplished by providing pageable memory segments, supporting external pagers for any segment, and clustering pagers.

The mapping of the elements of a file into local segments of the processes of a cluster is performed by external pagers, which themselves form a cluster, called a *clustered memory agent*. If the application attempts to access an element in its segment that is not resident, a page fault occurs, which has to be handled by the external pager on that node. The clustered agent can then access the file blocks, and distribute all elements they contain to the appropriate nodes through the user channels.

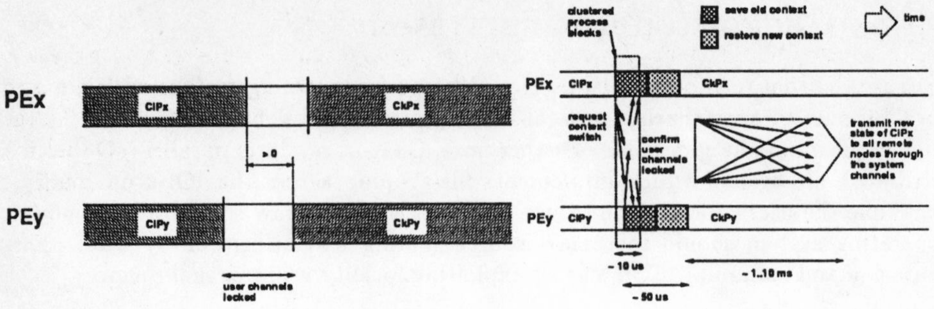

Figure 6: *Isolating clusters with respect to user channel access (left). Fast cluster switching with the torus synchronization unit (right).*

5.3 Structure of the scheduler

User channels, processors and the processors' local memories are the three resources present in the CU that have to be shared by clusters. Since the execution time slice of a particular program is considerably shorter than the time spent residing in memory, a two-level scheduler is appropriate. The *short-term* scheduler controls context switches of processes and entire clusters while the *long-term* scheduler controls memory allocation and thus swapping of entire processes or clusters between local storages and disks.

Because of the distributed nature of Chagori, the actions controlled by the two schedulers, namely cluster switching and cluster swapping, are performed locally on the nodes. Switching and swapping clusters can therefore be seen as switching and swapping (local) processes by the nodes simultaneously.

5.4 Dispatching parallel jobs

Parallel process clusters must be dispatched such that a process (e.g., CiPx, see figure 6, left) of one cluster (e.g., Ci) can never send data to a process (e.g., CkPy) of another cluster (e.g., Ck) through the user channels. That is, *the execution phases of processes running on neighboring nodes and belonging to different clusters shall never overlap.*

A cluster dispatching scheme based on fixed and predefined time slices and synchronized clocks limits the maximum achievable torus utilization ratio, because it may result in many unnecessary context switches (if a too short time quantum has been chosen) or else long idle times caused by wait states and processor blocking on remote wait states within the time slices.

Chagori uses a variable time slice scheme to achieve a good utilization of the CU. A cluster switch can be initiated when any clustered process blocks or when all processes of a cluster either have blocked or are attempting to read from an empty user channel connected to a process that has already blocked. The task of dispatching clusters is divided into two subtasks, i.e., the determination of the precise instant of a switch and the shipping of scheduling information to determine the sequence of clusters to be activated (see figure 6, right).

The torus synchronization unit allows any node to initiate a switch and to get the acknowledge from all other nodes that they have performed a critical part of the switch.

It furthermore allows any node to raise an exception signal in the case it does not know yet which cluster to run next. Exception signalling is necessary because process state changes are broadcasted through the system channel network. In particular, the ready queues of the nodes are ordered by means of a protocol that implements a distributed short-term scheduler. It guarantees that all nodes either see a process belonging to the same cluster at the head of their local process queues or that some nodes see an empty queue.

5.5 Chagori compared with general-purpose distributed systems

Chagori resembles large distributed systems like Amoeba[19] or Mach[20]. In fact, the kernel is replicated on each node and provides only minimal functionality, such as supporting processes and multiple threads, local memory management and message passing for interprocess communication. Chagori differs instead from other distributed operating systems in the following points.

- In order to support fine grain communication Chagori must implement an efficient gang scheduling [21, 22]. While Amoeba does not support anything comparable, the gang scheduling of Mach [23] is not enough architecture-specific to be effective on K2. The control architecture suggested in [24] solves a more general scheduling problem; however, and contrary to the latter, Chagori takes into account all kinds of process wait states since transitions to wait states suspend a cluster.
- Multithreading under Chagori (which is provided mainly to allow servers to overlap I/O and computation) always yields pseudo-parallelism, contrary to Mach and other operating systems for shared memory multiprocessors which offer threads as a means to achieve real parallelism.
- Contrary to Amoeba, virtual memory and demand paging is provided; however, distributed memory sharing is not acceptable as a communication method.
- Chagori supports distributed objects (blocks of a file distributed over multiple disks) and distributed servers that are able to perform parallel I/O.

6 Project status and evolution

The hardware of the machine has been completely designed and single units have been tested successfully at full speed. Several CNs and IONs boards will be manufactured and tested in the next months. System backplane, chassis, power supplies, fans, etc. have been integrated together. New versions of Oxygen will include more sophisticated data-dependence analysis, following the philosophy of Parafrase-II. The first release of Chagori will be limited in its goals; in particular, it will support multiprocessing, multithreading, virtual address translation, but no paging. It will also feature an improved system channel communication mechanism.

References

[1] D.L. Slotnick et al. The Solomon computer. In *Proc. AFIPS - Joint Computer Conference*, volume 22, pages 97–107, 1962.

[2] G.H. Barnes et al. The Illiac IV computer. *IEEE Trans. on Computers*, C-17(8):746–757, August 1968.

[3] H.T. Kung. Memory requirements for balanced computer architectures. In *Proc. 13th Symposium on Computer Architecture*, pages 49–54. IEEE-ACM, June 1986.

[4] M. Annaratone, E. Arnould, T. Gross, H.T. Kung, M. Lam, O. Menzilcioglu, and J.A. Webb. The Warp Computer: Architecture, Implementation, and Performance. *IEEE Trans. on Computers*, December 1987.

[5] M. Annaratone, C. Pommerell, and R. Rühl. Interprocessor communication speed and performance in distributed-memory parallel processors. In *Proc. 16th Symposium on Computer Architecture*, Jerusalem, May 1989. IEEE-ACM.

[6] C. L. Lawson, R. J. Hanson, D. R. Kincaid, and F. T. Krogh. Basic linear algebra subprograms for Fortran usage. *ACM Transactions on Math. Softw.*, 5(3):308–323, September 1979.

[7] M. Annaratone and R. Rühl. Interprocessor communication mechanisms on distributed memory multiprocessors for the efficient execution of compiler-generated parallel code. Technical report, Integrated Systems Laboratory, Swiss Federal Institute of Technology, September 1990.

[8] S. Borkar et al. Supporting systolic and memory communication in iWarp. In *Proc. 17th Symposium on Computer Architecture*, pages 70–81, Seattle, May 1990. ACM-IEEE.

[9] S. Borkar et al. iWarp: an integrated solution to high-speed parallel computation. In *Proc. Supercomputing 88*, November 1988.

[10] M. Annaratone, M. Fillo, K. Nakabayashi, and M. Viredaz. The K2 parallel processor: Architecture and hardware implementation. In *Proc. 17th Symposium on Computer Architecture*, Seattle, May 1990. IEEE-ACM.

[11] M. Wolfe. Automatic detection of concurrency for shared memory multiprocessors. Technical report, Kuck and Associates Inc., October 1987. 1987 ESUG meeting.

[12] C. Polychronopoulos et al. Parafrase-2: An environment for parallelizing, partitioning, synchronizing, and scheduling programs on multiprocessors. Technical report, University of Illinois, CSRD, 1989.

[13] S.C. Eisenstat, M.C. Gursky, M.H. Schultz, and A.H. Sherman. Yale sparse matrix package I: The symmetric codes. *International Journal for Numerical Methods in Engineering*, 18:1145–1151, 1982.

[14] S.C. Eisenstat, M.C. Gursky, M.H. Schultz, and A.H. Sherman. Yale sparse matrix package II: The nonsymmetric codes. Technical Report 114, Computer Science Department, Yale University, 1977.

[15] R. Rühl and M. Annaratone. Parallelization of fortran code on distributed-memory parallel processors. In *International Conference on Supercomputing*, pages 342–353, Amsterdam, June 1990. ACM.

[16] P. Beadle, C. Pommerell, and M. Annaratone. K9: A simulator of distributed-memory parallel processors. In *Proc. Supercomputing 89*, Reno, Nevada, November 1989. ACM.

[17] R. Rashid et al. Machine-independent virtual memory management for paged uniprocessor and multiprocessor architectures. Technical report, Carnegie Mellon University, July 1987.

[18] M. Young et al. The duality of memory and communication in the implementation of a multiprocessor operating system. In *Proc. 11th Symposium on Operating System Principles*, November 1987.

[19] S.J.Mullender et al. *The Amoeba distributed operating system: selected papers 1984-1987*. Centrum voor Wiskunde en Informatica, 1987.

[20] A. Tevanian Jr. and R.F. Rashid. Mach: A basis for future UNIX development. Technical report, Carnegie Mellon University, June 1987.

[21] J. K. Ousterhout, D.A. Scelza, and P.S. Sindhu. MEDUSA: An experiment in distributed operating system structure. *Comm. ACM*, 23(2):92–105, February 1980.

[22] P. Emrath. Xylem: An operating system for the cedar multiprocessor. *IEEE Software*, 2(4), July 1985.

[23] D.L. Black. Scheduling support for concurrency and parallelism in the Mach operating system. *IEEE Computer*, May 1990.

[24] D.G. Feitelson and L. Rudolph. Distributed hierarchical control for parallel processing. *IEEE Computer*, May 1990.

European Declarative System (EDS): Architecture and Interprocess Communication

G. Watzlawik
Siemens AG, Otto-Hahn-Ring 6, D-8000 München 83
E. H. Robinson
ICL, Wenlock Way, Manchester M12 5DR

Abstract

The consortium of Bull, ECRC, ICL, Siemens and their associates is currently designing a MIMD parallel computer with distributed store architecture. This work is being done in the framework of ESPRIT II projects. It is a scalable machine with up to 256 Processing Elements connected by a Multistage Interconnection Network. This paper describes the system and the hardware architecture of the machine and discusses the hardware support of the interprocess communication.

1 Introduction

The European Declarative System (hereafter called EDS) project is an ESPRIT II project (EP2025). Its main focus is towards the parallel support of applications written in declarative languages where the greatest market in the near future is expected in the field of databases with SQL as the standard interface. Parallel versions of Lisp and Prolog are the two other languages which will be developed within the project. The project has a timeframe starting in 1989 and ending in 1992.

The aim of the project is to build a MIMD-type parallel computer with distributed store architecture. This architecture is different to shared memory machines like the Butterfly GP1000 [1], the IBM RP3 [2] or the NYU Ultracomputer [3] which share a common physical address space. Nevertheless, the EDS machine will not be a pure message passing engine like the Intel iPSC/2 [4], but will also support a distributed virtually shared memory. This approach was conceptually described in [5] based on a prototype implementation of a LAN interconnecting workstations. In the EDS project, the processing elements are tightly coupled over a high speed network and the communication is embedded in the operating system of the machine.

In section 2 an overview of the system architecture of EDS is given. Section 3 describes in more detail the hardware architecture of the system. Section 4 details the interprocess communication facilities where emphasis is put on the description of the store copying mechanism which supports the implementation of the distributed virtually shared memory. Section 5 gives a summary.

2 EDS System Architecture

Figure 1 shows the system diagram of the EDS machine. Up to 256 elements

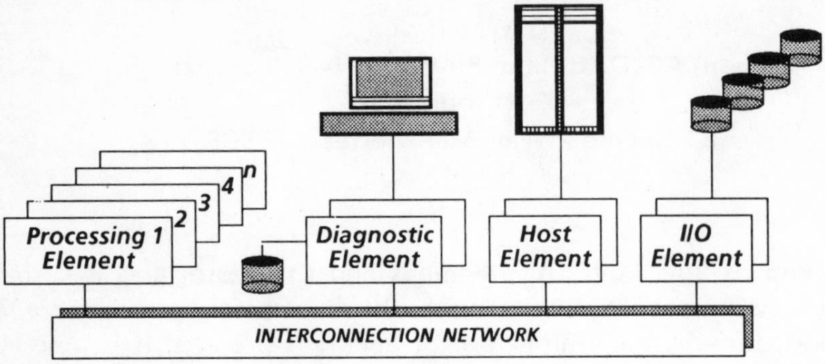

Fig. 1: System Diagram

can be connected to a multistage interconnection network. The machine is scalable for a wide range of applications depending on the selection of elements which are offered: Processing Elements which give computing power, I/O Elements which provide local disk access, Host Elements which form the connection to a host machine and Diagnostic Elements which provide all the facilities for power on and maintenance.

The EDS machine will be used as a backend machine and host accelerator (e.g. database server) and will therefore not provide any user interfaces. The user is connected to EDS through the host machine. The host may be either a mainframe or a workstation.

3 EDS Hardware Architecture

To achieve good scalability, a modular design approach was chosen for the EDS machine. The main building blocks are described below.

3.1 Multistage Interconnection Network

A Delta network forms the communication media. It offers up to 256 full duplex channels with a bandwidth of 20 Mbytes/sec in each direction. It is built with VLSI semicustom circuits each forming an 8x8 crossbar switch with independent input buffers [6]. Extensive simulations have shown that a throughput greater than 3 Gbytes/sec can be maintained with low blocking probability.

The EDS network is a packet switched network with variable packet sizes up to 128 data bytes plus 16 header bytes. The "virtual cut through" scheme is implemented to give low latency figures of the packets at moderate network load.

3.2 Processing Element

Figure 2 shows a sketch of the Processing Element of the EDS machine. This

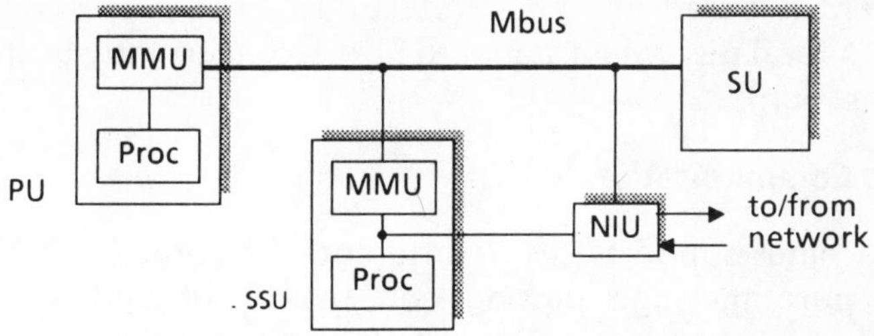

Fig. 2: Block Diagram of the Processing Element

element provides the computing power in the system. It has a dual processor construction. The main CPU is the Processing Unit (PU) which is supported by a System Support Unit (SSU) which offloads some of the operating system tasks from the PU, especially the workload imposed by interprocessor communication. Both CPUs are connected via MMUs to a common memory bus (Mbus). The caches of both CPUs are kept consistent by hardware (bus snooping). The two CPUs are standard RISC processors from the SPARC family.

Tightly coupled to the SSU is the Network Interface Unit (NIU). It is a DMA device which is under complete control of the SSU. It forms the physical link between the main store and the network. The NIU can read data from the store and transfer it over the network to a remote processing element. At the same time, it can receive packets from the network.

The Store Unit (SU) forms the local memory on each PE. It is a two-way interleaved dynamic memory with a size of 64 Mbytes. Therefore, a 256 element EDS machine can have a total memory capacity of up to 16 Gbytes. Besides the data and Hamming error detection and correction bits the memory holds some tagbits. They allow a finer grain management of the paged physical memory. Each 4 Kbyte page (the minimum size is fixed by the used CPU-MMU chips) is divided into smaller units of 128 bytes, called sectors. Each sector has an associated tagbit which provides a valid / invalid flag (see subsection 4.3 for more details).

3.3 Other Elements

The other elements connected to the network (see Fig. 1) build the various links from the EDS machine to the "outside" world.

The Diagnostic Element connects the EDS machine to a maintenance, service and diagnostic console. During the development of the prototypes it will support the debugging of the machine and serve also as a preliminary Host Element and I/O Element.

The EDS machine is a backend machine. It is attached to a host via the Host Element. Depending on the communication needs, several Host Elements can be used to fulfill the bandwidth requirements.

The I/O Element is based on the architecture of the Processing Element. It offers access to local disks via a standard interface (currently SCSI2 and IPI are under consideration).

4 Interprocess Communication

The EDS machine supports two different interprocess communication mechanisms: pure message passing and the distributed virtually shared memory. Both use the very same basic communication scheme which is supported by hardware.

4.1 Basic Communication Mechanism

As already mentioned in the description of the EDS hardware architecture, the Processing Element has two CPUs. One is the PU and the other is the SSU which supports the PU and serves as a communication processor. It is tightly coupled with the NIU which is used as a DMA unit and interfaces the network with the main memory.

If the PU has to communicate with a remote processing element, it installs an entry in the SSU's job queue in main memory. Afterwards, the PU can execute a process switch and is no longer concerned with communication. As soon as the SSU detects an entry in its job queue (polling or interrupts are possible) it sets up the appropriate parameters in the NIU's output queue. The NIU then starts the transfer. On the remote side the NIU receives packets from the network, stores them in a FIFO buffer (large enough for several packets) and informs the SSU about the reception of a packet. The SSU analyses the header and starts the actions depending on the type of the packet (short-message, page-request etc.) and sets up an acknowledge packet. It is important to mention that most of these actions can be accomplished without interrupting the PU.

All communication requests are held at the originator's side in the SSU's job queue until they are acknowledged or a time out occurs. This scheme allows the safe retransmission of packets in case of temporary problems in the network or at the remote Processing Element.

4.2 Message Passing

The EDS machine supports explicit interprocess communication by message passing through "ports". Short messages (less than 128 data bytes) or long messages can be transmitted. The message passing is embedded in the kernel software of the system. Synchronous and asynchronous protocols can be invoked by message passing primitives. For a more detailed description the reader is referred to [7].

4.2.1 Short Messages

Short or unsolicited messages are transmitted with a protocol depicted in

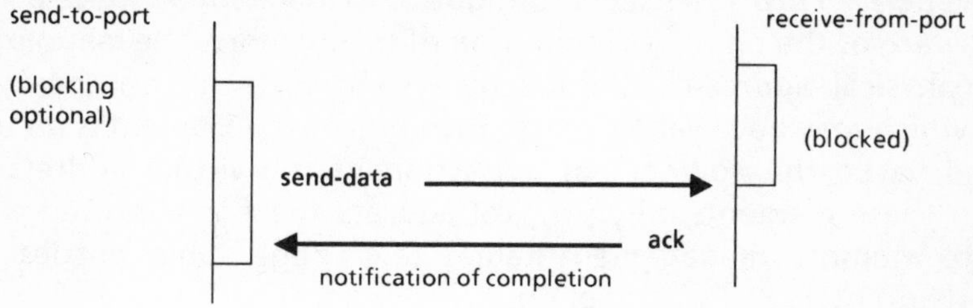

Figure 3: Short Message Protocol

Figure 3. They have a maximum size of 128 bytes which is the size of a network packet. The sending process is blocked in the synchronous version of the protocol until the ack comes back from the receiving side. If the "receive-from-port" operation occurs after the message has been delivered to the port, the receiving process is not blocked.

4.2.2 Long Messages

Long or solicited messages are used if the size of the transferred data is larger than 128 bytes. For these messages, the protocol in Figure 4 is used. The "send-

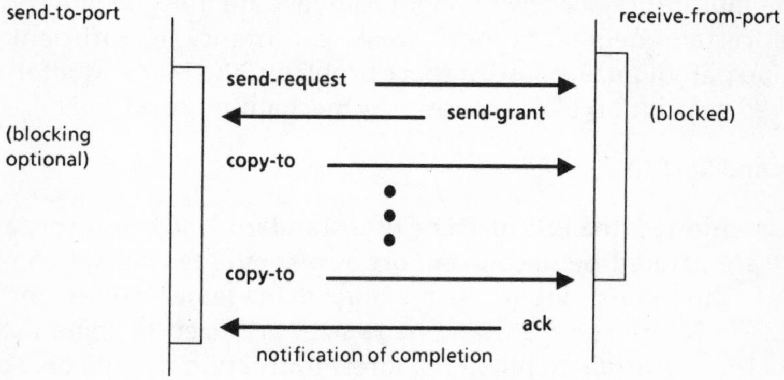

Figure 4: Sending Long Messages

request" requests a buffer space at the remote element. The allocation of a buffer is notified by a "send-grant packet". After having received the grant the sending element copies the data to the remote side with several "copy-to packets" until the data are transferred completely. It is important to notice, that only at the end of the transfer is an acknowledge sent. Again, the protocol can be used synchronously or asynchronously.

4.3 Store Copying

The EDS machine supports a distributed virtually shared memory. In this scheme, the parallel processes see a contiguous virtual address space and need not to be aware of the physical distribution of the memory. The mapping from virtual to physical addresses is done by system software on the basis of "regions" which may have variable size. Each Processing Element is annotated on demand to be the "owner" of a fraction of the virtual address space. Initially, on these elements only physical address space is allocated and the appropriate memory management tables (e.g. page table entries (PTEs), intermediate pointers (PTPs)) are set up.

The access of a virtual address will be handled initially by the MMU. If the mapping from virtual to physical address cannot be found in the TLB a table walk has to be initiated. The page which corresponds to the virtual address may be marked invalid. If this happens on a Processing Element which is not the "owner" of the associated region, the page will be copied from the owner and put as a "cache" copy into the local memory. It can be accessed there as fast as data which are "owned" by the Processing Element. This scheme is in some sense similar to a demand paged virtual memory management. The requested pages are not copied from disks, but they are fetched from a remote memory.

The main difference to a standard virtual memory management is imposed through the multiprocessor environment. Global data must be in a consistent state to a certain degree even if weak consistency is sufficient for a programming paradigm. Because of space problems, the reader is referred to a more detailed description of the consistency mechanisms in [8] and [9].

4.3.1 Pages and Sectors

As already mentioned, the EDS machine uses standard RISC processors as CPUs. These CPUs are offered by silicon vendors as a complete chip set comprising integer units, floating point units, memory management units and cache controllers. The MMU's segment and page sizes are fixed to some extent. In the case of EDS, the virtual to physical address translation is made on a basis of 4 kbyte pages.

Simulations showed that this size of an atomic unit to be copied over the network is too large. A page is therefore again divided into smaller subunits, called sectors. The management of the sectors is supported in hardware by the Store Unit. It exists as an additional level of store management. The MMU still manages pages, but as soon as an access to a non-copied sector is made (the tagbit of this sector is invalid in the Store Unit), the current bus cycle is aborted and the missing sector is copied from the remote memory. Afterwards, the tagbit is set to valid and the memory access can be tried again.

4.3.2 Sector Size

To determine the appropriate sector size for the EDS machine several address traces of parallel Lisp and Prolog program emulations were analyzed. Table 1

sector size in Bytes	hit rate of remote accesses in % over all PEs			# of copies over all PEs			utilisation in % over all PEs		
	min	max	aver.	min	max	aver.	min	max	aver.
128	53	85	71	9	117	67	7	22	13
256	56	88	75	9	96	56	4	13	8
512	59	90	78	8	80	47	2	8	5
1k	68	93	83	7	57	35	1	6	3
2k	68	94	85	7	51	30	1	3	2
4k	68	95	86	7	39	25	1	2	1

Table 1: "Hit Rates" at different Sector Sizes

shows the results of the parallel version of the Boyer-Moore benchmark. It indicates that even with small sectors the "hit rate" is sufficiently good. It is important to note that hit rate here means how many of the remote memory accesses are turned into local memory accesses if a sector with size n bytes is copied. The utilization of a sector is still quite poor. But this is due to the programming style (side effect free) and the fact that the traces contained data addresses only and no code addresses.

In Table 2 the last column shows that the network load can be drastically

	sector size	hit rate in %	# of copies	transport. data	difference in %
Boyer-Moore	128 4k	71 86	67 25	8576 102400	8,4
quicksort1	128 4k	88 95	20 8	2560 32768	7,8
quicksort2	128 4k	91 97	28 9	3584 36864	9,7
quicksort3	128 4k	91 97	47 8	6016 32768	18,3

Table 2: Data Transfers at different Sector Sizes

reduced with sector copying as only about 10 % of the data have to be transported compared to copying full pages. The transfer time over the network without any blocking is 6.4 usec for 128 bytes, the transfer time for a page is 204 usec. With sectors the blocking probability in the network is reduced as the links are used for shorter time periods. Prolog traces showed a similar behavior.

Therefore, 128 byte sectors seem to be a reasonable choice. Additionally, one sector can be transported over the EDS network within one packet which reduces the protocol overhead. Nevertheless, multiple sector copies can be requested. This feature can be used if bulk data has to be transported, e.g. code pages.

But why not use even smaller sectors? The utilization figures increase with smaller sectors, e.g. 32 bytes. But there are a several arguments which indicate that too small a sector size is not the best:

- The overhead increases: there is a 16 byte header for each packet. For 32 bytes the overhead is 50% (12% for 128 bytes).
- The network uses fixed sized buffers of 128 bytes even though it allows the sending of smaller messages. Therefore the blocking probability in the net will remain the same. The transport time only will be reduced from 6.4 usec to 1.6 usec.
- The determining factor is the software overhead. The utilization of sectors is not linear. It is about 40% for 32 byte sectors, about 20% for 128 byte sectors. Thus, two 32 byte sectors have to be copied on average instead of one 128 byte sector. Then the software overhead (about 20 usec for each transfer) dominates.

4.3.3 Store Copying Protocol

Figure 5 shows a schematic diagram of the actions performed if a sector is copied from a remote memory. After the PU has installed a copy request in the SSU's job queue both CPUs can operate fully parallel. The SSU acts as a communication processor. It is worth mentioning that the PU is not interrupted at all on the remote element. The remote SSU can handle the sector request completely. The PU can continue with the execution of the application program. The only interference with the sector copying performed by the SSU may be collisions on the memory bus.

In the case of the store copy protocol which is also built up on the basic communication mechanism the returning data are used as the acknowledge. This saves two packet transfers over the network and gives the security that no requests are lost.

On the initiator side, the PU is notified of the completion of the sector copy at the very end of the data transfer after the requested sector is completely written into the local memory.

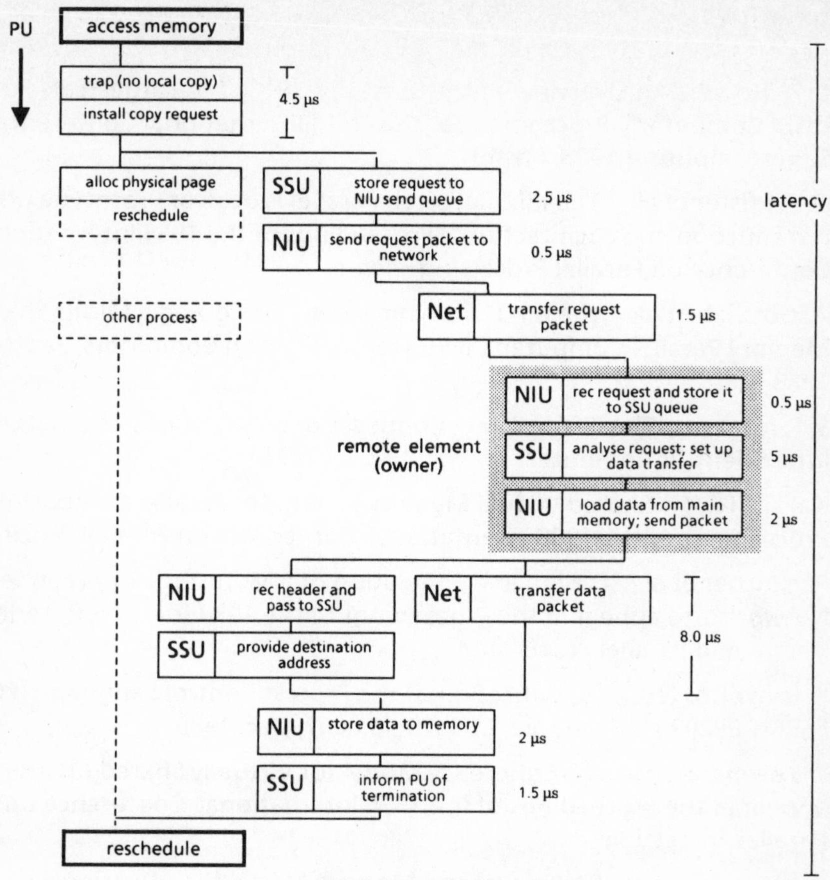

Fig. 5: Store Copying Protocol

5 Summary

The EDS machine is a multiprocessor of type MIMD with distributed store architecture. Pure message passing and the implementation of a distributed virtually shared memory is supported by hardware through a communication processor. Both interprocess communication facilities are built on top of a basic and common communication mechanism. The performance of the implementation of the distributed virtually shared memory is enhanced further by introducing hardware supported sectors.

Acknowledgement

The work described in this paper was done within the framework of the EDS ESPRIT II project. The authors would like to thank their colleagues in the hardware and the kernel software team at ICL and Siemens for their contributions to the project and helpful discussions.

References

[1] C. D. Howe, "An Overview of the Butterfly GP1000: A Large-Scale Parallel UNIX Computer", Proceedings of the Third International Conference on Supercomputing 1988, Boston

[2] G. F. Pfister et al., "The IBM Research Parallel Processor Prototype (RP3): Introduction and Architecture", Proceedings of the 1985 International Conference on Parallel Processing

[3] A. Gottlieb et al., "The NYU Ultracomputer - Designing a MIMD Shared Memory Parallel Computer", IEEE Transactions on Computers, February 1983

[4] S. F. Nugent, "The iPSC/2 Direct Connect Communications Technology", Intel Scientific Computers

[5] Kai Li, "IVY: A Shared Virtual Memory System for Parallel Computing", Proceedings of the 1988 International Conference on Parallel Processing

[6] R. Holzner et al., "Design and Simulation of a Multistage Interconnection Network", to appear in the Proceedings of the 1990 Joint Conference on Vector and Parallel Processing

[7] P. Istavrinos (ed.), "Specification of the Process Control Language (PCL)", ESPRIT EP2025 Deliverable, EDS.DD.1S.0007, Dec. 1989

[8] L. Borrmann et al., "A Coherency Model for Virtually Shared Memory", to appear in the Proceedings of the 1990 International Conference on Parallel Processing

[9] P. Istavrinos et al., "A Process and Memory Model for a Distributed-Memory Machine", to appear in the Proceedings of the 1990 Joint Conference on Vector and Parallel Processing

DAMP - A Dynamic Reconfigurable Multiprocessor System With a Distributed Switching Network

Andreas Bauch, Reinhold Braam and Erik Maehle

Universität-GH-Paderborn, Fachgebiet Datentechnik
Pohlweg 47-49, D-4790 Paderborn
Fed. Rep. of Germany

Abstract: In this paper the dynamic reconfigurable multiprocessor system DAMP is introduced which is currently under development at the University of Paderborn. Its architecture is based on a single type of building block (DAMP-module) consisting of a transputer, memory and a local switching network. These building blocks are interconnected according to a fixed topology with restricted neighborhood (octagonal torus). Circuit-switching is used to establish and to release communication paths between nodes dynamically during runtime under program control. Currently an 8-processor prototype is operational, a redesign for a 64-processor system is under way. After describing the basic architecture of the DAMP system the paper concentrates on its reconfiguration properties (especially blocking problems). Finally the implementations of centralized and decentralized switch control on the prototype system are presented and first measurements of communication setup times are discussed.

0. Introduction

As conventional sequential supercomputers are more and more approaching their physical limits the interest in parallel computers has grown considerably in the last years. Among the broad spectrum of parallel architectures, MIMD-systems with distributed memory are especially promising. Being based on mostly standard VLSI-components they offer a very good price/performance ratio. Furthermore the lack of global resources, which always carry a potential for a bottleneck, make them easily expandable to a large number (hundreds or thousands) of nodes.

Usually a processing node consists of a (standard) microprocessor (plus eventually numerical coprocessor), local memory and communication links to the other nodes in the system. A central role plays the interconnection network between nodes and the internode communication strategies. As a full interconnection is impractical for a large number of processors, topologies with a restricted neighborhood like rings, trees, meshes, pyramids or hypercubes have been proposed. Especially hypercubes have become very popular and are used for several commercial machines, e.g. Intel iPSC, Ncube or Ametek [Ree87].

Today communication between neighboring nodes is usually done by bitserial message passing (synchronous or asynchronous). But also memory coupling by local multiport or dualport memories has been employed successfully (e.g. in the EGPA and DIRMU systems of the University of Erlangen-Nürnberg [Hän85] or the Japanese PAX computer [Hos89]). In both cases communication between neighbors is rather fast (or even very fast in the case of memory coupling) while communications between non-neighbors has to be implemented by some routing scheme via intermediate nodes. The two most important techniques are *store-and-forward* and *wormhole routing* [Dal87]. In store-and-forward routing a message is completely buffered in an intermediate node before it is forwarded to the next one. This of course causes a considerable message latency. In wormhole routing special routing hardware forwards a message as soon as the head of the message containing the routing information has arrived, i.e. a message is spread over several nodes leading to a very short latency even for long communication paths. Unfortunately the link protocol of current transputers [INM88b] forbids wormhole routing. However, this is announced to be changed for the next generation, the H1 [Pou90].

Especially if store-and-forward routing has to be used, mapping schemes must be employed which try to map application tasks to nodes in such a way that not only load balancing is achieved but also the overhead by non-neighbor communication is minimized. For wormhole routing this point is no longer of that importance, but minimization of network traffic is still desirable to keep the blocking probability of messages small.

In order to support the mapping of different application problems to a distributed memory machine the interconnection topology can be made more or less reconfigurable. This leads to the following classification:

- *Static topologies:* Fixed point-to-point links between neighboring nodes which are either hard-wired or at best can be replugged by hand. Examples for this kind of systems are DIRMU, simple transputer systems or most hypercube machines.
- *Quasi-static topologies:* A switching network allows to establish a topology specified by the application program *before* its execution starts. During the runtime of the program the topology remains unchanged. Examples are more recent transputer systems like Paracom Supercluster [Küb88].
- *Quasi-dynamic topologies:* The application program can be divided into several phases which require different topologies. Before a new phase starts the switching network is reconfigured, within phases the topology remains fixed.
- *Dynamic topologies:* The communication topology can change nearly arbitrarily at runtime, i.e. it can be easily matched to the communication requirements of the application program. Another advantage is the potential for fault-tolerance: faulty nodes or links can easily be bypassed and spare nodes be switched in. The MULTITOP system from Max Planck Institute Garching [Her89], Esprit P1085 Supernode [Ada90] and our DAMP (Dynamic Adaptable Multi-Processor) belong to this category.

In the following we will now describe the basic architecture, communication capabilities and some implementation issues (especially switch control) for the dynamically reconfigurable transputer system DAMP.

1. Basic Architecture of the DAMP System

For non-static topologies a switching network is required which can be either implemented in a centralized way or can be distributed among processing nodes. As a single global switch easily becomes too complex and is difficult to expand a cluster approach is often taken. For example in the Paracom Supercluster there exists a NCU (96 X 96 crossbar switching unit) for each cluster of 16 transputers which allows to configure any topology of degree four (number of transputer links). 32 links are leaving the cluster NCUs and are connected to higher-level NCUs forming a supercluster with 64 processors. For even larger systems the free NCU links of the higher level can be connected to further NCUs etc. The control of the NCUs is done by separate control transputers which is sufficient for quasi-static topologies but easily becomes a bottleneck for dynamic ones (which currently are not supported). Furthermore a fault in the NCU or its control transputer can affect large parts of the systems which contradicts the requirement for fault-tolerance.

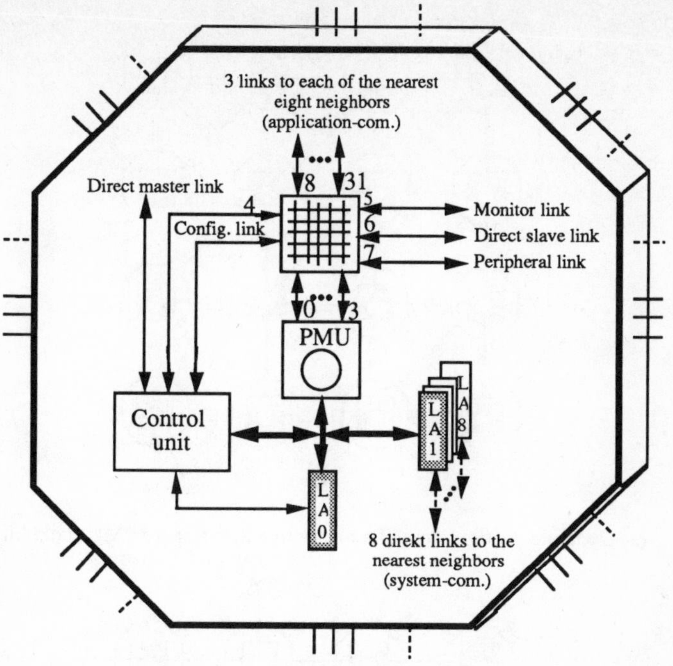

Fig. 1: DAMP module

Therefore in the DAMP system a *distributed switch* has been chosen. This leads to one single node type (fig. 1) consisting of a Processor/Memory Unit PMU (transputer T800 plus up to 8 MB of memory), a local switching network based on a 32x32 crossbar switch (C004) with its control logic and several link adaptors LA (C012). The LAs are parallel-serial converters which convert byte parallel data into a serial data stream according to the transputer link protocol. In the DAMP system they are used only for system communication (e.g. control of the crossbar switch). In the current design only LA0 and LA1 are provided. In the redesign however, another seven LAs will be added. Note that all application communication is always carried out over the four transputer links. From the 32 links of the local crossbar

- 24 are used for the interconnection to neighboring nodes
- 4 are connected to the transputer links in the PMU
- 2 are provided for control purposes (see chapter 3): e.g. to establish communication via LA0 between a master and a subordinate slave node (direct slave link)
- 1 allows to connect an external performance monitor (monitor link)
- 1 is used for (optional) I/O (peripheral link).

There exist two possibilities to control the configuration link of a local crossbar switch: from an external master over the direct master link (only for hierarchical configurations to be described later) or locally by the PMU itself via LA0. The switch can be set for connecting the 4 transputer links of the PMU to the neighbors as well as for transferring incoming data from one neighbor directly to another without affecting the PMU (except perhaps for setting the switch in the beginning).

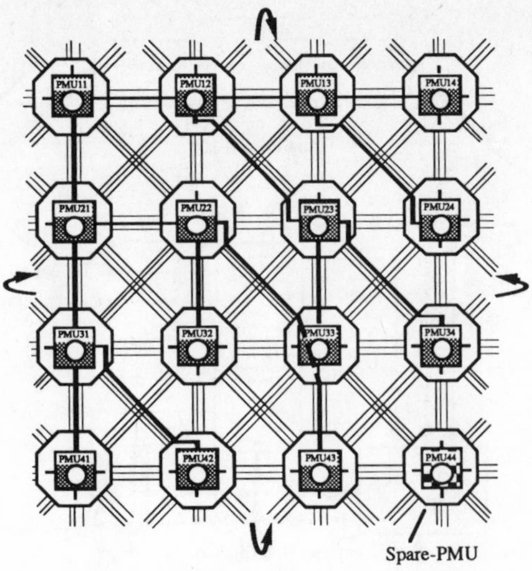

(a) Dynamic configuration of a binary tree with a spare PMU (bold lines)

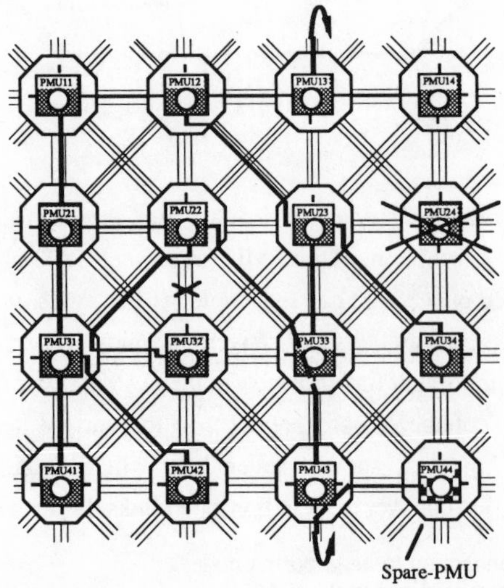

(b) Reconfiguration in case of a failure of PMU24 and all three links PMU22 - PMU32

Fig. 2: Static interconnection network of the DAMP system (octagonal torus).

A DAMP multiprocessor system is formed by connecting several DAMP-modules according to a physical fixed topology (static interconnection network). In our prototype we have chosen an octagonal torus (fig. 2). Note that there are 3 links to each of the 8 neighbors. Being fully passive the fixed interconnection net can easily be implemented by a backplane. The choice of the torus was mainly for practical reasons. In our theoretical studies other topologies (e.g. DeBruijn graphs) will be considered as well.

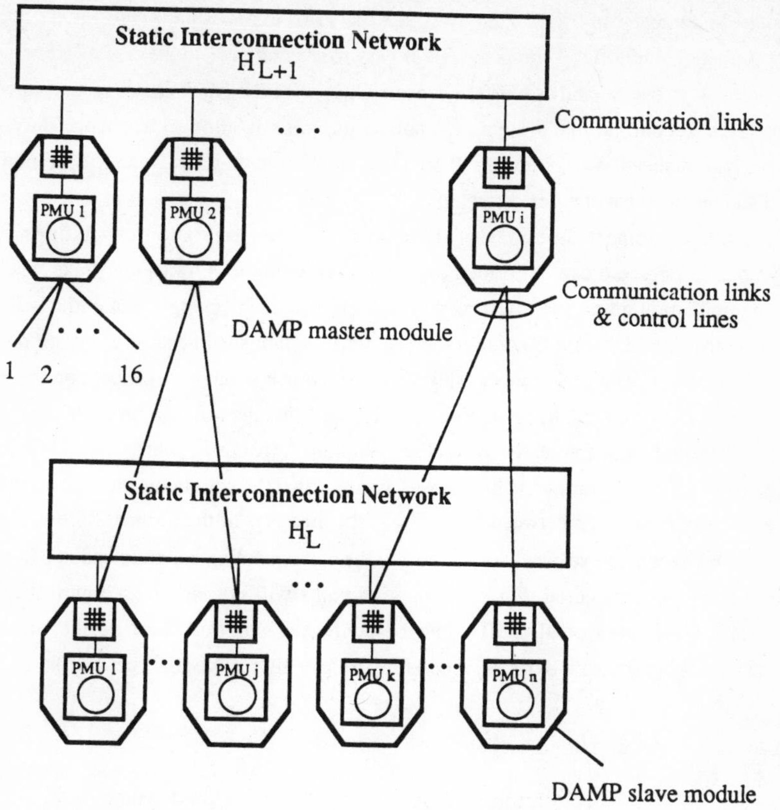

Fig. 3: Hierarchical DAMP systems

Optionally hierarchical DAMP systems can be built as well (fig. 3). In addition to the static torus network within each layer, up to 16 modules of a layer H_L can be connected by further communication links (direct master link and direct slave link in fig. 1) and control lines to a master PMU at layer H_{L+1}, these again to H_{L+2} etc. yielding a pyramid-like structure. As to be described in chapter 3 master PMUs can be used for centralized switch control schemes.

2. Dynamic Reconfiguration

The DAMP system is able to support quasi-static as well as dynamic reconfiguration schemes. As an example fig. 2a shows a binary tree with 15 nodes (application graph) configured on a 4x4 octagonal DAMP-torus (machine graph). The root of the tree is mapped to PMU11. The bold lines indicate paths which are switched with aid of the local crossbar switches between the respective transputer links. As can be seen lines between immediate neighbors mostly suffice. The connection from PMU22 to PMU43 via the local crossbar of PMU33 is an example of a communication path between physical non-neighbors. However, once a path is built it can be used in the same way as a direct link connection. The only difference is a small additional delay (about 180 nsec) per local crossbar switch.

In our example PMU44 is used as a spare. Suppose now that PMU24 as well as all three links between PMU22 and PMU32 have failed. In this case the local crossbar switches can be reconfigured as shown in fig. 2b: the spare is switched in for PMU24 by a path via PMU43 and a path via PMU31 bypasses the broken links. As there are no central components it is easy to see that even in the case of arbitrary multiple failures the system stays operational as long as a reasonable application graph can be reconfigured.

Being a dynamic reconfigurable system the application graph is allowed to change during runtime according to the communication requirements of the parallel program. In fully dynamic operation paths can be established and destroyed at any time in an unpredictable way.

Of course there are some restrictions in these dynamic reconfiguration capabilities. First only application graphs of degree 4 can be formed due to the limitation to 4 transputer links. Second it can happen that an application graph can not be configured because of blocking, i.e. a communication path corresponding to an edge in the application graph can not be established because there are no more free links in the static network. The probability of blocking is of course strongly dependent on the application graph and will increase with a growing number of processors. To get a first impression of the blocking behavior of DAMP simulations for nearly worst case conditions were carried out.

For square octagonal tori of various sizes N it was assumed that the communication distance D between all nodes is uniformly distributed between 1 and D_{max}, the diameter of the torus or follows a decreasing distribution ($\approx 1/D^2$). Nodes are selected at random and the corresponding communication paths according to their distributions are configured. For simplification paths will not be released until the end of the simulation run. If all 4 links of all PMUs can be connected without blocking the run terminates successfully, if a blocking occurs it stops unsuccessfully (max 9 alternative trials per path).

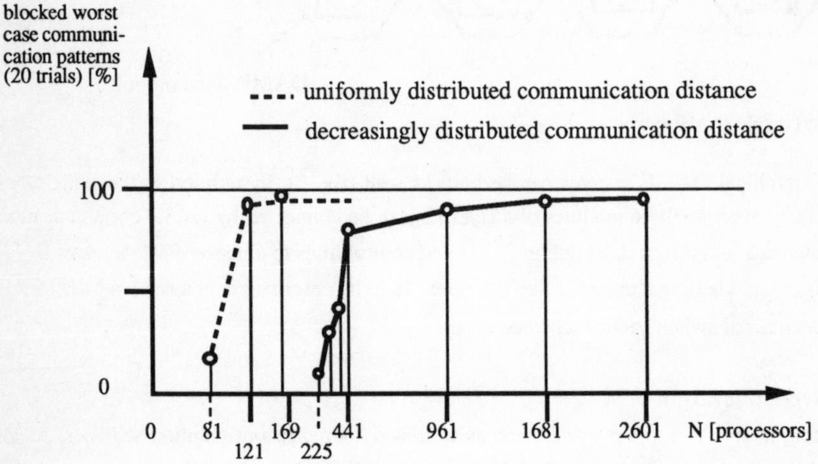

Fig. 4.: Simulation results for worst case blocking behavior of DAMP tori

The results of these simulations (20 runs per torus size N) are shown in fig. 4. As expected blocking is observed at smaller torus sizes (≥81 nodes) for the uniform distribution than for the decreasing one (≥225 nodes). In both cases the probability of blocking increases rapidly for larger N. However, it must be stressed that these are worst case considerations. In real applications not all 4 links of each PMU will always be used at the same time and communication paths will be released as soon as they are no longer required. Nevertheless blocking will be an important issue for further experiments with real applications.

3. Implementation of Dynamic Configuration Control

On our prototype system with 8 DAMP-modules (2x4 octagonal torus) we have implemented a centralized and a decentralized control scheme for dynamic reconfiguration in the programming language Occam 2 [INM88b].

Centralized Switch Control

As mentioned before hierarchical DAMP configurations can be formed optionally. In our prototype one of the torus nodes can take over the role of a master, the other 7 PMUs are slaves. In the centralized mode the master is responsible for controlling the switches of its slaves by the extra communication links and control lines provided. The corresponding software consists of a Master Management MM for the Master PMU and Local Managements LM for the slaves (fig. 5a). In our scheme only communication channels have to be identified (e.g. P0.to.P1), the locations of the corresponding processes are determined at runtime.

Let us assume process P0 in PMU i wants to establish a communication path to process P1 in PMU k. In this case P0 and P1 must open a communication channel by calling appropriate routines with the same channel identification P0.to.P1 (open.ch.for.write, open.ch.for.read respectively). This causes the corresponding local managements LM to send an event (interrupt) to the master management MM. By these events MM can identify the current PMUs of P0 and P1. Note that MM waits until both partners have called their open-routines, user processes are descheduled during eventual waiting times. As MM has a complete knowledge of the switch settings of its slaves, it can compute an optimal route and set switches in PMU i, PMU k and all intermediate nodes PMU j (if any) accordingly. The open-routines return with a pointer to the actual transputer link (link.pt0, link.pt1). Over these links the new communication path can now be employed in both directions from Occam as if the links were directly connected. The path exists until it is explicitly closed, which causes MM to free the corresponding links and switches.

Measurements have shown that building up a path in this centralized way takes some time (2 msec on the average for a 4x4 torus) [Rol89]. The main reason for this is the algorithm for finding optimal routes. Furthermore MM as a central resource can soon become a bottleneck if many paths must be established at the same time and it also contradicts the demand for fault tolerance.

Decentralized Switch Control

An alternative is to set the switches in a fully distributed way. In this case the identification of the destination PMU must be known. Let us assume in fig. 5b the same scenario as in fig. 5a. Now only local managements LM exist which also control the local switches in their nodes. In order to build up a path LMs in neighboring nodes must be able to communicate with each other (system communication implemented by link adaptors LA, see chapter 1). In the current prototype there exists an event line to each of the 8 physical neighbors. If an event signals that a neighbor wants to start a system communication, both partners switch their LA0 to one of the three communication links (which has to be reserved for this purpose). Thus control information about the path to be established can be exchanged.

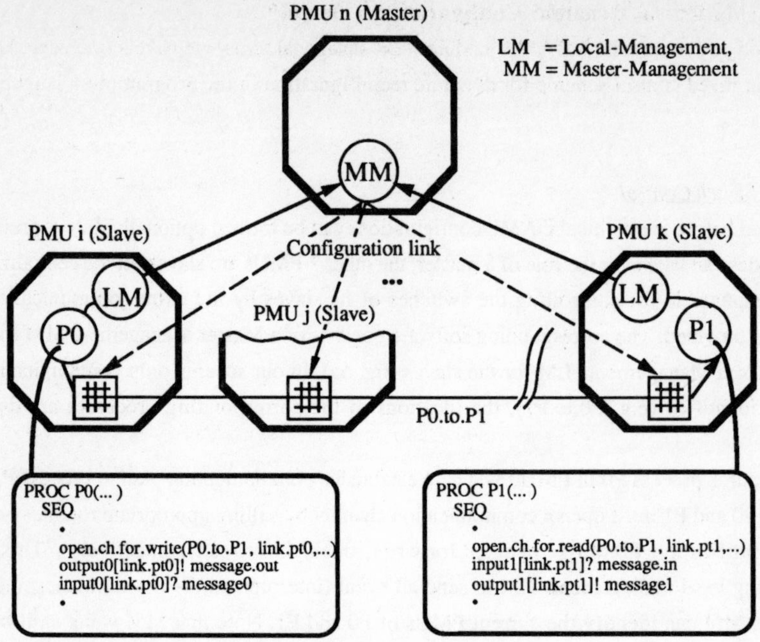

(a) Centralized switch control

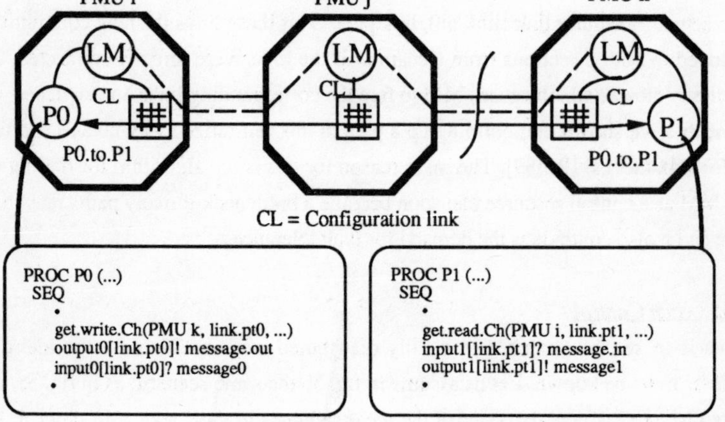

(b) Decentralized switch control

Fig. 5: Dynamic configuration control in the DAMP system

In the redesigned node there will be one dedicated LA for each neighbor which is directly connected according to the torus topology. System communication then only requires writing data into the corresponding LA which is immediately transferred over the LA's direct connection to the neighboring LA. As LAs are able to generate an event when data arrives, event lines are no longer required. So this new scheme is not only faster, it also has the same wiring complexity (links instead of event lines) and leaves all three regular links for application communication. In addition a fast broadcast mechanism is supported by writing to all LAs simultaneously.

In decentralized mode paths are built up from node to node in a backtracking fashion supported by routing tables [Dam90]. PMU i first communicates over the system communication links with an appropriate neighbor PMU j selected from its routing table. Then the two switches are set accordingly and the next hop of the path is established in the same manner until the destination node is reached. If all suitable routes from one node are occupied backtracking to the last but one node takes place and an alternative route is tried. This procedure ends successfully if the destination node PMU k is reached or terminates without success if either a preset counter for the number of steps is exhausted or there are no more alternatives to try (blocking). Note again that once a path is built it can be used in a bidirectional way like a direct link. The only penalty is the small signal delay per switch. As in the centralized case paths exist until they are explicitely closed by the application processes.

Measurements on the prototype have shown that the overhead is about 800 µsec per hop [Dam90]. As most of this time is taken for event handling and switching link adaptors we expect it to be reduced to 300 µsec for the redesigned DAMP module.

One advantage of the decentralized scheme is that many paths can be built up simultaneously. This however rises the danger of deadlocks which can e.g. be prevented by appropriate routing schemes [Dal87, Dam90]. Furthermore distributed routing is well suited for fault-tolerant operation as it does not require any central facility and can easily bypass faulty nodes or links.

In both schemes there exists a considerable overhead for establishing a path. The main consequence is that it is too costly to change the communication topology very frequently (e.g. for each message). Instead paths should only be switched if either a large amount of data has to be transferred or if they will be used for several subsequent messages. As due to the circuit switching nearly the full communication bandwidth is available, the overall communication can nevertheless be very efficient.

4. Concluding Remarks

The main feature of the DAMP multitransputer system presented in this paper is that it implements dynamic reconfiguration by a fully distributed circuit-switch. The switch control can either be centralized (hierarchical configurations) or decentralized. The decentralized schemes offers more advantages especially if fault tolerance is required. Measurements on a first prototype showed that path set up times can be rather high (in the millisecond range) making too frequent switching inefficient.

This contrasts our approach to wormhole routing as it is e.g. employed in the Intel iPSC/2. For this machine a setup time of 390 µsec for a one-hop message of hundred bytes or less and 697 µsec for longer ones is reported [Dun88]. Note that this overhead has to be paid for *each message*. The advantage however is that it is rather independent of the path length while for the DAMP system about 800 µsec (redesign 300 µsec) have to be paid for *each hop*. But once a DAMP path is built it can be used with the low message setup times of transputers in the range one microsecond [INM88b].

Of course the real performance of the DAMP system will also depend very much on the parallel application programs. First experiences with a parallel simulation program for the pressure distribution in partly contacted joints (e.g. human knee) together with the Department of Anatomy, University of Cologne on our prototype have already shown promising results [Bra90]. Currently we are building the redesigned 64-processor DAMP system. Further work will e.g. consist of:

- Implementation of further parallel application programs
- Integration of a hybrid monitor
- Application of a dynamic distributed scheduling algorithm [Ros90]
- Development of fault tolerance techniques.

References

[Ada90] Adamo, J.-M.; Bonello, Ch.: TéNor++: A Dynamic Configurer for SuperNode Machines. Proc. CONPAR 90-VAPP IV, Lecture Notes in Computer Science 457, 640-651, Springer-Verlag, Berlin 1990

[Bra90] Braam, R.; Mockenhaupt, J.; Pollmann, A.: Simulation von Beanspruchung und Verformung biologischer Gelenke auf dem dynamisch adaptierbaren Multiprozessorsystem DAMP. To appear: Proc. TAT'90, Transputer-Anwender-Treffen, Aachen 1990

[Dal87] Dally, W.J.; Seitz, C.L.: Deadlock-free message routing in multiprocessor interconnection networks. IEEE Trans. on Computers, vol. C-36, no. 5, 547-553, May 1987

[Dam90] Damsz, J.: Softwaremodul für den dezentralen Verbindungsaufbau im dynamisch adaptierbaren Multiprozessorsystem DAMP. Interner Arbeitsbericht Nr. 35, Fachgebiet Datentechnik, Universität-GH-Paderborn 1990

[Dun88] Dunigan, T.H.: Performance of a Second Generation Hypercube. Oak Ridge National Laboratory 1988

[Hän85] Händler, W.; Maehle, E.; Wirl, K.: The DIRMU Testbed for High-Performance Multiprocessor Configurations. Proc. First Int. Conf. on Supercomputing Systems, 468-475, St. Petersburg FL, 1985

[Her89] Hertweck, F.: Vektor- und Parallel-Rechner: Vergangenheit, Gegenwart, Zukunft. Informationstechnik it 1/8, 5-22, Oldenbourg-Verlag 1989

[Hos89] Hoshino, T.; Sekiguchi, S.; Yuba, T.: Parallel Scientific Computer Researches in Japan. Informationstechnik it 1/8, 23-30, Oldenbourg-Verlag 1989

[INM88a] Occam 2 Reference Manual. Prentice Hall, New York London 1988

[INM88b] Transputer Reference Manual. Prentice Hall, New York London 1988

[Küb88] Kübler, F.D.: A Cluster-Oriented Architecture for the Mapping of Parallel Processor Networks to High Performance Applications. Proc. Int. Conf. on Supercomputing, 179-189, ACM 1988

[Pou 90] Pountain, D.: Virtual Channels: The Next Generation of Transputers. BYTE, 4/90, McGraw-Hill 1990

[Ree87] Reed, D.A.; Fujimoto, R.M.: Multicomputer Networks - Message Based Parallel Processing. The MIT Press, Cambridge MA, 1987

[Rol89] Rolfsmeier, D.: Implementierung eines Software-Moduls zum Aufbau beliebiger Kommunikationspfade innerhalb des Multitransputersystems DAMP. Interner Arbeitsbericht Nr. 10, Fachgebiet Datentechnik, Universität-GH-Paderborn 1989

[Ros90] Rost, J.; Maehle, E.: A Distributed Algorithm for Dynamic Task Scheduling. Proc. CONPAR 90-VAPP IV, Lecture Notes in Computer Science 457, 628-639, Springer-Verlag, Berlin 1990

Posters

D. Deserable: Diffusion on a Recursively Scalable Honeycomb Network,
INSA, Rennes (F)

V. Fack: Total Exchange Algorithms on "Sandwich Graphs",
Rijksuniversiteit, Gent (B)

P. Fraunié: Periodic Ambulent Flows calculation using transputers,
I.M.S.T., Marseille (F)

J. Höfener: 3-D image preprocessing by discrete fast Hartley transform using transputers,
RWTH, Aachen (D)

G.N. Howard, K. Maguire: Solving Banded Systems on Distributed Memory Systems,
University of Liverpool (U.K.)

P. Jacobson: Algorithm Development for Distributed Memory Computers using CONLAB,
Univ. of Umeå, Umeå (S)

G. Koller, A. Stein: Virtual Shared Memory Based on an Object Oriented Communication Controller,
TUM, München (D)

G. Mando: Parallel Image Processing,
Université Jose H. Fourier (F)

C. Neusius, D. Scheerer: Efficient Distributed Thinning on DATIS-P,
Univ. des Saarlandes, Saarbrücken (D)

T. F. Pena: Simulation of Semiconductor Devices in Hypercube Computers,
Univ. de Santiago de Compostela, Santiago de Compostela (E)

M. Smith: Dynamic Load-Balancing on a One-Dimensional Mesh,
Edinburgh Parallel Computing Centre, Edinburgh (GB)

B. Tourancheau: Matrix Multiplication and Matrix Transpose: Fixed topology vs. switching Network,
Ecole Normale Supérieure de Lyon (F)